Canadian Politics in the 1980s

Canadian Politics in the 1980s
Second Edition

Edited by

Michael S. Whittington
and Glen Williams

⬡ Methuen

Toronto   New York   London   Sydney   Auckland

Canadian Politics in the 1980s
Copyright © 1984 by Methuen Publications
A division of The Carswell Company Limited

Canadian Cataloguing in Publication Data

Main entry under title:
Canadian politics in the 1980s

Includes index.
ISBN 0-458-97610-5

1. Canada — Politics and government — 1980-*
I. Whittington, Michael S., 1942–   II. Williams,
Glen, 1947–

FC630.C36 1984   971.064'6   C84-098564-9
F1034.2.C36 1984

Printed and bound in Canada

3 4 5   84   89 88 87 86

Contributors

MICHAEL M. ATKINSON, Associate Professor, Department of Political Science, McMaster University, Hamilton, Ontario

DAVID V.J. BELL, Professor of Political Science and Dean of Graduate Studies, York University, Downsview, Ontario

FRANÇOIS BREGHA, Energy Analyst, Ottawa, Ontario

M. JANINE BRODIE, Associate Professor, Department of Political Science, York University, Downsview, Ontario

DAN BUTLER, Chief Research Officer, Professional Institute of the Public Service of Canada, Ottawa, Ontario

FREDERICK J. FLETCHER, Associate Professor of Political Science, York University, Downsview, Ontario

JANE JENSON, Associate Professor, Department of Political Science, Carleton University, Ottawa, Ontario

JACK LAYTON, Professor, Department of Politics, Ryerson Polytechnical Institute and Senior Alderman, Ward 6, Toronto City Council

BRUCE D. MACNAUGHTON, Senior Policy Advisor, Ontario Ministry of Municipal Affairs and Housing, Toronto, Ontario

PATRICIA MARCHAK, Professor, Department of Anthropology and Sociology, University of British Columbia, Vancouver, British Columbia

DAVID MILNE, Associate Professor, Department of Political Studies, University of Prince Edward Island, Charlottetown, Prince Edward Island

WILLIAM MISHLER, Professor, Department of Political Science, State University of New York at Buffalo

MAUREEN APPEL MOLOT, Associate Professor, Department of Political Science, Carleton University, Ottawa, Ontario

JON H. PAMMETT, Professor, Department of Political Science, Carleton University, Ottawa, Ontario

LEO V. PANITCH, Professor, Department of Political Science, York University, Downsview, Ontario

A. PAUL PROSS, Professor, Department of Political Science, Dalhousie University, Halifax, Nova Scotia

RICHARD SCHULTZ, Professor and Director, Centre for the Study of Regulated Industries, McGill University, Montreal, Quebec

DAVID E. SMITH, Professor, Department of Political Science, University of Saskatchewan, Saskatoon, Saskatchewan

GARTH STEVENSON, Professor, Department of Political Science, University of Alberta, Edmonton, Alberta

DAPHNE GOTTLIEB TARAS, Research Coordinator, Canada–China Relations Project, York University, Downsview, Ontario

GLEN TONER, Assistant Professor, School of Public Administration, Carleton University, Ottawa, Ontario

REGINALD A. WHITAKER, Professor, Department of Political Science, York University, Downsview, Ontario

MICHAEL S. WHITTINGTON, Professor, Department of Political Science, Carleton University, Ottawa, Ontario

GLEN WILLIAMS, Associate Professor, Department of Political Science, Carleton University, Ottawa, Ontario

RICHARD J. VAN LOON, Deputy Secretary, Ministry of State for Social Development, Ottawa, Ontario

Contents

Introduction

Now near its mid-point, the 1980s has proved to be an unpredictable and turbulent decade. On the international scene, there has been a frightening escalation of the arms race and cold-war confrontation, with both the Soviets and the Americans becoming increasingly belligerent and bellicose. As well, the world economy has at times threatened an eclipse as dark as that of the 1930s. In the developed countries, we have faced unprecedented unemployment and inflation. Widespread political repression, economic bankruptcy and increasingly intolerable levels of absolute deprivation and even starvation were the lot of much of the rest of the planet.

In Canada, our 1981 prediction of "changes aplenty" in the introduction of the first edition of this reader seems at this juncture to have been, if anything, understated. Canadians have witnessed the Queen's signature on a new Constitution, the emergence of new leadership in both our major political parties and the addition of pressing new items to the political agenda of both the provinces and the federal government. Indeed, so many new factors have recently come into play on the Canadian political scene that we felt compelled to bring out a second edition just three years after the initial publication of this volume. Four of our chapters discuss completely new material, and, of the remaining sixteen, most have required very substantial revisions in order to keep pace with this decade's remarkable rate of change in Canadian political life.

Some of the major controversies likely to shape our political discourse in the remainder of the decade are included in our first section. Its list of topics is by no means meant to offer an exhaustive preview of all that will come to dominate the political agenda in the next few years. Whatever the efforts of political scientists to understand it, the future will obviously set its own agenda. However, this selection is meant to provide background on a broad range of partisan, regional and economic concerns from which more specific issues will undoubtedly emerge.

Authored by Butler and Macnaughton, the first chapter of this section places the current heated debate over government cutbacks into a wider political context. They remind us that those who have called for "spending restraint" and "fiscal responsibility" have presented a highly oversimplified picture of how, how much and why governments have grown and have fudged on the question of which sectors of society will benefit and lose if their vision of a smaller state is realized.

The chapter by Whitaker sets out the post-referendum and post-Constitutional settlement position of Quebec within the Canadian federation. Examining the rise and fall of the electoral fortunes of the Parti Québécois, he shows why it is likely that future Quebec politicians will stress economic and social issues over nationalism.

Whittington's analysis of the north also has a regional focus. Although the general public is probably less well informed on politics north of the 60th parallel than some of the other areas examined in our first section, the last decade has seen this vast hinterland's concerns approaching ever closer to centre stage. This is because, as Whittington shows, the recent debates of northern politics have encompassed many of the other broad trends that we have identified in this introductory part of the volume—continentalism and the environmental issues of energy and renewable resource extraction, public sector growth and province building, and ethnic conflict and native rights.

A venerable topic in Canadian politics, Canada's relationship to the United States, is given a fresh look in a chapter co-authored by Molot and Williams. Employing the political economy approach, they consider the implications of continentalism and foreign investment for the integrity of Canadian nationhood in a decade of world-wide economic dislocation and readjustment.

While Molot and Williams pay special attention to the many difficulties of industrial policy making as we move toward the 1990s, the subsequent two chapters examine topics related to Canada's traditional role as a resource producer. Toner and Bregha attempt to come to grips with the political and economic significance of Canadian energy policy in the wake of the National Energy Program. The politics of petroleum, they demonstrate, will likely continue to catalyze some of our most intense east–west regional and government–private sector disputes.

Finally, Marchak plots the squandering of our "renewable" resource heritage. No resource is automatically renewable, she reminds us, and both governments and business have failed to adjust to an environment in which the technology of extraction far exceeds the ability of the resources to replenish themselves. Consequently, we are racing toward the destruction of both our fishing and forestry sectors.

The second section of our volume shifts the focus from the broad trends that will likely determine the agenda for political decision makers in the remainder of the decade to four aspects of the sociocultural milieu within which the Canadian political process must operate. The chapter by Bell outlines the basic political attitudes and values of Canadians—our political culture—with a view to identifying potential changes. In the same vein, Mishler examines the immediate behavioural reflections of our political culture in the levels and kinds of political participation that will continue to characterize Canadian liberal democracy. Panitch looks at the Canadian social structure in terms of class. He addresses himself to the role of elites and discusses the way economic and political power is distributed in our society.

Moving from this more generalized focus, Fletcher and Gottlieb analyze one of the most important institutional forces in Canadian society, the media. They argue that the role of the media, always significant, will continue to expand, and they attempt to identify some important forces which may alter the nature of the press and electronic media in the future.

The third section of our book contains three chapters that survey the main "linkage" institutions that connect the political system with its environment. These linkage institutions are important because the manner in which they operate can significantly affect the issues that are brought to the attention of the political elites. Brodie and Jenson discuss Canadian political parties from a new perspective and attempt to come to terms with the recent structural and ideological changes in our partisan politics. Pammett uses the data from the most recent federal elections to suggest how the trends that emerge from his analysis may be manifested in future partisan contests. He sees significant forces at work in Canadian society which are reflected in the electoral process and which could have far-reaching implications for subsequent elections. The final chapter by Pross investigates the increasingly important role of pressure groups in the policy process.

The concluding section of our book concentrates on governmental structures and institutions, the traditional meat and potatoes of political scientists. Constitutional reform has been near the top of the Canadian political agenda for decades. In an important new chapter, Milne identifies the major actors in the constitutional debates of the 1970s and early 1980s and shows how their bargaining positions were reflected in the Constitutional settlement of 1981. He also looks forward to how the new Constitution is likely to change the nature of the Supreme Court and affect the future of intergovernmental conflict in the federation.

Atkinson's chapter outlines the current role of the Canadian Parliament and forecasts how that role may evolve and change. Recent reforms in parliamentary practices, he points out, could lead to the House of Commons becoming a more relevant part of the policy-making process as we move toward the 1990s. In a complementary chapter, Smith places the leadership role of the Cabinet in the parliamentary system within its historical context. He concludes that the central importance of the Cabinet now lies in its governing and representative functions.

In a chapter dealing with federalism and intergovernmental relations in Canada, Stevenson surveys the basic trends of the past decade in this area from a perspective that is unique in Canadian political studies. Professor Stevenson not only provides a political economy approach to his topic but views intergovernmental relations from a centralist vantage point. His work serves as a refreshing departure from the traditional literature on this well-analyzed subject and gives the reader a different glimpse of what may be in store in the next few years.

Layton, as well, provides a fresh look at the growing importance of urban politics from a political economy perspective and, in so doing, succeeds in putting life into what has frequently been a dry and overlooked subject. Being both a professional political scientist and a serving elected official in Canada's largest city, Layton is uniquely qualified to comment on his field.

The final pieces in our collection deal with two of the more bureaucratic aspects of our political system and are written, appropriately, by political scientists who have had extensive practical experience inside the Canadian bureaucracy. Van Loon examines the role of the central agencies in the policy process and identifies trends which began in the late 1960s and projects them into the coming decade. Schultz focuses on what has become one of the major functions of government, the making of regulations. While the regulatory process has been studied extensively elsewhere, his chapter sheds new light on the subject, projects current trends into the future, including an assessment of the debates on deregulation, and identifies possible implications for Canadian political life.

Although this volume includes articles on social and economic trends and on institutions and processes that characterize Canadian politics today, the reader must keep in mind that the subjects discussed are not mutually exclusive. In fact, all the chapters are interrelated in a number of complex ways. Moreover, as editors of the book, we must emphasize again that our chapters do not represent an exhaustive catalogue of all the important issues likely to face Canadians in the next few years. However, we do feel that the subjects addressed are important and very current and that all of them, in one way or another, will be found on the agenda for political decision making as we move toward the 1990s.

The contributors have deliberately written in a clear and uncluttered way. The goal here has not been to dazzle the reader with extensive footnotes or elaborate theoretical frameworks. Rather, our objective has been to present often complex and always extremely important issues to people who, while aware of Canadian politics, do not have the training of professional political scientists. Our aim has been to simplify a complex set of problems so that a wide readership can benefit from the analytical skills and substantive knowledge of our authors.

Michael S. Whittington
Glen Williams

Canadian Politics in the 1980s

Part 1
Political Agenda to the 1990s

Chapter 1
More of Less for Whom? Debating Directions for the Public Sector
Dan Butler and Bruce D. Macnaughton[1]

Introduction

By many indicators of economic performance, the recession experienced in Canada beginning in the spring and summer of 1981 marked the country's most dramatic economic crisis since the Great Depression of the 1930s. For six consecutive calendar quarters, the Gross National Product declined in real terms, shrinking by over 7 percent in total. Business and farm failures reached unprecedented post-war levels, corporate profits and investment contracted sharply in many sectors, and residential construction plummeted. Few elements of the market escaped the wrenching impact of a recession unforeseen by many economists, a recession whose severity and persistence came to startle even the most pessimistic of forecasters.

The real dimensions of the downturn of 1981–82 are revealed most compellingly in the staggering toll of human costs and personal dislocations experienced during this period. For many Canadians, the events of 1981 and 1982, following fast on the economic shocks of the turbulent second half of the 1970s, rekindled haunting images of Depression-era food kitchens and long lines of the unemployed. By early 1983, when the first faint glimmers of a recovery in production had appeared, over 1.5 million Canadians, almost 13 percent of the labour force, were officially out of work. More realistic unofficial measures which included the thousands of other individuals who had abandoned as futile the search for employment estimated the jobless rate at more than 16 percent. For young Canadians entering the labour market for the first time, the picture was even bleaker, with one in four Canadians between the ages of 15 and 25 unable to find work. To them, the prospects for any early secure footing in the job market seemed remote, as employers continued to pare down their labour forces, sell off accumulated inventories and search for labour-saving productivity measures.

For many Canadians still at work, the future must have appeared only marginally brighter. Average real earnings had declined every year since 1978. Double-digit inflation and crippling consumer and mortgage interest rates in excess of 20 percent had only recently abated. Residential and rental accommodation were in critically short supply, and basic shelter costs for many Canadians consumed 40 percent or more of their disposable incomes. Taxes levied by all levels of government seemed to continue to grow, and the price of important durable consumer products appeared beyond the reach of significant numbers of families. Not surprisingly, polls sounding out the economic confidence of Canadians during this period revealed high levels of uncertainty about future prospects, widespread fear for job security, and little faith in the capacity of governments to achieve a speedy and lasting economic recovery.

In the political crucible of the recession, public officials across the country faced daunting tasks. As more Canadians were driven out of the workforce and as hundreds of thousands found themselves in pressing need of social assistance, perhaps for the first time in their lives, the demands placed on public support programs strained the fiscal capacities of many governments to the extreme. On the federal scene, government subsidies to the unemployment insurance system burgeoned from an already high $1.05 billion in fiscal year 1981–82 to $2.18 billion in fiscal year 1982–83, and were projected to reach even higher levels in 1983–84. Similarly, Canada Assistance Plan payments by Ottawa in support of provincial welfare programs grew by 21 percent to $2.78 billion in 1982–83 and were forecast to rise almost one-half billion dollars more in 1983–84. Key revenue-producing tax sources, conversely, exhibited virtual stagnation and in some areas showed absolute declines. The very recession that had served to increase demands on the public purse so rapidly was at the same time drying up revenue sources as many individuals and corporations experienced substantial reductions in their incomes and expenditures susceptible to taxation. At the federal level, once again, total outlays by the government grew by 16.8 percent between 1981–82 and 1982–83, yet budgetary revenues increased by only 1.5 percent over the same period. Almost all provincial administrations across the country were confronted by a similar dilemma. Public sector fiscal planners, as a result, either found themselves facing substantial deficits for the first time or struggled with very significant increases in already large fiscal shortfalls. Ottawa alone anticipated a deficit of $31.3 billion in 1983–84 on a Public Accounts basis, $6.0 billion more than in 1982–83 and fully $17.6 billion higher than the deficit for 1981–82.

In response to their deteriorating fiscal positions, governments characteristically redoubled their efforts to control or cut operating costs. Each level of government sought new ways of shifting the burden of expenditures and the accompanying political costs to other levels: Ottawa re-examined the basis of its system of tax and revenue transfers to the provinces hoping to compel the latter to accept a "fairer" share of program costs. Many provinces, in turn, attempted to pass on their fiscal problems to municipalities, hospitals, universities and school boards by imposing rigid ceilings on revenue assistance and stricter controls on the use by local authorities of provincial funds. Perhaps most dramatically, public employees in almost all jurisdictions found themselves subject to statutory wage controls or wage guideline programs, often more restrictive and clearly of a more selective nature than under the Anti-Inflation Act of 1975–78. For most public employees, controls appeared to promise real wage losses without the benefit of any accompanying price controls. At the federal level, the "6 and 5" controls program embodied in the Public Sector Compensation Restraint Act (Bill C-124) constituted the political flagship in a fight against inflation deemed so crucial as to justify the unilateral suspension of collective bargaining rights for 500,000 employees. In Quebec, the government of René Lévesque legislated temporary public employee wage rollbacks averaging almost 20 percent, and imposed unilaterally new multi-year contracts strictly limiting or reducing many terms and conditions of employment. More recently in British Columbia, the Social Credit administration took wage controls one sweeping step further by extending controls indefinitely, by providing the arbitrary means to reduce nominal income levels across the entire public sector, and by ceding all public employers the right to fire employees without cause—all in the name of fiscal responsibility and economic recovery.

What effect has the experience of steep recession had on the content of political debate in Canada? What do Canadians believe that governments can or should do to bring about economic recovery? The objective of this chapter is to raise some of the questions and issues frequently posed in the current debate over the role to be played by the public sector in confronting the pressing economic problems of the 1980s. In important respects, the contours of today's debate reflect many of the same concerns which marked public discussions in the latter half of the 1970s. During this period, political pundits often talked of a "shift to the right"—a "new conservatism"—in the attitudes of Canadians. This "shift," ostensibly parallelling developments in the United States, Britain and other western liberal democracies, was said to be characterized by increasing public attention to a series of critical concerns: (1) the size of government deficits and the proportion of budgetary resources required to service the public debt; (2) a fear that public expenditures were "out of control" and beyond the influence of most citizens; (3) opposition to new government spending programs, in particular in the area of social assistance, coupled with a passion for revealing "waste" in existing services; (4) disenchantment with the burden of government regulations and the level and scope of public taxes; and (5) a conviction that public workforces were too large and public employees overpaid for jobs performed inefficiently and ineffectively.

These concerns clearly persist. In a sense, however, there appears to have been something of a qualitative change—more than just a greater intensity—in the way the debate over such issues is framed. At the risk of greatly oversimplifying a very complex public opinion climate, it might be argued that concern has shifted somewhat in the early 1980s from the emotive question, "Has government grown too large?", to a perhaps more basic debate over the underlying issue, "What roles *should* the public sector play? What *should* be the nature of public sector intervention in the economy?" In somewhat the same fashion that the Great Depression of the 1930s launched a re-evaluation of the role of government in regulating the economy—out of which emerged the new Keynesian "consensus"—so too are there signs that the experience of a far-reaching recession in the first part of the 1980s may be serving to crystallize debate again, at least among opinion leaders, over the fundamental orientation of the public sector to the economy. "Neo-conservative" appeals for fiscal responsibility and expenditure cutbacks, heady wine for some in 1978, now no longer seem novel. Government restraint has become a virtually universal reality, yet economic prosperity seems as far away as ever. Increasingly, observers question whether government can, in fact, do anything about the economy. Economists wonder whether the usual "fine-tuning" tools of fiscal policy favoured by governments are really very useful at all when only very blunt measures—a deliberate policy to engineer a recession—seem to have had a significant impact on inflation. Some critics ask whether it might not be better to change course radically and reduce to a very pronounced degree government intervention in the economy. Might it not be time to go beyond the public belt-tightening of recent years and determine whether the very existence of many types of government programs is in fact justified?

Responses to these questions vary widely across the political spectrum—from the unabashed Canadian adherents of Reaganomics and Thatcherism to critics on the left arguing for new forms of state intervention; from the orthodox monetarists and free marketeers of the right to the social conscience of the Roman Catholic Bishops' Declaration; from the advocates of further public workforce reductions and permanent public sector wage controls to the proponents of more public sector spending and job creation programs. Whether a new "consensus" can or will emerge from the interaction of these viewpoints is at this point far from clear. Indeed, it remains to be seen whether the "debate" itself will continue and intensify or, with a return to more expansive economic conditions, recede from the agenda of public discussion.

To place the debate over the role of the public sector in perspective, several basic questions must first be broached: What is the "public sector"? How and why has the size of the public sector changed in recent years?

What Is the Public Sector?

During the federal election campaign of 1979, the Progressive Conservative party promised to reduce the size of the federal public sector by some 60,000 positions. After the election, the new Treasury Board President began planning for this task with a vigour and dedication which unsettled many public employees and greatly upset their unions. As the first few months of nervous anticipation passed, however, it became apparent that the promise of sweeping personnel reductions was fading in the face of political and logistical pressures. The original language of "decisive restraint action" was soon replaced by one of "gradual attrition" and "rationalization."

Besides attesting to the practical problems confronting any government party which attempts to pare the size of a large and politically resourceful bureaucracy, the events of 1979-80 illustrate important aspects of the public sector definition problem. Where earlier Conservative statements implied that reductions would be exacted primarily in the central departments and agencies of the federal government—the traditional "civil service"—later pronouncements suggested that the cutbacks would be spread more widely across a range of regulatory bodies, crown corporations and public enterprises. Thus, although initial reports had hinted at plans to eliminate 60,000 positions from a public sector perhaps as small as 280,000 employees (i.e., a 20 percent decrease), later revisions enlarged the universe affected to include perhaps as many as 575,000 workers (thereby reducing the proportionate cutback by half). Either scenario would certainly have yielded a significantly reduced government workforce, yet the political costs and benefits for the Conservatives of trimming a 575,000-position "public sector" by 60,000 versus those of paring a much smaller 280,000-employee universe by an equivalent amount would have in all likelihood been quite different. The range of activities affected as well as the severity of individual program reductions would have varied greatly from one scenario to the other. In the end, of course, a second election intervened. No comparably sweeping proposals for federal public sector personnel reductions have since surfaced, at least in official party positions.

Definitions of the public sector are, if anything, more fickle in the provincial sphere. On the one hand, it may be argued that the provincial public sector comprises only the executive departments of the Crown (once again, the more traditional notion of the "civil service"). On the other, some analysts contend that the concept of the "provincial public sector," if it is to have any real meaning at all, must also include a large number of commissions, Crown corporations and other bodies created by government, as well as institutions involved in the performance of the so-called "parapublic" services. The latter pre-eminently include education and health care activities which, taken together, account for a major proportion of current provincial expenditures and much of the real growth in provincial spending in the post-war period. Undoubtedly, inferences about changes in the size and character of the provincial public sector based on a broad definition will differ substantially from conclusions reached in examining narrower "civil service" trends. Political arguments supporting or challenging expenditure trends will choose whichever formulation of the public realm best conforms to a particular set of ideological predispositions and/or partisan needs.

Efforts to establish objective criteria by which a common, satisfactory definition of the "public sector" may be derived almost inevitably encounter severe problems. It has been suggested, for example, that a good working definition of the public sector, either federal or provincial, would be obtained if all government agencies or activities funded from a common source under the same budgetary regime were gathered together under a single rubric. The "federal public sector" might, accordingly, be construed as including all public programs requiring support from the Consolidated Revenue Fund. While such a definition would certainly encompass most major areas of federal activity, it would nonetheless exclude a number of important appendages of the federal government. For instance, proprietary crown corporations which normally operate on a self-financing basis largely independent of parliamentary appropriations (e.g., Eldorado Nuclear Limited, Air Canada) would fall among the entities excluded by such a definition. Conversely, a literal interpretation of the "common source of funding" criterion might logically contend that activity formally under provincial jurisdiction but jointly financed by the federal government could be considered in a sense part of the federal public sector. Certainly, the large-scale financial involvement of Ottawa in a range of ostensibly provincial activities must be taken into account if trends in real federal public sector growth are to be comprehensively evaluated. Indeed, those who criticize the size of the federal government rarely consider that approximately 20 percent of federal expenditures are required annually to support provincial programs. In this sense at least, boundaries separating the "federal public sector" and respective "provincial public sectors" often become very indistinct.

Another definitional criterion sometimes advanced in discussions of the nature of the public sector centres about the issue of "decision-making autonomy." In brief, public and para-public bodies judged to enjoy decision-making autonomy from their parent governments are, by virtue of this "independence," considered by some analysts to lie effectively outside the public realm. Following this line of reasoning, it might be contended that provincially established hydroelectric utilities which are autonomous in direct administrative and managerial terms do not form part of the "provincial public sector" in the conventional sense of the term. Ontario Hydro, for example, might be viewed as an institution separate from the Ontario public sector and an entity whose expansion need not be reckoned in assessing general patterns of provincial public sector growth. However, equally persuasive reasons can be found for treating Ontario Hydro and other institutions similar to it as integral components of the provincial public sector despite apparent decision-making autonomy. Many observers in fact assert that the autonomy of such bodies is sometimes more symbolic than real, and that basic policy priorities guiding their operation are decided beyond their boardrooms in the highest bureaucratic and political councils of government. If this assertion is accepted, Ontario Hydro and other comparable agencies must be construed as belonging to the same decisional universe as the rest of the more conventionally understood "public sector." In summary, the effective locus of decision-making authority in many public and parapublic agencies is often difficult to establish, making judgments about autonomy and sectoral status rather hazardous.

The problem of defining the public sector, it would seem, is less than straightforward. Equally perplexing at times is the task of selecting appropriate indicators for measuring public sector size, however one may choose to delimit the public realm. Different indicators—of expenditures, deficits, public debt, employment levels, public wage bills—reveal various faces of the public sector. Once again, the choice of the "best" measure or measures often reflects a judgment as much political as it may be analytic. As the following section will seek to show, discussions about public sector trends frequently bring together different types of evidence, sometimes conflicting, and often too readily accepted at face value.

How Much Has the Public Sector Grown?

Government Expenditures

One of the most commonly employed means of assessing trends in public sector expansion and restraint is to evaluate changes in the level of government expenditures in constant dollars expressed as a proportion of the Gross National Product (GNP), also in constant dollars. This expression provides an approximate indication of the relative size of government compared to the size of the economy as a whole after the confounding effects of inflation have been removed. Data portraying the growth over time of total government expenditures in Canada as a percentage of the GNP are presented in Table 1.1.

Table 1.1 shows that real government spending as a proportion of GNP rose from 28.6 percent in 1947 to 40.8 percent in 1981. More comprehensive time series data reveal that the largest increase in fact occurred over the ten years beginning in 1965, with little significant change subsequently. Figures from 1982 and, when they become available, from 1983 will show new, temporary increases in the percentage of GNP accounted for by government, not because government has necessarily grown anew but because the rest of the economy has contracted.

Table 1.1
Total Government Expenditures in Canada
(All Levels), by Type for Selected Years,
as % of GNP
(Constant 1971 dollars)

Year	Total Expenditures	Exhaustive Expenditures	Transfer Expenditures
1947	28.6	17.7	10.9
1950	26.4	18.4	8.0
1955	31.3	22.9	8.4
1960	32.5	21.2	11.3
1965	31.9	21.8	10.1
1970	36.9	23.7	13.2
1975	41.0	22.6	18.4
1980	40.7	20.2	20.5
1981	40.8	19.7	21.1
1982	45.5	21.1	24.4

Source: Statistics Canada, *National Income and Expenditure Accounts*, various years, and calculated from Government of Canada, Department of Finance, *Economic Review 1982*, Tables 4, 43 and 50 and *Economic Review 1983*, Tables 4, 42 and 49.

The total expenditure ratios outlined in Table 1.1 serve only as very general measures and have little direct economic significance in and of themselves. More useful insights perhaps follow from the question "What do governments actually purchase with their expenditures?" An important distinction frequently used in this vein divides expenditures into those which consume goods and services which might otherwise be available for other uses in private sector activities ("exhaustive expenditures") and those which merely shift income from one individual to another within the private sector ("transfer expenditures"). The former category includes government purchases of equipment and material and spending on public infrastructure; the latter subsumes income maintenance programs such as old age pensions, family allowances and unemployment insurance. In the case of transfer expenditures, governments decide who will receive support as well as the means for collecting required revenues, but the recipients of payments, not governments, determine how the money is ultimately to be spent. In this sense, transfer expenditures may not represent a direct claim on economic output in the same way as do exhaustive expenditures on goods and services. When critics argue that the growth of government reduces the economic resources controlled by the private market, they probably have exhaustive expenditures more directly in mind. As shown in Table 1.1, however, this category of spending has increased only marginally as a percentage of GNP since 1947. On the other hand, the proportion of GNP represented by transfer payments has more than doubled, increasing from as low as 8.0 percent in 1950 to 24.4 percent in 1982. It would appear that assertions of sustained government growth in the post-war period are only accurate with respect to the transfer expenditure category. If spending in this area does not in the final analysis "remove" resources from the private market, then charges that public sector expansion has constrained the economy may be misleading.

The information presented in Table 1.1 portrays expenditures for government in Canada treated as a single entity. It is also important to identify and examine spending trends for each level of government in the country to permit more exact delineation of growth patterns. Table 1.2 disaggregates total government expenditures into federal, provincial and local categories and expresses each as a percentage of GNP over time.

Table 1.2
Expenditures by Level of Government
Selected Years
(as % of GNP)

Year	Federal	Provincial	Local
1947	14.1	5.2	4.4
1950	11.5	5.7	4.9
1955	15.3	5.2	5.8
1960	15.0	7.3	7.3
1965	12.9	6.8	8.1
1970	13.8	10.2	9.4
1975	16.8	12.2	8.8
1980	16.5	12.7	8.6
1981	17.5	12.4	8.5
1982	20.1	13.6	9.4

Source: Richard M. Bird, *Financing Canadian Government: A Qualitative Overview* (Toronto: Canadian Tax Foundation, 1979) and calculated from *Economic Review 1982*, Tables 3, 52, 57 and 59 and *Economic Review 1983*, Tables 4, 51, 56 and 58.

Expenditures trends reported in Table 1.2 indicate clearly that provincial spending has experienced the most pronounced increase of the three levels of government in the post-war period, followed by growth in local and federal government activities. This conclusion accords closely with earlier observations about the rapid expansion of provincial services, particularly in the education and health care fields. Note, however, that intergovernmental transfers are assigned in these tables to the level of government that actually spends the money rather than the level that provides the funds. The figures in these tables consequently do not reflect the extent of federal funding of provincial programs or of provincial funding of local governments. The "local" public sector includes spending by boards of education, municipalities, police commissions and other institutions which are frequently required to provide certain mandatory services by provincial statute.

Table 1.3
Federal Fiscal Transfers to Other
Levels of Government, Selected Years

Year	As % of GNP	As % of Federal Expenditures	As % of Provincial Revenues
1947	1.4	9.2	14.4
1950	1.4	10.5	19.9
1955	1.6	9.2	11.0
1960	2.5	14.3	25.6
1965	2.4	15.9	27.4
1970	3.8	21.6	31.1
1975	4.5	21.2	33.8
1980	4.4	21.1	27.7
1981	4.3	19.7	26.8
1982	4.4	18.8	27.3

Source: Bird, *op. cit.*, and calculated from *Economic Recovery 1982*, Tables 3, 52 and 66 and *Economic Review 1983*, Tables 4, 51 and 65.

Federal transfers to the provinces, as depicted in Table 1.3, increased as a percentage of GNP and also as a percentage of federal expenditures and provincial revenues throughout most of the post-war period, although they have declined slightly since 1975. Federal transfers to the provinces currently represent about one-fifth of federal expenditures and over one-quarter of provincial revenues. Given the large federal budgetary deficit and the fact that many provinces, at least until recently, have experienced surpluses or much lower shortfalls, it is perhaps not surprising that the federal government has attempted of late to reduce its fiscal transfers to the provinces. The actual dollar amounts involved have become very substantial and constitute a crucial component of the revenues available to provincial governments. Indeed, for provinces with weak economic bases, federal transfer payments may be the major revenue source supporting important program activities. The impact of fiscal transfers and the dependence which results must be closely considered in any evaluation of comparative federal and provincial growth patterns.

Deficits and the Public Debt

One of the most deep-seated and cherished ideals that Canadians seem to associate with "good government" is the "balanced budget"; that is, a budget free of any deficit. Although many economists view government deficits with equanimity, the public and the business community generally appear to link deficits to a lack of government discipline, to fiscal irresponsibility, to waste and even (for some) to rampant socialism. While some critics grudgingly regard deficit financing as a temporary evil to be tolerated, others argue that governments must move *now* to "balance the books" and "live within their means." Government expenditures must be reduced, public payrolls cut and a policy of "pay as you go" adopted.

What in fact does the deficit measure? It appears that the meaning of the terms "deficit" and "surplus" are quite different in the public and private sectors. Senior levels of government, for instance, treat "capital expenditures" exactly like "current expenditures," a practice not followed elsewhere. When the federal government purchases airplanes or constructs a building, the total cost is treated as an immediate expenditure regardless of the continuing value of the assets acquired or the real initial outlay. If the total value of these acquisitions in a given year plus the total value of regular operating expenses for that year exceeds current receipts, then the government is considered to have a "deficit." By way of contrast, a householder (or business) who buys a $100,000 home and takes out a $60,000 mortgage to finance the purchase would normally claim only $40,000—the actual amount immediately invested—as expenditures in an accounting of earnings and outlays for the year of purchase. Subsequently, the householder's budget would be said to be in balance if his or her current earnings equalled current expenditures plus annual amortization costs. Were the federal government the purchaser instead, using the same method of financing, the entire $100,000 would be treated as an expenditure in the year of purchase, and the balance of revenues and outlays for that year would take on a very different appearance. This unusual feature of public accounting practices is partially reconciled by the fact that governments generally do not charge themselves depreciation on their properties nor treat payments on the principal of their debts as a normal charge in their annual budget, as do most private enterprises. Nevertheless, if major capital expenditures were recorded in the Public Accounts more in line with orthodox private sector practice, it seems probable that government deficit figures would be substantially reduced even after adding capital depreciation costs.

A further noteworthy feature of government accounting is the customary exclusion from budget balance calculations of the transactions of certain major social insurance and government pension funds (e.g., the Unemployment Insurance Account, the Canada Pension Plan) as well as the profits/losses which emanate from government enterprises and from various other loans, investments and advances. Such items *are* included under a different and less publicized accounting system, the National Income and Expenditure Accounts. Deficit or surplus figures using this system can vary significantly from those calculated on a Public Accounts basis. In 1981, the federal budgetary deficit was reported at $11.4 billion in the Public Accounts but stood at only $7.5 billion on a National Income and Expenditure Accounts basis (calendar year). While this difference might seem merely the result of some accounting sleight-of-hand, it does in reality point to the arbitrary nature of the definition of the government deficit so widely imbued in the public consciousness. Indeed, it seems clear that we have come to apply considerably more rigorous accounting criteria to the public realm than we ordinarily expect of most private sector undertakings.

If our understanding of government deficits is based on somewhat arbitrary figures, how sound is our appreciation of the closely associated notion of the "public debt"? Governments must, of course, borrow to meet requirements arising from budgetary deficits, but their debt transactions are not quite like those of a family or small business which borrows from a bank, or a corporation which sells bonds on the financial market. Where the resulting debt in the latter cases is to some outside actor, government borrowing, at least at the federal level, draws largely from its own shareholders—the people of Canada. Approximately 90 percent of the national debt is "owned" domestically. In 1981, the Government of Canada raised $12.1 billion to meet its debt, $8 billion of which flowed from sales of Canada Savings Bonds while only $300 million (U.S.) was borrowed on foreign bond markets. The frequent charge that every man, woman and child in Canada carries a legacy of over $5,000 in national debt (1982) is thus interesting but not particularly meaningful. Every man, woman and child (or their institutions) also on average owns credits of virtually the same value in the form of treasury bills, marketable bonds and Canada Savings Bonds. The public debt, from this perspective, might almost be construed as representing shareholder equity rather than individual liability. Moreover, interest payments made to the Canadian citizens and corporations who hold most of the public debt are subject to taxation. A significant proportion of government debt interest payments thus returns to the public treasury in the form of tax revenues. (Note that the debt situation *may well* be more serious in the case of some provinces, provincial enterprises, municipalities and utilities. Here, deficits are financed to a far greater degree through borrowings on foreign bond markets. Such transactions incur significant external liabilities which must be repaid in the currency of the lender with possible adverse consequences for the value of the Canadian dollar. Moreover, as non-residents, most foreign bondholders do not pay taxes in Canada on their capital income. Public concern for these situations ironically seems much less acute than anxiety for the highly visible federal government deficit whose form, as we have seen, bears quite different implications.)

Much of the above points to the difficulty of interpreting the meaning of deficit and debt statistics, and to determining their actual impact on the economy. Can we at least stand on firmer ground by placing current public financing "problems" in some historical perspective?

It is frequently argued that deficits are the rule rather than the exception in government finance, with the unwarranted implication that this is not the case outside of government. In actual fact, the federal government has experienced a deficit on nineteen occasions since 1947— only approximately half the time—and provincial governments as an aggregate have similarly failed to "balance their books" during twenty of the intervening fiscal years. Significantly, fourteen of the nineteen federal government deficits occurred in the years 1958–1963 and 1975–1982, both periods of very slow economic growth or recession. The record of continuing deficits at the federal level in the latter of these periods has apparently done much to create the impression that budgetary shortfalls are now natural or inevitable. Critics allege that this development reflects the recent "excessive spending" of governments. Recalling Table 1.2, however, it would appear that governments have experienced a period of expenditure restraint since 1975, suggesting that it is unlikely that "excessive" spending increases have contributed significantly to government deficits. Government expenditures in fact grew most rapidly prior to 1975 when budget surpluses rather than deficits were the norm.

For many observers, the cost of servicing the debt rather than the sheer incidence of deficits represents a prime concern. Canadians, it would seem, have come to believe that interest payments on the public debt consume an ever-increasing share of government expenditures and of the Gross National Product. At least with respect to the most recent period, their concerns are probably well founded. Data expressing interest payments on the public debt as a percentage of both total government expenditures and of the GNP reveal a gradual decline between 1947 and 1975 but a relatively dramatic increase thereafter. By 1981, debt service payments accounted for 15 cents out of every government dollar spent and approximately 6 percent of GNP.

During prosperous periods, government revenues tend to equal or exceed expenditures, and the resulting surpluses can be applied to reduce the outstanding debt. In times of slow growth or recession, government budgets move in the direction of a deficit as financial demand outpaces revenues. The concept of a "cyclically adjusted" budget balance, a measure of the budget balance that would have prevailed if the economy had been operating at an average level of activity, has been developed to take these trends into account. Application of this measure suggests that recent government deficits would be substantially reduced or would even become surpluses if an assumed "average" level of economic activity had occurred. In 1981, for example, had real GNP increased by 3.1 percent,

Table 1.4
Interest Payments on the Public Debt
as a Percentage of GNP and Government
Expenditures

Year	Total Government		Federal Government		Provincial Government	
	% of GNP	% of Expenditures	% of GNP	% of Expenditures	% of GNP	% of Expenditures
1947	4.1	17.5	3.4	21.7	0.5	8.5
1950	2.9	13.3	2.3	18.0	0.4	6.1
1955	2.3	8.8	1.7	10.1	0.3	5.1
1960	2.8	9.6	2.0	11.2	0.4	4.0
1965	3.0	10.1	1.9	12.3	0.5	4.3
1970	3.8	10.4	2.1	12.2	0.8	5.4
1975	4.0	9.6	2.2	10.4	1.1	5.8
1980	5.4	13.0	3.3	15.9	1.4	7.3
1981	6.2	14.7	4.1	19.0	1.5	8.0
1982	7.2	15.3	4.7	19.1	1.8	8.7

Source: Calculated from *Economic Review 1982*, Tables 10, 50, 52 and 57 and *Economic Review 1983*, Tables 4, 49, 51 and 56. Reproduced by permission of the Minister of Supply and Services Canada.

unemployment remained at 6.3 percent and labour productivity grown by 0.5 percent (all according to longer-term averages), it has been estimated by the Department of Finance that the federal government deficit on a National Accounts basis would have been only $3.2 billion as opposed to the actual result of $7.5 billion. To be sure, the veracity of these "assumed" indicator values is very much open to question. The actual employment rate has *not* fallen below 6.3 percent since 1974, and real GNP has *not* increased by as much as 3.1 percent since 1978. Nevertheless, it does seem quite likely that a significant proportion of government deficits is a product of cyclical trends in economic activity rather than government spending and taxing policy.

The impact of inflation on deficits and debts is particularly important to note. Inflation causes a decline in the real value of the stock of outstanding debt. Interest payments on the debt must therefore be viewed as consisting of both a premium for the erosion of the real value of the lender's asset and a real return on investment. The greater the rate of inflation, the higher debt interest payments will be pushed. To measure the effect of inflation on the deficit, economists have developed the concept of an "inflation-adjusted" deficit. Operationalizations of this concept provide some indication of the budget balance that would have prevailed in the long run in a non-inflationary environment. It has been calculated that the inflation premium on debt interest payments in 1982 comprised approximately 80 percent of the total cost, thus reducing the share of GNP devoted in real terms to this item from 4.7 percent to roughly 0.8 percent. The fact that high interest rates dramatically increase the cost of servicing the debt is, of course, to be expected. The irony is that recent high interest rates are the deliberate consequence of the government's own anti-inflation program. Its policy has consisted essentially of tight monetary and fiscal restrictions and changes in the Bank of Canada discount rate in lockstep with rates established by the Federal Reserve Board in the United States. Although the economic recession and high interest charges "explain" a large proportion of the deficits experienced in the early 1980s, it is entirely unclear whether the federal government will be willing or able to change the very policies which have led to its deficit "problem" in the first place.

Public Employment and Wages

Trends in public sector expansion and restraint are also frequently evaluated through an examination of changes in the aggregate level of public employment. The proportion of the total labour force employed in public programs is viewed by many analysts as a leading indicator of the impact of government in the economy. Unfortunately, public employment studies are troubled not only by the lack of a common definition of the "public sector" noted earlier, but also by disagreement over the best source of public employment statistics.

Several prominent attempts to enumerate the complete "public" component in the Canadian labour force have found that almost one-quarter of the labour force works in the public sector. A recent Fraser Institute estimate for 1981 identified 1.02 million Canadians in direct government employment (federal, provincial and municipal) and a total of 2.24 million individuals in the broader public sector including teachers, school board employees, hospital workers, and employees in public enterprises. Notably, these figures accord closely with a detailed accounting undertaken by Richard Bird of the situation as of 1975. It would appear that the relative size of the public sector has not changed significantly over the years separating the two studies, suggesting that restraint policies practised by most governments have apparently succeeded in limiting public workforce growth, but have seldom accomplished significant reductions. The initiatives launched by the Social Credit government of British Columbia in July 1983 may, however, mark a new and more ominous phase for public employees. Claiming a new election mandate, the Bennett administration announced a series of unprecedented measures, some of which could result in the elimination of 25 percent of provincial public service positions (through firings rather than attrition).

By any standard, one-quarter of the total labour force in the public realm is an impressive figure and one which clearly underscores the very major role played by the public sector in the Canadian labour market. Certainly, when dependants of public employees are entered into the calculus and/or estimates made of the number of individuals who receive the majority of their income in the form of government transfer payments, the overall proportion of the Canadian population directly or indirectly supported by the public sector would be very substantial indeed. Does this then imply that the public sector is *too* large? Such a question, of course, is essentially political and ideological. No set of data can prove or disprove the allegation that government is too big. Data *can* be gathered, however, to test the closely related charge levelled by public sector critics that government has grown at a disproportionate pace in recent years. Historical figures for the last two decades yield little support for this proposition. Indeed, the percentage of total employment accounted for by the public sector has remained almost constant over this period, standing at 22.2 percent in 1961, 23.4 percent in 1971 and approximately 24 to 25 percent in 1981. The public sector, it would appear, is only marginally larger in *relative* employment terms today than it was twenty years ago, despite very substantial increases in its *absolute* size over the same period. The composition of public employment by level of government has, however, changed to a pronounced degree. Beginning in the mid-1960s, the federal government component of total employment began to experience a relative decline as growth occurred most rapidly in the provincial sphere and, in particular, in the para-public services. Many studies have confirmed this pattern and suggest that allegations of disproportionate federal government expansion are either misinformed, or if relevant to any sector, more appropriate to discussions of provincial and local governments, and their associated services.

Observers who charge that public workforces have become too large often express a parallel opinion that public sector positions tend to be overpaid compared to similar jobs in the private sector. The merits of this allegation are difficult to establish, particularly inasmuch as adequate points of comparison for many public sector roles cannot be found in the private employment market. Where intersectoral comparisons are feasible, problems in appraising different compensation practices, benefit provisions and job classification standards frequently prevent the drawing of firm or reliable conclusions. Varying rates of sectoral unionization, differences in workforce demographic and educational profiles, and regional income variations also inhibit the calculation of valid wage differentials. Fortunately, several studies have begun the task of accounting for the effects of these and other factors. Their analyses generally suggest that the purported compensation advantages available in the public sector frequently are of a marginal nature and are neither consistent across occupational categories nor between different levels of government. A widely publicized 1980 Conference Board study evaluating public sector–private sector income differentials was able to identify higher public sector rates only in certain provincial public enterprises and at the local government level. In other public employment settings, pay rates for public workers either parallelled those of private industry or, in a number of cases, lagged behind. It is interesting to note, nonetheless, that there is some long-term evidence that public payrolls are increasing as a proportion of total labour income. In 1961, the category "public administration and defence," albeit a very narrow construction of the "public sector," accounted for approximately 6.9 percent of labour income in Canada. By 1982, preliminary estimates show the comparable contemporary figure to be 9.2 percent.

In the final analysis, the political importance of public employment and wage data should perhaps be viewed with caution. Where governments judge that there is a political profit to be made, experience suggests that public workforces and public employee salaries will be targeted for special restrictive treatment regardless of the "reality" documented in data. The example of the spread of informal and formal wage controls across most government jurisdictions in 1982 and 1983 arguably provides a strong case in point. Wage settlement figures bear little or no evidence that public sector workers had either received increases greater than their private sector counterparts or had succeeded in keeping pace with inflation since the 1978 termination of Anti-Inflation Board controls. Public employee incomes, however, were isolated by successive governments across the country for selective inflation-fighting controls "for the sake of economic recovery." In the political world of "six and five," it would seem, actual labour market statistics assume no greater importance than public decision makers are willing to accord them.

Why Has the Size of the Public Sector Changed?

Just as various approaches are taken to the problem of measuring changes in public sector size, so too do analysts provide a range of responses to the question, "How is public sector expansion explained?" At least three principal types of explanatory models are available. *Socio-economic* approaches stress the importance of external economic and social factors as key determinants of the growth of government. *Organizational* explanations of public sector expansion focus attention on pressures originating within the bureaucracy rather than on external social and economic factors. *Political* explanations, finally, underline the importance of such factors as party competition, elite ideology and pressure group demands as determinants of expenditure and employment levels.

Socioeconomic Explanations

The impact of inflation on expenditure growth has been widely recognized, though it is sometimes overlooked in popular debate. If figures representing total government expenditures in current dollars are "deflated" to account for the effects of the pronounced price increases which have occurred over the postwar period and particularly in the 1970s and early 1980s, then the "real" rate of government growth for these years declines appreciably.

Inflation influences the level of public expenditures in several ways. The first, often termed the "relative price effect," acknowledges the fact that the price of many goods and services purchased by government has risen at a much faster rate than prices in general. Even if the public sector continues to purchase the same package of goods and services from year to year, total public spending as a relative proportion of the economy may tend nevertheless to increase given the "relative price effect." Another consequence of inflation involves the revenue generation system. Under a progressive tax regime, increases in nominal personal income caused by inflation may force individuals into higher tax brackets even though their real income may not have changed. Barring effective tax adjustment formulae, moderate inflation and economic growth will thus generate higher government revenues without a change in actual tax rates, allowing governments to spend more while avoiding the political penalties associated with a formally announced tax increase. (We should note that the federal government moved in 1982 to place limitations on the indexation of personal income tax income brackets for two years, a move designed to bring extra funds into federal coffers.)

Population growth rates and demographic change are also important determinants of public expenditure levels. The costs to government of various health care, education and pension programs are particularly sensitive to variations in the age composition of the population. Expenditures on pensions, for example, are escalating rapidly as the number of eligible recipients and the average duration of support both increase proportionately. In addition, normal population growth in itself brings about greater government spending as public officials seek to maintain existing levels and types of services for an expanding universe of users.

A further socioeconomic factor is the level of real personal disposable income. According to some arguments, government spending
tends to increase over time because the demand for public expenditures
rises with upward movement in real personal disposable income. The
reason for this relationship is said to lie in an increased preference among
citizens for "publicly" rather than "privately" supplied goods as real after-
tax incomes rise. Once basic needs for food, shelter and clothing have
been satisfied, public demand for such services as parks, improved roads
and cultural facilities is thought to increase. Public expenditures consequently expand at a disproportionate rate as governments attempt to
satisfy increased requests for public goods and services.

The suggested relationships between public sector expansion and
various socioeconomic factors outlined to this point are normally
associated with studies written from a liberal ideological perspective.
Analysts assessing government growth from a non-liberal viewpoint,
however, also frequently stress the salience of social and economic
variables. In particular, political economists influenced by the Marxist
tradition discern an inherent historical link between public sector growth
and the functional requirements of social and economic organization
under capitalism. The historical expansion of state activities is seen as the
product of the ever-increasing need for public agencies to assist private
sector economic ventures, to maintain the social relations which define
control over production, and to assume the social costs which attend the
process of capitalist development.

Organizational Explanations

Unlike socioeconomic explanations which stress the influence of external
environmental factors, organizational explanations look to pressures originating within government as the primary case of public sector expansion. According to this perspective, bureaucracies judge their "success"
principally in terms of their own growth. Internal influences and
patterns of behaviour characteristic of bureaucratic organizations tend
to promote a constant increase in the scope of activities undertaken by
component agencies and, in doing so, expand the possibilities of greater
monetary and non-monetary rewards for the bureaucrats themselves.
As more resources are channelled into an area of activity over time,
public employment levels grow, leading in turn to additional demands for
further program expansion from the burgeoning public workforce and
from the beneficiaries of the program who are seen as allies of the public
employees who deliver the service.

A related line of argument holds that governments inherit a long
legacy of past decisions and statutory commitments which make very
difficult all but gradual modifications of existing programs in the short

run. Many contend that the only modifications which will be seriously entertained are those which incrementally enrich rather than reduce the existing level of expenditures. The underlying implication of this "incrementalist" interpretation is that policy makers have neither the time, the information nor the resources required to evaluate all or even most programs every year. Policy makers proceed incrementally because to do so reduces the difficulty of decision making and serves as an aid to calculation.

Political Explanations

Political explanations of public sector spending and growth emphasize the key role played by pressures generated within the political system in influencing the expansion of public expenditures and employment levels. It has been argued, for instance, that electoral competition induces governing parties to increase public expenditure levels to ensure their re-election. According to this view, electorally insecure governments spend more than secure governments, and increases in spending levels mandated by concerned politicians are generally greatest in the period immediately preceding an election contest. Furthermore, taxes or borrowing required to finance such election-year largesse will normally be postponed until after an election in order to avoid adverse voter reaction. Pre-election "years of plenty" may be followed by post-election "years of famine" as the governing party times its public expenditure decisions so as to maximize political support.

In contrast to the electoral competition thesis which de-emphasizes the role of ideology, other political explanations suggest that public expenditure policies are best understood as a function of party ideology. In this vein, several inquiries indicate that social democratic and labour parties have expanded the "welfare state" at a much faster rate than more conservative parties. The implicit theme running through such works is that more pronounced public sector growth and, in particular, more rapid increases in the level of social security expenditures should be expected where government embraces a leftist or redistributive ideology.

A variant of the political approach to explaining public sector expansion argues that the changing strength and activities of interest groups contribute directly to government growth. As pressure groups have become organizationally more resourceful and politically more vociferous in their representations to government, their influence on policy makers has been greatly enhanced. The principal expression of this influence takes the form of increased public spending in programs designed to satisfy the membership of active groups. A number of studies, for instance, suggest that the expansion of social security programs in a number of western liberal democracies is closely related to the growing strength of organized labour acting as a vigorous pressure group not only in the industrial relations setting but directly in the political system as well.

Each of the three types of explanations of the growth of the public sector discussed above directs our attention to particular aspects of empirical reality. In this sense, the three general approaches identified should be seen at least to some extent as *complementary* rather than necessarily antagonistic.

The principal difficulty with many socioeconomic explanations is that they frequently beg the question of exactly *how* the demographic and economic variables translate into policy outputs. Clearly, political and bureaucratic institutions mediate between changes in the environment and changes in policy outcomes, but most socioeconomic explanations make little attempt to describe the nature of this mediation. Similarly, arguments which purport to explain the rise of public expenditures as a function of rising incomes often fail to specify how citizens make government aware of the quantity of public goods and services they are willing to "purchase." Proponents of the "relative price effect" argument also seem to avoid dealing with the intervention of political actors and mechanisms. Governments are not compelled to maintain service levels regardless of rising costs. Socioeconomic explanations, in sum, neglect the role of the decision maker in the policy-making process and assume that politicians and bureaucrats enjoy very little discretion in the decisions they must make.

Organizational explanations, in contrast, do bring bureaucrats back into the policy process by identifying as central determinants of current expenditures "the number of years a program has been in operation" and "the previous year's level of expenditure," to name only two. It is unclear, however, that passage of time can in any way be considered in and of itself a fully satisfactory "explanation" for the growth of the public sector. Nor is it entirely evident why current expenditure levels are "explained" by the previous year's rate of spending. Even apparent stability in aggregate expenditure levels from year to year may in fact mask greater changes occurring within individual programs or departments. Many observers thus regard "incrementalism" as a descriptive rather than an explanatory approach, and allege that its proponents frequently move back and forth from description to prescription, making it difficult to distinguish between the "is" and the "ought."

Political explanations of public sector growth also display certain serious weaknesses. Authors who stress interparty electoral competition as a key determinant of public sector expansion assume without evidence that governing parties are aware of voter preferences and, more importantly, the intensity of these preferences. This approach also presumes that political parties compete for votes by increasing expenditures rather than lowering taxes, an equally reasonable possibility.

Ideological explanations stress the importance of party ideology as a determinant of public sector growth and allege that social democratic or labour parties will spend more and have different expenditure priorities than more conservative or right-wing parties. Support for this proposition has been mixed. Even if findings were more uniformly positive, however, it remains questionable that a larger public sector will necessarily be a more redistributive one. If, as some critics contend, much public spending and employment consists of subsidies to the already well-to-do, then it seems as reasonable to expect that conservative parties will spend more than social democratic ones.

Finally, the thesis that public sector growth can be explained by the strength of pressure groups or the organization of the political market merits criticism on several grounds. Proponents of this argument normally avoid specifying the mechanisms whereby increases in the strength of pressure groups lead to greater public expenditures in the program fields sought by such groups. The intervening role of decision makers in the policy process is largely neglected, as is an explanation of why some groups are more successful than others in having their demands satisfied.

The Debate: More or Less for Whom?

A number of basic issues of definition, measurement and explanation have been emphasized to this point. Much of the discussion has underscored the complexity of trends in public sector expansion and restraint, and points to the need for care in evaluating allegations which are frequently made about the impact of government on the economy. With these notes of caution in mind, the final section returns to look in more detail at the debate over the future of the public sector. What are some critics saying about the roles played by government, and what are the implications of the changes they propose?

As mentioned at the outset, various themes and catch-phrases mark the popular face of criticism of the public sector: "Governments are living beyond their means—or rather, beyond *our* means." "Bureaucrats are fat and pampered." "Politicians try to buy our votes with our own money by spending more and more." "We're not getting our money's worth from the public sector, and we'll never be able to pay back what governments owe." "Public services should be run on a far more businesslike basis." "Politicians are interfering far too often in people's lives, and giving too much to those who don't want to work and get ahead themselves."

These themes obviously have substantial emotive appeal for some groups in society. All imply that governments spend too freely, and often on the wrong types of services. Many bear evidence of a concern that public programs are too redistributive, subsidizing "freeloaders" at the expense of working taxpayers. To this extent, the basic charge that governments "spend too much" most often masks a more selective criticism directed against the growth of the "welfare state" and the programs of social assistance which are its foundation. Resentment of taxation and expenditure policies thus characteristically singles out for its most vehement censure the perceived role of the state as a redistributor of resources to the poor. Alleged abuses of social insurance schemes and the purported impact of welfare spending on both work incentive and the rate of inflation receive particular attention. Expenditures on defence or subsidies to the business community, by way of contrast, are seldom criticized as vigorously.

What are the remedies viewed from this standpoint? As critics of the public sector have grown more vocal, prescriptions for change appear to have taken firmer and harsher shape. General appeals for "spending restraint" and "fiscal responsibility" have been supplanted by a more determined advocacy of fundamental "reform." Despite some sense that vaunted Reaganite and Thatcherite models have not entirely succeeded elsewhere (or, where successful, have exacted some unfortunate social costs), the "reformers" nevertheless argue that the time has come in Canada to reverse public sector spending patterns in a more radical fashion by enforcing significant expenditure cutbacks, by restricting or terminating certain public programs and functions, particularly in the social services, and by selling off costly public enterprises. Government, in their opinion, has shown itself incapable of solving economic problems by spending more money and creating new programs. Initiatives to turn the public sector in the opposite direction are now imperative.

Responses to the question "Where do we go from here?" are very much dependent on answers to the basic issue "How did we reach the current state of affairs in the first place?" Prescription reflects explanation. Critics who are prone to link the contemporary growth of the public sector principally to economic factors tend to suggest that the basis for continued government growth or even maintenance of existing public functions no longer exists. The economic expansion of the 1960s and early 1970s permitted the public sector to increase in size, to add new programs and to undertake some social redistribution of resources; today's altered economic reality demands an entirely different approach—a scaling down of government to match the scaled-down economy. Those who prefer to emphasize the primary culpability of bureaucrats and bureaucratic behaviour for the alleged increasing public penetration of the economy inevitably stress the need to reduce public workforces significantly and to place bureaucrats under much tighter political control. Others who believe that the expansion of the public sector can be explained primarily in ideological terms decry the purported embrace by recent governments of political norms of intervention and redistribution, and call for a change in leadership to reflect the increasing "conservatism" of the public at large. Once again, these different "explanations" are not mutually exclusive but more often than not reinforcing. The "prescriptions" which they support are similarly complementary and often tend to come together in public appeals.

Every debate, of course, has at least two sides. If the debate over directions for the public sector has indeed intensified in the 1980s, and evolved toward a more fundamental questioning of the very existence and legitimacy of certain types of public sector roles, how are the defenders of the public sector responding? Significantly, it would appear that the defence is not finding a strong and common voice with ease. Faced with public opinion sympathetic to "conservative" criticisms of government, at least on an emotive level, political groups and interests in society who traditionally support a strong public sector role seem to be searching with difficulty for an effective counter-appeal. The dilemmas they face cannot be denied: How are the abiding liberal–social democratic concerns which fostered and sustained the growth of the welfare state in the post-war era now to be geared to the new, probably persistent reality of constrained economic growth or recession? How are some of the centrepiece social programs of the welfare state—unemployment insurance, the Canada Assistance Plan, medicare, Old Age Security, the Guaranteed Income Supplement—to be protected, let alone expanded, in the face of a public mood perhaps still sensitive to norms of social justice and equity but increasingly less willing in practice to pay the price to achieve such objectives? How are Keynesian fiscal policies which call for increased public sector spending in order to confront high unemployment during recessions to be "sold" to a populace which believes we cannot afford more support, which sees inflation as the greater evil, which seems preoccupied by the size of current deficits and the accumulated debt, and which apparently accepts the appeal that we must now "live within our means"?

The dilemma is perhaps nowhere better illustrated than in the problems faced by the New Democratic Party. Federally and provincially, the party struggles simply to retain its existing electoral support at a time when it might otherwise have hoped to make substantial new inroads. Moderate constituencies potentially attracted by NDP social justice and economic issues turn away from the party fearing that it would spend even more than other parties in pursuing its solutions. Long-standing policies supporting public enterprise gain few new converts as repeated press reports recount the financial strains experienced by many highly visible crown corporations. Opposition to wage controls and to other measures targeting public employees similarly yields few political benefits for the NDP in most regions, not least among the labour movement itself. Confronted by a potential Tory sweep at the national level, more radical elements in the party urge adoption of more distinctive democratic socialist policies; the pragmatic party establishment in contrast searches for ways of accommodating the public's commitment to government economy while retaining the party's ability to champion social justice and welfare causes. To this point at least, the party seems not to have fully succeeded in finding its new "voice," and its electoral fortunes sag accordingly.

New Democrats are not alone in their frustration. Defenders of the public sector in other political parties find it even more difficult to influence policy in the rush of their colleagues to gear partisan appeals to the prevailing anti-public sector mood. The labour movement, for its part, struggles to regroup its forces against unprecedented political challenges to its public component and severe economic threats to its industrial membership. Organizations on the left focus public attention on specific social and economic issues, but have largely failed to build a strong and continuing constituency capable of shouldering the public sector's defence. Surprisingly, the appeal to protect public sector social programs which has garnered greatest attention in the recent period originated in the Catholic Church. The January 1982 publication by the Social Affairs Commission of the Canadian Conference of Bishops of its statement "Ethical Reflections on the Economic Crisis" startled many observers, and won praise from many opponents of public sector cutbacks for its passionate advocacy of strategies "which place primary emphasis on the goals of combatting unemployment by stimulating production and permanent job creation, developing a more balanced and equitable program for curtailing inflation and maintaining health care, social security, and special assistance programs."

The debate over the public sector has thus been joined, although the forces for the defence appear to face a large task indeed to win over public opinion to their views. Their success may depend most critically on their ability to increase public awareness substantially about the real social and economic impact of public sector cutbacks. This impact, however, is not always easy to establish with certainty. If politicians decide that government should be significantly reduced, what will be the actual effect on various groups and classes in society? Who benefits and who loses as a result of existing public expenditure and tax policies, and how might movement to a smaller public sector amplify these costs and benefits?

Most studies of budgetary policy in political science have concentrated on an investigation of factors which affect the pattern and magnitude of public expenditures and taxation. The question of the *impact* of spending and tax policies on the population has only recently received similar attention. One reason for this situation lies in the difficulty of expressing the effects of government policy on the population in quantifiable terms and, especially, in the common denominator of dollars. While the Public Accounts record all government revenues and expenditures in precise amounts, there is no comparable enumeration of the effects of government spending and taxes on people, nor may any accurate accounting be possible. Critics of policy output studies contend that assessments of *aggregate* spending patterns reveal only one dimension of policy, and certainly provide little real insight into the actual content and impact of government programs. In particular, it is argued that much of the literature studying spending levels lacks an understanding of the *redistributive* dimension of expenditure and tax practices, and thus yields scant evidence of who actually benefits and who pays for public programs.

Few, if any, public policies distribute equal net benefits to all. Instead, most goods and services provided by government confer differential benefits. Some individuals are net contributors, while others are net beneficiaries from government activity. Analysis of the distributive effects of public policy poses difficult problems for political scientists. Most of the detailed research in this and related areas has been conducted in the field of economics, and political scientists interested in the issues of distribution and redistribution are often compelled to borrow from work in this discipline. In general, these studies conclude that the overall effect of public programs is a *modest* redistribution of resources toward lower-income groups. Moreover, the redistribution which does take place is found to result more directly from spending policy than from taxation measures.

Despite the image of scientific rigour and precision conveyed by many economic studies of the effects of the public sector on the distribution of personal income, major conceptual and methodological problems undermine the validity of some of their findings. Before any quantitative assessment can proceed, authors must make particular assumptions about who *benefits* and who *loses* from different types of tax and expenditure policies—assumptions whose accuracy is unknown. For instance, analysts may be compelled to determine who benefits from spending on the police and armed forces. Some observers will conclude that arms manufacturers are the principal beneficiaries, others will identify "protected" property owners, and still others might single out police and military employees supported by spending in this field.

Similarly, there are inherent difficulties in determining which groups in society bear the *costs* of particular taxes. The burden of a tax formally collected from one person or group of persons may frequently be passed on to others through various channels and mechanisms. To cite only one such case, controversy surrounds the issue of who really pays the corporate profits tax. While the tax is nominally levied on the profits of firms (and therefore their shareholders), many observers argue that companies are able to pass all or a significant part of the tax forward to consumers in the form of higher product prices or backwards to their employees through lower wages.

Apart from all the difficulties discussed above, income distribution studies can never reliably ascertain whether income distribution changes and effects supposedly "observed" or "demonstrated" are indeed the product of public sector tax and expenditure policies rather than any other set of factors. Redistribution *can* result from budgetary initiatives taken by government, but it may equally be a function of other non-budgetary public policies (e.g., wage and price controls, competition policies) or of any number of changes occurring in the private sector (e.g., technological change, unionization). If a study discovered that there had been little change in income distribution over time, it would be incorrect to infer that the redistributive impact of public sector budgets had remained constant, unless and until it could be determined that no other significant changes in the economy or in non-budgetary public policies had taken place during the same period.

What, then, can we say about the possible implications of large public sector expenditure cutbacks and program reductions for the welfare of different groups in society? The comments outlined above regrettably suggest that we know very little that would allow us to predict with assurance the precise impact on various social classes of a decision to reduce government spending and cut back public services. Although it seems clear that such policies will directly jeopardize low-income groups and undermine the position of those in society who are most dependent on public spending (the poor, the unemployed, the handicapped, the elderly), the exact nature and extent of such effects are very difficult to estimate. If the redistributive properties of existing public sector activities are largely unknown, then the probable consequences for relative income levels in society of the spending and program reductions advocated by "fiscal conservatives" may be equally unclear. To be sure, such an admission is difficult for any observer disturbed by the directions that conservative critics wish the public sector to follow. Public sector defenders argue on the assumption that smaller government will be a less redistributive government. On the other hand, long-term income-distribution data suggest caution in presuming that more public spending necessarily means greater redistribution of income. Clearly, more and better information on the precise social impact of different types of programs is urgently required.

Whatever the potential social costs of significant reductions in certain public services, the more vociferous proponents of cutbacks suggest that they must be accepted if governments are to be restored to a sound (i.e., deficit-free) fiscal position. From this perspective, most of our current economic problems are alleged to stem directly from the misguided propensity of governments to spend more than they earn. No further progress and growth to the benefit of *all classes* in society will be possible without a "balancing of the books." This line of reasoning usually reflects several basic assumptions about the impact of public finances on the economy as a whole: The government is viewed as a disruptive competitor on the financial markets. The greater its require- ment to borrow, the smaller will be the pool of available capital for private sector investment given that government needs, it is claimed, tend to take priority over those of the private sector. The activities of govern- ments in capital markets are thus alleged to "crowd out" private investors. Since government expenditures are assumed almost by definition to be "non-productive," critics contend that public borrowing ultimately constricts the potential for productive economic growth and for increases in real social well-being. Many assert that government competition in bond markets also drives up the price of money. Interest rates rise as a result and eventually translate into higher product prices creating destructive inflationary pressures in the economy.

Arguments abound over the plausibility and empirical accuracy of many of these assumptions and allegations. It is highly debatable, for example, whether Canadian government deficits are to any significant extent responsible for higher interest rates in this country. For better or worse, Canada is integrated into North American capital markets, leav- ing little scope for independent movement of Canadian interest rates. It may well be that high interest rates in this country are due more to the Canadian government's slavish imitation of U.S. Federal Reserve Board tight money policies than to the economic impact of its own debt. As to the alleged "crowding-out" effect of government borrowing, the Cana- dian economy is not even close to full employment, full capacity utiliza- tion situation. New business borrowing and residential mortgage financing remain sluggish while accumulated private sector savings stand at record levels. Under such circumstances, it is difficult to accept the argument that public borrowing will "crowd out" private investment. Unless the economy enters into a period of very robust recovery with much increased private competition for investment financing, govern- ment activities in the financial market are unlikely to affect private investors in any prohibitive fashion.

Attempts by governments to reduce deficits indeed represent some- thing of a paradox because they frequently result in even larger deficits. In order to reduce their fiscal shortfalls, governments in various juris- dictions have reduced spending, introduced new taxes, raised existing tax rates and/or resorted to legislated public sector wage controls. Spending reductions and public sector wage restrictions probably serve to increase unemployment and to reduce the real personal disposable incomes of public employees and public sector dependants. Government workers lose their jobs, as do persons employed by firms which sell goods to

governments as governments buy less. Unemployment insurance payments increase, while those with jobs earn and spend less and are able to
pay less in taxes.

Increases in tax rates and the imposition of new ones likely have the
same effect. Increased taxes can result in lower consumer spending.
Businesses similarly have less to invest and, because of reduced post-tax
profits, they have less incentive to invest. The decline in consumer
spending and business investment means the unemployment rate
increases. The unemployed pay less tax than before as do businesses as
their profits shrink. Government revenues thus diminish while their
costs rise for unemployment insurance and welfare. In sum, attempts to
reduce the deficit may in fact cause it to increase.

A significant source of deficits less recognized in popular debates is
government policies which reduce revenues. A good case in point is the
federal government's decision to partially index the tax system mentioned earlier. In 1974, Ottawa indexed basic personal exemptions and
tax rate brackets to the rate of inflation as measured by the Consumer
Price Index. Without such indexation, nominal increases in income would
have pushed individual taxpayers into higher tax brackets, thereby
causing their real tax liabilities to rise. While the policy introduced in
1974 did protect individual taxpayers from this effect, it also resulted in a
very significant decline in government revenues. In an effort to reduce
this outlay, the federal government moved in 1982 to limit indexation to
6 and 5 percent for fiscal years 1982–83 and 1983–84. Notwithstanding
this initiative, it has been estimated that the cost to the federal treasury
in 1982–83 of the indexation of the tax system was approximately 15
billion dollars. This is not to suggest that indexation is without merit, but
rather to illustrate the very substantial costs of this type of policy in
terms of lost revenues.

"Tax expenditures" represent another important source of revenue
losses to the public treasury. Tax expenditures are provisions in the tax
system that give preferential treatment to certain groups of individuals
or businesses in the form of tax exemptions, deductions, reduced tax
rates or tax credits. They exist for a variety of diverse purposes such as
aiding particular types of taxpayers (aged, those with children, the blind),
and encouraging saving for retirement (RRSPs), natural resource exploitation and charitable donations. Tax expenditures thus represent a form
of forgone or postponed government revenue. The evidence suggests
that these expenditures increased greatly in number and value during the
1970s and early 1980s.

Unfortunately, tax expenditures also do not often receive the same
public scrutiny as direct government outlays even though they frequently violate principles of *vertical* and *horizontal* equity. Vertical equity
refers to the desired relative tax treatment of individuals at different

income levels. Citizens or corporations with incomes which are so low that they pay little or no tax receive few benefits at all from most tax expenditures. Given the progressive personal income tax system, higher-income taxpayers conversely receive the largest benefits from tax deductions, as their marginal tax rates are highest and they typically enjoy the disposable income required to take advantage of various tax shelters. *Horizontal* equity refers to equality in the tax treatment of individuals with similar total incomes. For example, an individual who receives a total income of $25,000 in dividends should in principle incur the same tax liability as an individual with $25,000 income from employment. This, however, is not currently the case, as investment income from capital frequently enjoys preferential treatment. Some observers indeed have argued that the "progressive income tax" is better viewed as a "progressive wage tax" since much or most income from capital escapes taxation.

The existence of many exclusions and deductions from income both for individuals and corporations thus results in a narrowing of the tax base and changes in the social incidence of taxation. As a consequence, higher tax rates must be imposed on those who *do* pay in order to generate a given amount of revenue. A federal government study indicates that, for the 1979 taxation year, those personal and corporate tax expenditures which could be quantified resulted in a revenue loss of approximately $30 billion to the federal government. This compares with total federal government spending for the same year of $50 billion. Moreover, the $30 billion figure does not include consequent revenue losses incurred by the provinces given that nine of the ten provincial governments base their personal income tax directly on the federal tax base.

In brief, tax expenditures, whatever their merits, yield a significant loss in tax revenue, very often through reduction in the taxes paid by high-income individuals and corporations. Not surprisingly, these same individuals and corporations frequently are the most vigorous proponents of efforts to reduce the deficit and government spending, though *not* the existence of tax expenditure benefits. The postponement or reversal of many provisions to limit tax expenditures proposed in the now notorious November 1981 MacEachen budget vividly testifies to the influence of those determined to preserve existing benefits in the tax system.

If nothing else, the comments advanced in our analysis should point to the complexity of government spending and tax policies and the need to think closely about who benefits and who loses as a result of various types of spending and tax programs. Many participants in the debate over directions for the public sector regrettably make it sound as if the solutions to current problems are apparent and straightforward: "If only we could eliminate the deficit by cutting back costly and inefficient programs, then the economy would pick up again! If only we recognize that the private sector is the primary engine of growth, and that government should allow business to go about its task without interference, then everyone will benefit! If only the public sector would live within its means like the business world, then we would all be a lot better off!"

For better or for worse, the solutions are *not* apparent and straightforward. Changes in the roles played by the public sector or alterations in the proportion of society's resources devoted to public sector functions potentially yield very significant costs and benefits—but for whom? Advocates of government cutbacks and defenders of the public sector alike bear a responsibility to ensure that the current debate avoids simplistic assumptions and catch-phrases and seeks instead to address the most basic and important issue, "more or less government *for whom?*" An informed debate around this issue will benefit all involved, and may serve to advance the possibility of forging a new consensus about future directions for public sector activity.

Notes

1. The views expressed in this chapter are those of the authors alone and do not necessarily reflect the opinions of the Ministry of Municipal Affairs and Housing of the Province of Ontario or the Professional Institute of the Public Service of Canada.

Further Readings

Bird, Richard, ed. *The Growth of Public Employment in Canada: Causes and Consequences.* Scarborough: Butterworths, 1979.

_____. *Financing Canadian Government: A Quantitative Overview.* Toronto: Canadian Tax Foundation, 1979.

Bossons, John, and D.P. Dugnan. "The Government Deficit: Too High or Too Low?" *Canadian Tax Journal* 1, (January–February 1983): 1–29.

Borg, Sten G., and Francis G. Castles. "The Influence of the Political Right on Public Income Maintenance Expenditure and Equality," *Political Studies* 29: 604–21.

Bruce, N., and D.D. Purvis. "Fiscal Policy and Recovery from the Great Recession," *Canadian Public Policy* 9, (March 1983): 53–67.

Canadian Conference of Bishops, Social Affairs Commission. "Ethical Reflections on the Economic Crisis." January 1983.

Daniel, Mark J., and William A. Robinson. *Compensation in Canada: A Study of the Public and Private Sectors.* Ottawa: The Conference Board in Canada, 1980.

Davis, Otto A., M.A.H. Dempster and Aaron Wildavsky. "A Theory of the Budgetary Process." *American Political Science Review* 60 (September 1966).

Dodge, David A. "Impact of Tax, Transfer and Expenditure Policies of Government on the Distribution of Personal Income in Canada." *Review of Income and Wealth* 21 (1974).

Foot, David K., ed. *Public Employment and Compensation in Canada: Myths and Realities.* Scarborough: Butterworths, 1978.

Gillespie, W. Irwin. "On the Redistribution of Income in Canada," *Canadian Tax Journal*, July/August 1976.

Howard, John, and William Stanbury, "Measuring Leviathan." Exerpt from Fraser Institute study reproduced in *The Vancouver Province*, March 27, 1983.

Klein, Rudolf. "The Politics of Public Expenditure: American Theory & British Practice." *British Journal of Political Science* 6 (October 1976).

McCallum, John S. "Canadian Finance and the Federal Deficit." *Business Quarterly*, Winter 1982.

O'Connor, James. *The Fiscal Crisis of the State.* New York: St. Martin's, 1973.

Reuber, Grant. "The Impact of Government Policies on the Distribution of Income in Canada." *Canadian Public Policy* 4 (Autumn 1978).

Rousseau, Henri-Paul. "The Dome Syndrome: The Debt Overhanging Canadian Government and Businesses." *Canadian Public Policy* 9 (March 1983): 37–52.

Wilensky, Harold L. *The Welfare State and Equality.* Berkeley: University of California Press, 1975.

Department of Finance, Government of Canada. *The Federal Deficit in Perspective.* Budget paper. Ottawa: 1983.

Chapter 2
The Quebec Cauldron
Reginald A. Whitaker

The Quiet Revolution, the FLQ, "bilingualism and biculturalism," "special status," *"égalité ou indépendance,"* the 1970 October Crisis and the War Measures Act, the Parti Québécois and "sovereignty-association," the May 1980 referendum.... For twenty years Quebec has been constantly in the headlines, a bomb always seemingly about to explode, an enigma and a question mark always hovering on the Canadian horizon. "What does Quebec want?" has become a cliché of English Canadian political discourse in the sixties and seventies, and no doubt will continue through the eighties. It is surely impossible, if not absurd, to try to understand the dynamic and the rhythm of Canadian political development without understanding the forces which have gone into the Quebec upheaval.

The first problem is inherent in the question, What does Quebec want? With remarkable consistency, while working at complete cross-purposes, both the Quebec nationalists and their English Canadian opponents have operated on the assumption that there is something called "Quebec"—a monolithic, collective Leviathan which speaks with the united voice of six million Québécois. Whether as a mythical construct of nationalist yearnings or the equally mythical nightmare of anglophone bigotry, "Quebec" does not in reality have a concrete, material existence, any more than does "Canada." This is not to say that one cannot speak of a Quebec nation, which we surely can; nor does it mean that we cannot speak of Quebec nationalism as a force and a passion which far surpasses Canadian nationalism, for it certainly does. It is to say that the dynamic of events in Quebec, the explanation of the vast changes which have taken place within the past two decades, can only be understood when "Quebec" is viewed as a forum or framework within which conflict and struggle between contending forces, class, linguistic and ethnic, have taken place and continue to take place. Far from being a monolith, Quebec's extraordinary dynamic in recent years derives from its status as a battleground for conflicts perhaps more bitter and more profound than the contentions which have riven English Canada.

Any analysis of Quebec which locates events solely within the framework of nationalism tends to be tautological and ultimately void of explanatory power. Nationalism, in the sense of a strong feeling of national identity and, at least since 1960, a tendency to formulate demands on the political system grounded in concepts of the national interest, is a force which permeates almost all areas of Quebec life and which cuts across class and other social divisions. But to explain why Quebec has become such a disruptive and contentious force within the Canadian Confederation since 1960, "nationalism" tells us very little. After all, Quebec nationalism can be truthfully called a constant of Quebec history. The real question is why nationalism has taken the particular forms which it has assumed since 1960. And to answer that question one has to examine the conflicting forces at work within Quebec and how various formulations of nationalism have expressed the class and other interests of these conflicting forces. Thus, when one analyst of Quebec politics writes that the Parti Québécois is not merely a party but "the embodiment of the national identity and the collective will,"[1] he is writing nonsense. And those who assumed that the evolution of Quebec was an inevitable, irresistible flowering of the Quebec nation into the status of sovereignty failed to remember that history is innocent of "inevitabilities" imposed upon it by ideologists. At the same time, it would be equally fallacious (and equally tempting to those seeking simple answers) to assume that the 60 percent "no" vote in the 1980 referendum means that "Quebec" has single-mindedly rejected sovereignty-association and the independence option. The forces continue to contend and the options remain open.

Let us begin where Quebec itself begins as a nation, with the Conquest of New France by the British in 1760. A possible fate of the French-speaking Catholic inhabitants was assimilation or worse by their English-speaking Protestant conquerors. After all, such has indeed been the fate of numerous other people unlucky enough to have fallen under foreign military domination. In the event, the French language and certain French customs, such as the Civil Code, were preserved, along with the Catholic Church and the educational system which went along with the Church's domination of Quebec cultural life. As a result, what had begun as a tiny colony four centuries ago is today a modern, wealthy and confident nation poised, many would say, at the brink of national sovereignty. This long odyssey from conquered colony to a nation within the Canadian Confederation might seem to speak well of the tolerance and generosity of the conquerors. In fact it speaks more strongly of the courage and tenacity of this small people who would never give up what has made them distinctive in North America. For the survival of Quebec, and of French Canada, has been above all a story of *resistance* to pressures for assimilation or repression, resistance which has forced the English and then the English-speaking Canadians to make compromises and concessions over time which have taken form in various shifting accommodations. The simple reality of New France at the time of the Conquest was, as Pierre Trudeau once wrote, that the French were to weak to become themselves an independent nation, and yet too strong to be crushed by the conquerors. There is a sense in which this basic paradigm has remained true down to the present day.

It is in examining the bases of the various accommodations which have been arrived at over time that one can begin to understand the logic of Quebec's relation to Canada. And these accommodations have been above all economic accommodations of class alliances cutting across the two ethnic and linguistic communities. Following the Conquest a tacit alliance was struck between the English military and the English-speaking merchants who had come in the wake of the Conquest, on the one hand, and the Catholic clergy and the seigneurial landlords who benefited from the feudal land tenure system of New France. The core of this alliance was to be founded on a fateful tradeoff of mutual elite interests: the English were to be left formal political control and major economic activity, i.e., the "dream" of opening up a transcontinental economy along the "empire of the St. Lawrence"; the clergy would be left with "cultural" matters, such as religion and education. This guaranteed that the two dominant elites of New France would retain their privileges, but at the expense of economic development. At the same time, the English bought economic superiority at the expense of leaving the major institutions of the conquered people intact. Under these circumstances Quebec would find it very difficult indeed to develop an indigenous bourgeoisie, so necessary for autonomous capitalist development, and would be saddled with internal elites dependent upon the English, and with a vested interest in fostering economic backwardness and political subservience among the mass of the population.

The first and greatest manifestation of discontent spilling over into revolution against the English came with the rebellions of 1837-38, which were much more serious and sustained than the rebellion in Upper Canada, where discontent lacked the reinforcement of ethnic division. But the rebellions themselves were the desperate end product of a growing resistance symbolized by the deadlock in the government of the colony between the ruling anglophone clique and the assembly domi-nated by francophones. The latter group were led by a class element which had been generated by the anomalies of the accommodation referred to above: professionals such as lawyers and doctors who had been educated above their largely peasant origins but who could find no place in the state administration controlled by anglophone patronage. Forced to return to their places of origin, these "new middle class" elements remained close to the people but had the voice and education to agitate on behalf of French grievances in the assembly.

When worsening economic conditions and growing reaction among the English and the ruling clique finally forced matters to open rebellion, there was a further polarization between left and right within the rebellious *patriote* movement itself. Just as in the American Revolution over a half century earlier, events drove many rebels toward more radical liberal and democratic views—although in this case always within the context of a strong sense of nationalism, which reinforced in some *patriotes* a radical drive to overthrow the internal elites which were perpetuating their national subservience.

The movement failed, however, to develop the kind of mass base which could eventually drive out the English. The final defeat of the rebellion in 1838 had fateful consequences: not only did it confirm English hegemony in Quebec, but it also confirmed the dominance of the Church over Quebec life, a dominance which was to last for well over a century. For this period, French Canadian nationalism was largely stripped of the liberal democratic promise of 1837 and was instead characterized by social and political conservatism, under the close tutelage of the Church, which had become perforce the only institutionalized defender of the French language and culture. The general aversion of clerical nationalism to anything smacking of economic "radicalism" left the English-speaking capitalists more or less free rein. And the latter were only too happy to leave the Church in charge of educating a population which was more and more to provide a cheap and docile labour force for English, American and English Canadian capital.

At the same time, French Canadians were showing considerable skill in utilizing English parliamentary institutions to ensure national survival. The legislative union of Upper and Lower Canada in 1840 was designed to sink the francophone majority in Lower Canada into an overall minority, but this scheme immediately foundered on the capacity of the French members to act as a cohesive ethnic bloc which had to be accommodated by the warring partisan factions among the anglophone members, if they wished to form a government. It was partially out of a desire to break this stranglehold that anglophone politicians finally agreed to set out on the road to the Confederation agreement of 1867, but along the way they were forced to concede provincial status to Quebec, along with considerable powers over education and culture, and recognition of the French language in Quebec at least.

Moreover, it was soon apparent that in practice a French Canadian presence would have to be granted in the makeup of the federal Cabinet and other federal institutions, since any national government without Quebec support would prove precarious indeed. Yet the old economics-culture tradeoff, implicit in the tacit bargain struck after the Conquest and made explicit in the provisions of the BNA Act, which granted almost all important economic responsibilities and all important revenue sources to the national government, was itself reinforced in the elite accommodation of the Cabinet: until the 1960s no important economic portfolio was given to a French Canadian minister. Indeed it was well over a century until a francophone was appointed minister of finance, in the late 1970s. In addition, the two greatest crises of English–French relations in Canada's first half century—the hanging of Louis Riel and the imposition of conscription on an unwilling Quebec population in World War I—demonstrated that the West would be an exclusively anglophone preserve (thus clearly tilting the balance of Confederation), and that when an issue sharply divided the two communities, the English majority would always win. These events also sealed the fate of the Conservative party as a vehicle of accommodation of francophone political elites, thus ultimately ensuring that only one party, the Liberals, could effectively play this role.

By the early twentieth century two main variants of nationalist ideology had emerged. One was symbolized by Henri Bourassa, politician, journalist and founder of *Le Devoir*; the other by the historian Canon Lionel Groulx. The former was founded on the vision of *French Canada* and saw the best protection for the French Canadian nation in equal partnership with English Canada along bilingual and bicultural lines. The latter variant increasingly saw *Quebec* as the only viable basis of French Canadian nationhood and often looked to right-wing corporatist and authoritarian movements as the way to success—as opposed to the more liberal politics of Bourassa. Yet both variants finally failed to address themselves to the real core of the problem of French Canadian inferiority: their economic subservience. And it must be said that Bourassa's pan-Canadian liberalism, just as much as Groulx's more inward-looking nationalism, drove English Canadians to near-violent opposition—as during the World War I conscription crisis.

Consequently, by the 1940s and 1950s Quebec was increasingly the scene of insupportable contradictions. The francophone majority was manifestly worse off than the anglophone minority by virtually any measure one wished to use. At the same time they were mired in an ideology which had little or no connection with reality, a backward-looking rural vision of Catholic and anti-materialist values. The irony was that Quebec had early in the century become the most heavily urbanized of all the Canadian provinces. But in this case urbanization did not mean modernization, but instead the production of a cheap labour force for English Canadian and American capital.

There was a saying that in Quebec capital speaks English and labour speaks French. This not only caught the essence of the situation, but also indicated exactly how in the long run class and nationality would become mutually reinforcing characteristics. But so long as the traditional elites—the clergy, the politicians and the local notables and petty bourgeoisie—kept up their tacit alliance with English Canadian capital and the Canadian state, the situation remained frozen. Thus under Maurice Duplessis's Union Nationale government (1936–39, 1944–60), political corruption, patronage and intimidation helped maintain a regime which in fact challenged capital and the Canadian state only at the rhetorical level. Rural votes were mobilized to maintain a regime which was turning its energies to selling out Quebec's natural resources and encouraging industry seeking low labour costs.

Yet enormous changes were in the making. The 1949 asbestos strike drew five thousand miners out in defiance not only of the American company, but also of the Duplessis government, in a four-month confrontation widely viewed at the time as "quasi-revolutionary," and which drew the support of a number of journalists, labour leaders and academics—presaging in a small but dramatic way the coming cataclysm of the 1960s.

This was on the surface. Underneath were far-reaching changes in the very structure of Quebec society. As industrialization and urbanization proceeded, it was inevitable that the political and ideological superstructure would suffer increasing tension and pressure from new forces which had no place in the antiquated world of politics. Corporate capital requires a certain kind of labour force; it also requires a growing middle stratum of technical and professional white-collar workers. Slowly, inefficiently, the Quebec educational system was beginning to respond to the demand for more technical, professional and commercial skills.

Yet the emergent "new middle class" found precious little scope for their ambitions and talents. The corporate world was strongly anglophone and largely impervious to the advancement of francophones past the middle range, at best. The Canadian state presented an equally hostile face. And the Quebec provincial state under Duplessis presented little scope to any technical–professional middle class, whether francophone or anglophone, since it avoided economic intervention of the Keynesian variety and left social programs to the Church and the private sector. In fact, it was very much in this latter location that the new middle class was taking shape. The Church-controlled educational and health sectors required the services of a growing number of lay persons with technical qualifications to staff the schools, hospitals and other social institutions which in English Canada were under public jurisdiction. These people were generally underpaid and had very little say in running the institutions which they staffed. During the 1950s there was a notable increase in the number of Catholic lay organizations seeking a voice in the direction of their society. Much of this activity remained largely apolitical and well within the bounds of Catholic orthodoxy. Yet even in the 1950s—the era which later became known as *le grand noirceur* (the dark ages)—there were those who began to question more deeply. The review *Cité libre* carried on a long war with clerical and political reaction, featuring a roster of future "stars" of Quebec life in the sixties and seventies, from Pierre Elliott Trudeau to future *indépendantiste* intellectuals. And the Quebec Liberal party, shut out by Duplessis as well as by the federal Liberal party in Ottawa, began a "democratization" of the party structures in the late 1950s which had the effect of opening up the party to the new forces brewing beneath the surface.

The death of Maurice Duplessis in 1959 was like the breaking of a spell. First, the Union Nationale under Duplessis's successor, Paul Sauvé, appeared to be about to undergo changes itself, but Sauvé's untimely death left the UN without new direction, and in 1960 the Liberals under Jean Lesage returned to power after sixteen years of opposition. For once, a change in government was much more than a mere change in faces at the top and patronage to supporters below. The Liberal victory signalled the so-called "Quiet Revolution," a massive *déblocage* which opened up Quebec's great springtime. The Lesage government drastically revised the role of the provincial government in Quebec life, from the nationalization of private hydro-electricity (under then-Liberal minister René Lévesque) to the secularization of the educational system, to the reform of the civil service, to the setting of a whole new host of demands on Confederation which shook Canadian federalism to its roots. But this was by no means a period of change from the top down. Political events moved to a new rhythm: the seething demands and desires of a population suddenly liberated from generations of constraint and backwardness. For a while it seemed as if everything was in question, and that everything was possible. All the promise of modernity which had lain before English Canadians for so long appeared as a kind of revelation to this people so long repressed. Young people, intellectuals and artists in particular responded, and the early 1960s became a festival of innovation in culture and ideas. It also became a time of violence, when radical demands for independence took the form of demonstrations and even terrorist groups like the FLQ which took to bombs.

Revolutions, quiet or otherwise, are in the nature of things more or less civil wars. Not everyone in Quebec was swept away by enthusiasm for what was happening. Many elements, particularly from the older, rural and more traditional Quebec, were increasingly worried by the onrush of change and by their place in the new Quebec. In part this was masked by the fact that the new regime clothed its policies in the garb of nationalism, now given a brighter and more modern hue by a willingness to dispense with the age-old tacit bargain which had traded off economics for culture, and to make demands which struck at the very heart of the "unequal union," in Stanley Ryerson's phrase, of English and French in Canada. To this extent the Lesage Liberals were the most potent champions of the fundamental desire for national survival who had yet appeared on the scene, and they were thus able to mobilize widespread support behind policies which might otherwise have proven highly divisive. In retrospect, however, it is quite apparent that the nationalism of the Quiet Revolution was above all a nationalism of the new middle class, expressing their demands for a place in the sun in a language which was no doubt sincerely nationalist in its cultural identification but which was at the same time an expression of their self-interest as a class or, more precisely, a class fraction.

In fact, the entire logic of the modernization of the Quebec state and its transformation from a laissez-faire operation of local notables to Keynesian interventionism was predicated upon the ascent of the new middle class. Locked out from both the corporate world and the national state, the francophone middle class would build a state in Quebec which would be open to its talents. The nationalization of hydro, for example, created Hydro-Québec, a vast state enterprise staffed from top to bottom by a francophone technical and professional middle class. The reform of the civil service, the attack on the old patronage system of appointment and the expansion of technical tasks on the state's agenda all served to transform the provincial state apparatus into a pole of attraction for ambitious young francophone university graduates. The demands of the Lesage Liberals for control of the pension plan and medicare legislation being introduced by the federal Liberal government in the 1960s arose not so much from a traditional Quebec aversion to state social services but rather from a desire to control the vast investment funds which come with such schemes so as to strategically influence the economic development of the province.

This *étatist* orientation not only effectively renegotiated the terms upon which accommodation between the elites of English and French Canada took place, but it also tended to redefine the very subject of nationalism itself. "French Canada" increasingly began to give way to "Quebec" in nationalist discourse. In part this reflected a realization that the future of francophone communities outside Quebec was dim and that efforts would be best concentrated on the one jurisdiction where francophones formed an indisputable majority and could control the machinery of government. But in a deeper sense it was a reflection on the ideological level of the fact of the Quebec state's emergence as a powerful bureaucratic actor on the Canadian stage. That nationalism would increasingly be seen as Quebec rather than French Canadian nationalism symbolized the drawing together of nationalist ideology with the interests of the state middle class and other elements who saw their interests closely identified with the Quebec state. The interpretation of nationalism in generalized cultural or ethnic terms fails to grasp the specific class interests which had appropriated nationalist discourse for statist purposes.

If we accept this nationalist-statist discourse on its own terms, we simply see a kind of collective self-fulfillment, an *épanouissement* or flowering and the popular slogan *maîtres chez nous* (masters in our own house). In reality we find class conflict and the heightening of contradictions. Just who were to be the new *maîtres*? The 1960s saw the growth of working-class consciousness and increasing labour militancy, as the previously excluded workers sought their own share. Ironically, given the statist orientation of Quebec development, this increasing labour militancy bore most heavily upon the swollen state sector, so that by the 1970s the political leadership in Quebec, including the PQ after 1976, found themselves in an adversarial position with the teachers and other organized state employees. It is impossible to disentangle the developing class consciousness of Quebec workers from their developing national consciousness; in many ways the two were mutually reinforcing phenomena. Yet it would also be a mistake to simply subsume working-class consciousness under the rubric of nationalism: first, because nationalist demands articulated by the working class always differ in significant ways from nationalist demands articulated by the new middle class; second, because the confrontation with the Quebec state as employer pitted working-class francophones against a francophone elite, with both sides appealing to public opinion. This is a familiar enough scenario elsewhere in the Western world, but it fits rather uneasily into a simplistic nationalist schema.

In fact, the Quebec union movement has displayed an even more adversarial attitude toward the Quebec state than many English Canadian unions have displayed toward the federal or provincial states. This has remained true even when the PQ, closer to a social democratic party than any previous provincial party, came to power. Why this should be so may become clearer when we examine the deepest failing of the Quiet Revolution and its successors, the inability to actually confront the structures of English Canadian and American capital in any significant way. Apart from the nationalization of hydro, which indeed only followed the example of the Conservative government of Ontario which had created Ontario Hydro a half century earlier, the Lesage Liberals never made any real inroads into the power of capital. Like moderate reform governments everywhere, they were cowed by the necessity to maintain business confidence, to retain their credit rating in the bond markets, to encourage investment and to prevent flights of capital and consequent disappearance of jobs.

The Quebec Liberal party was in no way a vehicle for the mobilization of a mass working-class movement which might have formed an alternative centre of pressure and direction. The long-term result was that *maîtres chez nous* became an empty slogan when matched against the commanding power of "foreign" capital in making the really crucial decisions about the shape of Quebec development. To be sure, the

Quebec state gained a greater leverage than before in setting guidelines, in regulating and in exercising its own voice in deploying the investment funds which it now controlled. But this was a long way from mastering the Quebec economy in the name of the people who elected the provincial government. It also meant that the Quiet Revolution ultimately satisfied neither the new middle class elite of strongly nationalist persuasion, nor the working class who began more and more to see the Quebec state as an ally of their enemies, or in some cases as the enemy itself.

In any event the Lesage Liberals were themselves driven out of office in 1966 by a revivified Union Nationale under Daniel Johnson, who had quietly built up an alliance of all the elements in Quebec society which had reason to fear and mistrust the Liberal thrust toward modernization, especially in the rural areas and small towns. Johnson's problem, and that of his successor following his death, Jean-Jacques Bertrand, was an inability to construct a viable modern version of the old UN nationalism. With a social base in the old Quebec and no means of building a new base on the forces unleashed by the Quiet Revolution, the UN remained suspended uneasily between rhetorical nationalism and aggressive demands for equal partnership in Confederation (*Egalité ou l'indépendance* was the name of a book which Johnson authored). This came out most acutely in the crisis set off by the UN's attempt to enact language legislation with the ostensible purpose of strengthening the position of French: in fact they ended by antagonizing both francophones and anglophones without meeting either set of demands.

Meanwhile, another event of historic significance had taken place in 1965 when Pierre Elliott Trudeau, Jean Marchand of the CSN union federation, and the journalist Gérard Pelletier announced their adherence to the federal Liberal party and were elected to Parliament in the federal election of that year. This act indicated in a dramatic way that the new middle class was by no means united in its nationalist ideology. Some elements of the provincial Liberals, such as René Lévesque, were clearly moving in the inexorable direction of *indépendantisme*, the logical result of the philosophy of *maîtres chez nous*. Trudeau, Marchand and Pelletier went to Ottawa to create a federalist counter-pole of attraction.

When Trudeau won the leadership of the Liberal party three years later and a landslide victory in the general election which followed, this became in effect the official policy of the national government. The passage of the Official Languages Act and the promotion of bilingualism in the federal civil service were two prongs of a policy of attempting to renegotiate a new basis of elite accommodation between English and French Canada. Another was the concerted attempt to revitalize the federal Liberal party in Quebec, to appoint francophones to economic portfolios in the Cabinet hitherto reserved to anglophones, and to promote a francophone presence at the highest levels of the federal public service. Underlying all this was an ideological appeal to *French Canadian* nationalism, as opposed to Quebec nationalism, and an appeal to the pride of francophones to seek their fulfillment within the wider sphere of a federal system in which the rights of the French language and French Canadian culture would be guaranteed. The figure of Pierre Trudeau himself, the francophone who became one of Canada's most electorally successful prime ministers and a statesman of world status, was assiduously cultivated to symbolize the potential for French Canadians within the federal system. And indeed, opinion polls over the last decade have consistently shown Trudeau to be the most respected public figure among francophone Québécois.

The new-found confidence in Ottawa was parlayed into a new toughness on behalf of federal interests in negotiation with Quebec governments, putting an end to the apparent slide of the Pearson Liberals toward giving Quebec *de facto* special status. In some ways, the Trudeau style rather belied the reality that Quebec did continue to be treated somewhat differently than other provinces, in recognition that it is, after all, in Trudeau's own phrase, the "homeland and centre of gravity of the French Canadian nation." But there would be no *formal* recognition of special constitutional status: Trudeau has always been adamant on the fundamental philosophical point that the best guarantees of the French Canadian language and culture are through *individual* rights, unlike recognition of *collective* rights, which would be discriminatory and illiberal.

When René Lévesque left the provincial Liberal party in 1967 to form a new grouping which ultimately became the Parti Québécois, he tended to take away with him not only the more nationalist elements of the Liberal party but also the more socially progressive as well. This left the Liberals as a much more right-wing grouping than before, as most of the dynamic thrust of the Quiet Revolution left with Lévesque. But it also served to realign Quebec politics. Lévesque incorporated two fringe groupings, the RIN, a left-wing separatist force which had contested the 1966 election, and the smaller right-wing RN. As well, some of the more nationalist elements of the UN also joined in. Yet even in its initial formulations the PQ was notably moderate in its version of independence: the idea of linking political independence with economic association was not a later adjustment to political reality but a founding idea.

Shortly after the PQ had contested its first election in 1970—the same election that saw the Liberals under Robert Bourassa come back to power in a landslide—a series of events unfolded that dramatically highlighted the forces at play in the Quebec cauldron and also indicated the direction of the 1970s. What has been called the October Crisis began when the terrorist FLQ kidnapped a British diplomat and later kidnapped and murdered the Quebec minister of labour, Pierre Laporte. The response of the federal government in invoking the War Measures Act against an "apprehended insurrection" and the subsequent arrests and incarceration of numerous persons, few of whom had anything to do with the FLQ, remains a hotly debated question of public policy. What is relevant here is that the entire affair was in fact played out between different factions of Québécois: the federal Liberals, the Bourassa regime, and the Montreal government of Mayor Jean Drapeau on the one side, and on the other, the FLQ and their public sympathizers, such as the labour leader Michel Chartrand or the revolutionary theorist Pierre Vallières. In the event, the clear superiority of the federal government over the provincial state was demonstrated. Moreover, the might which the federal government could thus array in effect broke the back of the tiny terrorist organization which failed to mobilize popular resistance or even much public support. By the end of the crisis the field had at least been cleared. The PQ, with its moderate, constitutionalist approach of respecting the democratic electorate and observing due process, would be henceforth the only voice of *indépendantisme*.

The Bourassa regime turned to an economic development strategy which emphasized above all the attraction of private investment and the promotion of large public works projects—one of which, the James Bay Hydro development, was an immense success that gives Quebec a solid renewable energy resource base for the future, and another of which, the Olympic Games project, turned out to be a financial disaster and an administrative fiasco. In a sense, the Bourassa regime represented a reversion to the Duplessis era, inasmuch as everything was subordinated to the encouragement of private investment and business was given a distinctly privileged place in dealings with the provincial government; at the same time, union bashing became more or less official policy. Another aspect of Duplessism came to the fore as well: political patronage and corruption. Moreover the apparent servility of Bourassa to his "big brothers" in Ottawa began to grate on the nerves of nationalists, even those who were far from being separatists. This was particularly true when an anti-bilingual backlash developed in English Canada, calling the viability of Trudeau's national bilingualism into question, a dilemma symbolized by the strike of airline pilots over the use of French in air traffic control in Quebec and by the apparent capitulation of the federal government in the face of an anti-French backlash.

When the Quebec Liberals were still able to paint the PQ as a dangerous party which threatened the economic stability of Quebec by their "separatist" designs, they were able to mobilize public support, winning a huge landslide in 1973. But when the PQ hit on the strategy of promising a referendum on sovereignty-association and ran on the platform of competence and honesty in government, as well as on a mildly social democratic program, an electorate sick of scandals and sellouts turned the Liberals out of office. The coming of the PQ signalled the gravest crisis yet of Canadian federalism.

The PQ government which took office in 1976 appeared on the surface to be the true heirs of the Quiet Revolution; the Cabinet was a who's who of the Quebec political, administrative, academic and media elites. It must be said that the PQ has in its terms of office largely delivered on its promise of good government, in the sense of administrative compe-tence and efficiency, along with a reasonable degree of public honesty. A pursuit of the policy of *maîtres chez nous* was now given a much more hard-nosed economic and political thrust than it had had in the days of Lesage. Attempting to pursue the goal of sovereignty while operating a provin-cial government within the context of the existing Canadian federation is not, however, without its ironies.

One of the greatest ironies of all is that what may be the PQ's most enduring achievement probably undermined its own independence option. The PQ language legislation succeeded where the Liberals and the UN had failed before them: to make secure the position of the French language in Quebec life. By contrast with its predecessors, Camille Laurin's language act was clear in intention and followed through its aims with rigorous consistency, avoiding the anxiety-producing uncer-tainties of earlier acts. A wild uproar in the anglophone community led to streams of affluent refugees fleeing to Toronto and parts west. Among those who stayed there is now a much greater acceptance of the predom-inantly French character of Quebec. The immigrants, despite long-simmering conflicts with Montreal working-class francophones with whom they were competing, have adjusted for the most part with sur-prising good grace. Once the situation was made clear, those who had already made a decision to live their lives in a new language showed that they could adapt as well to French as to English. And since it was above all the immigrants overwhelmingly adopting English who had been the real threat to the linguistic balance, the PQ thus neatly defused what had been an explosive situation of ethnic conflict.

Now the francophones of Quebec feel a new security: Quebec is to remain unmistakably French in character. Hence the mere existence of an anglophone minority tied to an anglophone majority outside Quebec began to lose the threatening quality it once posed to the integrity of Québécois culture and identity. In short, the PQ reversed what had been one of the most significant weaknesses of Trudeau's official languages policy: a cultural and linguistic insecurity which it had actually encour-aged in Quebec. The profound irony for the PQ is that this achievement may well be seen as a necessary condition for Quebec's continued place within Confederation. Without it the case for independence would cer-tainly have been much stronger. With the substantive and psychic victory of the language law, Quebec may well feel more confident about playing a continued role in Confederation.

In economic policy, the PQ has been severely restrained in its approach, even to the extent of downplaying in office its moderate social democratic philosophy. In part this reflects a general disillusion with the statist ventures of the Lesage period, many of which (Hydro-Québec aside) have not proven to be particularly effective. Partly it reflects the unpleasant economic realities of the 1970s and 1980s, when inflation and unemployment have combined to discredit much of the earlier Keynesian interventionism. But above all it represents the conundrum of a party dedicated to seeking a major structural change in the national and constitutional status of Quebec. Since business fears uncertainty more than anything else, and since the PQ project was premised upon the maintenance of existing living standards and investment levels in Quebec, the PQ government was forced to go to lengths to reassure business which less "dangerous" governments can avoid. The PQ thus turned out to be very cautious and conservative in its fiscal and monetary policies.

In the case of its economic development strategy, the PQ represents, if anything, a step back from the Quiet Revolution. Apart from the more or less symbolic nationalization of the asbestos corporation (a ritual bow to the memory of the strike of 1949?), which was in any event a declining industry, the PQ has been notably loath to engage in direct state intervention. In fact, their development strategy has been largely along Bourassist lines: a heavy reliance on private investment by multinationals based upon the availability of natural resources and energy (James Bay), state agencies as facilitators of private enterprise, and a reduction of regulatory and control devices over business. The one area where they have differed from the Liberals is in the vast program of assistance and encouragement of small and medium enterprises (which of course are those most strongly francophone in ownership). Even this emphasis, strong in their first term, has begun to weaken in their second, with the realization that small and medium enterprises make only a small dent in the unemployment picture. As well they have begun emphasizing that the rationalization and consolidation of certain aging sectors of the economy will also be necessary, even at the cost of short-term dislocations. In short, they seem to be moving more and more into the kind of development strategy, heavily dependent upon large multinational capital and tied to resource sectors, which is characteristic of other provincial governments in Canada.

This raises another crucially important point about the nature of the PQ project for sovereignty: its economic base. Some have viewed the PQ as *merely* a vehicle for "new middle class" nationalism, rooted in the state elite. Yet the PQ has not behaved as if it were a mere reflection of a bureaucratic class fraction. Is this just a failure of will in the face of the power of "foreign" capital? It was, in fact, no longer true in the 1970s that francophones were shut out of the corporate sector. The emergence of a francophone bourgeoisie—not located in the small business sector alone—is obviously of critical importance for evaluating the relationship of Quebec to its Canadian, and North American, environment. That elements of a francophone bourgeoisie do exist is no longer a matter of much dispute; the hotly debated question has to do with its relationship to North American capitalism. Is it a "French Canadian" bourgeoisie linked to a pan-Canadian economy, a regional Quebec bourgeoisie offering a potential base for sovereignty-association, or is it itself divided into different fractions, with fragmented political projects?[2] These and other questions (such as the relationship between this bourgeoisie and the state elite located in such crucial positions as Hydro-Québec and the various investment funds) await definitive answers. Suffice to say for now that the PQ project for a sovereign Quebec seems to have been predicated upon some concept of a francophone bourgeoisie, assisted by the state, developing its place in the sun through a renegotiated settlement with English Canada and even, perhaps, through an eventual common market relationship with the United States. A sovereign Quebec was not seen as a socialist Quebec—although there have always been minority elements in the PQ which have retained more radical perspectives than the conservative and technocratic leadership. In any event, the support of business, including francophone business, for the "no" side in the referendum was a sign that this emergent bourgeoisie did not see itself as having *indépendantiste* aspirations, at least at this time.

If the PQ never saw its role as that of a socialist party mobilizing the working class against foreign capitalist domination, it did see its role in relation to the organized working class as distinct from that of the Liberals. The PQ began with a more conciliatory line in labour relations, including the passage of an "anti-scab" law more progressive than anything existing in any other North American jurisdiction. While it has generally shown more adroitness and finesse in handling labour relations than its predecessors, it has never gained the formal allegiance of the unions, who have no official affiliation with the party—although the majority of working-class voters appear to vote PQ. The fiscal crisis of the Quebec state, in part exacerbated by the PQ's studied largesse in encouraging its state-sector supporters in the years leading up to the referendum on sovereignty-association, came home to roost in 1982–83 when the PQ was forced into a confrontation with its own employees which has done severe damage to its image as progressive in labour relations. While the federal and other provincial governments have frozen or limited salaries of public employees, the Quebec government actually rolled back wages, under the authority of special legislation. The refusal of the teachers to accept the government's terms brought down on their heads one of the most draconian pieces of special anti-labour legislation passed in recent years in any Canadian legislature, including the specific exemption of the legislation from the provisions of both the federal and Quebec Charters of Rights. It now seems very doubtful whether the PQ can repair its relations with the organized labour movement in time for the next election.

The PQ has attempted to reconcile the contradictions of its labour policy by pushing for a series of quasi-corporatist-style government–business–labour advisory bodies. Although they hoped that common nationalist aspirations might overcome class divisions, not much has in fact come of these initiatives, nor is much likely to come. Nationalism does not in fact override the structural division of a capitalist economy, when bread and butter issues, as opposed to nationalist symbolism, are in question. On the other hand, the reaction from the labour leaders and from the political left in the wake of the PQ's cutbacks and special anti-labour legislation has gone to such extremes as to label the party as a reactionary betrayer of the working class. Since the PQ never claimed to be a workers' party in the first place, the degree of disillusion seems exaggerated.

Indeed, in continuity with its past, the PQ today seems to be pursuing a populist line, in which it portrays itself as the defender of the "little people" against the special interests, even where these interests include the unions, and especially when they include the "privileged" ranks of the state employees. Of course, this may damage its support among the new middle class, and particularly the participation of new-middle-class activists in the party organization. On the other hand, the party may become a different kind of organization, eschewing its former role as a mass party and instead coming to resemble a kind of modernized version of the old Duplessis Union Nationale: nationalist, populist, firmly rooted in a network of local supporters tied together by patronage and shared partisan identity, and solidly under the control of *le chef*. Of course, there are many differences with the old UN, but so too there are some striking similarities. The fact that the PQ began as a reformist party is no surprise; so too did the UN (Duplessis was allied with young left-wing nationalists and promised the nationalization of hydroelectric power). In both cases nationalism was the predominant thrust, and in both cases social reformism was always secondary. It might be added that in the case of the UN, the combination of populism and nationalism was sustained by substantial working-class support at the polls, even in the face of repressive anti-labour activities by the state.

If the PQ has a blurred conservative image in its economic and social policies, its constitutional formulation of its nationalist position has been even more riven with hesitation and contradiction. Despite hysterical anglophone allegations that the PQ are "racist" and that their independence project resembled some variant of "fascism," the truth is far different. Faced with the thorny problem of expressing a francophone nationalist vision in a society where about one in five does not share in this cultural and linguistic identity, the PQ (not without some hesitations and self-deceptions) never officially supported an *exclusionary* definition of nationality, but instead generally opted for a *liberal* interpretation, which left membership open to all those willing to participate voluntarily in the national culture, along with guarantees for minorities. Indeed the entire ethos of the PQ has been so permeated with a full acceptance of liberal democratic principles as to make any allegations of "totalitarianism" laughable—as well as to sharply differentiate the PQ from older reactionary and authoritarian expressions of Quebec nationalism. A close reading of the official documents produced by the PQ in power—from the constitution to culture to economics—indicates a liberal democratic discourse to which various nationalist themes are rhetorically wedded in an uneasy and contradictory manner. In some cases, as in the official economic development strategy (*Bâtir le Québec*), nationalist themes virtually disappear. In others, like the White Paper on sovereignty-association, the tension is reflected in glaring inconsistencies.

Partly out of its basic inability to define clearly its own nationalist direction, partly out of the constraints of trying to reassure business and voters, the PQ's constitutional option was very blurred. Since they insisted on linking political sovereignty with economic association, that is, to argue that national independence was a constitutional superstructure unrelated to the economic base, they were in effect putting a double proposition to the voters: first, that there was a will to seek political sovereignty; second, that this will to independence was linked to the continuance of existing economic relations with English Canada, in some cases on a new basis, in some cases on a basis suspiciously like the present. The problem with this was that the first part could be a unilateral expression, with which English Canada would have to deal; the second was a matter for negotiation, which cannot be unilateral. Yet the first was linked to the second. The paradox for the PQ was that Quebec opinion, as revealed in the government's own polls, was contingent upon English Canada's reaction; this was summed up neatly in a cartoon in *Le Devoir* showing Quebec as a boxer in the corner saying, "We're ready to come out and fight, if English Canada allows us to win." Trudeau paraphrased the referendum question as: "Do you want to have your cake and eat it too?" Even worse was the PQ promise that the economic association would be based upon the principle of equality (*égal à égal*). Why English Canada, representing 70 percent of the population, should agree to a 50/50 relationship with 30 percent of the population in Quebec was never very obvious. Presumably the *formal* equality involved in bilateral relations between sovereign nations would be in effect, but formal equality between materially unequal nations is an empty equality.

What the referendum result revealed was an underlying reality of Quebec's relationship to Canada which appears to have escaped the attention of the most militant *indépendantistes*. Quebeckers have a long history—and, doubtless, a long future—of demanding more power and autonomy for the province. *Péquistes* made the mistake of assuming that this was a cumulative process which would inevitably lead to sovereignty. The problem is that demands made *in the provincial sphere* for provincial goals are not the same as demands made *in the federal sphere*. Hence the sometimes bizarre contrasts between provincial and federal voting in Quebec (PQ in Quebec and Liberal in Ottawa). In pursuing apparently divergent ideological and constitutional paths in federal and provincial politics, Quebeckers are not necessarily being irrational. Quite the contrary. A strong voice for the province of Quebec in federal–provincial negotiations need not be in contradiction to a strong Quebec presence in Ottawa—the irrationality may perhaps be discerned in the *structures* of federalism which set one political elite from Quebec against another elite in an adversarial bargaining confrontation, but that is another story. Pierre Trudeau *and* René Lévesque were both perceived by the bulk of voters in Quebec as champions of Quebec interests. And so they were.

The PQ's fatal error was to demand in effect that the people of Quebec be forced to choose, definitively, between two levels of government to which they were still, by and large, attached. If the federalist option had been successfully portrayed as a unitary centralism, within which the Quebec provincial state would inevitably disappear, then the PQ option could have won considerable support. A small number of *Péquiste* zealots aside, such a scenario could gain little credibility. Anyone with much of a memory could see tangible evidence that the Quebec state, under federalism, had gained enormously in fiscal power and responsibility over the twenty years since 1960. The real choice was between federalism, with its two levels of government, and sovereignty, with its one level. Of course the PQ hastened to muddy this with its arguments about sovereignty-association and its curious recreation under different names of federalist structures (although as decisively *bureaucratic* structures without the legitimation of direct popular election). But in order to mobilize support for the "yes" vote it was necessary to rhetorically identify loyalty to Quebec exclusively with a sovereign Quebec, thus excluding the notion of attachment to the federal dimension.

When the "no" strategists devised the slogan "*Je suis fier d'être québécois et canadien*," they quite brilliantly distilled the quintessence of the reluctance of the mass of the population to make the choice demanded by the PQ. Although a vast majority unsurprisingly agreed with a mid-referendum questionnaire statement that "I am profoundly attached to

Quebec," it was perhaps less expected that 76 percent of the same sample agreed with the statement "I am profoundly attached to Canada"— including an extraordinary 47 percent of those who intended to vote "yes."[3]

As the "no" campaign gained in confidence, an interesting phenomenon came to the fore. The display of Canadian flags and the singing of "O Canada" became features, not only in predominantly anglophone gatherings but in francophone ones as well. The point to be made here is not that Quebec francophones are really Canadians first; rather it is that the steady growth over recent years of popular identification as "Québécois" has not necessarily meant that "Canadian" has suffered an equivalent elimination. Obviously, for a body of *indépendantiste* activists and perhaps for certain occupational categories such as intellectuals and artists, Quebec and Canada have tended to become mutually exclusive categories. But for a sizeable section of the population, the intensification of emotional, nationalistic attachment to Quebec which began with the Quiet Revolution did not in itself subvert an attachment to federalism and a Canadian identification which no doubt lacks the warmth and sentimentality of loyalty to Quebec, but still maintains tenacious roots. Perhaps Pierre Trudeau's notion that passionate national loyalties to French Canada are matched by a cooler, more "rationalist" or functionalist base of loyalty to Canada as a whole may have some relevance here.

This raises another question. It has been argued, especially by left-wing independence supporters, that the "no" campaign was largely one of fear, in which pro-federalist forces combined with the big corporations to intimidate working-class and vulnerable middle-class voters into backing away from sovereignty-association under the threat, implied or direct, of a flight of capital. This charge has an element of truth, but it can be exaggerated. The PQ hardly posed a radical alternative to capitalism in its referendum question. Moreover it suggests a deep contempt of the Quebec people themselves to argue that federal anti-alcohol ads with the theme *"non merci"* somehow stampeded impressionable voters into the "no" side. In any event the PQ had four years of control over government advertising in the media to drive *their* point home.

Despite some rather tortured attempts to argue that the majority of francophone voters had actually voted "yes" (it being necessary to assume a sharply higher turnout among anglophones than among francophones *and* an extraordinarily high "no" percentage among all non-francophones), it seems likely that in fact more francophones voted "no" than voted "yes." It should also be obvious that the percentage of francophones who did vote "yes" was quite high, even if not a clear majority. Although the referendum was run on a simple majority basis, with no distinctions formally being made between francophone and anglophone voters, the political reality was, of course, quite different. An overall "no" majority of, say, 51 percent would clearly have lacked any legitimacy, since under such circumstances it would have been obvious that the francophones had voted decisively "yes." The resulting crisis would have been extremely volatile and dangerous for relations between the two communities in Quebec and would have left matters hanging intolerably for the rest of Canada. A clear result, one way or another, was obviously preferable, and in the event, this was in fact produced.

The question remains whether the result of the referendum can be seen as *definitive*. Predictions about the long run are best left to astrologers, but there has been a growing sense in the years since the referendum that in the short run—say, the next decade or so—the result will be determining. Despite the increasingly ritualistic reiterations by government leaders that sovereignty remains just around the corner, and despite repeated promises to run the next general election as a referendum on sovereignty, there is a pervasive feeling in Quebec that *indépendantisme* is yesterday's issue. There are a number of reasons for the waning of this question which so dominated Quebec politics for so many years.

The referendum was, in some ways, a moving example of a people undertaking a collective decision which would determine their destiny for the future. The debate penetrated into levels of society normally left untouched by party politics, and in some senses represented a moment of true democracy rarely witnessed in Quebec or elsewhere. The other side of this coin is that it was a traumatic event for many, to those whose families and personal relations were rent by political divisions, and above all to those who threw themselves body and soul into the "yes" campaign and then saw their dream rejected by 60 percent of their fellow citizens. The historic moment arrived and the vision suddenly shattered. It may be very difficult for this generation of *indépendantiste* activists to put themselves again through that kind of traumatic public vulnerability for some time.

Apart from psychological suppositions, there are deeper reasons to suspect that the referendum has settled matters for a good while. There is, for instance, growing evidence that the ancient complaint of francophones that they have no future in the corporate sector is becoming less credible as capitalism adjusts to making profits in French as well as in English. Moreover, there is a marked shift among francophone students toward commerce and business administration, which is eliminating differences with anglophones in career orientation which had remained apparent until recently. A study published in 1981 under the sponsorship of the *Conseil de la langue française* revealed that when age is taken into account, there is little if any evidence of higher income among anglophones than among francophones in their forties and younger in similar occupations in Quebec; indeed, there is marginal evidence that some francophones now make more than their anglophone counterparts.[4] In short, the generation which came of age at the time of the Quiet Revolution has moved through a historic alteration in the old pattern of unequal accommodation between the two language groups. The generation coming of age in the 1980s faces fewer of the blatant aggravations which galvanized an earlier generation into militant *indépendantiste* politics. Lévesque claimed on referendum night that his sovereignty-association option had been defeated by *"le vieux Québec."* The assertion that the younger voters are naturally *indépendantistes* and that opposition to the PQ option will pass away with time—an assertion repeated once again for the benefit of the French media on Lévesque's 1983 visit to France—appears to be another comforting, but insubstantial, PQ myth. PQ support is in fact weakening among the very youngest voters, and 18–21-year-old voters appear to have divided pretty much in the same proportions as their elders in the referendum.

The problematic character of Quebec youth's attachment to independence was dramatically highlighted in August of 1983 when a summit meeting of youth organizations voted against a resolution expressing support for an independent Quebec. As some of the delegates made clear, this result arose perhaps not so much out of positive support for Canadian federalism as from disillusion with an *indépendantiste* government which, instead of solving problems whose solution already lay within provincial jurisdiction, persisted in trying to use these problems as a means of mobilizing support for sovereignty as a panacea.

The backdrop to the referendum and to the subsequent confrontation between the PQ government and Ottawa over the new constitution has, of course, been the continued economic recession which has cut even deeper in Quebec than in some other parts of Canada, given the historically limited nature of Quebec's industrialization. The PQ has attempted to fix the blame for this squarely on the federal government's policies and to argue that salvation can only come through independence. Yet far from intensifying popular support for sovereignty, hard economic times seem to have deepened *disinterest* in nationalist adventures. In part this disinterest derives from fear of more political uncertainty driving out investment and jobs, and in part it derives from a desire to see both levels of government stop their petty conflicts over place and prestige and get down to the job of cooperating for economic recovery.

The PQ's role in the constitutional negotiations following the referendum must also be critically scrutinized to understand their waning prestige within Quebec as the defenders of the Quebec nation. Having misfired their own constitutional option, the PQ proved singularly inept in negotiating a new constitutional arrangement within Canada. Lévesque actually signed an accord with the premiers in opposition to Trudeau's unilateral initiative, which failed to recognize a special veto for Quebec on amendments (the federal government's proposals did include a Quebec veto), and then bitterly denounced Ottawa for denying Quebec's "historic" right to a veto when the accord to which he had agreed was accepted. At a premiers' conference in the 1970s, Lévesque had offered a reciprocal exchange of minority language rights in education with the English Canadian premiers—and then vehemently denounced the exact same agreement, when written into the new constitution, as an attack on Quebec's linguistic rights.

Lévesque's negotiating tactics only make sense if they are seen as resulting from *une politique du pire*, that is to say, a policy of ensuring defeat in order to demonstrate that things are so bad under federalism that sovereignty is the only salvation. If that were indeed the plan, the effect on public opinion may have been badly misjudged. Quebec voters have always wanted their provincial government to stand up for Quebec in federal–provincial relations. While some may interpret the Canada Act of 1982 as a sign that there is no future for Quebec within Canada, a great many more may well conclude that the PQ are simply poor negotiators on behalf of Quebec interests. Moreover, while the absence of a Quebec veto is dangerous in a binational state, things are not so dark as the PQ would have people believe. Provinces can, after all, opt out of constitutional amendments of which they disapprove, and, where such amendments have to do with educational or cultural matters, they can receive fiscal compensation—a clear indication of a special status for Quebec. The main lines of the Quebec language law (French as the language of work, a French language environment in terms of signs and advertising, etc., and the assimilation of the non-anglophone immigrants into French language education) are now preserved by the constitution, with only such marginal matters as bilingual statutes and debate in the National Assembly, and the right of anglophones coming from other provinces to send their children to English schools open to change by constitutional interpretation. In exchange, there has been a major concession to French language rights in education in English Canadian provinces, and the extension of official bilingualism to New Brunswick, with its large Acadian minority.

In fact the new constitution does clearly recognize the linguistic and cultural duality of Canada, that is, the duality of English and French Canada. What it does not do is to recognize duality of the Quebec and Canadian *states, qua* states. In short, the constitutional resolution of 1982 was a victory for Pierre Trudeau's long-standing belief that the question was one of individual rights of English and French Canadians, and a defeat for the *péquiste* position that linguistic and cultural survival demands a sovereign state as its only sure guarantee. Time alone will tell if the Trudeau solution will actually work; just as obviously, it is requisite to the PQ's survival as a force that it *not* work. The conundrum for the PQ is whether *la politique du pire* is a defensible strategy to sell to the people. For instance, the PQ, alone among the provincial governments, has opted to invoke the "notwithstanding" clause on each and every piece of legislation it introduces into the National Assembly, thus exempting Quebec from the Charter of Rights. Can it, in the long run, justify to its own citizens the denial of the protection of individual rights, in the name of a (negative) defence of the rights of the Quebec state?

The difficulties encountered by a government attempting this kind of strategy were painfully highlighted in the immediate aftermath of the constitutional accord, at a PQ congress. After escalating the rhetorical level to suggest that Quebec was being virtually raped by the federal government and the English Canadian provinces, Lévesque in effect incited the extreme nationalist wing of the party to push for an out-and-out sovereignty position. Aware at the same time that this extreme reaction would be rejected by the voters, Lévesque refused to accept the majority decisions of the congress, and subjected the party to the humiliating exercise of a mailed ballot (the so-called *"Renérendum"*), in which party members were asked to recant their views or to force *le chef* to resign. Obedience to *le chef* won over party democracy. The confusion in all this is profound, and the contradictions may well be insupportable. Certainly doubts must remain that the PQ will actually fulfill its stated determination to fight the next provincial election on the sovereignty issue, or, if it does, that it can be anything other than a suicidal decision. In 1970, 1973 and 1980 the PQ was the party of sovereignty, and was rejected by the voters. In 1976 and 1981, it was the party of good government, and was endorsed.

An interesting feature of the 1981 election was the decline in ethnic polarization. More anglophones and especially other ethnics voted PQ than before, and two anglophones were elected as PQ members in predominantly francophone seats. In the Montreal civic elections of 1982, ethnic and linguistic polarization seem to have broken down entirely under the counter-pressure of a struggle between the old Jean Drapeau machine and a francophone–anglophone reformist party. It is possible that in the future Quebec politics will become more oriented toward economic and social issues and less dominated by an overarching concern for nationalism without social content. Ironically, the PQ will have helped bring this about, both through creating a legislative framework conducive to the enhanced position of francophone identity in Quebec, and by finally stretching the nationalist issue to near breaking point. How well the PQ can itself survive its ironic success is another matter.

Beyond party politics, there remains the deeper and more significant question of the relationship of Quebec society to Canada, and North America. The problem to be addressed for the 1980s is that of the integration of Quebec into the economic structures of North American capitalism. To what extent this process will continue, to what effect on the class structure of Quebec, and to what effect on Quebec culture and identity—these are questions which will ultimately determine whether the referendum of 1980 was the last gasp of the kind of nationalism unleashed by the 1960s or merely another shot in a gathering campaign. Of course English Canada's *political* responses to Quebec will play a role in this, but not so important a role as the structural changes in Quebec itself. To return to where this essay began: one thing alone is certain, that Quebec nationalism will continue; what specific form and expression that nationalism will take will ultimately be a product of forces deeper than politics alone.

Notes

1. Henry Milner, *Politics in the New Quebec* (Toronto: McClelland and Stewart, 1978), p. 148.
2. Some of this debate has been translated into English in *Studies in Political Economy*. See Jorge Niosi, "The New French-Canadian Bourgeoisie," 1 (Spring 1979); Gilles Bourque, "Class, Nation, and the Parti Québécois," 2 (Fall 1979); Pierre Fournier, "Parameters of the New Quebec Bourgeoisie," 3 (Spring 1980).
3. Maurice Pinard and Richard Hamilton, poll reported in *Le Devoir*, May 17, 1979, p. 9.
4. Robert Lacroix and François Vaillancourt, *Les revenus et la langue au Québec (1970-1978)* (Québec: Government of Québec, 1981).

Further Readings

Bourque, Gilles, and Anne Legaré. *Le Québec—la question nationale.* Paris: F. Maspera, 1979. The best introduction to a Marxist view.

Clift, Dominique. *Quebec Nationalism in Decline.* Montreal: McGill-Queen's University Press, 1982.

Dion, Léon. *Quebec: The Unfinished Revolution.* Montreal: McGill-Queen's University Press, 1976. A collection of writings by one of the doyens of Quebec's intellectual life on the period from 1960 to the present.

Guidon, Herbert. "The Modernization of Quebec and the Legitimacy of the Canadian State." In *Modernization and the Canadian State*, edited by D. Glenday, H. Guidon and A. Turowetz. Toronto: Macmillan, 1978. One of the best succinct treatments of "new middle class" nationalism in the Quiet Revolution and beyond.

McRoberts, Kenneth, and Dale Posgate. *Quebec: Social Change and Political Crisis.* 2nd ed. Toronto: McClelland & Stewart, 1980. The best English-language source for an overview of Quebec since the Second World War (and in some ways more comprehensive than anything in French).

Milner, Henry. *Politics in the New Quebec.* Toronto: McClelland and Stewart, 1977. On the PQ.

Monière, Denis. *Ideologies in Quebec: the historical development*. Toronto: University of Toronto Press, 1981.

Murray, Vera. *Le parti québécois*. Montreal: Hurtubise, 1977. On the PQ.

Rioux, Marcel. *Quebec in Question*. Toronto: Lorimer, 1971. A nationalist interpretation.

Trofimenkoff, Susan Mann. *Quebec: The Dream of Nation*. Toronto: Macmillan, 1982. A historical view of nationalist ideas.

Trudeau, Pierre Elliott. *Federalism and the French Canadians*. Toronto: Methuen, 1968.

Chapter 3

Canada's North in the Eighties
Michael S. Whittington

A cursory glance at a map of Canada will reveal that a very large percentage of our total land mass lies north of the sixtieth parallel and outside the boundaries of the ten provinces. However, while Yukon and the Northwest Territories make up almost 40 percent of Canada, their combined population is less than 70,000. Long viewed as a trackless wasteland or barren wilderness by Canadians living in the ten provinces, during the 1950s these northern territories came to be viewed both as a frontier and as a vast storehouse of mineral and petroleum resources. The goal of "opening up the North" and tapping its resources for southern industries was made explicit during the 1960s and 1970s, and federal government policies such as Diefenbaker's "Roads to Resources" were directed at conquering the northern wilderness. The seventies, however, also witnessed an awakening of people's consciousness that the North, while a wilderness to southern Canadians, was in fact home to the Indians, Inuit and many long-term white residents. The Berger Inquiry in the 1970s revealed to southern Canadians that the people of the North are very committed to their land and feel a deep and justifiable resentment that their homeland is seen simply as a resource warehouse for southern industries. The fate of the North, its resources and its people, and the ultimate relationship that will exist between the northern territories and the rest of Canada became a central policy concern toward the end of the seventies, and the settlement of these issues will likely be a dominant item on the agenda for political decision making up to the turn of the century.

The Northern Environment: Population and Resources
The population of the North, while tiny numerically, is extremely diverse culturally and linguistically. The total population of the Northwest Territories is approximately 46,000, of which 17 percent are Dene, 35 percent Inuit, 6 percent Métis, and 42 percent non-native. A significant percentage of the white population of the Northwest Territories is composed of people who are only temporary residents or transients and who will ultimately return to southern parts of Canada. The population

of Yukon is approximately 23,000, of which slightly more than one-quarter are Indians and Métis and the remainder white. One significant difference between the whites in Yukon and those of the Northwest Territories is that a much larger percentage of the former are, in fact, long-time residents of the North.[1]

A common error made by southern Canadians when they speak of the North is lumping the non-white population of the territories together in the category of "natives." This leads to a very distorted perception of the diversity, both cultural and linguistic, that exists among the native communities. In the first place, the Inuit and the Indians have very little in common with each other and traditionally were bitter enemies when they came into contact. The Inuit language, Inuktitut, is as different from the Athapaskan or Dene languages spoken in the Macken-zie Valley as English is from, say, Finnish. On the other hand, while there are several distinct dialects of Inuktitut spoken in Canada's North, in fact they are similar enough that communication is possible among members of various dialect groups. There are several Indian languages spoken in the Mackenzie Valley, all of which share the Athapaskan root. However, Dogrib, Hare, Slavey, Chipewyan and Loucheux (or Kutchin) are distinct languages which are related to each other in the same way that the romance languages of Europe are related to each other. In Yukon, while there are virtually no Inuit, there are several Athapaskan dialects spoken, as well as Tlingit, which is a completely different language related to the languages spoken by the natives of Alaska. Moreover, of the Athapaskan languages spoken in Yukon, only one, Loucheux, is shared by natives of the Northwest Territories.

A second common error committed by southern Canadians is to try to generalize about Yukon and the Northwest Territories. As we shall see in the remainder of this chapter, while there are some similar problems shared by the two northern territories, there are also signifi-cant differences in the patterns of constitutional and political develop-ment and in the economies of Yukon and Northwest Territories.

The economies of Canada's northern territories, while only begin-ning to develop, are very diverse but generally founded upon primary resources. The traditional economy of the Northwest Territories and Yukon was based on hunting and fishing. In other words, before the whites arrived the northern economy was one of subsistence, depending on renewable resources such as wildlife, fish and wild plants to provide food, fuel, shelter and clothing to the original inhabitants. The first exposure to Europeans occurred in the north-east, where whalers and explorers, and later missionaries, made the initial intrusions. While these contacts produced some important cultural changes among the Inuit, they did not significantly alter the basic subsistence economy.

In the western Arctic, by contrast, the first exposure to whites was through the fur trade. Here, contact with the European culture actually had a very immediate effect on the traditional economy, for the fur traders taught the natives that they could exchange pelts for goods unattainable locally, such as metal tools and weapons, manufactured textiles and rum. In effect, the subsistence economy was modified to the extent that the notion of furs as a medium of exchange that could be used to obtain valuable commodities was introduced to the Athapaskan peoples. Nevertheless, basic needs such as food and shelter were still supplied by the subsistence economy, and in fact the fur trade was compatible and even complementary to the traditional way of life of the northern people. Again the missionaries, and later the RCMP, wrought significant cultural (and, it is alleged, genetic) changes on the people of the Mackenzie Valley but had little independent effect on the traditional economy.

The first direct exposure to white people in Yukon came considerably later, and, as with the natives of the Mackenzie Valley, the Yukon Indians had their subsistence economy altered to some extent by the incursion of the fur trade. The significant economic changes in Yukon, however, occurred with the discovery of placer deposits of gold in 1896, and the subsequent "gold rush" of 1898. This brief period of large-scale white immigration was to alter the economy and the lifestyle of the Yukon natives profoundly and (some would say) irreversibly. Where in the rest of the North the native contact with European culture was through "the Bay," the Church and the RCMP—and the individuals associated with these three venerable institutions tended to be only transient residents of the North—in Yukon, a significant number of the whites who migrated to the territory with hopes of "striking it rich" in the gold fields actually stayed on after the bonanza days.

In the Northwest Territories, the churches had come to bring the natives "salvation," the RCMP had come to bring them "law and order," and "the Bay" had come to exploit them in a commercial relationship. In Yukon, the whites who stayed set about to "civilize" the territory itself without much serious concern for the original inhabitants at all. Thus, in the Northwest Territories the whites were there to a large extent *because* of the natives, whereas in Yukon the natives tended to be an incidental fact of the environment and often were thus effectively ignored and left alone by the permanent white settlements in Dawson and Whitehorse.

In the Northwest Territories there was very little change in the basic lifestyle of the natives throughout the first half of the twentieth century. The discovery of oil at NormanWells in the 1920s did not produce significant changes in the economy, though the Canol pipeline was built from Norman Wells to Alaska during World War II as a stratetic response to the possibility of a Japanese invasion of the west coast and consequent severing of supplies to Alaska. Gold was discovered near Yellowknife in the 1930s, and since that period mines have operated at varying levels of production in the Great Slave Lake region of the territory. However, while these enterprises may have had localized effects on the natives in the immediate vicinity of the projects, there was no attempt to include the local inhabitants in the workforce. In the eastern Arctic there was still less development and, in fact, with the exception of some mineral exploration and the occasional visit of an RCMP patrol (sometimes with a public health nurse in tow) the Inuit were left to the tender mercies of either the Anglican or Roman Catholic Church (depending upon who got there first). As a result, the economy of the Inuit did not alter very much. However, where there was contact with the Church and where, therefore, the Inuit received some European education and exposure to the values of Christianity, a number of the traditional values of their culture may have been weakened or erased.

Again, the experience of Yukon was different. While there was constant gold mining throughout the early decades of the century, and while there was a permanent white population throughout the period, significant new development did not occur until the building of the Alaska Highway. The construction period itself caused social disorientation in the native communities along the way, partly because many settlements were physically relocated along the highway by the government so that they would be easier to administer. The more significant impacts, however, were to occur as a result of Yukon becoming accessible by road to the south. Not only did this open up opportunities for mineral exploration, but tourism began to evolve as a significant component of the economy of the territory. The local white inhabitants welcomed this development as an opportunity to "civilize" still further their chosen homeland. A new wave of white immigration occurred after World War II, and as before, while there was no intentional meddling with the native culture or economy, the incidental impacts were fairly extensive.

By the 1960s, the pace of northern development had speeded up considerably. The construction of a string of defensive radar bases across the far North, the Distant Early Warning (DEW) line and related military operations in the Arctic had brought white people into local contact with native communities. As well, the Conservative government's "Roads to Resources" program had helped stimulate the construction of all-season roads to once-remote communities such as Inuvik in the Mackenzie Delta (the Dempster Highway, completed in 1978) and Yellowknife, Pine Point, Hay River, Fort Smith and Fort Simpson in the Great Slave region (the Mackenzie Highway). Moreover, a series of Canadian governments had come to the realization that there were vast and significant potential petroleum and mineral resources in the far North that could be utilized to supply the raw materials for growing industries in southern Canada. Here, the presumption was that such development was to the advantage of *all* Canadians and that, in fact, it would even be welcomed by the natives of the North, who would benefit from being brought into the mainstream of Canadian life with all of its economic, health and cultural benefits. This presumption has proven to be simply presumptuous. To the amazement of southern Canadian politicians, the northern natives have not always welcomed this southern-style development and, in fact, have often become outspoken in their opposition to it.

The economic development of the North is continuing, but as we look to the decade of the eighties, the problems of "opening up the North" transcend the engineering and technological problems of building roads and pipelines through regions of discontinuous permafrost, of operating heavy and delicate machinery in extremes of temperature and of building tankers that have "class ten" icebreaking capacities. These problems of technology and engineering have in many cases become second order, incidental problems when compared to the social and political obstacles of developing and transporting resources when the indigenous population is vehemently opposed to such projects from the outset.

Native Values: The Land

Southern white Canadians have all too often assumed that the value system of the natives was very close to their own. On the contrary, there are great cultural differences not only between the white and native communities but even among the various native groups in the North. Perhaps the most significant difference between white and native values is that the natives, in this case the Dene as well as the Inuit, place a far higher value on the collectivity and the community. The notion of private property is extremely underdeveloped, and the principle of community sharing of the wealth of the band, settlement or extended family is very important. The concept of possession, which is such an important cornerstone of liberal societies, is replaced as well by the simpler notion of "use" of things valued. The sharing ethic and the replacement of the liberal notion of private ownership with the shared inherent right of individuals to use a resource are nowhere more prominent than in the native concept of *the land.*

In the native culture, Dene and Inuit alike, the land holds a very special place, for it is the land upon which the community must depend for its survival. All of the requirements for existence must somehow be extracted from the land. Conversely, in a mystical way, the native peoples feel a "oneness" with the land. Unlike the whites' view of the North as a wilderness and a frontier to be pushed back and altered to serve their needs, the natives of the North view it as a homeland to which they must adapt in order to survive. The native religions all espouse the notion of human respect for the land and of the spiritual connections between people and the land that provides their livelihood. Thus the native culture has difficulty accommodating the very idea of extracting *non-renewable* resources from the wealth of the land. For the most part, the native economy extracted only resources *which could be renewed*—in this sense the natives *use* the resources of the land but they do not permanently alienate any of its wealth.

Finally, the natives of the North have been opposed to many of the resource development schemes, not simply because the notion of resource extraction is culturally alien to them, but for very practical reasons. The natives have learned from hard experience that all too often the whites leave a trail of waste and destruction behind them when they undertake to develop the North. (It has been said in ironic jest that the symbol of the North should be a forty-five gallon fuel drum because of the large numbers of them abandoned even in the most remote parts of the North.) In this respect the natives have been suspicious of development, not simply because the concept of non-renewable resource extraction is foreign to them, but because the activity associated with resource development can alter or even destroy the renewable resources—the fish, wildlife and flora—upon which the native economy and the traditional way of life ultimately depend. In this matter the natives often share the views of southern-based environmental groups such as the Canadian Arctic Resources Committee (CARC), but, as we shall see, for quite different reasons.

The Native Political Culture

Southerners often mistakenly assume that the natives of the far North have no indigenous political culture—that until the coming of the Europeans the North lacked political institutions. However, the northern people have governed themselves since their arrival on this continent centuries before the European explorers. While the native political cultures are less institutionalized than ours, the fact remains that the basic political functions were performed in traditional native communities. One of the features that distinguishes our political culture from that of the Dene and the Inuit is their egalitarianism. An extension of the "sharing" ethic described above, when transposed into the political context—the right of all members of a community to express their views and to have an influence on the decisions that affect them—is an ancient and deeply rooted political value.

The egalitarianism, however, does not eliminate the need for leadership in the traditional communities. But, where we tend to think of political leadership as a highly unitary concept—that is, a concept that features a sovereign institution or individual with the ultimate power to make final decisions on all aspects of social and political life—the native concept of leadership is both *diffuse* and *functional*. It is diffuse because native communities follow different leaders for different kinds of community activities. There are often totally different power structures in a traditional native community, depending upon whether the decisions to be taken involve hunting, war, spiritual matters, settlement of internal disputes or punishment of wrongdoers. Native leadership is functional because the choice of leader in any given situation depends upon who is best suited to lead in that particular circumstance. There are the top hunters in the communities who will dominate decision making in one area, shamans who will dominate in another and tribal elders who may assume authority for still others. These leaders are not elected in the sense that democratic politics defines elections, but rather they come to lead almost automatically, through a sort of community consensus that they are the people most able to do so. Thus it is that sometimes even the most well-meaning attempts of white people to give the natives the best of our political institutions—institutions such as representative democracy—have met with only marginal acceptance. The partial failure of some of these experiments, such as elected municipal councils, must be viewed not so much as an indication of the lack of political development of the native peoples, but more as simply a reluctance to replace the political values that they have applied for centuries with a new set imposed from outside. This point must be kept in mind when we discuss the basic political institutions which operate in the North today.

Constitutional History of the North

Although it would be possible to write an extensive article on the constitutional development of the North, the aim here is simply to outline the major events in order to place the current situation in context. Ironically, both the Northwest Territories and Yukon have enjoyed a status closer to responsible government in the past than they do today. The older Northwest Territories, composed of Yukon and the modern Northwest Territories as well as territory that is now the provinces of Alberta and Saskatchewan, had a fully elected legislative assembly by 1881 and responsible government from 1897. In 1898 the Yukon territory was carved out of the Northwest Territories and a commissioner was appointed. Originally the commissioner was advised by an appointed six-member council, but gradually the number of elected members of the council was increased until, by 1908, all members were elected. The territory seemed virtually on the brink of full responsible government and well on the way to provincial status at this time. But after the Klondike boom collapsed, the population declined, and by the end of World War I the territory had come to be administered almost totally at the whim of the federally appointed commissioner.

Although the Yukon Territorial Council declined in size as the boom period faded away, the council continued to be wholly elected, and both the commissioner and the council continued to sit in the territory rather

than in Ottawa. Any hope for a gradual evolution to responsible government and ultimately provincehood was shelved effectively until the
decade of the seventies when the slow movement in that direction began
again.

The modern Northwest Territories enjoyed an even shorter period
of boom than Yukon. When the provinces of Alberta and Saskatchewan
were created in 1905, the remaining lands of the territory and the people
who lived there reverted to full colonial status, ruled by public servants in
Ottawa. In 1921 a council was appointed to advise the commissioner, but
all six of the councillors as well as the commissioner himself were federal
bureaucrats in the national capital. This status remained essentially
unchanged until 1951 when the first members were elected to the council
and the first sitting of the council was held in the territory. The territorial
franchise was originally limited to the residents of the Mackenzie Valley,
but in 1966 three ridings were created in the eastern Arctic. However,
the commissioner still ruled very much as a colonial governor, residing in
Ottawa and dividing his attention between his responsibilities as commissioner and other obligations as a senior bureaucrat in the Department
of Northern Affairs. Moreover, in his decisions regarding the territory,
he listened to his elected councillors more as a matter of protocol than
through any constitutional obligation. In 1965, a three-member commission was established to look at the political future of the territory. The
"Carrothers Commission" made a number of recommendations about
the conduct of government, with the result that the council was enlarged
to sixteen members in 1967, and the seat of government and the commissioner of the territory took up permanent residence in Yellowknife. By
1975 the Northwest Territories had the first totally elected council since
1905, and since then the council has been converted to a legislative
assembly.

Political Institutions of the Northern Territories

In spite of all the pressure for more responsible government emanating
from the territories and in spite of the gains that have been made in that
direction, constitutionally the territories are still subordinate entities.
Much of the administrative responsibility continues to reside with the
Department of Indian Affairs and Northern Development (DIAND). The
legislative assemblies, although now fully elected in both territories, do
not have sovereign powers. Their authority is a result of delegation to
them by the Parliament of Canada and by DIAND, and can be taken away
at the whim of the federal government. In this sense the constitutional
status of the territorial legislatures is analogous to the status of a municipality vis-à-vis the province.

The Yukon legislative assembly is composed of sixteen members
elected by constituency, and the Progressive Conservatives form the

current government in Yukon, holding nine seats. The official opposition is the NDP, with six of the seats in the assembly. There is one Independent member who is also the Speaker of the assembly. The Executive Council in Yukon is composed of five ministers and the commissioner. While the system is not yet one that can be called full responsible government, the practice on the executive council at the present is very close to that. As a result of a letter from the PC minister of northern affairs in 1979, the commissioner is now instructed to operate as though he or she is a lieutenant-governor and must take the advice of the elected executive. In fact, the commissioner no longer even sits on the executive council, which is chaired by the Government leader. As a result of this letter of instruction from the minister, the commissioner of the day, Ione Christenson, resigned, stating, in effect, that she did not wish to be merely a figurehead. The subsequent defeat of the federal Conservatives has not in any apparent way reversed the trend toward full responsible government in the territory, and in fact the legislative assembly is operating today as though it possessed the power of voting non-confidence in the executive in the same way that a legislature can defeat a government in the provinces.

The Northwest Territories has not progressed quite as far as Yukon along the road to responsible government, but it is not far behind. Its legislative assembly is composed of twenty-four members elected by constituency from across the territory. While political parties have not yet evolved in territorial elections, a large number of the current crop of MLAs are active in and committed to *federal* political parties. There was a short-lived attempt before the 1983 election to form a "Northern Party" out of a coalition of Liberal and PC candidates. However, the idea did not receive much support outside of Yellowknife and was ultimately abandoned when the PC Association in the Territory refused to endorse it. While future territorial elections may eventually be fought along party lines, the current divisions in the territorial assembly are factional ones, reflecting regional, ethnic, and urban–rural differences rather than partisan ones.

There is an executive council in the Northwest Territories as in Yukon, which is composed of eight elected members chosen by the legislative assembly; however, unlike Yukon, the commissioner of the Northwest Territories is still an active member of the executive council and in fact still acts as the chairperson of that body. The deputy chairperson of the executive council is the Leader of the Elected Executive, a position established during the Ninth Assembly and clearly designed to ultimately evolve into a "proto-premiership." While, unlike the case of Yukon, there was no magical letter from Ottawa instructing the commissioner of the Northwest Territories to "back off" and let the elected people take the initiative, because of the personality of the current commissioner, John

Parker, who generally favours responsible government, the position of the commissioner in the territory is gradually evolving toward a role very similar to that of the commissioner of Yukon.

Possibly the most significant obstacle to the development of full responsible government in the Northwest Territories is the lack of a party system in the legislative assembly. The system in place, often referred to (perhaps ironically) as "consensus government," sees the selection of the members of the executive council through a wide open "election at large" within the "caucus" of the assembly. The caucus, in the absence of political parties, includes the entire assembly sitting *in camera* and casting votes as twenty-four Independents. This means that the members of the executive council sit there as Independents—there is no collective responsibility and consequently no clear procedure for voting non-confidence in the government. Unless the members of the executive can be held collectively responsible for their actions there can be no responsible government in any conventional sense.

But having said this, it must also be recognized that the current system *is* working. The various regional, ethnic and urban–rural factions form issue-specific coalitions within the caucus before controversial matters are raised formally in the assembly. As a result there is a constantly shifting pattern of alliances and sub-coalitions within the legislature and within the executive council itself which permit the continuation of the government and the conduct of the legislature's business on an issue-by-issue basis.

The composition of the legislative assemblies of the Northwest Territories and Yukon is reflective of the ethnic and regional diversity of the two territories. There are three members of the Yukon assembly who can claim native ancestry, two on the opposition side and one on the government back benches. However, the executive council of Yukon is composed entirely of non-natives. The legislative assembly of the Northwest Territories has eight Inuit, six Dene and ten non-native members. The Executive Council is composed of two Inuit, two Dene (one of whom is the Leader, Richard Nerysoo from Fort McPherson) and four whites. However, what is more interesting in the Northwest Territories is the *regional* distribution of the members of the executive council. The communities of Yellowknife, Hay River and Fort Smith, which contain one third of the population of the Northwest Territories, are not represented at all on the executive, while the Mackenzie Delta Region, with a population of only 6,000, has three ministers and the Keewatin Region, with a population of less than 4,000 and only two seats, has both of its members on the executive. It would appear, then, that the dominant coalition within the Tenth Assembly reflects a large centre–small centre cleavage rather than the east–west split which dominated the deliberations of the Ninth Assembly.

There are three federal constituencies in the North: one in Yukon, which has been the virtual fiefdom of Conservative Erik Neilson for decades; Western Arctic in the Mackenzie Valley, which is currently held by Dave Nickerson of the PCs; and Nunatsiaq in the eastern Arctic, which is held by Peter Itinuar, the first Inuk ever to be elected to the Canadian Parliament. Itinuar, who was elected as an NDP candidate, crossed the floor of the House in November 1982 to join the Liberal caucus, where he felt he could have a greater influence on federal policies affecting the North. While the representatives of the Northwest Territories and Yukon are only three out of 282, they have been able to score some points for their constituents from the back benches. In the case of Erik Neilson, who is a PC front bencher, it seems quite likely that the initiatives taken in 1979–80 by the short-lived Progressive Conservative government toward responsible government and provincehood in Yukon were influenced significantly by him. Finally, although the Senate is not a particularly dominant institution in the business of government in Canada, it must be noted that Yukon and the Northwest Territories are each represented by a senator, and the one from the Northwest Territories, Willie Adams, is in fact an Inuk, appointed by the Liberals in 1977.

Having reconciled the gradual but perceptible evolution of the territories toward responsible government and the extent to which the territories are represented in the Parliament of Canada, it is still necessary to point out that the relationship of the territories to the federal government remains essentially colonial. Ultimately we must ask, does it matter if there is responsible government *within* the Northwest Territories and Yukon if neither territory possesses any real power vis-à-vis its colonial parent in Ottawa? The issue of primary concern to northerners in the long run will be that of *devolution of authority* to the territorial governments and ultimately the achievement of provincial status. The most promising trend in that regard can be seen, perhaps ironically, in the growth of the territorial bureaucracies.

Bureaucracy in the Territories

A dominant if declining bureaucratic force in the Northwest Territories and Yukon to this day is the federal Department of Indian Affairs and Northern Development (DIAND), which functions as a kind of "colonial office" for the North. It is a vast, sprawling organization, sometimes at war with itself when its "Development" mandate collides with its "Indian Affairs" mandate, but with extremely comprehensive responsibility within the two northern territories.

Until the Carrothers Commission, DIAND was virtually unchallenged in its control over all matters in the Northwest Territories. Some specific functions were performed by branches of several federal departments such as Transport, Health and Welfare, and DND, but, where "provincial-type" responsibilities had to be carried out, it was Northern Affairs that dominated. Until 1967 there was virtually no territorial bureaucracy at all, for the simple reason that the territorial government was given very little to do. As a result of recommendations of the Carrothers Report, the federal government began a policy of gradual devolution of legislative authority to the territorial council. Naturally this meant that there would have to be an expanded territorial public service to carry out the ordinances of that council, and, since then, we have seen a fairly rapid growth of the territorial bureaucracy. In Yukon the territorial bureaucracy evolved earlier than in the Northwest Territories. Because there was a significant number of white residents who demanded a level of political control closer to what they had been used to in southern Canada, the federal government was forced to make concessions in the name of the principle of self-government.

By 1981 the territorial assemblies had been delegated responsibility for education, social development, municipal affairs, public works and the administration of justice. In the economic areas, the territories have been given control over some matters such as tourism, small businesses, and the regulating and licensing of sport fishing and hunting.[2] While traditionally the budgets of Yukon and the Northwest Territories were passed as part of DIAND's estimates, as of 1980 the territorial councils submit their estimates directly to the Treasury Board in Ottawa. Currently the territorial governments and Ottawa are working out a new system of formula financing whereby the Northwest Territories and Yukon will simply receive a block grant from the federal treasury that can be spent entirely at the discretion of the legislative assembly. If and when this more autonomous system of funding is implemented, we can anticipate some expansion of the territorial bureaucracy in the general areas of finance and administrative support. Although the organization of portfolios varies both over time and from one territory to the other, basically the bureaucracies are reflective of their legislative mandates, and the principles of departmentalization are similar to those that prevail in the provinces.

Not surprisingly, a significant implication of the growth of the territorial bureaucracies has been a reduction of the dominance of DIAND. While this has been achieved as well by marginal increases in the northern establishments of other federal agencies such as DOE and EMR, the DIAND presence in Whitehorse and Yellowknife has continued to grow in terms of human resources. When this is coupled with the rapid growth of the territorial public service and with the fact that white southerners tend to monopolize the positions in both the federal and territorial bureaucracies, the result has been a shift in the ratio of whites to natives in both territories. The realization that they might one day soon become a minority in their own land has been an important catalyst in the evolution of Indian and Inuit political movements. It is to a consideration of this and related issues that we must now address ourselves.

The North in the Eighties: Issues and Dilemmas

The North has been evolving very slowly over many decades, and while changes have occurred, there was never perceived to be any real rush about dealing with northern issues. Why then, one might well ask, is there any urgency today, and why could this series of chapters on Canada in the mid-1980s suggest that northern development is going to be a significant item on the agenda for decision making in the remainder of the decade? The answer is simply that, at last, the mainstream Canadian economic and political elites now see a need to develop the resources that for more than a century have been permitted to lie in "cold storage," undiscovered or at least unexploited. The North (and its people), traditionally ignored by southern politicians, has become economically significant to the rest of Canada.

The initial assumption of southern Canadians was that development would be welcomed by the people of the North, who at last were to be given the full benefits of southern industrialized society and all of the luxuries associated with "civilization." When the first development schemes were unwrapped, the objections of a few outspoken northerners were dismissed as the bleatings of a minority of cranks—crackpots who dared to stand in the way of progress. However, the process of the Berger Inquiry clearly brought home the point that the northern natives were very much in agreement in expressing their fears of large-scale development projects. The natives of the North wish to ensure that resource development projects will not destroy their way of life and ultimately wipe out the native culture. The native culture is very fragile when compared to the cultures of complex industrial societies, and in fact the social and economic uniqueness of the native culture rests to a large extent upon the land. If the land and its resources are taken away or destroyed by large-scale development, the culture, the traditional economy and the way of life of the native people will perish.

While the original position of the Northern native groups was that there should be no development until land claims are settled, there are some indications that that position has softened. All of the major native groups in the North have set up development corporations which are becoming involved directly in resource development projects. As examples, the economic arm of the Committee for Original Peoples' Entitlement (COPE), the Inuvialuit Development Corporation, has become involved in joint ventures with the oil industry in the Beaufort Sea and Mackenzie Delta, the Denendeh Development Corporation has entered a joint drilling venture with Esso Resources in the Norman Wells Area, and the ITC's Nunasi Corporation has established a number of small businesses and has become directly involved in oil and gas exploration and mining enterprises in the eastern Arctic. While this heralds a radical departure from the strongly anti-development position of the native groups in the mid-1970s, the efforts to reap some benefits from what they see as inexorable trends has not lessened their commitment to a fair settlement of land claims.

While settlement of land claims is the central issue in northern development for the natives, the white northerners have a different axe to grind. The long-range goal of the non-native northerners, particularly the PCs in Yukon, is for control over land and resources and ultimately provincial status. The northern whites, while generally favourable to economic development, also want to ensure that, as residents of the North, they reap the economic benefits of resource development. As a full-fledged province, for instance, Yukon would have the ownership of all natural resources, which would mean that Yukoners would be the prime beneficiaries of the royalties and resource taxes that normally would accrue to a province. However, a downturn in the Yukon economy, particularly in the non-renewable resource sector, has somewhat dampened the demands for immediate provincial status. Without a stable mining sector, Yukon would have difficulty financing itself, and so the thrust of territorial demands has been to begin the transfer of lands from the federal government to the territory, and to institute a formula for royalty sharing. There are steps in the general direction of province-hood, but the final thrust cannot proceed until it is clear that such a move will not impose inordinate fiscal demands on an already beleaguered economy.

In the past it has been on the question of provincial status that native and non-native northerners have disagreed fundamentally. The natives fear provincial status if it occurs before the settlement of land claims. In Yukon, the Indians see that they are in a minority situation and that provincial status would put them at the mercy of the territory's white majority. They prefer to negotiate the land claims with the federal government and to secure some kind of political guarantees of native representation in any provincial scheme before they accede to provincial status. In the Mackenzie Valley, the feelings of the Dene are much the same. The bureaucratization of the northern government and non-renewable resource development projects have led to an influx of southern whites and reduced the native people of the western Arctic to a minority situation. Further development would only accentuate this trend, and provincial status for the Northwest Territories without guarantees of native representation in local institutions would put the Dene in a position where they would be unable to control their own destiny. In the eastern Arctic, the Inuit are still a comfortable majority. What they are asking initially is for a new territory, Nunavut, to be set up in the eastern part of the Northwest Territories and for a timetable for the evolution to provincial status then to be established. Here the land claim *per se* is not as important, because the Inuit feel that if they have provincial status they will, by virtue of their majority position, control the provincial government. As the "Crown in right of the province of Nunavut" they would hence collectively *own* all the lands in the territory outright. As we can see, there are a great many points of view about the appropriate direction and timetable for political and constitutional development in the North, and many of these are mutually exclusive.

There is one further point of view—that expressed by southern environmentalists. They share with the natives of the North a fear of the consequences of rapid resource development on the fragile northern ecology. Their solution is, at a minimum, to ensure that "wilderness," as a disappearing resource, be protected from thoughtless and unnecessary reduction on the part of resource developers, and, in the extreme, to oppose outright *all* development in the North. One of the policy options being pressed for by many southern environmental groups is the creation of vast wilderness parks or reserves in the North. The problem with this particular option is that the natives resent the alienation of their traditional hunting and fishing territories for the creation of parks as much as they resent the alienation of their lands for purposes of building pipelines, mines and highways.

The Land Claims

There are four basic aboriginal land claims in the North on the agenda for settlement by the political decision makers in the coming years. The smallest of these involves 2,500 Inuit of the Mackenzie Delta and the western Arctic coastal region who call themselves the *Inuvialuit*. These people are the descendants of Alaskan Eskimos who migrated east along the northern coast of Yukon, and who finally settled in the region around the Delta. They are represented by the Committee for Original Peoples' Entitlement (COPE), and they are close to a final agreement on their land claims. The deal hinges on the willingness of the Inuvialuit to give up all aboriginal claims in return for outright ownership of 700 square miles in and around their settlements, the control over and surface rights to another 32,000 square miles comprising their traditional hunting, trapping and fishing territory, and a large cash settlement. The key to the agreement is that the COPE negotiators agreed to *extinguishment* of aboriginal title to the land, a concession that is hotly opposed by the other native claims negotiators.

The other three land claims in the North involve the Yukon Indians, the Dene and Métis of the western Northwest Territories and the Inuit of the eastern Arctic. Only the Yukon claim is close to settlement. The representative of the Yukon natives in the land claims negotiations is the Council for Yukon Indians (CYI), which was formed as an umbrella organization of separate Indian and Métis associations in 1973 for the purpose of getting the land claims negotiations underway. The basic position of the Yukon native people was set out in a paper entitled "Together Today For Our Children Tomorrow," which asks for an affirmation of native title to their traditional lands, cash settlements to repay Yukon natives for resources that have already been removed from Yukon by the whites, social and economic development programs to help the natives adapt to changes brought about by development, and guaranteed political rights to protect the Indians as a minority within the eventual province of Yukon. The most significant aspect of the Yukon claim, which has not changed much since 1973, is that the CYI is completely opposed to large-scale development projects such as the Alaska Highway pipeline, and to provincial status until land claims are settled. The natives of the Yukon now realize that they must gain recognition for their land claims through negotiations with the federal government, because the government in Yukon tends to be pro-development and unsympathetic to native claims for special status.

It appears that the final settlement of the CYI claim will involve extinguishment of aboriginal title despite the opposition of the natives. On the other hand the Yukon government has been opposed to a number of the provisions of the agreement, especially the granting of a preference in contract tenders for northern native development corporations. However, it would appear that the lines of a compromise have been drawn, and settlement of the remaining differences is only a matter of time.

The Dene of the Mackenzie Valley are represented by the Dene Nation, an organization that grew out of the Indian Brotherhood of the Northwest Territories. The Métis of the Valley are represented by the Métis Association of the Northwest Territories, who until very recently were at odds with the Dene Nation. The federal attitude to the natives of the western Arctic was that the Métis and the Indians had to get together before there would be any negotiations. This may have been a ploy on the part of the federal government in order to put off negotiations, but a reconciliation has been achieved at least in part, and the process of dealing with the claims of the people of the Mackenzie has begun. The essence of the claim of the Dene Nation is that they are seeking more than simply a settlement of land claims. They are looking for a political settlement as well which will guarantee to the Athapaskan peoples of the western Northwest Territories permanent control over their destiny. They are seeking "special status" in Confederation, a recognition of

Indian sovereignty, control over traditional lands, constitutional guarantees of language and education rights, and the affirmation of aboriginal rights rather than an extinguishment of them.

The Dene claims are in many ways the most radical. The political philosophy of the leaders of the Dene Nation as stated in the *Dene Declaration* of July 1975 is rooted in principles of national self-determination, and many of the earlier pronouncements of the organization were couched in terms of national liberation and independence. It is clear that the over-enthusiastic espousal of concepts and language rooted in Marxist and Maoist rhetoric stiffened the federal opposition to the Dene proposals during the seventies, but times have since changed. The Dene have abandoned the policy of boycotting the Legislative Assembly as a "colonial institution" and now are an active if not a dominant force in its affairs. Similarly, in the economic context, the Dene have moved from strident opposition to all non-renewable resource development in the Mackenzie Valley to joint ventures with multinational subsidiaries.

However, the basic delay with finding an acceptable settlement to the Dene claims stems from the fact that the Dene and white communities are not geographically isolated from one another. In the larger communities there are both whites and natives living together, and even in the smaller hamlets in the Mackenzie Valley there are permanent white residents who have to be considered. Simple majority rule in the Mackenzie Valley would likely spell assimilation and the end of the native way of life because of the white majority. On the other hand, to grant special status to the natives by setting up separate native and white communities with separate systems of representation has been opposed by many because it looks too much like "apartheid." Thus, the "land" part of the Dene claim could be settled fairly easily if both sides were willing to compromise, but the settlement of the "political rights of the Dene" part of the claim involves two mutually exclusive sets of political values that have to be incorporated in a single settlement. Negotiations are beginning, not only in the North but in the national constitutional arena as well, but consensus on guaranteed political rights for native people is not even close.

The original land claims proposal of the Inuit of the eastern Arctic, entitled *Nunavut*, was presented to the federal government in 1976 by the Inuit Tapirisat of Canada (ITC), the organization that represents the Inuit. While ITC originally included the Inuvialuit, COPE eventually broke away from ITC and proceeded with its own land claims proposal. The Nunavut proposal demanded approximately 250,000 square miles of land in the eastern Arctic, along with royalties and compensatory payments for the past use (and abuse) of Inuit lands. The document was received with considerable criticism from the regions of the eastern Arctic because it saw the land claim settlement as ultimately extinguishing aboriginal title and because it did not provide for political and constitutional guarantees of the rights of the Inuit after settlement of the land claims. The result was what amounted to a withdrawal and redrafting of the original proposal.

The position of the ITC today is based on the simple fact that the Inuit form a solid majority in the territory above the tree line in the eastern Arctic which the people themselves refer to as *Nunavut*. The solution, as the Inuit see it, is simply to secure the *division* of the current Northwest Territories into at least two separate territories, with the creation, in the east, of the territory of Nunavut. The ultimate goal of the ITC is for Nunavut to eventually become a province with all of the rights of other provinces in Confederation, which of course implies the ownership of "Crown lands." The Inuit foresee fixing the franchise for elections in Nunavut to ensure that only people who have resided in the region for a set number of years and who have indicated a long-term commitment to living there may vote. In this way the Inuit majority would be protected for a number of years, and the potential danger of dilution of the native political presence by the sudden influx of southern whites would be eliminated. While the Inuit are realistic enough to see that they are not ready yet for economic or political independence, they do feel that the creation of a new *territory* can be achieved fairly quickly. The current proposals of the ITC also include a demand for an elaborate land use planning system that would prevent resource development projects in Nunavut Territory from proceeding before provincehood without full consideration of the economic and cultural needs of the people of Nunavut.

The federal response to the division of the Northwest Territories was at the outset rather quiet. The Drury Commission on constitutional development in the Northwest Territories came out in opposition to such a plan, and in the 1970s the territorial government was also cool toward it. However, the territorial assembly voted in late 1980 to approve in principle the ITC proposal for a divided territory. A plebiscite was held in the Northwest Territories in 1982, and a majority of the voters were in favour of division. The Honourable John Munro announced in November 1982 that the federal government was "in favour in principle" of division, but set the following strict conditions on its implementation: (1) land claims must be settled first; (2) a boundary must be agreed upon; (3) there must be continued support for division by the people of the Northwest Territories; and (4) there must be a general agreement on the basic governmental structure, location of the capital, etc., within the new territories. While research, public hearings and negotiations between the eastern and western Northwest Territories' representatives have been proceeding through the auspices of the Nunavut Constitutional Forum (NCF) and the Western Constitutional Forum (WCF), the progress toward division still faces the major hurdle of finding consensus on a boundary. The stakes here are high, and neither the people of Nunavut nor the people of the western Northwest Territories are willing to give up the potential resource wealth in the region where the boundary demands overlap.

Thus the land claims of the Northern natives, none of which have been settled finally and some of which are at a fairly early stage of negotiations, will have to be settled in the 1980s if division is to occur. Moreover, the urgency from an economic perspective is that Canada needs the potentially vast petroleum and mineral wealth of the North to improve its international balance of payments, and ultimately to become self-sufficient in oil and gas production. However, far more important is the fact that we are defined internationally and in terms of our own consciences by the way we deal with our minorities, and specifically with our aboriginal peoples. If we wish to maintain the notion that we are a "just society" through the decade of the eighties, it is essential that the federal government settle the legitimate claims of the northern native peoples fairly and without undue delay.

Provincehood

The ultimate goal of political and constitutional development in the North is full provincial status for the people who live there. Of all the various "proto-provinces" in the North, Yukon appears to be the closest to achieving provincehood. In fact, the short-lived Conservative government of Joe Clark promised the Yukoners that his government would speed up that process considerably and had taken the first steps by reducing the role of the commissioner of the territory to something akin to that of a lieutenant-governor in a province. The termination of the brief Conservative interregnum and the return to power of the Liberals, coupled with the severe downturn in the Yukon economy, have at least temporarily dashed the hopes of the provincialists in the Yukon, although there is a general recognition by all parties in the House of Commons that provincial status is the bottom line in territorial constitutional development. Realistically, however, a number of criteria have to be met in order to elevate the territory to provincehood, and these criteria have varying levels of importance to the federal politicians.

The most important of these criteria is that the potential province possess a tax base to support itself. According to federal government assessments, both Yukon and the Northwest Territories have higher per capita revenue potentials than the Canadian average. In other words, in good economic times, if the territories were given full tax powers over their natural resources, personal income tax, etc., they would be better off than all provinces except Ontario, British Columbia and Alberta. The problem, however, is that the per capita expenditures of both Yukon and the Northwest Territories are much higher than any of the other provinces. The conclusion of the federal government's analysis of the territorial tax base is thus that the territories cannot now support themselves, nor can they be expected to in the immediate future, and thus should not become provinces. The provincialists in the territories counter this by claiming that if the federal government subsidizes them now it could continue just as easily to do so if they were provinces. Moreover, they argue, the new discoveries of gas, oil and other minerals will eventually expand the revenues of the territories so that they will be able to pay their own bills.

The truth of the matter lies somewhere between these arguments, but it must be recognized that the root of the tax base argument against provincehood is, in effect, an argument about population size. Even tiny Prince Edward Island has a population of 120,000 by contrast to Yukon's 23,000, and even without taking into account the higher costs of running a government in the extremes of climate and physical distance that are the rule in the North, and the boom–bust cycles of the northern economies, the northern territories are the victims of negative economies of scale. The fact is that there is likely a threshold minimum population beyond which the per capita cost of providing the sorts of services provided by provincial governments in Canada is simply too high. Furthermore, in a related way, the small population of the northern "proto-provinces" would make it difficult or impossible to staff the provincial public services from within. It would be necessary to hire a lot of outsiders to assist in running the show, which in the case of Nunavut, for instance, would mean a significant threat to the Inuit majority in the long run and, given the power usually assumed by bureaucracies in modern political systems, a loss of local control over much of the process of government in the short run. Thus, while it is extremely distasteful to put a size limit on self-government, the fact remains that paying the bills to maintain an effective provincial bureaucracy and a high quality of services delivered might end up placing an unreasonable per capita tax burden on the people of the territory.

The second criterion which must be assessed if provincial status is to be feasible is the level of political development in the potential province. In Yukon, there is a long history of political involvement by the whites, and with the evolution of a party system in elections it would appear that there is sufficient political sophistication and sufficient political awareness among the people to warrant self-government. However, this would not be very successful until the native people of the territory can be guaranteed a place in the political process as well. In the Northwest Territories, the political institutions have not evolved as quickly or as far as they have in Yukon, but it would appear that the territorial assembly is on the brink of party politics. Many of the members of the assembly are politically capable of assuming the new responsibilities of provincial status if that were the only consideration. If and when the separate territory of Nunavut should be created, it is not likely that the people of the territory would have the level of political sophistication to enter into a provincial form of government immediately. The Inuit, as with the Dene in the West, have gone through a very rapid process of political mobilization, largely due to the threats to their livelihood presented by major resource development proposals. However, while there is now a high level of awareness of political issues that affect them directly, the level of broad political sophistication required to run a provincial government and to bargain as equals with the other provinces and the federal government has not yet been attained. This said, it must be emphasized that the northern natives are learning the ropes of liberal democratic politics very rapidly, they already have a number of very capable leaders, and there is no question that by the end of the decade they will have attained the level of political sophistication necessary for coping with the burdens of provincial status. In sum, the lack of political development as an argument against provincial status in the North is not a strong one today, and it will be virtually irrelevant by the end of the 1980s.

The third criterion for provincial status is that the people in the territory must themselves want provincehood. This criterion can be met most simply through a referendum in the given proto-province in which all of its citizens are permitted to vote. This technique would work very well in the eastern Arctic, where there is relative cultural and ethnic homogeneity, but in Yukon and the Mackenzie Valley there is some danger that a simple referendum might impose a tyranny of the majority. The problem in each of these parts of the northern territories, as we have seen, is that there are significant minorities, specifically the Indians, who do not want provincial status until there are some guarantees of their rights as a unique group with special status.

The likelihood of securing these rights after provincial status is achieved seems remote to them, and given the general orientation of the whites in both the Mackenzie Valley and Yukon, native fears appear to be justified. Hence, one of the reasons cited, particularly by the Liberals in Ottawa, for rejecting provincial status at this time is that it would deal a death blow to the native way of life in the North. The natives and the more enlightened whites in the North agree, even though some of the latter feel that the sacrifice in terms of traditional lifestyles is one that must be made in the interest of what they see as a greater good—economic development.

The fourth criterion that must be met if the federal government is to agree to provincehood for any of its northern territories is that the move must be politically advantageous. Given the problems the federal government has had recently in dealing with the energy-producing provinces, it is naturally not at all that enthusiastic about creating new resource-rich provinces with which to spar. While this is perhaps a cynical view of the motives of the federal politicians and bureaucrats, the fact remains that they have a lot more to lose than to gain if they meet the demands of the provincialists in the northern territories. Furthermore, it is easy for the federal government today to justify its lack of enthusiasm for provincehood in terms of the tax base or political development argument, or still more convincingly by posing as a defender of the native way of life. As usual, when the issues are not clear, as they are most definitely not in this situation, the easiest thing for a government to do is nothing.

When the issues gel, as they likely will within the next few years, the federal government will be forced to take at least some action. While it is dangerous to speculate, the most likely scenario is for Ottawa to move on the division of the Northwest Territories and for the creation of the territory of Nunavut in the eastern Arctic. This is likely to occur because the territorial legislative assembly has agreed to it in principle, the ITC is pressing for it, the other native organizations, the Dene and the CYI are generally favourable or neutral to the proposal, and it does not mean a significant transfer of authority from the Parliament of Canada to the territorial legislature. Provincial status is the next likely scenario, but that will not likely occur until the economic recovery is in place and federal policies have changed significantly. However, given a satisfactory land claims agreement and some guarantees of political representation for the native population, the elevation of Yukon to provincehood might be politically feasible fairly quickly. There is a higher level of political development generally in that territory than in the rest of the North, and as well, the possibility of vast petroleum and mineral resources in Yukon does not at the present time seem as likely as in the Northwest Territories, so that the "feds" would not be giving up as much power as they would be elsewhere. The thorniest problems will occur in the late 1980s in the Mackenzie Valley. Here, the settlement of native claims in such a way that the interests of the white residents and the development interests are accommodated to those of the Dene will be very difficult indeed. Ironically, it is in the Mackenzie Valley, where the demands for a transportation corridor including gas and oil pipelines reflect the growing energy needs in the rest of Canada, that the urgency for a settlement of the issues is the greatest.

The North is important to Canadians as a whole because it is a land of vast potential wealth, not only in terms of natural resources, but also in terms of a cultural and linguistic diversity that has become a hallmark of the Canadian political identity. The manner in which future generations of Canadians define their worth as a nation may well come to rest upon the manner in which the present generation of political leaders resolves the poignantly human dilemmas of northern development in the latter half of the 1980s.

Notes

1. It must be noted that the figures relating to the ethnic and linguistic distribution of the populations of the North vary widely depending upon who you ask. While I have attempted to stick fairly closely to those figures provided by Statistics Canada and by the governments of the Northwest Territories and Yukon, the native groups themselves usually state statistics which show a much larger native population. For instance, the Council of Yukon Indians normally claims that Indians and Métis make up approximately one-third of the residents of Yukon and a majority of those who have lived there at least ten years.

Further Readings

Berger, T. *Northern Frontier, Northern Homeland: The Report of the Mackenzie Valley Pipeline Inquiry.* Vol. 1. Ottawa: Supply and Services Canada, 1977.

Brody, H. *The People's Land.* Toronto: Penguin, 1975.

Dacks, G. *A Choice of Futures.* Toronto: Methuen, 1982.

Dene Nation, The. *The Dene: A Statement of Rights.* Yellowknife: The Dene of the N.W.T., 1977.

Drury, C.M. *Constitutional Development in the Northwest Territories: Report of the Special Representative.* Ottawa: Supply and Services Canada, 1979.

Inuit Tapirisat Canada. *Nunavut.* Ottawa: I.T.C., 1976.

Lotz, J. *Northern Realities.* Toronto: New Press, 1972.

Lysyk, K.M. *Alaska Highway Pipeline Inquiry.* Ottawa: Supply and Services Canada, 1977.

Nunavut Constitutional Forum. *Building Nunavut.* 1983.

Yukon Indian People, The. *Together Today for Our Children Tomorrow.* Whitehorse: The Council for Yukon Indians, 1977.

Chapter 4

The Political Economy of Continentalism
Maureen Appel Molot and Glen Williams

Very little of significance can be said about either political or economic development in Canada unless it is recognized that the two processes have always been inextricably fused by the search for metropoles to consume our resource staples. As the nature of the staples trade progressed, from fish and fur to lumber, wheat and eventually fuel and non-fuel metals and minerals, so did the major purchaser of these staples change with the passage of time from France to Britain and, lastly and most significantly, the United States.

Interest in the United States as an important market for Canadian staples developed early. Once colonial producers lost their privileged position in the British market as a result of the introduction of free trade in 1846, they began to press the Colonial Office to negotiate a reciprocity treaty with the United States under which staple commodities such as fish and lumber from the Maritimes and wheat and other agricultural products from the United Canadas could enter the American market duty free. The Reciprocity Treaty, in effect from 1854 to 1866, was abrogated by the United States for a number of reasons, not the least of which was opposition to the treaty from its own resource producers in New England and New York and unhappiness with the Galt–Cayley tariff of 1859 which had the effect of making certain American manufactured goods less attractive to Canadian buyers.

Whatever the real benefits of the Reciprocity Treaty in trade terms, it had an enormous psychological impact on Canadian primary producers and on those who made their money in the carrying trade. There remained for some decades, particularly in Ontario and Montreal, a strong belief that the future of Canada lay in some kind of formal commercial ties with the American metropole. This belief found political expression in a free-trade-oriented Liberal party prior to the election of 1896 and emerged full blown as a desire for a new reciprocity treaty in the 1911 Liberal platform.

It is perhaps one of the great ironies of the political economy of Canada–U.S. relations that the failure to agree upon reciprocity after

1866 did not impede continental economic integration. Prior to Confederation and in the years immediately thereafter, the bond that linked the two economies was staples: first, primary products of the sea, forest and farm and later, and of greatest significance for the contemporary relationship, extractive resources such as iron ore, copper and oil and gas. U.S. investment in the Canadian resource sector began as early as 1860 and has continued unabated, with great spurts of development activity in the years following both World Wars.[1]

By the turn of the century the second prong of the continental link was clearly evident—American investment in manufacturing capacity in Canada behind the security of the Canadian tariff wall. It is this dual attractiveness of Canada to the United States, both as a source of staples *and* as a market for U.S. developed manufactured goods, that makes the North American economic linkage unusual and of great consequence for the Canadian economy. Unlike other metropole–hinterland relationships where foreign investment is concentrated in either the resource or the manufacturing sector, there are significant levels of U.S. investment in Canada in both sectors.

The introduction of a tariff in 1879 to protect nascent Canadian manufacturing industries against inroads from American goods was part of a trio of policies designed to consolidate a new national economy. It was the expectation of the Macdonald government that goods manufactured in central Canada would be purchased by Canadians across the country, that the export of the wheat staple of the developing Prairie economy would generate capital to allow for consumption of domestically produced manufactures and for the further construction of the transcontinental railway system, and that the railway would carry staple commodities east for export and manufactured goods west for sale. This did happen; however, what is crucial for our purposes is an understanding of the way in which Canadian manufacturing capacity evolved.

Modern Canadian industry was just gathering steam at a period when American industry had already largely made the transition to efficient national firms using sophisticated technology.[2] Although after the introduction of the tariff there was limited American investment in Canadian manufacturing, it grew markedly only after the beginning of the century, as American entrepreneurs looked for new locations in which to invest their surplus capital. The contrast between levels of industrialization in Canada and the United States affected the pattern of Canadian industrialization in two ways: the availability of American technology and of American surplus capital for investment abroad. Canadian manufacturers, desirous of producing goods most cheaply and efficiently for sale in Canada, looked to American manufacturing processes rather than developing their own. In contrast to industrialists in other countries who initially borrowed technology and then innovated and adapted what had been borrowed for their own domestic purposes, this use of foreign machinery and production processes in Canada became a permanent part of our industrial pattern, thus tying it in an important structural way to the evolution of industry in the United States.

This pattern of industrialization is termed "import substitution industrialization" (ISI), that is, an industrialization strategy characterized by unchallenged technological dependency and a disinterest in production for anything but domestic consumption. Most Canadian industrialists were simply not interested in exporting manufactured goods, with the result that they, unlike their counterparts in the United States, Sweden and elsewhere, never developed specialized product lines which would be competitive in world markets. Moreover, Canadian industrialists did not recognize the long-term economic significance of a strong machinery sector. With the exception of farm machinery, the growth of a dynamic Canadian machinery and industrial equipment sector lagged far behind that of other industrializing countries.

The choice of this ISI strategy was influenced by considerations of Empire and the availability of investment capital. Both pointed Canadian state and economic elites toward deepening and intensifying our role as a supplier of food products for British industrial workers. The opening of the West and the program of railway construction then in place consumed so much capital—some 40 percent of all capital then available for investment (1901-1915)—that there was little left for investment in heavy industrial equipment and machinery. In fact, the share of capital (7 percent) invested in developing the industrial infrastructure (machinery) approximated that invested in agricultural implements.[3] As we will demonstrate below, the long-term implication of this approach to Canadian industrialization has been to constrain severely the economic options available to governments.

With its protected domestic market and trade preference within the British Empire, Canada was an obvious location for the establishment of American branch plants. Through takeovers of existing Canadian manufacturing firms, such as those in the automotive industry, or by the incorporation of new subsidiary firms, for example in the electrical sector, American industrialists consolidated a place of prominence in Canada's most dynamic industrial sectors by the 1920s. Canadian-owned manufacturing became concentrated in the technologically backward and less capital-intensive industries such as textiles, clothing and footwear, food processing and furniture manufacturing. By the onset of the Depression, the structure of the Canadian economy as one based on the duality of the export of staples and the provision of manufactured goods for the domestic market by ISI had been clearly established.

The post–Great Depression era was marked by a tremendous expansion in the capital stock of direct foreign investment in Canada. In the decades of the 1940s and 1950s, its book value increased by over five and a half times and its share of the total Canadian economy (excluding agriculture and finance) grew from one-fifth to one-third. Two central economic sectors, manufacturing and mining, moved from a position of majority Canadian ownership to majority foreign ownership with two-fifths foreign control at the beginning of the period and three-fifths at its conclusion. Indeed, the most dramatic growth can be discovered in the minerals sector (including mining, smelting, oil and natural gas) where foreign investment increased more than twenty-five fold.[4]

The peak of the post-war boom in foreign investment was reached in the early 1970s. As can be seen in Table 4.1, a moderate decline has since set in. This has been the result of mergers, takeovers (mainly governmental), and a few controversial reclassifications by Statistics Canada of the nationality of some large corporations. This decline also reflects a wider international trend which has seen the worldwide growth in direct foreign investment, particularly the wholly owned subsidiaries of the Canadian variety, slowing considerably.

Was all of this foreign investment necessary, as was commonly claimed at the time it was taking place, for the expansion of the Canadian economy? The answer would appear to be no, because by far the greatest part of the foreign investment splurge was generated within Canada. The Gray Report on Foreign Direct Investment demonstrated that only 25 percent of the 1946–1960 expansion in foreign-controlled enterprises was funded from foreign sources. A similar analysis of the last two decades indicates that this portion has fallen to under 20 percent.

To a significant extent, therefore, the existing pre–Depression complement of branch plants, especially in the growth consumer industries of the manufacturing sector, simply expanded in step with the remarkably strong post–war domestic economy. Funding came mainly from retained earnings on operating profits made in Canada, loans from Canadian financial institutions and investors, and investment incentives built into the tax system. It is important to note, however, that the advantage of access to the relatively small share of new imported foreign capital Canada utilized must be balanced against the inevitable return of dividends to sources, U.S. parent firms. During the 1970s, for example, the value of interest and dividends on old direct foreign investments leaving Canada was approximately twice as much as the value of new direct foreign capital entering it.

Rather than recognizing that foreign investment had advanced naturally in step with the wartime and post–war economic booms, governments at both the federal and provincial levels began to ascribe the successes of economic growth to its main beneficiaries, the branch plants. As one particularly forthright Ontario minister of trade and development put it in 1968, "We'd still be chasing Indians if it were not for foreign

Table 4.1

Foreign Control of Canadian Industry, 1970 and 1980 (percent of total)

	Assets		Sales	
	1970	1980	1970	1980
Food	44	29	33	27
Beverages	32	32	30	35
Tobacco products	86	100	82	100
Rubber products	93	91	91	90
Leather products	22	23	20	20
Textile mills	53	54	49	54
Knitting mills	21	15	18	14
Clothing industries	14	14	11	13
Wood industries	33	19	23	17
Furniture industries	21	12	19	11
Paper and allied industries	45	35	47	38
Printing, publishing and allied	15	12	13	12
Primary metals	43	13	41	15
Metal fabricating	45	34	43	37
Machinery	75	52	77	59
Transport equipment	85	71	90	84
Electrical products	68	54	66	62
Non-metallic mineral products	63	70	53	60
Petroleum and coal products	100	70	99	82
Chemicals and chemical products	80	77	83	76
Miscellaneous manufacturing	51	43	50	42
Total manufacturing	**59**	**48**	**56**	**51**
Mineral Fuels	82	53	91	74
Total Mining	**70**	**45**	**75**	**59**

Sources: Statistics Canada, *Annual Reports*, 1971 and 1980; Corporations and Labour Unions
      Returns Act, Part I, March, 1974, and December, 1982.

investment." It is a short step from this kind of identification of foreign investment as the motor of economic growth to a belief that the promotion of foreign direct investment will produce even more economic growth which, in turn, will pay large electoral dividends to the government or political party able to most closely associate itself with it.

The politicians found further inspiration in the academic economic orthodoxy of this epoch set forth by such prominent authorities as W.A. Mackintosh, H.G. Johnson, A.E. Safarian and the Economic Council of Canada, who championed an intensification of continental integration of investment, production and trade.[5] Most recently, the Senate Standing

Committee on Foreign Affairs has enthusiastically picked up the continentalist mantle. Thus, the postwar period has featured a parade of
short-sighted politicians falling all over themselves to create a "climate"
favourable to foreign investment. Among the most famous of these was
C.D. Howe, who held a number of posts in successive federal Liberal
governments during the 1940s and 1950s and was the driving force
behind taxation and investment policies designed to lure U.S. dollars to
Canada. Those few outside the centres of state power who worried about
the long-term consequences of foreign economic domination were
accused of attacking the standard of living of ordinary Canadians and/or
of trying to turn Canada into a northern "banana republic."

This kind of upside-down jingoism was effective only so long as the
glue of economic fortune could prevent the cracks in its foundation from
swelling. With the economic dislocations of the last decade, however, the
enterprise has begun to crumble along a number of policy stress points
which we will now briefly examine.

Trade and Industrial Policy

When the anatomy of our international trade is profiled, Canada defies
her status as a developed industrialized nation. In spite of the towering
progress in manufacturing made in this century, we have maintained our
traditional role as primarily a resource exporter. This is at great variance
with the experience of other industrialized countries. Where 50 to 70
percent of their total exports are the finished products of their manufacturing enterprises, we can only manage about 32 percent.

Yet even this low proportion is greatly inflated by the peculiar
effects of the 1965 U.S.–Canada Auto Pact free trade agreement. While
massive in volume, this trade in automobiles and parts tells us little about
Canada's ability to sell her manufactures in world markets. For one thing,
the Auto Pact provides mainly for the intrafirm transfers of goods
between U.S. firms and their Canadian branches which incidentally pass
over an international frontier. For another, Canada has been losing
heavily on these exchanges, with a near 7 billion dollar deficit over the
seventeen-year life of the agreement. If, then, an adjustment is made to
remove the Auto Pact exchanges, Canada's proportion of fully manufactured exports falls to 22 percent. This places us firmly in the company
of such semi-industrialized countries as Brazil, Mexico and India.

On the other side of the coin—imports—Canada has fared just as
badly. Where highly industrialized countries, without exception, export
more manufactured goods than they import, Canada, along with Brazil,
Mexico, and other semi-industrials, maintains a negative trade balance in
finished goods. In fact, Canada has for many years held the unenviable
distinction of being the world's largest importer of manufactured goods

on a per capita basis. In recent years, the trend has accelerated. Our trade deficit in fully manufactured end products totalled a shocking 87 billion dollars during the 1970s, 60 billion of which were suffered in the last five years of the decade. As the economic downturn of the early 1980s deepened, the trade prospects for the remainder of this decade could only be viewed with alarm. In its first four years alone, our end product deficit totalled 64 billion dollars.

While the cause of Canada's industrial export impotence can be traced to the import substitution industrial strategy of the late nineteenth century, in the current era, the factor most strongly linked to the problem is the overwhelming dominance of direct foreign investment in our branch plant sector. Very simply, branch plants were never established in Canada to become independent entities capable of competing with their parents in world markets. Rather, they were components of an international marketing strategy established by U.S. firms to capture and hold a share of the Canadian domestic market for products developed at the multinational's head office. Typically, an administrative division of the North American market would establish a Canadian "satellite" plant to satisfy regional demand in this country, just as, say, a Chicago plant would fill demand in the U.S. midwest, while research and development as well as exports were centred in the U.S. parent plant.

The importation of most of the technology necessary for branch plant production, including machinery and components, means that Canadian manufacturing is far more dependent on purchases than on sales abroad. Over three-quarters of the imports of foreign branch plants in Canada are procured from their parent companies. In turn, these imports of capital equipment make a weighty contribution to our deficit in fully manufactured end products. In addition, they largely explain why Canada has perhaps the worst record of technological innovation among all developed nations. By itself, this dismal industrial research and development record is preventing Canada from developing products unique enough to compete on world markets.

Whereas other governments in western Europe and Japan have found it expedient to adopt leadership roles in the development of industrial exports, the Canadian state, in keeping with its favourable attitude toward foreign direct investment, has avoided directly confronting the problem. It has found it safer simply to throw money at the manufacturers in the form of trade promotion and research and development programs. The federal government, for example, carries out a larger proportion of national research and development activities than is true for any other major capitalist country. Our Trade Commissioner Service, which offers information and advice to interested exporters, maintains offices in nearly seventy countries. These policies have satisfied the demands of the constituency which they service as well as created the impression that government was at work to correct our problem in this area. However, to the extent that such policies leave undisturbed the underlying structural weaknesses that they appear to address, they are merely makeup on a corpse.

Regulation of Foreign Direct Investment

The creation of the Foreign Investment Review Agency (FIRA) in the early 1970s to screen takeovers of established Canadian companies and applications for foreign direct investment marked a significant policy departure for the federal government in its handling of what was becoming a contentious issue in Canada. In contrast to previous foreign investment restrictions, which had as their purpose the regulation of levels of foreign ownership in certain key sectors of the economy such as banks, communications media or uranium extraction, with FIRA, Ottawa opted for a more global instrument to examine and control the entry of foreign direct investment into Canada. However, for reasons of restricted mandate, lack of enforcement capacity and vacillating political direction, FIRA's impact on the overall problem of foreign investment in the Canadian economy has been very limited.

FIRA was a child of the 1972 Gray Report. This Report was commissioned as a Liberal Government policy response to growing public disquiet over both the level and impact of foreign investment in this country and the recognition that very sizeable amounts of new direct foreign investment in Canada were being financed domestically. The task force concluded Canada was not deriving sufficient benefit from such investment and suggested alternative policies by which the level of benefit might be increased. The authors of the Gray Report discarded two policy options, a buy-back of some foreign-owned industry and a mandatory increase in the number of Canadian directors of subsidiary companies, in favour of a third, the creation of a review agency. This last proposal, and the legislation embodying it, were opposed by virtually all economic interest groups, save for labour, on the grounds that the establishment of such a review agency would constitute unwelcome government interference in the economy. The perspectives of these economic actors reflected their historic belief that Canada needed foreign investment for continued economic growth. Most provincial governments also criticized the proposed regulatory agency, arguing that foreign investment was crucial to the establishment of new industry and employment within their borders. Those who supported the agency did so cautiously and expressed concern that the federal government not use it as a tool to alleviate regional disparities. After extensive parliamentary consideration of the legislation, the act creating FIRA was passed in December 1973 and came into effect in two stages, April 1974 for the review of takeovers and October 1975 for the review of new investment.

The mandate under which FIRA operates suggests rather strongly that, despite opposition to it, the agency was more an exercise in symbolic politics than a genuine effort to regulate foreign investment coming into Canada. Eligible for review are new direct investments initiated by a foreign investor not previously active in Canada and expansion by foreign-owned companies already in Canada into areas "unrelated" to their ongoing activities. What remains free of the review process is the most obvious means by which foreign control of the economy continues to grow, namely expansion, by subsidiaries, of existing plant capacity as well as their movement into areas of "related" business.

Permissiveness with respect to all investment applications has characterized FIRA's decisions since its inception. During the 1970s, the approval rate varied from a low of 83 percent to a high of 96 percent. In the early years of the eighties an increasing number of investment applications have been allowed, with approvals in 1983 of 94 percent and in the first few months of 1984 of over 95 percent.

FIRA cannot monitor properly, nor can it do anything about, what might be termed the "ripple effects" of foreign ownership—that is, the negative impact on Canadian sourcing that results from takeovers. When Canadian manufacturing firms are purchased by American-owned companies, a switch from Canadian to U.S. suppliers of the components of the manufacturing processes almost invariably occurs as the formerly Canadian-owned companies are integrated into the framework of the multinational enterprise. This, in turn, has the effect of weakening and sometimes closing former Canadian suppliers.

FIRA also lacks the capability to enforce the conditions under which it approves an investment. The agency reviews applications according to a number of criteria, such as job creation, increased trade, Canadian sourcing or research and development, and allows the investment on the condition that the foreign company agrees to certain undertakings which will benefit the Canadian economy. When investors default on some of these promises, which has happened on a number of occasions over the years, FIRA has only two remedies: force the investor to leave the country for failing to meet commitments or take the company to court to force implementation of the undertakings. In all its years of operation, the agency has never resorted to either of these alternatives. Rather, it has "renegotiated" corporate commitments, a procedure which can only lessen the benefits of the investment for Canada. Moreover, the failure of some investors to effect investment promises has not led FIRA to establish stricter review procedures.[6]

The cabinet debate over two policy initiatives announced in 1980 by the then recently re-elected Trudeau government illustrates the difficulties of imposing restrictions on the entry of direct foreign investment into Canada. The first of these was the proposal, mooted during the election campaign and then contained in the 1980 Speech from the Throne, that FIRA's mandate be expanded to include performance reviews of large foreign-owned firms and the right to publicize prospective foreign takeovers with a view to soliciting counter-offers from Canadian companies. This proposal was but one component of a highly interventionist discussion paper drafted by then Industry, Trade and Commerce Minister Herb Gray and presented to cabinet in the summer of 1980.[7] In criticizing the performance of subsidiary corporations, Gray argued that the branch plant character of much of Canadian industry imposed significant structural barriers to the realization of Canada's economic potential. These structural barriers could not be overcome by expenditure programs alone. The government would have to both *monitor* the performance of subsidiaries and consider the introduction of regulatory guidelines to "ensure that MNEs [multinational enterprises] perform to world standards in terms of innovation and export freedom."

This expansion of FIRA's authority never materialized. Gray's document was not well received in the Trudeau Cabinet and was soon vying for attention with a much less interventionist paper prepared by Economic Development Minister H.A. Olsen. Canadian criticism of efforts to enhance FIRA and even more vociferous opposition to the proposals from the United States strengthened the hand of Gray's opponents and resulted in a cabinet decision to leave the agency's powers as they were. As noted earlier, Canadian economic elites were wedded to the idea that foreign investment generates growth. Indeed, in time of recession uninterrupted infusions of new foreign investment were seen as essential to economic recovery. American objections to the strengthening of FIRA centred on the discriminatory treatment of foreign capital relative to Canadian (an issue also in U.S. antipathy to the National Energy Program, to be considered below) and on the performance requirements demanded of potential investors. U.S. animosity with respect to FIRA was such that the Reagan administration eventually requested an international body, the General Agreement on Tariffs and Trade (GATT), to investigate whether FIRA's activities violated its regulations on international trade. In little more than a year the Trudeau government had done a complete about-face on the issue of regulating the entry of foreign investment into Canada and had moved from threats to toughen the agency to an active effort to promote FIRA as a friendly arm of government anxious to facilitate the approval of new investment applications.

In contrast to its reversal on FIRA was the government's stance on the second important policy innovation, the National Energy Program (NEP). The essence of this program was to increase Canadian ownership of the critical energy fuels sector by offering more lucrative exploration subsidies and protected exploration rights on Canada Lands (those areas such as Crown land in Yukon, the Northwest Territories and off-shore sites) to companies with a minimum of 50 percent (for some benefits the percentage of Canadian ownership required was as high as 65 percent) Canadian ownership. Despite considerable bilateral tension, including threats of economic retaliation from both the White House and Congress, the federal government did not alter the basic tenets of the NEP.[8]

Why did the Trudeau cabinet remain firm on one option while capitulating on the other? The crucial difference lay in domestic political realities. The Trudeau cabinet was deeply committed to the National Energy Program as a tool to redress what it increasingly viewed as a serious imbalance within Canadian federalism that had its roots in the post–1973 rises in oil prices. Moreover, there was a strong sense that greater Canadian control over the oil and gas industry should be actively encouraged. These perspectives were shared in large measure by officials in the Department of Energy, Mines and Resources who also saw in the NEP an opportunity to improve their department's position within the bureaucratic hierarchy. By promulgating the National Energy Program and establishing Petro-Canada (in 1976) Canada was emulating other industrialized political economies desirous of exercising greater national control over this key sector of their economies. In contrast, there was no similar coalition of support, political or bureaucratic, for a broadly nationalist position on the foreign investment issue.

Sensitivity to foreign and domestic criticisms of FIRA and the NEP shaped the context of the continuing discussion over economic policy and reinforced the position of those in the cabinet opposed to regulating foreign investment and increasing Canadian control over various sectors of the economy. An ad hoc cabinet committee chaired by then Finance Minister Allan MacEachen was established to resolve the differing perspectives represented by the Gray and Olsen policy papers and to prepare a statement on economic alternatives for Canada in the eighties. Rather than addressing the problems of restructuring Canadian industry to face the competitive international trading environment, the resulting Cabinet statement, *Economic Development for Canada in the 1980s,*[9] stressed a reorientation toward *resource exports.* Convinced that the changing terms of trade in primary commodities in the 1970s had strengthened Canada's comparative advantage in staple exports, this policy document highlighted a return to the staple thesis of export-led growth. Canada's "leading opportunity" was to be found in the development of its "rich bounty of natural resources," which included energy, minerals, agricultural and forest products and fish. Spinoffs from resource extraction would stimulate industrial capacity, as Canadian manufacturers would supply the machinery and equipment required for both primary produc-

tion and the upgrading of resource commodities beyond the primary
stage. Manufacturing industries did receive some attention in the statement, but it was clear that resource exports were viewed as the prime
source of growth. Finally, the statement assuaged the fears of those
concerned about further Canadianization of specific sectors of the economy and overall restrictions on foreign investment by promising that
the format of the National Energy Program, would not be extended to
other areas and that no additions to FIRA's powers were contemplated.

This intense struggle over economic strategies in the early 1980s is
instructive for the lessons it provides about continentalism and the policy
process. First, the controversy over strengthening FIRA illustrated the
dominance of the traditional view of foreign investment and the arsenal
that supporters of this perspective could muster to fend off any chal-
lengers. Second, Ottawa's determination to stand firm with respect to
the National Energy Program despite strong pressures to weaken it
suggests that the state *can* act decisively to protect what it sees as vital
Canadian interests. Third was the impact of the intense critical assault
launched against the proposed strengthening of FIRA by the business
community, provincial politicians, the federal Conservatives and the
media on popular attitudes about the foreign investment issue. As the
Gallup Polls reveal, in the 1970s two-thirds of Canadians thought there
was sufficient U.S. capital invested in Canada and approximately one-
half were prepared to countenance schemes to buy back majority control
of U.S. companies operating in Canada *even if this were to reduce living
standards*. By the time the same questions were posed in November 1981
public opinion had begun to change dramatically. Not only did the percentage of Canadians wanting to see more U.S. capital in Canada increase
and the numbers disapproving of buy-backs rise considerably, but the
number of respondents answering "don't know" also fell. If popular
opinion had once supported restrictive policies on foreign investment
and, in fact, had led elite attitudes on the subject, the two were now again
more in concert than they had been for at least a decade. This was almost
certainly achieved by linking, in the public mind, the severe economic
recession of the early 1980s with the aborted Liberal Party challenge to
foreign investment represented by the strengthening of FIRA.

Federal-Provincial Relations

No discussion of the political economy of Canada–U.S. relations is
complete without some consideration of the competing tension between
the continental economic pull on the one hand and the development of an
integrated national political economy on the other. Whatever the hopes
of successive Canadian governments that their economic policies could
counter the attractiveness of north–south ties, the economies of the
provinces have all become closely linked to that of the United States. The

Table 4.2
Public Perceptions of Foreign Investment

"Now thinking about U.S. capital invested in Canada—Do you think there is enough now or would you like to see more U.S. capital invested in this country?"

	Enough Now	Like to See More	Don't Know
1983	57%	35%	8%
1982	56	36	8
1981	67	21	12
1980	64	20	17
1978	69	23	9
1975	71	16	13
1970	62	25	13

"Some experts are suggesting that Canada should buy back a majority control—say 51%—of U.S. companies in Canada. Even though it might mean a big reduction in our standard of living, would you approve of this or not?"

	Approve	Disapprove	Qualified	Don't Know
1983	37%	53%	1%	10%
1982	43	46	2	10
1981	45	43	1	12
1980	48	34	2	16
1978	52	34	2	11
1975	58	26	2	14
1970	46	32	3	19

Note: Percentages may not add exactly to 100, due to rounding.
Source: Canadian Institute of Public Opinion. *The Gallup Report*, Thursday, September 1, 1983.

U.S. is the primary export destination for the goods of all provinces except British Columbia, for which it ranks second (after Japan). As well, American investment, both direct and portfolio, has played a crucial role in developing provincial economies, particularly since World War II. In fact, U.S. investment in Canadian resource industries since 1945 had contributed significantly to the affluence and, in the context of Canadian federalism, the increasing aggressiveness, of the resource-rich provinces. Consequently, federal initiatives to restrict or regulate the entry of direct foreign investment into Canada have been met with almost uniform hostility by provincial governments which view this capital as necessary for economic diversification.

Not surprisingly, then, the economic health of individual provincial economies depends directly on the rate of growth in the American economy. The recent recession bore witness to this linkage insofar as unemployment in the Ontario automotive industry and the B.C. forest sector, to name but two, were a direct result of declining U.S. car purchases and a fall-off in U.S. housing construction, respectively. In both of these instances, as well as in many others, the federal government could do little to stimulate individual provincial economies which are more closely tied to the southern metropole than they are to the rest of Canada.

Many of the major issues of contention in Canadian federalism have been conditioned, at least in part, by the continental connection. Take the question of oil and gas exports, for example. Alberta has historically wanted to export more oil and gas to the United States at prices far higher than those paid by Canadian consumers while Ontario has argued that these resources should be preserved for domestic use and sold at prices below the world level to assist the competitiveness of Canadian industry in world markets. As noted in the previous section, a major motivation behind the National Energy Program was Ottawa's concern to reduce intergovernmental conflict over energy prices by asserting federal leadership in the energy sector. A second example can be found in attitudes expressed on the Canadian tariff. The Canadian manufacturing industry, which is located primarily in Ontario and Quebec, continues to press for protection against the importation of foreign-made consumer goods. On the other hand, consumers in the western provinces have traditionally criticized the tariff, maintaining that it forces them to purchase more costly Canadian-made commodities rather than cheaper items from the United States.

Balance of Payments Policy

The principle behind the balance of payments issue is relatively simple. Ideally, governments would like to ensure that the value of what is brought into the country is less than, or only as much as, the value of what is sent out. Otherwise, the resulting international indebtedness will force policy makers to divert energy and capital into a search for the means to repay the deficit. In extreme and long-term cases, failure to take corrective action may lead to dependence on international financial institutions such as the World Bank or International Monetary Fund and a consequent surrender of a measure of economic sovereignty as governments struggle to fulfil the conditions attached to their loans.

Since 1950, Canada has suffered from chronic balance of payments difficulties. Including 1983, in only six years in these more than three decades have we generated a surplus on our current account of our balance of payments. Between 1975 and 1983, our cumulative current account deficit was a staggering 25 billion dollars.

The current account is composed of two principal components—merchandise and service (items such as tourism or interest payments). The former measures the exchange of commodities while the latter describes the flow of capital on exchanges not directly tied to goods. While merchandise trade in the Canadian current account has been generally healthy, with only two deficit years in the last two decades, service transactions have been continuously in deficit since 1950.

The slight surpluses on merchandise trade are based mainly, as we might suppose, on resource and resource-based staple exports. But there seems little doubt that these relatively modest merchandise surpluses could potentially be far larger. The reader will remember that in our earlier discussion of trade and industrial policy we pointed to the structural weaknesses of our branch plant economy which make Canadian manufacturers far more dependent on foreign purchases of machinery and components to equip their plants than on the sales of their own products on international markets. The severe recession of the early 1980s has dramatically illustrated this point. In 1982 and 1983 we enjoyed freakishly large merchandise *and* current account surpluses not because we had made new breakthroughs in international markets, but simply because the economic downturn had encouraged Canadian firms to hold back on their traditionally high levels of capital goods imports.

Meanwhile, on the other side of the current account ledger, the perpetual deficits on service transactions are also directly related to the high level of foreign direct investment in Canada. Between 1975 and 1982, 64 billion dollars, over four-fifths of the total deficit on service transactions, was accounted for by payments to foreigners of interest and dividends on their Canadian investments as well as royalties, licensing fees, management and technical services and other intrafirm transfers.

Crippled by its relationship to foreign direct investment and staple production, the unfortunate structure of our balance of payments triggers a number of policy headaches for the Canadian state. To begin with, our vulnerability to the health of world resource markets is exaggerated. When commodity prices fall, the one bright spot in our current account dims. Exposed to the cruel winds of international economic fortune, crisis management, not forward planning, becomes by necessity the style of the Department of Finance.

Second, little can be undertaken to correct the balance of payments situation without presenting a historically unprecedented challenge to foreign direct investment in Canada. For example, any serious attack on the service accounts deficit would almost certainly involve some form of currency control in order to regulate the flow of foreign-controlled profits leaving Canada in any of the numerous direct or indirect forms they might possibly take (transfer pricing, management and royalty fees, etc.). Washington would almost certainly retaliate in a dramatic fashion. The horror of such a confrontation explains why Canadian politicians prefer to restrict themselves to bashing tourism, the one, albeit minor (about one-eighth of the total), portion of the service account deficit over which they feel they have some control. On the merchandise side, an improvement could be expected with the implementation of an industrial strategy which would force the branch plants to develop an export trade. We have already pointed to the unattractiveness of this option for Canada's economic and state elites.

Finally, on the theory that the disease is better than the cure, Canadian governments have in the past attempted to balance deficits on the current account by seeking surpluses on the capital account of the balance of payments. This account measures the international flow of productive investment funds—in this case, new foreign investment in Canada. This strategy is, however, wearing very thin in an era where, as we noted above, dividends are leaving the country twice as fast as new investment is entering it. And, in recent years, further problems in relying on capital account inflows to make up for shortfalls in the current account have emerged. This has been the result of large and unprecedented outflows of private and public Canadian capital used to purchase from foreigners control of their Canadian properties. The energy sector has been in the vanguard of this repatriation movement.

Monetary Policy

Canadian monetary policy is similarly affected by the political economy of Canada–U.S. relations. Capital ties between the two countries are so close and access to the New York capital market so important to Canadian borrowers that the Canadian government must remain constantly attentive to U.S. monetary policy and to capital flows across the 49th parallel, which, on occasion, it has found difficult to control. In years when Canada had a fixed exchange rate, for example between June 1962 and May 1970, the influence of American monetary policy on Canada's was profound. During the eight years in which the Canadian dollar was pegged in terms of the U.S. currency, the Canadian government found it virtually impossible to conduct a monetary policy geared to domestic rather than external considerations, in this case those dictated by the U.S. balance of payments programs. In return for guaranteed access to U.S. capital sources in an era (the 1960s) in which the U.S. was concerned about capital flows, Canada had to accept limits on the reserve level of U.S. dollars it could hold. This, in turn, meant that the government and the Bank of Canada had to manage Canadian monetary policy in such a fashion as to regulate the movement of capital into Canada rather than in a manner which would dampen the growing rate of inflation Canada was experiencing in the mid-sixties.

Under a floating exchange rate regime the Canadian government has enjoyed slightly greater flexibility with respect to monetary policy. However, the degree of monetary policy independence gradually lessened in the late 1970s and early 1980s as the government and the Bank of Canada battled inflation. By 1981–82 Canadian monetary policy and interest rates were once again paralleling those south of the border. Canada has traditionally maintained an interest rate slightly higher than that of the U.S. to attract portfolio capital into the country and, thereby, to protect the Canadian dollar. When, for short intervals (as in mid-February 1982), Canadian interest rates were allowed to fall below those prevailing in the United States, a wave of selling forced the Bank of Canada to intervene and raise rates so as to again draw short-term foreign capital into the country. With the decline in American interest rates that began in late 1982, Canadian rates also began to fall, although they remained higher than U.S. levels. The extremely high interest rates of 1981–82, and the demand from some sectors of the Canadian political economy that these be lowered, engendered a debate about the independence of Canadian monetary policy. The debate was brief— Canada could not unilaterally lower interest rates without either risking massive capital outflows to the U.S. in search of higher returns or exchange controls. The Governor of the Bank of Canada captured the essence of the strictures on Canadian monetary policy in his 1982 Annual Report:

> It seems to be a persistent faith of some Canadians that it should be possible to manage economic affairs in this country with little regard to what is happening in the United States. Given the high degree of inter-connection and interdependence between the two economies this is not possible. . . .[10]

If the flexible exchange rate broadens the government's monetary policy options vis-à-vis the United States, in theory at least, it also high-lights the vulnerability of the Canadian balance of payments position and the relationship between the strength of the dollar and the current Canadian trade picture. A rise or fall in the dollar's value routinely follows the monthly announcement by Statistics Canada of the Canadian trade balance. The dollar falls when the Canadian current account position is weakened by a drop in demand for our resource products abroad, particularly in the United States, and rises when the current account shows a surplus. Since the return to a floating rate, the value of the Canadian dollar has gradually slipped from a high of $1.04 relative to the U.S. dollar to its present (early 1984) psychological bottom of approximately 78 cents. At each step along the decline (or when the dollar has been under pressure because of large capital outflows), the government has attempted to maintain the dollar level by either intervening directly in the exchange market and buying dollars or by actively promoting exports. Very often in the past this export promotion took the form of massive new resource export projects. This, in turn, merely compounded Canada's economic dilemma because these resources were then no longer available for the development of future industrial capacity.

Employment Policy

We will conclude our review of policy problems related to direct foreign investment in Canada by a short examination of employment policy. To some degree, all that we have previously discussed has pointed us in this direction because the provision of meaningful jobs is, after all, the final adjudicator of economic performance.

Canada has been plagued with a disturbingly high rate of unemployment for the greater part of the last fifty years. Since the early 1960s, we have had the distinction of the highest rate of unemployment in any major industrialized capitalist economy. In addition to this high unemployment rate, Canada also has a somewhat different structure of employment compared to other industrialized economies, with relatively low (and declining) percentages of its workforce in manufacturing jobs (approximately 20 percent) and of Gross Domestic Product accounted for by manufacturing (approximately 21 percent). To illustrate, in 1981, Canada had 19.4 percent of its workforce in manufacturing employment, while the norm for OECD countries approached 25 percent. In that same year, the U.S. displayed a comparable 21.7 and Sweden 23.3 percent. At 21 percent, even Ireland bested Canada's miserable performance.

Here, again, our branch plant industrial structure is implicated. Employment in Canada does not reach the level which we might expect from our developed status because of three important gaps in the manufacturing process of the typical subsidiary. Management and research and development jobs are usually concentrated in the parent's operation outside the country. Further, branch plants have had little or no freedom to develop export markets and thus the jobs that go with them. Finally, the production process in Canada is incomplete, as machinery and components are most often imported from the foreign parent rather than made in Canada.

On this last point, some have suggested that as the economic woes of the U.S. economy multiply, parent firms will come under tremendous pressure to reclaim jobs from their Canadian branches by turning them more and more into "warehouse–assembly" operations or closing them completely.[11] U.S. federal and state governments' "buy-American laws," which demand that all public bodies purchase goods made in the United States, will compound Canadian employment woes as Canadian firms, desirous of selling south of the border, move their assembly plants to the United States.[12] A Science Council of Canada report has suggested that this problem is so serious that Canada is being "de-industrialized," and that we are in danger of "regression toward economies like that of Chile or Brazil."[13]

Conclusion

Speculation that Canada is drifting toward semi-industrialized under-development is premature at this juncture. The disastrous effects of resource export dependency which are so painfully obvious in Latin America are, in Canada, largely contained and modified by a developed economy with a high standard of living and an imposing industrial capacity. In turn, this developed economy is managed by a correspond-ingly developed state and class structure which has always demonstrated the ability to act in defence or promotion of what it perceives to be the national interest—capitalist accumulation with social harmony.

In the past, Canada's close ties with the United States have been seen by our economic and state elites to provide for their vision of the national interest. It is on this basis that they have supported the extension of these links. If the liabilities of foreign investment became too great—say massive unemployment (15–20 percent), aggravated social unrest and reduced investment opportunities—these elites could be expected to lead Canada along the road to greater economic independence. A military dictatorship, as in Latin America, to preserve the sanctity of foreign capital and those associated with it is not a realistic option in the Cana-dian case. However, a full-blown economic collapse is highly unlikely at this time. We are outlining the case for frustrated potential, not potential catastrophe.

If we assume that the worst-case scenario just sketched will not happen, what are the parameters within which the federal government will have to act to cope with Canada's nonetheless severe economic difficulties? Let us review our current position within the continental political economy. The U.S. presently accounts for nearly three-quarters of Canadian import and export trade. Continental free trade, vaunted as the panacea for Canada's economic problems by the Economic Council of Canada and by the Senate's Standing Committee on Foreign Affairs, is for all practical purposes already upon us. Between 1965 and 1978, the average rate of duty in Canada fell by nearly 40 percent. By 1987, 80 percent of current Canadian exports to the U.S. will enter that country duty free and up to 95 percent will be subject to tariffs of 5 percent or less. From the other side, 65 percent of U.S. industrial exports will enter Canada duty free, and 91 percent with rates of 5 percent or less.[14]

There are four main paths along which Canadian manufacturing firms have been trying to readjust their traditional ISI pattern of operations to meet the demands of this new freer trade environment. At one extreme of the continuum has been the shutdown. Whether through bankruptcy, or simply as the result of a judgment that Canadian demand could be more profitably met from a multinational's U.S. facility, there have been enough spectacular closures in recent years to cause real concern. Further along the continuum, other firms have attempted to cling to their long-established import–substitution approach by sacrificing a number of their most highly inefficient lines and by relying on the protection afforded against imports by our devalued 80-cent dollar.

A third option has been pursued by a growing number of branch plants. Following the example of the automotive firms under the Auto Pact, many subsidiaries have sought to rationalize their continental production by selecting a limited number of lines which can be manufactured or assembled in Canada for both the U.S. and domestic markets. Here, too, the 80-cent dollar appears to be crucial to the success of these schemes. As long as Canadians remain content through this monetary device to remain a relatively low-wage enclave within North America, some multinationals will find it both rational and profitable to concentrate a portion of their relatively labour-intensive assembly stage of production in Canada.

From the perspective of the Canadian national interest, such a continental division of labour is far less rational. As we have no control over the technological processes involved, and, indeed, remain highly dependent on U.S. imports of the capital, equipment and machinery necessary for assembly production, our firms are highly vulnerable to having their jobs recalled across the border as the result of either a shift in parent corporate priorities or the imposition of non-tariff barriers by the U.S. government. Because it does not build a base for world competitiveness, so-called continental rationalization is, at root, simply a replication of the worst features of traditional Canadian ISI on a somewhat larger stage.

This brings us to the last, and most hopeful, path being pursued by Canadian manufacturers in the mid-1980s: world competitiveness. Some factories, particularly Canadian-owned establishments with some measure of control over their innovative capacity, have been gearing up to claim their place in the North American and world markets now opened to them through freer trade and favourable exchange rates. Bombardier of Montreal is a spectacular example of a firm which has achieved considerable success through pursuit of this strategy. The multinationals also have their version of outward-oriented production— the world product mandate. In its full form, the mandate allows the Canadian subsidiary access to world markets in a particular line or lines, cuts the requirement of buying components from or through the parent, and develops independent Canadian research and development and international marketing capacities. Although hailed as the industrial wave of the future for some time now, it appears that only a small minority of branch plants have been ceded world product mandates, and even these arrangements have often been more symbolic than real as foreign firms have apparently used them as devices to impress the federal government with their commitment to promoting Canadian exports.[15]

It is still too early to say which of these paths is likely to emerge as our era's dominant industrial strategy. Of the four, however, only the last can give us any great optimism for the long-term future of Canadian manufacturing. Moreover, in the aggregate, the short-term picture emerging from the evidence brought forward in this chapter is extremely negative. For example, while it is true that Canadian manufacturers have recently enjoyed some success in allocating a larger proportion of their production to foreign customers as we have moved toward freer trade, imports have become, at the same time, increasingly effective in penetrating our domestic market. The unfortunate result has been a hemorrhaging trade deficit in end manufactures (150 billion dollars since 1970), that will likely continue well past the mid-1980s.

What about the resource sector as we move into the remainder of this decade? As we will recall from our earlier discussion, the 1980s opened with an important cabinet statement which represented a defeat for those within the state who favoured an industrial reorganization for Canada based on getting a better deal from the foreign investors who dominate our major manufacturing enterprises. However, even as it was being enunciated by the Liberal government in 1981, the vision of resource-led growth outlined in *Economic Development for Canada in the 1980s* as the panacea for Canada's economic problems was coming apart at the seams. The high prices fetched by resource commodities in the late 1970s dropped as the recession deepened and demand fell. Just as the rapid depletion of our timber lands is reducing our future capacity as a prime exporter of forest products, the recent trend on the part of multinational corporations to world-wide sourcing for resources has cast doubt on Canada's centrality as a producer of an important number of minerals. Finally, with the collapse of the oil price bubble, the massive energy mega-projects, potentially worth over 400 billion dollars and at the heart of this rather pathetic retreat into the staples past, were quietly extinguished.

Further, the cabinet's optimistic expectations of backward and forward linkages to our manufacturing sector from mega-project resource extraction were based on assumptions that were open to serious question—on the one hand the assumption that the Canadian capital goods sector was capable of developing and supplying the machinery and equipment necessary for resource production and processing, and on the other hand that there was some likelihood of resource upgrading before export. But, as we know, the weak Canadian capital goods sector has traditionally been able to provide only a fraction of the equipment for the fuel and minerals producers. Moreover, despite strenuous efforts during the Tokyo Round, the Canadian government failed to persuade its major trading partners to adopt a sectoral bargaining strategy which would have reduced tariffs on upgraded raw materials, and thereby enhanced Canada's position as a resource exporter. Even with progressively lower tariffs on processed exports, however, there would be little incentive for multinationals to change the locale of resource processing from foreign sites to Canadian ones, particularly given our relatively high-wage economy.

Finally, having reviewed Canada's trade and investment linkages within the continental political economy, let us conclude by speculating on how the state will likely respond in the remaining years of the 1980s to the profound structural difficulties we have identified in the Canadian economy. Unfortunately, the record we have set out here does not give much cause for optimism. Although the issues surrounding foreign ownership have been at the heart of much of our critique of continental integration, foreign investment by itself is not the problem. Rather, historically the Canadian state has not striven to get the most out of the country's resources and capabilities by seeking the best possible deal from foreign investors. The National Energy Program illustrates the *ability* of the state to intervene definitively to protect Canadian interests when it chooses, but such interventions have been the exception. While it is true that the leaders of both major national parties are currently not predisposed to address the structural imbalances of the continental relationship, the deteriorating Canadian political economy may yet force the state to adopt NEP-like initiatives in some industrial sectors before the end of the decade.

Notes

1. By 1897, U.S. direct investment in Canadian resources was 61 million dollars or 38.2 percent of U.S. investment in Canada at the time. For statistics on the growth of U.S. investment in Canada see Hugh G.J. Aitken, *American Capital and Canadian Resources* (Cambridge: Harvard University Press, 1961), Chapter 2.
2. Wallace Clement, *Continental Corporate Power* (Toronto: McClelland and Stewart, 1977), especially Chapter 3.
3. Computed from Kenneth Buckley, *Capital Formation in Canada 1896–1930* (Toronto: University of Toronto Press, 1955), pp. 22, 135, 136.
4. Aitken, *American Capital and Canadian Resources*, Chapter 2.
5. For example, *Looking Outward: A New Trade Strategy for Canada* (Ottawa: Information Canada, 1975).
6. *Globe and Mail*, October 6, 1983, p. B12.

7. Department of Industry, Trade and Commerce, *Framework for Implementing the Government's New Industry Development Policy During the Next Four Years and Proposals for Immediate Action*, July 3, 1980.
8. It agreed to alter the "back-in" provisions of the NEP and to amend the industrial benefits component to permit foreign suppliers to be competitive with Canadian ones. For details on the NEP, see Stephen Clarkson, *Canada and the Reagan Challenge* (Toronto: Lorimer, 1982).
9. Government of Canada. *Economic Development for Canada in the 1980s*, November 1981.
10. Bank of Canada, *Annual Report of the Governor to the Minister of Finance 1982* (Ottawa, 1983), p. 8.
11. J. Laxer, "Canadian Manufacturing and U.S. Trade Policy," in *Canada Ltd.: The Political Economy of Dependency*, ed. R. Laxer (Toronto: McClelland and Stewart, 1973).
12. For example, Bombardier Inc. of Montreal, a manufacturer of urban transportation equipment, established a plant in New Jersey to assemble passenger railway cars. *Ottawa Citizen*, July 23, 1980.
13. J. Britton and J. Gilmour, *The Weakest Link: Canada*, Background Study No. 43 (Ottawa: Science Council of Canada, 1978), p. 26.
14. Canada, Senate, Standing Committee on Foreign Affairs, *Canada–United States Relations, Vol. 3, Canada's Trade Relations with the United States*, March 1982, p. 33.
15. *Globe and Mail*, December 30, 1983, p. B11, and January 30, 1984, p. B12.

Further Readings

Aitken, Hugh G.J. *American Capital and Canadian Resources*. Cambridge, MA: Harvard University Press, 1961.
Britton, J., and J. Gilmour. *The Weakest Link*. Background Study No. 43. Ottawa: Science Council of Canada, 1978.
Clarkson, Steven. *Canada and the Reagan Challenge*. Toronto: Lorimer, 1982.
Clement, Wallace. *Continental Corporate Elites*. Toronto: Macmillan, 1977.
Drache, Daniel. "The Crisis of Canadian Political Economy: Dependency Theory versus the New Orthodoxy," *Canadian Journal of Political and Social Theory*, Fall 1983.
Government of Canada. *Foreign Direct Investment in Canada*. Ottawa: Information Canada, 1971.
Hutcheson, John. *Dominance and Dependency*. Toronto: McClelland and Stewart, 1978.
Innis, H.A. *Essays in Canadian Economic History*. Edited by Mary Q. Innis. Toronto: University of Toronto Press, 1956.
Layton, Jack. "Capital and the Canadian State: Foreign Investment Policy, 1957–1982." Ph.D. thesis, York University, 1983.
Levitt, Kari. *Silent Surrender*. Toronto: Macmillan, 1970.
Mackintosh, W.A. "Economic Factors in Canadian History." In *Approaches to Canadian Economic History*, edited by W.A. Easterbrook and M. Watkins. Toronto: McClelland and Stewart, 1976.

Pammett, J., and B. Tomlin, eds. *The Integration Question: Political Economy and Public Policy in Canada and North America.* Toronto: Addison-Wesley, 1984.

Panitch, Leo. "Dependency and Class in Canadian Political Economy." *Studies in Political Economy,* Autumn 1981.

Safarian, A.E. *Foreign Ownership of Canadian Industry.* Toronto: McGraw-Hill, 1966.

Williams, Glen. *Not for Export: Toward a Political Economy of Canada's Arrested Industrialization.* Toronto: McClelland and Stewart, 1983.

Wright, Gerald, and Maureen Appel Molot. "Capital Movement and Government Control." *International Organization* 28 (Autumn 1974): 671–88.

Chapter 5

The Political Economy of Energy
Glen Toner and François Bregha

Since the 1973 OPEC crisis and the federal–provincial confrontation which followed in its wake, energy politics in Canada have been marked by conflict. October 1980 signalled a major escalation in this conflict with the introduction of the National Energy Program (NEP). The NEP was a centralist, nationalist and interventionist political and policy initiative which at its core was intended to substantially restructure the key relationships of power and the sectoral and regional distribution of wealth in Canadian energy politics. The main features of the NEP were: the unilateral imposition of a new four-year pricing regime for oil and natural gas; the establishment of a new revenue-sharing scheme which would increase Ottawa's share of petroleum revenues by levying several new taxes, including a new tax on natural gas sold in Canada or exported; the launching of a massive energy substitution program to reduce oil imports; and the creation of a program to increase Canadian ownership in the petroleum industry.

In a prime-time provincial television reply to the Liberal Budget, Alberta's Conservative Premier Peter Lougheed charged that "the Ottawa Government has, without negotiation, without agreement, simply walked into our home and occupied the living room."[1] He also unveiled Alberta's three-pronged retaliation to the federal actions: a challenge to the legality of Ottawa's proposed tax on natural gas, a further delay in the approval of new tar sands and heavy oil projects, and the reduction of oil shipments to eastern Canada by 15 percent over a period of nine months. In addition, Lougheed stated, "I don't think it's unfair to say that if the oil was owned by the Province of Ontario, that we in Alberta . . . know that we would in fact—in terms of the history of Canada—be paying world prices for our oil today."[2]

In the months leading up to the budget, Alberta and British Columbia were emphatic in their opposition to the introduction of an export tax on natural gas. Robert McClelland, the B.C. Social Credit government's Energy Minister, charged that "the budget statement that there will be no export tax is a lie," and that "the budget is a money grab by Ottawa, more extensive than any we thought they might dare attempt."[3] Saskatchewan's New Democratic Premier Allan Blakeney claimed "Ottawa's energy taxes are every bit as bad as we thought they would be."[4] Federal Progressive Conservative leader Joe Clark asserted "this is an anti-Alberta, anti-B.C., anti-Saskatchewan energy policy," and that "the budget is designed to cause a division, perhaps for constitutional reasons."[5]

On the other hand, William Davis, Ontario's Conservative premier, responded to Alberta's plan to reduce oil shipments with:

> It is both sad and of deep concern that one provincial government, presiding over what is the most rapidly expanding economy in the country should respond to a continued and prolonged disagreement by imposing deep economic penalties on the working men and women, the pensioners, the businessmen, the people of Canada.[6]

Prime Minister Trudeau reacted to Alberta's energy plans by suggesting that they "beg a fundamental question about our economic union: should provinces interfere in the free movement of goods—especially strategic goods such as oil—within Canada?"[7]

Predictably, the predominantly foreign-owned industry reacted angrily to the restrained price increases, to the decrease in the industry's share of petroleum revenues and to the National Energy Program's plan to ensure that the industry was 50 percent Canadian owned by 1990. To the industry's subsequent threat to transfer a number of drilling rigs from Alberta to the United States, federal Energy Minister Marc Lalonde replied:

> How many oilfields have we found there in the last couple of years anyway? As far as gas discoveries go, what if we go for a year and don't discover any more gas? It will take more than a plunge of 90 points in the market one morning, or a few rigs . . . pack[ing] up and cross[ing] the border . . . to make us run for cover.[8]

The NEP was clearly a federal power play; it did not come, however, as a complete surprise. Rather, the NEP must be seen and can only be understood in the context of the broader policy agenda of the Liberal government and in the historical context of the conflictual energy politics of the previous eight years. Viewed in the context of the other high-profile initiatives undertaken by the recentralizing Liberal government within the first year or so of its new mandate, the NEP can be seen as part of an interrelated effort by the Liberals to reaffirm the central government's economic management powers and political visibility by checking the centrifugal forces of provincialism and foreign ownership. Seen in the historical context of energy politics, the aggressive "act first, talk later" strategy of the NEP was the latest stage of the ongoing eight-year energy battle which had already been marked by consultation, unilateralism, conflict, ploy and counterploy.[9]

The "raising of the stakes" in Canadian energy politics in 1973 with a quadrupling of the world oil price, and again in 1979 with a further doubling in the world price as a result of the Iranian revolution, revealed with shocking clarity the conflicting interests within each of the five major relationships of power in Canadian energy politics. These relationships are: government–industry, federal–provincial, interregional, Canadian–American and partisan. The source of these various power relationships can be traced to the four pre-eminent facts of political life in Canada: Canada is a country of regions and has a regionally unevenly developed capitalist economy; Canada has a federal system of government with a constitutional division of power; Canada shares a continent with the world's most powerful capitalist nation; and Canada has a liberal democratic parliamentary political system with a single-member plurality electoral system and an unevenly dispersed electorate. Hence, each of the partisan, state and private sector interests has its own structural basis of power from which to act.

In addition to these political and economic determinants, there is also the geographical factor. Namely, Canadians live in an intemperate climate and are separated by vast distances and consequently require and use a lot of energy—more per capita, in fact, than any other nation in the world. It is not surprising, then, that the politics of energy, perhaps more than any other public policy area, reveals the potentially conflicting constitutional, regional, partisan and state–industry relationships of power. In fact, Canada is unique in that its governments, industries and regions epitomize within one country the interests that on the global scale divide energy producers and consumers. Hence, there is a continuing struggle within each relationship, and among them, for the power to initiate and direct energy developments. Consequently, within each relationship there are times when the positions of the major interests coincide and times when they are in open conflict. With respect to the issues of pricing, revenue sharing and resource management since 1973, the fundamental interests of each of the contending actors in each relationship have often been in opposition. Not surprisingly, given the cumulative impact of five overlapping relationships, the dominant characteristic of Canadian energy politics over the past decade has been volatility.

This chapter is about energy politics and the policy which results from it. Specifically, the objective is to place the energy conflicts of the past decade within the global context of Canadian politics. In order to provide an understanding of the dynamics behind the energy conflicts, this chapter will review the constitutional powers of each level of government with respect to the administration of energy policy; the historical relationship of western and central Canada and the roots of western alienation; the formation of Canadian energy policy since 1947; and the reactions of the federal government and the producing provinces to events since 1973. In the final section we shall consider the implications of recent developments in energy politics for each of the five key relationships of power.

Division of Powers with Respect to Natural Resources

The constitutional division of powers is at once the essence of federation and an area of constant friction between legislative authorities. This is particularly so for the administration of natural resources as the constitution provides for both strong federal and provincial powers, while at the same time containing controversial areas of both overlapping and uncertain jurisdiction. Therefore, any discussion about control of natural resources demands an examination of the rights of the provinces as owners of the resources and a consideration of the ways in which the federal government might, in the exercise of its constitutional jurisdiction, restrict the exercise of those ownership rights.

Under the provisions of section 109 of the B.N.A. Act, all lands, mines, minerals and royalties belong to the provinces. This is a very important provision in relation to energy resource development, granting, as it does, authority to the provinces to manage their own energy resources. The provincial ownership power is reinforced by the property and civil rights clause 92(13), the power to levy direct taxes, 92(2), and the authority over the management and sale of public lands belonging to the province, 92(5). These powers together confer on the provinces far-reaching authority over the management of all lands in the province, even those that are not public lands. It has been conceded for many years that the provinces have primary responsibility for the regulation and management of natural resources and primary access to natural resource revenues. The federal government exercises these "provincial powers" of land ownership in the Yukon, the Northwest Territories and in off-shore areas.

There are a number of significant bases for federal involvement in the natural resources sector as well. The "trade and commerce" power gives Parliament jurisdiction over all aspects of interprovincial and international trade as defined in section 91(2). This includes interprovincial pipelines and oil and gas exports and consequently is an important authority with respect to marketing. The "declaratory power" as spelled out in section 92(10)(c) gives Parliament control over provincial works it "declares" to be "for the general advantage of Canada" or "of two or more of the provinces." The "emergency power" of section 91 gives Parliament extensive authority to legislate and maintain "peace, order and good government." Section 91(3) provides virtually complete freedom to employ any mode or system of taxation, the only limitation being the prohibition of section 125 against taxation of "Lands and Property" belonging to a province. This power is important with respect to the provision of incentive systems for resource development. The "spending power" is Parliament's power to make payments for purposes other than those for which it can legislate. This was used to provide direct grants to home owners for home insulation, notwithstanding the fact that jurisdictionally provincial governments are responsible for all aspects of this field. Finally, even though this power has not been used since the Depression, the federal Parliament may reserve or disallow provincial legislation.

In addition, in the wake of the 1973 energy crisis, the producing provinces and the federal government passed new legislation pertaining to the management and pricing of oil and gas. Ottawa's Petroleum Administration Act gives it the power to fix the domestic price of oil and gas in the absence of an agreement with a producing province. The Alberta government's Petroleum Marketing Act gives it the power to set oil prices within the province, and the Natural Gas Administration Act gives it the same power with respect to gas. The federal government passed twelve major pieces of legislation in establishing the legislative authority for the NEP.

After years of frustrated effort and hard federal–provincial bargaining the Constitution Act was proclaimed in April 1982. Canada's new Constitution consists of the Constitution Act of 1982 and the B.N.A. Act of 1867 and all the amendments thereto. While the Constitution Act of 1982 does affect jurisdiction over oil and gas directly through the resource amendment and perhaps indirectly through the Charter of Rights, the real substance of legislative jurisdiction is still to be found in the 1867 Act, the important features of which are described above. The resource amendment is found in Section 50 of the Constitution Act 1982, which adds Section 92A to the 1867 Act. It will suffice here to note only three subsections of 92A. 92A(2) enables a province to make laws in relation to the export from the province to another part of Canada of the primary production of a resource, with the qualification that such laws may not discriminate in prices or in supplies exported to another part of Canada. Subsection (3) states that nothing in Subsection (2) derogates from the authority of the federal government to enact laws in relation to the same matters. Most important in terms of provincial jurisdiction is section 92A(4), which expands the taxation power in respect of non-renewable natural resources. Whereas prior to the amendment the province was limited to direct taxation within the province to raise revenue for provincial purposes, it is now empowered to make laws in relation to the raising of money by any mode or system of taxation in respect of non-renewable natural resources, including indirect taxation of resources. Depending on how the courts interpret it, certain aspects of the Charter of Rights could also have ramifications for energy activities. All one can really do at present is acknowledge that the "stakes involved in jurisdiction over natural resources, both in terms of revenue and political power, are so astronomical that any changes or concessions will be made carefully and grudgingly," and that "the new Constitution has increased the legislative base of the provinces with regard to non-renewable natural resources, but has done nothing to shift the overall balance of power between the two levels of government."[10]

The History of Western–Central Canadian Relations

The debate over the management of energy resources illuminates the underlying tension that exists in the Canadian economy between the industrialized manufacturing core of central Canada and the natural resource staple producing western periphery. It is important to note that historically the manufacturing and resource sectors of the Canadian economy have been the two most dominated by foreign capital. Consequently, interprovincial conflicts may result in which various provincial governments defend the competing interests of various fractions of foreign capital.

The hostility exhibited by western Canadians and their provincial governments toward a number of Ottawa's energy policies in the 1970s was not unique. Rather it was a continuation of a decades-long tradition of regional dissent resulting from the region's frustration with its economic role. The pattern of economic development which cast Canada in the role of an economic satellite and marginal supplier of resource staple products to other more advanced cores, chiefly Great Britain and the United States, is roughly analogous to the historical relationship of western Canada to central Canada. Just as the United States and Great Britain had for Canada as a whole, central Canada acted as a source of capital, manufactured goods and immigrant labour as well as a market for the staple products of the West. The federal government, representing the ambitious business–state coalition put together by John A. Macdonald and his associates, played a major role in this developmental process by establishing policies designed to facilitate the production and export of staple products from the West. An example is the National Policy of 1879, which ensured the completion of the Pacific Railway, encouraged western settlement, and created a new frontier of investment opportunities for the commercial and financial interests of the St. Lawrence. Another feature of the National Policy was the provision of a system of protective tariffs which assured a captive market for the products of central Canadian manufacturing trusts.

In addition, control over the land of western Canada was instrumen-

tal to Ottawa's plan for transcontinental expansion and western agricultural settlement. Consequently, when the province of Manitoba was
created in 1870, it was given an inferior constitutional status. Specifically,
Crown lands in the new province were retained by the central government "for the purposes of the Dominion." When the provinces of
Saskatchewan and Alberta were carved out of the old Northwest
Territories in 1905, Ottawa once again retained control over natural
resources. It took nearly three more decades of protest and provincial
rights agitation before control over natural resources was transferred to
them in 1930.

By then, western Canadians already resented their colonial status
within Canada. The transfer of control over natural resources did little to
alleviate this resentment, for 1930 also marked the advent of the decade-
long drought which, together with the economic depression, had devas-
tating results for the Prairies. As the western economy expanded and
diversified, new grievances, largely focused on oil, gas, potash and
mineral wealth, joined the column of historical grievances. In addition to
the natural resource disputes, the tariff, and the activities of the banks,
transportation policy—particularly railroad freight rates—federal monetary policy and the regional distribution of manufacturing remain the
cornerstones of western economic discontent.

It should be noted that there is no general agreement about the
relative degree to which the West's disadvantages are the fault of federal
policy or simply the logic of market economics for a vast, sparsely
populated market geographically peripheral to the national and continental metropoles. Nevertheless, there is general agreement that, on
resource taxation and energy pricing, the West was placed in a uniquely
discriminatory position by national policy. The prime examples of this
discrimination were the federal government's two-price policy for oil and
its export tax on oil. The former kept domestically consumed oil below
its international commodity value. The federal government used the
revenues derived from the latter to help subsidize eastern consumers
who are dependent on imported crude. In an oft-cited quotation, then
Premier Allan Blakeney of Saskatchewan articulates a widely held
western view about federal policies:

> We in the West find it passing strange that the national interest
> emerges only when talking about Western resources or Eastern
> benefits. If oil, why not iron and steel products? If natural gas, why not
> copper? If uranium why not nickel? And to add insult to injury, we in
> the West are now being told that the national interest demands a rail
> transportation policy in which the user pays full cost. What user will
> pay the most under that kind of system? Landlocked Saskatchewan.
> Air transport is subsidized. The Seaway runs monumental deficits.
> Our ports are all subsidized. Truck transport is subsidized by many

provincial highway systems in Canada. But in rail transport—the one
upon which we depend, we are told the user must pay.[11]

In essence, however, it does not even matter that much whether the
West's economic grievances are carved in solid economic stone, but
rather that they exist, are part of the political culture and, as such,
influence political behaviour. Regardless of whether regional discontent
is subject to partisan manipulation by provincial political elites, there is
no question that in the past it has influenced political behaviour in the
West with respect to both the provincial and federal arenas. Moreover, it
continues to do so.

Since the Depression, with the exception of two brief "interregnums"
in the late 1950s and 1970s, the Liberal party has, as a result of its
domination of the large central Canadian electorate, dominated the
federal electoral scene. Westerners have developed a perception of the
Liberal federal government as, in the words of one of the leading
authorities on prairie politics, an "imperial government," which, when
necessary, will sacrifice western interests in the name of national unity,
but in reality, in the interests of central Canada.[12]

Perhaps not surprisingly, the Liberal electoral success in central
Canada has been matched by their lack of success in the West. Moreover,
the affiliation with the federal Liberals has proven to be a major thorn in
the side of western provincial Liberal parties; in 1983, there was not a
single Liberal MLA in the four western provinces. In the mid-1970s, in the
two major oil-producing provinces of Alberta and Saskatchewan, provincial Conservative and NDP governments, respectively, were returned to
office with increased majorities after fighting elections based on
strengthening provincial powers over resource management, in the
wake of political and constitutional conflicts with the federal Liberal
government. In the 1980 federal election, the Liberals returned only two
MPs from the West. Since westerners see themselves in a position of
permanent political disadvantage in federal politics, they have turned to
their provincial governments for protection.

The coincidence of international circumstance (the energy crisis) and
jurisdictional responsibility (control over resources) is providing western
Canada (and potentially the Atlantic provinces) with the opportunity to
redress the perceived historical economic and political inequalities within
the Canadian federation. The governments of the western provinces
wish to seize the opportunity to diversify their economies beyond the
historical boom–bust syndrome of dependence on the traditional staples
and to localize decision–making power over the region's economy and
society. The key to the provinces' economic development strategy is the
control over the management and revenues of the natural resource
sector, particularly the depleting reserves of non-renewable conventional oil and natural gas. The western provinces' intention to use the

considerable leverage provided by increased natural resource revenues to encourage a fundamental diversification of the regional economy has, as a concomitant, the alteration of its traditional role within the national economy and, hence, of the structure of the national economy itself.

Since the Leduc discovery, the Canadian society and economy have developed a way of life dependent upon both cheap and abundant energy. That energy, however, is not evenly distributed: Ontario and Quebec (which together used about 55 percent of the oil and gas consumed in Canada in 1981)[13] produced almost none of either fuel; conversely, the three western provinces supply virtually all of Canada's oil and gas. Depleting conventional Canadian supplies and rapidly rising international prices after 1973 saw the ill-prepared federal government attempting to reconcile the competing interests of the major energy–producing and energy–consuming provinces, while at the same time maintaining its own unique set of interests. The energy debate also saw the government of Ontario become increasingly critical of the western producing provinces and vice versa. It is within this historical context of the West's development within the Canadian political economy that the energy controversies which strained federal–provincial and western–central Canadian relations in the '70s must be viewed. Before reviewing some of the specific controversies, it is necessary to review the history of Canadian energy policy.

Canadian Energy Politics, 1947–1973

At the risk of oversimplification, Canadian energy policy since World War II can be divided into two distinct periods. The first period began in 1947 when oil was discovered at Leduc, Alberta, and the modern Canadian oil industry was born. This period—which lasted until 1973—was marked by a consensus of values between the federal and provincial governments over the management of Canada's growing oil and gas reserves. The overriding objective of Canadian energy policy was to encourage oil and gas production and to stimulate the growth of the domestic petroleum industry. This objective was achieved through the construction of major oil and gas pipelines from the producing provinces to consuming centres in both Canada and the United States,[14] the creation of a favourable tax climate to spur investment and an aggressive export policy. Within this policy framework, the oil and gas industry was given a wide latitude by both levels of government in the development of Canada's oil and gas reserves. The first period in Canadian energy policy was thus largely one of minimum government interference in the interplay of market forces. The second period stands in sharp contrast to the first. Whereas the period before 1973 was characterized by assumptions of abundance, the one since 1973 until recently has been marked by assumptions of scarcity. Price stability has given way to rapid inflation;

the objective of promoting growth has been superseded by that of conservation. Most strikingly, conflict has replaced the previous consensus.

The basic tension between a national and a continental petroleum policy appeared as soon as Alberta oil and gas reserves were realized to be significant. The arguments in favour of economic efficiency seemed to dictate that Alberta supply the American Pacific coast while eastern Canada continue to rely on American imports. This was a concept that the petroleum industry generally supported, as it meant greater sales and more certain markets.

The attitude of the federal government at that time toward the prospective integration of the Canadian and American energy economies was ambiguous. The government seemed content, for the most part, to leave the initiative in developing Canada's oil resources to the predominantly American-owned industry. Consequently, Canadian oil prices were determined in reference to the price of oil in Chicago. It was also the oil industry, led by Imperial Oil, the largest Canadian oil company and a subsidiary of Exxon, that decided to build the Interprovincial pipeline south of the Great Lakes in order to serve both the American Midwest and central Canadian markets. A noteworthy exception to this passive approach was the Canadian government's insistence in 1957 that the TransCanada gas pipeline be built entirely in Canada. In fact, Ottawa helped finance the pipeline in order to realize this objective.

It should be noted that American influence would have played a significant role in the development of Canada's hydrocarbon resources even if the federal government had explicitly followed a nationalistic policy. For example, transportation of oil or gas over large distances is expensive, thus exports, as a means of financing costs, are an attractive option to producers. Canada's reliance on exports to build projects for its own needs gave the United States an enviable bargaining position which it used to extract advantageous terms for itself. Perhaps the best example concerns the construction of Westcoast Transmission. Forced to export in order to achieve the economies of scale necessary to serve southern British Columbia markets, Westcoast committed itself to selling gas in the United States at a price one-third less than what it charged Vancouver residents.

This is only one, albeit an extreme, example of American leverage. The high level of American ownership of the Canadian oil and gas industry, the construction of Canadian pipelines across the United States (approximately 40 percent of the energy Canadians consume crosses the United States), the determination of Canadian oil prices in Chicago, and the rising level of Canadian oil and gas exports all contributed to greater North American integration, a development recognized as early as 1957 by the Royal Commission on Canada's Economic Prospects. The evolution of the continentalist flavour of Canadian energy policy resulted from more than the government's *laissez-faire* attitude and indeed reflected deep-seated values that were widely held, within both industry and government. The call for a continental energy policy was heard often through the 1960s, culminating in J.J. Greene's famous remark in Washington in 1969, when he was Minister of Energy, Mines & Resources, that he favoured continentalism so that "people will benefit, and both countries will benefit, irrespective of where the imaginary border goes."[15]

The rapid growth in the Canadian oil industry in the 1950s, as well as the controversy which had surrounded the construction of Canada's first two major gas pipelines—Westcoast Transmission and TransCanada pipelines (it was the 1956 TransCanada pipeline debate which contributed to the electoral defeat of the St Laurent government the following year)—underlined the need for an independent agency which would supervise the activities of the petroleum industry more closely, as well as depoliticize the volatile energy issue. It was also acknowledged at the time that little direct information was available to the federal government concerning energy matters. Accordingly, in 1957 the government named a Royal Commission on Energy (The Borden Commission) to study Canadian energy policy and make recommendations on the discharge of the government's responsibilities. The Borden Commission recommendations led to the creation of a National Energy Board in 1959. The Board was to act as a regulatory authority over pipeline certificates, tariffs, the interprovincial marketing of energy resources and portions of international energy trade, as well as to play a general advisory role over a wide range of energy matters.

The Borden Commission also recommended the adoption of a National Oil Policy. As a result of falling world oil prices, the Canadian oil industry in the late 1950s was encountering increasing difficulty in competing against imports of cheaper foreign oil. The National Oil Policy created a protected market for Canadian oil west of the Ottawa Valley, thereby allowing the industry to grow free from foreign competition while the five eastern provinces continued to be supplied from abroad.

The National Oil Policy became the cornerstone of Canadian energy policy for the next decade. By artificially restricting the size of the domestic market, it created an exportable oil surplus. Indeed, one of the unfulfilled objectives of Canadian oil policy through the 1960s was to gain greater access to the American market, which was protected by import quotas. The National Oil Policy also restricted the size of the domestic gas market, since Canadian gas could compete with Canadian oil, but not with imported oil, thereby creating a natural gas surplus. Canada used the existence of that surplus not only to increase its gas exports to the United States but also to bargain for greater oil exports as well, a policy that was largely unsuccessful until the early 1970s when declining American oil production led the United States to accept more Canadian oil. By then, Canada was forced to restrict its exports because of falling conventional reserves.

The National Oil Policy must therefore be seen as a key element in the growing integration of Canadian and American energy policies throughout the 1960s. It illustrates the dilemma of Canadian energy policy: Canada could choose either to pay a substantial economic penalty by building oil and gas pipelines all the way to the Maritime provinces, or it could accelerate the momentum of continentalism by importing oil into eastern Canada and exporting Alberta oil and gas to the United States. In energy, as in other commodities, the north–south flow of trade was more economically advantageous than the east–west routes of Macdonald's National Policy.

If the 1950s had been a period of rapid growth, the 1960s were a period of consolidation. With the main oil and gas pipelines in place, a National Energy Board to oversee the administration of Canadian energy policy and the National Oil Policy protecting the domestic oil industry, no new major policy initiatives were launched until the early 1970s. Canadian oil and gas consumption grew steadily, prices were stable and the country's hydrocarbon potential appeared unlimited. This uneventful decade made the adjustment to the energy crisis of the early 1970s all the more traumatic.

Energy Politics, 1973–1980:
The Crisis and the Controversies

Canada, as indeed most of the industrialized world, was completely unprepared to cope with the consequences of the four-fold increase in international oil prices and the partial oil embargo imposed by the Arab members of the Organization of Petroleum Exporting Countries (OPEC) in the wake of the 1973 Middle East War. The reasons for Canada's unreadiness were simple. First, the government had no direct access to information on which it could base policy. In 1974, Donald Macdonald, the Minister of Energy, Mines & Resources, was forced to admit that "one of the difficulties facing the Canadian government is that it is virtually dependent on major international companies for its sources of information."[16] Second, the government only had an embryonic policy-making ability. According to Bill Hopper, Petro-Canada's president, "You could [have] put the people in Energy, Mines & Resources who knew anything about oil and gas in one corner of Imperial's corporate economic department."[17]

With no means to gather information independently and, in any event, no means to digest it, the government predictably reeled from crisis to crisis in 1973 and 1974. Thus, in quick succession, the government imposed oil export controls, similar controls over the export of refined products, announced the extension of the Interprovincial oil pipeline to Montreal (only two months after having reaffirmed the National Oil Policy), froze domestic oil prices, levied an export tax on crude oil, developed an oil import compensation scheme to protect consumers dependent on imported oil, considered and rejected acquiring a subsidiary of one of the major multinational oil companies, and contemplated the imposition of oil rationing.

An additional response by the minority Liberal government to the events of the fall of 1973 was the decision to establish a national oil company, Petro-Canada. Contributing factors to this decision were: Ottawa's concern about the vulnerability of Quebec and Atlantic Canada to interruption in world markets; Ottawa's growing frustration with its lack of control over security of supplies; the growing popularity among the producing nations of state-to-state contracts; Ottawa's recently recognized lack of solid information with respect to Canada's indigenous supplies and reserves and the growing apprehension of being dependent on the foreign-owned industry for this information; and the dawning realization by Ottawa that the dictates of market forces, specifically, the pressure by commercial developers, for reasons of quick return on capital, to produce new discoveries even if it meant exporting, was not synonymous with the "national interest" of enhancing security of supply through frontier exploration and the retention of indigenous reserves.

The two important political factors which combined with these "policy" factors to ensure Petro-Canada's creation were the growing acceptance among the bureaucrats in the department of Energy, Mines & Resources that a state oil company could extend their control over the energy sector and expand their departmental influence and the fact that the minority Liberal government was dependent for its parliamentary life on the support of the NDP, who advocated the creation of a state oil company. It must be understood that Petro-Canada's creation was viewed as an alternative to nationalization, rather than an instrument of nationalization. The Liberals intended to utilize Petro-Canada as a policy instrument to encourage an autarkic energy policy, that is, a policy which emphasized meeting Canadian energy requirements by exploiting indigenous resources. Petro-Canada's initial mandate was to pursue self-sufficiency by expediting the timing of high-risk exploration and development and by supplementing private sector frontier exploration and tar sands research. Initially, Petro-Canada was not mandated politically, but had the legal authority, to undertake downstream activities such as refining and marketing.

Lacking the framework of an energy policy, Ottawa was forced to react to crises, such as the 1973 OPEC crisis, as they occurred. The consequent abrupt and often erratic formulation of policies resulted in hasty and improvised solutions which often directly impinged upon provincial control of resources, and in so doing commenced a period of confrontation between Ottawa and the producing provinces. At the same time, the western producing provinces realized that the rapidly changing international situation in the oil and gas trade had created a shift in bargaining power from consumers to producers. By moving to capture the major share of rapidly increasing energy revenues, the producing provinces felt they could gain the leverage to spur their transition to modern industrial economies. As noted above, it is precisely the link between the energy issues of pricing, revenue sharing and resource management and the wider economic environment which has made this issue one of the most acrimonious and complex constitutional and political confrontations since Confederation.

The stakes in the energy–economy debate during the 1970s were high. They included: jurisdictional questions over resource ownership, the transfer of huge sums of money from consuming to producing provinces, the implications of this income redistribution on equalization payments, the macroeconomic impact of the new policies on the Canadian economy and the country's competitive position internationally, questions of regional development, and the consequences for future policy formation of the relative shifts in power between the major actors. Each of the three aspects of the energy issue—pricing, revenue sharing and resource management—were a focus of bitter conflict between Ottawa and the producing provinces and between the western provinces and Ontario during the 1970s. H.V. Nelles has concluded about this volatile period that:

> The net effect of this vigorous federal intervention was to hold Canadian energy prices well below world levels, but thereby to internalize in the form of sharp federal–provincial conflict, the struggle raging internationally between oil importing and exporting countries.[18]

Generally speaking, federal policy initiatives throughout the 1970s were motivated by the following objectives: to cushion the impact of rapidly escalating international petroleum prices on Canada's industrial sector and, in doing so, to provide a comparative advantage to Canadian export manufacturers; to protect all Canadian consumers from OPEC-set world prices and to subsidize those Canadians who are dependent on offshore crude; to slow the interregional transfer of income from oil-importing provinces to the western producing provinces; to dampen the inflationary impact of rising energy prices on the Canadian economy; to protect the federal tax base and federal revenues with respect to equalization payments; to encourage the development of new supplies; to encourage conservation; and to ensure that the producing provinces, as owners of the resource, received an adequate price for their depleting resource. Throughout the 1970s, then, the primary focus of Ottawa–producing provinces conflict was not pricing, but revenue sharing and resource management.

Pricing, however, has been a particularly thorny issue in western Canadian–Ontario relations, as the producing provinces wanted higher prices while Ontario argued that prices should increase slowly. Quebec was also a large consumer, but chose as a matter of principle to side with the producing provinces and support unfettered provincial control over natural resources. Ontario feared that rapidly escalating petroleum prices would have severe repercussions for its industry's competitive position internationally and would increase unemployment. Ontario argued that it was irrational for Canada to follow blindly the monopoly price set by OPEC—a price which was totally unrelated to the cost of producing conventional supplies of Canadian oil and gas. Furthermore, Ontario charged, the price increases of the late '70s were not necessary to encourage the development of new energy supplies, but were simply the result of the competing appetites of the federal and provincial treasuries.

The producing provinces of the West argued that Ottawa's attack on western resource policies was not prompted by the belief that the provinces were acting beyond their powers, but rather by a desire to extend the central powers of the federal government at the expense of provincial powers. The western producers argued that by selling their depleting reserves of oil and gas at prices well below world price they were providing a massive subsidy to the rest of the country. Ottawa's various initiatives in this field were seen as further examples of federal willingness to displace negotiation by unilateral action, an approach which western governments charged smacked of traditional Ottawa arrogance and insensitivity toward the West.

Quite clearly, then, throughout the post-1973 period the major governmental actors exhibited diverging interests and objectives with respect to the control of energy developments and differing perspectives regarding the constitutional powers over resources.

The Politics of the NEP: 1980–1983

The two-year period following the release of the National Energy Program in October 1980 ranks as the most turbulent in the history of Canadian energy politics, surpassing even the turmoil which characterized 1973–1974. Overnight, energy policy became the priority item on the political agenda, defining partisan conflict, federal–provincial cleavages, government–industry relations and regional politics.

As the first comprehensive statement of Canadian energy policy, the NEP represented a unilateral intervention by the federal government into every facet of energy policy making. More significantly, the NEP consti-

tuted a conscious effort to fundamentally restructure the power relationships among the principal actors in the Canadian energy scene. Not
surprisingly, therefore, the NEP unleashed a passionate and, at times,
bitter response from those who stood to lose the most from the new
initiatives: the producing provinces, chiefly Alberta; and the oil industry,
principally its large foreign-owned element.

The NEP set three objectives for Canadian energy policy in the 1980s:

- fairness in petroleum pricing and revenue sharing. In its starkest
  terms, this objective entailed a redistribution of income from industry
  and the producing provinces to the federal government. It also implied
  the protection of Canadian consumers from rapid world oil price
  increases.
- opportunity for Canadians to participate in the petroleum industry
  and share in its expansion. The government set a target of 50 percent
  Canadian ownership of oil and gas production by 1990, Canadian
  control of a significant number of large firms and an early increase in
  public ownership of the industry.
- security, which was defined as the achievement of oil self-sufficiency
  by 1990.

The first two objectives in particular, and the policy and legislative
instruments introduced to implement them, implied an unprecedented
degree of government involvement in every phase of industry activity,
from determining the Canadian ownership ratings of individual companies to negotiating exploration agreements in the frontiers and
industrial benefit packages. In reviewing the at-times frenzied march of
events which the NEP set in motion, it is useful to focus on the
implementation of the NEP's three objectives and the conflicts they
engendered.

Fairness

Alberta retaliated only two days after the NEP's release, announcing it
would cut back 180,000 barrels a day in oil production to be implemented
in steps starting March 1, 1981. In addition, the province withheld final
approval of the Alsands and Cold Lake mega-projects which were to
represent 20 percent of Canadian oil supply in 1990. As a final measure,
Alberta challenged the legality of the gas export tax the federal government had proposed to levy. British Columbia, which is also a gas
producer, responded to the NEP by announcing it would refuse to pay the
federal government's export tax on natural gas.

In early March 1981, Alberta cut back oil production as threatened,
forcing the federal government to raise the price of oil to the consumer to
pay for additional oil imports. As the confrontation between the two
governments escalated, both sides sought to reconcile their differences in

a number of high-level meetings. After several false starts, they were able to reach a compromise in September 1981 in a Memorandum of Agreement which gave Alberta the higher prices it sought and the federal government the higher revenues it needed. Compromise was made considerably easier by the belief that the world oil price would continue its rapid climb, making the revenue pie to be divided among the two levels of governments and industry large enough to satisfy everyone. This breakthrough was followed in quick succession by pricing and revenue-sharing agreements with the other two main energy-producing provinces, British Columbia and Saskatchewan.

The premise upon which these agreements were based, however, was shown to be wrong soon after they were signed; that is, world prices did not continue to escalate at the rapid pace that was assumed. Both governments had gone too far in raising taxes on an industry whose revenues were rising much more slowly than predicted. Thus, by as early as April 1982 Alberta was forced to pump $5.4 billion back into the industry in the form of new revenue and incentive programs. In May, the federal government followed with its own $2 billion package in the NEP Update. These stopgap measures were not enough to cover the widening difference between expected and real prices. By mid-1983, the Memorandum of Agreement itself had to be renegotiated in the wake of the drop in world oil prices in the spring. By then, however, the Alberta and federal governments had a vested interest in making the Agreement work: both wanted to maintain stability for an industry that had been shaken up by the policy initiatives of the previous three years. The economic recession contributed further to their distaste for more confrontation, and the second round of negotiations was therefore accomplished in record time.

As well, all sectors of the industry had continued throughout the post-NEP period to lobby hard for changes to the NEP and Memorandum of Agreement pricing provisions, arguing that prices should move to world price or at least closer to world price. The new federal Energy Minister Jean Chrétien perceived his role to be that of re-establishing a measure of stability in the energy sector. Consequently, Chrétien acceded to higher prices for more categories of oil, arguing that the Liberals' "blended price" was still below world levels, and world levels for 1983 were much lower than it was assumed in 1981 they would be.

Opportunity

Elements of the Canadian industry, particularly the large Canadian-owned firms, reacted positively, but quietly, to the NEP. Some big and medium-sized firms both in and outside of the oil industry saw the NEP as an opportunity to expand within or enter the booming oil and gas business. The foreign-owned sector, on the other hand, reacted with varying shades of anger to the NEP's plan to ensure that the industry would be 50 percent Canadian owned by 1990. These companies significantly slashed exploration budgets for the coming year, while their parent companies exerted pressure on the U.S., British and Dutch governments to pressure Canada to change aspects of the NEP. Somewhat to Ottawa's surprise, many of the smaller Canadian-owned firms also reacted negatively to the NEP—in part on ideological grounds, in part in opposition to the NEP taxes which would affect their cash flow, and in part because the new incentive program encouraged exploration on the Canada Lands where few small firms were equipped or anxious to move. This element of the industry reacted by significantly curtailing drilling programs and by shifting a percentage of their exploration activity to the U.S.

Nevertheless, in early 1981, the federal government scored a first important success: Dome Petroleum, a largely foreign-owned though Canadian-controlled company, which was the most active explorer in the Beaufort Sea and, therefore, a key actor in Canadian energy policy, announced the creation of a new publicly owned company, Dome Canada, which would be entrusted with Dome's exploration activities. By establishing a Canadian-owned subsidiary, Dome was not only gaining access to the rich exploration grants the government was making available to Canadian corporations, but it was also publicly declaring its support for the Canadianization policy. The importance of Dome's announcement was underlined by the attendance of Marc Lalonde, the federal Energy Minister, at the Calgary press conference which unveiled Dome Canada.

In February 1981, Petro-Canada acquired Petrofina, an integrated, Belgian-owned company, for $1.46 billion. In April, Ottawa announced that beginning May 1, 1981, it would implement the special Canadian ownership charge provided for in the NEP on sales of petroleum products and natural gas to cover the costs of Petro-Canada's purchase of Petrofina. In June 1981, the partially federal government–owned Canadian Development Corporation acquired Elf Aquitaine, a French company, for $1.6 billion. Critics of these purchases argued that while they increased the level of Canadian ownership and control, the expenditures of vast sums of money did not find any additional oil or gas and thereby did not contribute to greater security of supply for Canada.

The general public's response to the NEP was overwhelmingly positive. Even the Canadian Petroleum Association's own confidential poll indicated that 84 percent of Canadians supported the move to make the oil and gas industry at least 50 percent Canadian owned. A December 1981 Gallup poll showed that 64 percent of Canadians would favour even more rapid Canadianization, specifically 75 percent Canadian ownership by 1985. This included a plurality of Canadians from all regions and age groups and both sexes. The same poll revealed that 55 percent of respondents favoured the acquisition by Petro-Canada of one of the four major foreign-owned oil companies—Imperial, Gulf, Shell or Texaco. In 1982 Petro-Canada acquired the refining and distribution assets of B.P. Canada for $347.6 million. Petro-Canada now had assets in excess of $7 billion, and the Canadian public continued to favour Petro-Canada. Petro-Canada's retail sales in 1982 were up by as much as 30 percent in a shrinking gasoline market.

At the height of the industry campaign against the new energy taxes, the discriminatory Petroleum Incentives Program, the Petro-Canada purchase of Petrofina, and other aspects of the NEP, the federal government released in March 1981 *The State of Competition in the Canadian Petroleum Industry*, a report by the Combines Investigation Branch of the federal government. This report charged that the major integrated firms had, as a result of following uncompetitive practices such as overpaying parent companies for imported oil and operating an inefficient gasoline distribution system, overcharged Canadians by $12 billion for petroleum products between 1958 and 1973 (in 1981 dollars). The report had the effect of placing the multinational majors, which had been employing a major media and lobbying campaign against the NEP, back on the defensive.

The government, however, also remained on the defensive, paradoxically, as a result of the runaway success of its own Canadianization policy. By mid-1981, acquisitions worth more than $6 billion had been made by Canadian companies in the wake of the NEP. Concerned about the impact of such a rapid transfer of assets out of the country, Finance Minister Allan MacEachen called on representatives of the major banks to help slow down the rate of takeover by Canadian firms by making loans less readily available.

One major additional acquisition worth noting was made before the year was out, this one by the Ontario Energy Corporation, a provincial Crown corporation, for a 25 percent interest in Suncor. This purchase was significant for the explicit support the Ontario government lent to the embattled federal energy policy.

Security
Like the other two NEP objectives, energy security met with wide public support. The issue which once again divided government and industry was not so much the objective itself as the means chosen to implement it.

In order to encourage Canadianization, the government replaced its previous tax-based exploration incentives system with one based on direct grants. This new approach not only represented a much more direct level of government involvement in industry affairs but it was also heavily biased in favour of Canadian companies, which led the U.S.

government and multinational companies to charge they were being discriminated against.

The Petroleum Incentives Program (PIP), furthermore, gave far larger grants to companies operating on the Canada Lands controlled by the federal government (the north and the offshore) than it gave to exploration in the provinces. In this way, the federal government hoped to reduce in time Alberta's leverage over energy policy by accelerating the development of oil supplies under its direct control.

As a result of these incentives, the oil industry in 1981 began redirecting a substantial portion of its exploratory effort to the Canada Lands. The drop in world oil prices, which had already necessitated the renegotiation of the Memorandum of Agreement with Alberta, was to have its most adverse effect on this objective: combined with disappointing exploration results in the three years immediately following the NEP, this drop was to frustrate the achievement of the self-sufficiency target of 1990. The prior collapse of the Cold Lake and Alsands projects, initially stalled by the Alberta government in its confrontation with Ottawa on oil pricing and revenue sharing and finally scuttled for being too risky economically, meant the federal government had run out of options in trying to achieve this objective.

Although industry argued that the self-sufficiency and Canadianization objectives were largely incompatible in the time frame the government had originally envisaged, the failure of international oil prices to continue rising constituted a much more fundamental reason for the problems that emerged. While the NEP was one of the first energy policies to explicitly highlight the role of conservation and substitution in achieving Canadian energy goals, the overwhelming ascendancy of the supply-side orientation remained. After an initial conservation thrust and a more important substitution initiative highlighted by the extension of the natural gas pipeline into eastern Quebec, furnace retrofits and some motor vehicle fuel conversion, the drop in the international price of oil dissipated much of the urgency attached to substitution in 1980. Consequently, demand-side solutions remain underdeveloped in Canada.

Summary

This review of the history of post-war energy politics reveals that since 1973 the fundamental interests of the major actors have, for the most part, been in conflict. The federal government and the petroleum industry have been at loggerheads throughout much of the decade on the issues of pricing and taxation. Provincial governments and the industry have quarreled over royalty rates. The major regional cleavage has been represented by the ongoing conflict between the governments of Ontario and Alberta over pricing and the distribution of energy revenues. Partisan conflict between the federal Liberals and Tories in particular over energy issues, escalated throughout the decade to the point where it became a key issue in the 1980 federal election. Indeed, the basic differences in philosophy and approach of all three major parties was reflected nowhere more clearly than in the energy policies they presented to the electorate in the 1980 election campaign. Canadian–American relations have been strained by energy issues throughout the 1970s as various U.S. administrations have attempted to more tightly integrate Canadian energy resources into the U.S. market in the face of declining domestic U.S. supplies. Canadian governments, on the other hand, have periodically tried to strengthen Canadian ownership within the U.S.-dominated Canadian petroleum industry, and to improve the industrial spinoffs for Canada of Canadian energy projects. Federal-producing province relations have since 1973 been dominated by conflicts over issues of revenue sharing, resource management and pricing. In the final section we will reconsider the impact of past developments on each of the major relationships of power in Canadian energy politics.

The Government–Industry Relationship

As outlined above, government–petroleum industry relations were not always characterized by conflict. From 1947 to the OPEC crisis, the powerful, predominantly foreign-owned industry enjoyed generous tax incentives and considerable autonomy in guiding Canadian energy policy, which was designed along continental lines. One major lesson of the shock of the early 1970s was that energy policy could no longer be made, by default, by the industry. Consequently, Ottawa and the provincial governments became increasingly more interventionist in the management of energy resources. All governments have reinforced their arsenals of regulatory powers and, in the case of a number of governments, have created Crown corporations and other public agencies to provide themselves with a presence in the heretofore exclusive private petroleum sector. The rapid rise in prices has made energy policy an integral part of the federal and provincial economic policy. In the resultant wrangling over pricing and revenue sharing, the industry has increasingly found itself caught in the squeeze, even though its revenues have skyrocketed since 1973 as a result of dramatic price increases.

In addition, the branch-plant nature of the industry has changed in the political environment of oil in the 1970s from an asset to a liability. On a number of occasions in the last decade, Ottawa has found itself attempting to formulate policy based on industry-supplied information that has been either inadequate or wrong. Perhaps the most embarrassing example was Energy, Mines and Resources Minister Joe Green, in 1971, attempting to convince Americans to import more Canadian oil and gas because Canada had 923 years of oil and 392 years of natural gas in the ground.[19] Within three years the industry was arguing that Canada was running out of both natural gas and conventional oil.

It was becoming understood in Ottawa in the late 1970s that foreign-owned and foreign-controlled subsidiaries worked within a policy mandate approved by their parent companies. Simply put, it was increasingly recognized that the commercial interests of private capital may not equate with the national interest. Given the dominance of foreign-owned companies in the Canadian petroleum industry, the federal government became concerned after the major international price escalation in 1979 that foreign-owned firms would use their increased cash flow and enlarged profits to take over companies in other sectors of the Canadian economy or repatriate the profits to their foreign shareholders to the detriment of Canada's balance of payments. Ottawa was also becoming concerned in the insecure and uncertain period of renewed Middle East conflict in 1979–1980 about being dependent on the oil pools of the multinationals.

The NEP was the first attempt by a federal government to invoke nationalist sentiment against a major foreign-owned industrial sector. Given the prevalent assumption in 1979–1980 that world oil prices would continue to escalate, the Liberals reasoned that the price rises for oil and gas would make the assets of the foreign-owned firms so expensive that Canadian firms would never be able to enter the industry or expand within it unless it was done soon and in conjunction with restrained price increases. The Canadianization proposals also had the objective of altering the internal balance of power within the industry by driving a wedge between sectors of the industry based on ownership nationality.

Interestingly, the reaction of the industry was mixed. Virtually all of the industry opposed the restrained NEP price increases, the increased taxes, the Crown Interest and the generally increased government intervention represented by the NEP. Two of the most important developments within Canadian energy politics in the 1970s were the emergence within the industry of (a) Canadian-owned and Canadian-controlled companies capable of competing meaningfully with the foreign majors and (b) nationalist voices openly critical of the foreign domination of the industry. A number of Canadian-controlled firms calculated that it was in their material self-interest to take advantage of the pro-Canadianization climate to buy foreign-owned companies. Indeed, some of the firms went far beyond what was suggested in the NEP and attempted to take over American firms in the U.S., angering American business and government in the process.

Yet the industry reaction to the Canadianization proposals of the NEP did not break down solely on national ownership grounds. In fact, the opposition of some small Canadian firms showed that these firms not only calculated that their material self-interest was not furthered by the chosen NEP instruments but that they opposed the thrust of Canadianization on philosophical grounds. Indeed, one of the major lessons of the reaction to the NEP was to show the strength of the shared belief systems within the industry across the major size and ownership divisions.

On the other hand, the strident reaction to the NEP of some of the key member firms and the executive of the Independent Petroleum Association of Canada (IPAC), the major industrial organization of the Canadian-owned sector of the industry, alienated some of the smaller Canadian firms which feared that IPAC's vociferous opposition was decreasing its lobbying effectiveness in Ottawa. As a result, a number of these small firms chose to distance themselves from IPAC and lobby for changes to the NEP independent of IPAC. It is acknowledged that their efforts achieved results in the NEP Update, among others.

However, by as early as 1982 there was a growing realization in Ottawa of the difficulty of forcing the pace of Canadianization. This was particularly true where Canadianization was conjoined with security objectives via frontier and offshore exploration. When faced with the combination of falling world prices for oil and gas and high interest rates, many Canadian-owned firms were found to be incapable of carrying the debt load involved in corporate acquisitions and mounting expensive exploration programs on the frontiers. The multinational majors have been, and continue to be, the best-financed and economically most powerful actors in the industry. The NEP never intended to totally displace the foreign companies but rather to challenge their heretofore overwhelming power within the industry. The emergence of a number of Canadian majors and their growth via NEP incentives has at least in part achieved this objective.

The Federal–Provincial Relationship

The root of this conflict can be traced to the differing perceptions of the federal government and the producing provinces about their constitutional powers over resources and their diverging objectives in controlling the development of these resources. Both levels of government want control over energy resources for two reasons: revenue, and management, or the ability to control the pace of development. Donald Smiley has suggested that perhaps the most crucial result of the 1973 energy crisis is that it has led to a resurgence of power and purpose by the central government.[20] The most outstanding example of the new-found federal Liberal assertiveness and centralism was the 1980 Budget and National Energy Program. The problem is that a central government–imposed national energy program can be extremely divisive, particularly when jurisdiction over many of the elements of a comprehensive energy program lies with the provinces.

Indeed, the NEP did spark a major federal–provincial conflagration, highlighted by the Alberta production cutbacks. The difficult negotiations between the Clark Conservative government and Alberta, the unilateral imposition of the NEP by the Liberals and the hard-fought agreements which followed it reflect the major conflicts of interest which characterize the relationship between a producing province government concerned solely with maximizing benefits from the sale of non-renewable natural resources, and a federal government which must balance the concerns of both energy-producing and energy-consuming regions. Given the considerable powers that each level of government can bring to this issue, it is not surprising that federal–provincial conflict is a natural feature of Canadian energy politics. Such conflicts can, however, create a great deal of uncertainty in the industries most directly affected and, in the case of major conflicts, for the economy as a whole.

A second major arena of federal–provincial confrontation throughout the last decade has been the eastern offshore. While the short-lived Clark Conservative government was willing to transfer offshore resource ownership to the coastal provinces, the Trudeau Liberals have insisted that the resources of the offshore are the property of all Canadians and must be managed by the federal government. In March 1982, Nova Scotia came to an agreement with Ottawa for a joint management system for the offshore oil and gas. After months of negotiations Newfoundland and the federal government were unable to arrive at an agreement, and in March 1984 the Supreme Court of Canada ruled unanimously that the offshore was owned by the Crown in right of Canada.

The Constitution Act has done little to clear up the ambiguity created by the division of power in Sections 91 and 92. However, this ambiguity is itself beneficial in that it imparts some useful flexibility to adapt to new situations while at the same time making both parties unsure of their bargaining positions. This sense of uncertainty has fostered an attitude of accommodation between the two levels of government and made each hesitant to engage in head-to-head confrontation in the courts. Despite the magnitude and intensity of the conflicts between the federal and provincial governments over the past decade, surprisingly few disputes have ended up in the courts. Accommodation by negotiation, while always difficult and sometimes seemingly impossible, has been the preferred and chosen way.

The Interregional Relationship

The underlying cause of both the central–western and central–eastern Canadian conflict over energy policy is the unevenly developed regional economy of Canada. As the section on the West's historical relationship with central Canada showed, the roots of western alienation, and thus the cause of the West's hostility to Ottawa's energy policies, run deep. This cleavage is relevant at present primarily because, as a result of escalations in the price of oil and gas and other resources over the last decade, the West has gained a measure of economic power. The four Atlantic provinces also resent their economically disadvantaged status. While the present federal Liberal regime will not transfer control over resources to the coastal provinces, the fact that their major political opponents were willing to do so is important. If at some point in the 1980s the Atlantic provinces do gain control over offshore resources, the possibility exists that the central-eastern version of the metropolis-hinterland reality could be challenged. Whether this would be a positive or negative development depends very much on one's view of Canada.

In addition to the historical economic relationships, a key institutional factor tends to exacerbate interregional conflict. Canada's unevenly dispersed electorate and single-member plurality electoral system allows for the election of a federal government with electoral support in only one region, central Canada. This provides potential for regionally based partisan conflict, which may, in turn, reinforce as well as reflect discontent.

The intensity of the conflict which periodically characterizes the interregional cleavage in Canadian energy politics is best represented by the open warfare that raged within the body of the Conservative party in 1979–1980, when Conservatives formed the governments of Canada, Alberta and Ontario. While the Conservative governments in Edmonton and Toronto had quarreled over price increases and the recycling of oil and gas revenues since the 1973 price shock, their conflict had often been mediated and deflected by the federal Liberal government. Liberal governments in recent years have had weak to very weak western representation, while the Clark Conservative government was well represented by Westerners. This shift in the interregional balance of representation in Ottawa had the potential to have an important impact on energy matters. Indeed, the Ontario government was shocked when it learned that the Clark government had offered Alberta a $6 per barrel a year increase in the price of oil in the 1979 energy negotiations. Concerned with the inflationary and employment as well as the redistributive implications of such "excessive and imprudent" pricing scenarios, the Davis government implemented a campaign to galvanize public opinion in Ontario against the federal Tory government's pricing and Petro-Canada privatization policies. And ultimately, it was the abandonment of the federal Tories by southern Ontario voters which sank the Clark government in the 1980 election. The Ontario–Alberta exchange during this period was vicious, with Ontario at one point advising the federal government to use its draconian constitutional powers if necessary to force a pricing and revenue-sharing arrangement. The Lougheed government, in turn, charged the Davis government with having a double standard and the Clark government with having capitulated to Ontario and its voters/consumers.

Within the Atlantic region, the nascent energy boom has revealed a competitive tension between the provinces of Newfoundland and Nova Scotia. Most fundamentally, Nova Scotia has decided to agree to an arrangement with Ottawa on the sharing of the management and revenues of offshore oil and gas while putting aside the ownership question, but Newfoundland has not. One important motivation of the Nova Scotia government in striking a deal was that it would give Nova Scotia an important advantage in the competition with Newfoundland to become the primary onshore supply base for the potentially very lucrative offshore exploration, development and transmission activity.

Finally the North–South interregional relationship is important as massive energy mega-developments in the North have been at the centre of Canadian energy politics for the last decade. The theme common to virtually all of these northern projects is that the oil and gas resources of the North will be exploited to serve the energy demands of southern Canadians or, where the export of oil and gas reserves are contemplated, foreigners. Consequently, decisions which may have a major impact on the lives of northerners are regularly made in Ottawa and corporate headquarters in southern Canada and the U.S. with little input from and often little consideration for the concerns of northerners. This is of particular importance because the North comprises a peculiar blend of environmental, social, economic and political systems. In 1977 the Berger Commission recommended a ten-year moratorium on energy developments in the Mackenzie Valley in order to provide native northerners, in particular, with the opportunity to prepare themselves for the onslaught of industrial and non-renewable resource development. In the intervening seven years the native community has developed politically and socially to the point where in 1983 the Dene formed a joint drilling venture with Esso Resources. Northern energy development issues have acted as a catalyst for other issues which may ultimately have a significant effect on the relationship of northern and southern Canada. Native land claims, territorial government lobbying for the transfer of jurisdiction over natural resources, and pressure for the establishment of provincial or at least more politically autonomous forms of government in the North are all legacies of fifteen years of intense energy politics.

The Canadian–American Relationship
Until the early 1970s, when both Canadian and American governments awoke to the importance of formulating national energy policies,

Canadian–American energy relations were largely determined by the actions of the oil and gas industry. The industry, almost by definition, planned its activities on a continental basis. When the Alberta oil boom began in the late 1940s, for example, corporate planning logically dictated that an oil pipeline should be built from the newly found fields to the U.S. midwest—which is located far from domestic U.S. sources of oil—before it was extended to Toronto.

The adoption of the National Oil Policy in 1961 constituted a major step toward a further integration of the Canadian and American energy economies. By erecting an artificial barrier at the Ottawa valley, the Canadian government created in effect an oil and gas surplus which was available for export to the U.S. The National Energy Board export recommendations throughout the 1960s were therefore made possible to a large extent by this arbitrary division of the Canadian energy market.

As early as 1957, the Royal Commission on Canada's Economic Prospects was reporting that "in terms of energy, our situation is beginning to blend more and more closely into that found across the border." Canadian policy makers saw this as a positive trend. Thus, two years later, the Borden Commission on Energy made the following remark:

> We mention the possibility of a continental policy not because we believe that it can necessarily be developed in the immediate future but because we feel that care should be taken to ensure that Canada, by actions and commitments now, does not jeopardize the subsequent development of such a policy.[21]

The National Energy Board, which was the main government energy policy maker in Canada throughout the 1960s, reflected this bias and played an important role in reinforcing the already strong continental ties binding Canada and the U.S. In determining exportable gas surpluses and the price at which these exports were to be sold in the U.S. market, the NEB developed an informal "amity and comity" test which stressed the value of developing closer relations with the U.S.

Ironically, throughout the '60s, it was Canada rather than the U.S. which promoted a continentalist energy policy. Faced with growing surpluses of oil and natural gas, Canada expressed on numerous occasions its frustrations at U.S.-imposed trade barriers designed to protect the U.S. oil industry. By the late 1960s, however, the drop in American petroleum reserves led the Nixon administration to extend oil import quotas from which Canada had been exempted until then, in order to pressure Canada into an energy-sharing agreement. Paradoxically, limitations to Canada's own supplies would frustrate the unrestricted access to the American market which Canadian policy makers had sought for so long.

The depletion of Canada's oil reserves and the fear of impending domestic gas shortages, coupled with the OPEC crisis, severely shook the until-then placid Canadian–American energy relationship. By cutting back its oil exports, considering possible cutbacks to its gas exports and, in particular, sharply increasing the price of its gas exports, Canada created a number of irritants for the U.S. The increases in gas export prices—to reflect the growing value of the fuel—were imposed despite contractual provisions which kept prices low, and led one American senator to accuse Canada of "un-American" actions. Canada was of course only acting in its self-interest as a gas producer, and gas pricing policy was designed more to protect its own consumers than to break with the continentalist momentum it had helped to create. In 1977, the Canadian government, by approving the Alaska Highway pipeline on an American-dictated schedule, offered Canada as a cheap land bridge for the construction of an American project. In 1980, the government even allowed the "prebuild" of the southern portions of the pipeline, and the export of large volumes of gas, in order to boost the pipeline's sagging fortunes.

Although the NEP was aimed at shifting political power from Alberta and economic rents from the oil industry to the federal government and was devised with scant regard for its foreign policy implications, the NEP objectives and chosen means of implementation became entangled with American electoral politics and developments in the private sector to contribute to an overall major souring of the relationship. Canada's "dirigiste" approach in energy policy contrasted sharply with the asser-tive laissez-faire thrust of the newly elected Reagan administration, revealing some of the underlying philosophical differences between the two governments. For a nationalist administration committed to reas-serting U.S. hegemony over the western world, the attempt by its closest ally and major trading partner to impose a nationalist and interventionist energy policy was philosophically and politically unacceptable.

The U.S. was particularly incensed at the Petroleum Incentives Program, which it considered discriminatory, and at the provision of a 25 percent Crown share in all oil and gas rights in the Canada Lands, which it deemed to be confiscatory. The U.S. also linked the NEP with other "objectionable" Canadian policies such as the Foreign Investment Review Agency. The Americans threatened retaliation against the NEP, though nothing of substance was done, ironically enough because the closely integrated trade relations between the two countries meant that retalia-tion would have hurt the U.S. as much as Canada. In response to the verbal threats of the U.S. government Ottawa did make some conces-sions on the NEP, though the NEP's basic thrust remained intact. Ottawa also forwent some additional nationalist initiatives it had been contem-plating in the manufacturing sector.

The relationship had returned by 1983 to a calmer state, though irritants on both sides continued to characterize the complex energy relationship. From the Canadian government's perspective, there was increasing concern about the continuing delays on the Alaska Highway Pipeline. The U.S. government in 1982–1983 once again criticized Canadian gas export pricing policy and exerted pressure on Canada to reduce the price, which the Canadians did, in part, in 1983.

The Partisan Relationship

The Liberals and Conservatives have, over the years, exhibited a political bipartisanship on most issues—the northern pipeline being one—affecting the oil and gas industry, an eloquent tribute to the effectiveness of the industry lobby. Nevertheless, by the late 1970s energy conflicts began to take on an increasingly partisan tone at the federal level. This was largely a result of the regional support bases of the various parties. For instance, western dissatisfaction with Liberal policies helped to elect a Conservative federal government in May 1979 whose main electoral base of support lay in the West. It was in the February 1980 election, which followed the Iranian revolution and the doubling of the world oil price, however, that energy policy really took its place as a high-profile partisan issue. The Conservative government's 18 cents a gallon increase in the excise tax on gasoline and its plans to "privatize" Petro-Canada were two of the major issues of the campaign. The Tories also promoted a "strong regions make a strong country" theme. The Liberals argued the need for a strong central government and opposed both of the Tories' energy measures. They designed an energy platform around the reassuring objectives of security and Canadianization, which would allow them to recapture the Ontario vote they had lost in 1979. Liberal support in Ontario in the 1979 election fell from 55 to 32 seats, but returned to 52 in February 1980. Together with their victory in 74 of the 75 Quebec seats, the Liberals returned to power with 86 percent of their parliamentary support in Central Canada. The resulting overlap in the partisan and regional cleavages helped to further strain already tense federal–provincial and interregional divisions.

Because there were no Liberal governments in the West after 1971, it is difficult to determine the degree to which the producing province–Ottawa battles over pricing, revenue sharing and resource management were partisan. The only hint we have of this is the brief period between May 1979 and February 1980 when Conservatives formed the governments of Canada and Alberta. While the Tories in Ottawa and Edmonton did allegedly arrive at an agreement, it was not done without considerable difficulty, even though Prime Minister Joe Clark and Energy Minister Ray Hnatyshyn were both westerners. This, however, is not atypical of the situation that exists when federal and provincial governments of the same party are negotiating on some matter. Each government represents a different set of interests and has its own set of electoral concerns. Each government must be seen as representing the interests of its constituents, and therefore the federal Tories could not be seen to be capitulating to Alberta and selling out Ontario and Quebec. Interestingly enough, a sellout is precisely how the Conservative government of Ontario portrayed the federal Tories' deal with Alberta, ultimately to the peril of the federal Conservative government. Regional interests here clearly outweighed ideological or partisan solidarity.

The NEP also sparked a major partisan confrontation in the House of Commons in 1982. The Liberals attempted to pass most of the enabling legislation for the NEP in one omnibus energy bill. Charging that the omnibus Bill C-94 was in fact eight different bills, the Conservatives employed a procedural tactic which resulted in keeping the division bells ringing for fourteen days. As party House leaders assailed one another daily before the television cameras in the corridors of Parliament with the ringing bells omnipresent in the background, energy policy disputes were once again thrust to the forefront of the nation's consciousness. Ultimately C-94 was broken into eight bills.

Even though the international energy situation is significantly different in 1984 than it was in 1980, energy issues, and the NEP in particular, promise to be important issues in the 1984 federal election as the western Conservatives will be encouraging the federal Conservatives to undo much of the NEP. It will be incumbent upon the Conservatives to have a coherent energy policy in place for the election campaign, as they dare not arrive in power with only a shadow of a policy as they did in 1979. However, developing an energy policy and deciding what to do about the NEP will not be easy for the Conservatives, since on virtually all the important energy issues the interests of the federal Conservatives' two power bases in Ontario and Alberta conflict. Furthermore, unlike the last time, the Conservatives cannot afford to be seen to be in opposition to the politically popular idea of Canadianization. In addition, the Mulroney Conservatives will have to carefully reconsider whether they want to maintain the Clark government's position of transferring jurisdiction over the offshore to the eastern provinces. This may be particularly difficult if the Supreme Court decision gives sole jurisdiction to the federal government. Governments of any stripe are not well known for giving away revenues (NEP taxes, for example) or jurisdictional authority.

Conclusion

Thus, it can be seen that each of the major interests in the five key relationships of power has its own structural basis of power from which to act to influence the outcome of energy developments. In turn, each of these interests is affected by important energy events and decisions. Energy politics in Canada are complex and volatile precisely because so many powerful interests—national and provincial governments, major political parties, some of the largest companies in Canada, a number of which are subsidiaries of some of the world's largest private corporations—interact in an ongoing set of relationships to determine what does and does not happen in the Canadian energy arena.

It is unlikely in the present situation of apparent abundance in international oil supply that Canadian decision makers will have to deal with the major supply and price shocks which confronted them in 1973 and 1979–80. Yet major domestic issues, such as the fate of the PIP program and frontier exploration, energy taxation and revenue sharing, and the eastern offshore jurisdiction question, remain to be dealt with by the party that forms the government after the next federal election. Moreover, these domestic issues are conditioned by a global energy situation that is potentially disruptive, particularly given the increasing political volatility of the world's major oil-exporting region. This complex of factors suggests that energy issues will seldom be far from the top of the agenda of Canadian politics throughout the remainder of the 1980s.

Notes

1. Premier Peter Lougheed, "Address to the People of the Province of Alberta," October 30, 1980, pp. 12–13.
2. *Ibid.*, p. 5.
3. *Globe and Mail*, October 30, 1980, p. 10 and November 15, 1980, p. 15.
4. *Globe and Mail*, October 30, 1980, p. 10.
5. *Globe and Mail*, October 31, 1980, p. 1.
6. *Globe and Mail*, November 1, 1980, p. 13.
7. *Globe and Mail*, November 1, 1980, p. 14.
8. *Globe and Mail*, November 1, 1980, p. 2.
9. For a comprehensive analysis of the NEP see G. Bruce Doern and Glen Toner, *The NEP and the Politics of Energy* (Toronto: Methuen, forthcoming).
10. John B. Ballem, "Oil and Gas Under the New Constitution," Inaugural lecture delivered at the official opening of the Canadian Institute of Resources Law, Calgary, Alberta, December 2, 1982.
11. Allan Blakeney, "Resources, the Constitution and Canadian Federalism," 1977 speech reprinted in *Canadian Federalism: Myth or Reality*, 3rd ed., ed. J. Peter Meekison (Toronto: Methuen, 1977), p. 181.
12. David E. Smith, "Western Politics and National Unity," in *Canada and the Burden of Unity*, ed. David Jay Bercusson (Toronto: Macmillan, 1977), p. 150.
13. Canada, Energy, Mines and Resources, *The Energy Statistics Handbook*, 1981.
14. The 1950s witnessed an explosion in pipeline construction as the oil and gas lines which serve most of Canada's needs were built. The Interprovincial oil pipeline was built from Edmonton to Sarnia in 1954. It was followed by the Transmountain oil pipeline from Edmonton to Vancouver and the U.S. Pacific Northwest. The Westcoast Gas Transmission line to British Columbia

was completed in 1956, and a year later the TransCanada gas pipeline from Alberta to eastern Canada was finished.

15. Quoted in James Laxer, *Energy Poker Game* (Toronto: New Press, 1970), p. 1.
16. *Oilweek*, January 21, 1974, p. 8.
17. *Financial Post*, August 5, 1978, p. 1.
18. H.V. Nelles, "Canadian Energy Policy 1945–1980: A Federalist Perspective," in *Entering the Eighties: Canada in Crisis*, ed. R. Kenneth Carty and W. Peter Ward (Toronto: Oxford University Press, 1980), p. 100. For a detailed description of federal–provincial conflict in this period, see our earlier version of this chapter in the first edition of *Canadian Politics in the 1980s* (Toronto: Methuen, 1981).
19. From a speech to the Petroleum Society of the Canadian Institute of Mining and Metallurgy at Banff, Alberta, June 1, 1971.
20. Donald Smiley, *Canada in Question: Federalism in the 70s*, 3rd ed. (Toronto: McGraw-Hill Ryerson, 1980), p. 202.
21. Canada, Royal Commission on Energy, *Second Report* (Ottawa: Queen's Printer, 1959), p. 135.

Further Readings

Bregha, François. *Bob Blair's Pipeline: The Business and Politics of Northern Energy Development Projects*. 2nd ed. Toronto: Lorimer, 1981.

Canada, Department of Energy, Mines and Resources. *The National Energy Program*. Ottawa: October 1980; *The National Energy Program: Update*. Ottawa: May 1982.

Clarkson, Stephen. *Canada and the Reagan Challenge*. Toronto: Lorimer, 1982.

Crane, David. *Controlling Interest: The Canadian Gas and Oil Stakes*. Toronto: McClelland and Stewart, 1982.

Dacks, Gurston. *A Choice of Futures: Politics in the Canadian North*. Toronto: Methuen, 1981.

Doern, G. Bruce, and Glen Toner. *The NEP and the Politics of Energy: The Development and Implementation of the National Energy Program*. Toronto: Methuen, forthcoming.

Dosman, E.J. *The National Interest: The Politics of Northern Development 1968–75*. Toronto: McClelland and Stewart, 1975.

Foster, Peter. *The Blue-Eyed Sheiks*. Toronto: Collins, 1979.

Laxer, James. *Canada's Energy Crisis*. Toronto: Lorimer, 1976.

Lyon, Jim. *Dome: The Rise and Fall of the House that Jack Built*. Toronto: Macmillan, 1983.

McDougall, John N. *Fuels and the National Policy*. Toronto: Butterworths, 1982.

Pratt, Larry. *The Tarsands: Syncrude and the Politics of Oil*. Edmonton: Hurtig, 1976.

———. "Energy: Roots of National Policy." *Studies in Political Economy*, Winter 1982, pp. 27–60.

Richards, John, and Larry Pratt. *Prairie Capitalism: Power and Influence in the New West*. Toronto: McClelland and Stewart, 1979.

Shaffer, Ed. *Canada's Oil and the American Empire*. Edmonton: Hurtig, 1983.

Simpson, Jeffrey. *Discipline of Power: The Conservative Interlude and the Liberal Restoration*. Toronto: Personal Library, 1980.

Voyer, Roger. *Offshore Oil: Opportunities for Industrial Development and Job Creation*. Toronto: Lorimer, 1983.

Chapter 6

The Political Economy of Renewable Resources
Patricia Marchak

The advertisements of the 1960s proclaimed that forests are like vegetable crops: perpetually renewing themselves with just a little tender loving care. Forests are not cut; they are harvested. Timber shipped out to more advanced economies is a net gain to we the sellers, because there will always be more in the Canadian wilderness from whence it came.

The advertisements stopped appearing about the time that the Canadian Forestry Service and provincial governments proclaimed an emergency in Canada's forests in 1980. How could it happen that Canada was running out of trees? And was it a coincidence that just as Canadian governments were puzzling over this, several of the largest American companies sold out their Canadian holdings?

Fish were disappearing as well. On both coasts catastrophes were announced as foreclosures on vessels occurred in unprecedented numbers and fishermen desperately tried to come up with solutions in briefs and petitions to the two commissions established to investigate the turn of events.

This chapter is concerned with identifying the causes of resource depletion in two industries that are supposed to have renewable resources, and considers how these crises might be dealt with in the 1980s. While specific details are drawn largely from British Columbia, it should be understood that the B.C. situation is but a variant on a general theme that is played in all Canadian provinces.

There are two general kinds of information we need to understand the non-renewal of renewable resources. The first is the nature of resources themselves. The second is the nature of commercial use of resources: private ownership rights, government licensing practices, international markets, and the organization of labour; in short, capitalism in the resource industries.

The Nature of the Resources
No resource is automatically renewable, and all have finite limitations on their tolerance for extraction. Many tree species require a century or

137

more to become mature, and to generate a new forest they require a range of soil and other natural conditions including a long period during which a cycle of different species grow, die, and enrich the soil before the great softwoods take root and flourish. They require clean air, rain, sunlight, shelter, and space, and they simply will not grow in response to the mass production needs of mills or political exigencies.

Fish are even more delicate. When herring roe or prespawning salmon are taken, there is finally a point at which the remaining fish cannot regenerate the species. They will not spawn in polluted waters, they may themselves become polluted by unhealthy water environments, and many impediments in rivers and streams can prevent them from reaching spawning grounds. If their habitats are polluted, the food chain may be broken; if smaller fish are removed, larger fish may starve: over time such conditions can so deplete the remaining stocks that the resource is in danger of extinction. Renewable resources can renew themselves only if they are cherished. And cherishing them is not what either the forest or fishing industries have been all about.

The nature of the resources create some limiting conditions on their commercial use. Trees, for example, require vast expanses of unpopulated lands, which is why Europe in the nineteenth century and the United States and Japan in the twentieth century looked to Canada for forest products. Not all trees produce wood suitable for construction, and those which are suitable for uses other than pulping are sometimes mixed up in forests with pulp-grade trees. When pulp has a high market value, there is a strong incentive to clear-cut forests and ship all timber to the pulpmills, forgoing the additional costs of selective logging. But trees are like minerals in at least one respect: they stand still, so that a company can stake out a claim and declare it as private property.

Fish are not so convenient in their habits; they roam the seas. For this reason they are called a "common property resource." They are particularly problematic because they are susceptible to disease and demise from pollution; thus a fishery is always in conflict with other industries and high population densities which may pollute waterways. Fish are unlike other resources in another respect as well: they are a food source, and on both the Atlantic and Pacific coasts they have been an important food in the subsistence of the local population. This creates a continuing tension between those who would eat and those who would sell.

To understand this tension and the reason that cherishing of nature has not been a fundamental component of North American attitudes, we must refer to the commercial impulse of resource extraction: the making of profits. Resources are not extracted only for purposes of building shelters and providing subsistence. They are extracted for sale. The objective is to harvest and process large quantities for mass consumption. The particular way in which this is done and the quantities processed are in the first instance obviously limited by the nature of the resource but ultimately determined by the market demand.

Markets and Companies

The markets for pulp, lumber and newsprint throughout the post-war period to 1980 were apparently insatiable. Canada was the largest national exporter of pulp and paper, accounting for 41 percent of the world's pulp exports and 69 percent of its newsprint. Most of these products were sent to the United States: 49 percent of pulp, 89 percent of newsprint and 79 percent of lumber.[1] The second largest market, particularly for British Columbia, was Japan.

The companies engaged in the forestry business are international in their operations, and they produce different forestry products in different regions. The primary products from Canada are the least advanced— dimensional lumber, raw pulp and newsprint. The more advanced products, such as finished construction materials, prefabricated houses, wooden furniture, other wood products and specialized and high-grade papers, are usually produced in parent companies elsewhere, particularly in the United States and Japan. In addition to lumber, pulp and newsprint, Canada sells even less advanced forestry products: raw timber and pulp chips. The sale of these latter products increased with the recession of 1981–83. The timber and chips were purchased by large processing companies in the United States and Japan, where they were manufactured into newsprint as well as further end products.

Fish have not generally enjoyed such international demand, and the product itself has generally had a much lower market value. Further, there is intense international competition over the resource because of its mobile nature. Large commercial trawlers from Norway, the United States, Russia and Japan fish in international waters for species that spawn in Canadian waters, thus limiting the Canadian catch and the international sales of Canadian producers. The capacities of these large offshore vessels so outstripped the capacities of the small inshore fishery in Newfoundland that by the 1940s the Newfoundland fishery could no longer support the population of that province as it had ever since European settlement. As well, the freezing technology available on the large vessels made the salting techniques obsolete and the Newfoundland salt-cod industry went into a continuing decline.[2]

In B.C., where salmon has always been the major fishery, a canned product did command international markets. As well, canneries moved into the fresh-frozen market so that the province did not suffer Newfoundland's fate. However, the returns on fish have never been in the same league as the returns on timber. For this reason, there has not been the same drive by foreign investors to buy into the industry. As well, since the processing is relatively simple and not much more can be done with fish beyond preparing it for a commercial food market, there were few advantages to be obtained by linking up firms in Canada and the United States. The exception to this was the B.C. herring roe fishery which blossomed in the early 1970s but was short-lived because the herring supply could not sustain the hectic overfishing. During this brief period, Japanese companies bought into the B.C. processing sector, thereby guaranteeing their supplies for a highly profitable gourmet market in Japan. The herring roe was "popped" in B.C. firms, shipped on Japanese vessels and repackaged and sold there by the Japanese. B.C.'s participation—and profits—were limited to the capture, the popping of roe and the sale of the raw material.

Public Property and Licensing in Forestry

Under the B.N.A. Act, the provinces retained jurisdiction over land, and forestry became a provincial matter. The federal government, on the other hand, gained jurisdiction over fisheries. The provinces sold some of their land to private forestry companies, but for the most part they chose instead to rent the land, receiving in return for public investments in infrastructure and servicing a royalty known as "stumpage." In theory, the stumpage should have paid for reforestation, roads, a Forest Service, silviculture and other nurturance of the forests, and the many services that governments have undertaken to facilitate the growth of the industry. As well, in theory, it should have been sufficient to enrich the public treasury, so that together with taxes it would permit governments to provide the vast range of social services the industry workers require. In fact, as we shall see, the historic development of provincial forestry policies has encouraged industry concentration, foreign ownership and relatively low rents for timber products, all of which have been detrimental to the wise management of this resource.

In the Maritime region, much of the timber land was sold. In B.C., very little was sold, although some grants of land to railways subsequently became extremely valuable commercial forest land under private ownership. Ontario, Quebec and Newfoundland forests are also overwhelmingly held by the Crown. In the western provinces there has been no strong pressure to introduce private ownership. From the perspective of the private companies, public ownership may be inconvenient if governments refuse to grant long-term harvesting rights, but since governments have generally been entirely agreeable to lengthy contracts this has never posed a serious problem. The benefits to the companies are considerable: they have no need to invest in all of the services, they obtain virtually guaranteed supplies, and the risks of a cyclical industry are shared by the public treasury. The "arrangement" is that the private companies obtain long-term tenures to harvest the resource, own the processing facilities and are free to sell their harvesting rights when they sell their mills even though they do not own the timber.

The first Forest Act in British Columbia (1912) was intended to regulate the harvesting and reduce the number of "cut and run" operations. But by 1940 widespread fears of resource depletion sparked a demand for nationalization by the CCF party (then in opposition) which resulted in the appointment of a Royal Commission by the Liberal–Conservative coalition government of the time.[3] The Commission recommended the adoption of "sustained yield" principles. These involved reforestation consonant with harvests over a five-year cycle, with allotted annual cutting rights which were flexible in response to changing market demands but which would provide conservation measures over time.

While these policies would theoretically conserve the resource, their more immediate impact was to oust many small logging and sawmill operations from the industry. Only the large companies could plan long-term harvesting cycles and implement the sustained yield principles. In recognition of this fact harvesting rights were assigned almost exclusively to the larger firms. In addition, smaller companies were unable to finance the technological changes required under the new government legislation. Accordingly, the larger companies bought out the timber rights of the smaller companies, and consolidated all of their timber operations together with both lumber and pulp facilities. Ironically, the increased size of the newly consolidated forestry firms, once seen as a boon to sustained yield, came, in time, to threaten the proclaimed conservation principle of the program. Since these firms were now able to process timber in such enormous quantities, and indeed, their mills required such enormous quantities in order to be profitable, neither they nor the Forest Service were able to reforest at the rate of depletion.

In the post-war period American penetration of the pulp and newsprint industries increased everywhere in Canada, along with American ownership of mineral, oil and manufacturing industries. Newsprint and pulp were identified in the Cold War–inspired Report of the [U.S.] President's Materials Policy Commission (the Paley Report) as among the strategic materials for long-term defence.[4] This report set out the position that Canada's resources were valuable and in strategic demand in light of the U.S. depletion of its own natural endowments. Long-term guarantees of forest and other natural resource supplies produced by U.S. companies in Canada were consonant with American interests, and exemption from import duties allowed these raw and semi-processed materials to move across the border without penalties.

In B.C., as industry consolidation and U.S. investment proceeded, the number of firms with licences steadily declined, though the cutting acreage more than doubled. By 1974, prior to the striking of another Royal Commission, the top ten companies controlled 83 percent of the harvesting rights. The same companies owned about 35 percent of the lumber, 74 percent of the plywood and veneer, 90 percent of the pulp, and all of the paper facilities.[5] The Pearse Commission was followed by the Forest Act in 1978. This entrenched in legislation many of the ad hoc practices that had evolved over the post-war period. Among these were preferential treatment of "established operators" for timber licences, meaning firms with plants in any region where new licences were up for bid. Forest licences and Tree Farm licences of twenty and twenty-five years' duration with clauses that allow for ten-year extensions accommodate future needs of the companies. Since it takes closer to ten years to amortize the cost of a pulpmill, these lengthy terms of licences do not really reflect the industry investment cycle. In fact, as many critics have argued, they permit the established firms to hoard the resource rights against future investments, and in the process they prevent other, smaller firms from entering the industry.

One of the historic curiosities of the relationship between provincial governments and the large companies throughout Canada is the low resource rent for harvesting rights. In B.C. this is estimated to be about a tenth the rate in neighbouring American states, though the comparison is difficult to make because in Canada the companies are supposed to provide a larger share of the maintenance and reforestation costs. This difference in burdens is used as an official explanation for stumpage rates that are so low that during the recession of 1981–83 the U.S. lumber manufacturers which did not have Canadian properties complained that they represented government subsidies to Canadian-based sawmills. The U.S. investigation of these charges led them to conclude that the Canadian rates were indeed the chief cause for Canada's ability to sell lumber at lower prices on the U.S. market, but that low stumpage rates could not be legally named as subsidies.[6] It is a fine line.

The stumpage formula in B.C. is particularly curious because it rests on a market price for logs and then allows the companies to deduct a range of costs for reforestation and maintenance (and possibly, as argued by Copithorne,[7] for increases in wage rates). Apart from the problem of over-cutting and under-reforestation—puzzling in the circumstances— there is the problem of a market price: there is no market for logs. The companies for all practical purposes own the timber and determine its value as it moves from their logging division through its sawmills and on to its pulpmills. Large companies also swap timber supplies according to their various regional needs. But very little timber is actually sold, with the result that the government does not really know how much it might be worth and what its fair return in the form of resource rent should be.

Where a region develops a pattern of dependency on a single resource, there is inevitably a tendency to extract as much of it as possible while it can command high market returns. But this tendency in itself does not explain why the high returns from timber were not ploughed back into transforming the economy so that, when the resource was depleted or the markets turned down, there would be secondary industry to maintain the population. To explain that, one needs to consider the prerogatives and rational calculations of investors. Throughout the twentieth century it has been very profitable to invest in the forest industries in Canada. Wood was used in construction of homes across the continent, and pulp and newsprint were increasingly valuable as advertising and newsprint businesses grew.

The exemptions of raw materials from the general U.S. tariffs were not matched by exemptions on manufactured materials. Furniture, prefabricated houses and the wide range of wooden items that timber can become, together with higher grades of paper, had to compete with American manufactured products for that market. Investors quite rationally—from their point of view—chose to invest in the raw materials production in most of Canada, and in the manufacturing of end products from the raw materials in the United States. The domestic market in Canada was always relatively small, and it remained small in part because no manufacturing jobs were established in the resource regions. It made more economic sense to companies to produce manufactured items in the United States and then sell a small portion of these in Canada than to go about the process in reverse. The same companies were in both countries, and in both the resource and the manufacturing sectors. Behind the companies were the same investors or others linked to them through a wide range of interlocking ownership arrangements, shared directorships and common economic interests.

If the investors could not be expected to voluntarily reinvest in the resource regions of Canada, could governments have done so? Theoretically there is no reason why they could not have been more active in pursuing our national interest in capturing a larger measure of the downstream benefits of this industry. They controlled the forest resource and determined how much harvesting could be done, by whom and under what conditions. Furthermore, when Canadian governments have decided to channel public funds toward public industries they have done so. Throughout the war years, for example, the federal government did so on a grand scale. More recently, the federal government established Petro-Canada in order to gain a measure of control over energy policies. But neither the federal nor provincial governments have taken action to control profits and investments in forestry, and in fact they have generally given away resource extraction rights at rock-bottom prices with minimal demands on companies to regenerate or nurture the forest.

The explanation provided by governments for their largesse to the large, international companies in the forest industry is that these companies can best withstand variable markets, can best provide high wages and job security, and are more likely to care for the resource because they have long-term horizons. But recent history shows that none of these beliefs can be sustained. The large companies can withstand variable markets, but they can also move their investments elsewhere when the resource is depleted or the long-term prospects for market recovery are poor, or simply when technology and products change. Four large American companies withdrew from British Columbia over the past decade, leaving behind them outdated mills, depleted forests and unemployed, dependent communities, but taking with them the profits they earned in B.C. while cutting its timber.

The explanation is not merely a crude coincidence of private interests between members of the government and the companies, though that is frequently the case. It has more to do with the line of least resistance, the place of a Canadian province within the continental economy and the apparent advantages of temporary affluence. Governments are charged with the task of providing the "investment climate" suitable for private industry to establish businesses which employ and maintain the regional population. Within the context of corporate capitalism, this is most easily done by cooperating with the large companies, providing them with access to the resource and various government aids and infrastructure. To do otherwise—to insist on higher rents, more reinvestment in manufacturing facilities, greater reforestation and more local control of resource extraction rates, for examples—would incur threats of capital strikes and loss of employment.

A government already committed ideologically to the rights and legitimacy of private enterprise would not willingly accept such risks. As long as the resource holds out and markets are strong, the firms will stay, employment and wages will be high enough to allow the employees a high standard of living, and a more-or-less acquiescent population will, with luck, express its electoral gratitude to the party in power. The problems of this line of least resistance, of a staples-dependent economy, become obvious to large numbers of residents only when the resource base is depleted, the companies begin to withdraw, and the markets slump. Such pain was encountered in B.C. beginning in 1981. By the end of 1982, close to 35 percent of the forestry labour force was out of work, mills were being closed permanently as well as temporarily, and communities throughout the province were left in limbo without employers or a resource base. The solution proposed by the B.C. government was the substitution of more renewable and non-renewable resources as staples industries. B.C.'s northern rivers were suggested as potential hydroelectric sources, and coal for Japanese steel mills became the high-priority development project. The stubborn, entrenched belief that "big is better" continues to govern public policy.

The same ideological predispositions affect the fisheries, but in that industry the scale of investments and the organization of the industry are quite different, even though the result for the resource is similar.

Common Property and Licensing in Fisheries

The federal government could not similarly sell or rent fish. But the limitations on the "common property resource" were greatly reduced by a licencing system which imposed conditions on entry to the fishery. As the commercial fishery evolved, so too did the number of restrictions imposed on fishermen. No one owned the fish, but only those with licences could catch them. At some periods, the owners were mainly the processing firms. But for most of the history of this industry, individual fishermen held licences, invested in vessels and gear and sold their catch to the processors. The processors increased their control of the catch by striking agreements with the fishermen, providing them with advance cash loans against catch to purchase gear, and with various services. In this fashion, the processors did not have to tie up their capital in the high-risk investments of vessels engaged in a variable and seasonal fishery; they could obtain their resource supplies and fishermen's labour at relatively low cost. They captured the fishermen instead of the fish.

By the 1950s, fears of depletion prompted drastic measures. The Davis plan was instituted in 1968 to deal with the problem.[8] It involved restrictions on licences, a buy-back program to reduce the number of vessels, and financial incentives to improve vessel standards and the quality of landed fish. As a result, an artificial market for licences evolved and licences originally attached to small vessels were purchased at high prices to be attached to much larger vessels. Fewer boats had vastly greater capacities to roam the seas, and they were able to stay out on the fishing grounds for long periods while fish were kept fresh with better icing and circulating sea water systems, or simply frozen in the holds.

The Davis plan, then, had reverse effects to its stated intentions. For a while the consequences were hidden by the lucrative returns on vessel capitalization. Both salmon and herring were caught in large numbers, dockside prices were good, and cash buyers put pressure on the established processors to increase the price. Vessels equipped for both fisheries cashed in on the bonanza. Inevitably, however, the fish stocks declined under the pressure.

The Department of Fisheries and Oceans, charged with regulation of the fisheries, responded by establishing severe restrictions on "openings" or time periods during which fishing would be permitted. The fishermen, in their vastly overcapitalized vessels and heavily in debt, began to suffer financial problems because they could not catch sufficient fish in these openings to meet their obligations. Even with these restrictions, the fish stocks were in such decline by the 1980s that the federal government established investigatory commissions on both coasts and threatened severe corrective action.[9]

During this same period, there were changes in the processing sector and in the relations between fishermen and the processing companies. Some of the changes were technological: the size of the plants increased, their capacities for freezing salmon and popping herring roe were much enlarged, and transportation systems were changed so that fish could be hauled overland if necessary and kept fresh in specially equipped reefer trucks. The net result of the technological changes was that small processing plants dotted along the B.C. coast became obsolete; the large vessels with their long-distance travelling capacities and on-board freezing and preserving equipment could deliver large catches to main plants at very few locations. One major firm took over many smaller firms and finally its major rival.[10]

In addition to technological changes, a major alteration in production relations was occurring. The cost of the vessels, the gear, and most particularly the licences had risen astronomically. In an earlier period, the companies had provided a large part of the financing for individual fishermen, thereby retaining their loyalty and their catch. But through the 1970s, they began to withdraw from the role of financier, investing instead in the processing sector. In their place came the banks.

The banks, unlike the companies, were not knowledgeable about fish or fishermen. Nor did they have an interest in a paternalistic system. Their interest was solely in the profits from the loan business, and they entered the fishing business in a major way during the 1970s. The indebtedness experienced by fishermen by the 1980s was largely to banks.[11] Some of the vessels were repossessed, bankruptcies were declared, but the crisis went beyond individual fishermen since for the banks a vessel without a fisherman and his licence was not particularly valuable property, and the licences suddenly lost their grossly inflated value as the stocks declined.

At first glance it would appear that the fisheries dilemma is a direct result of individual fishermen's greed. From the point of view of any individual fisherman, the decision to invest in new vessels and gear was rational enough, indeed was the best means to survival. But collectively, their individual decisions amount to such an onslaught that the fish could not survive. Yet blaming the fishermen does not explain the events. The question has to be raised: why did the banks provide the capital, and why did the federal government continue with a policy that was so destructive of the industry and the resource?

The answer to the first question is that the federal government backed the bank loans, even went out of its way, through the Fisheries Improvements Loans Act, various tax incentives, grants, subsidies and small business loans policies to encourage overcapitalization. Thus, while one federal agency was attempting to reduce the catch, and in the process punishing the fishermen, sister agencies were providing the wherewithall to increase the catch.

The answer to the second question is not easily obtained. It seems probable that the various arms of government simply operated on different principles and for different constituencies. While the Department of Fisheries and Oceans, staffed in large part by marine biologists, sought ways of reducing the catch by the only means they could devise—limitations on catching time—the other departments were defining the situation according to quite different considerations. The Department of Industry, Trade and Commerce, for example, was concerned with maintaining the viability of the Canadian shipyards, and paid subsidies for vessel construction or renovations. Indian Affairs provided loans to enable native fishermen to stay in the industry and to upgrade their vessels. Since many of the loans came from the chartered banks or were funnelled through them, those institutions were significant beneficiaries of the process as long as the large catches and "boom" period lasted. However, it would overstate the case to say that *all* of these financing schemes were simply ways of supporting the banks; they did that, but as well they served a variety of constituencies whose various needs were defined by government departments without extensive reference to either the total context or any long-range and integrated plan.

Technology and Marginal Profits

In both industries, the historical pattern is one of constant increases in the productive capacities of ever fewer economic units. The increases occur with changing technologies, and in each case the investment then demands increases in the amount of raw material regularly processed. The technologies of mass production always lead, eventually, to diminishing returns on investment. When one or a few companies introduce methods of increasing productivity or volume of materials, they reap the profits of the initiators. Other companies follow, and shortly all others must follow or their plants will become obsolete and their competitive capacities decline. When most or all companies have the technology, there are no longer advantages in its possession, and the remaining companies, each with a much expanded investment in plant (or vessels), have to keep producing the large volumes at decreasing marginal profits. Small plants which would have provided a modest profit with a smaller quantity of the resource have no viability once the process of mass production is in full operation, and the large companies cannot reduce their consumption of the raw materials and obtain a high return on their investment in the expensive technologies. Thus there is a vicious cycle which impels the companies toward ever-greater consumption and production, irrespective of the long-term damage to the resource.

In addition to the vicious circle, there is the problem of resource utilization standards. If a company has a small quantity of the raw material and no long-term guarantees of supplies, it has an incentive to utilize all of the material. If it has large quantities and guarantees, then it will utilize materials according to the most cost-efficient organization of its plant and labour force. In forestry, mass production virtually eliminates the cost-effectiveness of selective logging and utilization of the timber to the utmost degree. If saw-logs are mixed with pulp-logs, for example, and the labour and transportation costs of separating the two exceed the returns on the saw-logs (as would be the case when lumber markets are in a slump), there is no incentive to separate them. If cedar poles grow in pulp forests, there is no incentive to log them separately unless the market value of the cedar rises well beyond the extra cost of selective logging. In fishing, the mass capture methods similarly dissuade fishermen from time-consuming quality control work when the rewards in terms of price differentials are small. In short, mass production techniques not only deplete the resource by overconsumption, they also utilize resources inefficiently.

Mass production at the resource extraction level occurs in conjunction with mass consumption at the marketing level. Wood is logged with a view to its ultimate destination as dimensional lumber for construction and pulp for newsprint and paper within the dense urban markets of the United States, Japan and Europe. Fish are caught and canned or frozen for the food markets in these countries. Herring roe is an extreme example of a general process: it was worthless before the Japanese market emerged, and in response to that market demand herring were suddenly a most valuable resource and were soon fished almost to extinction.[12] These products are not designed for small, domestic markets or for specialized use by small populations. Thus their profitability comes from their volume, not from their quality.

This pressure to mass produce and mass consume raw materials inevitably means that private interests with private investments tied up in the process will attempt to obtain as much of the materials as they can, regardless of the long-term impact of their collective action on the resource base. It would be absurd to expect these individual companies to put conservation ahead of profits unless they were all obliged to do this simultaneously. Such an obligation could only be imposed by outside agencies with public support—governments—and so we must consider the role of governments in the resource sectors.

The Role of Governments

Although the scale is vastly different and the relationship to the United States and world economy are different, the forestry and fishery industries have in common a dwindling resource base and a history of legislation that persistently favoured those with the most capital to invest in plants or vessels. In both cases, the government under which the resource was to be regulated was either incapable or unwilling to conserve the resource or to preserve the livelihoods of workers, small boat owners, or communities dependent on the resource economy. In both cases, economic efficiency was defined as mass production (or mass catching power) and social effectiveness was ignored in the drafting of legislation and regulations.

This brief review of government legislation and regulatory decisions suggests that governments in Canada and British Columbia have not defined their roles relative to any long-term economic development program. In forestry, where there were multinational producers and multimillion-dollar sales involved, the only policy throughout the history of resource extraction was to enable these large corporations to proceed as quickly as possible. Such a dearth of imagination might best be explained in terms of the ideological predisposition toward large companies precisely because they were large and privately owned, but the explanation has to include as well a tendency of governments to avoid taking leadership roles. They react to pressures and crises, establishing Royal Commissions when crises become unmanageable and instituting stopgap measures in lieu of developing long-range resource management programs.

In so acting, they avoid public hostilities where these would arise from attempts to regulate resource extraction. There is certainly no evidence that the general population of British Columbia wanted better resource management guidelines and initiatives from their government during the boom period of the 1970s. Their standard of living was very high, wages were high in forestry and fish prices were good: very few individuals expressed reservations about the possibilities of resource exhaustion. As well, both the general population and the government accepted the shibboleth of private enterprise that somehow technological development would always overcome resource depletion. In forestry, there was a belief that discoveries would enable foresters to grow trees at a faster rate; in fisheries, that various forms of ocean ranching and hatcheries would make up for nature's deficiencies.

The fact that governments have short electoral horizons and that any form of regulation which reduces immediate profits incurs resentment and opposition is part of the explanation. The fact that the major companies provide corporate taxes, resource royalties (such as they are) and payrolls for the population is also part of the explanation. But beneath these explanations there is the further condition of liberal democracies: that governments are designed to facilitate the accumulation of capital for private investors rather than to foster the long-term stability, viability and sustenance of all sectors of the population. The argument is that in facilitating the accumulation process, the population is, in fact, cared for. But this argument holds only in the short run, when markets are strong for the resources of the hinterland. It fails as soon as the markets decline, or when substitutes are developed, or when the resource base disappears. Then the lack of long-term planning, regulation and development of secondary industries results in rapid economic deterioration.

Alternative Policies for the 1980s

Rather than learning from the inadequacies of their past renewable resource strategies, all levels of government presently seem content to compound the unfortunate errors of history. Apparently, they are currently attempting to simply shift their economic focus to the exploitation of as yet undepleted resource sectors. However, the damming of new rivers, the construction of new pipelines or, in general, the extravagant sponsoring of new mega-projects involving non-renewable resources will not solve any of the problems current in the renewable resource sector. Moreover, such strategies will not only decrease the capacities of small communities to survive but will, as well, further deplete existing renewable resources. Unfortunately, this is the direction most of the provincial governments in Canada are taking. As a supplement, they are also investing in the glamour "high-technology" research and development field, in spite of the fact that every other developed country is simultaneously investing heavily in high-technology industries and that Canada has never been a technological leader. To add to the futility, these industries are capital intensive and will not provide employment for Canadians displaced by the collapse of renewable resource industries.

In the fishing industry, the federal government is contemplating two recent Royal Commission reports which recommend drastic action to reduce the number of fishermen and further "rationalize" the industry. The basic assumption of these reports, that private profit for the most highly capitalized fleets and processing units should increase, has not yet been successfully challenged in the public debates on this issue.

Yet there is a case to be made for a dramatic shift of policy toward the development of small-scale enterprises designed to conserve the resource and sustain small populations. There is a good deal of evidence in favour of the argument that small populations dependent on a renewable resource base will develop their own conservation methods. Local resource management is practised by fishermen when they have reasonable tenure rights to a particular territory, and communities in the forestry sector have demonstrated similar concern for their resource base. What these small communities require in order to practise forest conservation is the withdrawal of outside companies; and in fisheries, the exclusion of large vessels from outside the region, combined with some form of marketing agency through which the locals can independently sell their produce. Obviously they would not sell in mass, and would not enjoy the returns of greater economies of scale, but they could at least survive—and in the circumstances that is a not inconsiderable "plus."

A policy of decentralization and reduction of scale would possibly involve the loss of employment in urban centres. A large part of urban activity—including universities and other cultural institutions—is carried on because such excessive wealth is generated in the resource regions and appropriated as well as managed by the urban populations. If these industries were scaled down and if the objective of public policy were to sustain the real producers, there would be less surplus to extract, and fewer urban folk could live on it.

The above impact, however, might be reduced in several ways. For instance, the number of people who would be required in conservation work if conservation were taken seriously could increase. The nurseries, replanting, silviculture, and general care of forests, and the Salmonid Enhancement Program, mariculture, and cleaning up of polluted or damaged streams would engage the energies of many workers. Similarly, a genuine industrial strategy would encourage the creation of a range of secondary manufacturing establishments, backed by government grants or loans or by umbrella marketing agencies, in sectors that could serve domestic or very specialized export markets. The objective of these would not be mass production and export, but rather specialized production. Finally, one of the possibilities which has yet to be seriously investigated is the development of what are known as "appropriate" or "intermediate" technologies—technologies suitable for relatively small-scale production which is labour intensive and capable of substituting goods for those presently imported. Indeed, Canada would be well situated to become a major innovator and producer of the technologies themselves, and much better suited to that role than to the role of competitor in the "high-technology" industries.

These suggestions ignore the ideological context of economic policy in Canada and in its provinces. There is, at this moment, no indication that policy makers are aware of the problems, let alone concerned with policy alternatives. They are aware that resources are diminishing, but their solution so far is to seek other resources for similar purposes. They are aware that employment is in dramatic decline with high-technology industries and with automation in the traditional industries, but their solution so far is to exhort the population to lower its expectations and its standard of living.

In both forestry and fisheries, the least well capitalized and the smallest units have gone or are going under; the remaining competitors are large—well beyond efficiencies of scale and too large to suit the resource base. This is an essential aspect of the problem, and it has to be faced before governments will develop policies that conserve the resource while still sustaining the population.

Notes

1. Pulp and Paper, *North American Industry Factbook, 1980–81* (San Francisco, CA: Miller Freeman, 1982). Also Province of B.C., Ministry of Forests, *British Columbia Forest Facts*, November 1979.
2. David Alexander, *The Decay of Trade: An Economic History of the Newfoundland Saltfish Trade, 1935–1965*, Newfoundland Social and Economic Studies No. 19, Institute of Social and Economic Research, Memorial University (St. John's: Memorial University).
3. Royal Commission on the Forest Resources of British Columbia, *Report.* (Victoria: King's Printer, 1945). Also, Royal Commission on the Forest Resources of British Columbia, *The Forest Resources of British Columbia 1956.* 2 vols. (Victoria: Queen's Printer, 1957).
4. *Resources for Freedom: The Outlook for Energy Sources.* Report of the President's Materials Policy Commission, Washington, DC. See, for extended discussion, Melissa Clark, "An Ear to Washington" (Ph.D. dissertation, Department of Sociology, McMaster University, 1979).
5. Royal Commission on Forest Resources, *Timber Rights and Forest Policy* (Victoria: Queen's Printer, 1976).
6. *Conditions Relating to the Importation of Softwood Lumber into the United States.* United States International Trade Commission, Report to the Senate Committee on Finance on Investigation No. 332-134, under Section 332 of the Tariff Act of 1930 (Washington, DC: April 1982).
7. Laurence Copithorne, "Natural Resources and Regional Disparities: A Skeptical View," Canadian Public Policy 5 (Spring 1979): 181–94.
8. The Davis Plan, named after the Minister of Fisheries at that time, was in large part based on an earlier study by Dr. Sol Sinclair, *License Limitation— British Columbia* (Ottawa: Department of Fisheries and Oceans, 1960). A discussion of the impact of the plan is given in Brian Hayward, "The B.C. Salmon Fishery: A Consideration of the Effects of Licensing," *B.C. Studies* 50 (Summer 1981): 39–51.
9. Peter H. Pearse, *Turning the Tide: A New Policy for Canada's Pacific Fisheries* (Vancouver: Queen's Printer, 1982). For the East Coast, Michael Kirby, *The Kirby Task Force Report,* prepared for the Department of Fisheries and Oceans (Ottawa, 1982).
10. For discussion of the different circumstances and strategies of the various processing plants in B.C., see Lyn Pinkerton, "The Dressed and the Undressed," paper delivered at the CSAA annual meetings, June 1983 (avail-

able from "Fish and Ships Research Project," Department of Anthropology and Sociology, U.B.C.).

11. Detailed data on indebtedness is provided in John L. McMullan, "Financing Fishermen: State, Capital and Debt in the B.C. Fishing Fleet," paper delivered at the CPSA annual meetings, June 1983 (also available from U.B.C.).

12. Neil Guppy, "The Roe-Herring Bonanza and its Impact on the Structure of the B.C. Fishing Industry," paper delivered at the CPSA annual meetings, June 1983 (also available from U.B.C.).

Further Reading

Forestry

Byron, Ronald Neil. *Community Stability and Economic Development: The Role of Forest Policy in the North Central Interior of British Columbia.* M.B.A. thesis, University of British Columbia, 1976.

———. "Community Stability and Forest Policy in British Columbia." *Canadian Journal of Forestry Research* 8 (1978): 61–66.

Copithorne, Laurence. "Natural Resources and Regional Disparities: A Skeptical View." *Canadian Public Policy* 5: 181–94.

Grainger, M. Allerdale. *Woodsmen of the West.* 1908. Reprint. Toronto: McClelland and Stewart, 1968.

Hayter, Roger. *An Examination of Growth Patterns and Locational Behaviour of Multi-Plant Forest Products Corporations in British Columbia.* Ph.D. dissertation, University of Washington, 1973.

———. "Corporate Strategies in the Forest Product Industries of British Columbia." *Albertan Geographer* 10 (1974): 7–19.

Lakehead University. *The Economic Future of the Forest Products Industry in Western Ontario.* Prepared for the Royal Commission on the Northern Environment. Toronto: Queen's Printer, 1982.

Lower, A.R.M. *The North American Assault on the Forest: A History of the Lumber Trade Between Canada and the United States.* Toronto: Ryerson Press, 1938.

Marchak, Patricia. *Green Gold: The Forest Industry in British Columbia.* Vancouver: University of British Columbia Press, 1983.

McKillop, William, and Walter J. Mead, eds. *Timber Policy Issues in British Columbia.* B.C. Institute for Economic Policy Analysis Series. Vancouver: University of British Columbia Press, 1976.

Nagel, George Shorten. *Economics and the Public Policy in the Forestry Sector of British Columbia.* M.A. thesis, Yale University, 1970.

Pearse, Peter H. *Timber Rights and Forest Policy, Report of the Royal Commission on Forest Resources.* Victoria: Queen's Printer, 1976.

Fisheries

Anderson, Raoul, and Cato Wadel, eds. *North Atlantic Fishermen: Anthropological Essays on Modern Fishing.* Newfoundland Social and Economic Papers, No. 5. Toronto: University of Toronto Press, 1972.

Barrett, L. Gene. "The State and Capital in the Fishing Industry: The Case of Nova Scotia." Paper presented at annual meetings of the Canadian Political Science Association, Dalhousie University, Halifax, May 1981.

Barrett, L. Gene, and Anthony Davis. "Floundering in Troubled Waters: The Political Economy of the Atlantic Fishery and the Task Force on Atlantic Fisheries." Gorsebrook Research Institute for Atlantic Canada Studies, Occasional Paper No. 1. St. Mary's University, Halifax, 1983.

Fraser, G.A. "Limited Entry: Experience of the B.C. Salmon Fishery." *Journal of the Fisheries Research Board of Canada* 36 (July 1979).

Kirby, Michael. *Navigating Troubled Waters: A New Policy for the Atlantic Fisheries.* Report of the Task Force on Atlantic Fisheries, prepared for the Department of Fisheries and Oceans. Ottawa: Supply and Services, 1982.

Pearse, Peter H. *Turning the Tide: A New Policy for Canada's Pacific Fisheries.* Vancouver: Queen's Printer, 1982.

Scott, Anthony and Philip A. Neher. *The Public Regulation of Commercial Fisheries in Canada.* Ottawa: Economic Council of Canada, 1982.

Scott, Gordon H. "The Economic Theory of Common Property Resource: The Fishery." *Journal of Political Economy* 62 (1954): 124–42.

Sinclair, Sol. *License Limitation—British Columbia.* Ottawa: Department of Fisheries of Canada, 1960.

Special Edition on the Canadian Fisheries. *Journal of Canadian Studies* 19 (Spring 1984).

Part 2
The Sociocultural Milieu of Canadian Politics

Chapter 7
Political Culture in Canada
David V. J. Bell

The Importance of Political Culture

Culture is a fundamental component of life because it affects how we perceive the world and how we interact with it. Culture provides a set of lenses through which people view the world. Beliefs about the world and individually held values shape both attitude and action. Culture also provides a way of doing things, a common stock of knowledge about appropriate and inappropriate behaviour in different settings. As we are socialized into a culture, we learn to behave in ways that others in the same culture will find acceptable and comfortable. We learn what to wear, what to say, and how to stand. We learn to distinguish between the public and private, how to say "hello" and "goodbye," how to indicate pleasure or unhappiness.

Political life is similarly affected by "political culture": beliefs and values related to politics, attitudes to the political system and to political issues, and commonly accepted standards of political behaviour. Frequently, political values, beliefs and attitudes are crystallized and represented by various symbols. In its simplest sense, a symbol is a kind of shorthand: something that stands for something else. In politics, symbols usually evoke both thoughts and feelings, and reflect long-standing traditions to which individuals become strongly attached.

Canadian political culture includes a number of symbols. Some, such as Parliament, the Crown, and Mounties in red coats, have been around for a long time. Others, such as the Charter of Rights and the National Energy Program, are much more recent. Political symbols can evoke images of consensus and cooperation—as does the idea of helping the poorer provinces, or furthering Anglo–French partnership. But symbols can also catalyze negative emotions and hatred or distrust, as does the phrase "forcing French down our throats," or the bitter accusation of eastern domination, symbolized in the phrase "freight rates." The variety and richness of these symbols demonstrate that Canadian politics simultaneously features harmony and disunity, conflict and cooperation. Politicians invoke symbols in their speeches to rally support for their parties and policies, to quiet discontent, or to inflame bitterness directed at their opponents. Members of the general public, for their part, often appear to need symbolic reassurances, to identify with symbols manipulated in public debate by their political leaders, and to find gratification in the symbolic aspect of politics even when more practical and material aspects are less than satisfactory.[1]

Because of its impact on individuals in their capacity as both citizens and subjects, followers and leaders, political culture (including symbols) affects the content and nature of what goes on in the "black box" that we call the political system. It helps transform the inanimate machinery of government into the living organic reality of politics. The foremost theorist of the systems approach, David Easton, points out that cultural inhibitors affect "what are to be considered culturally appropriate areas for political decision."[2] In any political system, the political culture demarcates the zone of appropriate action for government, and sets other areas beyond the realm of the legitimate. Thus, for example, Pierre Trudeau announced soon after his election as prime minister that "the state has no place in the bedrooms of the nation."

Conversely, the political culture provides a range of acceptable values and standards upon which leaders can draw in attempting to justify their policies. Unless a politically viable justification can be attached to a controversial policy, it will not usually be adopted. The political culture sets the parameters within which debate over policy justification takes place. The political culture further affects what people view as appropriate areas of governmental action. It shapes the perception of politically relevant problems, thereby affecting both the recognition of these problems and the diagnosis of their various aspects. It influences beliefs about who should be assigned responsibility for solving problems, and what kind of solutions are likely to work. This aspect of political culture is in turn related to more general notions about the general purposes of government and the kinds of processes and substantive decisions that are acceptable and legitimate.

In some instances, political values, attitudes and beliefs cluster together in a particular constellation called an ideology. Ideologies are more or less coherent and explicit, and tend to be held by people whose political involvement is unusually high. Such activists find ideologies useful guides to political action. Ideologies have a programmatic aspect insofar as they provide a diagnosis of the problems facing society and a prescription of solutions for these problems. Indeed the ideology in many instances amounts to a way of viewing the world (*Weltanschauung*).

Ideologies are often derived from or closely related to more profound and sophisticated statements as set forth in works of political philosophy. In this respect, ideology is like the *Reader's Digest* paraphrase of a great work. Compared to political philosophies, ideologies are more simplified and less profound. They emphasize action over thought and may stress emotions rather than cognitions.

Most of the great works on ideology assume that ideologies rest on a set of underlying interests and predispositions, often derived from one's class position in society. Thus, one speaks of the ideology of the ruling class, working-class ideology, bourgeois ideology and so on. This aware-ness of the connection between ideology and interests leads inexorably to a concern to "unmask" ideologies to discover their material base in social relations.

It is evident that relatively few people have coherent and explicit ideas about politics that deserve the designation "ideology." Many individuals lack a clear, consistent set of political views. They react in an ad hoc fashion or simply avoid thinking about politics altogether. They may have low levels of information, hold contradictory opinions, misunderstand basic concepts and so on. Still others do have politically relevant views which are, however, either implicit or contradictory. At this point the concept of political culture becomes useful. Indeed, an attempt to look at mass in addition to elite opinions and values regarding politics was a major consideration in developing the concept of political culture, which was viewed from the outset as a broader concept with wider application than ideology. A single political culture could comprise several ideologies: the Canadian political culture is thought to include the ideologies of conservatism, liberalism and socialism.

In short, the political culture is invisibly interwoven into all aspects of politics and government. One can isolate the cultural variable for the purposes of analysis, but to do so requires a sensitive appreciation for the techniques that can render the often hidden assumptions, values and beliefs visible and comprehensible. The study of political culture can therefore remain rather general and abstract, encompassing the broadly stated political values at their highest level; or it can be made much more specific and focused on beliefs and values related to specific issues or policies.

Approaches to the Study of Political Culture

Most students of political culture seem to agree on one point: culture is a collective phenomenon, the attribute of a group and not of an individual. An individual cannot make or possess a culture. However, she or he can learn a culture. For this reason, the components of a political culture—values, beliefs and attitudes among others—can be observed in the individual. Thus one might refer to X's religious values or Y's attitudes to abortion as aspects of a culture. But what does it mean to talk about a *group* value or attitude? Is a group merely the sum of those individuals who belong to it, and its culture the average beliefs of its membership? Or is culture something different again from majority opinion or a statistical average? In grappling with these questions, social scientists tend to fall into one of two camps: some opt for a "holistic" approach, while others insist on "methodological individualism."

The *individualistic approach* to political culture assumes that values and beliefs exist only in specific individuals, who may or may not resemble one another. To generalize about the values of any group of people requires reliable information obtained from a large sample of individuals who are representative of the population as a whole. These data are almost always obtained by survey research. Once these individual-level survey data have been gathered, the problem of how to aggregate them in order to make judgments about the entire population involves the use of statistical "modal" characteristics. The term "mode" refers to that point along a continuum where the largest concentration of attitudes is found.

The first and most prominent example of the individualistic approach to political culture is Gabriel Almond and Sidney Verba's study of five countries: the United States, Britain, Mexico, Germany and Italy.[3] The authors selected a sample of respondents from each country and administered a long questionnaire designed to elicit attitudes to the political system in general, to the role of the individual as both a citizen (i.e., a participant in the decision-making process) and a subject (i.e., someone on the receiving end of the laws and regulations enforced by the system.)[4] In analyzing their data, Almond and Verba introduced several categories that allowed them to generalize about the "modal" characteristics of each of the societies they studied. For example, they planned to use results of "citizen efficacy" and "subject competence" questions, together with questions about orientations to the system as a whole, to locate societies along a continuum from primitive political cultures, in which there is little awareness of the existence of the nation state or of the individual's role in the national political system; through "subject" cultures in which the individual responds positively to the system's outputs but has a low sense of personal citizen efficacy; to the most advanced "participant" cultures, displaying high measures of both efficacy and competence. Their survey results proved somewhat disappointing. The neat distinctions between participant, subject and primitive political cultures did not materialize. Instead Almond and Verba found a mixture of attitudes encompassing elements from all three categories. Consequently the term "civic culture" denoted the hybrid mixture of attitudes and values—some "modern," others pre-modern—found in what they believed to be the most highly developed democratic political system in their study: the United States.

Although Almond and Verba did not include Canada in their five-nation study, their survey has been applied (at least in part) many times in this country. Virtually every major academic survey conducted since 1965 has included one or more items from the civic culture survey. Researchers have emphasized in particular the questions on "efficacy" and "trust."

The questions measuring efficacy and trust include various versions of the following items:

Political Efficacy

1. "Generally, those elected to Parliament (Congress) soon lose touch with the people."
2. "Sometimes politics and government seem so complicated that a person like me can't really understand what's going on."
3. "I don't think that the government cares much what people like me think."
4. "People like me don't have any say about what the government does."

Political Trust

1. "Do you think that people in government waste a lot of the money we pay in taxes, waste some of it, or don't waste very much of it?"
2. "How much of the time do you think you can trust the government in Washington (Ottawa) to do what is right?"
3. "Would you say the government is pretty much run by a few big interests looking out for themselves or that it is run for the benefit of all of the people?"
4. "Do you feel that almost all of the people running the government are smart people who know what they are doing, or do you think that quite a lot of them don't seem to know what they are doing?"
5. "Do you think that quite a few of the people running the government are a little crooked, not very many are, or do you think hardly any of them are crooked at all?"[5]

The efficacy questions were included in Canadian national surveys done in 1965, 1968, 1974 and 1979. The trust questions were administered only in 1965, 1968 and 1979. Comparable data from the United States are available for both sets of items for 1964, 1968, 1972 and 1978. A comparison of the Canadian and American results is quite revealing. The following table indicates that on most items Canadians on average have as high a sense of efficacy as Americans; however, the statement "people like me don't have any say" elicited much more agreement from Canadians than Americans. Citizens from the two countries show similar levels of trust and distrust in government if we compare the 1972 U.S. average with the 1968 Canadian data. By 1978, however, Americans had become much less trusting of government than

Table 7.1
Political Efficacy and Trust in Canada and the United States*

Political Efficacy (% Efficacious)

	Canada				United States			
	1979	1974	1968	1965	1978	1972	1968	1964
Leaders Soon Lose Touch	33%	35%	39%	40%	30%	32%	44%	—
Government Complicated	32%	35%	28%	29%	28%	29%	28%	32%
Government Doesn't Care	45%	42%	54%	52%	50%	50%	56%	63%
People Like Me Have No Say	42%	45%	51%	49%	54%	64%	59%	70%

Political Trust (% Cynical)

	Canada			United States			
	1979	1968	1965	1978	1972	1968	1964
Government Wastes Money	75%	46%	38%	76%	68%	61%	48%
People in Government Crooked	35%	27%	27%	39%	38%	20%	30%
Government Run by Big Interests		90%	83%	65%	59%	44%	30%
People in Government Smart	29%	49%	57%	49%	42%	39%	28%
Trust Government to do Right	29%	39%	39%	67%	46%	37%	22%
Average	42%	50%	49%	59%	51%	40%	32%

*For the political efficacy questions, the entry in each cell is the percent giving an efficacious response. For the political trust questions, the entry in each cell is the percent giving a cynical response. No political trust questions were asked in the 1974 Canadian study. Four of the five were asked in 1979.

Source: Nathaniel Beck and John Peirce, "Political Involvement and Party Allegiances in Canada and the United States," *International Journal of Comparative Sociology*, March–June 1977, p. 29. 1978 U.S. data from American National Election Study 1978 (Center for Political Studies, U. of Michigan, 1979). 1979 Canadian data courtesy of Jon Pammett.

they had been earlier. Canadians, by contrast, had become on average more trusting.

One of the most useful and innovative applications of these concepts appears in the work of David Elkins and Richard Simeon. Instead of analyzing efficacy and trust responses separately, Elkins and Simeon combine them to form a new typology of orientations to politics, as follows:

Table 7.2
Typology of Orientations to Politics
(Elkins & Simeon)

| | | EFFICACY | |
		High	Low
TRUST	High	Supporters	Deferentials
	Low	Critics	Disaffected

Furthermore, in line with a general tendency among Canadian political scientists to pay much more attention to provincial politics and regional differences, Elkins and Simeon use the typology to analyze political orientations in each of the ten provinces, separating out anglophones in Quebec and francophones outside of Quebec. Using data from the 1968 federal election survey, they found some rather surprising results.

As Table 7.3 indicates, only about one-quarter of the total sample of respondents fell into the "supporter" category, while fully one-third are classified as "disaffected." Striking provincial contrasts emerge. Only in Ontario, Manitoba and British Columbia are there more supporters than disaffected. These provinces also, however, had the largest number of "critics." In the Atlantic provinces over half the respondents were disaffected. Nationally, and without exception in every province, the smallest group were the "deferentials."

While these and similar survey results are clearly interesting and illuminating, they also have important limitations. Surveys provide a *direct* measure of political culture, and have the advantage of forcing people to make explicit what may be otherwise obscure or implicit. In doing so, however, these measures sometimes distort or twist reality in subtle ways. We cannot be sure that survey responses validly reflect what people really believe or value. Furthermore, surveys and interviews can be used only in the present or recent past, and do not illuminate the period of earlier history that contains important clues to the development of political culture. Hence indirect approaches are critical supplements to interviews and surveys.

The *indirect approaches* are far more numerous and varied in their utility and validity. A number of techniques, usually involving content

Table 7.3

Four Citizen Types by Province-Language Groups, 1968 (Percentage Down)

	NAT	NFLD	NS	NB	QE	QF	ONT	MAN	SASK	ALTA	BC	Non-QFR
Supporter	26	8	17	10	29	17	31	32	26	30	38	14
Deferential	10	13	6	10	11	13	8	11	10	4	9	17
Critic	30	27	24	25	30	25	35	31	26	29	38	23
Disaffected	34	52	53	54	30	44	26	26	38	36	15	46
Total percentage	100	100	100	99	100	99	100	100	100	99	100	100
N=	2,767	48	110	76	122	632	927	133	136	235	247	84

Source: David J. Elkins and Richard Simeon, eds., *Small Worlds: Provinces and Parties in Canadian Political Life* (Toronto: Methuen, 1980), p. 45.

analysis, allow researchers to extract from written documents or
speeches the values and beliefs that are implicit in them. In the case of the
political values of the elite, a highly specialized "operational code"
approach has been used to reconstruct the outlook and assumptions of
key individuals.[6] Biographies and autobiographies shed light not only on
cognitive beliefs and values but on life experiences that reflect how
important those values are for behaviour. Indeed, by studying the
behaviour of individuals, or the collective behaviour of institutions (i.e.,
their adoption of various policies), skillful students of political culture can
excavate latent assumptions about politics and therefore create a picture
of the political culture of both the present and the past.

The latter kind of indirect approach often accompanies a "holistic"
conception of political culture. In the holistic approach, political culture
constitutes a kind of "ethos"[7] that envelops and conditions a society.
Certain values and predispositions are, figuratively speaking, "in the air."
For this reason, one sometimes speaks of a "climate" of opinion. Like
climate, these values influence behaviour invisibly but effectively. The
individual is born into this ethos and absorbs it through a kind of osmosis.
Though people may vary in the degree to which they absorb the culture,
everyone is exposed to these values to a great extent. An individual's
departure from the prevailing ethos, or social deviance, in no way
disproves the existence of the culture, because socialization is never
complete.

Descriptions of the ethos of Canadian political culture are many and
varied. Sometimes geography is credited with having produced a
distinctive Canadian ethos. Two years after Confederation, for example,
in a lecture about Canadian "national spirit" delivered to the Montreal
Literary Club, Robert Grant Haliburton stressed the formative influence
of Canada's "northern" geography and climate: "... may not our snow
and frost [he asked] give us what is of more value than gold or silver,
a healthy, hardy, virtuous dominant race? [For Canada] must ever be ...
a Northern country inhabited by the descendents of Northern races."[8]
Haliburton regarded the superiority of northerners as a fundamental
axiom of politics. Rhetorically he asked, "If climate has not had the effect
of moulding races, how is it that the southern nations have almost
invariably been inferior to and subjugated by the men of the north?"
From the felicitous marriage of racial inheritance and northern
environmentalism, there would emerge a Canadian people worthy of the
ideals of "the true north, strong and free."

Not all efforts to define a Canadian ethos are infected by the virus of
racial nationalism. Nor do they necessarily emphasize the formative
impact of geography. Seymour Martin Lipset explicitly posits the
existence of a national ethos in the following passage: "[V]alue differences between the United States and Canada suggest that they stem in

large part from two disparate founding ethos."[9] But for Lipset (as we will see below) historical events rather than geographical factors account for the variation.

The approach presented in this chapter draws on both individualism and holism. We are interested in the pattern of individually held values and beliefs, and thus examine relevant survey results such as those discussed above. We are aware, however, that the individualistic approach alone is insufficient. To appreciate the importance of the larger whole within which individuals operate (without, however, arguing that values and beliefs are somehow preserved in an invisible ethos, a kind of social formaldehyde) we draw attention to certain distinctively Canadian political institutions such as Parliament, the Constitution Act, federal–provincial conferences, the CBC, Air Canada, CN, elements of popular culture (novels, poetry, songs, films, etc.) that form part of Canada's political personality and illuminate the character of Canadian politics. They exist in important respects independent of the modal attitudes and values of individuals living in Canada at any particular moment in time. Some of these institutions present themselves to the outside world as quintessentially Canadian, frequently with explicit authorization to speak or act on behalf of Canada. Notwithstanding the range of possible variation within the country, there are times and places where a single voice speaks, and it calls itself Canadian.[10] In these settings, the individual or group that presumes to speak for the collectivity, insofar as it is effective, becomes the collectivity. Individuals who hold a different outlook become irrelevant, at least until they are able to project a dissenting voice or image. The world, in short, contains significant "institutional facts" that assume a different character and exist apart from the individuals that surround and inhabit them. Canadians, whatever their individual conceptions of value and purpose, live and breathe to some extent in a common political space dominated by institutions whose very design and functioning evolves from and gives shape to the complexities of Canadian political culture. Thus it is useful to examine the values promoted by and embodied in these institutions. Of particular interest are institutions that explicitly undertake a role in political socialization, described in the title of a recent textbook as the "foundations of political culture."

Political Socialization:
The Learning of Political Culture

Political socialization is the process of transmitting political values and attitudes through time and across space. Agencies involved in the process include families, schools, churches, political parties and, perhaps most importantly, mass media. These and similar institutions consciously attempt to inculcate certain values and foster particular attitudes toward politics. Political socialization is especially effective during the "formative stage" in the development of the individual's values and orientations (the early teen years), but political socialization can continue beyond adolescence.

Socialization and learning are not perfectly congruent. Socialization suggests a planned, controllable, linear pattern of acquiring knowledge and values. But people learn more than they are "socialized" to learn. They learn from unpredictable events in both the natural and the social environment. A flood can serve as a fundamental learning experience, as can a war, a hockey game or even a federal election. People learn from introspection and self-education, often despite what their socializers would like them to learn instead. They learn as well from individuals and groups whose values run counter to the prevailing political culture. In short, learning, unlike socialization, is a dialectical process full of contradictions and unpredictable outcomes.

Furthermore, socialization is not always a benign process. The attempt to preserve and transmit a culture can have a nasty side. Although the following observation exaggerates the extent to which coercion is used to "socialize" people in our society, it serves to remind us that cultural continuity should never be taken for granted:

> To maintain and transmit a value system, human beings are punched, bullied, sent to jail, thrown into concentration camps, cajoled, bribed, made into heroes, encouraged to read newspapers, stood up against a wall and shot, and sometimes even taught sociology. To speak of cultural inertia is to overlook the concrete interests and privileges that are served by indoctrination, education, and the entire complicated process of transmitting culture from one generation to the next.[11]

Societal Origins of Political Culture: Four Views

We may surmise, therefore, that an individual acquires political culture traits through a learning process, part of which is controlled by various socializing agencies. But where do the political culture traits embraced by these socializing agencies originate? In attempting to answer this question, students of political culture have adopted differing interpretations. One theorist, Louis Hartz, argues that societies like Canada and the United States, founded by immigrants from Europe, develop a political culture that reflects the values and beliefs of the groups that were dominant during the "founding period." Hartz contends that the "founders" are able to dominate the political culture of a "new society" by setting up institutions and myths that imbue their values and beliefs with a nationalistic flavour, thus making membership in the nation contingent on accepting the dominant ideology.[12]

Thus new societies, "fragments" of Europe transported to the New

World, tend to have a political culture that conserves and preserves the values, beliefs and attitudes of the founders of that society. The "fragment theory" was first applied to the United States. Hartz describes the political culture of the United States as "bourgeois," and points to its origins in British seventeenth- and eighteenth-century society. Applying the fragment theory to Canada is complicated by the fact that ours is a "two fragment" society. *La Nouvelle France* was founded by seventeenth- and eighteenth-century emigrants from feudal France. English Canada was founded by Loyalist refugees from the American Revolution, who were also largely bourgeois in outlook. Much of the present-day difference between Canadian anglophones and francophones can be traced back to the vast political culture differences between these two founding fragments.

Seymour Martin Lipset disagrees with Hartz's view that societies bear forever the cultural marks of their birth. For him cultural inheritance is less significant than the experiences that society undergoes. Indeed, he suggests that one can identify certain "formative events" in the history of a country which help mould or shape its values and consequently have a lasting impression upon its institutional practices.[13] When he applies his formative events notion to (English) Canada, however, the differences between him and Hartz shrink. For Lipset, the most important formative event in Canada's history is the obverse of that in the United States: the "counter-revolution" and subsequent migration north of the Loyalists, an event which he believes affected Canada's political culture as significantly as the American Revolution moulded the United States.

Thus both Hartz's "fragment theory" and Lipset's "formative events" notion focus attention on the Loyalist experience as a major source of English Canada's political culture. Yet the cultural consequences of the Loyalist migration are a subject of considerable controversy among historians and social scientists. Much of the debate has turned on defining the ideological outlook of the Loyalists. The main issue has been to what extent the Loyalists presented an "organic conservative" alternative to the "liberal" world view of the revolutionaries who expelled them and shaped the political institutions and culture of the new United States.

Lipset himself speaks of the Loyalists as "counter-revolutionaries" who helped make Canada more elitist, ascriptive and particularist, with greater emphasis on the collectivity, than the United States. To substantiate his claims, he examines not only survey results but also data comparing crime rates, educational practices, economic policies and even religious traditions in the two countries.

A number of scholars have criticized Lipset's interpretation of these data, and more fundamentally his failure to distinguish anglophones from francophones. Clearly the two groups have had different cultural origins and experienced different formative events. The French Canadians were relatively unaffected by the American Revolution. For them, the major formative event was undoubtedly the Conquest (described in their history books as the Cession, a term which reveals their profound sense of betrayal by France.) Even today French-language history books typically depict the events leading up to 1763 as a "catastrophe," and devote half of their space to the "golden age" which preceded it.

One advantage of Hartz's fragment theory is that it highlights the cultural uniqueness of the anglophone and francophone fragments. But despite a general consensus about the political culture of the francophone fragment, followers of Hartz have disagreed even among themselves about the impact of the Loyalists. Some have seen the Loyalists as primarily a bourgeois fragment, albeit "tinged with Toryism." Others have insisted that we not dismiss the "Tory Touch," which is deemed to have had an important influence on both policies and institutions.[14] While both perspectives on the Loyalists (i.e., the "liberal" interpretation and the "conservative" view) contribute important insights, they tend to ignore effects of the Loyalist migration that go beyond the usual categories of ideology. Although undoubtedly Canada's unique brand of conservative liberalism probably can be traced back to our Loyalist origins, so too can our profound identity crisis, our fascination with the mosaic, and our willingness to use the state for "interventionist" purposes that most Americans would reject. Furthermore, one can regard the Loyalist experience as having produced an "anti-fragment" insofar as it encouraged a prolongation of emotional and cultural ties to Britain instead of leading to the kind of cultural isolation that is a precondition to the "freezing" of the fragment culture. Consequently English Canada found no difficulty importing British-style parliamentary socialism in the twentieth century, whereas both Quebec and the United States rejected it as "alien."

Although the fragment theory, enriched by the introduction of Lipset's formative events notion, illuminates the otherwise baffling history of ideologies and political parties in Canada, political culture studies need not be confined by the categories of analysis that derive from the European ideologies of conservatism, liberalism and socialism. Much of the experience of the new world lies beyond these categories, and, in any event, the study of political culture can and should embrace virtually every aspect of political practice. Similarly, Almond and Verba's concern with efficacy and trust is too limiting. They chose to focus on those aspects of political culture because they were primarily interested in the problem of democracy. But the problem of democracy is not the central political problem in Canada. Therefore, there is no reason to stick with their concepts and concerns either. Instead, as students of the Canadian experience, we need to examine values, attitudes and beliefs that relate to more fundamental and pressing problems such as Anglo–French relations, regionalism and American domination, not merely to the problem of democracy or the problem of class and ideology which animated the work of those who pioneered in the use of political culture.

Furthermore, we need to supplement the rather idealistic approaches to political culture of Hartz and Lipset with approaches that have a much firmer appreciation of the structural bases of culture. For culture never exists in a vacuum, nor does it have an all-determining effect on politics. Rather, culture and its structural underpinnings are interrelated and interdependent. To understand this aspect of culture and trace it back to its societal origins, we need to examine the work of two additional theorists, Harold Innis and Karl Marx.

Although he did not consider himself a student of political culture, Harold Innis offers important insight into the process of cultural transmission.[15] Unlike Hartz and Lipset, who seem to treat values and beliefs as determinants of social and political structures, Innis reverses the causal arrow. It is not culture which shapes society. For Innis, cultures are heavily affected by the technology of production and distribution of ideas. Hence the culture of society is transformed when new developments take place in the technology of communication. The invention of the printing press revolutionized western culture, according to Innis. Recent revolutionary developments, dubbed by Alvin Toffler "the third wave," include the discovery of radio and television, the introduction of inexpensive copying machines, and the still-emerging technology of the microchip, including two-way video communication such as Canada's Telidon system. Unfortunately, Innis died before most of these innovations had become widespread, and thus he did not assess how they have affected Canadian political culture. But his insight concerning the importance to culture of the underlying structure of communication remains fundamentally useful.

Innis's insights can be elaborated to explain much of the crisis of Canadian identity in the twentieth century. Clearly the means of distribution of culture (including popular culture) are important determinants of what ideas get transmitted to the general public. Canada, unlike virtually any other country in the world, has a cultural transmission system that is almost entirely in the hands of a foreign power. Most Canadian children pass into adulthood without, for example, ever seeing a Canadian feature-length film. They watch American television and even read school textbooks that are produced and written in the United States. They listen to American records and eat food produced by mass-distribution food outlets owned in the United

States. They see American commercials and read American advertising. Little wonder then that they grow up with a very shaky sense of Canadian identity and relatively little knowledge about their own country and political institutions, much less any sense of what might constitute Canadian culture in the mass media, the arts, music and letters. So extreme has been the domination of our cultural networks that in a document prepared in 1977 to provide new directions for the Canadian Broadcasting Corporation, the then CBC President Albert Johnson commented, "Canada today faces its greatest crisis in history: the combination of national lifethreatening arguments over our nationhood and the relentless American cultural penetration."[16] Whether this cultural domination leads to economic domination, or the reverse, is perhaps immaterial: the massive U.S. presence on the cultural scene is matched by an equally dominant U.S presence in the economy. It is this aspect of the underpinnings of culture which is the primary concern of Marxist and neo-Marxist analyses of the Canadian dilemma.

According to Karl Marx, the material conditions under which a society produces its wealth is a major factor in determining the nature of the political culture. In his view, there are relatively few "modes of production": primitive, feudal, capitalist and socialist. Each limits the kind of political structures and culture which can exist. Within a given mode of production, however, variations will occur as result of different patterns of external trade relations and of internal control of production and distribution. Students of contemporary Canadian politics who have applied Marxist concepts to Canada emphasize the effect on our political culture of Canada's major economic structures. The fact that we are a capitalist country with a long history of economic dependence on foreign capital bears heavily on our current political difficulties.

Furthermore, the neo-Marxists have pointed out that within the dominant capitalist class are various "fractions" which have different perceptions of their interests and different orientations toward the economic system. They distinguish in particular between a mercan-tile/financial class fraction which makes profits on the circulation rather than the production of goods and services, and an industrial capitalist fraction which is more entrepreneurial and is interested in industrial development and expansion. Particularly in the crucial period of the late nineteenth century, the interests of these two class fractions were opposed. The Mercantilists did not favour the development of an indigenous heavy industry in Canada but instead sought to profit on the exchange of staple products from the hinterland for manufactured goods imported from the imperial centre (i.e., Britain and at a later point the United States). According to the neo-Marxists, the political culture of colonialism and imperial dependency was consciously fostered by the mercantile class fraction to support their economic interests. The dominant element of Canada's capitalist class, this group could not see themselves as rulers of a strong, independent nation-state. Burdened with a colonial mentality, they opposed any efforts to develop a true Canadian nationalism.[17]

Each of the above approaches to political culture sheds light on the social origins and development of culture. A comprehensive historical analysis must therefore take account of:

(a) the cultural genes implanted by the founding groups (Hartz)
(b) the kinds of formative events which affected cultural values and institutions (Lipset)
(c) the nature of the technology of communication (Innis)
(d) the economic infrastructure of society (Marx)

These four perspectives complement each other. Any one of them alone is insufficient. Yet, taken together, they illuminate the complexity and richness of a political culture. They show as well that a variety of institutions plays a part in transmitting political culture, including the family, schools, the mass media and work experiences.

Summary

It is possible to analyze the development of Canadian political culture in more detail using the four insights mentioned above. From the Hartzian perspective, we realize that Canadian political culture developed from the cultural genes implanted by the two major founding groups, the English and the French. These two groups embodied contrasting ideologies that would never easily mix together. The absolutism and feudal tendencies of the French fragment led to a preservation of that culture and an antipathy toward the modernizing impulses of the anglophones. The anglophones for their part were a very strange mixture of elements. Irrespective of how important the Tory touch was, the anglophone bourgeois culture had the ironic and paradoxical characteristic of being simultaneously liberal and anti-American. Because the United States had made liberalism into its national culture, the anglophones were prevented from doing so: thus the origin of Canada's never-ending identity crisis and the peculiar combination of celebration of the British connection and antipathy toward a culture which was ideologically very similar to that of English Canada. Furthermore, because of the failure to nationalize the political culture of the anglophones, and because of the pattern of settlement which led to a direct importation into the Canadian West of founding groups from Europe that did not become socialized to either anglophone or francophone Canadian culture before settling there, the Canadian West featured what some have called a process of sub-fragmentation in which new groups brought with them ideologies that reflected their European origin and that were much more progressive than those of the older fragments. Thus, socialism arose in Saskatchewan. The Alberta sub-fragmentation reflected the influence of the United States, from which many of the founding settlers of Alberta came. In general, the political culture of the Canadian West has shown noticeable differences from that of the older parts of the country and has featured the appearance of at least two ideological variants not found in much strength elsewhere: socialism and social credit.

The Lipset emphasis on formative events is similarly revealing. Canada had no single great nationalizing formative event. The events that are significant in our history show the strong influence of the colonial powers, because in almost every instance the events were the outcome of struggles taking place between England and France or England and the United States. These events include the Conquest of New France in 1763, the American Revolution in 1776 and the War of 1812. Two other events which were significant and had more of an indigenous flavour were the uprisings in 1837 and the passage of the B.N.A. Act in 1867. But even that latter event took place in England as a statute of the British Parliament, a fact which continued to bedevil attempts to patriate the constitution until 1982. A second insight from the formative events notion is that different regions and different cultural fragments have had a different perspective on these formative events and in effect a different kind of history.

The Innis approach suggests how important it is to have a national communications network which would be capable of binding the community together. This system would have to offset cultural fragmentation between anglophones and francophones and the enormous cultural influences from south of the border. But in several respects we have failed to carry out this task successfully. Despite the setting up of a national broadcasting network in the 1930s, the CBC has proved incapable of bringing together francophones and anglophones or of offsetting infusions of American culture. Furthermore, other important socializing agencies were not left in the hands of the federal government. Responsibility for education was assigned to the provinces, and political party organizations developed into quasi-autonomous provincial organizations with a very loose federal alliance at the top. Thus, two of the most critical socializing agencies have been under provincial control and have contributed to the development of provincial political cultures in some cases at the expense of a national culture. At present, Canada is facing a severe crisis over the control of new communications systems such as Cablevision, pay TV and Telidon. The provinces, aware of the potential of the communications system in controlling the thoughts and minds of the public, are determined not to let this control pass to the federal government.

Finally, from the Marxist perspective, we see immediately the important impact on our political culture of foreign dependency and the different alignment of capitalist groups around the dominant capitalist forces in the country. We see as well the effect that uneven economic development has had on the country in fostering regionalism and leading to the growth of regional economic interests and regional perspectives. Paradoxically, however, class divisions (supposedly the major determinants of political culture in a modern society) have had only a minor effect on Canadian politics, in part because the party system and the electoral system enhance sectional cleavages.

Conclusion

Political culture consists of individually held values, attitudes and beliefs concerning politics; symbols that catalyze sentiments and beliefs about politics and political action; politically relevant knowledge and perceptions, including perceptions of historical experiences and notions of identity; and finally ideologies as aggregations of values and beliefs that have coherence and internal cohesion. Political culture must be examined historically, and therefore one must use both direct and indirect techniques for measuring it. Political culture serves as an important filter affecting political action because of the way that it constrains perceptions about politics, notions of what constitute political problems, and prescriptions for resolving these problems.

Political culture is historically derived. It is affected by the cultural baggage brought to a society by immigrants, especially first settlers. It is moulded by the formative events a society undergoes in the course of its modernization. It is conditioned by such structural underpinnings as class relations, trade patterns, the flow of transportation and communications. It changes as a result of contact with other cultures.

Canadian political culture is besieged by several problems. It is in important respects fragmented along regional, linguistic and class lines. How well elites respond to these challenges through the remaining portion of this century will be heavily conditioned by the present political culture.

Notes

1. For a discussion of symbolism in politics, see the several books by Murray Edelman, including *The Symbolic Uses of Politics* (Urbana: University of Illinois Press, 1964); and Lowell Dittmer, "Political Symbolism and Political Culture: Toward a Theoretical Synthesis," *World Politics* 30 (1977).

2. David Easton, *A Systems Analysis of Political Life* (New York: Wiley, 1965), p. 101.
3. Gabriel Almond and Sidney Verba, *The Civic Culture* (Princeton: Princeton University Press, 1963).
4. The distinction between citizen and subject was first discussed by Jean Jacques Rousseau in his famous book *The Social Contract*, W. Kendall trans. (Chicago: Henry Regnery, 1954), p. 21. Rousseau says:
     The members of a body politic call it "the state" when it is passive, "the sovereign" when it is active, and "a power" when they compare it with others of its kind. Collectively they use the title "people" and *they refer to one another individually as "citizens" when speaking of their participation in the authority of the sovereign, and as "subjects" when speaking of their subordination to the laws of the state.* (Emphasis added)
5. As summarized in Nathaniel Beck and John Peirce, "Political Involvement and Party Allegiances in Canada and the United States," *International Journal of Comparative Sociology* 18 (March–June 1977), p. 28.
6. See, *inter alia*, Ole Holsti "The 'Operational Code' Approach to the Study of Political Leaders: John Foster Dulles' Philosophical Beliefs," *Canadian Journal of Political Science* 3 (1971).
7. The most extensive discussion of "ethos theory" has occurred in the literature on urban politics. In 1963, Edward Banfield and James Q. Wilson in *City Politics* (New York: Vintage Books) wrote about "two fundamentally opposed conceptions of politics" (p. 234), "two mentalities" (p. 46) found in U.S. cities. These two conceptions accounted for a great deal of political behaviour in urban settings. For a critique, see Timothy M. Hennessy, "Problems in Concept Formation: The Ethos 'Theory' and The Comparative Study of Urban Politics," *Midwest Journal of Political Science* 14 (November 1970).
8. Quoted by Carl Berger, "The True North Strong and Free," in Peter Russell, ed., *Nationalism in Canada* (Toronto: McGraw-Hill, 1966), p. 6.
9. S.M. Lipset, *Revolution and Counterrevolution* (New York: Anchor Books, 1970), p. 55.
10. By the same token, however, a number of important institutions are provincial, and they help foster and maintain a provincial outlook.
11. Barrington Moore, *Social Origins of Dictatorship and Democracy* (Boston: Beacon Press, 1966), p. 486. To validate Moore's point one need only review the history of cultural contact between whites and natives in Canada. The coercion that sometimes accompanies political socialization indeed proves, as Moore argues, that cultural inertia is not inevitable. But is also shows how difficult it is to engineer cultural change. This difficulty has complicated attempts to inculcate the "official" political culture in countries like Poland and Czechoslovakia where values from an earlier era continue to dominate. See Archie Brown and Jack Gray, eds., *Political Culture and Political Change in Communist States* (London: Macmillan, 1977).
12. Louis Hartz *et al.*, *The Founding of New Societies* (New York: Harcourt, Brace, 1964).
13. Lipset, *Revolution and Counterrevolution*.
14. See especially Gad Horowitz, *Canadian Labour in Politics* (Toronto: University of Toronto Press, 1967).

15. See, for example, the following works by Harold Innis: *Canadian Economic History* (Toronto: University of Toronto Press, 1956); *The Fur Trade in Canada*, rev. ed. (Toronto: University of Toronto Press, 1970); *Empire and Communications*, revised by Mary Q. Innis (Toronto: University of Toronto Press, 1972). Also see James W. Carey, "Harold Adams Innis and Marshall McLuhan," *Antioch Review*, Spring 1967.

16. Albert Johnson, *Touchstone for the CBC* (mimeo, 1977), p. 2. See also John Redekop, "Continentalism: The Key to Canadian Politics" in *Approaches to Canadian Politics*, 2nd ed., ed. John H. Redekop.

17. Gary Teeple, ed., *Capitalism and The National Question* (Toronto: University of Toronto Press, 1972). For a critique see Glen Williams, "The National Policy Tariffs: Industrial Underdevelopment Through Import Substitution," *Canadian Journal of Political Science* 12 (June 1979).

Further Readings

Bell, David V.J., and Lorne J. Tepperman. *The Roots of Disunity*. Toronto: McClelland and Stewart, 1979.

Black, Edwin, *Divided Loyalties*. Montreal: McGill-Queens University Press, 1975.

Christian, William, and Colin Campbell. *Political Parties and Ideologies in Canada*. Toronto: McGraw-Hill, 1974.

Clarke, Harold, *et. al. Political Choice in Canada*. Toronto: McGraw-Hill, 1980.

Elkins, David, and Richard Simeon, eds. *Small Worlds: Provinces and Parties in Canadian Political Life*. Toronto: Methuen, 1980.

Hartz, Louis, *et al. The Founding of New Societies*. New York: Harcourt Brace, 1964.

Lipset, Seymour Martin. *Revolution and Counterrevolution*. New York: Anchor Books, 1970.

Pammett, Jon, and Michael Whittington, eds. *Political Socialization: Foundations of Political Culture*. Toronto: Macmillan, 1976.

Chapter 8

Political Participation and Democracy
William Mishler

Few aspects of Canadian government reveal as much about its political character as the way in which Canadian citizens participate in the political life of the country. Widespread, informed and effective participation is a hallmark of democracy. Participation provides citizens with the means to influence the selection of their political leaders, communicate their needs and aspirations to government and hold government accountable for its performance. It also enables citizens to express dissent and ventilate their grievances with government, thereby regulating political conflict and promoting stability.

As well, democratic theory holds participation to be important for the individual. Liberal democrats believe the ability to participate effectively in decisions affecting one's life gives citizens a sense of self-esteem. It enhances human dignity and self-respect and contributes to the individual's civic education and moral development. To a substantial degree, therefore, the extent to which Canada conforms to the democratic ideal is revealed by the nature and extent of the political participation of its citizens. How do Canadians participate and how extensively? Who participates and in what activities? Why do some citizens participate but not others? What is the quality of citizen participation? How effective is participation in influencing the course of government action? And what are the prospects for promoting still higher levels of better-informed and more effective participation in years to come? The answers to these questions reveal a great deal about the health of democracy in Canada in the mid-1980s and beyond.

How Do Citizens Participate?
Political participation may be defined as voluntary activities by citizens which are intended to influence the selection of government leaders or the decisions they make.[1] In an open society such as Canada there are many ways in which citizens can attempt to influence government, directly or indirectly, individually or in groups, legitimately or illegitimately. Many of these activities are complementary; others are not.

Voting is the most common and widely recognized avenue for citizen participation in Canada, as it is in most of the western democracies. Although Canada does not hold as many elections as the United States, the federal structure of Canadian government combined with the competitiveness of political parties provides citizens with opportunities to vote in federal, provincial or municipal elections on an average of almost once a year. Citizens also have occasional opportunities to vote directly on public issues. Although the use of plebiscites is rare, when used, such contests can generate considerable political interest and activity, as illustrated most recently in the vote on sovereignty-association in Quebec.

Voting, however, is only the most visible means by which citizens participate in politics. Elections inevitably produce political campaigns which in Canada are relatively expensive and labour-intensive contests. As a consequence, campaigns provide virtually unlimited opportunities for voluntary activity such as ringing doorbells, canvassing neighborhoods, mailing campaign literature, distributing posters and the like. Moreover, parties and candidates are always willing to allow citizens to participate with their pocketbooks by contributing money to campaigns.

Political parties also depend heavily on volunteer labour between elections. For a few citizens, parties provide opportunities to participate in relatively glamorous activities such as screening candidates for party nominations, developing party policies, and attending party conferences. However, parties provide many more opportunities for citizens to perform a myriad of routine and frequently boring tasks such as organizing party files, updating membership lists, stuffing envelopes and licking postage stamps.

Of course, opportunities for citizen participation are not confined to the electoral process. Citizens frequently have interests that cannot adequately be expressed through the simple choice that voting provides or cannot await the next election at some uncertain date perhaps five years in the future. Thus, many citizens attempt to influence government directly. One way they do this is by contacting public officials to express an opinion or request assistance. Government officials at all levels receive a steady flow of letters, telegrams and telephone calls, and are contacted directly by constituents in shopping centres, on street corners, at hockey games or wherever citizens gather.

Other citizens find it more comfortable, or think it more effective, to try to influence government as part of a group. Some are members of formal, voluntary organizations or interest groups which lobby government on behalf of members' interests. Others join informal groups such as neighborhood organizations which also pressure government for group or community concerns.

The most direct means for citizens to influence government is by becoming part of it, by running for elected office or seeking an appointed post. Opportunities to hold office are severely limited, not only by the small number of available positions and by the time and money required for successful campaigns, but also by the practical necessity of securing a party's nomination and ultimately the approval of Canadian voters. Nevertheless, although the ascent to public office is a slippery slope, there are always ample volunteers to attempt the climb.

Despite abundant opportunities to participate in conventional forms of political activity, citizens sometimes perceive a need to use more forceful and dramatic means either to register their political opinions or to protest government action. Protest may be individual or collective, legal or illegal, violent or passive. Citizens may march in peaceful demonstrations to protest public policies; they may disobey specific laws in an effort to have them changed; they may even attempt to stop government actions directly through the use of force or violence. Over the past two decades, protests in Canada have run the gamut from bombings and kidnapping by advocates of independence for Quebec to the passive resistance of conservation groups attempting to stop government-sanctioned hunting of baby seals.

How Extensively Do Citizens Participate?

Opinions vary on the extent of citizen participation in Canada.[2] Some argue that Canada is a nation of political spectators whose citizens are content to observe the political spectacle from the sidelines, rarely becoming involved directly. Others maintain that Canadians are relatively active, especially in comparison to citizens of other democratic nations. Few deny, however, that opportunities for participation far exceed current levels of actual citizen involvement.

Those who hold that Canadians are relatively active usually point to the comparatively high levels of voter turnout in both federal and provincial elections. Given the opportunity to vote, most citizens do so. Over the past thirty years an average of 75 percent of the citizens on the voters' lists have voted in federal elections. In fact, turnout has fallen significantly below average in only two elections since World War II, in 1953 and, again, in 1974, both of which were held during summer months when many citizens were away from home on vacation. Similarly, the mid-winter 1980 federal election had a lower than typical turnout.

Turnout in provincial elections is on a par with that in federal contests. Moreover, because enumeration is a government responsibility, except in British Columbia, more than 90 percent of the voting-age public are included on the voters' lists. In British Columbia, it is the citizen's responsibility to register to vote, and only 75 percent of those who are eligible do so.

Excluding nations where voting is compulsory and enforced by legal sanctions, Canada ranks near the top among western nations in terms of voter turnout. In the United States, for example, only about 70 percent of those who are registered turn out for presidential elections, and fewer than two-thirds of those who are eligible are registered to vote. Still fewer Americans vote in congressional and state elections, and turnout in all elections has been declining for a quarter century.

The extent of voter participation in Canada is even more impressive when examined over time. There are many reasons that a citizen may fail to vote in any single election: bad weather, illness, the need to be out of town on business. However, the available evidence from voter surveys suggests that fewer than 10 percent of the public are habitual non-voters. Another quarter fail to vote in an occasional election, but nearly two-thirds of all citizens vote regularly whenever elections are held.

Underlying the national average, turnout in both federal and provincial elections varies substantially between provinces. Generally, these differences are tied to variations in the competitiveness of party politics. Competition makes elections interesting and gives voters a sense that the voting matters. Prince Edward Island and Saskatchewan traditionally have enjoyed the most competitive party systems and have experienced the highest levels of voter turnout in both federal and provincial elections. On the other hand, Alberta, Quebec and Newfoundland (until recently) have been among the least competitive and have had the lowest turnout.[3] It is interesting to note, however, that turnout increased dramatically in Newfoundland in the early 1970s with the rise in competition that accompanied the end of Joseph Smallwood's more than twenty-year domination of provincial politics. Similarly, turnout in Quebec traditionally has been higher in provincial elections where issues and candidates are more relevant to French Canadians. Indeed, in the plebiscite on sovereignty-association, turnout in Quebec exceeded 80 percent.

Although most citizens take advantage of their opportunities to vote, substantially fewer participate in other aspects of political life. For example, despite abundant opportunities, most citizens never participate in political parties or campaigns. Indeed, the available evidence, summarized in Table 8.1, indicates not only that fewer than half of the voting-age public participate in any campaign activity but also that most of those who are active in campaigns take part in relatively "passive" activities such as attending political rallies, or talking with friends and attempting to influence how they vote. Only one citizen in ten actually has worked in a political campaign or has contributed money. Political parties are even less successful in attracting volunteers between elections. Fewer than 5 percent of the public are active party members, and many who are members work sporadically, devoting an average of less than an hour a week to party affairs.

Part of the reason that citizens do not participate more extensively in political parties and campaigns may be that many are unaware of the opportunities that exist. Surveys indicate that greater numbers are willing to contribute both time and money, but have never been contacted by parties or candidates and asked to participate. In Canada, as in

Table 8.1
The Extent of Citizen Participation in Canada

Type of Activity	Percentage Participating	
1. Voting		
a) Votes in most federal elections	90	
b) Votes in most provincial elections	86	
2. Election Campaign Activities	*Federal/Provincial*	
% who often or sometimes:		
a) Try to influence friends' votes	20	20
b) Attend political rallies	19	18
c) Work for party or candidate	11	9
d) Contribute money to party of candidate	8	10
3. Active Member of Political Party	4	
4. Sometimes Contacts Public Officials	17	18
5. Ever Worked with Others to Solve Community Problems	34	
6. Actual Protest Activities		
a) Has signed political petition	36	
b) Has attended protest meeting	18	
7. Attitudes Toward Protest		
a) Believes political strikes sometimes justified	80	
b) Believes boycotts sometimes justified	81	
c) Believes legal demonstrations sometimes justified	80	
d) Believes illegal but peaceful demonstrations sometimes justified	47	
e) Believes violent protests sometimes justified	9	

Sources: 1. Thomas Atkinson, Bernard Blishen, Michael Ornstein and Michael Stevenson, *Social Change in Canada: Trends in Attitudes, Values and Perceptions* (1979, Phase 2).
2. Harold Clarke, Jane Jenson, Lawrence LeDuc and Jon Pammett, *The 1979 Canadian National Election* and *Panel Study.*
3. Allan Kornberg, Joel Smith, and Harold Clarke, *Citizen Politicians: Canada* (Durham, NC: Carolina Academic Press, 1980).

the United States, political parties are poorly organized and highly inefficient in recruiting volunteer political activists.

Among the various opportunities for participation in non-electoral
activities, citizens are more likely to sign petitions, write their public
officials or work with others on community affairs. However, despite the
fact that writing a letter takes little time or energy, less than a quarter of
the Canadian public have ever written to a public official. Nor do many
citizens respond to most of the questionnaires that elected officials
occasionally distribute or take advantage of the other opportunities to
communicate directly with public officials. What makes this all the more
surprising is that the overwhelming majority of citizens—indeed, more
than 75 percent—believe that public officials do pay attention to
constituents' letters and try to respond to their requests.

About one citizen in four participates in informal groups sometime
during adult life. Moreover, although 60 percent or more of adult
Canadians are members of one or more formal voluntary organizations
such as labour unions and professional groups, only a fraction of these
members play an active role in group affairs. Still fewer are interested in
or even aware of the political activities of their groups, most having
joined for social, economic or professional concerns rather than for
political reasons. Thus the number of citizens who can be said to
participate politically through groups probably is quite small.[4]

Finally, although Canada has a long tradition of periodic political
protest and violence, what little evidence is available suggests that only
small minorities of citizens have ever taken to the streets to express their
political discontent. During the 1960s, a period of relatively high political
discord, it has been estimated that Canada experienced more than 40
significant protest demonstrations and riots which resulted in fewer
than 10 deaths. In the United States, by comparison, the '60s witnessed
more than 700 riots and demonstrations which were responsible for
more than 250 deaths. Even controlling for the difference in their
population sizes, Canada experienced less than one-quarter of the
political protest and violence than occurred in the United States during
the same period.[5]

Nevertheless, for a small minority of citizens, protest is, or can be, an
important avenue of political expression. In a recent survey, for example,
nearly 20 percent of those interviewed reported having taken part in a
protest rally or march. Eighty percent of those questioned indicated that
they thought that legal protests were sometimes justified as a means of
political expression. And nearly 40 percent believed that even illegal
protests could be justified under certain circumstances. Moreover, these
figures do not include those citizens who express their protest by
dropping out of politics or who register their dissent by voting for
extremist political parties.

In determining how much citizens participate, it is important to remember that different types of political activity appeal to different individuals. The 25 percent of the Canadian public who write letters to public officials are not necessarily the same 25 percent who participate in informal groups. When the accumulated evidence on different types of participation is aggregated, the picture that emerges is one of a surprisingly active Canadian public. Although it is true that upwards to 10 percent of the public do not participate in political life, and another 25 to 30 percent confine their activity to voting, it also is the case that nearly two-thirds of adult Canadians participate at least occasionally in one or more political activities in addition to voting.

Who Participates?

Because they believed that the interests of less active citizens are ignored by government, classical democratic theorists advocated high levels of participation among all segments of society. Although political activity in Canada is widespread and includes participants from virtually every social and economic group, citizens from certain walks of life enjoy greater political opportunities, possess superior political resources, and are exposed to more intense political stimuli which, taken together, lead some citizens to participate more than others. Some of the most important of these differences are illustrated in Table 8.2.

In Canada as elsewhere, the higher a citizen's social position, the more likely the citizen will be to participate in politics. Social status influences participation in several ways. In addition to determining the social and economic resources available for political investment, social status influences citizens' perceptions of their personal stakes in politics and their ability to influence government decisions. High-status citizens also are the neighbours of the political elite. They are more likely to know and be known by political decision makers and are viewed by the public and by politicians alike as opinion leaders in the community.

Social status in Canada is determined by a variety of factors, principal among which are occupation, income and education. Since work typically is the central experience of adult life, it is not surprising that occupation has important consequences for citizen participation. Generally, individuals in higher-status occupations participate more than those holding lower-status jobs. Although this relationship holds broadly for all types of political activity, differences based on occupation are most pronounced for the more difficult and demanding forms of participation. This is illustrated most graphically among those elected to public office. Although lawyers, businesspeople and other professionals constitute fewer than 20 percent of the Canadian workforce, they hold more than 75 percent of the seats in Parliament and in the ten provincial assemblies.[6]

Table 8.2
Who Participates and in Which Activities?

	Voting	Campaigning	Contacting MPs	Community Work
Occupation				
Professional/Managerial	89%	38%	30%	25%
White-Collar	88	45	24	19
Blue-Collar	83	36	21	18
Farmer	82	39	23	31
Income				
$20,000+	88	46	35	21
$10,000–19,999	86	40	25	21
Less than $10,000	84	38	19	19
Education				
College Graduate	86	42	32	22
High School Graduate	88	46	26	22
Did Not Grad. from H.S.	83	37	21	19
Ethnicity				
British	88	38	26	26
French	82	43	19	15
Other	83	42	26	20
Sex				
Male	88	42	28	23
Female	84	39	20	19
Age				
66 Years +	85	38	20	20
36–65 years	86	44	25	24
22–35 years	82	36	26	16
18–21 years	86	43	14	13

Source: William Mishler, *Political Participation in Canada* (Toronto: Macmillan, 1979).

Income and education reinforce the political advantages of occupation. Although it may not be true that money can buy political power in Canada, it can buy a variety of political opportunities and resources which give the relatively affluent decided advantages in political life. Money can "buy" the leisure time necessary to pursue politics as a hobby or career, it can buy the political information which whets the political appetite and increases awareness of political opportunities, and it can buy the contacts with party leaders and public officials which facilitate both political communication and influence. Consequently, wealthy citizens participate more extensively in all forms of political activity. Although they enjoy only marginal advantages in voting and community work, affluent citizens are considerably more active in political party and campaign activities, correspond more frequently with public officials, and nearly monopolize elected office. From the meagre evidence available it also appears that the well-to-do are above-average participants in political protests. Not only were student activists in the 1960s disproportionately from wealthy families, but many of the leaders of the separatist movement in Quebec and of other protest movements have been members of the upper strata of Canadian society.[7]

Education also conveys important political advantages, increasing political interest and awareness, expanding opportunities, and developing the political skills necessary for effective participation. Interestingly, however, although a college education has become a virtual necessity for holding high public office and facilitates, as well, contacts with public officials, people with only a high school education are more frequent voters and more likely to participate in political campaigns. College-educated citizens, apparently, are more skeptical of the effectiveness of voting and of other forms of collective participation and tend to concentrate their political energies on more demanding and, presumably, more effective activities.

Although occupation, income and education are the principal determinants of a citizen's position in society, other factors such as ethnicity, religion, sex and age also condition relative social standings and influence levels of participation. Consistent with their traditional dominance of Canadian society, citizens of Anglo–Celtic descent participate more extensively in most areas of political life. Although French Canadians are especially active in political campaigns, they tend to neglect most other forms of participation at the federal level and concentrate their efforts on provincial activities. Religious differences have very similar political consequences. Protestants are more likely to vote, work in the community and contact public officials, but Catholics are more active in political campaigns. Jewish citizens, however, are most active in all these areas.

Traditionally, the most consistent differences in participation have been those based on sex. Because women until quite recently have been viewed as a politically inferior group, politics has tended to be a man's world. Women were denied the right to vote in federal elections until 1918 and in some provincial elections until 1940. And numerous informal barriers to women's participation persist today. In particular, it is argued that women are disadvantaged in two important ways. First, women bear disproportionate responsibilities for managing home and family— responsibilities that reduce political opportunities and drain political energies. Second, women frequently are socialized into a set of political roles which emphasize subservience and passivity. Whatever the reason, however, women do participate less extensively in virtually every form of political endeavour. Although these differences are shrinking in the face of the women's movement and other changes in society, women still have some distance to go to achieve equality in political activity.

Finally, politics traditionally has been the preserve of the middle-aged. Younger citizens, especially those aged 21 to 35, tend to be preoccupied with the demands of starting jobs and families and establishing life's routine. As a consequence they have been slow to take advantage of the political opportunities available to them. Because older citizens frequently are burdened by ill health or a debilitating sense that they are no longer contributing members of society, they, too, participate less frequently in most activities than citizens in their middle years. The principal and somewhat surprising exception to this pattern is apparent among the very youngest group of adult citizens, those aged 18 to 21. Although substantially less likely than their elders to contact public officials or to participate in community affairs, these youngest citizens have been quick to exercise their recently acquired right to vote and have been among the most active participants in political campaigns.

In sum, although the ranks of the political activists in Canada include representatives from all segments of society, certain groups of citizens participate more than others. The wealthy and well educated, men and the middle-aged, Protestants and members of the English "charter" group all enjoy modest but significant advantages in political activity.

Why Do Some Participate More than Others?

The extent of citizen participation in political life is determined by the interplay of two general forces: motivation and opportunity. Before citizens will participate in any activity they must both want to participate and possess sufficient ability legally and personally to translate motivation into action.

Restrictions on political opportunity are of two broad types: formal restrictions such as age and residency requirements which are established by law; and informal restrictions which stem from a citizen's lack of political resources or from the inconvenience a citizen experiences attempting to participate. Although political opportunities in Canada once were severely circumscribed by laws restricting the participation of the poor and property-less, Indians, Inuit, and members of certain religions, most legal impediments to participation have been eliminated.[8] It remains true, of course, that political resources vary substantially between groups and that informal impediments such as the weather, the length of voting lines or the inconvenience of working in campaigns continue to deter many citizens from participating. However, most citizens possess reasonable opportunities to participate in a wide range of political activities. Therefore, differences that persist in the political participation of different groups now appear to be better explained by differences in political motivations.

Motivations to participate are determined by a complex set of individual attitudes and beliefs about politics, society and self. At the core of these beliefs is a cluster of related attitudes, called psychological political involvement, which refers to an individual's awareness of, interest in and concern about politics and political affairs. It should come as no surprise that participation varies with political interest. Although even a passing interest in politics usually is sufficient to motivate most citizens to vote, political interest of a more absorbing kind is required for other types of activity. Few citizens, however, possess an abiding interest in politics. In one survey, conducted in 1974, barely 10 percent of the public reported high levels of political interest and more than 40 percent claimed to have no interest at all.[9] Even political campaigns with all their conflict and excitement generate little public enthusiasm. The problem, simply, is that for many citizens politics seems irrelevant and remote. It intrudes upon their daily lives every year or two when they are called upon to vote in an election, but otherwise has little direct or immediate effect on their workaday lives.

Compounding the problem of marginal interest is the fact that many citizens are poorly informed about politics and do not understand how government works. Political information and psychological involvement are closely related and mutually reinforcing. Just as citizens who are interested in politics attend more closely to public affairs and are likely to be better informed, those who understand government are more sensitive to political stimuli and are more likely to develop strong incentives to participate. The latter also are more likely to acquire the political resources needed for effective participation and to comprehend, as well, the range of political opportunities available to them. Most citizens, however, possess only a superficial understanding of Canadian government and politics. Although virtually everyone can identify the prime minister and most recognize the name of their member of parliament, substantially fewer citizens understand the structure of

Canadian government or can identify the stands taken by the different parties even on major issues.

For many citizens, of course, the motivation to participate stems from loyalty to a political party or candidate or from a commitment to political ideals. Partisanship, or a sense of loyalty to a political party, is a prime motive for numerous political activities, especially those related to elections. Citizens with strong psychological attachments to political parties or their leaders are more likely to vote and participate in campaigns. Theirs also are the backs on which the burdens of party work disproportionately fall.

Although few citizens hold intense opinions on political issues or possess well-developed ideologies, those who do are among the most active members of the polity. However, because political parties in Canada typically favour pragmatism over ideological consistency, citizens with strong ideologies frequently encounter difficulties finding appropriate outlets for expressing their views. Citizens motivated by ideology often identify with one of the smaller, more radical or programmatic parties such as the prairie protest parties of the 1930s or 1940s. Those who cannot find appropriate parties or other suitable outlets for their points of view ultimately may express their frustrations through political protest or abstain from politics altogether.

Whatever the initial impetus for political activity, citizens are unlikely to maintain their interest or continue to participate unless they are convinced also that participation holds reasonable prospects for success. *Political efficacy*, or the belief that one can influence political decisions through personal action, is a necessary if not sufficient condition for nearly all forms of participation. Although it appears that Canadians perceive voting to be a civic obligation to be performed irrespective of its likely impact, few citizens are willing to take part in more demanding activities unless they believe not only that opportunities for effective participation exist but also that they personally are capable of exploiting those opportunities. Even the discontented must be convinced that dissent will make some difference before they will express their dissatisfaction through protest.

For many citizens, however, government appears far too large, too complicated and too remote for them to understand, much less for them to influence. In a survey conducted in 1974, two-thirds of those interviewed complained that government was too complicated, more than half thought that government did not care about their opinions, and a majority concluded that they did not have any influence over government actions. Indeed, a majority of citizens doubt that even government officials know what they are doing. Most believe that government in Canada is dominated by big interests, and nearly a quarter of a 1965 sample thought that those in charge of government are crooks.[10] Given such widespread feelings of powerlessness, cynicism and distrust, it is no wonder that so many citizens are unwilling to sacrifice their leisure time to participate more extensively in politics.

What Is the Quality of Participation?

Classical theories of democracy require not only that citizens participate extensively in politics but also that they be informed, rational and tolerant of dissenting views. Although surveys indicate that Canadians compare favorably on most of these criteria with citizens of other western nations, in absolute terms, the quality of democratic citizenship in Canada falls well below the democratic ideal. We already have observed, for example, that citizens are only moderately informed about politics. Most recognize prominent political leaders, but considerably fewer are informed about current government activities or the issue positions of competing parties.

Still fewer citizens exhibit high levels of rationality. With respect to voting, for example, the rational citizen is one who studies political issues, evaluates the parties' programs and platforms, and votes for the party whose positions on important issues are closest to the voter's own. Although election surveys indicate that voters do tend to vote for the party they think is closest to them on a few, highly salient political issues, these studies also indicate that citizens are concerned only with two or three leading issues and that their conceptions of the issues are vague and superficial. Moreover, citizens are at least as likely to ignore issues and to base their voting decisions on partisan loyalties or prejudices, or on candidates' styles and personalities.[11]

Little systematic evidence is available on political tolerance in Canada. However, the history of the extension of political and civil rights provides important clues and suggests a mixed pattern. For example, although Canada extended the franchise to women relatively early in its history, pockets of political discrimination against women persisted until quite recently, and subtle forms of both civil and political discrimination against women persist today. Similarly, the Inuit were denied the right to vote until 1950; Indians on reserves were excluded from the franchise until the early 1960s, and until even more recently in some provinces; citizens of Asian descent suffered widespread political and civil discrimination, especially in British Columbia, well into the 1940s; and it is only recently that formal restrictions of political rights based on race and religion have been abolished. Moreover, it is at least arguable that non-legal forms of political and social discrimination based on age, sex, race, religion, ethnicity and a variety of other factors remain significant and widespread.

If, however, the average citizen falls somewhat short of the democratic ideal, there is increasing evidence that the failures of democratic citizenship stem partly, at least, from widespread feelings of powerlessness, cynicism and distrust.[12] These feelings of *alienation*, as they are called, appear to be linked, in turn, to the frustration many citizens feel at being excluded from significant opportunities to participate in important decisions which affect their lives outside the political arena, at home, in school and on the job.

Participation in non-political institutions, it appears, provides training for political life. Citizens reared in homes where family decisions are shared and those educated in schools where student opinions are solicited and taken seriously acquire confidence in their abilities to influence government and to develop more democratic personalities. Opportunities to influence decisions at work appear to be even more important. Relatively limited participation in the workplace appears sufficient to increase political interest and efficacy, to promote tolerance and thus to enhance both the quantity and quality of citizen participation.

How Effective is Participation?

Underlying all that has been said thus far is the assumption that participation matters—that who participates, how and how extensively has real consequences for the selection of political leaders and the substance of public policy. Democratic theory, we have noted, is predicated upon the belief that participation is the most effective way citizens have to express their interests to government and, consequently, that inequalities of political participation distort the representation of citizen interests and undermine the fundamental basis of political equality. Little evidence is available regarding the consequences of participation for leadership selection and public policy in Canada. However, the evidence which is available suggests that participation does, indeed, matter, and that government is most responsive to the interests of those who participate most extensively and in the most demanding political activities.

Although opportunities for citizen participation in Canada are numerous, the effectiveness of certain forms of political activity is tenuous at best. This is particularly the case for election-related activities. Despite widespread participation, the practical value of voting and campaigning is severely limited by the absence of effective competition in many elections combined with the relative homogeneity of the major parties on fundamental political issues. Because they fail to provide realistic alternatives to incumbent parties and leaders and offer little meaningful choice even where competition is robust, elections frequently are little more than political rituals. They permit citizens to participate symbolically but provide little influence in the selection of political leaders or the development of public policies.

In contrast to elections, other avenues of political participation provide substantial influence but are dominated by social and economic elites. Political parties, for example, play obvious and important roles in leadership selection and policy development. However, despite continuing attempts to expand their memberships and encourage wider participation by the rank and file, the major parties have been careful to ensure that the nomination of party candidates for public office and the formulation of party programs have remained the exclusive preserve of party leaders, who are not elected and who differ significantly from party members in social background and political opinion.[13] Interest groups, too, have substantial influence in Canadian government and politics. Even more than political parties, however, interest groups are dominated by elites whose backgrounds and interests may be very different from group members'. And despite the trappings of democracy, interest group leaders are only nominally accountable to their membership for actions taken on the group's behalf.[14]

Nor does political protest provide a viable alternative to other, elite-dominated, activities. Although it is arguable that political protest can heighten public consciousness of neglected interests and lay a foundation for gradual, long-term changes in public policy, in the short run, the usual response of government has been to suppress political protest and resist taking any actions that might be interpreted as capitulation to protest demands.[15]

Given the ineffectiveness of the more popular electoral forms of political activity combined with the domination of more demanding and effective activities by social and economic elites, it is not surprising that the composition of Canada's political leadership continues to be elite dominated or that the tenor of Canadian public policy appears to many observers to manifest an elite bias. At the same time, however, although the composition of Canada's political leadership has changed very little in this century despite broad changes in the nature and extent of citizen participation, even relatively modest changes in the composition of the politically active strata of society have been sufficient to stimulate significant changes in government policies and priorities. In particular, it appears, the gradual expansion of opportunities for working-class participation in political life has provoked somewhat greater attention to the interests of the disadvantaged, especially in those provinces where political competition has been comparatively high and where working-class–oriented political parties such as the CCF/NDP have enjoyed their greatest success.

On balance, the available evidence suggests that the nature and extent of citizen participation does have important consequences for political accountability and responsiveness. There is also increasing evidence that political participation has intrinsic value for citizens, enhancing individuals' self-esteem and fostering more democratic personalities. The problem, however, succinctly stated by Robert Presthus,[16] is that:

> In the context of democratic participation, the going system produces some questionable consequences. Participation tends to be restricted to those groups that possess the greatest amounts of resources. . . . The majority are unable to compete effectively in the political arena, for lack of such resources . . . [which] tend to be monopolized by those we have defined as political elites. Government in responding to [the elites] is placed in the somewhat anomalous position of defending the strong against the weak.

Summary

Assessments of the democratic character of political participation in Canada, perhaps inevitably, depend upon one's perspective. Although it is obvious from this brief discussion that the structure and quality of citizen participation in political life fall far below the democratic ideal, it also is apparent that Canada approaches much closer to this ideal than the great majority of the world's nation-states. Indeed, in many respects, the structure of citizen participation in Canada is surprisingly wide and deep. Most citizens regularly accept the responsibility to vote and a small majority take part in more demanding political activities, as well. Moreover, although many citizens display little interest in politics and manifest relatively strong feelings of cynicism, intolerance, alienation and political incompetence, there are good reasons to believe that both the quantity and quality of citizen participation would increase if political competition were strengthened and if more citizens were accorded more effective opportunities for participation both in the political life of Canada and in such basic social institutions as the family, school and workplace.

Political participation is a tonic. It is healthy for the individual and therapeutic to the state. Political activity in Canada would enhance the political interest and knowledge of its citizens, promote feelings of political competence, and strengthen citizens' attachments to society. Increases in the political activity of disadvantaged citizens especially also would foster more equitable representation of all political interests and strengthen political equality.

It is unrealistic, of course, to expect all citizens to participate extensively in every facet of political life. There are obvious, practical reasons for limiting the number of citizens who can hold elected office and for restricting violent forms of political protest. Notwithstanding such limits, however, there remain abundant opportuntities to increase citizen participation in a variety of middle-level political activities, thereby increasing the quality of democratic citizenship in Canada and achieving a closer approximation of the democratic ideal in the 1980s.

Notes

1. This definition is adapted from Sidney Verba and Norman H. Nie, *Participation in America* (New York: Harper and Row, 1972), p. 2.
2. For contrasting perspectives see Richard Van Loon, "Political Participation in Canada," *Canadian Journal of Political Science* 3 (September 1970): 376–99; and Leon Dion, "Participating in the Political Process," *Queen's Quarterly* 75 (Autumn 1968): 437–38.
3. Howard A. Scarrow, "Patterns of Voter Turnout in Canada" in *Voting in Canada*, ed. John C. Courtney (Scarborough: Prentice-Hall, 1967), pp. 104–14.
4. On interest-group membership and participation see Robert Presthus, *Elite Accommodation in Canadian Politics* (Toronto: Macmillan, 1973); and Robert Presthus, *Elites in the Policy Process* (London: Cambridge University Press, 1974).
5. Data are from Ronald Manzer, *Canada: A Socio-Political Report* (Toronto: McGraw-Hill, 1974), pp. 74–84.
6. Harold D. Clarke *et al.*, "Backbenchers" in *The Provincial Political Systems*, ed. David J. Bellamy *et al.* (Toronto: Methuen, 1976), pp. 216–19; and Allan Kornberg, "Parliament in Canadian Society," in *Legislatures in Developmental Perspective*, ed. Allan Kornberg and Lloyd D. Musolf (Durham, NC: Duke University Press, 1970), pp. 55–128.
7. See, for example, Michael Stein, *The Dynamics of Right-Wing Protest: A Political Analysis of Social Credit in Quebec* (Toronto: University of Toronto Press, 1973).
8. The nature of legal impediments to voting are discussed at length in T.H. Qualter, *The Election Process in Canada* (Toronto: McGraw-Hill, 1970), especially Chapter 1.
9. Data on the 1974 election are from *The 1974 Canadian National Election Study*. The data were originally collected and made available by Harold Clarke, Jane Jenson, Lawrence LeDuc and Jon Pammett.
10. Data on the 1965 Canadian general election were made available by the Inter-University Consortium for Political Research and were originally collected by Phillip Converse, John Meisel, Maurice Pinard, Peter Regenstreif and Mildred Schwartz.
11. For a different perspective see Harold Clarke *et al.*, *Political Choice in Canada* (Toronto: McGraw-Hill, 1979), Chapters 8, 11 and 17.
12. See, for example, the evidence cited in William Mishler, *Political Participation in Canada* (Toronto: Macmillan, 1979), pp. 142–45.
13. F.C. Englemann and M.A. Schwartz, *Canadian Political Parties: Origin, Character, Impact* (Scarborough: Prentice-Hall, 1975); and Allan Kornberg *et al.*, *Citizen Politicians: Canada* (Durham, NC: Carolina Academic Press, 1979).
14. Presthus, *Elite Accommodation*, pp. 286–87.
15. Judith Torrance, "The Response of Canadian Governments to Violence," *Canadian Journal of Political Science* 10 (September 1977): 473–96.

16. Presthus, *Elites in the Policy Process*, p. 461.

Further Readings

Kornberg, Allan, Joel Smith and Harold Clarke. *Citizen Politicians: Canada: Party Officials in a Democratic Society*. Durham, NC: Carolina Academic Press, 1979.

Mishler, William. *Political Participation in Canada: Prospects for Democratic Citizenship*. Toronto: Macmillan, 1979.

Qualter, Terrence H. *The Election Process in Canada*. Toronto: McGraw-Hill Ryerson, 1970.

Schwartz, Mildred A. "Canadian Voting Behavior." In *Electoral Behavior*, edited by Richard Rose. New York: Free Press, 1974.

Van Loon, Richard. "Political Participation in Canada," *Canadian Journal of Political Science* 3 (September 1970): 376–99.

Chapter 9
The Mass Media and Politics: An Overview[1]
Frederick J. Fletcher and Daphne Gottlieb Taras

The mass media have become in modern industrial societies the primary communicators of politically significant images. The capacity of these media—newspapers, magazines, radio, film, television—to reach large audiences and to select which ideas and images will have wide popular currency gives them a great deal of potential influence. In large part, the media form our psychic environment, especially with respect to matters beyond our direct personal experience, a realm into which most aspects of politics fall. The average Canadian adult spends more than three hours watching television each day, a little less listening to radio and more than fifty minutes reading a daily newspaper. Very few Canadians avoid these media altogether.[2] Indeed, television viewing takes up more of the average Canadian's time than anything but work and sleep.

The mass media are in the business of attracting audiences to sell to advertisers (or, in the case of the CBC, to convince Parliament of its worth). In the process, the media also sell a view of the world. While informing and entertaining us, "the media ... define what is normal and respectable in a society, what is debatable and what is beyond discussion by decent, respectable citizens," as Anthony Westell puts it in *The New Society*.[3] In choosing among the vast array of drama scripts, news items and other materials available to them, key media personnel have a great deal of influence on the beliefs and perspectives presented to the citizenry. These choices help to determine the available role models, images of reality, definitions of what is political and the role of citizens in the political process, subjects of conversation, things to worry about (from the threat of nuclear war to bad breath) and information on a wide range of subjects.

The importance of this gatekeeping function[4] derives in large part from the fact that gatekeepers tend to share assumptions about what makes appropriate media content. These assumptions can be traced in a general way to cultural norms about what is acceptable and appealing and more directly to the policies of media organizations, professional training of media personnel, current fashion and the requirements of media technologies. Government regulations also play a role.[5] Within the boundaries of acceptability, the gatekeepers are primarily concerned about what will attract audiences. While each medium has its own special requirements, they all tend to prefer the immediate, the personal and the concrete to long-term social processes or abstract ideas. Media consumers are conditioned to accept these standards as well, making it difficult for messages which do not fit the media mold to get a hearing.

Television is a particularly powerful shaper of values, not only because of its popularity, but also because people tend to use it non-selectively, watching whatever attracts them most at the time they want to relax. As a leading American communication researcher has put it:

> After more than 10 years of intensive research into its social function, I have concluded that television is best seen and studied as a ritual, as a virtually universal new religion that tends to absorb viewers of otherwise diverse outlook into its own "mainstream."[6]

He goes on to argue that television crosses social, religious, generational and class lines in an unprecedented manner, with the result that most viewers come to "share a great deal of cultural imagery" and that "the most recurrent patterns of the ritual tend to ... become the assumptions we make about the world." These patterns include the stereotyping of minority groups, a great exaggeration of the amount of crime and violence in society (television has ten times that of the real world), and an unwarranted emphasis on conflict and risk. All of these distortions have potential consequences for the legitimacy of political institutions and their capacity to function effectively.

In attempting to understand the role of the media in Canadian politics, analysts generally draw upon elements of two competing schools of thought: the liberal democratic and neo-Marxist approaches. The two perspectives share the view that the mass media, though for the most part privately-owned, have important political functions. Both believe that the media have significant "social power" and reject the argument advanced by some media executives that they merely reflect the values and tastes of their audiences.[7]

In liberal democracies like Canada, the media are seen by many as a "fourth branch of government," meeting the needs of citizens by presenting the information necessary for effective political participation and by providing a forum for debate on public issues. In this process, they are expected to help governments disseminate vital information about public services—and government accomplishments—while providing opportunities for opposition parties to criticize government and propose alternative policies. Ideally, they provide commentary on public affairs from a wide variety of perspectives, including those of unpopular minorities. An important tradition in the Anglo-American democracies holds that the news media should serve as watchdogs, sniffing out abuses of power—especially by governments—and barking out the alarm. Similarly, they are expected to be unofficial ombudspersons for the average citizen. Indeed, official ombudspersons rely primarily on publicity to restrain government power and are themselves, therefore, dependent on the media. In short, news organizations have a duty to "help keep democracy alive in societies too populous and too complex for face-to-face exchange. . . ."[8]

An alternative view, drawing on neo-Marxist thinking, sees the media as an important part of an ideological system which effectively promotes the dominant ideology of society, providing a justification for the economic and political status quo, thus serving the interests of the rich and powerful. By establishing the limits of debate, the media screen out radical critiques and reinforce existing values, values defined by the powerful and communicated from the top down. In North America, the mass media are seen as promoting consumerism, which supports the economic system, and the myth of "middle-classness," which holds that society's advantages are equally available to all and that critics of the system are failures, with only themselves to blame, or promoters of "foreign" ideologies. Private ownership of property is presented as an inviolable norm. When criticisms of the economic and political system are presented, the approach is generally reformist rather than radical. In short, the media are seen as "a powerful ideological weapon for holding the mass of people in voluntary submission to capitalism."[9]

Wallace Clement has demonstrated clearly that those who control the mass media in Canada are closely integrated with the economic elite, and argues that, therefore, the owners and media have a stake in the perpetuation of the existing power structure.[10] "Freedom of the press," as the American media critic A.J. Liebling said, "is guaranteed only to those who own one."[11] The late Roy Thomson, founder of the extensive Thomson newspaper chain, once observed that a television licence is "like having a licence to print money" and added that ownership of a daily newspaper confers similar benefits without the need for a licence.[12] The extent to which corporate control of media organizations actually influences content remains a matter of controversy and is examined below.

The Canadian Mass Media System
From their earliest beginnings in the eighteenth century, Canadian newspapers were political, with close ties to government or opposition parties. In the nineteenth century, they often served as personal vehicles for editor–politicians like George Brown, William Lyon Mackenzie, Etienne Parent, Joseph Howe and Amor de Cosmos. During the upheavals of the late 1830s, the press was a thorn in the side of those in

power, and the reformist strain of Canadian journalism was firmly
established along with a tradition of press freedom. After the 1838
rebellion in Upper Canada, Attorney-General John Beverley Robinson
lamented the principle of a free press but could do little about it:

> It is one of the miserable consequences of the abuse of liberty that a
> licentious press is permitted to poison the public mind with the most
> absurd and wicked representations, which the ill-disposed, without
> inquiry, receive and act upon as truths.[13]

During the nineteenth century, newspapers were small operations,
locally owned and highly partisan, often relying on government patronage or party financial support. They engaged in vociferous competition
and denounced political opponents with vigour, contributing much to the
vitality of political debate but often little to public enlightenment.

By the 1870s, the growth of urban centres and the emergence of new
technologies—mechanized printing, cheap newsprint, the telegraph for
rapid newsgathering—contributed to the proliferation of newspapers
and the creation of a mass press, which emphasized strictly political
matters less and social issues of broad interest more. Newspapers tried to
broaden their appeal to serve two distinct but related markets: readers
and advertisers anxious to reach them. Newspapers were no longer
primarily vehicles for political debate among competing elites. In the
competition for mass audiences, weaker publishers fell by the wayside
and, by the turn of the century, successful publishers were buying out
those in financial difficulty. The Southam and Sifton chains were well
established by 1920. For example, the Southam family purchased the
Ottawa *Citizen* (1897), the Calgary *Herald* (1908), the Edmonton *Journal*
(1912) and the Winnipeg *Tribune* (1920). The trend toward concentration
of ownership has continued to the present.

The quest for mass audiences, the growth of newspaper chains and
absentee ownership, and the advent of wire services selling news to a
wide range of clients all contributed to the decline of the partisan press.
More interested in profits than politics, the larger publishers moderated
their partisanship to appeal to broader audiences. The wire services,
wishing to sell to newspapers of all partisan stripes, sought to make their
copy as neutral as possible. Publishers were delighted to subscribe to
news services and to purchase syndicated features because they were so
much cheaper than staff-written material. The costs were shared by
many clients. For these reasons, the era of objective journalism emerged,
spreading gradually in the years following the Depression.

The major Canadian wire service, the Canadian Press (CP), was
founded in 1917 as a national cooperative, owned collectively by the
major daily newspapers. Set up as a giant clearing house for news gathered by Canada's dailies, CP provided an effective—and inexpensive—

mechanism for exchanging news among member papers and for bringing in up-to-date foreign news. CP expanded with its members and remains today the primary source of non-local news for all but the largest Canadian dailies. Increasingly, it uses its own reporters to cover major stories within Canada. It has few foreign correspondents, however, and continues to import foreign news from the world's major news services. Criticized by the Royal Commission on Newspapers (1981) for its lack of foreign coverage, CP increased its allocation for international coverage to $500,000, less than 2% of its total budget.[14] Given CP's heavy reliance on American sources—primarily its U.S. counterpart, the Associated Press (AP)—Canadians continue to see the world "through U.S. eyes."[15] Radio and television newsrooms, most of which lack the resources to do significant newsgathering on their own, rely on similar sources. Two CP subsidiaries, Broadcast News (BN) and Press News Ltd., supply much of the news and feature material used by Canada's approximately 450 radio and television outlets. They in turn rely on CP and the major international news services to establish their news priorities. The television networks derive much of their foreign coverage from the three U.S. networks and from Visnews, dominated by the British Broadcasting Corporation (BBC). Only the CBC makes a real effort at independent foreign coverage. The French media rely on these same sources, with a heavy dose of material from Agence France-Presse (AFP), the Paris-based service.[16]

From the beginning, the development of Canada's magazine and motion picture industries was hindered by competition from the United States. Since the 1930s, the Canadian government has employed tariffs, tax measures, subsidies and government agencies, including Crown corporations, to assist Canadian enterprises to survive competition from the large and well-funded American industries, which regarded Canada as a convenient additional market. The consistent view of Canadian governments has been that to permit American-based media to dominate Canadian markets would threaten Canada's cultural identity and siphon off revenues needed by Canadian enterprises to perform their public duties. For motion pictures, the federal government created the National Film Board (NFB) in 1939. Though receiving international acclaim for its documentaries, it has had little impact on Canadian popular culture. More recently, the Canadian Film Development Corporation (CFDC) was created to help finance Canadian feature films. It has created jobs for Canadian actors and technicians but there has been little that was Canadian about the content of the films. American images continue to dominate the country's movie screens.

In the early 1970s, the government moved to assist the magazine industry, with more success. Although Canadians continue to buy more Canadian than American magazines, federal legislation which withdrew tax deductions for advertisements in foreign-owned publications by

Canadian businesses for Canadian audiences appears to have helped a few Canadian magazines, such as *Saturday Night*, to survive. The law was aimed particularly at magazines which competed for Canadian advertising but offered little Canadian content, such as *Time*, which added four to six pages of Canadian news to its U.S. edition. Unable or unwilling to meet the requirement that it be 75 percent Canadian owned and have at least 80 percent distinctive content, *Time* closed down its Canadian edition, opening the way for *Maclean's* to become a weekly newsmagazine. *Reader's Digest* was able to adjust and remains Canada's best-selling magazine (with much more Canadian content).[17] In theory, at least, these magazines provide a Canadian view of national and world events.

Canadian radio and television services were founded in direct response to the spillover of signals from the U.S.[18] Government intervention was made necessary not only by the need to allocate frequencies and to negotiate an agreement with the U.S. government for a share of the airwaves, but also by the high cost of reaching Canada's scattered population. Faced with a choice between a government-owned system and a U.S.-dominated commercial one with little Canadian content which would serve only the major cities, the Conservative government of R. B. Bennett opted in 1932 for a Crown corporation, the CBC, which now provides nation-wide signals in both French and English. The radio network was joined by a television service in the 1950s. In 1958, the Board of Broadcast Governors was created to regulate both the CBC and the growing private sector. It oversaw the end of the dream of a single integrated broadcasting system and the growth of parallel public and private systems. The most important product of this evolution was CTV, a national private English-language television network formed in 1961. It now has seventeen affiliated stations covering most of the country. More recently, a number of independent stations and regional networks have been licensed. This proliferation of outlets fragmented the Canadian audience but provided relatively little in the way of increased Canadian content.

In 1968, a new Broadcasting Act was passed which changed the name of the regulatory agency to the Canadian Radio–Television Commission (later the Canadian Radio–Television and Telecommunications Commission, or CRTC) and set out some ambitious objectives for the broadcasting system:

> the Canadian broadcasting system should be effectively owned and controlled by Canadians so as to safeguard, enrich and strengthen the cultural, political, social and economic fabric of Canada; the programming provided by the Canadian broadcasting system should be varied and comprehensive and should provide reasonable, balanced opportunity for the expression of different views on matters of public

concern, and the programming provided by each broadcaster should be
of a high standard, using predominantly Canadian creative and other
resources.

Both public and private broadcasters were expected to contribute to
these goals, and the CRTC was to implement them. The new act, it was
hoped, would "help maintain the existence of a broadcasting system
intended to serve Canadian needs despite the influence everywhere of
American television and films."[19] Federal government objectives have
also included provision of coast-to-coast service in both official
languages, reflecting the diversity of Canadian cultural and social values
and, for the CBC, contributing to the development and maintenance of
national unity and Canadian cultural identity.[20]

In attempting to fulfill these objectives, the CRTC has promulgated
Canadian content regulations for both radio and television and has
required cable systems, which came into being to deliver clear U.S.
signals, to give priority to Canadian stations.[21] These regulations have
caused considerable controversy, especially where a popular U.S. station
has been removed to make way for a minority language or multicultural
station. U.S. border stations have complained that Canadian regulations
removing tax deductions from Canadian businesses advertising on non-
Canadian stations and requiring cable systems to carry only the
Canadian station when a program is broadcast simultaneously on a U.S.
station are interfering with the free flow of information.

In fact, of course, the station owners are primarily concerned with
their own profits. The conflict between open borders and cultural
sovereignty is not unique to Canada, of course, and in the Canadian case
virtually no U.S. programs are denied entry to Canada. The objective is
not to shut out U.S. programming but rather to preserve a place for
Canadian content.[22] Canadian audiences demonstrate an interesting
ambivalence on the issue. While showing a strong preference for U.S.
entertainment programs, they generally prefer Canadian documentaries
and news and public affairs shows. Moreover, there is clear evidence
from public opinion surveys that Canadians want to have a substantial
amount of Canadian programming available, even if they reserve the
right not to watch it.[23]

When the CRTC licenced pay-television in 1982, having resisted cable
company lobbying for a decade, it also sought to promote Canadian
content. The Commission awarded five-year licences for one national
general-interest service, requiring it to provide programming in both
official languages, three regional services (for the West, Ontario and the
Atlantic provinces), one national specialty service (to provide "cultural"
programming) and a regional multilingual service in B.C. A French-
language regional service for Quebec was licenced a few months later.

The major services were required to: (1) devote a minimum of 30 percent of total broadcast time to Canadian content, rising to 50 percent in later years; (2) allocate 50 percent of total revenues and 50 to 60 percent of total expenditures to acquisition of or investment in Canadian productions; (3) obtain certification from government officials for content claimed as Canadian. In addition, they were forbidden to show commercials or produce their own programs. In a statement accompanying the decision, CRTC Chairman John Meisel said the Commission's aim was to create a framework of relatively loose regulation that would encourage innovation. He said the CRTC view was that the market could support all of the new services but that regulatory adjustments would be made as needed, with tough action possible if the licencees did not meet their obligations to buy and invest in Canadian content.[24] In addition to meeting the Canadian demand for diversity of programming, the Commission optimistically expected that the new services would generate vast new revenues for Canadian independent producers, ushering in a golden age of Canadian film and television production.

The major services began broadcasting in the spring of 1983, amid considerable regulatory confusion and conflict with the cable companies that were to deliver the signals. By the end of the year, the national "cultural" channel, the Atlantic service and the B.C. multilingual system had folded, and the other services were in serious financial difficulty. The expected audiences had not subscribed, and there had been no bonanza for Canadian producers. The dissenting opinion by CRTC members Jean-Louis Gagnon and John Grace had been prophetic: "How many pay television channels can Canadians afford? How many do they need? How many of these birds will fly?"[25] Predictably, many critics blamed the Canadian content requirements for the problems, but the fault was clearly excessive competition in a market which was much smaller than the applicants and the CRTC had anticipated. Many U.S. systems also overestimated the potential audience.

On the whole, despite CRTC regulations and the best efforts of the CBC, the Canadian broadcast media have failed to develop an array of entertainment programs attractive enough to compete effectively with the flood of images from the great image factory to the south (which produces more than half of the world's films and television programs). Although Canadian content regulations have had considerable success in promoting an indigenous recording industry and coverage of sports and public affairs, private broadcasters have generally preferred to import popular U.S. shows rather than to commit the resources to develop competitive Canadian programs. The American imports are proven winners and much cheaper than home-grown shows of comparable quality, because their costs have already been recouped in the U.S. market. Thus it is that CTV is the only national television network in the industrialized world that does not produce a single dramatic series.[26] The bright side is that the regulations encouraged the development of good-quality news and public affairs shows that are now popular money makers. In addition, the CBC has in recent years been able to improve its audience share with an increasingly Canadian lineup. However, it has been suffering from financial cutbacks and has had its traditional role in the broadcasting system questioned by new government policies.[27]

Despite regulatory efforts, Canadians continue to be inundated with the values of American commercial television. Even on Canadian stations, U.S. programs dominate prime time.[28] English-speaking Canadian children spend more than 80 percent of their television viewing time watching U.S. programs. As then CBC President A. W. Johnson told the CRTC in 1978:

> The plain truth is that most of our kids know more about the Alamo than they know about Batoche or Crysler's farm. They know more about Davey Crockett than they do about Louis Riel. They talk about "taking the fifth" rather than about Canada's Bill of Rights.[29]

American images crowd out Canadian ones. Even when we watch television primarily for relaxation, much incidental learning takes place. Canadians who watch mainly U.S. programs could easily become confused about aspects of Canadian life, such as the judicial, federal and parliamentary systems, which differ markedly from their U.S. counterparts.[30] Many believe, as Meisel has put it, that television "has contributed significantly to the loss of regional and national identities" and to the Americanization of Canada.[31] This pattern of communication reduces our capacity to come to grips with our own particular problems and to preserve our distinctive values (civility, order, compassion, community responsibility). Frank Peers asks: "How many . . . Canadians want to concern themselves with the special concerns of Quebec or the Inuit when their eyes are fixed on *Dallas*?"[32] The question is, how far can the American occupation of the Canadian imagination go without threatening the foundations of Canadian society?

The extent to which the mass media system can contribute to promoting national unity and identity is also affected by two other enduring issues in Canadian politics: regionalism and cultural dualism. Canada's dispersed and culturally diverse population has always presented a formidable barrier to the development of national consensus. As with transportation, the creation and maintenance of a national mass media system has required federal government initiative. A series of court decisions awarded the federal government primary jurisdiction over broadcasting and cable, though the provinces have been making inroads with active educational broadcasting systems such as TVOntario and Radio Quebec and Saskatchewan's cablevision network.[33] Recently, some provinces have challenged federal jurisdiction over pay-television and other cable-delivered services. The challenge facing the two levels of government is to agree on a division of jurisdiction that allows provinces to use the new communication media to promote internal cultural and community development without reducing the capacity of the national system to communicate common perspectives of nationhood throughout the country and interpret each region to the others.

On the whole, the present national system has been only moderately successful in fostering interregional communication. Most newspapers and local radio and television have a distinct regional flavour, despite the efforts of wire services, syndication services and network feeds. Editors tend to select items with local appeal. Only the CBC offers national radio newscasts, and the national television newscasts attract only about half as many viewers as the local supper-hour shows. National magazines reach relatively limited audiences, as does the national edition of the *Globe and Mail*.[34] Although important advances in cross-regional communication have been made in recent years, primarily through improved regional coverage by the *Globe*, in the fourteen Southam dailies through its news service (SN) and on the CBC, the news still tends to originate in the Ottawa–Toronto–Montreal triangle. The commerical wire services and national syndicates, which distribute news and features, tend to draw heavily on the Toronto papers. The reporters in the regional bureaus of the *Globe*, SN and CBC write for Toronto- or Montreal-based editors. The system's combination of parochialism and central Canadian domination of national coverage has done little to strengthen the ties of Confederation.

Cultural dualism has been an even greater barrier to effective communication. As Brian Stewart has noted, "the physical system is consciously designed to increase the volume of communication transactions between English-Canadians wherever they live, and again between French-Canadians wherever they live."[35] The two language groups tend to live in separate media worlds.[36] The CBC French and English services are distinct in both personnel and content, with the exception of a few cooperative projects. Although the French service of CP has been improving, it is still relatively weak, and the French press tends to rely on its own personnel and AFP.[37] Until recently, most Quebec outlooks concerned themselves primarily with Quebec issues, and few had correspondents beyond Ottawa.

However, political developments of the past decade appear to have increased interest in the rest of Canada, and coverage has improved. The major English dailies have had correspondents in Quebec since the 1960s. Frequently, major political events are given sharply different interpretations in French and English media. For example, the near defeat of the Trudeau government in 1972 was widely interpreted in the French press as a rejection of French Canadian influence in Ottawa, while English-language journalists blamed it on economics and a lacklustre Liberal campaign. In 1979, however, Quebec journalists covered the federal campaign much more closely and tended to reject cultural explanations for the Liberal defeat.

Nevertheless, the separate media worlds remain. Studies over the past decade show that cross-cultural communication in both news and entertainment programming remains limited. French and English newscasts have relatively few items in common and each tends to focus on its own language group. The same tends to hold true for newspapers.[38] Entertainment programs are also distinct, with virtually no anglophones in French programming, nor francophones in English programming.[39] Each cultural group has its own celebrities and common perspectives, with little overlap. The French media tend to focus on the political and cultural interests of Quebec, thereby promoting a sense of distinctiveness.[40]

Ownership and Control

In the early 1980s, the trend to large-scale corporate ownership of the media seems to be accelerating.[41] By 1983, twelve groups owned 89 of the country's 116 dailies. The six largest controlled nearly 80 percent of the 5.5 million total circulation. In the English daily press, two major chains—Southam and Thomson—own 54 dailies with more than half the daily circulation. The largest independent, the *Toronto Star*, with a circulation of more than 500,000, is itself a media conglomerate, owning virtually all of the community weeklies in the Toronto area. As for the French press, three chains own all but two of the dailies and control more than 90 percent of circulation. Media conglomerates such as Southam have substantial and expanding holdings in magazines, radio, television, cable and electronic publishing, and other firms in these areas are also taking over smaller enterprises. Maclean-Hunter, which recently added the Toronto Sun Publishing Company to its empire of magazines and broadcast media, seems poised to grow. Control of our information media is being concentrated in fewer and fewer hands.

Even more troubling, perhaps, for those concerned about corporate control of the press is the tendency for media owners to have other business interests which far outweigh their media holdings in financial significance. The Thomson interests, for example, are involved in travel companies, real estate, oil and gas, insurance, electronic publishing and large-scale retailing (The Bay, Simpsons, Simpson-Sears and Zellers).[42] The Power Corporation, one of three groups which own all but one of the French-language dailies in Quebec, is involved in many economic activities unrelated to the media.[43]

In eight of the ten provinces, one publisher controls at least 65 percent of daily newspaper circulation and, in many cases, this dominance is
accompanied by control of key broadcast media as well. In New Brunswick, for example, the K.C. Irving interests own all five English-language
dailies, plus a radio station, television station, regional magazine and
book publishing company.[44] In Saskatchewan, the two major dailies and
important broadcast outlets are owned by a single group. Such cross-
media ownership certainly carries with it the potential for abuse.
Another cause for concern is absentee ownership: in three of the four
western provinces, all of the major daily newspapers are owned by chains
with headquarters in Ontario.

At the same time, direct competition among daily newspapers has
been declining rapidly. There are now only six cities in Canada where
there is any form of competition among dailies published in the same
language. In three of these, the second paper trails substantially in
circulation, so that the Calgary *Herald*, the Edmonton *Journal* and the
Winnipeg *Free Press* dominate their markets. In Vancouver the two dailies
are owned by Southam. Only in Toronto and Montreal (and to a lesser
extent Quebec City) is there full competition, which survives mainly
because the newspapers have been able to find distinct audiences.[45]

Until 1980, two major chains—Southam and FP—competed
vigorously across Canada. They had competing dailies in Vancouver,
Calgary, Winnipeg, Ottawa and Montreal and operated competing news
services based in Ottawa. Not long after the Thomson interests
purchased FP in January 1980, a series of manoeuvres took place which
ended the competition. The Montreal *Star* had already ceased publication
in September 1979, leaving Southam with the English-language market
there. In July 1980, Thomson abandoned competition in Calgary, selling
the failing *Albertan* to the Toronto Sun Publishing Co., which renamed it
the *Sun*. On August 27, Thomson closed the Ottawa *Journal*, leaving the
Southam-owned *Citizen* alone in the market. The same day, Southam
folded the Winnipeg *Tribune*, leaving the *Free Press*, owned by Thomson,
the only daily there. (The Winnipeg *Sun* came into being a few months
later and was eventually purchased by Quebecor.) At the same time,
Thomson sold its 50 percent interest in Pacific Press to Southam, leaving
the latter in control of both Vancouver dailies. While there may have
been sound financial reasons for these transactions, they clearly marked
the end of meaningful newspaper competition for most of English
Canada and alarmed politicians and the interested public to the point that
the Royal Commission on Newspapers was set up and a parallel investigation was begun under the Combines Act.[46] (The Kent Commission is
discussed below.)

Charges of conspiring to lessen competition and unlawful merger
were subsequently laid against Thomson and Southam in May 1981.

Although court testimony made it clear that the two giant chains had exchanged information and discussed the future of the newspapers to be closed, the court found no public detriment, and the charges were dismissed in late 1983. It has proven exceedingly difficult to demonstrate harm under the Act and, in practice, it presents no real barrier to concentration of media ownership.[47]

Whatever one's views on concentration of ownership, there is little doubt that the media present a rather similar picture of society, in general terms. Observers agree that the media tend to reinforce the dominant institutional and cultural patterns of authority. As Edwin R. Black has pointed out, "the effective range of public debate is limited in even the freest of countries."[48] By setting the limits for public debate, the media generally exclude serious challenges to the status quo, whether from the left or the right. Even as mild a challenge as that mounted by the New Democratic Party (NDP) is too much for most editorial boards. Editorial endorsements for the NDP are so rare as to be newsworthy. In addition, most newspapers are reluctant to challenge in any direct way the dominant interests in their communities.[49] However, there is a reformist thrust to the media, both private and publicly owned, that angers some conservatives.[50] Both business and labour tend to feel aggrieved about their coverage and can cite evidence of biased coverage.[51]

What causes this status quo orientation? One explanation cites the fact that all major private media are owned by members of the business community and that it is unreasonable to expect them not to use the means at their disposal to defend their class interests.[52] Alden Nowlan has pointed out that "wherever the capitalist system exists, the newspapers will be owned by capitalists," suggesting that while they may not interfere directly in editorial operations, they can hardly be expected to mount campaigns against themselves.[53] However, many well-informed observers discount the argument that the media elite use their outlets in any direct way for propaganda purposes, noting that few if any media operations are kept operating at a loss to serve an ideology.[54] Nevertheless, it seems that journalists do learn the limits of tolerance in their newsrooms and therefore avoid submitting materials likely to be rejected. The Davey Committee suggested that the unwillingness of many newspapers to challenge existing power structures

> is the result of a certain atmosphere—an atmosphere in which boat-rocking is definitely not encouraged—and of news editors trying to read the boss's mind. This leads to journalistic sins (of omission, mostly) that result from lassitude, sloppiness, smugness, and too chummy a relationship with the local power structure. One-newspaper towns are the most frequent victims.[55]

An additional explanation, perhaps the most persuasive, is that the media cling to the "extreme middle" of the political spectrum not so much because their owners and managers are tied in with the country's power structure—though, as noted above, such ties are well-documented—as because their profits depend upon attracting mass audiences to sell to advertisers, and mass values tend to be middle-of-the-road. By reflecting these values, the mass media reinforce them, a cycle which is most frustrating to those who seek change.

News Coverage of Government and Politics

Much of what Canadians know about the political process comes from the day-to-day news coverage of government. Most major news organizations have arrangements for obtaining reports from city hall, their provincial capital and Ottawa. The news and commentary from these centres of political activity are important for the quality of public debate. Question Period in Parliament and most provincial legislatures is largely determined by the contents of the major daily newspapers each day,[56] and the attentive public also tends to take its cues from the press.[57] Parliamentary debate would be an empty ritual without the media to tell the country about it. Opposition parties rarely can mobilize support to modify government policies without media attention. The informational role of news outlets is even more important in municipal politics, where there are no political parties to mobilize voters and organize support for policies.

The largest and most important group of political reporters is in the parliamentary press gallery in Ottawa. As an "adjunct of parliament," in Mackenzie King's terms, gallery members are given special access to government documents and the activities of Parliament[58] and are expected to inform the public and represent them by holding the government accountable for its actions. As one study for the Royal Commission on Newspapers put it:

> The gallery correspondents play an important role in deciding what aspects of the political process will be communicated to the citizenry, both by screening the information presented to them by government and the [opposition] parties ... and by deciding which additional stories and features to pursue. They also provide ... interpretations of events.[59]

By 1982, the gallery had about 240 members, including reporters, editors, columnists and broadcasters, having more than doubled in size over the previous twenty years.

The gallery's growth and the arrival of a new generation of better-educated journalists have helped the gallery provide more and better coverage of federal politics than it did two decades ago. Yet much government activity goes unreported as the majority of reporters concentrate on Question Period and government announcements (with opposition reactions). Because most editors give priority to routine coverage, reporters rarely have the time to dig behind the scenes for the real story of how decisions are made. As Anthony Westell has observed, "The question period ... is almost a perfect media event. *Public personalities* come into *Conflict* over current *Controversies*, providing in one neat package the basic ingredients of a news story."[60] These stories meet the standard criteria of news but provide little information about policy development or the philosophic differences between parties. The courts, regulatory agencies and the inner workings of the civil service and cabinet are rarely covered adequately.

The work of the gallery also reflects a high rate of turnover and the fact that most reporters are generalists. Some news organizations send reporters for no longer than two or three years to avoid having them coopted into the Ottawa scene. While this approach has some merit, new reporters often lack the background to understand fully what they are covering. Even more important, perhaps, is the tendency for reporters, after a few years in the gallery, to go into government, where pay is higher and security greater. Reporters have little opportunity to specialize. Robert Fulford has commented that

> most [political] reporting, on TV or in the papers, is done by men and women who appear innocent of serious knowledge in the fields they describe. You have a sense, as you listen to them or read them, that all they know of the subject is what they heard from the last expert they met.[61]

In fact, most major news organizations—CP, SN, the *Globe and Mail*, the *Toronto Star*, *La Presse* and one or two others—do have specialists on such subjects as finance and economic affairs, energy policy, social issues, federal–provincial relations, and so on. However, they are few and they tend to shape the coverage in their areas. Since the gallery often operates according to a kind of "herd instinct," mainly because editors complain if their staff coverage differs in significant ways from that provided by the wire services, the major stories of the day are generally identified collectively and often given a common interpretation.[62] A consensus often emerges in the gallery as to what is important and how it should be presented. This pattern, combined with the rather narrow ideological range represented by the major columnists,[63] means that diversity of perspectives one would hope for in a healthy media system is often absent.

The general situation at the provincial and municipal levels is even worse. The provincial galleries face many of the same problems as the Ottawa gallery but are much smaller, allowing even less opportunity for specialization. As in Ottawa, reporters are expected to cover not only the legislature, including committees, but also the civil service, regulatory agencies and tribunals, federal–provincial negotiations and especially political parties and elections.[64] City hall reporters are rarely specialists in local government and tend to focus on personal conflicts at the council level, ignoring important committees and boards. Yet, local coverage is vital to effective citizen participation in the absence of alternative sources of information and analysis. Some observers hold the poor quality of local coverage partly responsible for the low turnouts in municipal elections.[65] In smaller centres, there appears to be a marked reluctance on the part of local media to dig into issues which might embarrass local officials or the business community.[66]

An important aspect of political reporting is the mutual dependence of reporters and their sources. Politicians need publicity to promote themselves and their programs, and reporters need information and quotes for their stories. Even the prime minister needs media attention to maintain political popularity, which is an important resource when dealing with the cabinet, negotiating with provincial premiers, or trying to persuade a private group to support government initiatives. The prime minister, on the other hand, as Ottawa's chief newsmaker, also has considerable capacity to manage the news, by timing announcements and rewarding sympathetic journalists by granting interviews, for example, and can also bypass the gallery by requesting network television time. Other prominent political figures, including the premiers, cabinet ministers, and opposition party leaders, have similar resources, but none can match the "clout" of the prime minister.[67] In all news management situations, the government has the advantage of being able to act, while opposition parties can only react or suggest. Governments often use the media to test public opinion by leaking proposals to a reporter who will value the "scoop." A positive public response often strengthens the position of those in government supporting the policy, while a negative reaction might cause it to be abandoned.[68]

The advent of the electronic Hansard in the House of Commons in October 1977 has reduced the dependence of radio and television reporters on direct access to the prime minister and other leading politicians. While such access is still sought for various reasons, reporters can now obtain clips for their stories from the audio and video tapes. Politicians can expect more media exposure but, except for the relatively few citizens who watch the proceedings on cable, the focus remains on Question Period, for both newscasts and special programs on Parliament. While no empirical studies have been done, the general view is that the advent of television in the House has increased the visibility of the opposition party leaders and critics, putting them on a more equal footing with the prime minister and cabinet.[69]

Recently, governments have turned to advocacy advertising to bypass the gallery. Using mainly television, governments have employed spot commercials to promote everything from energy conservation and physical fitness to national unity and constitutional reform. An ancillary objective, it seems clear, is to improve the government's image at public expense. Such advertisements played a major role in the 1980 Quebec referendum campaign.

While some observers feel the gallery is credulous and easily manipulated,[70] others feel that too many journalists have come to see themselves as commentators and critics rather than reporters, rendering judgments instead of reporting the arguments of the contending parties. Some see the automatic hostility to authority of many gallery members as an unjustified extension of the appropriate stance of skepticism; others say that politicians have given reporters much to be cynical about. Anthony Westell argues that the parliamentary system has an institutionalized opposition and does not need an adversarial press. Paraphrasing Walter Lippmann, he says "the central business of the press is to facilitate communication between the institutions which do the business of democratic society and the publics which are supposed to oversee them."[71]

The focus on conflict and "win/lose patterns" in political coverage, most evident in the broadcast media,[72] has led some observers to attribute a decline in popular support for Parliament to negative media coverage.[73] Press hostility to government agencies and Crown corporations shows up clearly in content studies of English-language newspapers.[74] There is also evidence of a leadership cycle in which the media select a champion and then become disillusioned as time reveals a less-than-perfect (i.e., human) leader.[75] Certainly, the media treated Prime Minister Trudeau's "peace initiative" of 1983 with considerable cynicism, with many portraying it as either a ploy to gain popular support for a government at an all-time low in the polls or as an attempt to gain a Nobel Peace Prize. There is a concern that the journalistic emphasis on conflict creates a sense of continuing crisis that alienates citizens from the political process. However, Marxist critics argue that the conflicts emphasized are not the significant conflicts in society and that the adversarial approach to government is superficial and personalized rather than aimed at the real issues of class conflict.[76]

From a liberal, democratic perspective, election coverage is particularly important. Modern campaigns depend upon extensive media coverage. Although many daily newspapers continue to endorse candidates and parties on their editorial pages, overt political bias is now rare. Nevertheless, reporters and editors, through their selection and presentation of news, help to shape the images of party leaders, define campaign issues and influence the tone of the coverage. In many respects, campaigns are contests in which media attention is the prize. The parties attempt to use the media, especially television news, to focus attention on their appeals to voters.[77]

The dominant role of television has become particularly evident in recent campaigns, primarily because party strategists believe that it is the best medium for reaching uncommitted voters.[78] The party leaders' tours are tailored for television, with speeches written to produce a ninety-second clip for the television news and cameras given the best vantage point at rallies. The commitment to "image politics" also shows up in the increasing use of television advertisements, mainly thirty- or sixty-second spots, with time to communicate symbols but not arguments. The new electoral law which partially subsidizes broadcast advertising encourages the image-making approach (while making it possible for the less well-financed New Democratic Party to join in).

The main consequence of television's dominant role is that style tends to overwhelm substance. Campaigns become contests of television performance, favouring some leaders over others on attributes which have no significance for capacity to govern. Former Conservative leader Joe Clark is a good example of a politician whose weaknesses—awkward-ness, nervousness, slight pomposity—are magnified by television. It seems likely that his "image problem" cost him a majority in the 1979 federal election and, ultimately, the party leadership (though there were many other factors involved as well). Influenced by television, the national campaigns tend to focus on party leaders, downplaying local candidates and potential cabinet ministers, as well as issues.[79]

In the end, the campaign presented in the media is a product of the interaction of media and parties. As long as the parties play by the media rules, focusing on the leaders and a few central issues and presenting their appeals in brief and dramatic fashion, they can set the campaign agenda. Only a few of the major news organizations have made any real effort to get the leaders to address issues they might wish to ignore. In the 1979 and 1980 campaigns, much of the coverage failed to relate the public debate to the concerns of average citizens. As Clive Cocking put it in reviewing the 1979 coverage: "The media did not ... generally approach this election from the standpoint of the problems facing ordinary Canadians or the major challenges facing the country."[80] In recent elections, at least, the interaction tended to produce simple flashy promises and snappy one-line put-downs of the opposition rather than thoughtful exposition of policies.[81]

Because it can make policy announcements and has a record to be examined, the governing party normally gets more than its share of media attention. But the negative tone of recent coverage, especially on newscasts, has made this a mixed blessing. In 1979 and 1980, the two major parties and their leaders received a remarkable amount of unfavourable coverage,[82] reflecting the cynical tone of political coverage noted above. Robert Fulford has commented on the "contempt," "casual insults," and "disdain" that a number of political commentators direct at politicians.[83] As Cocking notes:

> the normal journalistic reaction is not to praise but to criticize. There is a tacit understanding among journalists that to write favorably about events or people is, if not perverse, at least gutless and certain to harm one's career. Criticisms, charges and accusations produce the most jolts on television news and the biggest headlines in the papers.[84]

Much of the criticism, especially in one-liners on radio and television, is not penetrating but rather simply capricious.

Although some analysts feel that the media, by focusing on conflicts between regions and language groups, have increased hostility to the Canadian federal system,[85] research on election coverage shows that for a few weeks at least the political agenda has been much the same across the country, with few regional differences and only minor variations between French and English media.[86] Moreover, the coverage of constitutional issues also seems to have been generally integrative,[87] except when hot regional issues like language policy and energy pricing are at stake. As noted above, however, sharp differences in coverage by region and language do emerge and more research is needed on the question of the national political agenda.

The actual effect of media coverage on election outcomes remains a matter of controversy. What is clear is that the media cannot deliberately swing elections. For example, there has been a consistent drift of editorial support away from the Liberals since 1972 and in 1980 only two major dailies endorsed them. Broadcast commentators also reflect this shift. Yet the Liberals were returned to office. If the swing to the Conservatives on the nation's editorial pages is a function of concentration of ownership, it does not appear to be much of a threat. In more general terms, the most comprehensive study of voting in a Canadian election to date suggests that there is considerable potential for campaign and media effects on voting choice. The study found that less than 40 percent of Canadian voters have strong and stable party ties, and 45 percent made their voting choice during the campaign (63 percent of those who switched parties). However, the study found no significant relationship between paying attention to campaign coverage and switching parties between 1972 and 1974.[88] Nevertheless, the coverage may have reinforced voting decisions or helped to form images of leaders and perceptions of issues, regardless of attention to media, which triggered vote decisions.

The Kent Commission: Ownership and More

The previously discussed chain manoeuvres of 1980 triggered the most extensive investigation of the newspaper industry in Canadian history. The Kent Commission, given a tight ten-month deadline for fear of additional takeovers, spent more than $3 million and produced a 296-page report supplemented by eight volumes of research. The central issue—the pros and cons of chain ownership—had been debated for many years in Canada and elsewhere with no clear resolution. The Commission brought the work of the Davey Committee[89] (1970) up to date, but did not advance the debate very far.

Working from a liberal, reformist perspective, the Commission began with the assumption that the daily newspaper's importance to the democratic process means that it cannot be treated as just another business. The Commission argued that radio and television cannot perform the central functions of the daily newspaper as (1) the medium of record, (2) the primary gatherer and originator of news and commentary, (3) the agenda setter for the other media and the attentive public.[90] In examining the economics of the industry, the Commission found that: (1) competition could not be restored nor concentration rolled back without unacceptably radical measures; (2) under the circumstances, market mechanisms would not protect consumers because, with revenues derived primarily from advertising and circulation not dependent in any significant way on the quality of public affairs coverage, there was little economic incentive for publishers to spend money on quality journalism; and (3) the issue for the 1980s was the disappearance of the newspaper industry as such, as newspapers became mere profit centres in large conglomerates.[91]

The Commission took the view that conglomerate ownership is a particularly potent threat to the public service functions of newspapers. Of particular concern was the tendency it identified for conglomerates to make return on investment their highest priority, with little regard for editorial quality. The commissioners also doubted that corporate owners could be counted on to take a hands-off approach to their newsrooms—as owners had claimed they did in Commission hearings—and worried that in any case the mere possibility that a newspaper would fail to investigate abuses by its parent company would damage newspaper credibility.[92]

Having determined that competition could not be restored by government action and that breaking up the chains was not feasible, the Commission sought other remedial measures. While arguing that conglomerate control was as much of a threat to democracy as government control, it was anxious not to weaken the traditional press freedom from the state, so it developed a number of indirect measures in a search for balance. After suggesting to the industry that it "professionalize" journalism by opting for higher educational standards and more autonomy for journalists, as well as adopting self-policing mechanisms (press councils and ombudspersons), the Commission turned to possible government action, through a proposed Canada Newspaper Act. With respect to ownership, it recommended a number of restrictions designed to prevent further concentration of ownership, including cross-media ownership, and some compulsory divestiture to "correct the very worst cases of concentration that now exist."[93] These recommendations would have broken up some existing groups, limited the emergence of new ones and prevented conglomerates from purchasing newspapers.[94] The Commission also recommended a series of financial incentives to "encourage newspapers to devote more of their resources to the provision of information," to promote local private investment in newspapers and to assist wire services.[95]

On the apparent assumption that conglomerate owners are less susceptible than others to community and employee pressures for community service, the Commission recommended a series of measures to enhance journalistic independence within such chains and to open their editorial practices to public scrutiny. The "individual proprietor" whose principal business was the newspaper would be unaffected, but the "editorial autonomy" of journalists working for chain or conglomerate owners would be protected by law. In such a situation, the proposed Canada Newspaper Act would provide for a written contract for the "editor-in-chief," outlining his or her full responsibility for editorial content and guaranteeing an adequate budget. The editor would make an annual report on the newspaper's performance measured against the objectives set out in the contract, to be published in the paper and received by an Editorial Advisory Committee representing the publisher (two members), the staff (two) and the local community (three), which would discuss objectives and performance and report annually to a national Press Rights Panel within the Human Rights Commission. The three-member panel was to be appointed by Cabinet and responsible to Parliament. It was to monitor press performance and have broad powers to gather information and to approve sales and mergers of newspapers or order divestitures.[96]

When the Kent Commission *Report* was released on August 18, 1981, the industry response was hysterical denunciation, with more measured commentary coming only when the research reports began to appear a few weeks later. The most extreme criticisms saw the recommendations as a deliberate attempt to bring the press under government control.[97] More moderate critics accepted some of the diagnosis, but viewed the attempts to protect journalistic autonomy as unworkable. Many working journalists.privately supported many of the recommendations but were reluctant to speak out.

When the report was received by the Privy Council Office in July, the officials responsible felt that the report called for too much government intervention to be widely accepted and foresaw the editorial outcry. They had hoped for a more direct attack on concentration and a less bureaucratic approach to ensuring journalistic independence. They agreed with Siegel that the proposals would create a system for second-guessing journalistic decisions that would inhibit rather than promote journalistic independence.[98] While some academic observers viewed the recommendations as "mild" and felt "stronger measures might have been expected," others saw them as "draconian" and a threat to press freedom.[99] The key issue was whether one viewed the state or the conglomerates as a greater threat to democracy.

Subsequently, a task force of three senior civil servants was appointed to review the report and the research upon which it was based and to consult with the industry and working journalists before preparing recommendations. The result of this consultation was a proposed National Newspaper Act, announced by then Minister of State James Fleming in May 1982. The proposal abandoned many of the more controversial recommendations. There was no requirement that chains sell off newspapers, no tax incentives to raise editorial quality (subsidies for out-of-province correspondents were substituted), no measures to ensure the independence of editors of chain-owned newspapers, and no cabinet-appointed press rights panel.

Instead, chains were to be restricted to no more than 20 percent of national circulation, non-media companies would be required to demonstrate to the Restrictive Trade Practices Commission that any newspaper purchased would be operated independently of other interests, cross-media ownership was to be banned, except under special circumstances (a policy already in place under a Cabinet directive to the CRTC), and a Canadian Advisory Council on Newspapers was to be established. The latter was to be a fifty-member, nationally representative body insulated from government influence by an endowment and charged with hearing public complaints and reporting bi-annually on the state of the industry (based on its own research). The Minister suggested that the Council proposal might be abandoned if most dailies joined voluntary press councils.[100] By the end of 1983, most dailies were members of press councils, and critics of the monitoring proposal were hoping that no further action would be taken.[101] Defenders of the Kent Commission, like Peter Desbarats, however, pointed to the need for "a coherent program of news media research and public education" to promote quality journalism and called for a national media centre.[102]

Underlying the Kent Commission's arguments and the proposals of the federal government is the assumption that concentration of ownership, particularly in the hands of conglomerates, is bad for the democratic process. The Commission stated:

In a country that has allowed so many newspapers to be owned by a few conglomerates, freedom of the press means, in itself, only that enormous influence without responsibility is conferred on a handful of people. . . . It is as important as ever that the press should be free from the interference of the state. But it should be free from other pressures too. The purposes of freedom can be achieved only if undivided, if it withstands all the forces that tend to restrict information and opinion.[103]

Critics charge, however, that the Commission failed to demonstrate that chain or conglomerate ownership resulted in a decline in editorial quality or a reduction in the free flow of information.[104] What can we say about these key questions?

On the positive side, the Commission recognized that chain ownership does have benefits. For example, the big chains can use their resources to cross-subsidize faltering units, though there are clear limits on their willingness to do that, as the 1980 closures reminded us. Their economies of scale and access to capital permit them to take advantage of technological advances too costly for most independents and to provide chain-wide services to individual dailies. Southam, for example, operates an excellent news service, with an Ottawa bureau, including two highly rated columnists and specialist reporters, a network of regional correspondents across the country and a number of foreign correspondents, as well as staff training programs, which no individual daily could afford.[105]

The disadvantages of ownership concentration stem primarily from the possibility that a select few can exercise control over the content and operation of powerful institutions, as noted above. The Commission found little definitive evidence that chain and conglomerate ownership reduced quality or that owners interfered to protect their own interests. But they did discover a number of trends and portents that pointed in those directions. The most compelling argument, perhaps, stems from the editorial concentration that comes with ownership concentration, with important editorial decisions being made by fewer gatekeepers.[106] The chain news services, for example, while beneficial in many ways, contribute to the homogenization of coverage and comment, reducing the range of information and opinion available to the citizenry.[107]

In addition, by establishing budgets, hiring personnel, and setting standards of success, chain management clearly, though indirectly, sets the tone of its newspapers. There is good reason to believe, as the Commission did, that conglomerates are more likely than independents to promote the domination of the "bottom line" over considerations of journalistic excellence or community service than local publishers subject to community pressures.[108] Such conclusions are very difficult to prove, however. Certainly, the involvement of large corporations with diverse economic interests in media ownership exacerbates the inevitable tension between public responsibilities and private economic interests.

There is little evidence that chains dictate an editorial line on key issues from the centre, though some individual instances have been cited. In election editorials, for example, region has generally been a more powerful predictor of issue emphasis and editorial position than ownership.[109] In general, newspapers seem to reflect community norms more than ownership. Indeed, direct owner interference seems more frequent when local ownership is closely tied into the community power structure.[110]

With respect to quality, the picture is mixed. While several chain takeovers resulted in a deterioration of journalistic quality, some led to improved performance.[111] Focusing on competition, there are some measurable negative effects when a newspaper is left in a monopoly situation. For example, a recent study found that, after the folding of the Winnipeg *Free Press* and the Ottawa *Journal*, there was a clear "overall decline in the quantity and quality of municipal government news in both the surviving papers."[112] While competition can have negative effects, (promoting sensationalism, for example), it can also serve as an incentive for more comprehensive and penetrating journalism.[113]

In many respects, the battle over freedom of the press stirred up by the Kent Commission recommendations was, as Siegel says, "in actuality a conflict over power between big business and big government."[114] The citizen is in some sense a spectator, though it is really the citizen whose right to be informed is at stake. At the end of 1983, it seemed unlikely that the federal government would proceed with any form of newspaper act, though the new minister in charge, Judy Erola, suggested that there might be a new competition act to restrict concentration of ownership in many sectors of the economy, including newspapers. She also suggested that some form of national media centre might be established.[115] In the meantime, the social responsibility of the news media is enforced only by the CRTC (which has authority only over the broadcast media), the consciences of the owners and key journalists, public scrutiny through voluntary press councils, and the limits of audience acceptance.

The Political Significance of Media Patterns

Because the effects are often long term or obscured by other influences, media effects on individual attitudes and behaviour are frequently hard to trace, as we saw with voting. Nevertheless, most observers agree that the contents of the media do set the agenda for public discussion and influence the basic value system of society. The priorities of the media do tend to become over time the priorities of the public.[116] However, these priorities are largely byproducts of the quest of the media for audiences and profits. Conspiracy theories which attribute vast malevolent influence to the media through sublimal advertising and deliberate slanting of the news have had to give way to those which view the process as a form of social interaction. Media priorities emerge from the organizational needs of the media and from their interaction with political parties, interest groups, advertisers, boards of directors, government regulators, and so on. The political bias which excludes radical criticism of the status quo is more a function of the perceived limits of public tolerance than of the preferences of corporate owners. The relative absence of tough-minded investigative journalism can be explained more readily by reference to the unwillingness of publishers to spend the necessary funds and take the risk of libel suits than to corporate ideologies.[117]

As we have seen, there are certain systematic biases in our media system which may well have significant political effects. For reasons of both convenience and ideology, journalists prefer official sources and established images to more unconventional approaches. While it is true that effective mass communication is difficult without reference to widely known personalities and ideas, the resulting status quo orientation means that audiences are rarely asked to question society's basic assumptions. The media's focus on public rather than private sector abuses of power lends support to the dominant ideology of "welfare capitalism." These tendencies—found in entertainment programming as well as news and public affairs—probably promote political stability at the expense of social progress.

Other patterns, such as the weaknesses in communication across regional and linguistic lines, along with the stress on conflict and the personal side of politics, may well damage the fabric of Confederation. The denigration of political leaders and institutions in the quest for media jolts may hamper their capacity to cope with the strains in the system. The crowding out of Canadian images on television by popular American programming appears to be weakening our sense of ourselves. The scarcity of journalists with the genuine expertise to gain credibility with policy makers impoverishes public policy debate in Canada. While the individual level effects of these patterns are difficult to demonstrate, the larger effects seem clear enough.

Given the long-established involvement of government in the Canadian mass media system, many of the patterns described above pose public policy dilemmas. The problem of preserving a degree of Canadian content in the broadcasting system is increasingly serious, especially with the advent of new technologies which make cultural regulation less and less feasible.[118] With new satellite and video systems making American programs readily accessible to nearly all Canadians, private broadcasters are trying to survive primarily as distributors of U.S.

materials.[119] New strategies are obviously necessary. As Minister of Communications Francis Fox put it recently:

> If Canada does not want to create an electronic curtain, but prefers to compete vigorously in the international marketplace, we must insure that our own industry is strong and can compete against the best in the world.[120]

The new federal government broadcast strategy is, in essence, to strengthen the private production sector by subsidy, through a Broadcast Program Development Fund, and by ensuring access to CBC facilities and air time, for programs that are distinctively Canadian.[121] The new strategy also proposes to permit cable companies to import U.S. specialized channels—all-news, all-sports, all-weather, all-health, etc.—only if paired with a Canadian service for subscription.[122] Whether or not these measures will preserve Canadian content remains to be seen.

In general terms, the tensions between forces calling for government intervention and those defending private interests will continue. Because of the high cost of television broadcasting, there seems little likelihood that market forces alone will protect Canadian cultural interests or provide the diversity audiences want. The audiences for special-interest programs tend to be too small for them to be economic.[123] The dilemma faced by the Kent Commission of balancing freedom from the state and the need for state action will remain. The balance between the demands of the provinces for a larger say in communications policy and the need for a national system will also be hard to strike as we move toward 1990.

The individual reliant on the news media for information also faces dilemmas.[124] The major ones are how to find the information needed to participate effectively in the political process and how to assess the information provided. The triumph of style over substance in much coverage means that the serious citizen must seek out a mix of public affairs radio and television programming and a variety of print sources in order to obtain adequate information. Even then, the citizen might reasonably conclude that the range of information and comment is too narrow. For those generally satisfied with the economic and political status quo, the information provided by the major outlets may be sufficient, since most provide a variety of points of view within the dominant ideology. For those not satisfied with reformist approaches, however, the range of options will inevitably be too narrow. Within their accepted limits, however, several news organizations devote considerable resources to public affairs coverage and perform a valuable public service.

As we look ahead to 1990, we must note that the present media system is likely to undergo some profound changes. Since the power of the mass media derives from the capacity to decide what will be presented to mass audiences, we can expect it to diminish in the 1980s as new technologies usher in an era of audience liberation. Government regulations and market forces permitting, Canadians will have access to many channels of specialized entertainment and information programming, through cable or satellite pay-television, superstations transmitted over thousands of miles by satellite and a variety of other business- and leisure-oriented services. It may well be that in the long run the concept of a mass audience served by national networks will disappear, with networks dissolving into more specialized operations, but to date consumers have been reluctant to pay the costs of most such services. Newspapers may be transformed into information packages tailored to the interests of each subscriber.[125] Two-way communication will transcend the telephone, and special-interest groups operating their own high-tech information exchanges over thousands of miles may become common. For the immediate future, however, rapid adoption of new systems is likely to occur primarily for new technologies which expand on or make more convenient the services we are used to, like video recorders and satellite dishes.

In social terms, the new technologies will probably promote both diversity, permitting better service for minority tastes, and privatization, as people are able to withdraw into their own individual media worlds. This may mean that local communities will regain their importance. Or it may mean that communities of interest will emerge over wide areas, reducing the importance of geographic localities. In any case, maintaining a pan-Canadian perspective is likely to be an increasing challenge. Given the cost and complexity of the new technologies, class differences in the distribution of information may become more pronounced, with the information-rich having a clear advantage over the information-poor in coping with social and economic change. We are already seeing the emergence of a division between elite and mass newspapers, with the tabloids dominating one end of the market and the *Globe* and *Le Devoir* the other.

Despite these likely changes, the political implications of which are far from clear, the major patterns and issues discussed above are likely to remain. The whole apparatus of gatekeepers will continue to exist because most people will be unable to process all the information available for themselves. Market forces will continue to influence the availability of information and entertainment. For example, the question of whether or not there is a market for serious political journalism will remain. Commercial and public service norms will continue to pull in opposite directions in many areas and government intervention will still be needed to preserve Canadian input. The new information technologies will be as susceptible to monopoly and foreign control as the old. Old issues will simply reappear in new guises.

Notes

1. This is an extensively revised and updated version of "The Mass Media and the Political Process," which appeared in the first edition of this volume. Some of the ideas in this chapter were previously expressed in Fred Fletcher, "Priorities of the Media vs. Priorities of the Public," *UBC Alumni Chronicle*, Autumn 1980, pp. 4–7.
2. Leonard Kubas *et al.*, *Newspapers and Their Readers*, Research Studies on the Newspaper Industry, vol. 1, Royal Commission on Newspapers (Ottawa: Supply and Services Canada, 1981), pp. 11–12.
3. Toronto: McClelland and Stewart, 1977, p. 73.
4. See David Manning White, "The Gatekeeper: A Study in the Selection of News," *Journalism Quarterly* 26 (Fall 1950): 384.
5. A very useful discussion of gatekeeping and the factors affecting it may be found in R. H. Wagenberg *et al.*, "Media Agenda Setting in the 1979 Federal Election: Some Implications for Political Support," a paper presented at the Duke University Conference on Political Support in Canada: The Crisis Years, November 1980, pp. 13ff.
6. George Gerbner, "Television: A New Religion?" *London Free Press*, January 24, 1981. For a more detailed account of Gerbner's views, see G. Gerbner and L. Gross, "The Scary World of TV's Heavy Viewers," *Psychology Today*, April 1976, pp. 41–89, and a series of articles in *Journal of Communication*.
7. Denis McQuail, "The Influence and Effects of Mass Media," in *Mass Communication and Society*, ed. James Curran *et al.* (London: Edward Arnold, 1977), pp. 90–91.
8. John Westergaard, "Power, Class and the Media," in Curran, *Mass Communication and Society*, p. 97. Westergaard sets out this view to debunk it. For a more sympathetic treatment, see Fred S. Siebert, Theodore Peterson and Wilbur Schramm, *Four Theories of the Press* (Urbana: University of Illinois Press, 1956), pp. 39–103.
9. Ralph Miliband, quoted in Denis McQuail, "The Influence and Effects of the Mass Media," in Curran, *Mass Communication and Society*, p. 89. The general argument is taken from Wallace Clement, *The Canadian Corporate Elite: An Analysis of Economic Power* (Toronto: McClelland and Stewart, 1975), pp. 270–86.
10. Clement, *The Canadian Corporate Elite*, pp. 325–43.
11. Ibid., p. 343.
12. Special Senate Committee on the Mass Media, *The Uncertain Mirror*, vol. 1 of the *Report* (Ottawa: Queen's Printer, 1970), p. 74.
13. Paul Rutherford, *The Making of the Canadian Media* (Toronto: McGraw-Hill, 1978), p. 1. This discussion of the development of the Canadian media draws on Rutherford and W. A. Kesterton, *A History of Journalism in Canada* (Toronto: McClelland and Stewart, 1967).
14. Arthur Siegel, *Politics and the Media in Canada* (Toronto: McGraw-Hill, 1983), p. 194. See also Royal Commission on Newspapers, *Report* (Ottawa: Supply and Services Canada, 1981), pp. 119–33, hereinafter cited as Kent Commission.
15. Joseph Scanlon, "Canada Sees the World Through U.S. Eyes: A Case Study in Cultural Domination," *The Canadian Forum*, September 1974, pp. 34–39. A

re-examination of the issue in 1983 came to a similar conclusion: Joseph Scanlon and Al Farrell, "No Matter How It Sounds or Looks, It's Probably Not Canadian," paper presented at the Conference on Media and Foreign Policy, University of Windsor, October 29, 1983. It must be noted, of course, that the Southam News service (SN), and the *Globe and Mail* maintain a number of foreign correspondents of their own and devote significant resources to overseas coverage.

16. On radio and television news, see Scanlon and Farrell, "No Matter How It Sounds," pp. 5–12 and Debra Clarke, "Second-hand News: Production and Reproduction at a Major Ontario Television Station," in *Communication Studies in Canada*, ed. Liora Salter (Toronto: Butterworths, 1981), pp. 20–51.

17. The ten best-selling magazines in Canada in 1983 were *Reader's Digest, Chatelaine, TV Guide, National Geographic, Maclean's, Canadian Legion Magazine, Canadian Living, Woman's Day, Family Circle* and *Penthouse* (*Globe and Mail,* January 24, 1984, p. 3).

18. For details of these developments, see Rutherford, *The Making of the Canadian Media,* pp. 77–123; Patricia Hindley *et al., The Tangled Net: Basic Issues in Canadian Communications* (Vancouver: J.J. Douglas, 1977), Chapter 4; Frank W. Peers, *The Politics of Canadian Broadcasting: 1920–1951* (Toronto: University of Toronto Press, 1969) and *The Public Eye: Television and the Politics of Canadian Broadcasting* (Toronto: University of Toronto Press, 1979).

19. Peers, *The Public Eye,* p. 409.

20. Martha Fletcher and Frederick J. Fletcher, "Communications and Confederation: Jurisdiction and Beyond," in *Canada Challenged: The Viability of Confederation,* ed. R.B. Byers and R.W. Reford (Toronto: Canadian Institute of International Affairs, 1979), pp. 171–72.

21. For details, see Hindley, *The Tangled Net,* Chapter 5.

22. For a helpful discussion of these issues, see Katherine Swinton, "Advertising and Canadian Cable Television—A Problem in International Communications Law," *Osgoode Hall Law Journal* 15 (December 1977): 563. See also Hindley, *The Tangled Net,* Chapter 6.

23. This has been made clear in a series of Gallup polls over the past thirty years.

24. Canadian Radio-television and Telecommunications Commission, "Statement by Chairman John Meisel on CRTC Decision 82-240 (Pay-Television), Ottawa, 18 March, 1982." For details of the decision, see CRTC, "Decision 82-240," (Ottawa, March 18, 1982). For a useful summary, see Udo Salewsky, "Pay TV, Canadian Style" *Cable Communications Magazine* 48 (April 1982): 11–17.

25. CRTC, "Decision 82-240," p. 70.

26. CTV does produce a successful children's series, "The Littlest Hobo," and has recently been involved in several made-for-television movies. For a fuller discussion of the Canadian content issue, see Hindley, *The Tangled Net,* Chapter 6 and Robert E. Babe, *Canadian Television Broadcasting, Structure, Performance and Regulation* (Ottawa: Economic Council of Canada, 1979).

27. As part of a review of federal government cultural policy, which began with the *Report of the Federal Cultural Policy Review Committee,* the Department of Communications has asked CBC Television to reduce its dependence on

advertising, increase Canadian content significantly and fill 50 percent of its air time with programs purchased from independent producers, reducing substantially its own in-house production, among other reforms. See Canada, Department of Communications, *Building for the Future: Towards a Distinctive CBC* (Ottawa: Supply and Services, October 1983).

28. While anglophone Canadians spend about five hours per week watching CBC television, they still spend more than 75 percent of their viewing time watching non-Canadian programs. But then more than 75 percent of the programs available to Canadian households are non-Canadian. See Pierre Juneau, "A Report to Shareholders," notes for an address to the Broadcast Executives Society, Toronto, January 18, 1984.

29. A W. Johnson, *Broadcast Priorities for the 1980's*, CBC Corporate Statement to the CRTC, 1978, p. 3.

30. See, for example, E.D. Tate and R.L. Trach, "The Effects of U.S. Television Programmes upon Canadian Beliefs about Legal Procedure," *Canadian Journal of Communication* 6 (Spring 1980).

31. John Meisel, "Five Steps to Survival," speech at Conference on Mass Communication and Canadian Nationhood, York University, Toronto, April 10, 1981.

32. F. W. Peers, "Canada and the United States: Comparative Origins and Approaches to Broadcasting Policy," paper presented at the Canadian–U.S. Conference on Communication Policy, Centre for Inter-American Relations, March 11, 1983, New York.

33. Provincial governments have increasingly viewed the new communication technologies as tools for economic and cultural development within their jurisdictions. As one study put it: "In recent years, other provinces have joined Quebec in rejecting any notion that culture is primarily a federal responsibility or that national unity requires the development of a single dominant 'national culture.'" Fletcher and Fletcher, "Communications and Confederation," p. 172.

34. The *Globe* now offers home and office delivery of its national edition in most major cities and has nearly half of its total circulation outside of Toronto. However, from a national perspective it is essentially an elite rather than a mass medium.

35. W. Brian Stewart, "Canadian Social System and Canadian Broadcasting Audiences," in *Communications in Canadian Society*, ed. Benjamin D. Singer (Don Mills, Ont.: Addison-Wesley, 1983), p. 22.

36. Frederick Elkin, "Communications Media and Identity Formation in Canada," in Singer, *Communications in Canadian Society*, p. 150.

37. See Carman Cumming, Mario Cardinal and Peter Johansen, *Canadian News Services*, Royal Commission on Newspapers, Research studies on the newspaper industry, vol. 6 (Ottawa: Supply and Services Canada, 1981), pp. 51–60.

38. Many of the relevant studies are summarized in Andre H. Caron and David E. Payne, "Media and Canadian Politics: General and Referendum Applications," paper presented at the Duke University Conference on Political Support in Canada: The Crisis Years, November 1980, pp. 2–5 and 11–12. See also Andre H. Caron, Chantal Mayrand and David E. Payne,

"l'Imagerie politique à la télévision: les derniers jours de la campagne référendaire," *Revue canadienne de science politique* 16 (septembre 1983): 473-88. On the Quebec press, see Dominique Clift, "French Journalism in Quebec: Solidarity on a Pedestal," in *Canadian Newspapers: The Inside Story*, ed. Walter Stewart (Edmonton: Hurtig, 1980), pp. 205-18. See also Lysiane Gagnon, "Journalism and Ideologies in Quebec," and Florian Sauvageau, "French-Speaking Journalists on Journalism," in *The Journalists*, Royal Commission on Newspapers, Research Studies on the Newspaper Industry, vol. 2 (Ottawa: Supply and Services Canada, 1981), pp. 19-52.

39. Caron and Payne, "Media and Canadian Politics," pp. 4-5.
40. Siegel, *Politics and the Media in Canada*, p. 228.
41. The figures in this paragraph are drawn from Kent Commission, pp. 1-14 and 87-103 and Siegel, *Politics and the Media in Canada*, pp. 110-124.
42. Kent Commission, pp. 90-92.
43. The Power Corporation owns *La Presse* and three other dailies. Its other business interests are discussed in Kent Commission, pp. 94-95.
44. For details of the Irving holdings, see Kent Commission, pp. 95-96. See also Alden Nowlan, "What about the Irvings?" in Stewart, *Canadian Newspapers*, pp. 63-72.
45. The Calgary figures in 1983 were: *Herald*, 145,317; *Sun*, 52,190. For Edmonton, they were: *Journal*, 186,194; *Sun*, 66,626. The Winnipeg *Free Press* (196,065) clearly led the *Sun* (41,427). However, the three Suns all have substantial capital behind them. The Alberta tabloids are owned by the Toronto Sun Publishing Company and the Winnipeg tabloid by Quebecor, Inc., a major publisher of French tabloids in Quebec.
46. This paragraph is taken in large part from Frederick J. Fletcher, *The Newspaper and Public Affairs*, Royal Commission on Newspapers, Research Studies on the Newspaper Industry, vol. 7 (Ottawa: Supply and Services Canada, 1981), p. 2. For more details, see Siegel, *Politics and the Media in Canada*, pp. 135-36 and Kent Commission, Chapters 1 and 3.
47. See Kent Commission, pp. 57-60. The charges against Southam and Thomson were dismissed on October 28 and December 9 in judgments handed down by Mr. Justice William Anderson of the Supreme Court of Ontario.
48. E. R. Black, *Politics and the News* (Toronto: Butterworths, 1982), p. 54.
49. See Black, *Politics and the News*, pp. 54-56 and 140-45, for a penetrating discussion of these issues.
50. One observer suggests that there is an implicit agreement between reformist journalists and generally conservative publishers that newspapers may take a reformist stance on social issues as long as economic matters are treated conservatively. Conrad Winn, "Mass Communication," in *Political Parties in Canada*, ed. C. Winn and J. McMenemy (Toronto: McGraw-Hill, 1976), p. 132.
51. See, for example, Graham Knight, "Strike Talk: A Case Study of News," *Canadian Journal of Communication* 8 (June 1982) 3: 61-79 and Judy L. Gale and Mark N. Wexler, "The Image of Business in Canadian-Produced Television," *Canadian Journal of Communication* (Spring 1983): p. 15-36.
52. Clement, *The Canadian Corporate Elite*, p. 285.

53. Nowlan, "What about the Irvings?" p. 68.
54. Westell, *New Society*, pp. 77–78.
55. *The Uncertain Mirror*, p. 87.
56. In Ottawa, the key newspaper is the *Globe and Mail*. It "often writes the agenda for Parliament and for other papers which report on Parliament." Anthony Westell, "The Press: Adversary or Channel of Communication," in *Parliament, Policy and Representation*, ed. Harold D. Clarke *et. al.* (Toronto: Methuen, 1980), p. 27.
57. For example, when the minister of finance makes the budget speech, reporters are locked up with advance copies and given full briefings by government officials in an attempt to improve the quality of reporting.
58. Fletcher, *The Newspaper and Public Affairs*, Chapter 2.
59. Ibid., p. 50. Chapter 4 of this volume presents a general discussion of the press galleries in Ottawa and the ten provincial capitals.
60. Anthony Westell, "Reporting on the Nation's Business," in *Journalism, Communication and the Law*, ed. Stuart Adam (Scarborough: Prentice-Hall, 1976), p. 63.
61. *Saturday Night*, October 1977. Even with respect to the legislative process itself, only a dozen or so gallery members could be called expert.
62. Westell, "Reporting the Nation's Business," p. 63.
63. Fletcher, *The Newspaper and Public Affairs*, pp. 55 and 69.
64. For an overview of provincial press galleries, see Ibid., Chapter 4. One of the few case studies of a provincial gallery is Frederick J. Fletcher, "The Crucial and the Trivial: News Coverage of Provincial Politics in Ontario," *The Government and Politics of Ontario*, 2nd ed., ed. Donald C. MacDonald (Toronto: Van Nostrand Reinhold, 1980), pp. 245–71.
65. The argument is summarized in Fletcher, *The Newspaper and Public Affairs*, pp. 94–96.
66. The city hall reporter and managing editor of the Brampton *Sun* were recently fired for doing just that. Dave Silburt, "Local Journalists Eaten by Politicians—A Case Study that the Kent Commission Didn't See," *Content*, April–May 1983, pp. 4–7, 24. For a general discussion of the issue, see Black, p. 140.
67. See Frederick J. Fletcher, "The Prime Minister as Public Persuader," in *Apex of Power*, 2nd ed., ed. Thomas A. Hockin (Scarborough: Prentice-Hall, 1977), pp. 86–111, and Black, *Politics and the News*, 229–31.
68. A typical "trial balloon" was released in Ontario in 1979 when a cabinet minister let it be known that the government was considering allowing the sale of beer in the province's ball parks. Vociferous opposition from temperance groups and residents living near the parks led to the proposal's withdrawal, but it was later proceeded with when polls showed widespread support.
69. Richard D. Price and Harold D. Clarke, "Television in the House of Commons," in Clarke, *Parliament, Policy and Representation*, pp. 58–84.
70. See, for example, Walter Stewart, *Shrug: Trudeau in Power* (Toronto: McClelland and Stewart, 1971), pp. 203–21.
71. Westell, "The Press: Adversary or Channel of Communication," p. 49.
72. Carman Cumming, "The Coming Battle over Media Power," *Carleton*

The Mass Media and Politics   225

Journalism Review 1 (1977). See also Black, *Politics and the News*, Chapter 8.
73. Allan Kornberg and Judith D. Wolfe, "Parliament, the Media and the Polls," in Clarke, *Parliament, Policy and Representation*, pp. 35–58.
74. See, for example, James P. Winter and Alan Frizzell, "The Treatment of State-Owned vs. Private Corporations in English Canadian Dailies," *Canadian Journal of Communication* 6 (Winter 1979–80): 1–11.
75. Westell, "Reporting the Nation's Business," pp. 66–67.
76. See, for example, Philip Resnick, "Political Economy and Class Analysis: A Marxist Perspective," in *Approaches to Canadian Politics*, ed. John H. Redekop (Scarborough: Prentice-Hall, 1978), p. 362.
77. See Frederick J. Fletcher, "Playing the Game: The Media and the 1979 Campaign," in *Canada at the Polls, 1979 and 1980: A Study of the General Elections*, ed. Howard R. Penniman (Washington, DC: American Enterprise Institute, 1981), pp. 280–321.
78. This perspective emerged clearly in discussions with party strategists at the Conference on Politics and the Media at Erindale College, University of Toronto, June 12–13, 1980. See Margo Northey, ed., *Politics and the Mass Media* (Montreal: Reader's Digest Foundation, 1981). Some confirmation for this view may be found in Harold D. Clarke, Jane Jenson, Lawrence LeDuc and Jon H. Pammett, *Political Choice in Canada* (Toronto: McGraw-Hill, 1979), Chapters 9–12.
79. Content studies of campaign coverage tend to show that leaders are featured in about one-third of all national television items and more than half of front-page newspaper stories. They are mentioned in a much higher proportion. Local candidates get little attention. See, for example, Clarke, *Political Choice*, pp. 278–81, and Fletcher, "Playing the Game," pp. 295ff.
80. Clive Cocking, *Following the Leaders: A Media Watcher's Diary of Campaign '79* (Toronto: Doubleday, 1980), p. 295.
81. Fletcher, "Playing the Game," pp. 319–20.
82. On average, negative references to Liberal leader Pierre Trudeau and Conservative leader Joe Clark outnumbered positive ones by more than two to one. E.D. Briggs, W.I. Romanow, W.C. Soderlund and R.H. Wagenberg, "Television News and the 1979 Federal Election," paper presented at the founding meeting of the Canadian Communication Association, Montreal, June 1980, esp. Table 3, and Fletcher, "Playing the Game," pp. 306–12.
83. *Saturday Night*, October 1977.
84. Cocking, *Following the Leaders*, p. 111.
85. Rutherford, *The Making of the Canadian Media*, p. 122.
86. Wagenberg, "Media Agenda Setting," pp. 32–38.
87. W.C. Soderlund, R.H. Wagenberg, E.D. Briggs and R.C. Nelson, "Regional and Linguistic Agenda-Setting in Canada: A Study of Newspaper Coverage of Issues Affecting Political Integration in Canada in 1976," *Canadian Journal of Political Science* 13 (June 1980): 347–56.
88. Clarke, *Political Choice*, pp. 276, 290, 306.
89. Special Senate Committee on the Mass Media, *Report* (Ottawa: Queen's Printer, 1970). 3 vols. See especially vol. 1, *The Uncertain Mirror*.
90. Kent Commission, pp. 215–17. For a slightly different summary of the Commission's findings, see Siegel, *Politics and the Media in Canada*, pp. 139–46.

The reader should note that the authors of this article worked for the Kent Commission as contract researchers.

91. Kent Commission, p. 219.

92. Ibid., pp. 219–25, 233.

93. Ibid., p. 237.

94. Ibid., pp. 238–44.

95. Ibid., pp. 244–45, 252–55.

96. Kent Commission, pp. 245–52. The provisions summarized here are set out in considerable detail in the report and are hedged with measures to protect press freedom.

97. For a summary of industry response, see Donald C. Wallace, "The Kent Commission: The Fourth Estate Under Attack," in *Canadian Annual Review, 1981*, ed. R.B. Byers (Toronto: University of Toronto Press, forthcoming).

98. Siegel, *Politics and the Media in Canada*, p. 150.

99. The quotes are from Thelma McCormack, "The Political Culture and the Press of Canada," *Canadian Journal of Political Science* 16 (September 1983): 452 and Andrew Osler, "The Heart of Press Curbs in Canada is Still Beating," *Globe and Mail*, January 10, 1984, p. 7.

100. Jim Fleming, *Government Proposals on Freedom of the Press in Relation to the Canadian Daily Newspaper Industry* (Ottawa: Supply and Services Canada, May 1982).

101. Osler, *Globe and Mail*.

102. "A Media Centre Could Be a Saving Grace," *Globe and Mail*, January 10, 1984, p. 7.

103. Kent Commission, p. 217.

104. See Siegel, *Politics and the Media in Canada*, p. 147 and sources cited.

105. Kent Commission, pp. 93, 101–2, 177.

106. Kent Commission, pp. 166–68. For a fuller discussion of editorial concentration, see Fletcher, *The Newspaper and Public Affairs*, pp. 4–5, 114–15.

107. Kent Commission, pp. 166–67 and Fletcher, *The Newspaper and Public Affairs*, pp. 52–56, 67–68.

108. Kent Commission, pp. 101–3.

109. Studies of Canadian newspaper coverage and editorial comment on the 1972, 1974 and 1979 federal elections shows no tendency for chains to present a united front. The chain newspapers were no more likely to agree among themselves on the issues to emphasize on their news and editorial pages than with independents or dailies in other chains. These findings are summarized in a forthcoming book, *Media and Elections in Canada* (Toronto: Holt, Rinehart and Winston, 1984) by the University of Windsor group: E.D. Briggs, W.I. Romanow, W.C. Soderlund and R.H. Wagenberg.

110. See John A. Hannigan, "Ideology, Elites, and the Canadian Mass Media," in Singer, *Communications in Canadian Society*, pp. 55–61 and Fletcher, *Newspaper and Public Affairs*, pp. 35–48.

111. See Fletcher, *The Newspaper and Public Affairs*, pp. 36–37.

112. Katharine Trim with Gary Pizante and James Yaraskavitch, "The Effect of Monopoly on the News: A Before and After Study of Two Canadian One Newspaper Towns," *Canadian Journal of Communication* 9 (Summer 1983): 52. See also Daphne F. Gottlieb, "The Media and Local Politics Coverage in Victoria," report for the Royal Commission on Newspapers, 1981.

113. Fletcher, *The Newspaper and Public Affairs*, pp. 40–42.

114. Siegel, *Politics and the Media in Canada*, p. 149.

115. *Globe and Mail*, January 10, 1984, p. 7.

116. This is the thrust of the agenda-setting research in the U.S. For a summary, see D.L. Shaw and M.E. McCombs, *The Emergence of American Political Issues: The Agenda-Setting Function of the Press* (St. Paul, MN: West, 1977). For a Canadian case study, see J.P. Winter, C.H. Eyal and A.H. Rogers, "Issue-Specific Agenda-Setting: The Whole as Less than the Sum of the Parts," *Canadian Journal of Communication* 8 (January 1982): 1–10.

117. The proposition that the absence of hard-hitting (and costly) investigative journalism is more a reflection of tight editorial budgets than political timidity as such is supported by a wide range of anecdotal evidence. Veteran journalist and author Walter Stewart reports that

> those who work for FP noticed an immediate shift of emphasis after the Thomson takeover. Our communications with head office no longer concerned news coverage; we were debating instead whether our Edmonton correspondent could have two waste paper baskets, or confine himself to one. Our new bosses also killed plans for a Toronto bureau, and closed the Washington bureau. This was not because FP was losing money ... but because the drive to make more money superseded the drive to cover the news.

"No Virginia, There is no Lou Grant," in Stewart, *Canadian Newspapers*, pp. 17–18. In the end, the entire FP news service was closed down.

118. R. Brian Woodrow and Kenneth B. Woodside, "Epilogue," in *The Introduction of Pay-TV in Canada: Issues and Implications*, ed. Woodrow and Woodside (Montreal: Institute for Research on Public Policy, 1982), p. 226.

119. Peers, "Canada and the U.S.," pp. 29–30.

120. *Culture and Communications: Key Elements in Canada's Economic Future* (Ottawa: Department of Communications, November 3, 1983), p. 14.

121. See Department of Communications, *Building for the Future*. The CBC supports most of the Department of Communication proposals, while calling for more funds. See *The Strategy of the CBC* (CBC, 1983). Denis Harvey, new head of CBC's English television service, commented in an interview that: "Television is still bought by most people to be entertained, not to be informed. You can't just tell the story of this land through information programming [which does have high ratings]." He plans to produce more high-quality and popular drama "about this country, about our problems, our social issues, especially our triumphs," Rick Groen, "Harvey Tackles CBC Challenge," *Globe and Mail*, January 28, 1984, p. E1.

122. Val Ross, "A Strategy for Cultural Revival," *Maclean's*, November 7, 1983, pp. 76–77.

123. This argument is made for British television in Andrew Ehrenberg and Patrick Barwise, "Do We Need to Regulate TV Programmes," *Intermedia* 11 (July–September 1983): 12–15.

124. Some assistance for the individual may be found in "The Press and Politics: A Consumer's Guide," in *Canadian Politics Through Press Reports*, ed. D.C. Wallace and F.J. Fletcher. (Toronto: Oxford University Press, forthcoming). See also B. Zwicker and D. MacDonald, "A News Consumer's Guide," in *The*

News: Inside the Canadian Media, ed. Zwicker and MacDonald (Ottawa: Deneau, 1983), pp. 307–32.
125. See Thomas L. McPhail, "The Future of Canadian Communications," in Singer, *Communications in Canadian Society,* pp. 73–82.

Further Readings

Audley, Paul. *Canada's Cultural Industries: Broadcasting, Publishing, Records and Film.* Toronto: Lorimer, 1983.

Black, Edwin R. *Politics and the News.* Toronto: Butterworths, 1982.

Clement, Wallace. *The Canadian Corporate Elite: An Analysis of Economic Power.* Toronto: McClelland and Stewart, 1975.

Fletcher, Frederick J. *The Newspaper and Public Affairs.* Vol. 7 of Research Studies on the Newspaper Industry for the Royal Commission on Newspapers. Ottawa: Supply and Services Canada, 1981.

———. "Playing the Game: The Mass Media and the 1979 Campaign." In *Canada at the Polls, 1979 and 1980: A Study of the General Elections,* edited by Howard R. Penniman. Washington, DC: American Enterprise Institute, 1981.

Fletcher, Martha, and Frederick J. Fletcher. "Communications and Confederation: Jurisdiction and Beyond." In *Canada Challenged: The Viability of Confederation,* edited by R.B. Byers and R.W. Reford. Toronto: Canadian Institute of International Affairs, 1979.

Lyman, Peter. *Canada's Video Revolution: Pay-TV, Home Video and Beyond.* Toronto: Lorimer, 1983.

Peers, Frank W. *The Public Eye: Television and the Politics of Canadian Broadcasting, 1952–1968.* Toronto: University of Toronto Press, 1979.

Royal Commission on Newspapers. (Kent Commission) Ottawa: Supply and Services Canada, 1981.

Rutherford, Paul. *The Making of the Canadian Media.* Toronto: McGraw-Hill, 1978.

Siegel, Arthur. *Politics and the Media in Canada.* Toronto: McGraw-Hill, 1983.

Singer, Benjamin D., ed. *Communications in Canadian Society.* Don Mills, Ont.: Addison-Wesley, 1983.

Chapter 10

Elites, Classes and Power in Canada
Leo V. Panitch

"In Toronto there are no classes . . . just the Masseys and the masses." This little ditty, perhaps reflecting a centralist bias characteristic of Canadian politics itself, captures graphically the way political scientists have often approached the study of power in Canadian society. Inequalities of political and economic power are rarely denied and indeed are frequently a direct object of study. In general, however, political scientists have operated with a somewhat impoverished—and misleading—set of concepts in trying to understand these inequalities. As in the case of "the Masseys and the masses," they have tended to categorize society in terms of a gradation of rich, middle and poor, and to examine politics in terms of elites with power and masses without. In employing such imprecise and oversimplified generalizations, social scientists have obscured and mystified the real links between social, economic and political power in Canada.

Who, then, are these "elites" and "masses"? Occasionally, and most usually in the context of voting behaviour studies, the "masses" are divided into statistical classes grouped together on the basis of income, occupational status or the "common sense" self-perception of individuals themselves in class terms. Insofar as actual socioeconomic collectivities of people are dealt with, this has usually been done in terms of the concept of "interest groups"—formal organizations of farmers, workers, businesspeople, etc. Those who lead such organizations are usually designated as "elites" and differentiated from the "non-decision-making" mass of their members. In this view, *power* is seen in terms of *relations among elites.* It is extended to the study of relationships between elites and masses only through the highly structured contexts of elections, opinion polls and interest group "demands."

The problem with this approach is not that it sees politics as isolated from socioeconomic structure. On the contrary, the behaviour of elites is very much seen as conditioned by the socioeconomic "background" of the individuals who compose them, and by the highly structured demands coming through voting or interest groups from society. As in the

229

celebrated political system approach, which serves as a conceptual framework for Canada's most widely used introductory political science text,[1] the determinant of politics is seen as "demands" coming from the "environment" of politics.

It is often alleged that what is wrong here is that the political system is a "black box" which reveals little of the inner workings of government, where the most salient elites make their decisions. There is something in this argument, but what is even more striking is the "black hole"—the environment. We are told that scarcity prevails here and that demands are generated by conflicts over resources, but a systematic examination of the way in which our economy is structured to cope with material scarcity, of the social relations that result between people, and thus of the concrete material clash of social forces that goes on is seldom undertaken. References to individual competition or intergroup competition, as with rich and poor, elite and mass, may give us clues, but because of their "grossness" as categories, because of their abstraction from concrete social relationships between people in a capitalist society such as Canada's, they do not contribute enough to our understanding of what is acknowledged to be the determinant element of politics—the socioeconomic system in which politics is embedded.

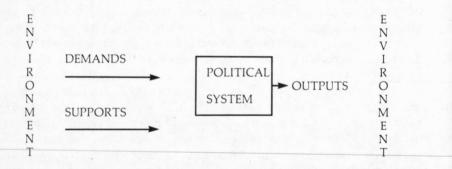

To properly understand the relationship between society and politics involves taking an analysis of society seriously, which itself entails going beyond categories such as elite, mass and group. It involves getting down to the material social relationships between people, their common experiences in terms of these relationships, and the actual collectivities they form and the struggles they enter into in handling these experiences. This is what a *class analysis* as opposed to an *elite analysis* of society and politics is designed to do. In Canada—and even in Toronto—there *are* classes, and it is their history of contradictory relations to one another, and the balance of power that results at given periods and instances, that establishes the foundation of politics, including setting the extent and limit of the power of the Masseys, or that of any other "elite."

Elite Analysis in Canada

There is fairly widespread agreement among political scientists that what is meant by the term "democracy" as applied to a contemporary political system is "that institutional arrangement for arriving at political decisions in which individuals acquire the power to decide by means of a competitive struggle for the people's vote." The people themselves do not decide, and therefore power does not immediately reside with the people, but rather "the people have the opportunity of accepting or refusing the men [sic] who are to rule them."[2] This is an "elitist" conception of democracy which does not require or expect high citizen participation in public affairs beyond the act of choosing between competing teams of leaders. A degree of *elite-pluralism* is guaranteed in this system, at least with a view to elections and formal parliamentary opposition, by a two-party or multi-party system. Moreover, in the case of a federal system like Canada, the elite-teams compete for votes in various jurisdictions, and this further tends to multiply the extent of elite-pluralism. Finally, insofar as freedom of association prevails, it is recognized that the decision-making elites may be subject to a process of interest group competition for influence upon them.

This system of "elite-pluralism," however much it may be demarcated from broader, more mass-participatory conceptions of democracy, is not to be sneezed at as a minimal description of "actually existing" liberal democracies. It captures, albeit in too formal and unhistorical a fashion, some of the basic differences between a polity such as ours and an authoritarian regime. Yet serious students of power in Canadian society have understandably not been willing to rest content with minimal descriptions of this sort. They have wanted to know *who* these competing teams of leaders are in socioeconomic terms and the extent to which they reflect in their competition and decision making a narrow or broad range of approaches to public issues and concerns. They have wanted to know the relationship between the democratically elected political elites and those decision makers in institutional spheres, such as the private corporations that dominate our economy, which are not democratically elected. To speak of elite-pluralism properly, they have recognized, entails examining the degree of *autonomy* political elites have from, at least, the elites that exercise power (in the sense of decision making) in the economic sphere.

John Porter's *The Vertical Mosaic*[3] is the classic Canadian study which asks these questions within the elite-pluralist conceptual framework, and it is for the most part better than similar studies of other liberal democratic societies. Porter began with an examination of the broad social differentiations between people in Canada in terms of demographic patterns, occupational and income distribution, and ethnic and educational inequalities. Although he discerned persistent "class" inequalities in Canada, in keeping with the elite–mass dichotomy of his conceptual approach, he tended to treat class as merely a "statistical category" imposed on society by the researcher rather than an actual collectivity of people with real social cohesion and power. Instead, he reserved the study of social cohesion and power only to the "elites"—to those identifiable individuals who occupied decision-making positions at the top of all the major institutional orders which might be said to perform "essential tasks" for Canadian society. Society is seen to be composed of institutional power centres in the state, the economy and the ideological sphere, with a set of elites in each (political and bureaucratic; corporate and labour; mass media, educational and religious) which have power by virtue of the necessity of institutions to be "directed and coordinated," itself entailing "the recognized right to make decisions on behalf of a group of people." Thus turning the question of power into a matter of "authority," Porter went on to isolate the principal authority roles in each institution, to locate the individuals who filled these roles, to examine their social backgrounds, and to study the degree of elite cohesion within each power centre and among them. His test of Canada's claim to democracy rested, then, not on popular involvement in, or resistance to, the exercise of power, but rather on whether the elites came from different social backgrounds and whether they were autonomous from, and competitive with, one another.

Porter's findings, covering the 1940–1960 period, substantially undermined the conventional wisdom of treating Canada as an "elite-pluralist democracy." Examining the boards of directors of the 183 corporations which dominated the Canadian economy in terms of assets and sales, he found an internally cohesive and concentrated elite characterized by extensive interlocking directorships between corporations, recruitment on the basis of "upper-class" family ties and exclusive private school education, common ethnic (Anglo-Saxon) origins and religious (Anglican) affiliations, common membership in exclusive social clubs, and a shared commitment to a "free-enterprise" capitalist value system.

In contrast, the political and bureaucratic elites (federal Cabinet ministers, provincial premiers, Supreme Court and provincial chief justices in the first case, and highly paid civil servants in the second) were somewhat less exclusive in terms of social backgrounds, although still drawn from a narrow "middle class" excluding some 90 percent of most Canadians. The political elite was characterized by a high degree of cooptation from other elites, lacked a discrete internal career structure, and Cabinet membership itself often served as a stepping stone for entry into the corporate elite. In terms of values it was ideologically cohesive, but with an obsession with national unity ("From Sea to Sea" as the formative credo of politics) which was innately conservative in terms of failing to express substantive values ("Liberty, Equality, Fraternity," "All

Power to the People") that could challenge the economic elite's private property-oriented value system. As such he saw Canada as burdened with an "avocational" political elite, particularly weak as a base for guaranteeing pluralism. As for the ideological elite, neither the mass media, nor religious leaders, nor intellectuals had the independence or the inclination to challenge critically the power of the economic elite.

Porter concluded that the Canadian system of power relations was best seen as a "confraternity of power" rather than as a set of competing, autonomous elites. The various elites were "operating more or less within the same value system, a condition brought about in part by the establishments of kinship and class. Any examination of career interchanging, the membership of boards, commissions and councils, and the structure of political parties would probably show the dominance of the corporate world over the other institutional systems."

Labour was the one elite Porter studied that was marked off from this "confraternity." Alone in being drawn from "lower-class" social backgrounds, the labour elite was questionably an elite at all in that they operated in the economic sphere as an oppositional element, excluded from decision-making positions. In any case, their role did not much extend beyond collective bargaining in the economic sphere, since they "rarely shared in the informal aspects of the confraternity of power." They were on "the periphery of the overall structure of power, called in by others when the 'others' consider it necessary, or when the labour leaders demand a hearing from the political elite." Defining democracy as entailing equality of opportunity for individuals, and competition among elites, Porter concluded: "Canada ... has a long way to go to become in any sense a thoroughgoing democracy."[4]

Studies more recent than Porter's have produced similar conclusions. Wallace Clement's examination of the corporate (and mass media) elites in the early 1970s[5] found a greater degree of corporate concentration (with 113 firms now dominant in the economy), even more extensive interlocking directorships among them, and a higher degree of social exclusiveness in terms of "upper-class" family background than there had been twenty years before. Clement stressed the greater structural differentiation within the corporate elite, distinguishing between a dominant fraction of Canadian-controlled corporations in the financial, utilities and transportation sectors, and a predominance of foreign-owned corporations in the manufacturing and resource sectors, with Canadian corporate executives located there as "compradors." But the interlocks between these "fractions" were extensive, as Canadian bankers were allied with American multinational capital. As for the mass media elite, Clement showed that they functioned as part of the corporate sphere. And he demonstrated that some 40 percent of the corporate elite themselves had, or had close relatives who had, occupied positions in the important political or bureaucratic offices.

Dennis Olsen's recently published study *The State Elite*, covering the 1961–1973 period, found marginal changes from what Porter had described, particularly pertaining to greater French and "other ethnic" representation. In the case of the political elite, he found that the elite had changed only "very slowly and not at all in some respects," in that it was still dominated by those from a narrow band of middle- and upper-middle-class origins and still lacked a discrete political career structure. As for the bureaucrats, he found that "the new elite is more open, more heterogeneous and probably more meritocratic, than the old," but that "the overall pattern is one of the marked persistence of both social class and ethnic preferences in recruitment." And he concluded that the "middle class state elite sees itself in alliance with business, or at least not in any fundamental opposition to its general interests."[6]

Robert Presthus's study of the accommodation between political, bureaucratic and interest group elites in Canada, although more oriented to a survey of the attitudes of the elites, is not in sharp variance with the above findings of elite analysis in Canada with regard to socioeconomic backgrounds or general ideological disposition. He too found an absence of institutional cohesion within the political system which would facilitate it acting as a counter-elite to business. He demonstrated that it is difficult for new or substantively weak interest groups to penetrate the decision-making process as "functional ties and established clientele relationships tend to crystallize existing power relationships." Significantly, he found that the senior bureaucrats showed a marked lack of enthusiasm for state welfare activities, although he still contended that the state elite "plays an equilibriating role in welfare areas." But "much of its energy is also spent in reinforcing the security and growth of interests that already enjoy the largest share of the net social product." Of particular note, in terms of the continuity of findings of elite studies, is that organized labour still "fails to enjoy the legitimacy imputed to other economic groups" and remains "marginal" vis-à-vis established elite arrangements.[7]

These exercises in elite analysis, while not gainsaying the value of liberal democratic institutions, are valuable for piercing the myths that tend to accompany these institutions, such as equality of opportunity, competitive pluralist power relations, the state as autonomous from corporate capital or neutral between "interest groups." But while useful in this sense, the very mode of analysis also obscures many aspects of power that require study, and tends toward either viewing power as monolithically exercised at the top of our society, or suggesting that more equality of opportunity would resolve the problem of power. The mode of analysis, sometimes against the inclinations of the researchers themselves, is thus both too radical and too liberal in the conclusions it tends to produce.

There is an implicit tendency in elite analysis toward seeing power in terms of a metaphor of "representation." Social groups are spoken of loosely as being "represented," not in the sense of election, accountability and control by the groups in question, but rather in the sense of elites having similar social backgrounds to the groups that are thus "represented." Yet there is no *necessary* link between someone who comes from a particular class or ethnic background and the behaviour he or she will exhibit as a member of the elite. Only if a person has a social base in a given collectivity, and only if her or his position in the elite is dependent upon this base and accountable to it in some significant respects, can we properly speak of representation. Much less valid is the notion that, by virtue of state personnel being more or less recruited from "middle-class" social origins, we can speak of the middle class as a social force engaging in alliances or conflict with other classes on the basis of state elite behaviour. This is a form, not so much of "class reductionism," as of "class substitutionism," in that it substitutes individuals of certain social backgrounds for a class which is not even specified in terms of its own social relations, associations, struggles, etc.

Turning to the tendency for elite analysis to treat social, political and economic power in relation to equality of opportunity, it should be apparent that problems of domination and subordination are not reducible simply to patterns of recruitment. Even a perfect meritocracy implies a social division of labour with people in authority and people subject to their authority. Authority positions, positions of control, set structural limits to what individuals can do in occupying decision-making roles within these institutions. If the president of INCO were to change places with a hard-rock miner, the structural position of the *place* occupied by each individual would strongly condition their behaviour. Elite analysis, in general, gives too much credence to the autonomous ability of "elites" to make unconstrained decisions. An awareness of individual social backgrounds and values is not unimportant in trying to understand behaviour. But neither should one overestimate their importance. Replacing one set of politicians or bureaucrats or capitalists by another is just that, unless the *social base and purpose* of the institutions in which they are located change simultaneously.

It may be said that the main shortcoming of elite analysis is that it tends to ascribe *too much power*, indeed exclusive power, to those at the top. Restricting the concept of power, by definition, to authority in institutions obscures the fact that *power is a fluid social process* which, if stopped dead and anatomized in institutional terms, constantly evades analysis. The very private property market economy which corporate elite members seem to dominate by virtue of their institutional authority and cohesiveness is at the same time a limit on their authority and cohesiveness. Their positions are dependent on maintaining a rate of profit relatively high in relation to other corporations. Even if corporation executives don't lose their positions by the corporation going bankrupt, capital will flow from the less profitable corporations to the more profitable, and thus those in the less profitable will lose a good deal of their power. It is less institutional control than control over capital, a much more fluid thing, that is the foundation of the power of the corporate elite.

Similarly, by looking for power only among the elites one is forced to treat the masses as inert political clay, without self-activity (except perhaps in the highly structured context of elections). Yet the ways in which collectivities outside the "confraternity of power" engage in struggles to further their interests both limit and influence the decisions of institutional office holders. Indeed, in the very definition of democracy that introduced this section it may be noted that the political elites' power finds its source in "the people's vote." This already implies that the power in question cannot be anatomized only by examining the elites but must instead be seen in terms of a relationship between masses and elites. This would mean paying attention to the social collectivities that make up the "masses," enquiring whether these have modes of activity, of exercising power, outside of the electoral process—as indeed they do. It would also mean examining whether and where the relations between the collectivities intersect and overlap within and between the spheres of economy, state and culture that the elite theorists only look at in terms of those at the top.

It is one of the ironies of elite theory that it often takes its intellectual root in the argument that Marxist class analysis assumes an all-powerful ruling class which does not fit twentieth-century reality. Yet elite theory ends up seeing power much more monolithically than class analysis ever does. For class analysis entails seeing power as a *relational* concept, involving the necessity of tension, conflict and struggle between social classes. The economy, the state and culture are not seen here merely as hierarchically structured institutions (with the rational bureaucracy becoming the model for society as a whole), but rather as fields of competition and struggle among the social classes that compose a society such as ours. It is an approach which, despite the metaphor "ruling class," does not see power as the unconstrained prerogative of certain individuals at the top, but as a quality of conflictual social relationships that runs through society as a whole.

Class Analysis

The concept of class which finds the significant determinant of social and political behaviour in the ability or inability to dispose of labour—

one's own and others'—demonstrated its value in nineteenth-century historical and sociological analysis, but has been rather scorned of late years. No doubt it is inadequate in its original form to explain the position of the new middle class of technicians, supervisors, managers, and salaried officials, whose importance in contemporary society is very great; yet their class positions can best be assessed by the same criteria: how much freedom they retain over the disposal of their own labour, and how much control they exercise over the disposal of others' labour. Nor is this concept of class as readily amenable as are newer concepts to those techniques of measurement and tabulation which, as credentials, have become so important to modern sociology. Yet it may be thought to remain the most penetrating basis of classification for the understanding of political behaviour. Common relationship to the disposal of labour still tends to give the members of each class, so defined, an outlook and set of assumptions distinct from those of the other classes.

This does not necessarily mean that the members of a class, so defined, are sufficiently conscious of a class interest to act mainly in terms of it in making political choices. Nor need it mean that their outlook and assumptions are a conscious reflection of class position or needs as an outside observer or historian might see them.

These words by C.B. Macpherson, from *Democracy in Alberta*,[8] are as relevant today as when they were written almost thirty years ago. The central notion here is that it is people's *relationship* to property, to the ownership and control of the means of production, that is the main guide to the social composition of society and to the power relations that pertain therein. Macpherson has noted in another context that a "... somewhat looser conception of class, defined at its simplest in terms of rich, middle or poor, has been prominent in political theory as far back as one likes to go."[9] It is this looser definition of class that is employed in elite analysis in Canada. Insofar as the object of attention is the elite and its characteristics, the 80–90 percent of the population that is excluded from the upper or middle class (defined by elite family backgrounds, private school or university education, fathers with professional occupations, or an income above a certain level—$8,000 in Porter's case), remains an undifferentiated "mass." Thus, even though Olsen and Clement insist that "class is defined objectively by relationships to the ownership and control of capital and other valued resources,"[10] this definition stands external to their elite analysis, which rests on the categories of upper, middle and "below middle" (the rest) as defined above. While this is appropriate to gaining a sense of limited mobility in our society, it runs counter to the way they say classes must be objectively defined. Unfortunately, they sometimes slip into referring to those who are in the "below middle" category as "working class," and it is thus often confusing to the student which operative definition of class they are working with at different points of their analysis.

A class analysis always begins with *social relationships* that people enter into, or are born into, in producing their material means of livelihood. For production to take place in any society—and without it no society can exist—three elements are necessary: producers—the people doing the work themselves; objects of labour—the natural materials to work on (land, minerals, fish, etc.); and means of labour—instruments to work with (hoes, nets, tractors, boats, machines, computers, etc.).[11] These elements may be owned by the producers themselves (collectively as in many primitive tribal societies, or individually as in the case of the family farm or the craftsperson's workshop) or by someone else, who is a non-producer. In a slave society, all the elements—including the producers—are predominantly owned by slave-owners. Under feudalism, the most important object of labour—the land—is predominantly owned by landlords. In a capitalist society, the means of labour—the machines, factories, offices, etc.—are predominantly owned by capitalists individually or as groups of capitalists (as in the modern corporation).

Thus, the relationships between owners and nonowners, producers and non-producers, vary in different modes of production. Under slavery, the direct producers are in a position of servitude to the non-producers and can be bought and sold, or born into servitude. Under feudalism, the peasants are not themselves owned and possess their own tools, but are legally tied to the land and required to pass over a portion of their produce to the landlord. Under capitalism, the producer is free, in the sense of having a proprietary right over his or her own labour, but is dispossessed of proprietary holdings of the objects and means of labour. In order to obtain the wherewithall to exist, therefore, the producer must sell his or her labour for a wage or salary to those who own the means of production and who control this labour directly—or indirectly through managers—in the production process. On this basis we can locate the predominant social classes of each society.

> Classes are large groups of people, differing from each other by the places they occupy in a historically determined system of social production, by their relation (in most cases fixed and formulated in law) to the means of production, by their role in the social organization of labour, and consequently, by the dimensions of the share of social wealth of which they dispose and the mode of acquiring it. Classes are groups of people one of which can appropriate the labour of another owing to the different places they occupy in a definite system of social economy.[12]

It will be seen immediately that classes as approached in this fashion are not ordered in a higher and lower fashion, as rungs on a ladder, but rather in terms of people's *relationship* to one another. And it is a multidimensional relationship in that people are dependent on one another (the elements must be brought together in order for production to take place), yet it is an unequal dependence in that one class appropriates the labour of another. Because the mutual dependence is therefore one of dominance of one class and subjection of another by the appropriation of labour, the social relationship is a *contradictory* one, entailing the potential of antagonism, of conflict, between the classes. This is not to say that the permanent condition of society is one of strikes, demonstrations, revolts and revolutions. These are but the more explosive outcomes of the contradictory relations in question. But in the sense of an irreconcilable *basis* of conflict, over how much and under what specific conditions labour will be appropriated from the direct producers, the system is a conflictual one. This has historically been expressed in struggles over control of the labour process, over the length of the working day, over remuneration, over new machines that displace labour and/or require labour to work more intensively.

But if these kinds of struggles have been more common than struggles to "change the system" itself, this reflects the balance of power between the classes. Class analysis is precisely about assessing that balance of power. This does not mean that those who sell their labour to others—the working class in capitalist society—only have power at the moment of social revolution. For it will be seen that what is operating in the relations between classes is never all power on one side and the lack of it on the other. Because the classes are constituted in terms of their mutual, contradictory dependence on one another, both sides always have power. The balance of power may be unequal, and may structurally favour those who own and control the means of production, but depending on given economic, cultural and political conditions, the balance may change. This may alter the terms and conditions of the appropriation of labour, and it may give rise to struggles over changing the historically structured relations between classes themselves. But all this is the object of inquiry within a class analysis.

It should be stressed that in talking about classes in this way, we are talking about actual historical groups, real collectivities of people, who therefore cannot ever be examined in terms of economic categories alone. Classes, as societies, are constituted on a material basis in terms of producing the material means of livelihood, but they exist simultaneously in terms of culture, ideology, politics, consciousness. Insofar as we speak of classes in terms of statistical economic categories (so many owners, so many workers, etc.), we miss the point that we are dealing with real men and women. This is usually seen to be important—and it is—in terms of assessing the degree to which class relations as defined above are expressed in cultural, political and ideological differentiations and conflicts. But it is important as well in terms of understanding the basis of social cohesion and stability of a society in the face of the inherently contradictory relations between classes, since the maintenance and reproduction of the relations of production is itself dependent not only on economic relations but on the degree of cultural, political and ideological homogeneity which keeps these contradictory relations in check. This too, then, is part of the balance of power, which means that to undertake a class analysis of society we do not just map out economic relations, but rather examine the totality of cultural, ideological and political, as well as the economic relations between classes as the relevant "variables" in the overall balance of power.

Elite studies have certainly provided us with a window to the constitution of the capitalist class in Canada (albeit only the most dominant fractions of it) as a social force along all of these dimensions. However, recent work in Canadian labour history has begun to reclaim for contemporary students of Canadian society the fact that it is not the "corporate elite" alone which is an active historical actor, with the "masses" but mere statistical categories. In a study of the formation of the working class in Hamilton in the latter half of the nineteenth century, Bryan Palmer has written: "Class is inseparable from class struggle. The process of confrontation conditions an understanding of class and of people's place in the larger social order, an understanding mediated by a particular cultural context. Class is thus defined by men and women as they live through the historical experience. It is class struggle and culture, not class itself, as an analytic category, that are the primary concepts upon which classes themselves arise and assume importance. One task of social history ... is to address the class experience in such a way as to force consideration of the central place of conflict and culture in any historical and/or theoretical discussion of class."[13] Palmer's study shows that through baseball clubs, firehalls, benevolent societies, and above all through the union hall, skilled workers created for themselves an associational network and a discrete culture which both grew out of and sustained the conflicts they engaged in with their employers. These struggles, taking place both in industry and politics, were about the very organization of workers into their own unions, about control over the labour process, about the ten-hour working day, about wages and conditions, in short about how much and under what conditions labour would be appropriated from the workers by the capitalists.

Studies such as these provide an antidote to other recent accounts of late-nineteenth-century Canadian society which, while freely and loosely employing the term "class," in fact have more in common with the tradition of elite analysis than class analysis proper. In particular, Tom Naylor's *History of Canadian Business*[14] sought to locate the roots of Canada's limited and dependent industrialization in the dominance of financial capitalists over other fractions of capital and the state. Characterized by an ideology which impelled them toward making profits through commercial transactions, rather than appropriating labour directly through industrial production, these capitalists are seen to have frozen out Canadian industrial capitalists and constructed a National Policy which encouraged resource exports and branch-plant industrialization with the Canadian banks as a source of loan capital. Yet in concentrating on the values and political power of one fraction of the capitalist class, Naylor replicates the shortcomings of elite analysis in his one-sided perception of power. By looking at interclass relations, especially by examining the extent of class struggle between workers and capitalists in industry, we may discern discrete limits to the accumulation potential of Canada's indigenous manufacturers, apart from those allegedly imposed by the values and machinations of the bankers (many of whom invested in industrial production where it was profitable to do so and thus became industrial capitalists themselves).

Given Canada's later start toward capitalist industrialization than that of the United States, and given our more limited domestic market, the only way capitalists could have competed successfully with American capitalists was through a higher degree of exploitation of the working class than in the United States. Thus the very struggles of Canadian workers, emboldened by the ready possibilities of migration to the United States and by the example of relatively high incomes in Ontario farming, put limits on the potential competitiveness of Canadian capitalists. These limits were constantly tested in struggles by both sides, but given this balance of power (as opposed to the presumed monolithic power of capitalists alone), it was scarcely surprising that Canadian capitalists (industrial and financial) and politicians turned to tariff barriers, new staple resource exports *and* foreign investment in industry as a means of promoting economic growth in Canada. Insofar as this entailed a clear strategy at all, it was arrived at more through the push and pull of contending social forces rather than emerging from the heads of a fully conscious and cohesive class of mercantile capitalists, and its development was conditional upon its ability to mediate between interests of the full array of class forces in Canada, including those of the working class (who after all, had an interest in obtaining jobs in Canada at as low a rate of exploitation as possible). If Canada's entry to the modern world of capitalist industrialization has proved to be based on the shifting sands of resource export dependence and foreign ownership, a class analysis of the roots of this sorry state of affairs has to go beyond the mercantile mentality of our leading capitalists.

This example will perhaps help to dispel one of the major misconceptions that commonly pertains to what class analysis is about in political science—that it is a sectarian attempt to confirm Marx's famous aphorism that the state is but "the executive committee of the whole bourgeoisie." Apart from the fact that what Marx may have written on any given occasion can scarcely be taken as the last word on anything (either by proponents or detractors of class analysis), the charge is unfounded. Because capitalism is a competitive system, and because capitalists are competing with one another, for the state to pursue policies in the interest of the *whole* capitalist class entails it having a degree of *autonomy* from the dictation of particular capitalists.

But the state's "relative autonomy" from the capitalist entails more than this. It will be recalled that, whereas in a slave or feudal system class relations are *legally* constituted and hence *directly* dependent on the state's coercive force, in a capitalist society individuals are free and classes are constituted on the ability to dispose of labour in the economy. This separation of the state from the constitution of classes and from the economy is also the basis of the state's "relative autonomy." To speak of the state in a capitalist society as a capitalist state means only that, to use Porter's phrase, the "essential task" of the state is to maintain the necessary social conditions for economic growth and the reproduction of classes in a way consistent with the dynamics of an economy that is capitalistically structured. This will mean the promotion of the profitable accumulation of capital, for economic growth is *dependent* on how much capitalists invest, but also on the containment and mediation of the contradictory class relations that might give rise to disruptive social conflict. This does *not* mean that the state is to be conceived of as a perfect planner, an all-seeing "collective capitalist," which balances the provision of favourable conditions for profit against the necessity of throwing the occasional crumbs to the working class. Rather, because the state is not the preserve of one class, it means that *the state is a field of class struggle itself.*

The capitalists are a "ruling class" only in the sense that the condition for the economy's growth is conditional on private profit, on the capitalists' structural position as investors and organizers of production on which all other classes and the state are dependent. But the degree to which the state is "relatively autonomous" from the capitalist cannot be given in the abstract. It can only be assessed through a concrete class analysis. And such an analysis of the balance of class forces must not only look at the political field directly (in terms of parties, interest groups making demands on the state, etc.) but also at the economy and culture, for the balance of forces here also constrains, limits and provides guidance to the possible choices of the state in any particular instance.

A second misconception that often arises regarding class analysis is that it only produces a bipolar, two-class model of society: workers–capitalists, peasants–landlords, etc. For the sake of exposition in relation to the bipolar elite–mass distinction of elite analysis, I have myself given this impression to this point. But this is incomplete. Because societies are products of history, not of analytic models, the various ways in which people are related to each other in material production allow for a wide variety of relationships. Although one may still discern the predominant social relationships that mark off one stage of history from another, each stage contains within it older forms of such relations and newer developing ones.

Thus in Canada it is commonplace to observe that for a very large part of our history, and to some extent even today, extensive groups of people have neither sold their labour nor directly appropriated the product of other people's labour through employing them, but have rather been independent producers—owning their own means of production and working on it themselves, engaging in commodity and credit exchange relations with the other classes. This is the traditional middle class, the old "petite bourgeoisie," of independent craftspeople, family farmers, etc. It is sometimes alleged that such a class exists only as an analytic category, not as a real historical actor through culture and struggle, because the independent nature of the activity begets no common bonds between these producers. Yet history, and above all Canadian history, demonstrates the contrary. From the great rebellions of 1837–38 to the Prairie radical farmer movements of this century, we have seen that this class was significant in the overall balance of social forces, with its own culture, institutions and ideologies whose effects were very strongly felt historically and whose influence can still be felt today.

To be sure, the development of capitalism, entailing as it does an increasing concentration and centralization of production as the forces of competition tend to squeeze out the weak and less capital-intensive units, orients class relations more and more toward a worker–capitalist dimension. In Canada, as elsewhere, the working class has been drawn, apart from immigration, from the displaced members of the class of independent producers. But Canada's history over the past century was distinctive in that the very industrialization of the country was in good part dependent on the successful exploitation of the wheat staple, which historically entailed the growth of the petit bourgeois farmer class in the western frontier simultaneously with the development of the working class (primarily located in industrial Ontario in terms of manufacturing, although more widely dispersed in relation to mineral and forest resource extraction.) This multidimensionality of class in twentieth-century Canada, characterized as it was by uneven regional location and salience of the various classes, produced a cacophony of interlocking but distinct struggles in the economy, polity and culture. Whereas an identity of class opponents sometimes united the farmers and workers, their different class experiences also divided them, as the farmers focused on conditions of credit, commodity prices, transportation costs and the tariff itself rather than on wages and conditions of employment or control of the labour process as the main terrains of conflict. Thus, even on those occasions when farmers and workers went so far as to identify the capitalists, the capitalist parties and even the capitalist system as their common enemy, the concrete struggles of each revealed a far more complex and ambiguous pattern of relationships at work.

At first glance it might appear that this situation has now changed, that today a bipolar set of class relations more nearly obtains. With the decline of the importance of Prairie wheat in the economy as a whole, and with the stark decline in the number of independent producers over the century, wage and salary employees now constitute over 80 percent of the economically active population. But not all wage and salary earners can be unambiguously identified as working class.[15] This is not primarily due to differences in income, status, etc., between white-collar salaried employees and manual wage workers, as the stratification approach of elite analysis would have it. These differences have more and more proved ephemeral and temporary, as the clerks in the office and the steelworkers in the mill are increasingly aware. Nor is it so much because many white-collar workers are located in the state and commercial sectors which are not directly a source of the profits on which the economy continues to depend for its dynamic.

For here as well, the main criterion is the ability to dispose of labour that is at issue, and this criterion traverses the industrial, commercial and state sectors of the economy. Indeed, the extensive unionization and militancy of so many white-collar employees would seem to suggest increasingly that they are indeed well into the process of class formation along the dimensions of culture and struggle that compose real social classes. But in terms of the disposition of labour, it is also clear that within both the private corporations and the public sector there has developed over this century a stratum of employees who, without ownership or control of the means of production, nevertheless dispose of labour in terms of managing, supervising and controlling the labour of others. Although there is some theoretical disputation regarding the "class position" of such employees, it does seem that in the terms within which we have been speaking these people might be properly conceived of as a (for want of a better word) "new middle class," who by virtue of their function in the labour process stand in a contradictory relationship both to capital and labour, as salaried technocrats, managers and professionals.[16]

It has indeed become one of the favourite themes of contemporary political science in Canada to identify many political changes in terms of this "new middle class" as a social force. In particular it has been seen as a dominant force underlying both the Quiet Revolution and the Parti Québécois in Quebec and the aggressive Lougheed Conservatives in Alberta. However suggestive these analyses, it must be said that there tends to be a rather cavalier attitude toward clearly delineating this class.

To take the example of Alberta, in John Richards and Larry Pratt's *Prairie Capitalism* this class is variously referred to as an "arriviste bourgeoisie" and an "upwardly mobile urban middle class," which includes not only "upper-income" professionals and managers but also indigenous Alberta entrepreneurs (capitalists) and a "state-administrative elite." There is a vague set of criteria operative here, borrowing rather indiscriminately from elite analysis and class analysis proper. It is possible that in terms of the culture and struggle that bind these groups together one might find the basis of a cohesive social force in class terms. But much more needs to be done in this respect before the case is convincing, not least involving the attempt to define more clearly the common social relationships with other classes that give this disparate "new middle class" its unity.

It is one of the ironies of *Prairie Capitalism* that it takes C.B. Macpherson to task for treating Alberta in the first three decades of this century as a "single-class society" in terms of the overwhelming predominance of the independent farmers. As against this, Pratt and Richards argue: "Alberta has never been as homogeneous and free of internal class conflict as is argued by Macpherson . . . in Alberta tensions among rival metropolitan centres, between urban and agrarian interests, between ranchers and farmers, mine-owners and coalminers, between indigenous and external capital, and between capital and labour are recurring, not occasional, themes in the various stages of the province's development; and they can be ignored only at the risk of distortion."[17] However, within the account of modern Alberta that Pratt and Richards give us, the broad perception of internal class conflict that they require of Macpherson is paradoxically absent. We are given an account of conflict between indigenous and external capital and, less clearly so, between urban and agrarian "interests," but little else. Are there no conflicts between capital and labour in contemporary Alberta? Are conflicts between the men on the rigs and the oil companies more or less salient than between miners and coal companies in the 1930s? What are we to make of the public sector strikes in that province in recent years, whether by nurses, teachers or manual municipal workers? Are these people— some or all—to be assimilated to the new middle class or arriviste bourgeoisie? Presumably not, yet what is the pattern of social relations and social forces in that province?

Class and Party

There is a tendency in much "new middle class" analysis, moreover, to posit a very close identity between class and party, whether it be the Lesage Liberals, the Parti Québécois, or the Lougheed Conservatives. This has, to be sure, long been a bane of class analysis in Canada, revealing an inclination to think that class analysis only has relevance if it receives an unequivocal party political expression. A number of points may be made in this regard. Although it is easy to locate the social backgrounds of a party's leading personnel, one must be careful to avoid the trap of "sociological representation" that we saw in elite analysis. Without representation in the sense of social base, control, delegation and accountability in the expression of common class interests, the socioeconomic origins of leaders may be quite misleading as indicators of class interests. *If* the party is one of the places through which the class is united as a social and cultural entity, one may speak of it properly as a party of a certain class. It well may be, and the evidence is suggestive, that this is the case for the "new middle class" with the PQ and the Alberta Tories.

But one should still be careful of treating the party *as* the class. Precisely because parties aim at state office (and even when they get there are only a part of the state as governing parties) their project entails a relative autonomy from specific classes, since a political party, as Gilles Bourque puts it, "poses the question of power amidst the whole process of the class struggle.... By definition, it cannot assert itself as the unilateral, unequivocal instrument of just one class or class fragment. The struggle between parties, in liberal democracies, is not a tournament with as many teams as there are classes or fragments."[18] Bourque goes on:

> Involved in a party is social space in its totality. A party undertakes not only the promotion of specific, multiple and heterogeneous interests, but also the reproduction of the totality of the social formation. In it unfolds the whole domain of hegemony, alliances and compromises. A party seeks to create those political and ideological conditions which are most favourable to the promotion of the economic interests it defends, whether or not these interests are dominant within the social formation. While it is true that a party does not enjoy the same autonomy vis-à-vis its hegemonic class, or even subordinate classes and fragments in its midst, as the state vis-à-vis the totality of classes, a party is less directly controlled than is a corporative organization by the short-term economic interests of its members. The program of a party, much less the policy of a government, cannot be unequivocally identified with the specific interests of its hegemonic class. While the legislation of a government may be used as an indication of the class interest defended by a party in power, this is not a demonstration of the operating social force.

This issue has relevance to a broader one in the domain of class analysis. It is often argued that class analysis is irrelevant *in Canada* because there is no major working-class party (often defined as Bourque warns us not to) on the national scene, or because voting behaviour does not exhibit a distinct pervasive cleavage along class lines. But it is a major mistake to arrange parties along ideological or policy dimensions of "left" and "right" and then hypothetically assign classes to them in a bifurcated fashion. If voters are found not to conform with this procedure, this may say as much about the brittleness of the analytical construct as about the flexibility of the voters. As Bourque suggests, every party seeks to contain within it the totality of social relations in a society.

Thus, when John A. Macdonald's Conservative party constructed a "Tory-Producer" alliance around the tariff and mildly progressive industrial relations legislation, it did so not by ignoring class (although certainly by decrying class conflict) but by incorporating working-class demands, interests and leaders in their project, mediating them in a way consistent with the hegemony of the capitalists in the party. When the Mackenzie King Liberals constructed their industrial relations and welfare state program in 1944–45, they did much the same thing. (How far a simple voting behaviour test of the relevance of class in Canadian politics departs from capturing reality may be noted in the fact that the Communist party supported the Liberals rather than the CCF in the 1945 election.) And Pierre Trudeau, seeking to end his dependence on the NDP in a minority government, and faced with the opportunity of the Stanfield Conservatives calling for an incomes and prices freeze, went to Sudbury during the 1974 election campaign and shouted: "So what's he going to freeze? Your wages! He's going to freeze your wages!"[19] Here again was the incorporation of class, the expression and mediation of working-class interests, within the framework of the Liberal party.

To be sure, the way in which politicians employ language and symbols is enormously important to whether the electorate itself explicitly perceives politics, and elections in particular, to be about class. People who have but recently engaged in militant and protracted strikes may very well fail to perceive that a subsequent election is about class struggle, much less connect either their strike or the election to the question of "socialism versus capitalism." It is parties that structure the symbols of the electoral battle, not the voters that do so (although the concrete promises contained within these symbols are certainly shaped by the balance of class forces). As Jane Jenson and Janine Brodie have argued in an analysis that applies as much to the CCF/NDP as to the Liberals and Conservatives:

> From the beginning, mass political parties have integrated voters into a system of partisan relations but in this process of integration, parties have also provided voters with a *definition of politics*. They define, for the electorate, the content of politics and the meaning of political activity. In other words, at the level of ideology, *political parties shape the interpretation of what aspects of social relations should be considered political, how politics should be conducted, what the boundaries of political discussion most properly may be and what kinds of conflicts can be resolved through the political process.* From

the vast array of tensions, differences, and inequalities characteristic of any society, political parties choose which will be treated as political alternatives in the electoral process and, thereby, how the electorate will divide against itself. This role of parties is profoundly important because before electoral cleavages come into being, a definition of what is political must exist. Whether a social problem is considered to be a religious, economic or political question is something that is set by this definition. A conspiracy of silence can exist around matters which parties, for whatever reason, choose not to elevate to the level of partisan.[20]

It can certainly be appreciated that the ability of a party to catalyze the working class around a class definition of politics, and reciprocally for the working class to construct a party in which it is the hegemonic class while successfully integrating other classes, is something that contributes very much to the cohesion and strength of the working class in society. But here we have to return to the balance of class forces. The inability to do so does not invalidate class analysis, but rather necessitates it all the more to cut through the veil of appearances that confronts the social scientist. (The sun *looks* like it is moving around the earth, even though we know that not to be the case. Indeed we explain why it looks that way through scientific analysis.) It is only when class analysis is thought to be a teleological exercise that involves the claim that the working class exists only when it has full consciousness and political expression of its "revolutionary destiny" that class analysis is invalidated. But this precisely fails to grasp that class analysis entails not imposing abstract categories (whether statistical categories or pristine parties) on real social relations, but rather concerns actually examining the many ways in which contradictory social relations between people take historical expression, through culture and struggle.

In Canada it has usually been the case that the struggle of the working class finds direct expression more in the arena of work and in union struggles than in electoral politics or in the "elite accommodation" of interest groups. Although this is not immediately promising in terms of replacing capitalism with socialism, neither is social democratic electoral politics or the elite accommodation of labour leaders. For in those countries where labour leaders have indeed been assimilated to the "confraternity of power" through these mechanisms, this has often not carried the class struggle to a higher plane but weakened it as labour leaders, as a condition of their entry into the confraternity of power, have acted as agencies of social control over working-class demands "in the national interest." If it appeared in the 1950s that such integration foretold the final "end of ideology" and the "embourgeoisement" of the working class, the resurgence of industrial militancy after the mid-1960s (of which Canada was one of the most prominent examples) belied such predictions. In Europe this rendered social democratic parties' "consensus" politics unstable. In Canada, given the lesser importance of such parties, this particular effect of industrial militancy has been less visible. But it has nonetheless had real political effects.

Let me conclude with a contemporary example of the political effects of industrial class struggles, effects which do not depend on explicit political "demands" coming to political elites from the working class. In 1981, a leaked discussion paper of the Department of Finance considered the options available to the government in fighting inflation.[21] It was a document produced very much by the "upper-middle class" bureaucrats of Porter and Olsen's state elite. (The fact that the anchovies disappeared off the coast of Peru was adduced as an example of what forced up food prices in the 1970s!) And it was clear that the labour elite had not been consulted in the process of framing the document. Yet the document was centrally about the power of the working class. This was not because the document provided an ideologically biased account of the causes of inflation. It was recognized that (unlike 1974–75) Canada was not experiencing a wage-driven inflation, as real wages had fallen over the previous few years.

Yet on each strategy proposed, the central variable used to assess its viability was its potential to provoke future demands of workers in the public and private sectors and what their response might be to changes in economic policy by the government. Would a given policy increase militancy or weaken it? Would it contain wage pressure so as to permit higher investment through higher profits and lower taxation, or would it produce a backlash which would contradict this goal and/or undermine the popularity of the government? If stronger groups of workers could not be contained, could the government compensate for this by concentrating harder on holding down the wages of weaker, less well-organized groups of workers, such as by refusing to participate in compulsory arbitration for such groups? To what extent were capitalists in the private sector prepared, in light of the state of the economy, their competitiveness, sales and profits, to resist workers' demands? How much would they need or appreciate supportive action by the state—whether by setting guidelines or setting an "example" by resisting the demands of public sector workers? In trying to answer such questions, the state was surveying the *balance of class forces* regarding an anti-inflation strategy. Of course, they are not the only social forces that have to be weighed on this or any other assessment of politics. But one wishes that political scientists, at least those outside the bureaucracy, and whatever their sympathies on either side, would undertake more of this essential social scientific practice in their work.

Notes

1. R.J. Van Loon and M.S. Whittington, *The Canadian Political System*, 2nd ed. (Toronto: McGraw-Hill, 1976).
2. J.A. Schumpeter, *Capitalism, Socialism and Democracy*, 5th ed. (London: George Allen and Unwin, 1976), pp. 269, 285.
3. J. Porter, *The Vertical Mosaic: An Analysis of Social Class and Power in Canada* (Toronto: University of Toronto Press, 1965). For two useful critiques of Porter's approach, especially his conception of class and power, see J. Heap, "Conceptual and Theoretical Problems in *The Vertical Mosaic,*" *Canadian Review of Sociology and Anthropology* 9 (May 1973), and J. Hutcheson, "Class and Income Distribution in Canada," in *(Canada) Ltd., The Political Economy of Dependency*, ed. R.M. Laxer (Toronto: McClelland and Stewart, 1973).
4. Porter, *The Vertical Mosaic*, pp. 532, 539–40, 557.
5. W. Clement, *The Canadian Corporate Elite: An Analysis of Economic Power* (Toronto: McClelland and Stewart, 1975).
6. D. Olsen, *The State Elite* (Toronto: McClelland and Stewart, 1980), pp. 82, 124.
7. R. Presthus, *Elite Accommodation in Canadian Politics* (Toronto: Macmillan, 1973), pp. 348–49, 169.
8. C.B. Macpherson, *Democracy in Alberta: Social Credit and the Party System* (Toronto: University of Toronto Press, 1st ed., 1953, 2nd ed., 1963), p. 225.
9. C.B. Macpherson, *The Life and Times of Liberal Democracy* (Oxford: Oxford University Press, 1977), p. 11.
10. Clement, *The Canadian Corporate Elite*, p. 10.
11. See J. Harrison, *Marxist Economics for Socialists* (London: Pluto, 1978), p. 30.
12. V.I. Lenin, "A Great Beginning" (1919), *Selected Works*, Vol. 3 (Moscow: 1971), p. 231.
13. B.D. Palmer, *A Culture in Conflict: Skilled Workers and Industrial Capitalism in Hamilton, Ontario, 1860–1914* (Montreal: McGill-Queen's University Press, 1979), p. xvi; c.f. G.S. Kealey, *Toronto Workers Respond to Industrial Capitalism 1867–1892* (Toronto: University of Toronto Press, 1980).
14. T. Naylor, *The History of Canadian Business 1867–1914* (Toronto: Lorimer, 1975).
15. See L.A. Johnson, "The Development of Class in Canada in the Twentieth Century," in *Capitalism and the National Question in Canada*, ed. G. Teeple (Toronto: University of Toronto Press, 1972).
16. For important attempts to "map" the contemporary class structure in these terms see: G. Carchedi, "On the Economic Identification of the New Middle Class," *Economy and Society* 4 (1975) 1, and *On the Economic Identification of Social Classes* (London: Routledge and Kegan Paul, 1977); E.O. Wright, *Class, Crisis and the State* (London: New Left Books, 1978). For a good example of the cultural dimension entailed in the relation between this new middle class and the working class, see A. Gorz, "Technical Intelligence and the Capitalist Division of Labour," *Telos* 12 (Summer 1972), especially pp. 34–35.
17. J. Richards and L. Pratt, *Prairie Capitalism: Power and Influence in the New West* (Toronto: McClelland and Stewart, 1979), pp. 150–51. On Quebec in this vein, see K. McRoberts and D. Postgate, *Quebec: Social Change and Political Crisis*, rev. ed. (Toronto: McClelland and Stewart, 1980).
18. G. Bourque, "Class, Nation and the Parti Québécois," *Studies in Political Economy* 2 (Autumn 1979): 130.

19. Quoted in the *Toronto Star*, October 18, 1975.
20. M.J. Brodie and J. Jenson, *Crisis, Challenge and Change: Party and Class in Canada* (Toronto: Methuen, 1980), p. 8.
21. "Discussion Paper on Anti-Inflation Policy Options," January 9, 1981. Incomplete reports of the document can be found in the *Toronto Star*, March 24, 1981, and the *Globe and Mail*, March 25, 1981.

Further Readings

Brodie, M.J., and J. Jenson. *Crisis, Challenge and Change: Party and Class in Canada.* Toronto: Methuen, 1980.

Clement, W. *The Canadian Corporate Elite.* Toronto: McClelland and Stewart, 1975.
_____. *Continental Corporate Power.* Toronto: McClelland and Stewart, 1977.

Hunter, Alfred A. *Class Tells: On Social Inequality in Canada.* Toronto: Butterworths, 1981.

Macpherson, C.B. *Democracy in Alberta: Social Credit and the Party System.* Toronto: University of Toronto Press, 1963.

Miliband, R. *Marxism and Politics.* Oxford: Oxford University Press, 1977.

Olsen, D. *The State Elite.* Toronto: McClelland and Stewart, 1980.

Palmer, B.D. *A Culture in Conflict: Skilled Workers and Industrial Capitalism in Hamilton, Ontario, 1860–1914.* Montreal: McGill-Queen's University Press, 1979.

Panitch, Leo, ed. *The Canadian State: Political Economy and Political Power.* Toronto: University of Toronto Press, 1977.

Porter, John. *The Vertical Mosaic.* Toronto: University of Toronto Press, 1965.

Schumpeter, J.A. *Capitalism, Socialism and Democracy.* 5th ed. London: George Allen and Unwin, 1976.

Teeple, G., ed. *Capitalism and the National Question in Canada.* Toronto: University of Toronto Press, 1972.

Wright, E.O. *Class, Crisis and the State.* London: New Left Books, 1978.

Part 3
Canada's Political Structures

Chapter 11
The Party System
M. Janine Brodie and Jane Jenson

Canada's federal party system provides a somewhat perplexing case for students of politics in liberal democracies. Some sociological theory, drawing on western European experience in particular, predicts that as changes in social structure induced by urbanization and industrialization occur, the traditional electoral cleavages of religion, language and region are eroded by the politics of class. In so-called "modernized" party systems, a class cleavage differentiates the electoral support base of the parties as well as their major policies. From this perspective, the Canadian federal party system does not appear to have "modernized." Instead, religion, language and especially region continue to differentiate the Canadian electorate's support for political parties. Studies of federal voting behaviour consistently depict an electorate which does not divide its support for political parties according to occupational position or even according to the location which voters think they occupy in a status ranking. In addition, the programs and policies of the two major parties reveal few differences in the class interests that they claim to protect and advance. Both depict themselves as guardians of the "national interest." As a result, they are most clearly distinguished by the differences in electoral support that they gain from Canada's major language groups and regions.

This is not to say that Canadian electoral politics has not witnessed at least some of the symptoms of a modernizing party system. From the earliest years, there have been social democratic or socialist parties active in the federal party system. Yet, all these parties, including the New Democratic Party, have never enjoyed anything near a majority of the support of their supposed constituency, the Canadian working class. Rather, the Liberal party gains more votes from workers than does the self-styled social democratic party, the NDP.

Students of Canadian political parties do not agree on how to explain or even describe this perplexing feature of our party system. One kind of study simply attempts to categorize the members of the federal party system so that they can be compared. For example, some typologies describe the federal party system according to the number of parties competing within it. Yet, even at this most elementary level of categorization, there is minimal agreement. Does Canada have a two-party system, since only the Liberals and Progressive Conservatives stand any reasonable chance of forming a government? Or, has there been a four-party system (until 1980) because there were four competitors which consistently won seats in Parliament? Or, should we count two-and-a-half parties, acknowledging the persistence of the NDP despite its remote chance of forming a national government? These questions have all been answered in the positive by students of party politics.

Another body of literature characterizes the federal parties according to their organization and electoral orientations. Here again, there is little consensus. Most observers agree, however, that there is a noteworthy difference between the two major parties and the NDP and its predecessor, the Co-operative Commonwealth Federation (CCF). The two major parties are generally described as cadre parties, pragmatic parties, or parties seeking consensus, while the CCF/NDP is depicted as a mass party and a party of program, principle or protest. Nevertheless, regardless of the basis of categorization, none of these typologies explains the anomalies of the federal party system, especially its apparent inability to "modernize" in predicted ways.

Party and Class in Canada

There are several popular explanations for the absence of pervasive class-based voting in federal politics. This absence has been attributed, by different authors, to the cultural cleavage between French and English Canada and the consequent lack of a sense of nation, to the conflict between central and peripheral regions and to constitutional biases which encourage regionalism. A familiar theme, however, is the notion that Canadian politics never has been characterized by class conflict because such conflict is irrelevant. Economic and geographic conditions, it is argued, have defused potentially divisive economic cleavages by promoting population movement and social mobility. A further deduction made by such observers is that Canada is a "middle-class" society where material and social benefits are widely shared and, thus, Canadian politics need not be affected by either class conflict or ideology. Partisan debate can focus on other issues.

Another suggestion about why class-based electoral politics has not flourished in Canada is based on observations about the nature of the federal parties themselves. Sometimes coupled with the "middle-class" view of Canadian society, this perspective describes the Liberals and Conservatives as "brokers," offering the electorate an aggregation and accommodation of the myriad of potentially conflicting interests that inevitably arise in any society. The parties' only concern, according to this analysis, is to accommodate diverse interests sufficiently to build an electoral coalition large enough to capture power. Instead of organizing the electorate around class interests, the major parties are said to engage in a politics of moderation which minimizes differences and restrains divisive tendencies. It is further argued that a beneficial consequence of such brokerage parties is that they can knit together diverse interests in a polity which is otherwise weakly integrated.

As appealing as the middle-class and brokerage theses may be, there are a number of factors which potentially challenge their validity as explanations of the absence of class voting. First, and most obviously, Canada is not and never was a "middle-class" society. In recent years, in fact, the distribution of wealth has grown even less equal. Similarly, there are ample reasons to question the accuracy of the brokerage conception of federal politics. If the major parties are solely concerned with accommodating social conflicts, then the federal party system is witness to their failures. For decades, large regionally-based third parties have occupied their own space on the partisan landscape, citing the neglect and biases of the "brokerage parties" as their reason for entering the electoral fray. Their existence suggests that not all interests are equally accommodated by the two major parties.

Finally, there is little evidence to suggest that brokerage parties are neutral and non–class-based organizations. Their major sources of campaign financing, their patterns of recruitment of members and candidates, and their policy orientations all suggest that the Liberals and Progressive Conservatives have a decidedly status quo and frankly pro-capitalist bent. Yet, paradoxically, these class parties find much of their electoral support among workers. Thus, we return to the question: why is there so little evidence of class-based voting in Canada's federal party system?

To begin answering it is helpful to return and re-examine the original prediction about the "inevitability" of class-based electoral politics in industrial societies. The principal assumption underlying the prediction is that there is a direct relationship between economic and partisan development. This view of the organization of class relations in liberal democracies arises from economistic Marxist analyses as well as from political sociology's observation that labour or socialist parties and class-based voting emerged and endured in industrialized countries. This formulation is also predicated on a further assumption—notably, that voters' political demands, attitudes and behaviour automatically reflect their class position.

According to these assumptions, electoral politics, organized around a class cleavage, will be concerned primarily with questions of control over economic production and distribution. In this view, competition between classes will lead to the general partisan organization of the bourgeoisie, and those supporting the interests of the bourgeoisie, into one party, and workers, and those supporting the interests of workers, into another. Partisan competition is thus assumed to develop between those who have, according to the rules of the private economy, control over the production process and its profits and those who have, according to the laws of liberal democracy, some control over the production process through the state.

The deduction that workers will be organized into one party and the bourgeoisie into another, however, is not the only one possible starting from an initial assumption about the political importance of classes in liberal democratic politics. In fact, what history has demonstrated in the last century of the joint development of capitalism and liberal democracy is the following: while capitalism has proceeded in all countries in similar directions toward centralization, monopolistically large corporations and an increase in state intervention in the economy, partisan expression of class conflict has differed widely in the several countries. Students of political sociology who have taken a rather deterministic view of the relationship between economic development and partisan organization, by and large, have been unable to explain the many variations of electoral politics in advanced capitalist countries. This is perhaps because they have tended to minimize the effects of specific national and historical contexts as well as the combined impact of elections, ideologies and political parties themselves in structuring partisan and class relations.

Historically, mass political parties came into being when franchise reform created large numbers of voters who had not previously participated in electoral politics. The way this integration occurred was important in structuring the subsequent partisan organization of class relations because parties primarily (though not exclusively) provided the electorate with a *definition of politics*. They defined the content of politics and the meaning of political activity by shaping an ideology. Most generally, *political parties have a major role in shaping the interpretation of what aspects of individuals' lives should be considered political, how politics should be conducted, what the boundaries of political discussion most properly may be, and what kinds of conflicts can be resolved through the electoral process.* From the vast array of tensions, differences, and inequalities characteristic of any society, parties are crucial to the selection of those which will be defined as political alternatives in the electoral process and thereby shape how the electorate will divide against itself. Whether a problem is considered to be a religious, economic or political question is set by this definition. This role of parties is profoundly important because *before* electoral cleavages come into being a definition of what is political must exist.

Elections are events of conflict and competition, but the substance of electoral politics is not automatically given. For example, politics may be described as the expression of conflict between classes or between ethnic groups or as the aggregation of individual preferences. Economic conditions, such as the level of industrialization, set parameters around the range of organization which is possible in any society, but they can never guarantee that particular classes will be politically active. Subordinate classes will not spontaneously recognize the political implications of their disadvantaged location in capitalist relations of production and vote according to their class position. Members of particular occupational sectors in capitalist society, whether they are farmers, blue-collar workers or office workers, do not and will not act cohesively as a class until they become aware that they are members of a class. The nurturing of this awareness demands, as a prerequisite, ideological and organizational activity. Classes as active and self-conscious social actors must be created, and, in turn, the extent to which they live politically as classes is largely the extent to which they behave as classes in elections.

At a very minimum, class-based voting must be preceded by the development of a class-based organization which challenges existing definitions of politics which interpret social and political relations in non-class terms. If the existence, characteristics and partisan implications of class conflict are exposed by the activities of a well-developed trade-union movement or a powerful and influential party of the left, then there will be evidence, at the level of voting, of class-based politics. Without these prior conditions, class cleavages will be submerged, distorted and rarely visible in voting behaviour.

Since the late nineteenth century, socialist parties have existed which have defined politics as the expression of conflict between classes and not as neutral aggregations of individual or group preferences. They have precipitated a conflict over definitions of politics as well as governmental policies. The existence of such a debate over definitions means that voters have been offered alternative bases for electoral alignment, and some of these threaten the very existence of one or more of the bourgeois parties. Not surprisingly, then, such parties struggle hard to maintain and recreate a definition of politics which denies the centrality of class differences and relations in capitalist systems. Time and again, confronted with a class-based definition of politics advanced by socialist parties, bourgeois parties have retorted that this definition is inappropriate and that politics is really about race or religion, and moreover that politics is not about conflict at all but about finding consensus so that the capitalist system can be managed successfully to the benefit of all.

If alternative ways of organizing the electorate are possible under the same economic conditions, and the nature of this organization affects the manner in which classes and individuals behave in electoral politics, we begin to see a way of unravelling the perplexity of the Canadian party system. The extent to which capitalist relations of production are debated politically depends in large part on how successfully either socialist or bourgeois parties organize the electorate behind their respective points of view. If politics is defined as conflict between language groups, it is more difficult to unite for partisan action members of the same class who have different linguistic backgrounds. In other words, some political cleavages are likely to be incompatible with others, as the dominance of one cleavage generally inhibits the growth of others. By examining this contest over the definition of politics, it is possible to arrive at a better understanding of the background to the contemporary Canadian party system, which is divided along lines of language and region.

Origins of the Federal Party System

In the early years of Confederation, Canada did not have a fully developed two-party system. For the first forty years, the federal government was engaged in a complex process of state building around the development strategy known as the National Policy. In essence, this policy was designed to achieve three goals. First was the promotion of railroad construction from the centre to the peripheries. Railroads linking all parts of the country would transport western products to the East and vice versa. The second goal was to foster immigration to the West, which would expand the number of agricultural exporters and provide an internal market for eastern manufactured goods. Finally, the National Policy imposed tariffs on imported goods, thereby protecting the Canadian manufacturing sector, concentrated in the central provinces, from foreign, especially American, competition.

These three aspects of the National Policy formed an integrated and mutually reinforcing whole. As the policy unfolded, however, it induced class-based tensions and the mobilization of partisan opposition which has continued to the present day. In order to trace the development of this opposition, it is necessary to understand the ways in which the party system organized relations between classes in the post-1867 years and the kind of political agenda and conflict which emerged.

The bourgeoisie was the moving force behind the establishment of the Canadian state, and this class was quite united in its support for the goals of the National Policy. In fact there was little ground for partisan competition among manufacturing, merchant and financial interests. All vigorously pursued in both their business and political dealings a strategy of nation building and railway building that facilitated further exploitation of an export-oriented, resource-extracting, staple-based economy. Westward expansion and the marketing of wheat were profitable to merchants and railroad investors; tariffs encouraged expansion in the manufacturing sector; and economic growth, in part stimulated by immigration, promised good returns for all, but especially for the financial community. In the early years of Confederation, these interests found their political home in the Conservative party of Sir John A. Macdonald, which held power virtually unchallenged for more than two decades.

There were isolated pockets of opposition to this particular strategy of economic development. Nevertheless, these disparate forces were unable to forge a cohesive partisan alliance against the "nation-building" Conservatives. In fact, it was not until the 1890s that the Liberal party managed to build a national party capable of competing on an equal footing with the Conservatives. It did this, however, not by contesting the Conservatives' vision of the national dream but rather by embracing it and emphasizing instead religious and linguistic differences within the electorate.

The transfer of the federal government in 1896 from the remnants of Macdonald's coalition to Laurier's Liberals is a watershed in Canadian partisan history. It marks the entrenchment of a definition of politics which has enabled the Liberal party to continue to dominate federal politics. It was never obvious in the first elections after Confederation what the substance of electoral conflict would be—whether class, language, religion or some other social differences would characterize the support base of the federal parties. The Conservatives, as nation builders, had a clear position to advance, but the Liberals had to find a viable way of distinguishing themselves from their competitors. In other words, they had to define and create their electorate. Eventually, the Liberal party came to realize the electoral potential of religious and linguistic allegiances as a basis for electoral cleavage.

Macdonald had recognized the need to defuse differences between English and French by forging strong links with the leadership of Quebec, through Georges-Etienne Cartier, and with the hierarchy of the Roman Catholic Church. In terms of its electoral support, then, the original Conservative party was an amalgam of Protestant and Catholic, English and French. But, by 1896 the party was unable to overcome the tensions which had erupted in its own ranks and which were a boon to the Liberals searching for a base. Capitalizing on the hanging of Riel, conflict over religious schools in the West, and increasingly vocal anti-French and anti-Catholic rhetoric in Ontario, the Liberals finally identified their issue, created their electorate and formed a competitive national party. In essence, they presented themselves as the only party still able to represent Quebec and thus guarantee the Confederation project.

The emergence of a bicultural definition of politics had a profound influence on the development of the federal party system. By the 1890s the two federal parties agreed about the pattern of economic development implied by the National Policy. Thus, the same bourgeois interests which had supported Macdonald's Conservatives easily could, and did, shift their allegiance to the Liberal party. They did this not because of any particular identification with the religious or language controversies of those years, but because the Conservatives had lost their electoral majority and, thus, their ability to govern in federal politics.

This particular form of partisan conflict had emerged partially as a result of an early decision on the part of Canada's trade unions, following the example of their American co-unionists, not to sponsor a "workers' party." By this decision they withdrew from the process of "creating" a working class at the level of electoral politics. In direct consequence, little expression of class conflict emerged in federal campaigns, at least not until the western farmers mobilized to contest the costs of the National Policy and the bourgeois interests which sponsored it.

When the two major parties first looked westward to the new provinces, there was ample reason to believe that a two-party system revolving around bicultural politics might be successfully transplanted there. A number of factors, however, made this transfer less than perfect. First, the eastern-based definition of the political, emphasizing nation building and the dual religious and linguistic composition of the new country, was largely out of tune with the western social fabric. More importantly, the western electorate grew increasingly disaffected with the National Policy embraced by both parties. It was especially difficult to maintain widespread support among farmers for the view that the National Policy was the optimal strategy for economic development.

Western farmers had only to compare the prices of their farm machinery and other products with the prices paid by their neighbours in the American midwest to realize that a large portion of the burden of tariffs (designed to encourage Canadian manufacturing by raising prices of imported manufactured goods) fell on them. Transportation, a second part of the National Policy, was also a source of mounting irritation. Railways were permitted to charge higher rates on the less competitive western lines than in the East, where competition from other modes of transportation made lower prices economically necessary. Because the federal government was the regulator of the railways, the level and characteristics of freight rates became a burning political question. Under such conditions it is little wonder that the western farmers began to press the two federal parties for adjustment of both tariffs and freight rates.

Additional explanatory factors must be added to help us understand how this potential for protest was mobilized. The complaints of the farmers had to be transformed into partisan differences, either within the existing two-party system or in the form of a separate party devoted to advancing the needs of farmers as a class. Farmers' organizations were crucial centres for both educating and organizing western discontent against the economic development strategies of the federal government. These farmers' organizations provided the foundation for opposition to the prevailing development strategy, an opposition which did not break along language and religious lines. The British-born, the anglophone Canadian, the German and eastern European farmers in unison criticized the eastern-based political parties for their seeming preoccupation with cultural issues to the exclusion of their economic grievances. Nevertheless, it was not until 1921 that these independent commodity producers, led by farmers' organizations, actually challenged the dominant cultural definition of politics with their own party, the Progressives.

The Progressive party is significant in the history of Canadian partisan relations because it was a class party with a class-based definition of politics rivalling the consensual definition which had dominated federal campaigns to that point. Given that the Progressives' critique threatened the very basis of their electoral support, both major parties went on the defensive against the Progressives' class-based conception of politics. They attacked the new party for being class-biased. Prime Minister Arthur Meighen, for example, described the Progressives as a misinformed class party which threatened to upset the fiscal balance of the country. The new leader of the Liberals, William Lyon Mackenzie King, urged the voters not to invite the awful unknown by experimenting with a discourse of class in matters of government. The western electorate in 1921, however, was unconvinced by these warnings. The Conservatives did not win any seats in Manitoba, Saskatchewan or Alberta, while the Liberals won only two, leaving the remaining thirty-seven seats to the Progressives. The Prairie provinces had rejected the politics of biculturalism and class consensus.

Perhaps because of their relatively short life, the Progressives have often been viewed as an isolated episode, a short-term regional deviation from the two-party system. Yet the Progressive experience was of fundamental importance in shaping the subsequent development of the federal party system. The federal system had been fractured regionally into two distinct components—one in the East revolving around the politics of language and religion and one in the West informed by the politics of class. After 1921 the Liberals and Conservatives would never be able to re-establish fully their preferred definition of politics. The experience of the Progressives left two distinct legacies. First, the success of the party in 1921 represented the mobilization potential of a class-based definition of politics with strong organizational resources. The Progressives claimed that the major parties' insistence that they represented the "national interest" was only a convenient myth which really protected and advanced the interests and needs of eastern capital, often at the expense of farmers and workers. In essence, the Progressives offered a redefinition of federal politics, one which allowed the interests of one subordinate class, the farmers, to be reflected in the party system.

The second legacy of the Progressive experience was that a space was opened for class-based politics in the federal party system. During the 1930s this space was filled by the Co-operative Commonwealth Federation. One of the curious anomalies of Canadian politics is that the most enduring party of the left emerged with support drawn from farmers located in an economic hinterland rather than from urban workers. While the CCF had its own organizational and ideological history, its success in the Prairie provinces cannot be isolated from the Progressive experiment, whose legacy was an electorate disengaged from cultural politics and open to the mobilization efforts of the CCF.

The Contemporary Party System

During the late 1930s and the war years, it appeared as if the CCF might successfully challenge, with the politics of class, the two major parties and their definition of politics. Some forty years later, however, it is apparent that neither the CCF nor the NDP has succeeded in this goal. The Liberal party, kept afloat by the politics of language, has won all but three federal elections since the Second World War. And, when that party momentarily faltered, it was the Progressive Conservatives rather than the CCF/NDP which replaced it in government. Confounded by a seemingly insurmountable electoral arithmetic, the CCF first moderated its policies, later forged a new organizational alliance with the trade-union movement and finally changed its name and formal structure in 1961 by reconstituting itself as the New Democratic Party. Each strategy was designed to enhance the electoral fortunes of social democracy in Canada. Yet, rather than expand the space for class politics, they tended to close it, leaving the NDP today weak and uncertain.

The reorientation of the CCF's socialism began during World War II when the party cautiously redefined its nationalization policy goals so as to avoid alienating the electoral backbone of the party, the western independent commodity producers. This strategy of moderation accelerated until, in 1956, the party adopted a new statement of principles, the Winnipeg Declaration, which provided the theoretical foundation for the NDP. An essential element of the CCF's moderation was its view of the state's role in social change. Departing from its earlier and more radical advocacy of state ownership of key sectors of the economy (in order to guarantee that production would reflect the public interest), the party increasingly proposed only Keynesian economics. It promised to pursue anti-cyclical policies to stabilize the economy and maintain full employment as well as to provide a comprehensive net of social programs to improve the lives of the disadvantaged. However, the Liberals and Conservatives, as did most bourgeois parties in the post-war

Canada's Political Structures

years, also promised most of the same policies. The CCF/NDP, therefore, did not represent a position sufficiently different from the Liberals, or even the Progressive Conservatives, to allow the electorate to distinguish their policies from what it was already getting from the other parties.

While it is clearly understood that the Liberal government was not "neutral" in its dealings with capital, the CCF argued that the state's biases could be eliminated by the installation of a new party and new elite in power. The CCF saw itself as forming that new elite, but it offered the electorate policies and options which were little other than more of the same. It proposed a better welfare program and more humanitarian leadership, but the party had no theory of how these social programs reinforced capitalism and no theory of how to break the capitalist state free of those tasks it performed for the reproduction and regeneration of capitalism.

The CCF's, and later the NDP's, failure to understand or explain the role of the state in the 1950s, which was a decade of relative economic prosperity, meant that the party did not constitute a clear alternative for the voters. With its liberal view of a basically neutral state, the NDP had only a single argument to rally support behind it—vote NDP for more honest and fair government. Moreover, the party's inability to recognize the contradictions inherent in the Keynesian state (that it benefited *both* capital and working people) was more debilitating in times of economic downturn, like those of the 1970s. The NDP had few policy alternatives to propose once full employment and investment policies came into conflict with each other. When the continued economic growth on which these policies were premised grew more and more difficult to achieve, the NDP was as confounded as the other parties. Its policies stumbled from "more Keynesianism" to an "industrial policy" to state-directed "investment" programs, but all without any solid theoretical grounding or presentation which could be credible to the voters of the 1970s and 1980s. It found itself competing with the bourgeois parties, especially the Liberals, more or less on their terms, and by the 1980s it began to look as if that competition would be lost as the Liberals proclaimed that their strategy was to pick up NDP supporters, especially in the western provinces.

A second factor accounting for the failure of the NDP to inject a viable alternative definition of politics into the federal party system followed from the strategic decision to construct a particular kind of organizational base for the party. In the 1950s the CCF thought that its decline could be halted only if it followed the example of the British Labour party and constructed a formal organizational link with the trade-union movement. Together with the newly formed Canadian Labour Congress (CLC) the CCF created a new social democratic party, the NDP, in 1961.

The anticipated surge of electoral support toward the NDP from

Canadian workers did not materialize, however. Overall, the union links with the party remained more formal and financial than designed for mobilization of the union membership in support of the NDP. The new party was largely a marriage of notables—designed by the leadership of the old CCF and the new CLC—and most of the organized workforce showed little interest in the new "party of labour." Canadian trade unionists were unfamiliar with, if not hostile to, social democracy, and neither the CCF/NDP nor the union movement had done much to persuade them otherwise. That portion of the labour force which was organized in unions in Canada was not yet interested in radical social transformation, and it was not about to undertake what it saw as a risk to its high wages and affluence for the promise of a new society.

The NDP did not replicate the successes of the British Labour party, largely because it failed to understand the importance of history and the dynamics of the partisan mobilization of the working class. The Labour party had grown out of a radical trade-union movement shortly after universal suffrage was achieved in Britain and had developed its electoral constituency with a critique of capitalism. Moreover, it had fifty years of political experience—including the implementation of the British welfare state—behind it. The NDP, however, was a new party created during the Cold War—when criticisms of capitalism were highly suspect—and with the help of unions representing only a small segment of the modern labour force. Further, they were the unions of the traditional working class. They were the unions of the industrial and craft workers rather than the unions of the rapidly expanding service and state sectors, which would have to be part of any successful left-wing party. The potential of these non-traditional workers as union members and left voters was not fully appreciated by the new party, which tended to assign them to the "middle class" and expect them to be hostile to the party's projects.

More importantly, the NDP's obsession with bringing about union affiliation meant that the union movement had to be accepted as it was—without political class consciousness, without a history of struggle for socialism, without a sense of responsibility for the creation of the welfare state or, for that matter, without political experience. This meant that the CCF/NDP felt compelled to moderate its program so as to gain the support of union leaders who, in turn, recognized the conservatism of their rank and file or who were politically conservative themselves.

What consequences did this moderation have for the NDP? With the Liberal party actively implementing a social program, NDP "moderation" meant more of the same. However, the Liberals were a "major" party while the NDP was the newcomer. Therefore, there was little reason to expect union members to support the NDP when they could have the same thing with the Liberals. There was no historic alliance between workers and a party which they themselves had built, as there was in

Britain. There was not a politically conscious working class in Canada, as the CCF/NDP ceased to address its anticipated electorate in a language of politics cast in class terms. The workers had not been organized into a class and they would not act as one in federal elections.

In essence, the NDP did not develop a language of politics which allowed it to construct a working-class alliance. It attached itself at the leadership level to a conservative and largely apolitical labour movement and accepted the existing language of politics rather than developing its own. Nor could it explain the actions of the state or the Liberal party in a way that reflected an understanding of the "welfare state." Doing these things, the NDP offered no alternative world view, no explanation of their conditions to either organized labour or the social groups and class fractions which advancing capitalism created. It could not explain, in terms much different than those used by the other parties, to the white-collar workers, the state-sector workers, the women workers, the workers in non-central regions, how their lives were affected by the capitalism of post-war Canada. By failing to understand the Canadian "case," the NDP could not be other than a left wing of the Liberal party—a more moral, a more democratic, but essentially a similar party. This position was, of course, a very vulnerable one. The Liberals were always tempted to "poach" in the NDP's areas of support, and the NDP suffered in consequence.

As a result of this failure to mobilize the subordinate classes behind a new definition of the political, federal elections by and large have revolved around the politics of religion and/or culture. Moreover, for most of the history of the federal party system there has been space for only one party of "the national interest" and only one strategy of national development. The continuing viability of the politics of culture has enabled the Liberal party to claim that space in the post-war years, although its strategy for development was altered from what it had been in the pre-war period. The Liberals, at least until very recently, pursued policies which facilitated the incorporation of the Canadian economy into the continental economy. This was a centre-oriented strategy because it encouraged the industrialization of the centre, largely via branch plant development, while the peripheries were seen as good sources of raw materials for central Canada or the United States. Since the American economy remained very buoyant throughout the 1950s and 1960s, the strategy of continentalization had few detractors in Canada.

Thus, with alternative definitions of the political weakly organized (if at all) and with a consensus about development strategies among the bourgeoisie, the Progressive Conservative party often was lost in a political wilderness. Time and again the party sought to create its own electoral space, but the logic of the party system, which grants the Liberals bloc support from Quebec, has proven to be a formidable obstacle.

The continuing search for a viable electoral strategy has been a constant source of tension for the Tories, a tension which was perhaps best exhibited in their decision in the 1940s to change the name of their party. Ironically, while the name chosen—Progressive Conservative—was obviously contradictory according to common ideological usage, it did in fact offer a relatively correct representation of the tension at the heart of the party. Historically, the Tories have subscribed to the same perspectives on development as the Liberals and sought to mobilize the electorate around a cultural definition of politics. Yet, as this is a difficult and usually losing strategy, another approach has sometimes been taken. At times the Progressive Conservatives have used a populist appeal designed to mobilize the electorate freed by the Progressives. While obviously rejecting the critique of advanced capitalism which that party (and the CCF/NDP afterwards) propounded, the Tories at times have tried to mobilize the electorate disenchanted with existing economic conditions.

This strategy was developed explicitly during the Second World War when the Conservatives adopted the prefix Progressive. At the same time, they proposed a series of social and economic reforms as their response to the ills of capitalism revealed by the Depression. With these policies they hoped to increase their electoral support, all the while maintaining a strong and clear commitment to the capitalist system. Their efforts to put a new face on the party ultimately failed, however, because the war brought another crisis in cultural relations which only strengthened the Liberals' base in Quebec and because the Liberals also revamped their policies at the same time. The Tories, therefore, dropped the populist strategy and rhetoric and, under the leadership of George Drew, returned to a more conservative electoral appeal. This experience revealed what was to be a continuing dilemma for the Progressive Conservatives. Each time the Tories staked out a new position for themselves the Liberals caught up with them. This produced both a constant dilemma for the party and created a party much divided by internal conflict over self-definition, policy and leadership.

In the 1950s populist elements once more gained ascendancy in the Progressive Conservative party, and with John Diefenbaker as leader the Tories succeeded in supplanting the politics of language sufficiently to sweep the country, including Quebec, in 1957. Diefenbaker made his appeal to the "little man" and to those with a vision of a new nationalism—pan-Canadianism and the prosperity which northern development promised. His populist appeals brought immediate electoral payoffs, but ultimately put him into conflict with interests within his party that favoured what was essentially the Liberals' centre-oriented strategy of heavy reliance on foreign investment to develop the manufacturing and resource sectors. Thus, vacillation in strategic thinking was revealed by the tension within the party and the public conflict which emerged during the Diefenbaker years. After only a brief time in office, Diefenbaker's spectacularly successful populism gave way to ignominious electoral defeat, party disunity and his public rejection as leader.

Once again the Tories were in the political wilderness, demonstrating that there was room in the party system for only one political party of "the national interest." By the late 1960s, there was very little room in which to manoeuvre. If the Progressive Conservatives were to dislodge the Liberals, they really had no choice but to accept the centre-oriented development strategy similar to that pursued by the Liberals and favoured by most of the Canadian economic elite. Since they were almost shut out of Quebec, they needed Ontario to provide electoral strength and organizational resources. No other option appeared apparent or plausible to Tory strategists. Therefore, taking guidance from opinion polls, the party tried to modernize its image to appeal to urban Ontario and at the same time accepted official bilingualism to appeal more to Quebec. Yet, because it remained so closed out of Quebec, any strategy which emphasized a bicultural definition of politics and used linguistic differences as a basis for party differentiation was one under which the Conservative party could only suffer. Therefore, in the late 1960s and early 1970s, the politics of biculturalism continued to favour the Liberals.

Since that time a number of factors have converged which have made it appear as if the Progressive Conservative party may be able to partially resolve its dilemma. First, the Liberals' centre-oriented development strategy began to unravel during the 1970s. Policies pursued by the American government to repatriate manufacturing jobs, as well as changes in the international economy more generally, dealt hard blows to the branch plant economy of central Canada. Several industries were forced to close and unemployment rose dramatically. The foundation upon which the Liberal party had based its promise of prosperity had eroded under pressure from a changing international division of labour. New space was opened up for debate and competition over the future course of Canadian economic development.

The most forcefully articulated alternative emanated from the "New West," whose immediate interests were in conflict with any new development strategy which maintained the unequal development which had characterized the relationship between Canadian regions since 1867. In the West, those actors whose interests were tied to the booming petroleum and other natural resource industries wanted to maintain the United States as a privileged market for their raw materials but they wanted the economic benefits of this continentalist relationship directed to the West rather than to central Canada as they traditionally had been. The governments of the western provinces, supported by local and resource capital, set out provincial development strategies to deepen and diversify their economies. These policies nurtured federal voters in the regions who were antagonistic toward the centrist orientation of the federal Liberal party. These voters were responsive to a party promising a new kind of economic development, as were the economic elites, whose future seemed to depend on a redistribution of economic activity westward. A rift existed, for the first time in a long time, within the Canadian economic elite over development strategies. The possibility appeared that there were enough voters and a divided economic elite to provide financial support and legitimacy so that two parties could promote different development strategies. These political changes, accompanied by a shift of population to the West, promised to change the electoral arithmetic such that a solid West would be created, similar to the Liberals' Quebec.

The late 1970s and early 1980s have witnessed the gradual but by no means certain process of recreating the Progressive Conservative party as representative of an alternative definition of "the national interest." Preliminary steps came during the leadership of Joe Clark, who brought together an unstable coalition of western capital and its supporters, province-building politicians and progressive elements (the so-called Red Tories) in order to gain power at the federal level. During the two elections of 1979 and 1980, this coalition offered policies which would have facilitated continentalism in the resource sectors, a looser federalism (a "community of communities") and, by implication, a national government less tied to central Canada.

The rhetoric of the Tories also drew upon some of the familiar themes of populism—the lack of western political influence in Ottawa, the centrist biases of federal policies, the power of giant corporations, etc. This strategy seemed attractive because it promised to combine populist electoral potential with an alternative and defensible development strategy for at least part (but a growing part) of Canadian capital. Unlike the Progressive experiment, however, it was not a redefinition of federal politics with an organizational base in a subordinate class. Instead, this new union represented one of the few times in Canadian history when regional protest and an alternate development strategy were combined by one of the major parties.

In 1979, the Tories appeared to have finally hit upon a winning formula, yet at the heart of it was a tension which would again throw the party into internal conflict. The Progressive Conservatives had built upon a growing malaise among the western electorate, but western alienation was no longer tied to progressivism, as it had been in the past. Rather, it was increasingly linked to neo-conservatism. The "twinned moods" of regionalism and conservatism, with their call for a return to free enterprise, had been manipulated by the western premiers to protect their jurisdiction over natural resources against federal incursions. Non-state intervention was often used as a shorthand for no federal intrusion in provincially-oriented and state-directed provincial economic policies. Nevertheless, the rhetoric was consistent with the growing right wing of the federal Progressive Conservatives which, regardless of provincial loyalties, wanted to see the winding down of state enterprises, social programs, and government regulation of business.

This electoral strategy and its ideological formulations created tensions within the Clark coalition. The pressures became manifest in Cabinet bickering and confusion over such issues as the privatization of Petro-Canada, cutbacks in the public sector, and, perhaps most dramatically, in the ill-fated Crosbie budget which brought the defeat of the Tories in Parliament in 1979. These ideological frictions also contributed to the resignation of Joe Clark, the Red Tory, after a party convention revealed deep division over his continued leadership.

The fundamental tension between progressives and conservatives within the Conservative party were even more evident as they were aired publicly at the 1983 leadership convention. Nevertheless, it is far from clear whether a new kind of unified party emerged from that process. The delegates rejected the candidates linked to the most right-wing positions but they also rejected the moderate progressivism of the candidates identified as Red Tories. Moreover, they rejected candidates based in peripheral regions, especially those from the West, despite that being where much of their electoral support is concentrated. Instead, the choice of the convention, Brian Mulroney, is not readily identifiable with any of the factions which divided the Clark coalition. He is a bilingual anglophone with strong ties to the eastern economic elite, and he gained support largely because he seemed able to make the politics of bicultural-ism work in favour of the Progressive Conservatives. Moreover, his low profile on policy matters makes him appear at the centre of the ideological spectrum, not far from the position occupied by the Liberals. It would seem, therefore, that the Tories are once again preparing to try to beat the Liberals at their own game. Their past problems with just this strategy suggests that it is hazardous, at best. Controversies over official bilingualism in Manitoba and Ontario remind us that the Liberal party is still able to manoeuvre to great advantage within a linguistic definition of politics.

The most difficult challenge in the study of political parties is to determine which among the constant flux of ideas, policies and partisan posturing holds lasting significance for the future development of the party system. Clearly, as the foregoing suggests, the past decade has witnessed changes which may alter the contours of federal politics into the 1980s and beyond. Population shifts have changed the basic electoral arithmetic of the party system. As a result of the last redistribution of federal constituencies, there are now more members elected from the four western provinces than from Quebec. Moreover, the severity of western alienation from the governing Liberals suggests that these seats will be divided between the NDP and the Progressive Conservative party.

The "New West," however, poses a challenge which if not met threatens the continuing viability of the NDP. Although the West has been the lifeblood of NDP support, the western electorate has increasingly rejected it in favour of the Tories. They, rather than the NDP, appear to be the current heirs of the space opened up by the Progressives' fracturing of the party system in 1921. In part this development flows from the NDP's decision to pursue votes in the Centre, especially from organized labour in Ontario, which resulted in the neglect of their traditional regional constituency. On each of the major issues which have pitted the Centre against the West in recent years—questions of oil pricing, divisions of powers in federalism, the National Energy Program, the Constitution and the Crosbie budget—the NDP seemed to side with the Liberals. Although there were loud protestations from the western wing of the party, to do otherwise would have threatened NDP support in Ontario. Considering that twenty-six of the NDP's thirty-one members elected in 1980 represented western constituencies, however, a Centre-oriented strategy can only encourage party disharmony and, perhaps, western revolt. The NDP's fiftieth-anniversary policy convention, held in Regina in the summer of 1983, revealed a growing regional cleavage, and resulting malaise, within the party.

The past decade has also witnessed significant alterations in the strategies of development promoted by the two major parties. Yet our analysis strongly suggests that it is uncertain at this point whether the Tories can afford unswerving support for the interests of the resource sector and western province builders. Clearly the party will have to make some commitments to declining industries in the East if it plans to challenge the Liberals in Quebec. Neither can we be certain that the Liberals will continue on the course of state intervention and Canadianization that they campaigned on in the 1980 election. American outrage and pressure over the NEP appear to have successfully pushed the party away from a similar strategy for other foreign-owned sectors of the economy. Moreover, the decline in world demand for natural resources, especially oil, effectively curtails the Liberals' proposed means to economic salvation through state-directed mega-project development. In other words, the situation in the international economy has effectively left the Liberal party without a clearly defined economic development strategy.

In many ways, then, it is an open question whether the Liberals or the Progressive Conservatives will be able to don the mantle of the party of "the national interest" in the immediate future. The Liberals, however, have a proven record as skillful opportunists who can manipulate bicultural politics to maintain their hegemony while at the same time changing their leadership and borrowing policies to maximize their support in other areas. If the history of the party system tells us anything, it is that Tory strategists would be well advised to keep in mind an old baseball expression: "The game isn't over until the final out."

Further Readings

Alford, Robert. *Party and Society: The Anglo-American Democracies.* Chicago: Rand McNally, 1963. Chapter 9.

Brodie, M. Janine, and Jane Jenson. *Crisis, Challenge and Change: Party and Class in Canada.* Toronto: Methuen, 1980.

Cairns, Alan C. "The Electoral System and the Party System in Canada, 1921–1965." *Canadian Journal of Political Science* 1 (March 1968).

Clarke, Harold D., Jane Jenson, Lawrence Le Duc and Jon H. Pammett. *Political Choice in Canada.* Toronto: McGraw-Hill, 1979.

Clarke, Harold D., Jane Jenson, Lawrence Le Duc and Jon H. Pammett. *The Politics of Discontent.* Toronto: Gage, 1984.

Laxer, James. *Canada's Economic Strategy.* Toronto: Lorimer, 1980.

Ogmundson, Rick. "On the Measurement of Party Class Positions: The Case of Canadian Federal Parties." *Canadian Review of Sociology and Anthropology* 12 (1975).

Penniman, Howard R. *Canada at the Polls, 1979 and 1980.* Washington DC: American Enterprise Institute for Public Policy Research, 1981.

Perlin, George. *The Tory Syndrome.* Montreal: McGill-Queen's University Press, 1979.

Przeworski, Adam, "Proletariat into Class: The Process of Class Formation from K. Kautsky's 'The Class Struggle' to Recent Controversies." *Politics and Society* 7 (1977).

Simpson, Jeffrey. *Discipline of Power.* Toronto: Personal Library, 1980.

Smith, David E. *The Regional Decline of a National Party: Liberals on the Prairies.* Toronto: University of Toronto Press, 1981.

Thorburn, Hugh G., ed. *Party Politics in Canada.* 5th ed. Scarborough: Prentice-Hall, 1979.

Wilson, John. "The Canadian Political Cultures: Towards a Redefinition of the Nature of the Canadian Party System." *Canadian Journal of Political Science* 7 (September 1974).

Winn, C., and J. McMenemy. *Political Parties in Canada.* Toronto: McGraw-Hill, 1976.

Chapter 12

Elections

Jon H. Pammett

Although the idea that the suffrage for elections should approach the universal is a product of very recent times, the notion that leaders should be chosen by voting is an ancient one. Some scholars have traced the practice back into prehistory to the fourth millenium BC, when a group of city-states was developing in ancient Sumeria, between the Tigris and Euphrates rivers in what is today Iraq. Detailed study of surviving myths and epics has led them to propose that the political organization of this "first civilization" was in the nature of a "primitive democracy," in which the leading men of the cities gathered in a general assembly in times of emergency and elected a leader to carry out its decision. This "war leader" evolved into the institution of kingship when the king ceased being the temporary servant of the council of elders and started governing by himself.[1] Elections, then, are one of humanity's most ancient political customs.

Elections have reached the status of virtually omnipresent institutions in nations of the modern world, no matter how authoritarian the actual regime is.[2] Elections are so popular because they serve a multiplicity of functions for almost everybody connected with them, as well as for the political system which sponsors them. Whatever complaints are registered about the time they take, the expense they involve, the choices they present or the results they produce, they are vital to the image that almost every country wishes to present to the rest of the world. And whether they are perceived to be "meaningful" or not, few individuals anywhere have recorded the wish to do away with them altogether.

Impressive catalogues of functions performed by elections may be compiled on all levels of analysis. For the *political system*, elections fulfill at the outset a recruitment function by providing an orderly way of choosing the rulers or elites which govern the society. Because of the complexities involved in so doing, the institution of elections facilitates grouping within the system, and thus participates in the creation and maintenance of a system of political parties. We have already mentioned the fact that elections are perceived to be symbols to the rest of the world about the democratic nature of the country concerned; within the bounds of the system, however, this legitimation function is also important. By the very fact of their having taken place and produced a result, elections create support for the political system (providing the result is seen as having been fairly arrived at) and a certain amount of legitimacy for the resulting government. "The people," it is often said, "have spoken." Not to be neglected is the important political socialization function discharged by elections. An election centres attention on the political system and provides opportunities for learning about it. It is often one of the few genuine communal experiences that people in a diverse country go through together, and simple participation in the same activity can be integrative for the system as a whole.

Political parties, for their part, are served by elections. They provide a ready-made occasion for a party to build or renew its internal organization; such activity can take place around an agreed-upon, short-term goal and thus galvanize all efforts. In some cases, elections may perform the function of allowing competing party elites to resolve internal power relationships and strategic conflicts within the party.[3] Elections can also provide the parties with policy guidelines or parameters, depending on how issues are seen by politicians as having affected the election result. These messages range from very specific policies which may be seen as having been accepted or rejected along with the party, to more general philosophical or ideological approaches to governing. Finally, the result of an election provides the party with a claim to the legitimacy of the status it achieved therein, whether that of victor, official opposition, major or minor party.

For *individuals*, elections serve the function of forging a link between them and the political system. This connection can foster a sense of support for the system or a sense of efficacy, a belief in the potential of provoking a response of the system to personal or group demands. It has been suggested that elections function as a protection for the individual, giving people control over those in power and "a voice in their own affairs."[4] Elections facilitate the socialization function by providing education and information about politics to individuals, as well as by affecting the partisanship they hold. Elections can also serve certain ego-enhancement functions for the individual personality by providing an opportunity to make a political statement, to impress others with political knowledge or disdain, and to feel in general infinitely superior to those politicans attempting to curry favour. Finally, political participation, stimulated by the election context, may advance a variety of functions, ranging from direct personal gain and advancement to ego-identity formation, to satisfaction in the involvement with other people.[5]

In keeping with the foregoing division of the functions of elections, analysis by political scientists takes place at both the level of the individual and that of the political system, and includes, as well, a considerable number of studies of the internal operations of political parties. The individual-level analysis consists of explanations of voting behaviour and of how individuals arrive at their decision to support one party or another at a particular time. Those working in this field have carried out numerous pieces of survey research to amass the interview data necessary to test their theories. The system-level studies have been less common and have generally been of two types. The first has been an effort to study intensively the "context" of a particular election—the party platforms and activities, the media coverage, the events of the campaign, the patterns of the results, etc.[6] The second has involved the attempt to use survey data to explain the outcomes of particular elections. We will explore this subject further after we examine some aspects of individual voting behaviour in Canada.

Table 12.1
Reasons Cited for Vote, 1974, 1979, 1980

(percentages)[1]

	1974	1979	1980
Party	41	29	23
Leaders, leadership	25	34	30
Local candidates	14	9	9
Issues:			
Inflation	23	8	8
Wage and Price Controls	7	4	—
Unemployment	—	11	5
The Budget	—	—	15
Mortgage Deductability	—	2	1
Other Economic	11	17	15
Energy	—	5	29
Health, Welfare, Pensions	8	5	3
Confederation issues[2]	—	18	11
Bilingualism	4	3	1
Majority Government	7	—	—
Other issues	16	9	14
Time For a Change	—	14	2
Give the PCs a Chance	—	—	6
Miscellaneous Other Reasons	19	13	11

1. Multiple response. Person could give more than one answer.
2. Includes references to national unity, separatism, Quebec independence, the constitution and federal–provincial relations.

Voting Behaviour in Canada

The fact that elections perform a variety of functions for the individuals who vote in them would lead us to expect considerable diversity in their reasons for casting ballots in any given election. All indications we have from the National Election Studies, which are conducted after most Canadian federal elections, are that this expectation is easily met.[7] To illustrate the varied reasons given by Canadians for their voting choices, Table 12.1 gives the distribution of answers after three recent elections to a question which asked voters to "take a moment to think over all the reasons why you decided to vote the way you did, and just briefly tell me the things that were most important to you."

The evidence presented in Table 12.1 shows that virtually any short-hand explanation of why Canadians vote is bound to be correct for only a portion of the electorate. Thus, one should be highly suspicious of the generality implied by such interpretations as "Canadians rejected wage and price controls in 1974," "Pierre Trudeau's unpopularity led to the Liberal defeat in 1979" or "The country voted against the Crosbie budget in 1980." Wage and price controls *were* cited by some as the main reason for their 1974 vote, a group of voters in 1979 thought Trudeau was "the issue," and the budget was important in 1980, but none of the clusters of voters choosing them comes anywhere close to constituting a majority.

Rather than being some monolithic entity, then, the electorate is composed of sub-groups of people acting for a panoply of different reasons. Some people say they are voting for the party as a whole, either because of long-standing loyalty or new-found conviction that it is time a new lot of politicians was given a chance to run the country. To another set of voters, the comparative evaluation of the leaders is a major factor; for some others it is the local candidate from their riding who makes the difference. A wide variety of different issues is cited, some of perennial concern (e.g., inflation during the 1970s) and others which emerge as important in one election but are scarcely mentioned in another (e.g., the national unity question, which dominated a lot of the election rhetoric in 1979 but was not a major issue five years earlier).

The question of the importance of issues in individual voting decisions has long interested political scientists. Because the electoral process involves decisions made by masses of people, and therefore by numbers of people who are low in political information or interest, there has always been scope for charges that voting decisions are not being taken for the "right reasons." Usually this involves assertions that voters decide on the basis of the personality or images of the leaders or candidates, or unthinking party loyalty, but not on "the issues." This kind of dispute often includes questions about the extent of "rational voting," voting on the basis of a reasoned consideration of the issues important to the voter. It does not seem particularly profitable to engage here in a discussion of whether Canadians vote rationally or not (and it would seem even less advisable to take a position on just what constitutes a rational motive for voting choice in the first place.) It is possible to state, however, that in Canada a considerable amount of voting does take place for issue-related reasons.

The extent to which voting choice is motivated by issue concerns can be more clearly seen if we look at the voters' rankings of the four factors of leaders, candidates, parties and issues in terms of importance to their vote decisions. To prevent setting up a direct choice between issues and these other factors in people's minds (we felt that the number citing issues might be artificially high because voting on the issues is a more socially approved answer), respondents to the National Election Surveys were asked to choose among the three factors of party, leader or candidate, and then asked whether or not there was an issue basis to their choice. The percentage of people ranking the four factors important in the 1980 federal election is shown in Table 12.2. When offered a choice between party leader, local candidate and party taken as a whole, the last emerges as the most important factor. Interestingly, however, while less than half of those citing party declared there was an issue basis to this choice, slightly more than half of those choosing leader as most important referred to the leader's stands on certain issues rather than his personal qualities. The same overall pattern as shown for 1980 in Table 12.2 holds for previous elections. In total, just slightly less than half of the electorate reports an issue basis for their voting decision, in contrast to glib election commentary which sometimes asserts that elections are just popularity contests between the leaders.

The sharp-eyed reader will likely have noted from the evidence about the reasons for voting cited so far that a large proportion of such motivating factors are distinctly "short-term" in nature. Leaders and candidates are subject to frequent change, especially if saddled with the

Table 12.2
"Most Important Reason" for 1980 Vote

(percentages)

Party Leader		Local Candidate		Party as a Whole	
36		20		44	
Issue Stand	Personal Qualities	Issue Stand	Personal Qualities	Issue Positions	General Approach
53	47	40	60	43	57

stigma of having lost an election or two, and issues can be quite differentially important from one election to the next, as we have seen from Table 12.1. Although Canadians are by no means bereft of general images of and loyalties to the political parties, a majority claim to make up their minds at each election on the basis of short-term factors operative at the time.

This picture of the Canadian electorate is supported by the evidence we have about the nature of partisanship in this country. A majority of voters develop party loyalties that are either weak, changeable over time or different at the two levels of the federal system. All three of these factors contribute to the *flexible* partisanship which characterizes the link of about 60 percent of Canadian voters to the federal political parties. Thus, for many, when we ask "To which party do you feel closest?" the answer we get may be different from the response we would have received to the same question last year or at the time of the last election.

Several facets of the political culture contribute to the flexibility of ties to political parties. The most basic is that Canadian political culture is relatively apolitical. While Canadians are moderately interested in politics, this interest does not translate for most into substantial political involvement. The amount of political information possessed by the average Canadian is low, reflecting both a general lack of desire for detailed knowledge and the inadequate presentation of political news in the public media. Studies of children's political learning, or socialization, show a relatively weak transference of preference for a political party from parent to child. Such transmission of enduring partisan ties from generation to generation is not the norm because these feelings may not be strongly or persistently held in the adult "socializer." Children are accordingly less likely to develop such feelings for themselves, and a culture is perpetuated in which partisanship is not strongly held, or is changeable.

Canadians are not often content with being apolitical; in many cases they are downright anti-political. In the 1974 national survey interview, the respondents were handed a blank map of Canada and asked to "write in five words or phrases which best describe politics in Canada." The replies revealed a considerable degree of negativism toward almost everything associated with the political system.[8] In particular, the public feels negatively about political parties and politicians. In such an atmosphere, it is no wonder large numbers of people are unwilling to stick with "their party" in perpetuity. When those people who changed their partisanship were asked their reasons, more talked of the negative qualities of the party they were changing from than mentioned the positive qualities of the party they were changing to. It is not hard to foresee that many may soon become disillusioned with their new party as well.

Because of the conflicts and regional loyalties associated with its founding and development as a nation, Canada is governed by an extremely complex federal system. By the 1980s it is clear that a complete understanding of our system of government requires information about and orientations toward several different political systems, as well as sophisticated notions about the interrelationships of these systems. While most people have a basic understanding of the constitutionally established functions performed by the various layers of the federal system, it would be unrealistic to expect detailed knowledge of intergovernmental relations on the part of the mass public. Lack of knowledge begets lack of interest. Further, the image of conflict surrounding the Canadian federal system contributes to the general public mood of exasperation with and cynicism about the political process.

Every Canadian is a member of a political community which possesses two systems of political parties. This situation does not necessarily further complicate the individual's political world, since in some areas those party systems are for all intents and purposes the same. For example, the provincial Liberals and Conservatives in Nova Scotia are really the same parties as their federal namesakes. In several provinces, however, this is not the case. In British Columbia, the only party common to both federal and provincial party systems which has any continuity in terms of its strength is the NDP. Quebec has contained several major provincial parties which have not existed in any form at the federal level. In other provinces, like Ontario, parties have different competitive positions at the two levels, and there are different strategic choices involved in casting votes.

This complex situation has produced the Canadian phenomenon of the "split identifier," where persons may consider themselves provincial Conservatives and federal Liberals (a common pattern in Ontario), or provincial Pequistes and federal Liberals (Quebec), and so on. The proportion of Canadians who can be classified as split identifiers has been increasing, largely due to identification with provincial-only parties in Quebec and British Columbia. By 1980, therefore, 26 percent of those identifying with parties in Canada chose different parties at the two levels of the federal system. By some complicated psychological process, being a split identifier seems to make it easier to change parties and votes within each level, as well, and contributes to the overall flexibility of partisanship.

Those whose ties to political parties are flexible have an enhanced potential to shift their votes from one election to the next, though only a minority of them do so at any given time. The reasons which influence such partisans, particularly those who switch their votes, are predominantly short-term in nature: liking for a political party at that particular time, feelings about a leader or candidate, concern for an issue, or some combination of these factors. We can pinpoint further types of flexible partisans who will be influenced by different factors if we sub-divide them on the basis of their political interest. In 1979, for example, one-third of the electorate was flexible in its partisanship while having a lower degree of interest in politics, while just over a quarter of the electorate was flexible in its partisanship with a higher degree of political interest. It is this flexible higher-interest group who will give relatively heavy weight to political issues in determining their voting choice; the parties aim to appeal to this group with their issue-oriented campaigns. The flexible lower-interest group, on the other hand, pays less attention to issues and more to general images of leaders and parties; the personal appeal of Prime Minister Trudeau worked well with this group in past elections.

The flexibility of partisanship in Canada, and the tendency for voting decisions to be determined by short-term considerations of the parties, issues, leaders and candidates active at any given time has meant that social cleavages which are sometimes thought to form enduring loyalties in the population and divide them in important ways are not very influential in affecting people's votes. One of these cleavages, religion, can still be discerned in voting patterns, specifically in that Roman Catholics tend to vote for the Liberals. Overall, however, the relationship between religion and vote has not been very strong and is seen by many analysts as either being in decline or being so difficult to explain in modern circumstances that it should be treated as a relic of the past.[9] Studies have consistently found that another important cleavage, social class, has virtually no relationship to voting choice at the federal level in Canada, though there is more connection between the two variables in some provincial elections. Ethnic factors affect voting behaviour only in the sense that there is a tendency for francophones to favour the Liberals; the overall effect of this factor is mitigated, however, since the Liberals get a lot of English-speaking support as well, particularly in Quebec where the tendency for anglophones to vote for that party is even stronger than it is for francophones. The votes of Canadians, then, are not heavily "preordained" by social or demographic factors as they evaluate an electoral situation, just as they are not predetermined by durable party loyalties.

One major consequence of this situation is that election campaigns can be of major importance in affecting the outcome. Almost half of the electorate claims to make up their minds which way to vote during the campaign period, and in 1974, 19 percent of the respondents to the National Election Study said they decided during the last week of the campaign or on election day itself. Given the short-term nature of the factors that are important in many voting decisions, and the potential impact of the campaign and its events, the Canadian electorate is a very volatile group of people. The potential for dramatic swings in election results is always present. We will turn our attention in the next section to why they have so seldom occurred.

The Outcomes of Elections

It may seem anomalous that a political system in which the electorate is characterized by such volatility appears so stable at the aggregate level of federal election results that it has at times been referred to as a one-party dominant system. The Liberal party, "the Government Party" as it has been called, has won the bulk of federal elections. The only governments formed by the Conservatives in the twentieth century have been those under Borden (1911–20, part of which was a wartime Unionist government), Meighen (1925–26), Bennett (1930–35), Diefenbaker (1957–63), and Clark (1979–80). In this century, under the long-term leadership of Laurier, King, St Laurent, Pearson and Trudeau, the Liberal party has dominated federal politics, forming governments with, for the most part, majorities of seats in the House of Commons.

The resolution of the apparent paradox between individual volatility and aggregate stability lies in our ability to differentiate between the effects of electoral conversion and electoral replacement. *Conversion* involves the extent of vote switching among those who are members of the "permanent electorate," people who are already in the electorate and who can be counted on to vote in every election. All parties, through their campaign appeals, attempt to get voters to switch over to them from a previous vote for some other party. We have seen that the potential for such conversion is high, since the incidence of durable party loyalty is relatively low. *Replacement*, in contrast, is the impact on the result that newly eligible voters will have, as well as a group of "transient" voters, who do not turn out in every election. The impact of the transient vote will be determined by the difference in behaviour of those leaving the electorate (who voted last time, but not this time) and those mobilized into the electorate from a past abstention. In a nutshell, the success of the federal Liberal party has been achieved because, whatever the patterns of conversion in any given election, they have consistently gained through the process of electoral replacement.

The three most recent Canadian federal elections, held in 1974, 1979 and 1980, illustrate the operations of the patterns of conversion and replacement. In 1974, the Liberals were able to increase their overall popular vote from 1972 and win enough seats to form a majority government. However, if the process of conversion had been the only one operating, the result of the 1974 election would actually have been *worse* for the Liberals than that of 1972. This is because vote switching from 1972 to 1974 among members of the permanent electorate favoured the Conservatives. The process of electoral replacement, however, worked quite differently from 1972 to 1974. The Liberals won the bulk of the votes of young voters who became newly eligible in 1974, and also the majority of support from transient voters, who had not gone to the polls in 1972. Thus, because those who did not vote in the previous election, either through choice or through lack of eligibility, favoured the Liberal party by wide margins, the party's losses through vote switching were more than offset.[10]

Table 12.3

Electoral Turnover 1974–1979[1]

(diagonal percentages)

		1979 Vote				
		Liberal	PC	NDP	Socred	Not Voting
	Liberal	26.9	8.2	3.1	0.3	3.3
	PC	1.5	17.6	1.3	0.1	1.6
1974 Vote	NDP	1.0	1.5	5.8	0.2	0.7
	Socred	0.4	0.3	0.1	1.0	0.2
	Not voting	2.3	2.6	1.3	0.3	2.2
	Not Eligible	5.2	3.5	2.2	0.6	2.7
						100%

1. As measured by 1974–79 panel and 1979 cross-section samples. N=2,396. Votes for other parties included in percentages but not shown in table.

The patterns of electoral turnover from 1974 to 1979 and 1979 to 1980 are presented in Tables 12.3 and 12.4. In determining the outcome of the 1979 election, in which the Conservatives came close to forming a majority government, conversion and replacement again operated differently. It can be seen in Table 12.3 that there was massive vote switching of 1974 Liberals away from that party toward the Conservatives. Fully 8.2 percent of the 1979 electorate switched from the Liberals to the PCs, whereas only 1.5 percent went the other way. In addition, the Conservatives managed a slight net gain in switches between their party and the NDP, a better performance than they had managed in 1974. Once again, however, electoral replacement was the Conservatives' Achilles heel. They did manage to win a slight plurality of the transient vote, important because of the high turnout in 1979. Newly eligible voters, on the other hand, still favoured the Liberals by a substantial margin, and this new-voter group was particularly numerous in 1979 because of the five-year interval since the previous election, and because the electorate is still mirroring the effects of the high post–World War II birth rate. Almost two-and-a-half million new voters had come of age since the previous election. The Liberals' ability to retain their appeal to this group, therefore, reduced the magnitude of their 1979 defeat, and the Conservatives' inability to win this new voter group was to have disastrous consequences for them in terms of denying them majority government status as well as the opportunity to renew their support among the young.

Table 12.4
Electoral Turnover 1979–1980[1]

(diagonal percentages)

		1980 Vote				
		Liberal	PC	NDP	Socred	Not Voting
	Liberal	30.4	2.5	1.3	0.1	2.4
1979 Vote	PC	3.9	24.0	3.2	0.1	3.7
	NDP	2.1	1.5	9.6	—	1.5
	Socred	0.7	0.4	0.4	0.6	0.5
	Not Voting	2.4	1.9	0.8	—	4.0
						100%

1. As measured by 1979–1980 panel. N=1,642. Votes for other parties included in percentages but not shown in table.

Table 12.4 reveals what happened a scant few months later. This time, the processes of conversion and replacement worked in the same direction, favouring the Liberals. The Liberals showed a net benefit in vote switching with the PCs and the NDP, and also regained their edge among transient voters moving into the electorate from a non-voting stance in 1979. Similarly, since voting turnout in 1980 was down from 1979, it is relevant to note that the Conservatives suffered disproportionately from the 1980 abstention of voters who had favoured them a year earlier. Thus, even though the Liberal party often loses voters through conversion (which is only natural since it is so often in power and in a position to disillusion voters) it makes up for that through infusions of new and transient voters, thereby creating a kind of "pass-through" effect. It is the ability to form a new electoral coalition of voters at each election that confirms the Liberal party in its dominant position in the centre of the Canadian federal political system.

Another reason for the success of the federal Liberal party has to do with the kind of political issues which emerge in Canadian elections.

More than any other party, the Liberals have managed to adopt as their own a cluster of political issues which can affect an election *outcome*, as opposed to simply affecting a number of individual voters. This distinction may not be immediately apparent, but it is extremely important if elections are to be analyzed as political events. An issue can affect an individual's vote simply by being important to that particular voter. To affect an election outcome, however, an issue must meet three conditions. First, an issue must be salient to an appreciable number of people—if few people think it is important they are not likely to act on it. Second, an issue must have a "skewed" distribution; in other words, it must be *valenced* in a certain direction, so that people are generally in favour of it or against it. If people are split on the general desirability of something like wage and price controls, to take an example from the campaign of 1974, then any shift of votes to one party on the basis of that issue is likely to be offset by a countervailing shift away from that party of those who do not care for the party's position. Third, an issue must be linked to one party. If no one party is particularly preferred on an issue, then voters may consider the issue to be important to their individual decisions, but voters switching to and remaining with all the parties will do so—and if it does not differentially benefit one party the issue will not affect the election result. This was the case with the inflation issue in 1974, and the energy issue in 1980. Lots of voters thought they were important, and they were agreed that inflation was bad or that plentiful, cheap energy was good, but no one party was perceived to have the solution to either the inflation or the energy problem, and therefore no party was differentially favoured.

It is difficult for economic issues, like those cited previously, to meet all three conditions for an effect on an election outcome. Although the public usually considers them to be important, they are often either not linked with a particular party (as with general problems like inflation or unemployment) or not valenced (as with specific economic issues like wage and price controls, or selling Petro-Canada, which had strong contingents both pro and con). The Liberal party, however, has managed to meet the three conditions on a set of Confederation issues including national unity, bilingualism, constitutional questions and issues involving Quebec. These issues, at least in their "national unity" manifestation, are valenced in that most people are concerned with keeping the country together and reducing conflict, and are definitely linked with the Liberal party in that the Liberals are seen as the one party with enough appeal to both English and French Canada to be able to work out solutions to the problems with Confederation. Such Confederation issues are not always front and centre in election campaigns, but in cases where they are, as in 1979, the Liberals benefit from them. The strategy of the Liberal party in 1979 was to try to emphasize the national unity issue, which they rightly felt would accrue gains to them if they could persuade the public of its salience at that time. They were at least partially successful in doing so, since as we saw in Table 12.1, Confederation issues were mentioned by 18 percent as the main reason for their vote. It is the facility of the Liberal party in turning Confederation issues to their advantage, as well as in maintaining a substantial edge in leader preference, which are instrumental in attracting new cadres of support and maintaining the party in power.

Conclusion

If we return to consider some of the major functions of elections referred to at the beginning of this article, it is apparent that federal elections in Canada perform some of these functions much better than others. Recruitment, for example, is reasonably well served; each election produces the requisite cadre of leaders to operate the ministries, though the scarcity of representatives from certain regions often causes concern to the parties. The function of creating support for the political system and legitimizing it in the eyes of its citizens is another matter. Because federal elections have produced in recent years highly regionalized patterns of support for the parties, there has been a tendency to regard governments as primarily representative of certain parts of the country at the expense of others. Liberal governments are spoken of as representative of the centre of the country, and particularly Quebec, and not of the periphery, whereas the Conservatives are seriously deficient in representing Quebec. This situation has the potential to affect the amount of support given to the central government, and thus to the present structure of the Canadian political system, but there is really very little evidence that discontent has penetrated to this deep a level as yet. Although many Canadians might favour some rearrangement of the existing federal system, particularly if some such proposal promised to alleviate the constant bickering between governments, very few favour basic changes to the system's structure or a serious weakening of the federal government. The 1980 referendum in Quebec was defeated largely because sovereignty-association was perceived as posing a serious threat to the overall Canadian political community.[11] A considerable amount of system support *is* being created in Canada, and elections play a part in this process; the continuity implied in the simple conduct of federal elections may in the long run be more important than the patterns of particular results.

Elections, we noted previously, perform functions for political parties as well. They certainly enable parties to revive and re-establish their organizations; since the Liberals and Conservatives (and also, to a large extent, the NDP) exist as political parties primarily for the purpose

of contesting elections, these events are their *sine qua non*. With regard to
the proposed function of setting policy parameters for the parties, or
sorting out the specific policies they will have a mandate to enact, the
Canadian election system does not perform very well. This is partly
because parties often seek to avoid specific policy stands during election
campaigns, knowing they would usually alienate as many voters as they
attracted by such pledges. Even if specific policies are proposed, recent
Canadian history shows that parties rarely feel themselves bound by
them. During the 1974 campaign, for example, the Liberals fought
strenuously against the idea of wage and price controls, and then
promptly introduced them once re-elected. Similarly, the short-lived
Clark government spent much of its tenure in office searching for ways
to alter or abandon its 1979 campaign promises on such matters as
moving the Canadian embassy in Israel, allowing mortgage interest
charges to be deducted from income tax, selling Petro-Canada, etc. Not
only does this behaviour of parties in power mean that elections provide
little opportunity for the public to affect policy, it also damages the credibility of politicians, increases political cynicism among the population,
and may have some negative impact on support for the political system.

Finally, with regard to serving functions for individuals, elections
also produce mixed results. They do affect the development of the
individual personality in many different ways, though whether these
effects contribute to a "healthy" personality is a judgment that had
perhaps better be left to psychiatrists. As to whether or not the institution of elections contributes to people feeling they have a say in controlling their own affairs or a sense of efficacy in dealing with government,
we can at the present time agree only partially. Most Canadians are not
very confident that they can understand and influence the political
system, and many are quite cynical about the possibility of producing any
significant change through elections. This situation may be mitigated
somewhat by the feeling on the part of most that their satisfaction with
their lives and material standard of living is not greatly affected by
government. Thus, the feeling that elections do not really accomplish
very much does not manifest itself in rage and destructiveness, but
rather in a bemused detachment from the whole political process, in the
apolitical political culture we noted earlier. Some people have argued that
this situation has been, on balance, beneficial in that elites are free to
govern and to implement some policies that might have been more
vigorously opposed in a more politicized society. That may be true, but
there are also inherent dangers in having a public so divorced from and
cynical about the political process in a country which depends so heavily
on politics to negotiate solutions to its numerous problems.

Notes

1. The "primitive democracy" thesis is particularly associated with Thorkild Jacobsen and his associates at the University of Chicago. See T.H. Jacobsen, "Primitive Democracy in Ancient Mesopotamia," *Journal of Near Eastern Studies* 2 (1943): 159–72, and Carl H. Kraeling and Robert M. Adams, eds., *City Invincible*, p. 65. It should be noted that this interpretation of the political organization of ancient Mesopotamia is by no means universally accepted. See the critique by Georges Roux in his *Ancient Iraq*, (London: Penguin, 1966) pp. 104–24.
2. In the early 1960s, data collected by Yale University showed that out of 100 countries for which information existed, 92 had held elections in the past six years. See Richard Rose and Harve Mossawir, "Voting and Elections: A Functional Analysis," *Political Studies* 15 (1967): 180.
3. Primary elections in the United States are an obvious example of this; however, it also takes place in other contexts. See Jane Jenson, "Strategic Divisions within the French Left: The Case of the First Elections to the European Parliament," *Revue d'integration européene/Journal of European Integration*, September 1980.
4. Norman D. Palmer, *Elections and Political Development* (Durham, NC: Duke University Press, 1975) p. 87.
5. Jon H. Pammett, "Adolescent Political Activity as a Learning Experience: The Action-Trudeau Campaign of 1968," in *Foundations of Political Culture: Political Socialization in Canada*, ed. Jon H. Pammett and Michael Whittington (Toronto: Macmillan, 1976) pp. 160–94.
6. This tradition in Britain produced the "Nuffield" series of election studies, such as David E. Butler, *The British General Election of October, 1974* (London: Macmillan, 1975). In Canada, the best examples are John Meisel, *The Canadian General Election of 1957* (Toronto: University of Toronto Press, 1962) and Howard Penniman, ed., *Canada at the Polls: The Canadian Elections of 1979 and 1980* (Washington: American Enterprise Institute for Public Policy Research, 1982.)
7. Large national surveys have been conducted after five Canadian federal elections. The studies of the 1965 and 1968 elections were organized by John Meisel, and the studies of the 1974, 1979 and 1980 elections by Harold D. Clarke, Jane Jenson, Lawrence LeDuc and Jon Pammett. The most complete report of the 1974 data can be found in Harold D. Clarke, Jane Jenson, Lawrence LeDuc and Jon H. Pammett, *Political Choice in Canada* (Toronto: McGraw-Hill, 1979.) For 1979 see Harold D. Clarke, Jane Jenson, Lawrence LeDuc and Jon H. Pammett, "The Impact of Issues and Leaders in the 1979 Federal Election,"*Canadian Journal of Political Science* 15 (September 1982).
8. The replies are analyzed in considerable detail in Chapter 1 of Clarke *et al.*, *Political Choice in Canada.*
9. See William Irvine, "Explaining the Religious Basis of Partisanship in Canada: Success on the Third Try," *Canadian Journal of Political Science* 7 (1974): 560–63. Also John Meisel, "Bizarre Aspects of a Vanishing Act: The Religious Cleavage and Voting in Canada," in his *Working Papers in Canadian Politics*, 2nd rev. ed. (Montreal: McGill-Queen's University Press, 1975) pp. 253–84.

10. A complete analysis of the outcome of the 1974 federal election can be found in Clarke *et al.*, *Political Choice in Canada*, Chapter 12.
11. Jon H. Pammett, Harold D. Clarke, Jane Jenson and Lawrence LeDuc, "Political Support and Voting Behaviour in the Quebec Referendum," in *Political Support in Canada: The Crisis Years*, ed. Allan Kornberg and Harold D. Clarke (Durham, NC: Duke University Press, 1983).

Further Readings

Beck, Murray J. *Pendulum of Power*. Scarborough: Prentice-Hall, 1968. Gives accounts of Canadian election campaigns to 1968.

Clarke, Harold D., Jane Jenson, Lawrence LeDuc, Jon H. Pammett. *Political Choice in Canada*. Toronto: McGraw-Hill, 1979. Abridged edition, 1980. The most extensive treatment of Canadian voting behaviour and partisanship currently available.

_____. *Absent Mandate: The Politics of Discontent in Canada*. Toronto: Gage, 1984. An analysis of voting behaviour in the climate of economic decline of the 1970s and 1980s.

Meisel, John. *Working Papers on Canadian Politics*. 2nd enlarged ed. Montreal: McGill-Queen's University Press, 1975. A series of perceptive, empirical analyses of Canadian elections.

Penniman, Howard, ed. *Canada at the Polls: The General Elections of 1979 and 1980*. Washington, DC: American Enterprise Institute for Public Policy Research, 1982. Articles by Canadian scholars on the campaigns waged by each of the parties, as well as such topics as campaign finance, nomination of candidates, mass media coverage, and the participation of women. A companion volume on the 1974 election is also available.

Regenstrief, Peter. *The Diefenbaker Interlude*. Toronto: Longmans, 1965. Based on the author's own polling during the Diefenbaker years, many of the conclusions about Canadian voting behaviour in this book have stood the test of time.

Schwartz, Mildred. "Canadian Voting Behaviour." In *Electoral Behaviour: A Comparative Handbook*, edited by Richard Rose. New York: The Free Press, 1974. An overview of voting behaviour, the electoral system and the nature of Canadian society. Includes a useful bibliography.

Chapter 13

Pressure Groups: Talking Chameleons
A. Paul Pross

The most difficult of all government's tasks is that of communicating with the public. Despite the millions of words expended in public debate every day, modern governments have great difficulty finding out what the public wants and needs, and what it feels about the work that the state is already doing. Equally, although its payroll is laden with press officers, writers and others skilled in the arts of communication, government has immense problems in explaining itself to the public, in reporting back to it and in persuading and leading it.

Pressure groups are one of three communications systems used by most modern states to overcome these problems. The other two are the internal apparatus of the government itself, such as the press officers and writers mentioned above, and the party system. Political parties are best equipped to transmit the demands and views of individuals and of groups of individuals concerned about specific localities. This is because political parties tend to be built around an electoral system created to fill a legislature that is territorial or *spatial* in orientation; i.e., each member represents the people who live in a specific area, or constituency.

Pressure groups have become prominent because they are effective where parties fail. They can identify and articulate the views and needs of individuals who may live far apart but who share common interests. In modern society, with its interdependent economy, its multinational corporations and its very large and specialized government bureaucracies, this *sectoral* approach of pressure groups is an essential complement to the spatial orientation of political parties. Even so, as we shall see later, the rapid growth and rising influence of pressure groups gives concern to many observers, some of whom feel that democratic government is threatened thereby.

Pressure groups are organizations whose members act together to influence public policy in order to promote their common interest.[1] Unlike political parties, they are not interested in directly wielding the power of the state, though sometimes a group representing a particularly large economic block (the Acadians are a good example) will decide to transform itself into a political party. In general, pressure groups are interested in exerting influence and in persuading governments to accommodate the special interests of their members.

To achieve this, pressure groups have to be more than mere assemblages of people. Their members have to be organized; brought together in structured relationships with one another and dragooned into identifying and expressing their common interests. Pressure groups are consequently distinct, clearly identifiable elements in the body politic. While their chief role, as far as the political system is concerned, is to provide a network for policy communication, in the following paragraphs we shall see that they have several other functions as well.

Pressure groups are also very adaptable members of the polity—so adaptable, in fact, that we can use their structure and behaviour as a guide to charting the policy process in a particular political system. We cannot look at this aspect of pressure group life in great depth here, but we shall try to use it to draw some comparisons between the manner in which the policy is made in Canada and in the United States. Furthermore, we shall use our understanding of the adaptive behaviour of pressure groups to set out a theory that explains the day-to-day relationship of pressure groups and their members to the policy system. Finally, we shall look at a couple of the very large issues raised by the growing influence of pressure groups in the policy system.

The Functions of Pressure Groups

Whenever we try to set down precisely what it is that pressure groups do, we have to remember that, like most institutions, they are different things to different people. Leaving aside for the moment those who feel that pressure groups are a curse and an abomination, let us look briefly at the ways in which government officials and group members relate to them.

Most of us are unaware of the number of pressure groups we belong to. Because we join many associations in order to share our interests and concerns with others, we tend not to think of them as pressure groups. Each September, as Canadian universities resume classes, thousands of students pay dues to their campus student associations. Most of that money supports local campus activity that has nothing to do with politics, but some of it is channelled to provincial and national federations of student associations which in turn devote considerable time and money to lobbying governments concerning matters such as tax breaks for students, university funding, tuition fees, student loans and national and international issues that have pricked the conscience of the university community. Acquiring a university degree is a serious business, and if government is to be deeply involved in education we should expect student associations to act as pressure groups.

We do not expect our leisure associations to camp as regularly on the doorsteps of government, yet they are among the most active pressure groups to be found in Canada. For instance, many a rural politician has trembled as provincial legislatures have debated hunting and fishing legislation; game laws have often been the most hotly contended items on legislative agendas, and provincial associations of hunters and anglers have been slow to forget the transgressions of politicans who have opposed their ideas. Similarly, associations of camping enthusiasts, naturalists, bird watchers and wilderness buffs have a surprising degree of influence with government agencies, such as Parks Canada, that cater to their interests. In fact the wilderness orientation of Canada's national parks system is in large part a reflection of the strength of this lobby.

These examples illustrate a basic point: very few pressure groups exist simply to influence government. Their members have joined in order to obtain some special benefit that each organization alone can offer. Yet, because government intrudes so much into our daily lives, these associations become a very convenient vehicle for communicating with government. While most associations inevitably develop some capacity in this role, the members often only very grudgingly allow this to happen—lobbying governments is an expensive business. But as the need to express their views becomes more urgent, they hire consultants, undertake studies, appoint "government liaison officers," meet with officials and politicians and generally join the babble of tongues that surrounds the policy process.

From the group members' point of view, then, the lobbying activities of their associations are first and foremost intended to *communicate*. People in government also see pressure groups in this light, though not always happily. Communication may take many forms, some of them violent, many of them distinctly noticeable to the general public—and therefore usually embarrassing. However, the great majority of them are unobtrusive, involving the careful negotiation of technical and regulatory details of policy. Although often unwelcome—after all, no official or politician likes to be told that a pet project or policy is faulty—pressure groups are frequently the most reliable and the best-informed link between government agencies and the portions of the public that they particularly serve. Indeed, so important is this function that governments have often gone out of their way to encourage the *creation* of special-interest groups. In the Maritime provinces the federal and provincial governments did exactly this in the late 1970s when they encouraged independent fishermen to form bodies able to participate in developing policies for managing Canada's newly expanded fishery. "If I had to write the manual for dealing with government," federal Fisheries Minister Romeo LeBlanc told one group, "I would put two main rules of the road: carry a flag—that is, have an organization—and sound your horn. Let people know you are there." By the early 1980s, the Eastern Fishermen's Federation, the chief product of the exercise, was a recognized actor in the fisheries policy community.[2] Similarly, core funding from the federal government was an important factor in developing the modern Canadian Indian movement.[3]

Nor does communication flow in only one direction. Most lobbying organizations present governments with a convenient means of reaching a special audience. Annual meetings can be addressed by ministers and senior officials intent partly on flattering and winning over a special clientele or constituency, but also on conveying various messages: a hint at policy change, an explanation of action, warnings, encouragement and so on. Eyes watering from cigar and cigarette smoke, perspiring under the television lights, wondering whether they can be heard above the clatter of coffee cups and the hum of comment, guest speakers drone through their after-dinner jokes, their compliments and their pious reminders, knowing that alert minds in the audience will soon have interpreted the speech's central message and passed it on to the less discerning. Similarly, organization newsletters, regional meetings and informal get-togethers offer government spokespersons networks for the rapid transmission of information.

If communication is the primary function of pressure groups, *legitimation* is not much less important.[4] That is, pressure groups play a very significant part in persuading both policy makers and the general public that changes in public policy are worthwhile, generally desired and in the public interest. Because pressure groups frequently speak for a significant proportion of the public that will be affected by a change in policy, governments find it reassuring to have their proposals endorsed by the relevant groups. As Romeo LeBlanc told fishermen in the speech we previously quoted, "Push the officials ... they like it." Cabinet ministers know how helpful it is to have a pressure group leader tell a legislative committee, as one did in 1975, that "we provided extensive comments ... with respect to the first draft. When we saw the new bill most of the corrections, changes or criticisms we had found with the first draft had been corrected, modified or vastly improved."[5] In a similar way, group leaders sell their members on the desirability of policy changes.

On the other hand, officials are aware that a disaffected group can use its many connections with the media, the opposition parties and perhaps other governments to attack policy and so undermine its legitimacy. The mining industry did this between 1967 and 1972 when it disagreed with the federal government over tax reform. Using a combination of general appeals to the government and behind-the-scenes lobbying with provincial governments, the mineral industries eventually forced the federal government to revise its proposals. One of the reasons for their success lay in their ability to persuade the public and the provinces that the new laws would discourage investment in the mining industry and so hurt the economy. In other words, they undermined the legitimacy of the proposed changes.[6] Similar interest group reactions to Finance Minister Allan MacEachen's 1981 budget had the same effect, ultimately leading to a number of changes and an attempt on the part of the finance minister, and his successor, to reform the budget-making process so that interests would have an opportunity to discuss possible tax changes before they become government policy. Fear of the embarrassment caused by such incidents, to say nothing of the disruptive effect on policy, gives government agencies a powerful incentive to consult with pressure groups that has become more pressing as our policy process has become increasingly diffuse.

Administrative and regulatory activities are much less prominent functions than communication and legitimation, but they occur often enough to deserve mention. Provincial administration of social services is often supplemented by the work of groups such as the Children's Aid Society or church-affiliated organizations. In the years when Canada was receiving large numbers of immigrants, voluntary associations provided many facilities which helped newcomers move to and settle at their destinations.[7] Today, as tight budgets constrain governments' ability to pay for services we once took for granted, we have begun to revive the practice of encouraging voluntary associations to provide supplementary services, particularly in education and in home care for the elderly. Often the groups involved in these activities are not thought of as pressure groups, but because they often do contribute to the development of policy in their areas of interest, we are justified in thinking of them in this way.

Groups perform administrative functions for several reasons. Often, as we have suggested, governments cannot afford to offer the services that they provide through a combination of volunteer and paid help. Sometimes governments are not willing, for policy reasons, to provide special services, though they are willing to help voluntary associations provide them. The community is so divided over many issues related to birth control, for example, that some governments prefer to support birth control counselling indirectly through general grants to organizations such as Planned Parenthood rather than to advocate directly one position or another. Finally, many groups administer programs that could as easily be carried out by government officials, simply because they have traditionally offered such services. Periodically, as in the case of the Children's Aid Societies in Ontario, these roles come under review and sometimes they are taken over by government.[8]

Regulatory functions are delegated to groups for quite different reasons. Lawyers, doctors, chartered accountants and other professional groups have been given considerable authority to govern themselves through their associations, largely because governments are reluctant to thrust themselves into the complicated and often treacherous debates that surround professional accreditation and ethics. As well, though, some professional groups have a great deal of influence, and, quite probably, that has been exerted to keep government at arm's length. Even so, we see governments increasingly cutting back on this autonomy—for instance, forcing the medical profession, by and large, to accept publicly approved fee schedules or, as in Quebec, by imposing a high degree of regulation on all professional groups.[9]

In summary, we have argued that as far as the political system is concerned, pressure groups serve four functions: they communicate, legitimate, administer and regulate, though to their members these are often the least important roles that they play. We have suggested that the communications function is the most important. In the following comments we shall concentrate on this aspect of pressure group life, looking especially at the way in which factors such as the need to communicate with government, the amount of resources available for communication and the level of understanding of policy systems combine to affect both the structure and behaviour of such groups.

Structure and Behaviour

The functions that pressure groups perform have much to do with both the organizational form they take and the way they behave. We might be tempted to claim that their form follows their function, were it not for the fact that structure is also greatly influenced by such things as the kind of resources made available by the group's members, their determination to promote their common interest through exerting influence and, always, the characteristics of the political system itself. We shall return to these influences after we have looked at the more fundamental aspects of pressure group structure and behaviour.

Earlier we defined pressure groups as "organizations whose members act together to influence public policy in order to promote their common interest." The fact that they are *organizations* is crucial. In political life there are many interests and over time a considerable number exert influence in the policy process, but unless they have access to more resources than most individuals and the majority of companies, they lack the ability to sustain their influence. Unaggregated demand, as political scientists call the political demands of individual persons and corporations, tends to occur sporadically and on a piecemeal basis. Often it is sufficient to achieve or avert specific decisions, such as a spot rezoning in a city plan, but it rarely influences public policy. This is because the process of policy formation is extremely complex, involving many participants, taking place over a long period of time and usually consisting of innumerable decisions.[10] For most of those who want to take part in this process the only feasible way to do so is to band together, to share costs, to deploy at appropriate times the different talents that participation requires, even simply to maintain continuity as the process unfolds—in other words, to organize.

Not all pressure groups organize in the same way or to the same extent. Much depends on what they want to achieve by engaging in the policy process, on the resources they can put into lobbying and on their understanding of the mechanics of policy making. Since the way in which all these factors come together has a lot to do with the policy consequences of the work of pressure groups, it is important to try to understand the relationship between the levels of organization pressure groups attain and their behaviour in the policy process.

Our goal here is not simply to understand the behaviour of pressure groups; the way in which they behave can also tell us a great deal about policy making in specific political systems and even about the political system itself. For example, as the introduction to this chapter implied, studies of Canadian pressure group behaviour have led some students to conclude that administrators in Canadian governments have a far greater influence in policy making than our earlier work on political parties, parliamentary institutions and legal frameworks had led us to believe.

To understand these aspects of pressure group life we must arrange what we know about them into meaningful patterns. There are various ways to do this. One that is used by many scholars is to classify all groups according to the *kinds of causes* they promote. This usually results in two broadly defined lists: in one, the groups that pursue the self-interest of their members; in the other, the groups that pursue more general, public interests. Some important insights have come from using this approach. For example, as a result of the debate triggered by studies such as *The Logic of Collective Action*,[11] which argues that interest groups only survive if they can offer their members advantages (selective inducements) that can be obtained nowhere else, we now know a great deal about the internal forces which motivate pressure group behaviour and we appreciate more than we ever have before the problems that beset public interest groups. A practical consequence of this improved understanding has been the trend in several countries toward giving public interest groups special assistance in arguing for the public interest before regulatory and policy-making bodies.[12]

Useful though this approach is, it has serious weaknesses. In the first place, the classification system itself is "messy," for there are far too many groups that work simultaneously for both selective benefits and the public interest, and it is often difficult to categorize them.[13] Again, there is often a very fine line between self-interest and public interest. (Bill Bennett and Richard Hatfield have both accused environmental groups of pursuing the interests of their members rather than the interests of the public at large.)

More important, however, this method takes a one-sided view of the relationship between pressure groups and governments. Although it admits that pressure group activity is often triggered by government action, such as the creation of a new program or the ending of an old one, it tends to explain the subsequent behaviour of such groups either in terms of competition between rival groups or in terms of what one writer has called their "interior life." In other words, the approach focuses on the effort group members are willing and able to make to convince policy makers of the rightness of their cause. This concern is very necessary, but it has to be put in perspective. The other partner in the relationship— government—affects pressure group behaviour just as much as does membership commitment, organizational sophistication and so on. In fact, most pressure groups are *chameleons*: those that take their lobbying role seriously adapt their internal organizations and structure to suit the policy system in which they happen to operate. That is why pressure groups working only at the provincial level in Canada are often quite different from those which concentrate their efforts at the federal level, and why both differ dramatically from their counterparts in eastern Europe, the Third World and even the United States.[14]

Several years ago this writer developed a conceptual framework which does try to look at pressure groups from the perspective of the *influence of government* as well as from that of the internal dynamics of groups. This approach starts with the assumption that pressure groups have functions to perform that are as necessary to the development of government policy as those performed by political parties, bureaucracies, executives and courts. However, the way in which they perform those functions is as much determined by the shape of the policy system as it is by the knowledge, the enthusiasm, the financial capacity and the other internal characteristics of individual groups.[15] For example, a policy system like Canada's, in which legislatures do not have a large say in policy development, will encourage pressure groups to develop quite differently from those that emerge in a system such as the U.S.'s, with its emphasis on congressional power.

Institutionalization, this approach argues, gives us the key to understanding pressure group behaviour. If we can come to understand how it is that some groups survive in a political system and become both influential and organizationally sophisticated, while others quickly disappear, then we can learn a great deal about their interior life and about their particular policy environment.

An institution is a sophisticated entity, one which not only works to achieve the goals laid down for it, as any organization should, but which actually embodies the values it is built around. Like any organization, it begins life as a collection of individuals gathered to achieve certain objectives. Sometimes such groupings have organizational shape—the members have structured relationships with one another which permit them to carry out specialized tasks—but often they are simply a group of people who want to accomplish something. Gradually, if they stay together, they elaborate an organizational structure, and if they are successful their organization develops into an institution, "a responsive, adaptive organism" which, to its members and many of those it deals with, has a philosophy, a code of behaviour and sense of unity related to the values it has come to embody. The Greenpeace Foundation is a good example of such an organization. It is not only sophisticated as an organization with an international structure, but it stands very firmly for certain beliefs and acts accordingly. As a pressure group it is highly institutionalized, even though it is not popular with governments.

When we apply the concept of institutionalization to pressure group analysis we must be very aware of a point made by an early student of institutions, Philip Selznick. "As institutionalization progresses," he maintains, "the enterprise ... becomes peculiarly competent to do a particular kind of work."[16] In the case of pressure groups this means that they must become "peculiarly competent" to carry out the four functions we have already discussed, especially the function of communication. The institutionalized group knows what government is thinking about, what it needs to know and how to get that information to it at the right time, in the right place and in the most acceptable form. This means a great deal more than simply buttonholing politicians at cocktail parties. It means the group must have an expert staff—or helpful, well-informed membership—able to communicate with government officials at bureaucratic as well as elected levels, on a continuing basis. The need for this particular competence has led this writer to claim that one of the defining characteristics of institutionalized pressure groups is "an extensive knowledge of those sectors of government that affect them and their clients." In its entirety that definition describes institutional pressure groups as:

> groups that possess organizational continuity and cohesion, commensurate human and financial resources, extensive knowledge of those sectors of government that affect them and their clients, a stable membership, concrete and immediate operational objectives associated with philosophies that are broad enough to permit [them] to bargain with

government over the application of specific legislation or the achievement of particular concessions, and a willingness to put organizational imperatives ahead of any particular policy concern.[17]

We cannot explain this definition completely here, but we should note several things about it. First, it is very unlikely that any real group could be described in these particular terms. It is an idealized version of a certain kind of group; it is a model with which to compare the various types of groups we come across. Second, because the idea of institutionalization suggests a progression and because this particular model can be used as a benchmark against which other groups can be compared, it becomes possible to think of pressure groups as falling along a continuum. At one extreme we can place institutional groups like those in our model, and at the other we can put those groups that have the opposite characteristics. These, we would argue:

> are governed by their orientation toward specific issues ... [and have] limited organizational continuity and cohesion, minimal and often naive knowledge of government, fluid membership, a tendency to encounter difficulty in formulating and adhering to short-range objectives, a generally low regard for the organizational mechanisms they have developed for carrying out their goals, and, most important, a narrowly defined purpose, usually the resolution of one or two issues or problems, that inhibits the development of "selective inducements" designed to broaden the group's membership base.[18]

We call these "issue-oriented" groups and can readily identify them. They spring up at a moment's notice, usually in reaction to some government action or a private sector activity that only government can change. (They are often seen in city politics confronting developers, highway builders and planners.) Usually they disband when their goals are either won or convincingly lost, but occasionally they keep on playing a part in politics and slowly become recognized voices in policy making. In order to do this they have to become more highly organized, developing their "peculiar competence" to communicate their policy views to government. Since the early 1970s a number of environmental groups have done this, in effect engaging in the process of institutionalization. They do not, of course, become institutional groups overnight. In fact, very few achieve that status, and most we could describe as either fledgling or mature, depending on how closely they seem to conform to the models at either end of our continuum.

Figure 13.1 sets out a visual guide to this continuum. In it we have tried to show how the organizational development of each kind of group helps define its relationship to the policy process. For example, the issue-oriented group with its supporters participating out of concern for a particular issue usually has a small membership which tries to make up in devotion to the cause what it lacks in resources or staff. Lack of staff is this type of group's most serious deficiency, at least in the Canadian setting, because it generally means that the group does not have expert knowledge about what government is doing or thinking about the issue concerning them. Its members tend, therefore, to work in an information vacuum. Not only do they not know what government is thinking, they tend not to know who in government thinks about their particular issue. Their reactions, therefore, tend to be gut reactions directed at the most likely figure in sight, usually a politician, and expressed vociferously in the media.

In the long run these methods do not work. A specific decision may be turned around, but to change policy—which is a mosaic of many decisions—groups need to be close to government thinking, able to overcome the barriers created by administrative secrecy and knowledgeable about where and when to intervene. In Canada, particularly, where public information legislation was until recently quite antiquated and group participation in policy making has been considered a privilege, not a right, government officials have in the past been able to undermine any groups too inclined to publicly attack policy simply by withholding vital information. It may be that recent changes in the policy process, particularly in the diffusion of power that has become the norm in Ottawa, is altering this condition. Nevertheless, for many years the authority of information control made government agencies the dominant partner in their relations with pressure groups and forced those issue-oriented groups that did survive to follow a pattern of institutionalization that took them very rapidly from the placard-carrying stage to the collegial and consultative relationship favoured by government.

Yet though confrontation has been and perhaps still is dysfunctional for groups in the long run, in their early life it can be very important, sometimes essential. Since they generally emerge in response to a policy issue, new groups cannot, by definition, have participated in the deliberations which led to the decision they are concerned about. Thus they enter the policy process at a stage when events are moving beyond their ability to stop them, and only the most drastic measures will have any effect. In these circumstances, confrontation may be the best available strategy, as it makes use of the media's ability to influence the only decision makers who may still be able to change the course of events—the politicians.

The group that outlives this early "placard-carrying" stage generally has done so by changing its relationship to its members and by adapting to the policy system. One of the first steps in this adaptation is that the organization must stop being concerned with only one issue and instead take up several causes. Many environmental groups took this route, starting up to prevent the destruction of a particular natural amenity,

Figure 13.1
The Continuum Framework

Categories	Group Characteristics							
	Objectives				Organizational Features			
	single, narrowly defined	multiple but closely related	multiple, broadly defined & collective	multiple, broadly defined, collective & selective	small membership/ no paid staff	membership can support small staff	alliances with other groups/staff includes professionals	extensive human and financial resources
Institutionalized				▨				▨
Mature			▨				▨	
Fledgling		▨				▨		
Issue-oriented	▨				▨			

then switching their concern to large issues. With a broader range of interests the group attracts a wider membership. While the new members may lack the fervent sense of commitment of the group's founders, and may be less inclined to sound a strident ideological note when the group tries to communicate with government, a wider membership base usually broadens the group's financial resources, bringing stability and a strengthened capacity to engage in the information game.

Levels of Communication with Government		Categories			
		Institution-alized	Mature	Fledgling	Issue-oriented
Access-Oriented	regular contact representation on advisory boards, staff exchange	▓			
	regular contact with officials		▓	▓	
	confrontation with politicians, officials			▓	▓
Media-Oriented	public relations; image-building ads, press releases	▓	▓		
	presentation of briefs to public bodies		▓	▓	
	publicity-focussed protests				▓

Here again group-oriented and policy-oriented developments may take place in tandem. With a steady budget the group may take on a modest staff, a move that usually ensures that finances are better managed and that the members are served more consistently. Financial capacity usually also means that the group can afford to hire professionals— lawyers, public administrationists, public relations specialists—who can help it acquire the information it needs to participate in the policy process. These are the first steps in institutionalization. From this point on, the nature of the organization does not change a great deal. It simply becomes more complex, more capable of adapting to changes in the policy system and, to the disappointment of founding members, more remote and professional, guided increasingly by its paid staff.

Once started on the road to institutionalization the pressure group more readily wins the attention of government officials and at the same time is more apt to adapt to meet shifts in government policy processes. This largely follows from the decision to hire professionals. Because they are familiar with the way in which policy is made, these people guide the group away from some lines of action and encourage others. In Canada and most European countries this generally means that groups become more and more intimate with the details of bureaucratic decision making and less and less inclined to use the media except when formal hearings necessitate the presentation of rather general briefs which are intended to create an image rather than promote a specific policy. In the United States, on the other hand, lobbyists can expect to have to argue both in public and in private. With these differences in strategy go differences in organizational structure.

As these comments suggest, the processes of pressure group institutionalization offer us a particularly useful way of discovering the differences between policy systems and even tracing the evolution of our systems over time. In Canada, for example, because we have pressure groups, we often mistakenly think that they behave in the same way as American pressure groups. This sometimes leads to the notion that our policy system is becoming more like the U.S.'s. It is quite true that in some respects, particularly when issue-oriented groups exploit the media, that there is more than a superficial resemblance between Canadian and American pressure group behaviour. As soon as we look at the behaviour of more established groups in both countries, however, we see major differences. For example, even well-established American groups readily take part in public debates over policy, while their counterparts in Canada see an appeal to public opinion as a last resort.

Why the difference? In the American system congressional politics plays a large part in policy development, with policy tending to be formed by the congressional committees responsible for a particular field, the administrative agencies carrying out policy, and the interest groups affected by it. Much policy discussion is conducted in private, but there is also an important public element involving committee hearings where rival demands are vigorously presented and where even the most secure, discreet and established lobby must put its case to the general public as well as to the policy makers.[19]

Canada has had no such public forum. Debate in Parliament has been tightly controlled by the government, and even committee hearings have offered few opportunities for airing grievances, much less changing policy. The basic form of public policy has been worked out between the political executive and senior administrators. Consequently, lobbyists and others wishing to influence public policy have chosen to do so by approaching and persuading civil servants and Cabinet ministers rather than parliamentarians. There are innumerable consequences to this, some affecting pressure groups, others the policy process itself, most of which we cannot discuss here. Suffice it to say that the end effect of this system is that "legitimate, wealthy, coherent interests, having multiple access to the legislative process, would tend to be much more influential than less legitimate, poor, diffuse interests, having few sources of access to the legislative process."[20]

It may be that changes in Parliamentary procedure, in the structure of policy making; in the availability of government information and in our constitutional framework are causing important modifications in this system of pressure group politics, making groups less dependent on bureaucracy and more capable of engaging in open and public debate. At the moment we have only a few hints that this is the case and no very clear idea as to what the future may bring. However, probably we can assume that a tendency for pressure groups to become more numerous and more publicly active will continue to grow.[21]

**Pressure Groups in the Policy Process:
The Role of Policy Communities**

We sometimes think of pressure groups in the singular, acting alone to bring off a policy coup or to thwart some scheme cooking in the "policy shops," as government policy analysis units are often called. At other times they are described en masse: collaborating, competing and generally rampaging across the policy stage. In general, however, their participation in the policy system is continuous, discreet and multifaceted.

The first responsibility of any pressure group is to attend to the immediate needs of its clients. This usually means dealing with quite routine problems: alleviating the too stringent application of regulations, negotiating a minor shift in policy, bringing about the slight extension of a service. Such minor irritations along the public sector–private sector interface bring pressure group representatives into daily contact with government officials and, while not inspiring in themselves, familiarize them with the subtle changes in administrative routine and attitude that eventually crystallize into a change in policy.[22] When formal policy discussions begin, the understanding developed through these routine contacts is of immense value.

The policy process itself is hard to define: the origins of policy are often obscure and the roles of those who take part are seldom exactly the same from debate to debate. Even so, we do have some general notions as to how the key policy actors—politicians, bureaucrats and lobbyists— relate to one another, and this helps us develop a rough picture of the part pressure groups play in the process.

The first point that we must bear in mind is that the entire political community is almost never involved in a specific policy discussion. Specialization occurs throughout the policy system. The existence of pressure groups gives us the most obvious evidence of this, but special- ization occurs elsewhere as well. Government departments, however large and multifaceted they may appear to be, are confined to a precisely defined territory. Even the political executive finds that only the really big issues are discussed by the entire Cabinet. All the rest are handled by individual Cabinet ministers or by specialized Cabinet committees. Richard Crossman, once a member of the British Cabinet, remarked in his diary that "we come briefed by our departments to fight for our departmental budgets, not as Cabinet ministers with a Cabinet view."[23] Only prime ministers and presidents play roles that encourage them to consider policy in the round, and they live with such tight schedules that only the most urgent and significant issues come to their attention.

Out of specialization come what we call "policy communities"— groupings of government agencies, pressure groups, media people and individuals, including academics, who for various reasons have an interest in a particular policy field and attempt to influence it. Most policy communities consist of two segments: the sub-government and the attentive public. To all intents and purposes the sub-government is the policy-making body in the field. It processes most routine policy issues and when doing so is seldom successfully challenged by interlopers. In the United States, sub-governments generally include the responsible executive agency, the congressional committee which oversees its activities and the most influential pressure groups concerned with the field. Each of these depends on the other for support of one kind or another, and out of their symbiotic relationship grows an extremely powerful institution.[24]

It is not clear what Canadian institutions can be likened to the American sub-government, though some combination of structures doubtless performs the same function. Since government agencies take such a very large part in the policy process, we would expect to find them somewhere close to, and possibly right at the heart of, the sub-government, with other power centres being the responsible Cabinet ministers, the most influential pressure groups and, very likely, where relevant, parallel agencies at the provincial level. Unfortunately, studies of Canadian policy making have not yet advanced far enough to let us say much more than that this inner circle–outer circle concept of the policy community is probably real enough.

The outer circle is partly described by the term "attentive public," which includes those who are interested in policy issues but do not participate in policy making on a frequent, regular basis. The academic community often plays this role, as do journalists working for specialized publications and, of course, a range of organizations and associations whose interest is keen but not acute enough to warrant breaking into the inner circle.

The attentive public lacks the power of the sub-government, but it still plays a vital part in policy development. Conferences and study sessions organized by professional and interest associations offer opportunities for officials at various levels to converse with the grass roots of their constituency and with journalists and academics who have been studying public policy. Most have views on government performance and are quick to put them forward. Though most are heard skeptically, sometimes patronizingly, they contribute to the process through which government and people gradually amend, extend and generally adapt policies and programs to the changing needs of the community. Similarly, the newsletters, professional journals and trade magazines which circulate through the policy community give both the sub-government and the attentive public plenty of opportunity to shore up, demolish and generally transmogrify the existing policy edifice. In this turmoil of theories and interests, officialdom—which is almost never monolithic, nearly always pluralistic and seldom at peace with itself—discerns the policy changes government must make if it is to keep nearly abreast of circumstance. The main function of the attentive public, then, is to maintain a perpetual policy review process.

In Figure 13.2, we have described the kind of policy community which might be active in a field in which the federal government is prominent. At the heart of the community are the key federal bodies involved: the agency primarily responsible for formulating policy and carrying out programs in the field; Cabinet with its coordinating committees and their support structures, the Privy Council Office, the Treasury Board, the Ministries of State, and so on. None of these are located at the very centre of the figure because no one agency is ever consistently dominant in the field. On average, though, because so much of policy making is routine, the lead agency tends to be most influential

Figure 13.2
The Policy Community

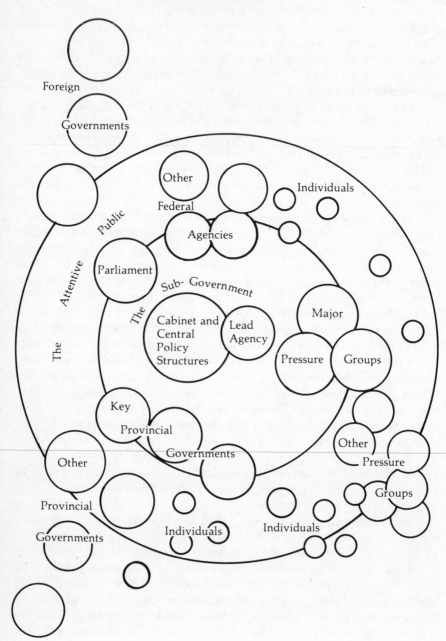

over time. Clustered around it are the pressure groups and provincial government agencies to which we have already referred, keeping a sharp eye on "the feds" and generally participating in the sub-government. Also involved are other federal agencies whose mandate overlaps that of the lead agency. These usually review agency policy, working through interdepartmental committees to do so, and often greatly alter it. For example, Canadian fisheries policy has often been influenced by External Affairs, worried about our relations with trading partners who fish off our coasts. Hovering on the edge of the sub-government is Parliament, perennially interested, intermittently involved, sometimes influential.

Also hovering on the edge of the sub-government are other provincial governments. Some of these might wish to be part of the sub-government but lack the resources to maintain a presence; others are simply not interested and are content to observe the activities of the sub-government, interfering when necessary. In the final analysis they may be no more influential than some of the major pressure groups active in the community. Some of the pressure groups are depicted as overlapping one another, because in fact they do overlap. They share membership, are often put together on advisory boards and frequently combine their efforts to present a common stand to government and the public. Finally we should note that foreign governments must also be included in Canadian policy communities. Canadian politicians and officials are great travellers, always aware of changing trends and conditions abroad—sometimes more alert to developments elsewhere than to developments in parts of Canada—and ready to import new ideas and approaches to the Canadian scene.[25]

The figure suggests an orbital movement around the lead agency and the federal executive, but that would be too static. Rather than revolving around the key agencies, the other members of the policy community are in constant motion. As governments and key personnel change, provincial government participation varies, or changing economic factors compel provincial agencies to retreat or advance into the sub-government. In the energy field, for example, Alberta became prominent after the Leduc discovery, and Newfoundland after Hibernia. Similarly, pressure groups come and go from the centre.

Pressure groups, along with individual members of the attentive public, are the most mobile members of the policy community. With their annual meetings, their newsletters, their regional organizations and, above all, their informal networks, they have an ability to cross organizational lines denied other more formal actors, such as government departments. They can, therefore, act as go-betweens, provide opportunities for quiet meetings between warring agencies and keep the policy process in motion. These services, together with their ability to evaluate policy and develop opinion, make pressure groups integral members of the policy community.

Before we conclude our comments on the policy community, we have to remember that the most prominent of its members are not primarily interested in making or reformulating policy. Rather, for them, the policy community is a protective device, limiting rather than expanding the opportunities for the public at large to achieve major policy changes. Thus, it is the goal of the sub-government to keep policy making at the routine or technical level. If it achieves this, the sub-government can keep interference to a minimum. Often, however, circumstances outside its control—economic changes, the development of new technologies, changing public concerns—are more than the sub-government can handle through its system of formal communications and informal networks. Controversy develops, new issues emerge, and more and more interests want to take part in policy making. Policy debate broadens as levels of conflict rise, so that eventually central issues are taken out of the hands of the sub-government and the policy community and resolved at the highest political levels—by Cabinet and by the first ministers' conference.[26] When this occurs, the policy community, as well as policy, is often vastly altered.

Pressure Groups and Democracy

Many people feel that pressure groups are a threat to democratic government. They distrust "special-interest groups," arguing that their special pleading circumvents the legitimate authority of elected representatives and unfairly competes with the average citizen who approaches government as an individual. They fear that the special-interest state is more easily corruptible than one which debates and settles policy in the open forum of parliament. "It is one thing," Robert Stanfield argues,

> for individuals to pursue their own interests as they always have: it becomes a qualitatively different kind of society when individuals organize to pursue their individual interests collectively. National life has become a struggle for advantage among large and powerful organizations—not simply corporations and trade unions. Organized pressures abound.[27]

Stanfield sees pressure groups supplanting political parties as the citizen's chief vehicle for communicating with government. John Meisel shares this view:

> Pressure groups are often unwilling to permit their interests to be expressed and transmitted only by parties, but wish to participate directly in making their voices heard and their influence felt. . . . Their numbers and means permit them to become rivals of political parties.

These rapidly proliferating groups and institutions can gain access to the decision-making process without having recourse to parties which thus become bypassed in the vital area of mediation between individual and group interests and the state.[28]

Not only does democracy suffer as the political party is undermined, but the country also loses "the only organization whose nature forces them to work towards a national consensus."[29] "National political parties are the only mass organizations we have which are forced to try to see the country as a whole and to reconcile regional and other differences."[30] Unless we act to check the spreading influence of pressure groups, Stanfield warns, we shall lose our capacity to discern the national interest. Similar fears have been expressed in other countries, particularly in the United States, where criticism of "interest group liberalism" suggests that pluralism, the touchstone of American government, has bred a monstrous, competitive and eventually self-destroying system.[31]

We cannot lightly dismiss these fears. There is no doubt that interest groups have proliferated in recent years, nor that the influence of political parties has abated. Nor does long study of their behaviour banish the suspicion that special-interest groups are capable of corruption and, however unwittingly, of destroying democracy. Ultimately special interests want special favours, and the logic of the relationship between groups and their clients countenances the unscrupulous use of influence.

The fact is, pressure groups have become necessary. In Canada and elsewhere governments have needed pressure groups so badly that they have encouraged their growth. They have given them moral encouragement and financial assistance, they have made places for them on advisory boards and regulatory agencies, they have created regulations which intentionally push those who are regulated into associations, and they have made many groups a part of the administrative process. None of these steps have been taken in order to destroy democracy, and although some challenged political patronage, they attacked corruption, not the party system.

The decline of the political party as an instrument for developing policy has come about because government itself has changed, not because of effete party leadership, rapacious pressure group activity or a declining sense of community among the public. The modern state delivers innumerable services, manages vast resources and attempts to direct complex economies, and to do all of these things it has organized itself into massive, functionally oriented, specialized bureaucracies. These agencies have great difficulty dealing with human beings. They deal with cases, with the partial needs of individuals. To develop policy they must talk with the public—not the public in general, but with the public they serve: their special public. What could be more natural than to persuade this public to organize itself, to adapt to the structure of modern government in order to communicate more effectively with it?

Nor does the trend to special-interest representation stem solely from the growing complexity of modern government. Equally important are the changes which have taken place in the economy over the last two centuries. The world of small enterprises whose fortunes were associated with the fortunes of particular places gave way during this century to a world economy vastly influenced by the giant corporation. Whether it is a multinational or not, the giant corporation is not very interested in what happens in specific localities. It has plants in many places, draws its resources from around the world and markets its products everywhere. In its own way it is just as concerned with specialized issues as are government agencies, and it is no accident that these two forms of human organization have achieved complexity together.

Equally, it is no accident that as these structures have evolved, political parties have declined. Political parties in most western nations, at least, have a territorial bias. They are designed to win control of legislatures, and thus political power, and as most legislatures are based on territorially demarcated constituencies, party organization must follow suit. This is in many ways anachronistic, for the reasons we have outlined: governmental bureaucracies and their clients deal with sectoral issues, not the local concerns that disturb constituency organizations. Hence the decline of party influence. Yet the party system is not as outdated as it may seem. Despite decades of organizational conditioning, human beings still exhibit tremendous attachment to specific places. Consequently, the spatial basis of political party organization provides an important antidote to the sectoral bias of the administrative arm and the machinery of the economy.

With the legitimacy of government rooted in a spatial orientation to political communication, and its effectiveness depending on sectoral organization, the modern democratic state contains a tension that is the most fascinating, most disturbing feature of modern political life. Out of it has come the decline, but certainly not the demise, of the political party and the rise of the pressure group, the ideal instrument for sectoral, specialized communication. Thus, while Robert Stanfield decries the growth of special-interest groups, his colleague Michael Forrestal hails this "most useful growing presence,"[32] and industrialized nations toy with Scandinavian ideas of corporatism,[33] a system of political communication which consciously structures organizations, like the pressure groups we know in North America, into highly formal relationships with one another in order to achieve not only policy communication but also the collective management of state, economy and society.

Whether we in Canada will ever achieve this ultimate form of pressure group life is a moot point. Prominent officials have urged it, important government publications have promoted it, and the federal, Quebec and Nova Scotia governments have experimented with it. But corporatism probably requires a much higher level of national private sector organization than Canadians would like, and it may also require a level of consensus about national goals and aspirations much higher than anything we have yet attained. For the moment we can expect pressure groups to continue to proliferate and to become a steadily more important partner in policy communication. In consequence, in the later 1980s we can expect that these "talking chameleons," these adaptive instruments of political communication, will find new ways to play their part in the policy process. We must make sure that our other institutions of policy formation, Parliament in particular, adapt equally well to the changing demands of modern society.

Notes

1. I have taken this definition from my earlier article, "Pressure Groups: Adaptive Instruments of Political Communication" in *Pressure Group Behaviour in Canadian Politics*, ed. Pross (Toronto: McGraw-Hill, 1975), pp. 1–26. There I explain more fully the institutional approach to studying pressure groups which I have only sketched here. Other aspects of the approach are presented in "Canadian Pressure Groups in the 1970s: Their Role and Their Relations with the Public Service," *Canadian Public Administration* 18 (1975) 1: 121–36 and more fully in *Group Politics and Public Policy*, forthcoming.
2. *Lunenburg Progress-Enterprise*, April 5, 1978, p. 16.
3. J. Hugh Faulkner, "Pressuring the Executive," *Canadian Public Administration* 25 (1982) 2: 240–44, 248.
4. See David Kwavnick, *Organized Labour and Pressure Politics* (Montreal: McGill-Queen's University Press, 1972) for a useful discussion of this aspect of pressure group life.
5. W.L. Canniff, Technical Director, Canadian Chemical Producers' Association, House of Commons, Standing Committee on Fisheries and Forestry, *Minutes of Proceedings and Evidence*, April 17, 1975, p. 18:4. (Re: "An act to protect human health and the environment from substances that contaminate the environment.")
6. See Arthur Drache, "Improving the Budget Process," *Policy Options* 3 (1982) 5: 15–19 and Douglas Hartle, *The Revenue Budget Process of the Government of Canada* (Toronto: Canadian Tax Foundation, 1982).
7. Freda Hawkins, *Canada and Immigration: Public Policy and Public Concern* (Montreal: McGill-Queen's University Press, 1972), p. 301.
8. The role of children's aid societies in Ontario has been vigorously debated in the last few years. See particularly *The Globe and Mail*, December 16, 1977, and, more recently, the debate over the provincial government's intervention in the operation of the Kenora District Office of the Children's Aid Society, in the provincial legislature. See also National Council of Welfare, *In*

the Best Interests of the Child: A Report by the National Council of Welfare on the Child Welfare System in Canada (Ottawa: The Council, 1979).

9. See René Dussault and Louis Borgeat, "La reforme des professions au Québec," *Canadian Public Administration* 17 (1974) 3: 407.

10. For example, in June 1983, officials in Ottawa sat down with representatives of the Canadian Chamber of Commerce, the Business Council on National Issues and the Canadian Manufacturers' Association to discuss revisions to federal competition legislation. On six previous occasions since 1971 government proposals to change the legislation had been set aside in the face of fierce opposition from business groups. (*Kingston Whig-Standard*, June 21, 1983.) The story of the long attempt to reform competition policy can be found in W.T. Stanbury, *Business Interests and the Reform of Canadian Competition Policy* (Toronto: Carswell/Methuen, 1978) and Irving Brecher, *Canada's Competition Policy Revisited: Some New Thoughts on an Old Story* (Montreal: Institute for Research on Public Policy, 1981).

11. Mancur Olson, *The Logic of Collective Action* (Cambridge, MA: Harvard University Press, 1965).

12. See Peter H. Schuck, "Public Interest Groups and the Policy Process," *Public Administration Review* 37 (1972) 2: 132–40.

13. Terry M. Moe, *The Organization of Interests* (Chicago: University of Chicago Press, 1980).

14. Suzanne D. Berger, ed., *Organizing Interests in Western Europe* (Cambridge: Cambridge University Press, 1981).

15. A similar view is put forward by Henry W. Ehrmann in *Interest Groups on Four Continents*, ed. Ehrmann (Pittsburgh: University of Pittsburgh Press, 1958).

16. Philip Selznick, *Leadership in Administration* (New York: Harper and Row, 1957), p. 139.

17. Pross, "Canadian Pressure Groups in the 1970's," p. 124.

18. Ibid.

19. See Randall B. Ripley and Grace A. Franklin, *Congress, the Bureaucracy and Public Policy* (Homewood, IL: Dorsey Press, 1976); Robert Presthus's two-volume comparative study on Canada and the United States, *Elite Accommodation in Canadian Politics* (Toronto: Macmillan, 1973) and *Elites in the Policy Process* (Cambridge: Cambridge University Press, 1974); and Mildred A. Schwartz, *The Environment for Policy-Making in Canada and the United States* (Montreal: C.D. Howe Institute, 1981).

20. Fred Thompson and W.T. Stanbury, "The Political Economy of Interest Groups in the Legislative Process in Canada," (Montreal: Institute for Research on Public Policy, Occasional Paper No. 9, 1979), p. viii.

21. The recent evolution of the Canadian policy process has caused a good deal of debate, which probably can best be followed in the journals *Canadian Public Administration* and *Policy Options*.

22. There are useful descriptions of these relationships in Kwavnick, *Organized Labour and Pressure Politics*.

23. Quoted in J.J. Richardson and A.G. Jordan, *Governing Under Pressure: The Policy Process in a Post-Parliamentary Democracy* (Oxford: Martin Robertson, 1979), p. 26.

24. Ripley and Franklin analyze the American sub-government system in

Congress, the Bureaucracy and Public Policy. My concept of the policy community will be presented in *Group Politics and Public Policy,* forthcoming.

25. For example, Canadian minimum wage policy has been influenced by the experience of other countries and the work of international organizations. See Chris Parke, "The Setting of Minimum Wage Policy in the Maritimes" (Halifax: Dalhousie Institute of Public Affairs, 1980).
26. This paragraph adapts to the Canadian scene concepts developed in E.E. Schattschneider, *The Semi-Sovereign People: A Realist's View of Democracy in America* (New York: Holt, Rinehart and Winston, 1960). The Canadian variant is looked at more fully in Pross, *Group Politics and Public Policy.*
27. Robert L. Stanfield, the Fifth George C. Nowlan Lecture, Acadia University, February 7, 1977, mimeographed.
28. John Meisel, "Recent Changes in Canadian Parties," in *Party Politics in Canada,* ed. Hugh G. Thorburn (Scarborough: Prentice-Hall, 1967), pp. 33–54.
29. Stanfield, Fifth George C. Nowlan Lecture.
30. Ibid.
31. Theodore J. Lowi, *The End of Liberalism* (New York: Norton, 1979).
32. *Halifax Chronicle-Herald,* May 11, 1971.
33. See Leo Panitch, "Corporatism in Canada," *Studies in Political Economy,* Spring 1979, and "The Development of Corporatism in Liberal Democracies," *Comparative Political Studies,* April 1977, p. 61.

Further Readings

Dion, L. *Société et politique: la vie des groupes.* Two volumes. Québec: Les Presses de l'Université Laval, 1971.

Kwavnick, D. *Organized Labour and Pressure Politics.* Montreal: McGill-Queen's University Press, 1972.

Lang, R.W. *The Politics of Drugs: A Comparative Pressure-Group Study of the Canadian Pharmaceutical Manufacturers' Association and the Association of the British Pharmaceutical Industry, 1930–1970.* Lexington, MA: Saxon-House and Lexington Books, 1974.

Presthus, R. *Elite Accommodation in Canadian Politics.* Toronto: Macmillan, 1973.

———. *Elites in the Policy Process.* Cambridge: Cambridge University Press, 1974.

Pross, A.P. *Governing Under Pressure: The Special Interest Groups.* Toronto: The Institute of Public Administration of Canada, Fourteenth National Seminar, 1981.

Schwartz, M.A. *The Environment for Policy-Making in Canada and the United States.* Montreal: C.D. Howe Institute, 1981.

Stanbury, W.T. *Business Interests and the Reform of Canadian Competition Policy.* Toronto: Carswell/Methuen, 1977.

Thompson, F., and W.T. Stanbury. "The Political Economy of Interest Groups in the Legislative Process in Canada." Montreal: Institute for Research on Public Policy, Occasional Paper No. 9, 1979.

Part 4
Structures of Canadian Government

Chapter 14
The New Canadian Constitution
David Milne

Constitution building is a uniquely difficult exercise for any people to put themselves through, and one not lightly undertaken. After all, constitutions are designed to be reasonably permanent instruments of state. They are foundational acts which define political institutions, declare national purposes, and instill legitimacy for a state's power arrangements and objectives. In the great modern examples of the American and French revolutions, the constitution has come to be seen as a people's covenant, a sacred declaration of national and democratic purpose celebrated thereafter in song and verse. That Canada was forced to begin again, to seek a national renewal of its constitution after barely completing its first centennial as a nation, seemed to betoken some grave original defect. Nevertheless, by the late 1960s millions of Canadians were convinced that their existing constitution was no longer a realistic foundation for the kind of federal state Canada had become. Moreover, thousands of Canadian citizens in the province of Quebec were looking toward a new homeland as a separate francophone state. Clearly, the Canadian constitution did not appear to be generating either loyalty or respect and did not function as an instrument of national unity.

To the student of Canadian history this may not seem surprising. The nation's birth was neither particularly fortuitous nor even memorable. The political accommodation of the French- and English-speaking peoples within British North America was a difficult and uneasy task. At best, it was a marriage of convenience. Maritimers would never have joined the union had they not felt imperial pressure to do so. Unlike the French or Americans, Canada did not become a people's state by virtue of a revolution, nor did Canadians endorse any stirring constitutional document which might have cemented their new political relationship. Their constitution, the British North America Act, was the product of colonial elites working in cooperation with the interests of the British Empire. It was conservative and elitist and totally lacked the popular legitimacy of the French or American revolutions.

Nor did the formal institutional arrangements intended to safeguard the Canadian union work as intended. While the founders had built a legally centralized union as a bulwark against the dangers of "states' rights" which might threaten Canada as it had the United States during the Civil War, Canada had by the 1960s become a highly decentralized federal state with increasing talk of "provincial rights" and even outright separatism. Some of the formal constitutional prerogatives of the federal government which were intended to keep the provinces in quasi-imperial subservience to the national government in Ottawa, such as its power to reserve or disallow provincial laws, had fallen into disuse. The economic focus had shifted from the mighty national projects, like the building of the transcontinental railway, to resource development projects in the provinces. The modern post-Depression state priorities in education, health and social welfare also had elevated the provinces from the "quasi-municipal" status which the fathers of Confederation had assigned to them. These developments, together with judicial review and multi-national penetration of the Canadian economy, had done much to undermine the founding fathers' plans for a powerful national government.

Nor was the constitutional formula used to foster effective territorial representation in the federal Parliament successful. Unlike the Senate in the United States or in Australia, Canada's second House, which was designed to ensure that the interests of the less powerful provinces would be heard and respected in national legislation, turned into a weak and ineffectual shadow of the Commons. The appointed members of the Senate, most of whom had received their seats as patronage gifts from the party in power, could hardly challenge a popularly elected chamber. Therefore, the provincial premiers became by default the only effective champions of the interests of the provinces and regions.

These institutional defects, by weakening the voice of smaller and less populated provinces concerning federal development policies, reinforced the problems of economic disparity in Canada. The political arrangements of the Canadian state came to reflect the unequal, lopsided nature of Canada's economy.

The colonial nature of Canada's constitutional genesis also meant that no thought went into the problem of a domestic amending formula which could be used after Canada acquired its independence. Britain might act as a referee in the event of intergovernmental conflict and a legal agent for changing the country's constitution so long as Canada remained a colony, but what was to be the formula after independence? As a federal nation, Canada would have to come up with a mechanism which specified a required level of provincial consent together with that of the federal Parliament before changes could be made—a task which proved to be impossible through all the years after 1927. Therefore, Britain retained the legal power to change the Canadian constitution even after Canada acquired political independence. This quasi-colonial anomaly was to remain unresolved until the 1980s.

But perhaps the most serious deficiency in the constitutional arrangements for Canada concerned the relations of the French- and English-speaking peoples. The British North America Act had merely provided guarantees respecting the use of the French language in Parliament and the French and English languages in the legislature and courts of Quebec. In addition, the founding fathers had relied on a paternalistic federal Parliament to watch over possible violations of the educational rights of denominational (hence, indirectly, linguistic) minorities. Section 93 of the Act permitted Parliament to make "remedial laws" with respect to legislation injurious to the educational rights of denominational minorities.

Apart from these provisions, of course, the rights of the French Canadians were expected to be preserved by the power of Quebec both within its own jurisdiction and within the federal Parliament itself. These provisions, too, failed to protect French-speaking minorities from legislative assaults upon their rights in English-speaking provinces. The conscription crises of the two world wars amply demonstrated that the power of Quebec was an insufficient counterweight to the interests of the growing English-speaking majority of the country. By the 1960s, when Quebec nationalism had moved well beyond its traditional defensive character, the Canadian constitution's compromise between the linguistic groups came to be seen as a totally inadequate statement of the French fact in the country. Indeed, the traditional guarantees to the English-speaking minority within the province were now attacked as threatening the linguistic future of the majority Québécois. It became evident that the 1867 constitutional bargain between the French- and English-speaking peoples in Canada had either broken down or would no longer be relevant to Canada's current circumstances.

It was in the light of these developments that the political elites of Canada began to gear up for major constitutional reform. The formal opening to the process came with the calling of a provincial Confederation of Tomorrow Conference by Premier John Robarts of Ontario in 1967, followed swiftly by a full-scale constitutional conference in Ottawa the next year. As a result of Quebec's quiet revolution, complete with its burgeoning nationalism and the rise of political terrorism, the constitutional status quo could no longer remain in its anomalous condition. Quebec's new political elite, which had come to power from the ashes of the Duplessis regime, now began to divide within itself. At least three major constitutional agendas arose to answer the new demands of the Quebec people.

Two of these constitutional options, arising out of the nationalist slogan *maîtres chez nous*, sought change by building up the power of the

Quebec state. One group, which might loosely be called the "decentraliz-ing federalists," argued that more powers over communications, foreign policy, social policy and the economy should be transferred from Ottawa to Quebec City in order that Quebeckers could be made to feel more at home and secure within the Canadian federation. Constitutional renewal meant increasing the new love affair between the Quebec people and its state which had begun with the quiet revolution. It meant enlarg-ing Quebeckers' new sense of themselves as Québécois rather than as French Canadians. While advocates of this option might differ on par-ticulars, some arguing for "special status" for Quebec and others for a *general* decentralization among all the provinces, their position followed a more or less consistent line from Premiers Lesage, Johnson and Bourassa to the later Liberal Opposition leader Claude Ryan.

The other option, looking to the Quebec state as the focus of consti-tutional change, was more radical. It responded to the new feelings of national awakening in Quebec by offering a new homeland, an independent Quebec state. This branch of the Quebec elite was a fusion of separatist and other extreme nationalist groups that splintered from the moderate nationalism fostered by Premier Lesage. The movement emerged as a powerful force with the founding of the Parti Québécois in 1968 under the leadership of René Lévesque, a former minister in the Lesage cabinet. Held together by a commitment to communal romantic nationalism, the PQ was actually a disparate party led by middle-class forces which could expect to be beneficiaries of the new state order they championed. They sought political independence from Canada within a common market arrangement. With the promise that it would put its constitutional option to the people in a referendum empowering the government to negotiate "sovereignty-association," the PQ won power in 1976.

A third agenda, sponsored by a branch of the francophone elite who came to Ottawa during the mid-1960s, challenged these two Quebec-centred constitutional programs. Championed by Pierre Trudeau, first as Justice Minister in the Pearson cabinet and later as Prime Minister, the federal Liberals sought to redirect the resurgence of nationalism among francophones in Quebec outwards toward the whole country rather than into what they saw as an inverted, dead-end option like separatism. Their objective was the creation of a genuinely bilingual country where respect for the French language and for equal opportunity for francophones would replace the prejudices and suspicions of the past. Their program was initiated with the establishment of the Official Languages Act in 1968, but it had a wider constitutional aim. This aim was the entrench-ment of a Charter of Rights which would simultaneously inject the popular liberal values of entrenched rights and freedoms into Canada's conservative constitution, while at the same time securing the French fact from coast to coast. In this way, the constitution could be considerably modernized and a foundation laid for a truly liberal democratic country, while francophone nationalism could be effectively defused.

These three Quebec elites and their respective agendas for constitutional change were to dominate Canadian politics through the 1960s and 1970s. Once allies in a common fight to topple Duplessis's regime, many of them were now bitter enemies, especially the federal Liberals and the separatists. Federal–provincial relations during this period came to be dominated by jurisdiction-defending state leaders in a competitive game known as "executive federalism." All that was needed to heat up this conflict was an escalation of the Quebec issue by the election of the separatists in 1976, together with a deepening and compounding of the contitutional grievances of other regional political elites. As fortune would have it, Canadians faced just that combination of troubles from the mid-'70s on.

The traditional discontents of the provinces of the east and west of Canada also were to take on a constitutional form during the 1970s. In part, this was simply a reaction to the nature of the power poker game, the bargaining over jurisdictions, which the Quebec–Ottawa feud had started. In part too it was simply an imitation of the impressive province-building policy of Ontario, which from the days of Oliver Mowat had always resisted federal leadership and power. But what really precipitated the discontent was the impact of the 1973 energy crisis, which pitted the interests of producing provinces in the West against those of central Canadian consumers and their governments in Ottawa and Toronto. Western alienation was fueled by the angry sense of blocked opportunity from national energy policies, by the region's lack of representation in the government in Ottawa, by Ottawa's legal attack on the resource powers of the provinces and by outrage over the West's treatment as a resource hinterland by central Canada.

The hinterland issue was really a deep-seated grievance not only of the West but of all the outlying areas of Canada. The Canadian union had not turned out to be economically attractive to all of its partners, even though that had been one of its chief objects. Regional economic disparity was a blight on Confederation, and the national government policies which had contributed to these inequalities were seen as unfair and illegitimate. The political elites of the have-not provinces became convinced that one remedy might be constitutional reform. Most, like the Quebec federal decentralists, argued for more power for the provinces on economic and other matters. Others, especially British Columbia and Prince Edward Island, also pushed hard for Senate reform. At the same time provincialists insisted that certain unacceptable federal powers permitting discretionary intrusions into provincial jurisdiction be removed or limited, and that the provinces play a more prominent role in developing federal policies affecting them.

Public concern over the "Quebec question" and the general matter of "renewing the federation" did not begin to manifest itself dramatically until after the election in 1976 of a Parti Québécois government committed to Quebec independence. However, subsequently there was a veritable torrent of constitutional proposals from provincial governments, professional associations and a special federal task force, as well as from many public interest groups. With the approach of the PQ government's referendum on sovereignty–association in May 1980, all of these festering unresolved constitutional issues finally boiled over.

As it turned out, the advocates of renewed federalism defeated the PQ's sovereignty–association platform. Almost 60 percent of Quebeckers decided to support the option being championed by the provincial Liberals under Claude Ryan, the federal Liberals under Pierre Trudeau, and all of the provincial premiers who visited the province during the campaign. The result was, however, clearer in its negative than its positive form. There was to be no mandate for any talk of Quebec independence, but precisely *which version* of "renewed federalism" was being endorsed by Quebeckers remained uncertain. After all, there was a vast distance between Trudeau's and Ryan's ideas about reforming the constitution and almost as wide a gulf between their views and many of the federalists among the provincial premiers.

In practice, although Ryan was the leader of the victorious "No" forces in the referendum, his was an empty mandate. He was not premier and therefore could not purport to represent the interests of Quebec in any constitutional discussions with other governments. It was the defeated advocate of the separatist option, René Lévesque, who was now saddled with the responsibility of negotiating a renewed federalism for the province. With the April 1981 re-election of the PQ, Quebeckers paradoxically reconfirmed Lévesque's anomalous position and formally excluded Ryan from any say in the constitutional bargaining. Pierre Trudeau and his brand of renewed federalism was now the only credible claimant to the winning "No" forces in Quebec. Nor was it only Quebeckers who had given Prime Minister Trudeau a decisive mandate to negotiate over the "Quebec question." In the February 1980 federal election he had been returned to power with a substantial majority in the House of Commons on a centralist platform which expressly rejected the provincialist "community of communities" rhetoric of Joe Clark and the Conservative provincial premiers.

This conjuncture of political forces at the beginning of the 1980s proved to be both explosive and ultimately decisive. Canadians first watched a historic referendum battle in Quebec, followed by a long summer of intergovernmental bargaining which produced no agreement among first ministers in September. They then witnessed a display of bravura when the federal government decided to act unilaterally in requesting Britain to amend our constitution so that their preferred constitutional program could be implemented without provincial consent. Almost a year later, on September 28, 1981, after a tumultuous and unprecedented period of intergovernmental conflict in Canada and in Britain, came a historic televised Supreme Court judgment on the legality, yet unconstitutionality, of the federal action, thereby forcing the governments back to the bargaining table. Finally, Canadians saw the process come to a bitter and ironic end with a constitutional agreement on November 5 between the federal government and nine of the provincial governments in the face of vigorous opposition from Quebec after its exclusion from the final stages of the process.

In stark contrast with the experience after the 1971 Victoria conference, when Quebec's opposition brought proceedings to a halt, the 1981 constitutional resolution proceeded with all-party consent through the Canadian and British Houses of Parliament accompanied by polite expressions of regret over Quebec's opposition. The new constitution was formally proclaimed by Queen Elizabeth before a flag-waving crowd in the rain in front of the Parliament Buildings on April 17, 1982, while protests were simultaneously mounted by some of Canada's native peoples and by disgruntled Quebeckers in Montreal. There was no room for any popular ratification of the constitutional changes, nor even for the modest legislative endorsement of the changes by all provincial legislatures, which had been the suggested procedure at Victoria in 1971.

The new constitution was adopted with virtually as narrow, legalistic and conservative a procedure as had been first used in the founding of Canada a little more than a century earlier, and with at least as much internal dissent and division. This was not the image of constitutional state building which the Canadian people had hoped for, nor certainly was it the result which Quebeckers anticipated after their referendum. Canada's political tradition seemed to be as far from the inspiring democratic models of France and America as ever, and its constitution just as mired in controversy. But that only underlined the fact that it was *Canada's constitution* with its own peculiar political logic and circumstances that was at issue. For both in style and substance the constitution must be seen as quintessentially Canadian.

Minority Rights, Bilingualism and National Unity

The Constitution Act of 1982 entrenches a substantial part of the Quebec federal elite's policy for updating and improving the position of French-speaking Canadians in Canada without concessions toward either the separatists or Quebec's decentralizing federalists. The language provisions in the new Canadian Charter of Rights and Freedoms make French and English the official languages of Canada. They also declare New Brunswick a bilingual province with the debates, statutes and records, government services and court proceedings of that province and of Parliament available in both French and English.

But, in the light of English Canada's long history of abuses to francophone minorities, and of the struggle in Quebec over Bill 101 and earlier legislative measures, it is the new provisions for minority language educational rights which are more important and controversial. Section 23 of the charter guarantees publicly funded primary and secondary schooling in the French language for the children of francophones in the predominantly English-speaking provinces "where numbers warrant." Equivalent rights are extended to the children of most English-speaking Canadians who either live in Quebec or might move to that province. This program of securing rights and breaking down barriers between the two major linguistic communities, even if flawed by compromises required to get intergovernmental consensus, was a central part of the program of Mr. Trudeau and his Quebec colleagues and at the heart of their idea of remaking Canada into an appropriate homeland for *both* English- and French-speaking Canadians.

It is not surprising that this particular constitutional agenda would be denounced by its rivals as a betrayal of Quebec's essential interests. For the independantistes who were engaged in a struggle to build a separate state in Quebec, the entrenchment of bilingualism could only be seen as an obstacle to their ambitions. Scoffing at this expression of francophone nationalism, which they regarded as ill-conceived and ineffectual, the separatists were convinced that without at least some additional powers for the Quebec state, Quebeckers could get nothing out of this linguistic arrangement.

Indeed, they were inclined to feel that to the extent that the new educational guarantees for the English-speaking minority in Quebec contradicted Bill 101, Quebeckers' own linguistic security in the province would be compromised. This was the argument which the PQ government had advanced for refusing to entrench minority language educational rights for the English-speaking minority even if they were to receive reciprocal guarantees for francophone minorities in the other provinces. Their opposition was steadfastly maintained despite Premier Lévesque's own acceptance of the minority rights principle in the 1977 St. Andrews declaration and despite widespread support for it by Quebeckers as a whole. Since there was no way that Lévesque's government would assent to the substance of this alternate program of nation building, these new minority rights were imposed on the province without the consent of its government.

Similar outrage over the substance and method of the constitutional reforms has been manifested by all of the Quebec provincial Liberals except for those representing largely anglophone districts. Not only were their preferred constitutional proposals for decentralizing the federal union largely ignored, but they have had to hear their own arguments about the separatists' unwillingness to participate in federal renewal come back to them as a justification for the imposition of the new constitution upon Quebec. It has been a humiliating dilemma for a party which spearheaded the referendum victory in 1980.

The new constitution therefore will certainly not end the rancour and division among Quebec's elites over the future of Quebec in Canada. On the contrary, it has served as a new battleground, worsening relations between Quebec City and Ottawa and even precipitating the entry of the PQ party machine into the next federal election in order to punish the federal Liberals for their "betrayal" of the province. Since the constitutional arrangement was arrived at in an evening bargaining session which excluded Quebec delegates and since it was subsequently imposed on the province without its government's consent, it is easy to see how the legitimacy, if not the legality, of the constitution can be called into question.

The matter is complicated, however, by the imprudent bargaining tactics of the Quebec government which partially caused its isolation from the eleventh-hour bargaining session that produced the agreement. As well, Lévesque's own support for much of the substance of the new constitution, including the ceding of a Quebec veto and the principle of minority language education rights, and legitimate doubts concerning any separatist party's willingness or ability to pursue federal reform must be considered. Moreover, with the PQ's own support dropping precipitately in the province, it is not clear that the party's nationalist rhetoric will prove as powerful as it might once have been. Caused in part by the massive economic recession of 1982 and the tough measures which the Quebec government has had to employ to deal with it, there has been a noticeable slackening of interest in Quebec nationalism. These developments have cooled the love affair between the Quebec state and its people and have cast considerable skepticism on the constitutional programs of all the Quebec state builders, especially the separatists.

In the short run, there will be direct collisions between the educational guarantees in the constitution and Quebec's Bill 101. These can be expected to spark new debates over the security of the French language in the province. But, since polls show that most Quebeckers support these rights and now feel much less threatened about the place of the French language in the province, the court cases may not be exactly *causes célèbres*. Opinion will certainly be inflamed, however, if francophone rights in English-speaking Canada are not at least as firmly protected by the courts as are anglophone rights. There will be difficulty too if there is not a gradual acceptance of this new dualism in English-speaking Canada. In that respect, the ugly and successful backlash against the Manitoba government's resolution to entrench bilingualism in that province in 1984 stands as a dark omen, suggesting considerable grassroots resistance to this new definition of the French–English relationship.

Even for the supporters of bilingualism there was dismay over the compromises and qualifications necessary to get substantial intergovernmental agreement over the policy. The chief beneficiaries, the linguistic minority groups, were disappointed that the measures didn't go nearly far enough. There was the niggling restriction "where numbers warrant" on the enjoyment of these rights; there was no explicit granting of minority control of its own school boards; nor was there any assurance that French schooling might not still go on in mixed or bilingual schools where the French language would always be at a disadvantage. More serious yet, Ontario, the province with the largest number of francophones, had failed to declare itself bilingual, thus leaving the language rights of this large minority to the discretion of the Ontario legislature.

All of these complaints, whether from linguistic minorities or from the various enemies of bilingualism, remind us again that constitutional politics can be exceedingly painful and divisive. They touch on the fundamental and conflicting beliefs and interests of virtually all citizens, especially when the constitution making is done *not* at a revolutionary moment of national unity before a people have developed a collective life together, but later in an existing state order with a real and bitter history to change and overcome. Under these circumstances, expecting the constitution to be a triumphant expression of national purpose or even expecting complete elite consensus on the nature of the changes may be unrealistic. It will take time to see whether the language provisions of the new constitution do succeed in cementing a new French–English partnership in Canada. It will also take time to decide whether all of the divisions created by the constitution-making process of 1980–82 were worth the risks.

It may therefore be premature to pronounce the constitution-making exercise a failure either because there is disappointment with its provisions or because certain powerful elites will not make peace with it. That is to demand too much. If it turns out that the Charter's recognition of bilingualism makes it more likely that Canada will survive as a common homeland for English- and French-speaking North Americans, history will not let today's opposition compromise the achievement. But it may all turn out to be too little too late. Whether bilingualism succeeds as more than a symbolic gesture will depend on a complex set of factors including demographics, economic changes, the experience with French-language immersion for anglophones, court judgments and the long-term political acceptance and expansion of the policy in Canada. But in the face of all of the pressures coming from a dominant English-speaking North America and from the grim record of assimilation of francophones outside Quebec and the bilingual belt of northern Ontario and northwestern New Brunswick, it will be a difficult gamble at best.

Regional Discontent and the New Constitution

The Constitution Act of 1982 included little from the list of demands which discontented premiers had put on the table in the summer of 1980. Virtually all of the arguments for a transfer of power from federal to provincial levels of government prominent in constitutional talks since the 1960s were swept aside following the fall 1980 unilateral initiative by the federal Parliament. So too did the provincial claims for repeal of federal discretionary powers like disallowance and the declaratory power to take over provincial works. These had always been the premiers' *quid pro quo* for any concessions they might make to the federal government regarding constitutional change. In the last-minute bargaining over a smaller package of matters all of federal choosing, they were now shunted aside. In effect, federal unilateral action had so shaken provincial governments that their priority now became to hold back the drive to patriation long enough to bargain over the contents of the resolution rather than to demand concessions over the division of power as a precondition to any constitutional change. This was clearly a major political victory for the federal Liberals.

Nevertheless, after the ambiguous Supreme Court decision of September 1981 on the legality of the unilateral road led the parties back to the bargaining table, it was clear that some part of the provincialists' constitutional agenda would have to be incorporated. There was already a declaration in the resolution concerning equalization. Even if it did little more than recognize the principle, this statement was of some value to the premiers from the have-not areas. There was also a section strengthening provincial control over natural resources, a matter of crucial importance, especially to the western provinces. Indeed, it had been included at the request of the federal NDP as part of its price for supporting the Liberals and to entice Saskatchewan to support the resolution. Apart from confirming the provinces' exclusive power over the exploration, development and management of their natural resources, Section 92A permitted the provinces to regulate interprovincial trade in their natural resources as well as to apply indirect taxes on their resources provided interprovincial discrimination was not the intention. Parliament could, however, override any provincial laws over interprovincial trade and already had paramountcy over the provinces in any conflict over taxing matters.

The section on natural resources therefore went some way toward accepting the Western premiers' principal demand for strengthened control over their natural resources, even if it was less than had been previously offered in the spring of 1979. What was critical now was to see how the provincialist demands could be accommodated in a smaller package of items containing a Charter of Rights and a new amending formula. In the end, the federal government decided that this could be best achieved by accepting a slightly modified version of the provincialist amending formula in return for the premiers' endorsement of a modified Charter of Rights containing firm guarantees over language and educational rights. This made up the bargain between the nine anglophone premiers and Mr. Trudeau.

The principal author of Canada's new amending formula is the government of Alberta. In place of the amending formula advanced by the government of Canada and its supporters granting a perpetual veto to the provinces of Quebec and Ontario, Alberta proposed a formula which removed any formal inequality of provinces by declaring that *no* province could exercise a veto over constitutional changes desired by most legislatures. Only the Parliament of Canada could hold up a constitutional amendment by refusing its assent. Constitutional changes in most areas could be achieved by securing the consent of the House of Commons together with that of seven provincial legislatures representing at least 50 percent of the Canadian population. To protect all provinces equally, however, Alberta proposed that provinces could opt out of constitutional amendments which reduce their own legislative or proprietary rights. Other sections required unanimous agreement for changes affecting the office of the Queen, the composition of the Supreme Court, the new amending formula, or any changes reducing the status of the French and English languages or of minimum provincial representation in the House of Commons. Constitutional changes affecting only certain provinces could be made by direct agreement of the affected province or provinces and of the Parliament of Canada.

The most serious political issue arising from the agreement over a new amending formula concerned the position of Quebec. Although Premier Lévesque had earlier supported the formula on the condition that there would be compensation to provinces opting out of amendments affecting provincial powers, the province did not in the end formally consent to it. With the agreement of the anglophone premiers, the federal government added a guarantee of compensation for education or other cultural matters in deference to Quebec. This, nevertheless, still left the province of Quebec with no veto and without the full compensation which its premier had sought. Since the formula did not recognize the principle of the duality of the two founding peoples, there were many who regretted this bargaining outcome.

From another perspective, however, the achievement of the principle of equality of provinces in the amending formula was not an inconsiderable victory for provinces seeking to overcome central Canadian domination of the federation. It had always seemed anomalous that Ontario and Quebec should each enjoy equivalent veto power to that of the national Parliament. Not only would such vetoes build in a protection for the historically most diehard province builders in the federation, but it would also set up invidious distinctions between provinces. Democratic requirements were handled by requiring a 50 percent population level. This provision gave Quebec and Ontario an advantage since the support of *either* of them would be necessary to meet this requirement under current circumstances. But building in permanent features of provincial inequality irrespective of future demographic change was unacceptable to most premiers outside central Canada. Indeed, in the light of the probable shifts in economic and political power which could be expected to take place in the country over the long run, it seemed especially unwise to graft on central Canadian legal dominance of the federation.

The other major issue of concern was the provision for provincial "opting out" of future constitutional amendments. Critics charged that this section would force the governments to seek unanimity for constitutional change since the Parliament of Canada would be unwilling to tolerate opting out. Others charged that the provision amounted to a system of "provincial sovereignty," since provinces could not be bound without their consent. But opting out applied only to a particular *class* of amendment and did not confer the usual attributes of sovereignty. Unlike a veto which would have granted provinces an ability to block constitution change on an equal footing with that of the national Parliament, the opting out provision was defensive and circumscribed. In effect, it enshrined two principles: first, that no province should have its constitutional rights and powers reduced without its consent; second, that no single province should be able to prevent others from making changes whenever there is a general will to do so. In this way a balance was achieved between the rule of consent and flexibility for constitutional change.

In summary, while the provincialists did not get their central demands for transfer of more powers, apart from the new section on natural resources, they did get the principle of equalization and the substance of their own amending formula accepted. Similarly, the federal Liberals achieved most of their bilingual objectives but not without political compromises and qualifications. The same pattern of mutual accommodation and blocking went on in every part of the constitutional settlement. Even the new Canadian Charter of Rights and Freedoms shows the same marks of negotiation and compromise. Indeed it is probably here where the contradictions are most glaring.

The Canadian Charter of Rights and Freedoms

Canadians are granted in the charter all the usual freedoms which liberals extol in an entrenched charter of rights—freedom of speech, assembly, thought or religion—except the right to property. That right was not included in order to retain needed support from the NDP in Parliament and some provincial premiers. The omission is, of course, anomalous since the protection of property has been held to be one of the fundamental rights of citizens in a liberal democracy.

Even more bizarre is the distinctly Canadian compromise concerning the conflict between entrenched rights and parliamentary sovereignty. After debating exhaustively and inconclusively the question of whether Canadians needed a constitutional charter of rights, Canada's political elites finally wrote in entrenched rights for all Canadians but then proceeded to grant a legislative override on some of those rights in Section 33. Once again politics defied logic or, rather, imposed its own logic on events.

It is necessary therefore to grapple with politics to get an understanding of the origin, issues and effects of the new charter. As we have noted, the idea of a constitutional charter of rights arose during the 1960s as the centrepiece of federal strategy toward Quebec nationalism and separatism. From the beginning, Pierre Trudeau, first as Justice Minister and then as Prime Minister, planned to place francophone language and educational rights within the framework of an entrenched national charter of individual rights and freedoms. This was a politically astute decision, since a rights charter was popular with the Canadian people, served to defuse any would-be anglophone backlash against the extension of francophone rights and channelled some of Quebec's nationalist drive outward toward the reform of the whole Canadian state rather than toward an inverted preoccupation with Quebec. The charter, then, was an essential part of federal state building which aimed to modernize and liberalize Canada so that Quebec nationalism could find a more progressive alternative to separatism. It offered Quebeckers a liberal theology of "rights" to replace what Trudeau had once called the secularized religion, the romanticized "tribalism" of Quebec separatism.

However, this program ran into ideological opposition from those opposed to protecting rights through an entrenched charter. To some extent, this rested on the respect which many English-speaking Canadians felt for the British tradition of parliamentary supremacy and the common law, but the case was also built on the charter's alleged deficiencies and undesirable side effects. There was, for example, little evidence to show that rights were better protected with a charter than without. A Charter would take many important political issues outside the democratic political process and drop them into the narrow confines of the courtroom, thereby granting exceptional power to an appointed judiciary to make fundamental choices for all Canadians. These and other arguments caused many of the anglophone premiers to offer stiff resistance to Trudeau's plan, especially after the mid-1970s. Nevertheless, beneath the rhetoric lay the premiers' usual preoccupations with defending provincial power.

In the end, the November 5 bargain might be seen as a draw. There would be an entrenched charter of rights. But at the same time, the legislatures and Parliament could expressly override fundamental, legal and equality rights by using the so-called *notwithstanding* clause in Section 33 of the agreement. In the spirit of compromise there would, however, be no recourse to a legislative override with respect to the other rights in the charter, namely democratic, mobility and language rights. These were to be "entrenched" rights which the courts would presumably defend from any interference from legislatures.

This compromise is instructive. It shows once again that language rights were at the essential core of the new entrenched Charter over which the federal Liberals would not compromise. Even entrenched "fundamental freedoms" were not nearly so important to their idea of reform of the Canadian constitution. From a classical liberal perspective, this is to say the least a curious set of priorities. For the language rights were not really individual rights at all; they were rights which individuals might claim *only by virtue of their membership in a distinct minority group or by the mere accident of their native language.*

Canadians at large did not find much to be enthusiastic about in the compromise and were disappointed over the potential legislative curtailment of certain individual rights. However, informed critics differed considerably over whether the notwithstanding clause seriously undermined the Charter. Some argued that the political sanctions against a government expressly overriding the Charter of Rights were so strong that the provision would be rarely used. In addition, the time limit of five years on any restriction meant that a legislature would have to face regular political sanctions for continuing to act against the Charter. Others argued that the override might even turn out to be a useful and politically popular means of overcoming narrow, conservative and politically unpopular court decisions. It would restore a needed political counterbalance to a pure system of judicial review. Further, because the override left the final decision up to the elected legislatures, it might even prod the courts into a more activist and liberal defence of rights than they would be otherwise inclined to take.

Many were not nearly as sanguine about the political hazards of overriding the charter. They pointed to the Quebec government's blanket use of the override or Alberta's threat in late 1983 to use it to overrule any court defence of the constitutional right to strike. There was also the politically aggressive attack on human rights in British

Columbia during 1983 under the guise of "economic restraint." These were all ominous signs that human rights could be politically attacked during a more conservative period of retrenchment. Under such circumstances these critics were inclined to feel that rights would be better protected by judges and not legislators.

What the new charter will actually do for Canadians' rights and freedoms is a subject best left to academic debate and dinner-speaking engagements for legal scholars, for it is a highly arguable, almost speculative, pastime. There is simply no way to know in advance how the Supreme Court will make use of the Charter. If American practice is any guide, however, we know that we can expect alternative periods of "conservative" and "liberal" courts more or less in line with shifts in general public mood. We know for certain that there will be a wide latitude for the courts to interpret the general clauses of the charter as they see fit—in effect, to interpret the constitution in the light of changing circumstances, to play a creative role in policy making. This will mean that the appointment process of the Supreme Court will be politicized and the political philosophies of judges scrutinized more thoroughly than ever. The court will need to reflect accurately the diversity and complexity of Canada as well as achieve a better balance between men and women on the bench.

For Canadian citizens who had accepted at face value the promises that their rights and freedoms would finally be "guaranteed" by the Charter, this discussion over the politics of the judiciary may seem unsettling. That is understandable, because their rights are not guaranteed in the Charter in any absolute sense. As Peter Russell has argued, these rights cannot be enjoyed "in this zero-sum fashion. We have more or less of them. What we have to settle about these rights and freedoms is not whether or not we will "have" them but what limits it is reasonable to attach to them and how decisions about these limits should be made."

With the entrenchment of the charter, we have agreed to grant appointed judges extensive power to define and enforce certain national values like freedom of speech and expression in scores of practical instances from pornography in books and films to political dissent. We have granted them the power to rule on the right-to-life principle concerning abortion or euthanasia. They will be singly responsible for defending the new educational guarantees for linguistic minorities against potentially hostile legislatures and publics and they are the final legal guardians of the new state policy on bilingualism. Their decisions will necessarily be national in scope and will prevail short of a constitutional amendment or the use of the notwithstanding clause over those matters where it applies. The courts are already facing an array of cases concerning many rights in the charter, the most celebrated of which is probably the legal challenge to the federal Cabinet's decision to permit testing of the guidance system of the cruise missile in Canada. Since overriding the courts in any of these matters will never be politically easy, the judicial branch is likely to be a far more important branch of government than ever before.

This will be true whether or not the courts live up to the expectations which have been placed upon them. If the courts attempt to evade their responsibilities by adopting a knee-jerk conservatism over the charter, that will have the effect of constitutionally sanctioning serious limits on rights and worsening the position of all Canadians. Alternatively, by using the charter creatively to impose their own policy choices upon the elected legislatures and the people, the courts threaten to embroil themselves in national politics in much the same way as the United States Supreme Court has often done. But even if they succeed in avoiding these extremes, the courts will be taking over some very contentious political issues which normally ought to be worked out in the democratic political process. Their decisions will therefore be judged not only for their technical merit but for their political wisdom. With the Charter, Canadians have, as Peter Russell observed, chosen "to judicialize politics and to politicize the judiciary."

Conclusion

Any commentary on the new constitution must stress the special role of the judiciary in shaping the future politics of Canada. Nor will this be simply a matter of enlarging the courts' power to define our rights and social priorities. The courts now have an opportunity to establish themselves as important *national* institutions rivalling Parliament and the local legislatures in popular interest and attention. Obviously their role will be critical in winning over the confidence of francophones in the new constitution. In this respect, the courts have replaced Parliament as the national guarantor and protector of minorities within the provinces. If they do not prove more effective than Parliament in protecting francophone minorities outside Quebec and the anglophone minority inside Quebec, the heart of the constitutional settlement will have been broken and the drift toward separatism increased. This judicial responsibility is even more critical in the light of the Quebec government's refusal to support the new constitution.

The courts will also play a pivotal role in the whole political modernization and state-building strategy of the federal Liberals. If they carry out their mandate to unify values around a national Charter of rights and freedoms, they will also make a significant contribution to overcoming regional divisions and loyalties. While there will be a great deal of political tension over the new court decisions over rights, the issues themselves will be genuinely *national* in scope and transcend the old regional cleavages of Canadian politics. By aggregating the interests of individuals and groups from across the country on such matters as the scope of police powers, abortion, pornography, affirmative action, compulsory retirement and labour rights, the new Charter will redirect political attention from the old regional and provincial–federal controversies. The charter will give Canadians an arena in which to fight out important national issues which do not call into question the legitimacy of Canada as a national political community.

The highest court will also set uniform national standards in place of the diverse array of provincial measures in areas like film censorship and employment practices. Provinces seeking to escape those national standards by using the notwithstanding clause against a Supreme Court judgment will find themselves in new and politically difficult circumstances where the rhetoric of regionalism is unlikely to be as successful as it might once have been. In all of these ways the nation-building potential of the Charter, as well as the critical role of the courts in shaping a new political alignment between themselves and the Canadian people, should become increasingly evident in the years ahead.

These are some of the new and important consequences of the 1982 constitutional provisions. Whether they will in the long run compensate for the political costs and shortcomings incurred in getting them entrenched in the constitution remains to be seen. For some, proceeding without Quebec's consent will seem too dangerous a deed, an ominous legacy for Quebec–Canada relations, and an everlasting stain upon the agreement. For others, the process by which the constitution was brought home may deprive the constitution of some of its legitimacy and may reinforce the anti-democratic traditions which have long contributed to a weak sense of national unity and purpose. For many, there will be disappointment over the somewhat limited substance of the agreement. Reform of the Senate and of the Supreme Court has been left undone, aboriginal rights remain undefined, the offshore question remains unresolved, and other festering problems over the division of powers between Ottawa and the provinces have simply been ignored. Some of these matters will doubtless be the subject of investigation by the new Royal Commission on the Economic Union and Development Prospects for Canada, but there is nonetheless a keen sense of lost opportunity from the restricted constitutional agenda after the summer of 1980.

These objections are understandable. But it must be remembered that politics is the art of the possible and never more so than during the attempted constitutional restructuring of a modern, complex and divided country like Canada. The suggestion that some of the most intractable problems of Canadian unity could somehow be amicably settled if only the constitution-making process were opened up to permit wider democratic participation by constitutional conference and referendum seems especially naive in the light of the ugly backlash in Manitoba in 1984 over entrenchment of francophone rights. It is quite possible that a national constitutional referendum on bilingualism, for example, would have deepened the divisions between the two linguistic communities in Canada and exposed the country to greater dangers than it faced with a closed system of bargaining between First Ministers. Similarly, it may be unrealistic to expect any constitutional reform process to have addressed and set right *all* the major constitutional grievances of the country. In short, political judgment concerning the constitution must start from the actual political conditions which determined its provisions and not from a reading of abstract and absolute principles.

Canadians, then, might well pause before joining the loud chorus of critics who have taken the measure of the new constitution and found it wanting by any number of rational yardsticks. For the politics of constitutional change are, by their very nature, difficult to achieve, resistant to the neat seductions of political theory, and almost invariably fraught with discontent and division. They come closest to expressing a single coherent vision only at special revolutionary moments of "unity" in the life of a country. In that respect, it may be well to remember that even France and America acquired their popular constitutional charters only by revolution and the forceful removal of dissenting individuals and classes.

Further Readings

Banting, Keith, and Richard Simeon, eds. *And No One Cheered: Federalism, Democracy and the Constitution Act.* Toronto: Methuen, 1983.

Cairns, Alan. "Recent Federalist Constitutional Proposals: A Review Essay." *Public Policy* 5 (1979): 348–65.

McWhinney, E. *Canada and the Constitution, 1979–82.* Toronto: University of Toronto Press, 1982.

Milne, David. *The New Canadian Constitution.* Toronto: Lorimer, 1982.

Russell, Peter. "The Political Purposes of the Canadian Charter of Rights and Freedoms." *Canadian Bar Review*, March 1983, pp. 30–54.

Russell, Peter. "The Effect of a Charter of Rights on the Policy–Making Role of Canadian Courts." *Canadian Public Administration* 25 (Spring 1982): 1–33.

Sheppard, R., and M. Valpy. *The National Deal.* Toronto: Fleet, 1982.

Simeon, Richard. *A Citizen's Guide to the Constitutional Question.* Toronto: Gage, 1981.

Zukowski, R. *Intergovernmental Relations: The Year in Review.* Vol. 2: *The Constitution.* Kingston: Institute of Inter-Governmental Relations, 1981.

Chapter 15

Parliamentary Government in Canada
Michael M. Atkinson

Parliament poses a problem for those who are comfortable only with clear, unambiguous categories. What, after all, is "Parliament"? Should the term be used to refer to all 282 MPs drawn together to oversee the conduct of the nation's business? If so, how does Cabinet fit into this definition? Are ministers simply MPs who have a slightly exalted status? Perhaps Parliament should refer to everyone except ministers of the Crown: this would recognize the ancient distinction between legislative and executive functions. But what would Parliament be without a ministry—without an executive to guide its activities?

To sort out this maze it is useful to begin by understanding that the most important principles of parliamentary government are built on conventions—rules of behaviour not enforced by the law courts or the officers of Parliament, but nonetheless considered binding by participants. Certain conventions (for example, that the governor general assents to all bills passed by Parliament) are adhered to more strictly than others; some are more important than others. A number of these conventions, taken together, form a coherent view of parliamentary government known as the Westminster model. It is a simplification, of course, and not the only model of parliamentary government, but so widely is it accepted that in Canada it is the starting point for almost all reform proposals. For many admirers of Parliament it is the genius of the British Constitution.

The first section of this chapter outlines the fundamental principles of the Westminster model. At the core of the model lies the view that strong executive leadership is the *sine qua non* of effective government. The cabinet, composed of ministers of the Crown, is understood to be the centre of legislative initiative. It is the government. Parliament is a lawmaking body only in a rather formal sense. It is, more accurately, a deliberating assembly—the arena in which the government is supposed to outline and defend its proposals while other members of Parliament sit in judgment and offer alternative ways of proceeding.[1] The government listens to criticisms and attempts to explain and justify its action. In the final analysis, however, cabinet retains the authority and the responsibility to act. Thus at first blush the Westminster model seems to provide a clear description of the essence of parliamentary activity and a compelling interpretation of what constitutes a responsible government.

But, whatever its virtues, the Westminster model is not a mixed and balanced constitutional formula. There is nothing in this system to ensure that Parliament will be an autonomous and vigorous political institution.[2] In fact, with the growth of government in the post-war period the natural tendency of the Westminster model toward executive dominance has been decidedly enhanced. The second part of this chapter examines relations between the government and Parliament other than those emphasized by the Westminster model. What emerges is a more complex picture of executive–legislative relations and perhaps some new directions for constitutional reform.

The Fundamentals of the Westminster Model

From the gallery of the House of Commons the scene below is a bewildering mixture of ritual, humour, incivility and solemnity. Most observers are unaware of the important formal rules that govern procedure (the Standing Orders) let alone the established, if informal, norms that govern personal behaviour. Yet a careful study of these rules and norms is not the place to begin to understand parliamentary government in Canada. The rules are important, of course, but primarily because they give expression to more profound principles upon which the Westminster model is based. In this section we examine two of these principles. They may strike readers as so elementary, so fundamental in fact, that little more than a brief mention is necessary. But as we shall see, problems arise when we are forced to give these principles some meaning. Not only are they at odds with one another, but they are often quite unrealistic in their expectations of politicians, public servants and the electorate.

1. The government is in charge of and responsible for the conduct of parliamentary business.

During the nineteenth century ordinary members of Parliament assumed much of the initiative for legislation by offering proposals in the form of private bills and private members' bills.[3] Even then, however, it was the government-sponsored public bill which was used to change the general laws of the country.[4] Now, almost all of the bills which Parliament finally adopts are government bills; that is, they have been introduced by ministers of the Crown. Moreover, only ministers are permitted to introduce bills which authorize the raising or spending of money. Parliamentary procedure has gradually tightened to give the government sufficient time to enact its legislative program and to curtail lengthy debates and dilatory motions.

The government has responsibilities other than the sponsoring of a legislative program. Every year, on or before March 1, the government lays before the Commons a request for funds to conduct business. These requests appear in the form of "estimates" followed by supply bills needed to give them legislative authority.[5] The minister of finance introduces a budget, usually in the spring of each year, which announces the government's overall financial plan and intended tax changes. The government house leader is responsible for orchestrating all of this activity, ensuring that deadlines are met, that important government bills are not postponed indefinitely and that the opposition is satisfied with the time that has been made available to discuss these measures. The prime minister is responsible for calling Parliament and, of course, for requesting that the governor general dissolve it. From the narrowest of details to the broadest of constitutional responsibilities, the government is in charge. Cabinet takes the lead, and the Commons usually follows, sometimes with reluctance.

How does a government acquire and retain these responsibilities? The formal and rather uninformative answer is that the Cabinet enjoys the confidence of the House of Commons and is therefore able to offer advice to, and act on behalf of, the Crown. But behind this expression of confidence lies the machinery of the electoral process and the politics of party organization and cohesion. The Cabinet enjoys, in the first instance, the support of its party colleagues in Parliament. This support has been garnered in the electorate, not in the House of Commons. It is the electorate that has chosen a political party and, in doing so, selected a prime minister who, in turn, has chosen a Cabinet. The House of Commons is normally involved in none of this. Expressions of confidence, in the form of votes on the floor of the House, whatever their symbolic value, are simply indications of support offered by the elected members of the governing party to that party's parliamentary leadership.

Called upon to extol the virtues of this system, one would surely point out that it concentrates authority and responsibility in the hands of elected representatives. A government created and sustained in this manner is able to act decisively and can accomplish a great deal without delaying and equivocating until problems have reached crisis proportions. In an era in which there is some concern that the overload of decision-making systems threatens to make democracies ungovernable,[6] the concentration of authority is sometimes praised as a means of avoiding deadlock and stagnation.[7] By the same token, the concentration of responsibility presumably aids in the assignment of blame. Since political parties remain cohesive parliamentary actors, the governors are easily identifiable and electors are able to sanction poor performance. It is little wonder that this type of system, with its focus on the effectiveness of centralized decision making, is often referred to as cabinet government.[8]

In spite of these advantages, certain problems have arisen in the practice of cabinet government in Canada. In the first place, the electorate may decline to give the governing party a majority of seats in the Commons. To have the confidence of the House, the government must, therefore, attract the support of at least some members of the opposition. Confidence motions, under these circumstances, are no longer routine demonstrations of party solidarity. Moreover, the assignment of responsibility for government actions is no longer as clear cut. It has been suggested, in their defence, that minority governments are likely to be sensitive to the House of Commons. What is lost in the concentration of authority is gained in a new responsiveness to Parliament. But there is nothing to guarantee this outcome, and during the Pearson and Diefenbaker years there was very little evidence of it.[9] Minority governments have their virtues, but the point is that they are not the same as those used to justify the Westminster model.

The second problem concerns the issue of whether Cabinet ministers are in any position to accept responsibility for government action. The fiction that ministers can comprehend the activities of enormous departments to the point of resigning in the face of administrative failure has been almost universally abandoned. Ministers simply will not accept personal responsibility for errors and omissions that occur at the hands of public servants. They retain effective responsibility for actions undertaken in accordance with their instructions or with their policies, but determining which actions are encompassed in this understanding can be very difficult.[10] Thus individual ministerial responsibility has come to mean little more than the requirement that ministers regularly appear in Parliament to answer questions and promise investigations. In short, one of the conventions central to the Westminster model has been seriously weakened in recent years.

In their attempt to make someone responsible for government actions, MPs and others have suggested that deputy ministers might accept responsibility for administrative matters and politicians responsibility for questions of policy.[11] If this type of reform were adopted, the accepted doctrine of ministerial responsibility, which contains the provision that senior officials offer politically neutral advice in exchange for anonymity, would be shaken but by no means toppled. Deputy ministers, and perhaps others, would be required to explain and justify how departments were managed, but they would not be held responsible for policy direction.

Of course, this implies that policy and administration can be neatly separated. It is somewhat ironic that the distinction between policy and administration should be pressed into service at a time when most books on the subject agree on the inadequacy of such a dichotomy, at least as a description of reality.[12] But, this problem aside, senior bureaucrats will always be expected to offer policy advice to ministers, and they have no intention of being held responsible for the advice given or the action taken. It is the quiet acknowledgment of this, on the part of both politicians and bureaucrats, that fuels the suspicion that ministerial responsibility is merely a polite subterfuge behind which senior officials and "superbureaucrats" silently govern. This interpretation is almost certainly incorrect, but there is ample evidence that, together, senior bureaucrats and ministers form a policy-making oligarchy in which the differences between them are sometimes hard to detect. As Colin Campbell and George Szablowski have observed, "the distinction between bureaucratic and political participants in the policy process simply does not exist in many crucial decision-making settings, even cabinet committees."[13] Thus the location of responsibility, far from being simplified in the Westminster model, remains an ambiguous issue.

The third problem concerns Parliament directly. In its heavy reliance on political parties to ensure responsibility, the established formula of cabinet government does not make it clear what role Parliament as a whole ought to play. Must all efforts to secure a representative and responsive government be filtered through the lens of partisan advantage? So it would seem, since the Westminster model does not countenance institutions or procedures that encourage and highlight the achievement of consensus. Political differences that are not partisan in nature find little room for expression in the Westminster model of parliamentary government.

Before parties had secured their grip on elected representatives, responsible government in Canada meant that the government was responsible to the legislative assembly in the crucial sense that, if provoked, the assembly could, and would, dismiss a government and install another without the benefit of a general election. From 1848, when responsible government first appeared in British North America, until 1864, when Confederation discussions began in earnest, a series of governments were made and unmade in the legislature with virtually no help from the electorate. Since members of the legislature were not faced with the propsect of their own dismissal on these occasions, defeat in the assembly was considered an obvious and constitutionally respectable manifestation of responsible government.

After Confederation, the term "responsible government" lost this meaning.[14] Between 1867 and 1873, John A. Macdonald suffered several defeats in the House of Commons but refused to resign. As political parties became cohesive in the electorate and in Parliament, the threat of defeat itself diminished considerably. Even the emergence of third and fourth parties and, in the 1960s and 1970s, a series of minority government situations did not spell immediate defeat for the government. And when defeat came, the government either refused to accept it (February 1968) or called an election immediately (May 1974, December 1979). Whatever responsible government meant in pre-Confederation Canada, it does not mean, in the 1980s, that the House of Commons can choose the government. That responsibility belongs to the electorate.[15] The House can still dismiss governments, but far from demonstrating that responsible government is alive and well, the defeat of a government in the House is often considered an abdication of responsibility, since the House cannot elect a new government to replace the one it has defeated.

If the cabinet is responsible, through the party system, to the electorate, how important is Parliament to the process of accountability? The answer is largely in the hands of the political parties around which Parliament is organized. The spectacle of a vigilant House of Commons constantly questioning and criticizing the government may be sufficient reassurance for some, but it is the actions of political parties, including the party in power, that determine how much of this is show and how much is substance. In this respect a great deal of emphasis is placed on the role of the opposition as an alternative government and a constant source of skeptical and critical pronouncements. We turn now to the consideration of a second principle of parliamentary government in Canada and an evaluation of the opposition's ability to hold governments accountable between elections.

2. *The opposition must have the right to criticize the government openly and the ability to make that criticism felt.*

In Parliament the government explains and justifies its action (or inaction), not to an audience sympathetic to the problems of governing and anxious to offer assistance, but to an organized, institutionalized opposition bent on demonstrating the inappropriateness and inefficiencies of government policy. Though it may never have the votes necessary to defeat the government, the opposition is nonetheless charged with ensuring that the responsibility of the government to the House of Commons is more than a formality. As John Stewart has put it, "It is this public testing of governance, with the government and the opposition as institutionalized adversaries, that is the hallmark of contemporary Responsible Government."[16]

The idea of opposition was not always so compatible with parliamentary government. Parliaments in Britain were originally meetings of nobles called to offer advice to the king and, it was hoped, to support the Crown in its ventures. Although an offer of advice often implied criticism, outright opposition could easily be construed as treason. In the seventeenth and eighteenth centuries, by which time Parliament had made good its claim to supremacy, the idea of opposition-in-Parliament was still resisted, this time by those who saw it as divisive—an expression of greedy factionalism. But, by then, efforts to create governments composed of the "best men" had failed, and observers had come to recognize that, while opposition to the government might be denounced as factional, the government itself was a "party."[17] Parties, moreover, might prove advantageous if they could be used as a bulwark against the danger of concentrated power. This bulwark would take the form of a recognized and legitimate opposition eager to secure office.

With the government facing the opposition in Parliament and two teams of party leaders struggling for support in the electorate, have we at last defined the essence of responsible government? Defined perhaps, but this system has to *work* before anyone can feel completely satisfied, and there are several obstacles to its effective operation.

First, the opposition in Parliament, because it is not in control of the parliamentary agenda, cannot insist that particular items be addressed on the floor of the Commons. Because of this, and the demands of government business, many issues of general concern are not debated in Parliament for weeks or months after they have come to the attention of the public. Thus, for instance, the Ocean Ranger tragedy was never properly addressed in Parliament and the McDonald Commission on the RCMP received no statement from ministers or any debate until months after the Report was tabled. Too often Parliament appears to be very ponderous, unable to react quickly or to act at all as a forum for the debate of serious political issues. Yet it is in this environment that the opposition must do the work assigned to it under the Westminster model.

Second, in Canada there are numerous bodies—interest groups, advisory councils and research institutes—which offer stimulating and informed criticism of government policy that is often more compelling than the criticism offered by the opposition in Parliament. In the economic sphere, for example, the C.D. Howe Institute, the Conference Board, the Economic Council of Canada and the Canadian Labour Congress provide short- and medium-term analysis of the economy complete with diagnoses and remedies. The opposition can use these studies, but in spite of approximately three quarters of a million dollars (1982–83) allocated to caucus research units, opposition parties have been unable (or unwilling) to generate their own economic analyses. They are without the information and expertise the government is able to marshal on virtually any specialized subject, and they appear to be convinced that the resources they do have ought to be used to exploit short-term partisan opportunities.

Nowhere is the irrelevance of opposition criticism more apparent than in the realm of federal–provincial relations. Because provinces own and control the development of most natural resources, debates on the floor of the Commons about, for instance, the price of oil have the quality of a sideshow compared to the negotiation and debate that take place between the federal government and the producing provinces in federal–provincial conferences and elsewhere. The major issues of centralization and decentralization in the Canadian federation are also debated outside Parliament at these meetings of ministers and officials. Not only is the opposition relegated to the sidelines in this process, but legislation determining federal–provincial fiscal agreements is barely discussed on the floor of the House of Commons. Thus, while a parliamentary system may concentrate authority and responsibility, a federal system disperses it. The result, in Canada, is that many subjects of national importance to the country are simply not addressed by the opposition in Parliament, and often the most effective opposition to federal policies is provided by the governments of the provinces.[18]

The third problem faced by the opposition in Canada is that of achieving policy distinctiveness. The institutionalization of opposition in Parliament was originally premised on an agreement among all participants not to question the foundations of the parliamentary system. Opposition parties have added to this their tacit agreement not to question the fundamentals of the social and economic order: *opposition parties offer voters not a new system, but a more effective operation of the existing one.* Consequently, the opposition is in no position to articulate dissatisfaction with the political regime. Parliament is not the forum for real ideological debate, for example, because certain important dissenting points of view are simply not to be found in the ranks of parliamentary opposition. Moreover, the opposition in Canada has not been at the forefront of efforts to reform Parliament or the electoral system, even though these institutions may not have served the opposition well in the past.

In Canada, an opposition committed to the present means of distributing economic resources, to the existing system of representation and to the structures of federalism faces an electorate deeply divided on regional and linguistic grounds. Policy innovation under these circumstances is, understandably, an uncommon occurrence. Yet without innovation, the opposition begins to surrender to interest groups and provincial governments the task of defining alternatives to government policy. Bernard Crick has described Parliament as, ideally, a "permanent election campaign";[19] but what good is that if the electorate perceives that there is nothing to choose between those two teams whose struggle is supposed to ensure responsible government?

Finally, what strength the opposition has in Canada is derived primarily from the fact that the government cannot ignore it. Ministers may make announcements and speeches outside Parliament (much to the consternation of the opposition), but it is Parliament that must eventually approve legislation and appropriate funds. In the course of doing so, opposition members engage in lonely debates in the hope that their ideas and reservations will be communicated beyond the chamber to an alert and interested public. Is this a reasonable expectation? Is electoral choice strongly influenced by the performance of the opposition on the floor of the House of Commons? A strong affirmative answer is impossible. In spite of the televising of Parliament (which is selective in content and distribution) there is no evidence that the electorate has an improved awareness of opposition policies and attitudes. The press gallery persists in concentrating on spectacular developments, scandals and human interest stories, while election campaigns continue to be contests among party leaders, not alternative ministerial teams. Opposition parties exacerbate the process by resisting the creation of a small and stable shadow Cabinet in favour of balancing regional claims to positions of prominence on the opposition front benches.

These observations on the opposition in Canada should not be interpreted simply as criticisms of opposition parties, the government or the media, whatever their shortcomings may be. The point is that the Westminster model of parliamentary government requires a great deal of the parliamentary opposition. Yet this opposition must work under severe institutional and political constraints not at all anticipated by the model.

In summary, the Westminster model promises decisive government, political accountability and the open debate of legislative changes, spending decisions and controversial government actions. It promises political stability in the form of a government-in-waiting should the present one falter. Unfortunately, as we have argued above, it cannot deliver on all of these promises. Since no model of government is perfect, and second-best solutions are frequently all that is available, a complete abandonment of the model is out of the question. For this reason the next section concentrates on additions to the model, additions that may ultimately change this part of our constitution but which, for now, constitute modifications.

Before leaving our discussion of fundamental principles, however, it is necessary to make mention of a new challenge to the Westminster model, the *Charter of Rights and Freedoms*. The *Charter*, introduced into the constitution in 1982, holds out the prospect that both legislative and executive actions will now be subject to the scrutiny of the courts. Without the *Charter*, the nature and extent of the rights possessed by Canadians was made concrete by the actions of Parliament and the provincial legislatures. With the *Charter* a portion of this task has been passed to the courts. This constitutional innovation will almost certainly result in some depoliticization of the public realm, as issues which were previously subject to political rhetoric are now to be interpreted via legal discourse.[20] How extensive this shift will be is very much in the hands of the courts.[21] But to the extent that it occurs, the claim that the

Westminster model delivers both decisive government and open political debate will be further undermined.

Executive–Legislative Relations

The Westminster model rests heavily on the clash of government and opposition forces. But to expect the opposition to assume the entire burden of ensuring a responsible and accountable government is, as we have argued, no longer realistic. In this section we explore relations between the government and the House of Commons which carry us beyond government–opposition confrontation. It is argued that the activities of members of Parliament, either as individuals or in concert with others, can complement the dominant adversarial style of politics in the House and supplement the work of the opposition. In fact, the activities of Parliament should be understood as a process of conflict and concession involving the government on the one hand and, on the other, three elements: the opposition, taken as a whole; small groups of MPs, both formal and informal; and private members, or MPs acting as individuals. Each of these relationships dominates parliamentary activities at a particular time, and each implies a different level and type of conflict and a different location.

The Government vs. the Opposition

At 4:20 p.m. on March 2, 1982 a member of the Conservative Opposition, Mr. Harvie André, moved that the House adjourn, and in so doing touched off what has come to be called "the bell-ringing incident." His motion was the culmination of unsuccessful efforts by the opposition to have an omnibus bill, the Energy Security Act, 1982, divided into more manageable parts. The division bells, which call members to vote, rang on and off until March 17, whereupon members from all parties appeared in the House to defeat the motion. In the interim the Conservatives had boycotted the chamber and debate had raged about what constitutes appropriate conduct on the part of both the government and the opposition. Should the opposition be able to bring parliamentary proceedings to a halt by simply moving adjournment and then refusing to appear to vote? Should the government be permitted to bring business to the floor of the Commons in precisely the way it deems fit even if this cripples the ability of the opposition to offer systematic criticism?

The bell-ringing incident had one immediate effect: members from both sides of the House demanded that a committee be established to recommend reforms to the operation of Parliament and its committees. No one, it appears, relished the prospect of a similar incident. But beyond that, the bell-ringing incident had the further effect of reinforcing the image of Parliament as a "bear pit." It showed the government and the opposition locked in a struggle over which of the principles of the Westminster model deserves to take precedence.

But the bell-ringing incident notwithstanding, this bear-pit image is a distortion. Even on the floor of the House of Commons agreement is more common than disagreement. The parliamentary leadership of both the government and the opposition parties are engaged in constant negotiation over the disposition of business, negotiation that ensures the smooth day-to-day operation of the House of Commons. Moreover, much of the legislation that passes the Commons does so with unanimous consent.

What can be said is that the Chamber is the stage on which the ritual and theatre of partisan antagonism is performed. It is the primary battleground of government and opposition forces, which usually means ministers or parliamentary secretaries, on the one hand, and members of the opposition front bench, on the other. The dominant style of debate is oratory, and backbenchers on both sides of the House are expected to provide an appreciative audience.

There are three important activities which take place on the floor of the House and have these combative and partisan qualities. Question Period is perhaps the most obvious: it is the opposition and the government at their most partisan. Under Joe Clark the Conservatives developed a systematic approach to Question Period which relies on an orchestrated series of questions. Ordinary backbenchers are discouraged from interrupting the flow until the front bench is finished. A similar quality of partisanship is found in the special debates which are scattered throughout the parliamentary year. The Throne Speech Debate (eight days) and the Budget Debate (six days) are opportunities for the opposition to criticize, and the Cabinet to defend, the government's vaguely worded legislative program and its more precisely formulated tax proposals. In addition, twenty-five "Opposition Days" are set aside in each parliamentary session during which motions proposed by the opposition parties form the basis for debate. These normally take the form of critical pronouncements on government policy, and six of these debates culminate in non-confidence votes.

A third occasion on which opposition and government traditionally confront one another is the second reading stage of government-sponsored legislation. The first reading is nothing more than parliamentary approval to allow the bill to be printed and placed on the order paper. Second reading is the stage at which Parliament debates "the principle" of the bill; no amendments are permitted and strict rules of relevance are enforced. It is here that the minister appears in the House to defend the legislation and the opposition spokesperson mounts a challenge. The government prefers to believe that once the second reading stage has been successfully completed, Parliament is obliged to concentrate on the details of the bill, the main battle over principles having been fought. This interpretation of second reading is entirely in keeping with the idea that legislation is a government–opposition affair.

It is not surprising that reform proposals designed to enhance the policy-making role of backbenchers hardly ever involve the floor of the House of Commons. The Special Committee on Procedure created after the bell-ringing incident succeeded in persuading the House to adopt, on a provisional basis, a set of reforms which would expedite the orderly conduct of government business and enhance the opportunities for opposition criticism. These reforms have the quality of a new orchestration for an old and familiar melody. There are now shorter speeches (normally twenty minutes) followed by a brief debate. There are no more evening sittings, no more votes on Friday and no more annoying mini-speeches under Standing Order 43. The government has agreed to announce its legislative intentions on a trimester basis and Parliament will sit for a determinate period each year, approximately 175 days. Most of the Committee's reforms were intended to improve, not alter, the quality of partisan debate.[22]

If all the business of Parliament were conducted on the floor of the Commons, there would be little more to add to this picture of executive–legislative relations. But with the growth of government activity and an increase in annual government spending to almost $90 billion (1983–84), the government has found it expedient to transfer some of its own business to standing and (occasionally) special commit- tees. In 1968, changes were made to the Standing Orders to require that detailed, clause-by-clause consideration of legislation be accomplished in standing committees. At the same time the opposition, somewhat reluc- tantly, agreed that the scrutiny of departmental spending estimates, previously considered under the heading of "Supply" on the floor of the House, could also be transferred to standing committees. Committees hold out the prospect of conflict as well, but not always on a strictly partisan basis.

Even without these changes to parliamentary rules, it would still be a distortion to think of Parliament strictly in terms of government–opposi- tion relations. Some of the most important political activity in Parliament takes place away from the floor of the House in the caucus of the governing party. It is in forums such as these—caucus and committees— that conflicts over policy are refined or redefined, that agreement is often achieved and that truly controversial matters are subject to a measure of conciliation.[23]

The Government vs. Formal and Informal Groups of MPs

For the government, one of the most important sources of criticism is the government backbench. Normally quiescent and polite in public, in private the backbench supporters of the government frequently clash with Cabinet on matters of policy. Open rebellion, though rare, can take the form of abstentions on important votes, minor media campaigns and cross-voting.

The disapproval of backbench supporters is a serious matter for the government. Occasional expressions of personal disgruntlement can be tolerated and many potentially disruptive issues can be assuaged by appeals to party loyalty. But when backbenchers refuse to respond to threats (e.g., no trips to Europe), to inducements (e.g., the possibility of a parliamentary secretary position), or to the rallying cry of party solidarity, the viability of the government itself is at stake. The opposition preys on suspected rifts within the governing party, and while cross-votes may not lead directly to government defeats, when a government has lost the confidence of its own backbenchers then it has lost the confidence of the House of Commons.

Government members, ministers included, meet in caucus every week when Parliament is in session. Because these meetings are always held *in camera* and MPs are very reluctant to expose to the public any sign of divisiveness in the party, the impression is sometimes one of Cabinet control and caucus deference. The reminiscences of MPs from the Diefenbaker and Pearson years have helped to confirm this image: denied any knowledge of the government's pending legislative program, MPs were forced to content themselves with issues such as parking spaces on Parliament Hill. In 1969, however, the Liberal caucus insisted that it be consulted on legislation and other expressions of government policy before these were announced in the House of Commons. A system of ad hoc caucus committees has been created to implement this consultative arrangement, and since 1970 the Liberal caucus has elected its own officers, including the caucus chairperson, without the direct interference of the parliamentary party leadership.

Caucus meetings are as closed as ever, but the noise of battle can occasionally be heard in spite of the secrecy. There is no doubt, for example, that some caucus members pressed hard for the resignation of ministers during the Judges Affair in 1976, and that others strongly opposed changes to the Unemployment Insurance Commission throughout the 1970s. Many amendments to the Liberal government's Crow Rate legislation in 1983 were accomplished at the insistence of caucus. In April of 1980, members of the Quebec caucus announced their support for General Dynamics' bid in the New Fighter Aircraft Program. It required a four-and-a-half-hour meeting with officials to convince the caucus to support the government's preference for the MacDonnell-Douglas offer. In short, the government must attempt to anticipate and answer caucus opposition to its proposals. A veteran of the Liberal caucus, Mark MacGuigan, has outlined the consequences of failure to do so: "From the beginning of my years in Parliament it has been apparent that strong caucus opposition to any government proposal imposes an absolute veto on the proposal."[24]

Like the meetings of caucus, committees of the Commons are vehicles with which smaller groups of MPs acting in concert can influence the direction of government policy. The potential of committees in this regard lies in their ability to study specific topics in depth and offer detached, and sometimes non-partisan, assessments. Unlike caucus, however, Commons committees are composed of representatives from all parties, and with one or two exceptions they conduct their hearings in public.

There are three types of committees: standing committees, which, as the name implies, are relatively permanent fixtures; special committees, which normally have a specific task and seldom last beyond a session; and joint committees composed of senators as well as MPs. Much of the time of standing committees is consumed in the clause-by-clause consideration of legislation and the scrutiny of departmental spending estimates. Since these are matters which the government has sponsored, Cabinet ministers naturally prefer that party lines be respected and that government supporters on each committee accept the direction of the minister (even though he or she is not a member of the committee) and the parliamentary secretary. This does not mean that changes to legislation cannot be accomplished, only that the government is normally the final arbiter.[25]

It is when standing committees begin to investigate problem areas such as the disposal of nuclear waste, Canada's foreign policy, or the income tax system that the partisan mould is often broken and committee members begin to act as a unit with less regard for partisan advantage. A classic example of this type of development occurred during the 30th Parliament (1974–1979) when a sub-committee of the Standing Committee on Justice and Legal Affairs explored in detail the state of Canada's penitentiary system. This sub-committee, composed of representatives from all parties, visited penal institutions in Canada and the United States, heard over four hundred witnesses and, finally, placed before Parliament a two-hundred-page report containing sixty-five recommendations which the committee had adopted unanimously.

Governments are ambivalent toward the launching of general investigations by parliamentary committees. On the positive side (from the government's point of view) public inquiries give the appearance of action without the substance. They ascertain the reactions of interest groups to government proposals without requiring that a formal commitment be made to introduce changes. MPs, particularly government backbenchers, are kept busy and given an opportunity to prove themselves. The Liberal government reiterated its interest in this type of parliamentary initiative when it announced early in the first session of the 32nd Parliament (1980-1983) the creation of six special committees, styled at the time as "task forces," composed of MPs from all parties who would study and offer recommendations on such subjects as regulatory reform, services to the handicapped and employment prospects in the 1980s.

On the negative side (once again from the government's point of view) committees eventually present reports, and committee members, not surprisingly, are usually eager to have their proposals discussed. If reports are tabled with the unanimous approval of committee members, the government will be facing a small body of informed opinion, usually supported by interest groups, which it might find difficult to ignore. The discussion of committee reports is also time consuming, in addition to which the government may calculate that it is not politically expedient to offer detailed responses to committee suggestions. The situation is all the more uncomfortable since appeals to government supporters on the basis of party loyalty are less compelling when reports are the product of considerable research and discussion among committee members. The opposition party leadership, for its part, is similarly reluctant to have opposition party supporters drawn heavily into investigations of this type lest unanimous committee reports compromise the opposition leadership in its struggle to establish itself as a viable alternative to the government.

In spite of the problems that committees pose for traditional government-opposition confrontation as sanctified in the Westminster model, it is safe to predict that throughout the 1980s governments will be called upon to respond to the studies and recommendations of small groups of MPs. In accepting the recommendations of the Special Committee on Procedure the government agreed, in November 1982, to automatically refer to standing committees the annual reports of agencies and departments and to respond within 120 days to committee reports. In its Fifth, Sixth and Seventh Reports the Special Committee returned to the subject of the committee system, this time recommending a significant transformation which would see much more specialization, especially in the area of financial accountability. These recommendations simply give further impetus to an established trend toward specialization both in the structure of committees and the behaviour of MPs. Since November 1982, standing committees consist of only ten to fifteen members, and the practice of using sub-committees is now widespread. Standing committees have gained considerable autonomy in the selection of committee leaders,[26] and the practice of wholesale substitution of committee members has been curtailed, thus increasing the likelihood that MPs will develop a genuine understanding of policy and practice in their selected areas.

How far can this be permitted to go? Critics of an expanded committee system have warned that once committees cease behaving as little replicas of the Commons, we can look forward to the decline of parliamentary traditions and a weakening of party ties that can only culminate in congressionalism. It is not at all clear, however, that this is the only path that Parliament must tread. Recent experience in the British House of Commons has shown that the defeat of government-sponsored legislation need not entail the defeat of the government itself. Both Labour and Conservative governments have witnessed a marked increase in the tendency of their own supporters to line up against them in formal Commons votes. Party leaders have responded by relaxing the convention that calls for the resignation of governments in the face of a defeat in the Commons.[27] Developments such as these suggest that there is another dimension to responsible government. The responsibility of a vigilant assembly to monitor closely the actions of a government need not be borne exclusively by the united opposition. Other groups of MPs, including the government caucus, standing committees and task forces of MPs can be reasonably expected to share that responsibility.

The Government vs. the Private Member of Parliament

In a government which spends enormous sums of money and employs hundreds of thousands of people, the private member of Parliament cuts a lonely figure. The vast majority of MPs owe their electoral victory to regional and national trends in the popularity of their party and its leaders. The machinery of party politics is such that very few of them will have made a critical contribution to their own election.[28] Once in Parliament they still have those privileges earned by their predecessors in the British House of Commons, but private members are no longer the source of legislative initiative that they were in the nineteenth century. A few hours every week are set aside for the consideration of private members' business, but attendance is generally poor and the vast majority of private members' bills do not even come to a vote at second reading. The arrival of cohesive political parties and the government-sponsored public bill long ago set the stage for the departure of the private member as law maker.

But as we indicated in the introduction to this chapter, neither the House of Commons as a whole nor private members should be judged as initiators of policy. While it is true that many items in the government's legislative program have as their precursors private members' bills, the task of private members, like that of the opposition and groups of MPs, is to prod, encourage, question and occasionally castigate the government with the intention of forcing it to justify in public its actions or inactions. For a certain range of matters the private member is in an excellent position to do that.

Each member of Parliament represents, on average, 55,000 electors. Representation implies, among other things, responsiveness to the needs of individual constituents, and many MPs spend most of their working time attending to their constituency caseload. This includes unemployment insurance problems, immigration cases and countless other instances in which the personal intervention of a member of Parliament is requested. While some MPs come to resent this combined role of social worker and ombudsperson, a 1983 Gallup poll showed that over 60 percent of respondents believed that looking after constituents should be the first priority of the MP. Moreover, it does keep members in touch with the concerns and problems of their constituents. For people who feel aggrieved in some fashion the government is the post office that has curtailed its service or the game warden who refuses to renew a fishing licence. The tendency to judge the House of Commons solely on the strength of its ability to affect the broad strokes of policy does a disservice to those MPs who labour to make sure that their constituents receive justice at the hands of the federal bureaucracy.

There are, in addition, those MPs who wage personal campaigns to secure a particular policy objective. Their names are virtually synonymous with their cause. In Canada, the name of Jed Baldwin, for example, will always be associated with the battle for freedom of information legislation. Anthony King has described this as the "private members' mode" of executive–legislative relations. MPs who adopt it, in his words, "come to see themselves simply as backbench Members of Parliament, concerned with investigating the quality of the performance of the executive (of whichever party), with protecting the rights of the citizen against the executive (of whichever party) and with asserting the prerogatives of backbench MPs (irrespective of party)."[29] Very few MPs can stand up to the demands imposed by this style of operation. Parliament is about political parties, not private members. Nonetheless, members of Parliament frequently feel the need to demonstrate their talents and to show that, in their case, the transition from backbencher to Cabinet minister would be an easy one. For this reason alone the government will always be confronted by the private member of Parliament.

Conclusion
The importance of Parliament does not lie in its capacity to be a centre for the detailed construction of public policy, for this capacity is meagre indeed. Parliament is, instead, a forum where the ideas and concerns of the government, the opposition, groups of MPs and individual representatives meet. The government, as we have emphasized, is in charge: its ideas and policies form the basis for the most important debates. But the government also listens. To be out of touch with the sentiments of backbench supporters or the opposition is to court disaster.

If the norms and rules which underpin responsible government continue to grow in complexity, and Parliament is strengthened in its ability to question and prod, governments will have to listen more closely. This will undoubtedly occasion some loss of flexibility, and demands on governments to inform and explain will tax ministerial and bureaucratic resources. But it is surely not too much to ask that a government which listens so closely to the pronouncements of the provinces, interest groups, OPEC and Washington also remain in touch with the country's elected representatives.

It is essential, however, that these representatives have something to say which merits attention. While strengthening Parliament's side in each of the relationships discussed above will help, it will also be necessary to challenge the fundamental principles of the Westminster model with a view to guiding its evolution. If ordinary MPs remain in splendid isolation, entirely neutralized by strictures of party discipline that very few Canadians understand, Parliament will increasingly become an irrelevant and obscure institution.

Notes

1. Although Canada's Parliament is a bicameral legislature containing an upper House consisting of 104 appointed senators, this paper will discuss only the House of Commons. For an excellent treatment of Canada's Senate, see Colin Campbell, *The Canadian Senate: A Lobby from Within* (Toronto: Macmillan, 1977).

2. See the argument developed in Mark Sproule-Jones, "The Enduring Colony?: Political Institutions and Political Science in Canada," *Publius* (Fall 1984).

3. On the various types of bills and the distinction between private bills and private members' bills see Robert J. Jackson and Michael M. Atkinson, *The Canadian Legislative System: Politicians and Policymaking*, 2nd rev. ed. (Toronto: Macmillan, 1980), pp. 89–92.

4. John B. Stewart, *The Canadian House of Commons: Procedure and Reform* (Montreal: McGill-Queen's University Press, 1977), p. 201.

5. The government is also authorized, under a variety of statutes, to make annual appropriations without submitting requests to Parliament. See Jackson and Atkinson, *The Canadian Legislative System*, pp. 91–92 and Stewart, *The Canadian House of Commons*, pp. 110–11.

6. Michel J. Crozier, Samuel P. Huntington and Joji Watanuki, *The Crisis of Democracy* (New York: Trilateral Commission, 1975).

7. It might also, however, be considered the antithesis of constitutionalism. See Carl J. Friedrich, *Limited Government: A Comparison* (Englewood Cliffs, NJ: Prentice-Hall, 1974).

8. For an excellent, balanced discussion of cabinet and prime ministerial government in Canada, consult R.M. Punnett, *The Prime Minister in Canadian Government and Politics* (Toronto: Macmillan, 1977).

9. Linda Geller-Schwartz, "Minority Government Reconsidered," *Journal of Canadian Studies* 14 (Summer 1979): 67–79.

10. Kenneth Kernaghan, "Power, Parliament and Public Servants in Canada," in *Parliament, Policy and Representation*, ed. Harold Clarke *et al*. (Toronto: Methuen, 1980), pp. 128–29.

11. Thomas d'Aquino, G. Bruce Doern and Cassandra Blair, *Parliamentary Democracy in Canada: Issues for Reform* (Toronto: Methuen, 1983), pp. 45–46, and Canada, Royal Commission on Financial Management and Accountability, *Final Report* (Ottawa: Supply and Services, 1979), p. 374.

12. V. Seymour Wilson, *Canadian Public Policy and Administration* (Toronto: McGraw-Hill, 1981), Chapter 4.

13. Colin Campbell and George Szablowski, *The Superbureaucrats* (Toronto: Macmillan, 1979), p. 209. For an extension of this argument in a comparative context see Colin Campbell, *Governments Under Stress* (Toronto: University of Toronto Press, 1983).

14. The transition is elaborated in Thomas A. Hockin, "Flexible and Structured Parliamentarism: From 1848 to Contemporary Party Government" *Journal of Canadian Studies* 14 (Summer 1979): 8–17.

15. Denis Smith, "President and Parliament: The Transformation of Parliamentary Government in Canada," in *The Canadian Political Process*, 2nd ed., ed. Orest Krulak *et al*. (Toronto: Holt, Rinehart and Winston, 1973), pp. 351–52.

16. Stewart, *The Canadian House of Commons*, p. 21.

17. Ghita Ionescu and Isabel de Madariaga, *Opposition* (London: Penguin, 1972), Chapter 2.

18. On executive federalism and parliamentary government see Donald V. Smiley, *Canada in Question: Federalism in the Eighties*, 3rd ed. (Toronto: McGraw-Hill, 1980), especially Chapters 2 and 4.

19. Bernard Crick, *The Reform of Parliament* (New York: Anchor Books, 1965), p. 201.

20. Harry J. Glasbeek and Michael Mandel, "The Legalization of Politics in Advanced Capitalism: The Canadian Charter of Rights and Freedoms," mimeographed (1983).

21. For two different interpretations see Peter H. Russell, "The Political Purposes of the Canadian Charter of Rights and Freedoms," *Canadian Bar Review*, March 1983, pp. 30–54, and A.F. Bayefsky, "Parliamentary Sovereignty and Human Rights in Canada: The Promise of the Canadian Charter of Rights and Freedoms," *Political Studies* 31 (June 1983): 239–63.

22. See the speeches delivered in Hansard, First Session, 32nd Parliament, November 29, 1982.

23. The role of legislatures in the management of conflict is often underemphasized. See the comments of Gerhard Loewenberg and Samuel C. Patterson, *Comparing Legislatures* (Boston: Little Brown, 1979), pp. 59–60.

24. Mark MacGuigan, "Parliamentary Reform: Impediments to an Enlarged Role for the Backbencher," *Legislative Studies Quarterly* 3 (November 1978): 676.

25. Paul G. Thomas, "The Influence of Standing Committees of Parliament on Government Legislation," *Legislative Studies Quarterly* 3 (November 1978): 683–704.

26. Michael M. Atkinson and Kim Richard Nossal, "Executive Power and Committee Autonomy in the Canadian House of Commons," *Canadian Journal of Political Science* 13 (June 1980): 287–308.
27. John E. Schwarz, "Exploring a New Role in Policymaking: The British House of Commons in the 1970s," *American Political Science Review* 74 (March 1980): 23–37, and Philip Norton, "The Changing Face of the British House of Commons in the 1970s," *Legislative Studies Quarterly* 5 (August 1980): 333–58.
28. William Irvine, "Does the Candidate Make a Difference? The Macro-Politics and the Micro-Politics of Getting Elected," *Canadian Journal of Political Science* 15 (December 1982): 755–82.
29. Anthony King, "Modes of Executive–Legislative Relations: Great Britain, France and West Germany," *Legislative Studies Quarterly* 1 (February 1976): 11–36.

Further Readings

Clarke, Harold D., Colin Campbell, F.Q. Quo and Arthur Goddard, eds. *Parliament, Policy and Representation*. Toronto: Methuen, 1980.

d'Aquino, T., G.B. Doern and Cassandra Blair. *Parliamentary Democracy in Canada*. Toronto: Methuen, 1983.

Jackson, Robert J., and Michael M. Atkinson. *The Canadian Legislative System: Politicians and Policymaking*. 2nd rev. ed. Toronto: Macmillan, 1980.

Kornberg, Allan. *Canadian Legislative Behaviour*. Toronto: Holt, Rinehart and Winston, 1967.

———, and William Mishler. *Influence in Parliament: Canada*. Durham, NC: Duke University Press, 1977.

March, Roman. *The Myth of Parliament*. Scarborough: Prentice-Hall, 1975.

Special Issue on Legislatures in Canada. *Legislative Studies Quarterly* 3, November 1978.

Special Issue on Responsible Government. *Journal of Canadian Studies* 14, Summer 1979.

Stewart, John B. *The Canadian House of Commons: Procedure and Reform*. Montreal: McGill-Queen's University Press, 1977.

Chapter 16

The Federal Cabinet in Canadian Politics
David E. Smith

In the year of Confederation, Walter Bagehot described the Cabinet as "a combining committee—a *hyphen* which joins, a *buckle* which fastens the legislative part of the state to the executive part of the state." Buckle and hyphen have proved durable metaphors with which to open discussions of cabinet government despite the fact that the functions and structure of modern cabinets are significantly different from those of Bagehot's time. The executive he had in mind, the Crown, has faded into obscurity in the public consciousness. For most Canadians, the Cabinet's central importance now lies in its *governing and representative* functions, while its role as advisor to the Crown is seldom considered and, when regarded, scarcely understood. Nevertheless, we should keep in mind that the Cabinet, through the prime minister, still formally advises the chief executive officer, the governor general, who always, or almost always, takes that advice, for not to take it would create a constitutional crisis.

Metaphors like Bagehot's are attractive when facts are hard to find, and, with notable exceptions, studies of the federal Cabinet are rare. There is no encyclopedic Canadian work comparable to Sir Ivor Jenning's *Cabinet Government* in Great Britain, nor even are there many less ambitious exercises.[1] Personal accounts of those in command at the Cabinet table go unwritten; of the sixteen prime ministers to date, only two (Diefenbaker and Pearson) have published their own memoirs, and these tell disappointingly little about Cabinet decision making or about the respective influences on Cabinet business of the bureaucracy, interest groups, political parties or the Parliamentary opposition.[2] In the twenty years since Lester Pearson formed a government, just two ministers (Walter Gordon and Judy LaMarsh) have written memoirs, though the revelations of Cabinet business contained in them are cause for regret that their contemporaries do not follow suit.[3] This reticence is not new. Mackenzie King's extraordinary tenure as prime minister for twenty-two years in this century proved no more productive of published accounts. If Pearson is excluded, only one of King's seventy-three other ministers dictated his memoirs.[4] In the first half-century of Confederation, when Cabinets were smaller and responsibilities less extensive, the selection is no better.[5]

The absence of memoirs is more than unfortunate for academics or for citizens who would like to know how government works. It is also revealing of a political system which produces politicians who are uncommunicative and incurious and who, according to Norman Ward and David Hoffman in their study *Bilingualism and Biculturalism in the Canadian House of Commons*, also lack ambition: "Only 24 percent [of the backbench MPs interviewed in that 1964–65 survey] indicated that they would be interested in a cabinet post at some time in the future; 50 percent said that they had no interest in any pubic office(s) in the future."[6] This reign of political silence and passivity stands in marked contrast to the situation in Great Britain in the last decade, where the then Prime Minister, Harold Wilson, had to resort to the courts to try to stop his ministers from publishing their memoirs, although some cynics suggested the prohibition had less to do with alleged violations of the Official Secrets Act than with allowing the Prime Minister to publish first!

While, then, we may not know as much as we might like about the inner operation of the Cabinet, we can begin our investigation by locating the process of Cabinet government within the context of the Canadian political tradition. This will prepare us for this chapter's subsequent examination of the role of Cabinet according to its two principal and historic functions: as an instrument of government and as a vehicle for representation.

Cabinet and the Canadian Political Tradition

Pragmatic Politics

Whatever label might be applied to the two political parties who have formed Canada's federal governments, doctrinaire is not one of them. Debates between these parties in Parliament and in the country do not reflect differences of principle so much as differences over how to implement policies of economic growth or social security. Within Cabinet this value consensus generally holds; only very occasionally are there intraparty divisions where the alignment of sympathies is as clear as it was between economic nationalists and continentalists in the Liberal party in the 1960s and the early 1980s. Significantly, one of the rare ministerial authors of memoirs was Walter Gordon, the gadfly of economic nationalism who held several portfolios in the Pearson government.

Walter Gordon was unusual less for the policy he advocated than for the arguments he used. He urged economic nationalism for its long-run concrete benefits, but promoted it first as a principle. From such studies of Cabinet as exist, the impression gained is that ministers are normally pragmatic in the positions they take. Perhaps, as will be discussed more fully later, this is inevitable in so large and diverse a group: matters of principle are simply less open to bargaining. And yet one must be careful not to underestimate the latent importance of values in Canadian politics. Walter Gordon was distinctive in publicizing his position. Most ministers do not. They may even act embarrassed when it is suggested that they hold an ideological stance on some issue. But the PC leadership contest in 1983 and the Liberal leadership contest in 1984 demonstrate, for instance, that candidates *are* forced to declare their position on such ideologically charged questions as medicare, Petro-Canada and bilingualism. Nevertheless, one reason Canadians are not used to thinking ideologically about such subjects is that their politicians have been reluctant to treat them this way.

The absence of a doctrinaire approach within the old political parties is revealed paradoxically enough in the resignations of ministers from the federal Cabinet. Not only do few resignations occur, but those that do are seldom attributed to policy differences. There are exceptions, of course. For example, Israel Tarte (Public Works) was ejected from the Cabinet in 1902 for publicly disagreeing with the government's tariff policy; Clifford Sifton (Interior) resigned in 1905 from the same government because he dissented from the original educational provisions of the Alberta and Saskatchewan acts; J.L. Ralston (National Defence) was fired by Mackenzie King in 1944 for advocating military conscription for overseas service before King, who long resisted this policy for fear of its detrimental effect on national unity, was ready to accept it; and Douglas Harkness (National Defence) resigned from the Diefenbaker Government in 1963 because he supported the arming of BOMARC missiles with nuclear warheads and his leader did not.

But even in instances such as these, the effect of the resignations was not to extend the political debate very far or for very long. Tarte and Ralston did not run at the next elections and Sifton and Harkness stayed on for at least one more Parliament but provided no voice for alternative policies, since the issues which led to their resignations quickly faded.[7] Much more typical is a resignation like that of John Turner (Finance) from the Trudeau government in 1975, which was publicly described as being for "personal reasons." Although Turner was subsequently labelled as more conservative than Trudeau on economic and social issues and although he was widely viewed as a major contender for the Liberal leadership when Trudeau retired, his resignation prompted little public debate over political principle either inside or outside the party. Certainly there was no massing of Liberal support behind competing interpretations of Liberalism. One consequence of this reluctance to inject policy differences into public debate as well as in the Cabinet is to depreciate political discourse within political parties and within the country, to the detriment of politics as an educative activity. In its place, the cult of personality seizes the attention of the media, the public and the politicians, and this is not, as we shall next see, an attitude conducive to the growth of professionalism in politics.[8]

Avocational Politics

Arguably, political debate is pragmatic because the politicians who take part in it are not professionals. Twenty years ago, in *The Vertical Mosaic*, John Porter wrote that a model political career implies

> a professionalizing of political roles where the individual devotes his life to politics and in the process develops a "love" for political institutions. . . . [But] where the political career is unstable and taken up for an interstitial period only, during a career devoted to something else, the political system will probably be strong in administration and weak in creativity.[9]

In the period he studied, Porter discovered that life at the top was peopled by ministers frequently coopted from other careers (for example, business or the public service) or after brief experience in the House of Commons, and that in either case their period in Cabinet was surprisingly short. In 1960, 47 percent of the ministers had served for less than six years. Porter's findings here were confirmed in a 1973 study by Dennis Olsen which found that 52 percent had served for five years or less and that 95 percent had served fewer than eleven years.[10] Moreover, given a House of Commons where the turnover rate is usually around 40 percent (in 1979 it was 38 percent and in 1980, only *nine months* after the previous election, it was 19 percent) and where another 20 to 35 percent of the MPs have less than five years' experience, Cabinet "timber" nurtured in a parliamentary environment is never a commodity in great supply when a prime minister sets about constructing a government.

There are other reasons why the Cabinet is deficient in political experience. The most important is the imperative of sectional representation, which will be discussed in more detail later in this chapter. At this point, it is enough to say that the practice of ensuring representation from all the provinces in Cabinet is now so strong—it is a convention or binding rule of prime ministerial behaviour—that it overrides considerations of political experience where the two criteria conflict. The depressing effect of this practice on those MPs who aspire to ministerial office but are excluded for geographic reasons needs to be recognized when explaining why Porter's model political career is infrequently seen in Canada. Conversely, the size of the Cabinet (thirty-seven in January 1984) increases the problem of finding sufficient personnel with satisfactory parliamentary experience.

One final word on the absence of professionals in federal politics concerns the party leaders themselves. During the Progressive Conservative leadership race in 1983, the Liberals liked to point out that one of the front-runners, Brian Mulroney, who eventually won, had no parliamentary experience. But Liberal leaders in this century since Mackenzie King have been remarkably innocent of backbench experience themselves: King had less than a year, St Laurent none, Pearson none and Trudeau seventeen months, fifteen of them as a parliamentary secretary. Norman Ward once wrote that "one excellent way of ensuring that one will not rise to the top of the Liberal party is to start at the bottom."[11] As well, one effect of leadership conventions in Canada has been to favour non-parliamentary over parliamentary experience, and this seems almost as true of the Progressive Conservatives as of the Liberals. Since 1942 and John Bracken's selection, the PCs have had six leaders, four of whom have had no parliamentary background.

Thus the Cabinet is not the kindergarten of political leadership in Canada that it is in Great Britain. (While no one knows, for example, who will succeed Margaret Thatcher, the probability that he or she will come out of the Cabinet's ranks is extremely high.) That reason—the fact that the Cabinet is not seen as the training ground of leadership coupled with the pragmatic nature of its politics already alluded to—helps explain the nature of Cabinet government in Canada. But there is a third factor, related to those already mentioned, that needs to be considered and that is the process by which major interests reach agreement through bargaining—brokerage politics.

Brokerage Politics

Brokerage theory, which has dominated Canadian political science, argues that national political parties must encompass all the essential interests in the country if both a majority is to be secured and minority rights guaranteed. This theory is both empirical and prescriptive. It purports to describe how parties actually practise their art, and it defends that practice. Parties, it is believed, are supposed to act as agents of consensus and as aggregators of interests rather than as instruments of choice. But despite its hegemony, the theory has its critics, none more pertinent than John Porter, who charged brokerage politics with stultifying "creative" political debate. The search for the middle ground in politics, he argued, too often excluded rather than included interests. The result was that parties and governments seemed always to pay undue attention to professional, commercial, middle-class concerns. "Seemed" was the operative verb, for as he noted: "We have in fact very little information about what interests political leaders take into consideration in making up cabinets."[12]

Unfortunately, we still lack the concrete information necessary to confirm Porter's judgment on the mechanisms of Cabinet selection.[13] But the belief that interests must be balanced, especially those geographically defined, remains strong. Currently, this can be seen in proposals to reform the electoral system or the upper house so as to bring to the centre a greater range of regional interests. More will be said of these proposals later. At this point, it need only be stated that institutional reformers assume the validity and utility of brokerage politics and, in the case of proponents of proportional representation, believe it would strengthen the Cabinet by presenting the prime minister with more choices when selecting ministers.

Brokerage politics cannot really be fully discussed in this chapter, for the scope of the discussion would go far beyond its effect on the Cabinet. However, it is necessary to recognize what its assumptions imply for a study of the Cabinet. Inevitably they suggest an analysis of the Cabinet in terms of how faithfully its members reflect the "elemental" divisions of the country. It is for that reason that so much research on the Cabinet presents in detail the geographic and socioeconomic characteristics of its members. But it is also the case that very few of these same studies explain why such "representation" is significant. Instead, it is assumed rather than demonstrated that the degree of fit between national and Cabinet characteristics affects the kind of policies and decisions made by government. There is a big jump here between *cause and effect*—not least over the conversion process whereby *balanced Cabinet representation leads to balanced policies.*

One of the most suggestive alternative theories about the Cabinet, federalism and political parties to appear recently in Canadian political discourse has come from abroad. This is the theory of *consociational democracy*, developed in small European countries like the Netherlands where the interests of strong sub-cultures require accommodation if national unity is to exist.[14] In the European experience, accommodation takes place at the elite levels and requires for its success integrated sub-cultures with clear patterns of leadership. From this brief description, the appeal of consociational democracy in Canada can be appreciated, especially since the 1960s, when the Canadian polity became increasingly fragmented as the Quiet Revolution spread in Quebec and as the other provinces increased their demands on Ottawa for greater financial and political control over economic and social policies. In addition, consociational democracy as a theory of bargaining among elites gave new respectability to brokerage politics. There was difficulty, however, in adapting a new theory to old Canadian practices. In the past, political parties had been the brokers while in the modern period governments, under the rubric of executive federalism, had gained the upper hand. But if governments, not parties, assumed prominence, then the politics of the federal Cabinet took on a new dimension too.[15]

Let us conclude this introduction by observing that the history of the federal cabinet is the history of Canada's evolution as an independent parliamentary democracy. Canadians are revolutionary neither in spirit nor in deed, and the best place to look for evidence of this gradualism is in the changing role of Cabinet. For it was here that the achievement of responsible government in the 1840s and the assertion of autonomy in external affairs over the next century took place. And so, having mapped the essential topography of the federal Cabinet within the Canadian political tradition according to its pragmatic, avocational and brokerage boundaries, we are now ready for a closer examination of the evolution of its governing and representative functions.

Cabinet as an Instrument of Government

A Colonial and Imperial Past

Colonial origins and imperial models determined the evolution of cabinet government. The idea that the Crown should heed the advice of those who command the support of the popularly elected chamber (which in the United Canadas was recognized in 1848 by Lord Elgin's acceptance of the Rebellion Losses Bill) implied more than a new parliamentary democratic value, as important as that was. It also signified a new organizing principle for the Empire, and Lord Durham's recommendation of a decade earlier that colonies should be responsible for their internal affairs was now to be implemented. The importance of this development for Canada cannot be underestimated. The conflict between Parliament and the king which had seen Parliament prevail in Great Britain a century before was now to be repeated in the colonies with the same result. However, there was something more here as well. To the extent that colonial Parliament prevailed over the king's representative, so did Canada prevail over Great Britain—responsible government thus ultimately led to independent government.

All of this is history, but it is history with a point as far as the development of the Canadian Cabinet is concerned. For it would be misleading to discuss the federal Cabinet's growth solely in terms of domestic politics, since the Cabinet and its leaders also gained strength and unity out of the colonial situation. Not only did external matters occupy Cabinet attention (especially military questions and their effect on domestic harmony—the Boer War and Laurier, the First World War and Borden, the Second World War and King), but the evolution of the Empire into the Commonwealth was accompanied by a transfer of power from imperial to Canadian authorities (in such forms, for example, as the power to make treaties, to declare war and, finally, to amend the constitution at home). Questions of status—colonial, dominion, national and international—have traditionally bulked large for prime ministers because of their implications for Canada's developing autonomy and prestige. This explains why until 1946 the prime minister acted as his own Secretary of State for External Affairs and why even afterward, in contrast to their British counterparts, Canadian PMs continued to play a leading role in foreign affairs.

If over time Canada's developing colonial status conferred new responsibilities on its Cabinet and enhanced the power of its prime minister, there were other influences derived from its colonial origins that affected the Cabinet right from the start. Indeed, some of these were pronounced well before Confederation. Responsible government arrived in the St. Lawrence lowlands when the Canadas, united since 1840 by a single set of political institutions but by little else, were already an embryonic federal system. In order to operate this unwieldy structure, practical adjustments were necessary, and from early on the cabinet proved especially useful as a mechanism for accommodating the social diversities of the colony. There were several reasons for this development. The myriad interests—religious, linguistic, legal, economic and military among others—which jockeyed for attention in the colony evolved through a period when they looked to the executive (the governor and his Council) to protect them. And there were no modern disciplined political parties. Instead, factions based on regional or social groupings were in a seemingly continuous process of formation and dissolution. The result was a series of coalition governments throughout the history of the United Canadas whose authority was frequently rejected by the elected legislators but who could look to their executive power as the Crown's advisors to give them the legitimacy they needed.

Old Traditions and Modern Practices

From the outset, Canadian cabinets were large because of the number of interests to be accommodated in a culturally bifurcated society, and because of the breadth of territory to be represented. The pressure to include rather than exclude affected the conduct of business too. From colonial days, the preferred practice was to confer rule-making power on the Council and not on individual ministers. In the modern era of expanded delegation from Parliament to the executive the same is true, for to do otherwise would favour with power or information some ministers over others—an act of discrimination which the sectional dimension of Cabinet membership particularly discourages. As an indicator of this volume, in 1976 there were 3,326 orders-in-council, of which the three largest categories concerned appointments (22.5

percent), regulations (19.6 percent) and property transactions (14.5 percent).[17]

A related effect has been to minimize traditional British distinctions as, for example, between Cabinet and Council or between Cabinet and Ministry. In Great Britain, where rank is one of life's organizing principles, such distinctions are accepted, but in Canada, where society is both more open and more heterogeneous, they are not. Here the governor's old Executive Council (after July 1, 1867 it was called the Privy Council) evolved into Cabinet with minimal distinction between the two. (By convention, membership in the Council is retained for life along with the designation Honourable, but even for ceremonial purposes the Council rarely convenes.) The Cabinet as a Committee of Council is a "masquerade," according to R. MacGregor Dawson, which it adopts "when it desires to assume formal powers."[17]

It is only since the Second World War and particularly since Trudeau became prime minister that the Privy Council Office has begun to have a life of its own. Although there has been a clerk of the Privy Council since Confederation, the office was (with rare exceptions) from Laurier through Diefenbaker seen as the fiefdom of the prime minister. Since Pearson's time the office of president of the Privy Council has been held by the leader of the House, and the Privy Council Office itself has become one of the so-called "central agencies," whose influence is derived from its position in the decision-making process and whose operation is described in more detail elsewhere in this volume.[18]

There was a similar reluctance, and for the same reasons, to follow British precedent and distinguish between Cabinet and Ministry. For although the number of ministers has always appeared large in comparison to the needs of a relatively small population, any attempt to introduce efficiency by streamlining structures (which usually has meant reducing numbers) has been resisted because of its exclusionary effect. In Great Britain the Ministry may be in excess of one hundred members and the Cabinet a quarter that number with an Inner Cabinet within that. By contrast, in Canada, except for the occasional exclusion of the solicitor general, the controller of Customs or the controller of Inland Revenue (all before 1926), *all* members of the Ministry have also been members of the Cabinet. Moreover, until the late 1960s when Cabinet committees were introduced, there has been nothing resembling an Inner Cabinet. Formally, that ceased to be true in 1979 when Joe Clark restructured Cabinet committees to create an Inner Cabinet and, practically, after the early 1970s creation of a Priorities and Planning committee by Trudeau introduced an approximation of an Inner Cabinet. It should be remarked that parliamentary secretaries (there were twenty-eight in February 1984), who have existed on a regular basis since the 1940s, when they were called parliamentary assistants, have never been considered part of the Ministry.

These changes notwithstanding, it is true that Cabinet government in Canada has meant, since Confederation at least, government by the full Cabinet—a body large in number and chosen to reflect the country's geographic diversity and cultural duality, although more recently its social base has broadened to include women (1957), someone not from one of the two founding cultures (1957) a non-Christian (1968) and a native Canadian (1976), a tendency that can be expected to continue as society changes.

The principal functions of the federal Cabinet are to direct the business of Parliament, to administer the individual departments of government, to formulate and discuss policy and to pass orders-in-council. Most importantly, it is "to furnish initiative and leadership" for the country and Parliament.[19] Essentially this is a joint enterprise of the Cabinet and the prime minister but, in truth, how well it is done and what character it assumes is the responsibility of the prime minister alone. In the Canadian system the prime minister enjoys inordinate powers by tradition and as a result of innovations in technology (e.g., television) and institutions (e.g., leadership conventions), which elevate the position vis-à-vis the Cabinet to the point where the oft-repeated claim that the PM is *primus inter pares* (first among equals) is no more descriptive of the position than Bagehot's buckle-and-hyphen metaphor is of the Cabinet.[20]

Three Models of Political Leadership

The Canadian system of government is party government, or more precisely party-in-government. The telescoping of these two features confers exceptional power on the leader of the legislative party that controls the House of Commons, but how that power is used is at his or her discretion. Since Confederation it is possible to discern three broad approaches to political leadership, each of which has affected the image Canadians have had of themselves and implied a different role and function for the Cabinet. For brevity's sake the three may be labelled as the personal, the accommodative and the pan-Canadian approaches. While historical events never fit exactly into time periods, it is possible to see each approach as the dominant characteristic of political leadership in the following major eras of Canadian history: personal (Confederation to First World War), accommodative (inter-war and immediate post–Second World War), and pan-Canadian (mid-1950s to the present).

The personal approach, in place up to the First World War, can be identified with the leadership of Macdonald and Laurier. Although of different political parties, each was concerned with national expansion: Macdonald basically with rounding out the Union by incorporating new provinces and territories and by welding the whole into one economic unit through his tripartite National Policy with its protective tariff, transcontinental railway and accelerated immigration; and Laurier by furthering that expansion through more aggressive immigration and settlement of the West. But though their policies were national, their political practices were local. As Gordon Stewart has shown, they pioneered patronage politics to create a national party system that was intensely local in its interests and profoundly personal in its management by the party leader.[21]

Under them, the Cabinet became a collective through which to channel gifts in the form of jobs and contracts from the government, which in this period was among the largest businesses (in terms of expenditure and employment) in the country. Unlike the United States, Canada had no giant capitalist corporations of national breadth, excluding perhaps the Canadian Pacific Railway, itself scarcely independent of the federal government. In the process Macdonald and Laurier created an "effective party structure" but not a "modern" one, and the First World War, with its economic and social dislocations, revealed just how inadequate the system was in adjusting to change. The rise of a strong third party in the form of the Progressives, who captured 65 of 235 seats in the 1921 election, vividly demonstrated the need for a new political response. That response had to come from the Cabinet and its leader, for among the functions of the Cabinet not listed earlier but of crucial significance to Canadian politics is its role as the "managing committee for the party in power."[22]

The new accommodative approach, initiated by Mackenzie King, became the hallmark of his long tenure as party leader and prime minister (as well as of Louis St Laurent's prime ministership) and differed from the Macdonald–Laurier style in several important respects. King was unusually alive to the divisive forces in Canadian society, in part because of his experience as a labour conciliator and in part because of events which preceded and accompanied his rise to office—the conflict in English–French elections from 1890 onward, culminating in the conscription crisis in Quebec and the Liberal party's split over it, and the farmers' revolt on the Prairies, which up to 1917 had represented safe Liberal territory. These factors and others, such as the civil service reforms of the former (Union) government which moderated patronage in federal politics and thus conformed more closely to King's personal disposition and political decision to be less directly involved in these matters than Laurier, help explain the source of King's consensual approach to leadership.

There is no dispute that King had no peer in the art of accommodation or compromise. Nor is there doubt that he used the Cabinet as one of his instruments and that he was supremely skilled in its use. He deflected the Progressives in the twenties in part by coopting two of their leaders (Forke and Crerar) and he similarly blunted the CCF threat in part by taking in Labour spokesman Humphrey Mitchell. Further, he defused a Quebec explosion over conscription through the help of his Quebec ministers, two of whom eventually resigned over this drawn-out question, and by the dismissal of the minister of National Defence (not from Quebec) who advocated conscription for overseas service before King believed the country was ready for it.

Under King and St Laurent, the Cabinet became not only the locus for resolving domestic tensions but the directing arm of the Liberal party. The ministers, when they were not former partisan opponents, were the chief Liberals of the day. A former provincial premier like J.G. Gardiner from Saskatchewan, for example, was as close to being a "pro-consul" in that province, and on occasion in the neighbouring prairie provinces, as could be found in Canadian political history. King and St Laurent respected departmental autonomy, and thus their ministers gained unprecedented independence at the same time as the growth of the Canadian government's activities and responsibilities increased their powers. But with power came costs. In the period of Macdonald and Laurier, party had penetrated the bureaucracy through patronage, and now the bureaucracy penetrated the party by transmitting its values, objectives and procedures to the politician. In the end the Liberals became what Reginald Whitaker has called "the government party."[23] And if the parties and governments of Macdonald and Laurier grew out of touch with national economic and social trends, the Liberal party and governments of King and St Laurent did the same, this time by failing to comprehend the growth of regionalism.

The pan-Canadian approach to leadership represented a response to this rise in regionalism, first by creating federal programs and departments to deal specifically with regional questions, and then, more distinctively, by promoting pan-Canadian policies—that is, policies that overarched constituency or group interests and touched individual Canadians wherever they might live in Canada. John Diefenbaker's "One Canada," his appeal to "unhyphenated Canadianism," his Bill of Rights, his national social policies (such as hospitalization) and other responses in the late 1950s and early 1960s took as their premise "equal rights for all, privileges for none." It was Diefenbaker who used the prime minister's appointment power to "recognize" distinctive groups in society, by placing the first woman and the first Canadian of Ukrainian origin in the Cabinet, by appointing the first Indian to the Senate and the first French Canadian as governor general.

But this initial attempt at a pan-Canadian approach of governing was cut short by the Quiet Revolution, for Diefenbaker's vision of his country did not sanction treating Quebeckers any differently from the rest of Canadians. His successors' visions, however, *did* see Quebec with a "special status." Both Lester Pearson and Pierre Trudeau accepted as a first principle that Canada was composed of two founding peoples. From this premise flowed a host of policies aimed at touching all Canadians through the medium of one or other of two official languages. Mr. Diefenbaker never accepted this Liberal view of Canada and, indeed, continued to fight it all of his political life in part because of what he interpreted as its anti-British connotations. But he did accept the implementation of other pan-Canadian policies, applauding, for instance, the federal government's national medical care and pension plans. In its National Energy Program, constitutional reforms and entrenchment of a Charter of Rights, Mr. Trudeau's government went further than either Diefenbaker's or Pearson's in breaking the consensual mould of national politics created by Mackenzie King. One cost of this approach for the Liberals was the loss for over two decades of major electoral support in the West, a region of the country where there had once been significant Liberal sympathy. The long-run implications for Canada of these policies remain unknown, but in the short-run the benefits to French Canadians of opening wider the institutions of the federal government are substantial. Nowhere else is this clearer than in the Cabinet itself. Under Pearson and Trudeau the number of French Canadian ministers has risen as has the importance of the portfolios they have held. In this century until 1963, the proportion of Cabinet ministers of French ethnic origin never rose above 30 percent, since then it has stood consistently above 40 percent, and while as late as 1970 it could be said that no French Canadian had ever held the Finance, Trade and Commerce or Labour portfolios, by 1984 French Canadians either did hold or had held all three.

This summary of models of leadership indicates the importance of political personality but also the different uses to which the Cabinet can be put, for as an instrument of government it is more than a body that passes orders-in-council or that superintends the administration of government. Because it combines political and governmental power, it occupies a unique position from which a leader can initiate and direct policies. What policies are chosen and how they are implemented is a function of many variables, but crucial among them is that leaders depend on the power they possess at the head of a disciplined party, caucus and Cabinet.

Cabinet as a Vehicle for Representation

The Cabinet is the pre-eminent institution of sectional representation in the Canadian parliamentary system. In practice that has meant the representation of the provinces and the historic linguistic and religious communities of Canada. Other minorities have been present in Cabinet, but the term "sectional representation" customarily refers to the foregoing interests. Whatever the expectations of the Fathers of Confederation, the Senate has never played this role. Appointment by governor-in-council, allocation of equal numbers of senators by regions and not provinces, separation from the executive which sat in the lower house, and infrequent membership in the Cabinet all saw to that. A province or a group (the English-speaking Protestants of Quebec or the Irish Catholics of either Quebec or Ontario, for example) who wanted to take part in the decisions of the day or to protect their special interests had to be represented in the Cabinet. Of course, there was not equal representation there either, since generally two-thirds of the ministers came from Ontario and Quebec, but a seat at the Cabinet table was believed to be more influential than any other federal office.

The Traditional Cabinet: A Federal Structure

The conviction that provinces must be represented was shared by leaders as well as followers, and the history of Cabinet building by any prime minister reveals the strength of this particularly Canadian article of faith. Where the electorate of a province was thoughtless enough to return no members to Parliament from the party which formed the government, then the prime minister had to perform as a political gymnast twisting his way around an inconvenient election result in order to fulfill one of the first commandments of cabinet making—that all parts of the whole must, if at all possible, be represented in the finished product. Generally speaking, he has had two alternatives: to run those who cannot get elected in their home province in a safe seat elsewhere (when the Liberals were shut out of Alberta in the 1921 election Mackenzie King brought the former Liberal premier of that province, Charles Stewart, into the Cabinet as Minister of the Interior by opening a Quebec seat for him) or to resort to the Senate route, where there are usually several Cabinet aspirants per province.

The former route is out of fashion today (although it was used in Canadian history to bring into Cabinet such outstanding ministers as Charles Dunning to Finance and Angus MacDonald to Naval Services, who were not electoral liabilities by any stretch of the imagination but for whom a federal seat elsewhere than in their home province was at the time convenient to them and the Prime Minister). The latter route is the preferred modern method (in 1980 Mr. Trudeau took in three senators from the three most western provinces where no Liberals had been elected), though it has little to recommend it other than its simplicity.[24] While the Senate continues to do some fine investigative work, it is not an institution in which the principle of democratic accountability is strong, and its members as Cabinet ministers experience and cause frustration. Senators are appointed to Cabinet where the governing party is weakest in electoral favour, yet the process does nothing to build the party and can indeed divide it by creating antagonisms and jealousies. The fact that recent prime ministers have resorted to this alternative in spite of its disadvantages is evidence of the strength of the convention that Cabinet must encompass representation from all provinces.

Sectional representation is not an abstract notion of symbolic value only, though this is not an unimportant consideration. In regard to certain matters, ministers *from* individual provinces are seen as ministers *for* those provinces. This is true particularly with respect to appointments but also to discussions of policy and its potential effect on provincial interests. It is misleading to depict the Cabinet as no more than a collection of sectional "veto groups"—some policies, labelled above as "pan-Canadian," are less regionally specific than others, and these, more characteristic of Liberal governments today than in Mackenzie King's time, are not susceptible to regional bargaining—but it is equally erroneous to ignore the durable effect of a federalized Cabinet on policy formulation.[25] Canada is still a country of sharply defined regions, with geographic and cultural boundaries that enclose distinctive ways of life, and the Cabinet continues, as it always has, to reflect this fact.

For much of the country's history particular portfolios were identified with particular regions or provinces. With the opening of the West, responsibility for agriculture went to a westerner until 1965. But the Liberals' dismal electoral record in that region altered this tradition, and in only four of the last twenty years has a westerner held that portfolio. As compensation, responsibility for the Canadian Wheat Board, the agency in charge of the prairies' staple industry, has been assigned either to a western minister with another portfolio or, in 1980, to a Minister of State who was a senator. The old Department of the Interior, which disappeared shortly after the transfer of the prairie provinces' natural resources from the federal government in 1930, was even more closely identified with that region's settlement and expansion. The prominence of that endeavour, which has been described as the most "far-reaching activity" in this century except for the prosecution of the wars, is indicated by the calibre of those who held the portfolio, among whom were Edgar Dewdney, Clifford Sifton, Frank Oliver, Arthur Meighen, Sir James Lougheed, Charles Stewart and T.A. Crerar.[26] Contrarily, Transport is seen as a portfolio associated with any province but Ontario. George Hees, who was given this portfolio in 1957 by John Diefenbaker, has commented that "a central Ontarian is not very much interested in Transport," and the list of ministers who have had this responsibility in the last half-century would bear him out. Only three other Ontario ministers for a total of seven years have held this portfolio. Transport has been the concern of Quebec or of the eastern and western hinterlands.

The above comments concern portfolios that have a specific regional impact; there are others (Fisheries is an example) of which the same could be said. But there are more portfolios, indeed including the great departments of state—Finance, Trade and Commerce (and its modern equivalents), Justice and External Affairs, which are marked by their lack of obvious geographic specificity. And yet these too have historically been allocated to ministers distinctive in part for their provincial origins but also for their language group. Finance until very recently has always gone to an English-speaking minister, and more often than not to one from Ontario, but sometimes from Quebec and occasionally from elsewhere. Justice on the other hand has tended to go to French-speaking Quebeckers. The concentration of the business community in Toronto and Montreal and the dual legal systems of Canada help to explain this distribution of portfolios in the same way that other reasons can be found for additional discernible patterns of portfolio allocation. What is perhaps most significant in the last two decades, however, is the decline in the boldness of geographic and cultural patterns. Sectional representation remains an indelible part of Canadian political practice; the segregation of portfolios to specific types of ministers does not.

The Modern Cabinet: A National Institution

The politics of the federal Cabinet, like the politics of the country, are more national than they once were. Ministers are less likely to be the party chiefs in their provinces than used to be the case in the time of Mackenzie King and St Laurent, and one looks in vain to find a Cabinet minister who can play the role of pro-consul as J.G. Gardiner did in Saskatchewan, or Stewart Garson in Manitoba, or Angus MacDonald in Nova Scotia. Canadian federalism has witnessed major changes since those days, none more significant than the growing separation between federal and provincial politics in the last quarter-century. The effect on political parties has been immense, not least on their claim to be institutions of national integration. The old structures of federated parties—national leaders dependent on a provincial base—require reform, and the Liberals more than the others (because they are in power in no province) have experimented with pan-Canadian structures to conform to their pan-Canadian policies. The Cabinet may remain the managing committee of the party, but the party it manages looks very different than it once did.

Federal–provincial relations are less a matter to be resolved through intraparty bargaining and more a subject for negotiation among governments. All ministers, but particularly the prime minister, find themselves meeting on a regular basis with their provincial counterparts. The description of Cabinet as party-in-government is still true, but in the federal–provincial realm the emphasis must today be placed more on the government side of this unique entity than on the party side. It is for this reason that federal governments in the modern period are so particularly concerned to have within their ranks authoritative spokespersons for the provinces with which they must negotiate. But it is because of the deterioration of the old party structures that they regularly find themselves deprived of this representation in some parts of the country. Here is the attraction of proportional representation, for under whatever guise it was implemented it would in all probability produce from each province at least a minimum of one popularly elected member of Parliament who, once admitted to the Cabinet, would confer on that body the imprimatur of a national government. Proportional representation was once promoted as a system of election preferable to plurality voting because it would make easier the representation of multiple interests in national legislatures. The national legislature would become a congress of more varied opinion than is produced by a system of election such as Canada at the federal level has always had. It is a measure of the strength of the belief in Cabinet—as an instrument of government and as a vehicle for sectional representation—that proportional representation has been turned on its head so that it is advocated not to make Parliament more diverse in the interests it embraces but to make Cabinet more powerful for its task of governing Canada.

Conclusion

Political attitudes and practices affect the operation of political institutions. In this article three attitudes and practices have been singled out for attention as regards the Cabinet: a reluctance to inject ideology into politics, an inclination to view politics not as a career in itself but rather as a temporary occupation into and out of which significant numbers of key personnel move and a belief that the primary aim of politics is to balance conflicting geographic and cultural interests. As an instrument of government the Cabinet has been crucially influenced as well by Canada's history, especially its colonial origins. The Cabinet as a collective body, in other words as a whole, has been favoured by tradition over its ministerial parts, which in turn has made Canadians place a great premium on leadership. At different times different models of leadership have dominated. In chronological sequence, these have been identified as personal, accommodative and pan-Canadian models. But while the Cabinet might be seen over time to have adjusted to a succession of leadership styles, at all times it has been expected to function as a vehicle of sectional representation, although here too an evolution in practice has occurred. Where once the Cabinet was pre-eminently a federalized structure, more recently this guise has been subsumed by a new emphasis on the Cabinet as a national institution.

Notes

1. The most useful Canadian sources are Thomas A. Hockin, ed., *Apex of Power: The Prime Minister and Political Leadership in Canada* (Scarborough: Prentice-Hall, 1971) and W.A. Matheson, *The Prime Minister and the Cabinet* (Toronto: Methuen, 1976).

2. From this count are excluded the many biographies, "life and times" studies, Henry Borden, ed., *Robert Laird Borden: His Memoirs* (2 vols., Toronto: Macmillan, 1938) and Mackenzie King's mammoth diary. The diary's importance is incalculable for the long period King was in office, but in published version it is available only in extracts as, for example, in the four-volume *The Mackenzie King Record* (Toronto: University of Toronto Press) covering the period 1939 to 1948. Volume 1 is edited by J.W. Pickersgill; the remaining volumes are jointly edited by him and D.F. Forster.

3. Walter L. Gordon, *A Political Memoir* (Toronto: McClelland and Stewart, 1977) and Judy LaMarsh, *Memoirs of a Bird in a Gilded Cage* (Toronto: McClelland and Stewart, 1968).

4. Norman Ward, ed., *A Party Politician: The Memoirs of Chubby Power* (Toronto: Macmillan, 1966).

5. The best is Sir Richard Cartwright, *Reminiscences* (Toronto: William Briggs, 1912).

6. N. Ward and D. Hoffman, *Bilingualism and Biculturalism in the Canadian House of Commons* (Ottawa: 1970), p. 125.

7. An exception among defectors was H.H. Stevens who resigned from R.B. Bennett's Cabinet because he believed Bennett was too soft on capitalists. He then formed the Reconstruction Party, which was devoted to the reform of capitalism and which in the general election of 1935 won 9 percent of the popular vote and one seat, Stevens's. See J.R.H. Wilbur, *H.H. Stevens* (Toronto: University of Toronto Press, 1977).

8. "In the adversary confrontation on the floor of the House, psychological issues may be more important than substantive ones." J.R. Mallory, "The Two Clerks: Parliamentary Discussion of the Role of the Privy Council Office," *Canadian Journal of Political Science* 10 (March 1977): 18.

9. John Porter, *The Vertical Mosaic* (Toronto: University of Toronto Press, 1965), pp. 405–06.

10. Dennis Olsen, *The State Elite* (Toronto: McClelland and Stewart, 1980), p. 130.

11. N. Ward, "The Liberals in Convention: Unrevised and Unrepentant," *Queen's Quarterly* 45 (Spring 1958): 1.

12. Porter, *The Vertical Mosaic*, p. 397.

13. An exception with a specific focus is Frederick W. Gibson, ed., *Cabinet Formation and Bicultural Relations: Seven Case Studies* (No. 6, Studies of the Royal Commission on Bilingualism and Biculturalism, Ottawa: Queen's Printer, 1970).

14. See Kenneth D. McRae, ed., *Consociational Democracy: Political Accommodation in Segmented Societies* (Toronto: McClelland and Stewart, 1974).

15. The literature on executive federalism is large. The best place to start is Richard Simeon, *Federal–Provincial Diplomacy: The Making of Recent Policy in Canada* (Toronto: University of Toronto Press, 1972).

16. *House of Commons Debates*, 17 October 1977, 8259. The durability of this practice

is confirmed in Canada, House of Commons, *Third Report of the Special Committee on Statutory Instruments* (1968–69) 35–7, though as the *Fourth Report of the Standing Joint Committee on Regulations and Other Statutory Instruments* notes: "Very few draft regulations are actually considered by the Cabinet as a deliberative body. By far the greatest number ... is recommended ... by the Special Committee of Council which consists of ten Ministers with a quorum of four." *Senate Debates*, 7 July 1980, 757–91 at 761.

17. R.M. Dawson, *The Government of Canada* (Toronto: University of Toronto Press, 1947), p. 201 in J.R. Mallory, "Cabinets and Councils in Canada," *Public Law* 2 (Autumn 1957): 244.

18. See Richard J. Van Loon, "Kaleidoscope in Grey: The Policy Process in Ottawa," in this volume. See, too, Colin Campbell, *Governments Under Stress: Political Executives and Key Bureaucrats in Washington, London, and Ottawa* (Toronto: University of Toronto Press, 1983), pp. 83–90.

19. Dawson, *The Government of Canada*, p. 233.

20. The Prime Minister's extensive powers are codified to some extent in a minute of the Privy Council (P.C. 3374, 25 October 1935), reprinted in Paul Fox, *Politics: Canada* (3rd ed., Toronto: McGraw-Hill, 1970). These include, among others, the calling of Cabinet meetings, recommendations for the dissolution and summing of Parliament, and recommendations for the appointment of such offices as Cabinet minister, lieutenant-governor and senator.

21. "Political Patronage under Macdonald and Laurier, 1878–1911," in *American Review of Canadian Studies*, 10 (1980): 3–12 and "John A. Macdonald's Greatest Triumph," *Canadian Historical Review* 43 (March 1982): 3–33.

22. Richard Van Loon, *The Structure and Membership of the Canadian Cabinet* (Internal Research Project of the Royal Commission on Bilingualism and Biculturalism, October 1966) p. 27.

23. R. Whitaker, *The Government Party: Organizing and Financing the Liberal Party of Canada, 1930–58* (Toronto: University of Toronto Press, 1977).

24. The Senate route is more popular now than at any time since Macdonald's day: "In the period 1867–1896 every cabinet portfolio except Finance, Railways and Canals, and Customs, was held at one time or another by a member of the Senate." Norman McL. Rogers, "Evolution and Reform of the Canadian Cabinet," *Canadian Bar Review* 11 (April 1933): 233.

25. The idea of the veto group is in J.R. Mallory, "The Two Clerks," p. 240.

26. Chester Martin,'*Dominion Lands' Policy*, ed. with introduction by Lewis H. Thomas (Toronto: McClelland and Stewart, 1973), p. xiv.

Further Readings

Foster, Sir George. "Getting Into the Cabinet." From *The Memoirs of the Rt. Hon. Sir George Foster, P.C., G.C.M.G.*, edited by W.S. Wallace, *Politics: Canada*, 4th ed., edited by Paul Fox. Toronto: McGraw-Hill, 1977.

Fox, Paul. "The Representative Nature of the Canadian Cabinet." In *Politics: Canada*, 4th ed., edited by Paul Fox. Toronto: McGraw-Hill, 1977.

Gibson, Frederick W., ed. *Cabinet Formation and Bicultural Relations: Seven Case Studies.* Studies of the Royal Commission on Bilingualism and Biculturalism. Ottawa: Information Canada, 1970.

Guide to Canadian Ministries Since Confederation, July 1, 1867–February 1, 1982. Public Archives of Canada. Ottawa: Supply and Services, 1982.

Hockin, Thomas A. *Apex of Power: The Prime Minister and Political Leadership in Canada.* 2nd ed. Scarborough: Prentice-Hall, 1977.

Matheson, W.A. *The Prime Minister and the Cabinet.* Toronto: Methuen, 1976.

Presthus, Robert. *Elite Accommodation in Canadian Politics.* Toronto: Macmillan, 1973.

Rogers, Norman McL. "The Introduction of Cabinet Government in Canada," "Federal Influences on the Canadian Cabinet" and "Evolution and Reform of the Canadian Cabinet." *Canadian Bar Review* 11 (January, February and April 1933).

Chapter 17

Federalism and Intergovernmental Relations
Garth Stevenson

Canada has had federal institutions since 1867, but the importance of intergovernmental relations is a fairly recent development, and one that has little or no explicit basis in Canada's written constitution. It is also at odds with the traditional theory of federalism, at least as federalism is understood in those countries that have been heavily influenced by British and American political thought. According to the traditional theory it is possible, and desirable, to distribute the functional fields of public policy between two levels of government in such a way that each level will have full power and responsibility to act within its own fields of jurisdiction without reference to the other level. Provincial governments may be assigned responsibility for education, natural resources and municipal affairs, while the federal government is assigned responsibility for banking, trade and the criminal law, but each can and should act unilaterally within its own sphere as though the other level of government did not exist. Once a constitution has divided up the spheres of jurisdiction, the only mechanism needed to maintain this harmonious equilibrium in virtual perpetuity is a Supreme Court that can decide in doubtful cases whether a particular policy or action falls within the federal or the provincial sphere.

This is not, of course, how Canadian government really works, but to a large extent the Constitution Act of 1867 did attempt to follow this model.[1] Parallel institutions of government were established, insofar as they did not already exist, at the federal and provincial levels. Each was given access to certain sources of revenue. The types of laws that could be made by Parliament and the provincial legislatures were listed in exhaustive detail, with no less than forty-eight enumerated categories. All but three of the forty-eight were assigned exclusively to one level of government or the other. According to the Colonial Laws Validity Act of 1865, neither Parliament nor the legislatures could legislate contrary to the terms of any imperial statute applying to them, and since the BNA Act was an imperial statute, this meant in practice that the Judicial Committee of the Privy Council would act as an arbiter in cases of disputed jurisdiction.

Insofar as the Constitution of 1867 deviated from this model, it did so by enabling the federal government to exercise power over the provincial ones, even if the latter remained within their own fields of jurisdiction. Thus the federal government appoints the judges to provincial superior and county courts, and also appoints the lieutenant-governor who is formally the chief executive officer at the provincial level. In the early days of Canadian federalism lieutenant-governors exercised real power: sometimes dismissing their ministerial advisors, refusing their assent to acts of the legislature, or reserving such acts for a final decision by the federal government on whether they would be allowed to come into operation. In addition, the federal government can disallow any provincial act within a year of its adoption, although this power was used very rarely after 1911 and has not been used at all since 1943. The federal government can also interfere in the provincial jurisdiction over education to protect the rights of certain minorities, although the one attempt to exercise this power in 1896 probably demonstrated that it was unusable in practice.

These admitted departures from the pure theory of federalism have little importance for modern intergovernmental relations. The powers of disallowance and reservation are unlikely ever again to be used. While provincial governments certainly complain loudly and frequently about federal "intrusions" into what they regard as their spheres of authority, it is usually the federal government's economic and fiscal policies that give offence, not the appointment of judges and lieutenant-governors. Moreover, and in complete contrast to the centralist preferences of the Fathers of Confederation, the provincial governments themselves now possess impressive means of complicating, frustrating, and interfering with policy making at the federal level, means which they are far less hesitant to employ than the federal government is to employ its virtually abandoned power of disallowance. Finally, a variety of institutional machinery not provided for in the formal constitution has been developed to facilitate interaction between the two levels of government.

All of this adds up to a remarkable and rather ironic transformation of Canadian federalism in the somewhat more than one century of its existence. Moreover it is a transformation that has been achieved largely without the aid of formal amendments to the constitution. As discussed in another chapter of this volume, formal constitutional change has been pursued at least intermittently by federal and provincial governments in recent years, and some provincial politicians have done their best to propagate the fraudulent fantasy that a rigid constitutional "status quo" presents an intolerable obstacle to the fulfillment of legitimate provincial aspirations. Yet any fair-minded observer must be impressed, whether favourably or otherwise, with the ability of the existing federal constitution to accommodate change in fact without appearing to change in form.

Much of the change which the Constitution has accommodated has been in the direction of increasing the power and importance of provincial governments, the larger of which now exercise powers that would be the envy of many supposedly sovereign members of the United Nations. Admittedly the power and importance of the federal government has expanded enormously as well, and it too performs functions that it was not expected to perform a century ago, but the growth of provincial power is more striking, whatever value judgment one may make about it.

The growth of the state is a ubiquitous phenomenon in the modern world, but Canada is unusual, and perhaps unique, in the extent to which that growth has taken place at the sub-national level. Economic development and external relations, the state functions that were considered most important in 1867 and probably still are today, were originally placed for the most part beyond the reach of provincial jurisdiction, yet today the provincial governments seek with some success to influence federal policies in these areas and with even greater success to conduct policies of their own.

Provincialists will respond that this change is counterbalanced by increasing federal involvement in such areas as health and welfare, environmental policies or the protection of consumers, but this response is unconvincing for two reasons. In the first place, these functions were not so much left to the provinces in 1867 as they were left to the private sector, so that the expansion of federal government activity has not really been at the expense of the provincial governments. Secondly, while these functions are certainly important, most observers would still consider them less fundamental to the raison d'être of the modern state than the more traditional functions of developing the economy and managing relations with the rest of the world. It is the performance of those traditional functions to some extent at the provincial level and to some extent at the federal level but in consultation with the provincial governments, that seems to distinguish Canada from most other modern states. The involvement of the central government in policies related to health, welfare and the "quality of life," while it too contributes to the complex pattern of Canadian intergovernmental relations, is a phenomenon not unique to Canada.

Causes of Decentralization
Although John A. Macdonald's hope that the provincial governments would dwindle away into insignificance was shown to be fallacious even

374 Structures of Canadian Government

before his death in 1891, it is only since about 1960 that the growth of provincial powers and the relatively limited capacity, or willingness, of the central government to act unilaterally in most areas of public policy have appeared to distinguish Canada from other modern states. During that time various Canadian political scientists, including the present writer, have attempted to explain these phenomena, although no real consensus has been achieved. Some observers, particularly in Quebec, continue to deny that the Canadian central government is significantly weaker than those of other federal countries. Even among those who recognize that it is, opinions differ as to which are the most significant reasons why this is so. Probably few would argue that any single explanation is significant. The main categories of explanatory factors that have been suggested may be summarized as follows:

Institutional

Some observers attach primary importance to certain features of Canada's federal constitution as explanations for the growth of provincial power, even though the Fathers of Confederation apparently designed it with quite a different intention. There are a number of specific explanations within this category. The adoption of British parliamentary government and an appointed upper house, rather than institutions on the American pattern, limited the ability of the central government to accommodate provincial interests and thus encouraged the growth of strong provincial governments as spokespersons for such interests. The explicit enumeration of provincial legislative powers, although designed to limit them, actually facilitated their expansion in practice by provincial governments and the judiciary, particularly since they included such broad categories as "property and civil rights." The very fact of having provincial governments at all facilitated "province building" and the development of separate identities. Provincial ownership of natural resources, although considered insignificant in 1867, strengthened provincial governments, most obviously in Alberta but in other provinces as well. Health, education and welfare, all entrusted to some extent to the provincial governments, proved to be more important areas of public policy than had been anticipated.

Geopolitical

Mackenzie King is said to have observed that Canada has "too much geography." Although sometimes taken for granted, Canada's vast physical extent, small and scattered population and geographical barriers such as the Laurentian shield, the Rocky Mountains and the Gulf of St. Lawrence tend to weaken national integration and perhaps to encourage emphasis on the provincial level of government as a supplier of services. The relatively small number of provinces in contrast to the fifty American states, the extremely large size of Quebec and Ontario which enables them to challenge federal power if they so desire, and the absence of metropolitan areas (apart from Ottawa–Hull) which spill across provincial boundaries may also be significant.

Sociocultural

Particularly in recent years, the literature on Canadian federalism has tended to emphasize, and often to celebrate, the allegedly distinctive cultural "identities" of Canadians in the different provinces. It is said that Canadians in different provinces are objectively different in terms of such categories as ethnicity and religion, and also that they are subjectively different in that they feel attachments to their respective provinces or "regions" more strongly than to Canada as a whole. According to this view, the provincial governments are strong in Canada because Canadians have distinctive needs and interests which cannot be accommodated within a single national government, and also because Canadians actually want strong provincial governments and a relatively weak federal one. This belief is often used as an explanation for the present state of Canadian federalism, but increasingly also as an argument for further weakening the central government through formal constitutional change.

While questionable in relation to most of the provinces, this line of argument is clearly more persuasive with respect to Quebec. Partly because they speak a language which is not widely spoken, and has sometimes been deliberately suppressed, in the other provinces, francophone Quebeckers tend to view themselves as a nation within a nation, whether they are federalists or separatists. Quebec's legal and educational systems are very different from those of other provinces. Public opinion polls consistently show much stronger support for provincial autonomy in Quebec than elsewhere, even though Quebec enjoys great influence in the federal Liberal party and even though Ottawa is physically closer to Quebec's main centres of population than to those of any other province. Thus some observers believe that the existence of Quebec by itself provides a sufficient explanation, or very nearly so, for Canada's failure to develop a centralized form of government. The fact that the centrifugal tendency in Canadian federalism became most apparent after 1960, when Quebec elected a provincial government more dedicated than its predecessors to active policies of social and economic development, lends some credence to the argument.

Political

While it may be more a symptom than a cause of the difficulties of Canadian federalism, the peculiar character of the party system has recently attracted some attention. Not only is the support for the major

federal parties distributed unevenly across the country, but this
tendency is grossly accentuated by the electoral system. Interestingly,
the two provinces most inclined to conflict with the federal government,
Quebec and Alberta, have the most idiosyncratic voting behaviour in
federal elections, both tending to give overwhelming support to a single
party. In the 1980 election Quebec gave 67.4 percent of its votes and all
but one seat to the Liberal party, while Alberta gave 64.7 percent of its
votes and all of its seats to the Progressive Conservatives. Moreover the
federal and provincial levels of party politics in most provinces appear to
be only tenuously related, with the dominant federal party having little
strength in the provincial legislatures (since 1979 no province has had a
Liberal government) and with some provincial governments controlled
by parties that are insignificant or non-existent at the federal level.
Conceivably, the uneven distribution of party support could deprive the
federal government of legitimacy in some provinces, while the separation
of federal and provincial party systems might contribute to
federal–provincial conflict and reduce the possibility of accommodation.

Economic

Recently there has been a revival of interest in political economy, a term
that has many meanings but that in Canada usually indicates a belief that
political and institutional phenomena can be largely explained by
patterns of economic development. Since the study of economic history
has been well established in Canada for many years and since Canadian
political scientists and economists were until recently affiliated with the
same university departments, this approach to the study of Canadian
government has deep roots.

Proponents of a political economy approach can cite many features
of Canadian economic development that might help to account for the
weakness of the federal level of government and the corresponding
strength of the provincial level. Mainly for natural reasons, but perhaps
partly because of federal economic policies, the provinces differ
considerably from one another in the structure of their economies, the
predominance of particular industries, and the nature and extent of their
trading and investment ties with foreign countries. Business interests
concentrated in a particular province may encourage the strengthening
of that province's government and the weakening of the federal
government. Interprovincial disparities of wealth and income are very
pronounced, and the rank ordering of the provinces in this regard has
changed very little since the 1920s. The importance of mining, petroleum
and forestry in the Canadian economy reinforces the provincial level of
government, which owns and controls these resources in accordance
with the B.N.A. Act. The relatively slow and limited development of

secondary manufacturing has restricted the mobility of population and thus reinforced provincialist sentiments. The dominant influence exercised by the United States over the Canadian economy has weakened the effectiveness of and lessened the support for the Canadian federal government. The domination of Quebec's economy by anglophones, at least until recently, stimulated Quebec nationalism and caused resentment to be directed against the federal government. The influence exercised over the federal government by financial, mercantile and transportation interests caused businesspeople associated with other industries to prefer the provincial level of government, particularly in Ontario. Recent economic changes in Quebec and Alberta have produced new and powerful classes in those provinces dedicated to strengthening the provincial level of government at the expense of the federal.

All of these types of explanations are of some value, although all have their weaknesses. The institutional and geopolitical explanations fail to explain why Canadian federalism has developed so differently since 1960 from the way it operated previously. The sociocultural explanation is undermined by the important diversities that exist *within* the provinces, the increasingly homogeneous character of Canadian society, including to some extent even Quebec, at the very time when demands for more power to the provinces are most strident, and the fact that, except in Quebec, provincial politicians appear far more committed to provincial autonomy than does the general public. The latter fact should be disconcerting to supporters of the sociocultural explanation since the politicians, unlike the general public, are overwhelmingly urban, upper-middle-class, Protestant and of British ancestry. Finally, the economic explanations, while the present writer finds them the most persuasive, are sometimes guilty of circular reasoning or of surreptitiously borrowing arguments from the other explanations.

In any event, and regardless of which explanations are preferred, the provincial level of government is clearly strong enough to ensure that there will be no uncontested supremacy by the central government, even within many of the fields of jurisdiction assigned to the latter under the B.N.A. Act. The federal government apparently cannot disregard the provincial governments and must bargain with them almost continuously in order to achieve its own objectives. The curious expression "the eleven senior governments," which has recently found its way into Canadian political discourse, is symptomatic of this factual equality of bargaining power, whatever the Constitution may say to the contrary. The remaining sections of this chapter will describe the actual, as opposed to formal, division of responsibilities between the two levels, the areas of conflict and the mechanisms of interaction, before turning to an evaluation and critique of the system.

Areas of Conflict

As an aid to understanding how responsibilities are actually divided between the two levels of government the Constitution Act of 1867, with its detailed and seemingly precise division of jurisdictions, is of very limited value. The categories overlap considerably, many subjects that preoccupy governments in the latter part of the twentieth century are not listed at all, and both levels of government have expanded their activities without much regard for the constitution.

The actual functional areas of public policy can be classified into areas occupied exclusively by one level of government with little or no objection by the other, areas where both levels of government are active but apparently without much conflict, and areas that give rise to federal–provincial conflict. The last category includes some areas that the Constitution Act of 1867 assigns primarily to the federal level, some that it assigns primarily to the provincial level, and some that it does not assign at all because they were insignificant or unknown at the time of Confederation. Naturally the extent to which particular subjects are shared or give rise to conflict changes over time: emphasis will be placed here mainly on the situation at the time of writing.

An examination of the names of government departments in the federal, Ontario and Alberta governments suggests what further investigation confirms: that very few areas of policy are now occupied exclusively by one level of government. The only exclusively federal areas appear to be military defence, veterans' affairs, the post office and monetary policy. The only exclusively provincial areas appear to be municipal institutions, elementary and secondary education and some areas of law related to property and other non-criminal matters.

Some fields of jurisdiction are partially occupied by both levels of government but are not areas of serious conflict, at least for the moment. These include agriculture and immigration, both areas where the Constitution says either level can legislate, and pensions, which were placed in the same position by subsequent amendments. Both immigration and pensions were the source of serious conflicts between the federal and Quebec governments in the not too distant past, but both seem now to have been resolved. Other areas of harmoniously shared jurisdiction, not mentioned explicitly in the federal constitution, include scientific research, cultural and recreational activities, tourism, and protection of the environment.

A number of areas assigned to federal jurisdiction have become sources of federal–provincial controversy, either because provincial governments have succeeded in becoming involved in them or because some of them are dissatisfied with federal policies and would like to do so. Freight rates and other aspects of railway transport policy have always been contentious in the Western and Atlantic provinces, and federal air transport policies are now becoming controversial as well. It may be noted that some provinces own railways or airlines while the federal government regulates them. The federal government has unwisely delegated the regulation of interprovincial highway transport to the provinces, although there was no legal reason for it to do so. Trade and commerce, including the external aspects of commercial policy, have also seen increasing provincial involvement and controversy. Provinces have established a variety of informal barriers to interprovincial trade, a few of which have been struck down by the Supreme Court, and have tried to become involved in foreign trade policy either by dealing directly with foreign governments or by seeking to influence the federal government. More recently Newfoundland and Nova Scotia have begun to demand at least partial provincial control over fisheries, another area assigned to federal jurisdiction. Relations with the native peoples are at least potentially a further area of controversy.

On the other hand, Alberta, Saskatchewan and British Columbia have argued that the federal government has intruded massively since 1972 into the field of natural resource policy, particularly with regard to oil and natural gas, despite the fact that provincial governments own the resources within their boundaries. While the federal government claims only to be using its power to regulate "trade and commerce," many western Canadians are unconvinced. The administration of justice, another area assigned to provincial jurisdiction, has also given rise to controversy over such matters as the RCMP campaigns against separatist organizations in Quebec and federal efforts to prosecute narcotics dealers in British Columbia. Federal policies that affect urban planning and the use of land also give rise at times to provincial unhappiness. Public health, an area conferred at least vaguely to the provinces, was the target of massive federal involvement between 1945 and 1970, followed by partial federal withdrawal for financial reasons in the late 1970s, and then a reassertion of the federal role again in 1984. The point here is that both the involvement and the withdrawal were resented equally by provincial governments.

Some of the most intractable areas of federal–provincial conflict are fields of jurisdiction that were not envisaged in 1867. A leading example would be the complex and arcane matter of "communications," which has grown increasingly contentious as technological change has blurred the once-familiar distinctions between telephones, telegraphs and broadcasting, while adding new and anomalous categories such as cable television and pay television. The situation is complicated by provincial ownership of some telephone systems, federal ownership of CN telecommunications and the CBC, the use of broadcasting (declared a federal responsibility by the Judicial Committee of the Privy Council in 1932) for purposes of education, and Quebec's desire to protect its language and culture.

Other "new" areas of jurisdiction that have led to conflict in recent years include worker training programs (regarded as part of economic development by the federal government but as part of education by some provincial governments) and income support programs such as family allowances. Family allowances were established by the federal government during the Second World War, but about a quarter century later the Quebec government began to complain that they were part of "social policy" (whatever that may mean) and should therefore be a provincial responsibility. This issue contributed to Quebec's rejection of the "Victoria Charter" in 1971, but subsequently the federal government agreed to share control over the program, though it continued to provide all the funds. Still more recently, legislation to protect the consumer has become a source of conflict, with both levels of government understandably wishing to occupy this politically popular (and financially inexpensive) area of jurisdiction.

A particularly important area of intergovernmental conflict, and one that exists to some extent in all federal countries, is that of finance and taxation. The constitution allows the federal government to impose any kind of taxation, while the provinces are restricted to "direct" taxation and to revenues from their natural resources. The Constitution Act of 1867 also provided for modest federal subsidies to provincial governments, but while these are still paid, they have been overshadowed since 1957 by massive "equalization" payments to provinces with below-average ability to raise revenue, a program whose annual cost to the federal treasury now exceeds four billion dollars. Since 1982 the obligation to make these payments has been entrenched in the Constitution.

Since both levels of government have constantly increasing needs for revenue, and since both ultimately rely on the same taxpayers to provide it, the need for coordination and the scope for conflict are obvious. Since the Second World War elaborate arrangements have been devised, and modified at five-year intervals, for sharing revenue from personal and corporation income taxes, which are now the most important sources of revenue. While these arrangements have been reasonably successful, there have been some eruptions of conflict, particularly involving the larger provinces, in the course of negotiating the five-year agreements. Apart from its obvious purpose of providing revenue, taxation is now viewed by governments as a tool for manipulating, regulating and stimulating the economy. Moreover, tax concessions to both individuals and corporations are important means of winning and keeping political support. Thus the "stakes" in financial negotiations are high.

Besides being an area of controversy in its own right, finance impinges on and exacerbates some of the other areas of controversy referred to previously. Responsibility for the costs of health and welfare programs, for example, has been a source of intermittent contention since the Second World War, and efforts to resolve this issue have become increasingly entangled with the five-year arrangements for tax-sharing. The conflicts over petroleum and other natural resources are also largely, although not entirely, financial in character. Provincial efforts to collect larger "royalties" from mineral and petroleum production in the early 1970s were viewed by the federal government as surreptitious efforts to violate the arrangements for sharing tax revenue from corporations, while federal efforts to keep the price of oil below international levels were resented by Alberta and Saskatchewan as depriving them of revenue that would otherwise be available for their provincial treasuries. An added complication is the previously mentioned practice of paying equalization to relatively poor provincial governments, which because of the formula employed could come to mean all except Alberta. Every increase in Alberta's revenue increases the amount which the federal government must pay to other provinces, while the federal ability to afford these payments is not improved in the slightest degree. This contradiction has already necessitated some adjustments to the equalization formula and has contributed to federal intransigence concerning the price of oil. Some observers have suggested that the Alberta government itself should assume partial responsibility for the costs of equalization, but few would hold their breath waiting for this to happen.

While it is increasingly fashionable to speak of "the provinces" as a collectivity, it should be remembered that the ten provincial governments are not identical in their interests, demands or behaviour. Indeed, if they were, the system would probably be unworkable, since their differences enable the federal government to make alliances with some against the others, and thus win more of the battles than it could hope to do otherwise.

The sources of these differences are various, and like the explanation for Canada's lack of unity, to which they are closely related, they may vary in relative importance according to the viewpoint and preference of the observer. While institutional self-interest (the tendency of any government to maximize its power at the expense of other governments) produces some common patterns of behaviour, its effect is lessened by differences in economic and social structure, size, level of affluence, party affiliation, the state of public opinion and even the personality of the provincial premier.

Ontario was traditionally a strong proponent of provincial autonomy, but in the past decade its relative economic decline and apprehension over the consequences for its vulnerable economy of policies pursued by certain other provinces have made it usually an ally of the federal government. Quebec's enthusiasm for provincial autonomy, even to the point of separatism in the case of its present government, is well known, but in the first few decades of the present century it was much less militant than Ontario. Alberta and British Columbia have traditionally been thorns in the side of the federal government while Manitoba and New Brunswick have been inclined to accept federal intiatives. Large size, prosperity, distinctive and specialized economic interests and an overwhelming majority in the provincial legislature tend to make provincial governments intransigent and uncooperative, while the contrasting attributes seem to encourage more accommodating behaviour.

In resisting or opposing federal initiatives, provincial governments make use of a variety of arguments. Sometimes they say that the provincial level of government is "closer to the people" and better able to understand their needs, sometimes that the federal government is seeking to impose "bureaucracy," centralization and excessive spending, sometimes that their province's allegedly distinctive "way of life" is in danger, and sometimes (more rarely in recent years) that the terms of the constitution are being violated. Western provincial governments often argue that federal policies discriminate in favour of Ontario and Quebec while Quebec governments argue that federal policies discriminate in favour of Ontario and the West. As the great economic historian Harold Innis commented in 1946:

> The hatreds between regions in Canada have become important vested interests. Montreal exploits the hatred of Toronto and Regina that of Winnipeg and so one might go through the list. A native of Ontario may appear restive at being charged with exploitation by those who systematically exploit him with their charges of exploitation, but even the right to complain is denied to him.[2]

Behind the rhetoric the interests at stake are often more specific than appears at first sight. Provincial politicians may need votes to win an election or provincial officials may want to expand the budget and clientele of their own "shop" by excluding the federal government from a contested field of policy. Interests in the private sector are also influential. Alberta's demands for higher oil prices and natural gas exports reflect the interests of the petroleum industry as well as the government. The Ontario government often lobbies against federal initiatives that are opposed by secondary manufacturing firms, such as the tougher restraints on corporate mergers and combines that were contemplated in the seventies. The differing positions of Alberta and Saskatchewan regarding the Crow's Nest freight rates reflect the predominance of ranchers and processors in one province and of wheat farms in the other. Provincial control over offshore resources, if achieved by the government of Newfoundland, would benefit the Water Street merchants of St. John's. Federalism provides regionally concentrated interests with a powerful defence against the possibility of being overriden by a national majority.

Intergovernmental Mechanisms

Because of the many ways in which the two levels of government affect one another's freedom of action, a variety of mechanisms and processes have developed for coordinating policies and resolving conflicts. A common characteristic of these mechanisms and processes is that none of them is provided for in the constitution. Those institutions that were provided for, the lieutenant-governors and possibly the Senate, have proved to be insignificant as means of facilitating the operation of the federal system.

As in most other federal states, the judiciary is an important, though sometimes controversial, mechanism for resolving problems of jurisdiction. Established in 1875, the Supreme Court only emerged from under the shadow of the Judicial Committee of the Privy Council when appeals from Canada to the latter institution were abolished in 1949. Most cases in the past in which the Court interpreted the terms of the federal constitution arose out of litigation between private parties and governments. Today, however, more and more are *reference cases*, in which a government seeks an advisory opinion on a question of constitutional law. A government may seek such an opinion either to forestall litigation directed against its own legislation, as a means of challenging another government's legislation, or simply to clarify an uncertain situation.

Since 1949, judicial opinions on constitutional matters have generally tended to uphold the authority of the central government, though the tendency has not been particularly pronounced. Since the mid-seventies, the Supreme Court has often been a subject of controversy and has even been accused, though unfairly, of anti-provincial bias. A number of controversial decisions concerning natural resources, official languages, communications, and the administration of justice have contributed to this trend, as did the high profile of the late Chief Justice Bora Laskin, a distinguished legal scholar who had expressed "centralist" views before his appointment to the bench. However, the Chief Justice has often been in a minority on a divided court, and a number of federal enactments, as well as provincial ones, have been struck down since 1975. (For two decades after 1949, when the Court was much less in the limelight, no federal enactments were struck down at all.) While the court upheld Parliament's power to enact wage and price controls in 1976, it did so on such narrow grounds that the scope of federal power was arguably diminished by its decision.

Politicians generally prefer political solutions, in which they can split the difference and provide partial satisfaction to both sides, to the clear-cut, "either–or" decisions produced by the judicial process. For some provincial politicians, this preference is reinforced by the belief, as noted above, that the Supreme Court has a centralist bias. In fact a great variety of informal political mechanisms for arriving at solutions are available. Federal and provincial governments interact at a number of different levels, ranging from relatively junior officials to premiers and the prime minister. Intergovernmental relations may also be distinguished in terms of which governments are involved: bilateral contacts between the federal government and one provincial government are a constant part of the process, and full-scale meetings of all eleven governments have become common. There are also interprovincial relations not involving the federal government, such as the annual Premiers' Conference, the Council of Maritime Premiers and bilateral contacts between Quebec and Ontario.

During the two decades that followed the Second World War, as the two levels of government began to have a greater and greater impact on one another's activities, there was a rapid development of collaborative relationships, including semi-formal and semi-permanent committees with representatives of both levels. Most of these involved officials, sometimes of relatively junior rank. Most were concerned with a few functional areas of policy in which there was a large amount of intergovernmental interaction: finance, health, welfare, agriculture, renewable resources and statistics. This pattern of intergovernmental relations came to be designated by the term "cooperative federalism." In many cases it was related to programs that were jointly financed by the two levels of government, though primarily administered by the provincial. It was characterized by a fragmentation of intergovernmental relations within each government, since departments with specific responsibilities were given a largely free hand to conduct their own relations with counterpart departments in other governments. Most of the officials involved were more concerned with resolving problems and running effective programs than they were with scoring points for their level of government in relation to the other level. In fact it is not easy to be certain, even in retrospect, whether cooperative federalism was centralizing or decentralizing in its overall impact. At the time, no one much cared.

Beginning in the late 1960s, and continuing in the '70s, this pattern of intergovernmental relations was transformed into a new pattern for which the more recent term "executive federalism," rather than "cooperative federalism," is more appropriate. Conditional grants, in which the federal government pays a fixed percentage of the cost of provincially administered programs which meet federally determined criteria, became unpopular as both levels of government sought to tighten control over their expenditures. Central agencies such as the Privy Council Office and its offshoot, the Federal–Provincial Relations Office, began to play a greater role in intergovernmental relations, riding herd on the activities of the functional departments. Political leaders, as opposed to appointed officials, also played an increasingly prominent role. For all of these reasons there was an increasing tendency, among both federal and provincial participants, to assign the prestige and power of "their" level of government a higher priority than the resolution of conflicts over the success of programs in delivering services to the public.

These changes were partly associated with the growth of Quebec separatism and with the energy crisis, developments that led to more conflict and less collaboration in federal–provincial relations. They were also encouraged by the popularity of "rational" approaches to decision making, which were based on the premise that each government could and should arrange its "priorities" in a centralized fashion and exercise a tight grip over its expenditures. Central agencies and elected politicians are more inclined than specialists in health, welfare or resource development to think in terms of maximizing their government's power in relation to other governments.

While ad hoc meetings and permanent committees of officials certainly continue to exist in large numbers, the proportion of intergovernmental contacts that involve politicians has increased considerably, and the autonomy of the administrative committees has thereby been reduced. There are now fairly regular and frequent meetings of finance ministers, justice ministers, welfare ministers, ministers of communications and so forth involving all eleven governments.

A characteristically Canadian institution that has assumed great prominence is the First Ministers' Conference, which brings together the federal prime minister and the ten premiers, assisted by a small secretariat of officials.[3] The building which served as Ottawa's railway station until 1966 has been remodelled into a conference centre where these and other federal–provincial meetings take place. The date perhaps reflects a not entirely accidental coincidence between the end of the age of steam and the rise of executive federalism. In the nineteenth century there were no conferences of all the heads of government, and until the 1960s they occurred only occasionally, usually in connection with proposed amendments to the Constitution or major changes in fiscal arrangements between the two levels of government. Since 1963 there has been at least one such meeting in most years, and in some years more. While it is possible that patriation of the Constitution in 1982 will prove to have lessened the need for so many conferences, this cannot be stated with certainty. The need, if any, for conferences on economic matters is not likely to be affected.

Some First Ministers' Conferences have been designated as Constitutional Conferences (theoretically a separate and distinct institution), others as conferences on the economy, while still others deal with a wide range of issues. A few, including some but not all of the constitutional sessions, have been televised, though it is generally agreed that serious negotiation is only possible when the sessions are closed and confidential. Preliminary meetings of subordinate officials, and sometimes of ministers concerned with particular fields of policy, are also considered essential if the First Ministers' Conference is to succeed. Increasingly it is also becoming common for some or all of the premiers to meet in advance, without the prime minister, in an effort to discover points of agreement.

Despite all the advance preparation, expense and ballyhoo, the record of First Ministers' Conferences in reaching agreements or solving problems is exceedingly poor. Consensus among eleven leaders representing different regions, political philosophies and jurisdictional interests is rarely possible, and decisions by majority vote may serve little purpose. There is certainly no respectable reason why the federal government, which represents all Canadians, should agree to be bound by a majority vote of the first ministers, and some provincial governments—Ontario with its large population, Quebec with its threat to separate, and perhaps Alberta with its oil—are powerful enough to exercise a veto in certain types of situations. The growing practice of seeking a common provincial position in advance of the federal–provincial bargaining is not only undermining the legitimacy of the federal state, but is making "executive federalism" increasingly unworkable.

While the attention of the public is directed toward multilateral conferences, particularly those involving the first ministers, much of the most important serious bargaining is bilateral in fact, if not always in form. For example, the negotiations over the Canada Pension Plan in 1963 and 1964 involved all eleven governments, but the most serious and important bargaining took place on a bilateral basis between federal and Quebec governments in April 1964, after three first ministers' conferences had failed to make any progress. Once those two governments agreed that Quebec could have its own pension plan, with the federal plan revised to make it more compatible with Quebec's, the objections of the other provinces quickly evaporated.

More recent negotiations over the price of oil also suggest the importance of bilateral bargaining. A First Ministers' Conference on the subject was held in January 1974, perhaps largely in order to demonstrate the lack of support at that time for Alberta's position, but the serious negotiation since that time has been essentially between the federal and

Alberta governments only; there would be little benefit to either side from involving the others. When the federal and Alberta governments finally reached agreement on oil and natural gas prices in September 1981, bilateral agreements with the other significant producing provinces, Saskatchewan and British Columbia, followed very quickly. When falling world prices led to divergent interpretations of the implications of the 1981 agreement, bilateral negotiations between the federal and Alberta governments resumed in 1983.

Conclusion

While Canada's problems may be slight compared to those of many other countries, and while the federal state has survived through a number of decades in which its future appeared less than assured, there is nonetheless some cause for concern about its present situation and prospects. Contrary to the myth propagated in some provincial capitals, the picture that Canada presents to the outside world is that of an increasingly loose collection of semi-sovereign provinces, with a central government unable or unwilling to exercise much control over the economy or to carry out coherent policies even within its own fields of jurisdiction. Compared with almost any other modern state, or with Canada itself as recently as the 1950s, the extent of provincial power and the passivity of the central government are remarkable.

It is too early at the time of writing to assess the impact on Canadian federalism of the various constitutional changes that took effect in April 1982, and there is no consensus on what their impact is likely to be. Some observers, particularly in Quebec, where the provincial government did not sign the agreement that led to "patriation," have argued that the changes on balance strengthen the federal government in relation to the provincial governments. It is true that the Charter of Rights and Freedoms will give the federally appointed Supreme Court more opportunities to review and strike down provincial legislation. Specifically, provincial control over education has been weakened by the new requirement to offer instruction in either English or French where numbers warrant under Section 23 of the 1982 Constitution Act. On the other hand, several provisions of the 1982 Constitution Act appear to strengthen the provincial level of government. These include the constitutional entrenchment of equalization payments (Section 36), obligatory provincial involvement in constitutional amendments (Sections 38 through 41) including the power to opt out of certain types of amendments, guaranteed fiscal compensation for dissenting provinces if an amendment transfers powers over education or culture to the federal government (Section 40) and a considerable extension of provincial legislative powers over natural resources (Section 50). In addition, the effect of the Charter of Rights and Freedoms is weakened by the provision in Section 33 that legislatures may override the Charter in the area of fundamental freedoms, legal rights and equality rights.

The conspicuous and frequent intergovernmental conferences since the early 1960s have possibly accustomed many Canadians to regard the central government as only one government among eleven that are more or less equal in status—a serious misreading both of Canada's constitution and of the requirements of a healthy political system. Harold Innis once wrote that provincial control over lands and resources was a survival of "feudalism" and a source of weakness for Canada.[4] Certainly the effort which the central government must devote to bargaining with quasi-independent provincial potentates both lessens its ability to function effectively and undermines its authority in the eyes of the public. The federal–provincial conference does resemble a meeting of a medieval king with his feudal barons more than it does the government of a modern state. The implicit assumption that regional divisions and interests are the most significant ones in Canada, and that only the provincial governments are capable of representing them, calls into question the authority and usefulness of the federal Parliament, which must often rubber stamp the results of intergovernmental agreements and which is prevented from legislating even in the areas assigned to its jurisdiction without interference by the provinces.

Provincial premiers and their allies in the media and the universities proclaim that the federal government under Prime Minister Pierre Trudeau has been rigidly centralist and even that its power is increasing. The reality is quite otherwise. Since the early sixties the federal government has surrendered so much taxing power to the provinces, and made such generous grants to them, that it now has chronic budgetary deficits while some provincial governments have comfortable surpluses. It has offered to surrender certain of its constitutional powers and has allowed others to fall into disuse; for example, Parliament's declaratory power to assume jurisdiction over "works" within the provinces has not been used since 1961. The federal government has effectively turned over control of family allowances to the provinces, withdrawn from any direct involvement with post-secondary education, offered to bargain away the power the Supreme Court gave it over cable television, allowed important provincial inputs into its foreign policy, and refused to proclaim the statutory provisions by which it could accept its responsibility for regulating interprovincial highway transport.

The provincial governments themselves have been allowed to get away with actions that would be considered outrageous, if not unbelievable, in any other federal country. Among these may be cited British Columbia's veto of the takeover of Macmillan Bloedel by Canadian

Pacific, Alberta's reduction of oil shipments to other provinces as a means of persuading the federal government to accept its position on the price of that commodity, Newfoundland's discriminatory measures to prevent mainland Canadians from working on the offshore oil rigs, the purchase by Alberta and Quebec of three out of the five regional airlines even though air transportation falls exclusively under federal jurisdiction, the increasingly flagrant departures from the principle of complete and universal health insurance, the proliferation of interprovincial barriers to trade and the establishment of more than forty quasi-diplomatic provincial missions in foreign countries.

A.V. Dicey, in his classic book on British constitutional law, described the constitution of Bismarck's Germany as being "too full of anomalies, springing from both historical and from temporary causes, to be taken as a fair representative of any known form of government."[5] Canada's ramshackle constitution, and the actual operation of its federal system, are beginning to take on a similar appearance, and the changes that took effect in April 1982 have not improved matters. A Supreme Court that is still only partially provided for in the constitution, an appointed Senate in which New Brunswick has more representatives than British Columbia, a complicated and confusing allocation of legislative powers, a Charter of Rights and Freedoms that can be overridden by legislative resolutions, not to mention the various qualifications inserted into it at the behest of particular provinces, and an amendment formula that might leave the federal Parliament able to exercise authority in some provinces that it could not exercise in others are only a few of the anomalies in the formal constitution. The recent practice of Canadian federalism is hardly more encouraging than the theory, for there are still very few initiatives that the federal government is both willing and able to undertake without involving one or more of the provincial governments. The provincial governments, on the other hand, show little or no disposition to reciprocate by allowing the federal government to become involved in their affairs, even when the federal government provides most of the money that supports the activity in question.

Canada is a relatively small industrialized country in a world where most of its competitors are larger, stronger and more centralized. If it is to survive in this environment and to overcome the divisive effects of its geographical barriers and its closeness to the United States, it may require a stronger central government than it has enjoyed in recent years, and a corresponding reduction in the powers of provincial governments. Moreover, a lessening of the Canadian obsession with provincial interests and jurisdictional controversies might direct attention to more significant issues, such as the unequal distribution of wealth, power and opportunity among the population.

Notes

1. The British North America Act of 1867 was officially redesignated as the Constitution Act of 1867 when the British Parliament surrendered its authority over Canada's constitution in 1982. The new designation is used throughout this chapter.
2. Harold A. Innis, *Political Economy in the Modern State* (Toronto: Ryerson, 1946), p. xi.
3. The term "first minister" came into use about 1970 as a generic term including both "prime minister" and "premier." It must be noted that in the French language these distinctions cannot be made, and the only possible equivalent for all three terms is "premier ministre."
4. Harold A. Innis, *Essays in Canadian Economic History* (Toronto: University of Toronto Press, 1956), pp. 277–78.
5. A.V. Dicey, *Introduction to the Study of the Law of the Constitution*, 10th ed. (London: Macmillan, 1961), p. 139.

Further Readings

Armstrong, Christopher. *The Politics of Federalism: Ontario's Relations with the Federal Government, 1867–1942.* Toronto: University of Toronto Press, 1981.

Banting, Keith G. *The Welfare State and Canadian Federalism.* Montreal: McGill-Queen's University Press, 1982.

Black, Edwin R. *Divided Loyalties: Canadian Concepts of Federalism.* Montreal: McGill-Queen's University Press, 1975.

Cairns, Alan. "The Governments and Societies of Canadian Federalism." *Canadian Journal of Political Science* 10, pp. 695–725.

Mallory, J.R. *Social Credit and the Federal Power in Canada.* Toronto: University of Toronto Press, 1954. Reprinted with additional preface, 1976.

Scott, Frank R. *Essays on the Constitution: Aspects of Canadian Law and Politics.* Toronto: University of Toronto Press, 1977.

Simeon, Richard. *Federal–Provincial Diplomacy: The Making of Recent Policy in Canada.* Toronto: University of Toronto Press, 1972.

Smiley, Donald V. *Canada in Question: Federalism in the Eighties.* 3rd ed. Toronto: McGraw-Hill, 1980.

Stevenson, Garth. *Unfulfilled Union: Canadian Federalism and National Unity.* 2nd ed. Toronto: Gage, 1982.

Trudeau, Pierre Elliott. *Federalism and the French Canadians.* Toronto: Methuen, 1968.

Chapter 18

City Politics in Canada
Jack Layton

City politics in Canada is in a state of turmoil. Civic leaders who were accustomed in the recent past to addressing the problems of rapid and uncontrolled urban growth now find themselves trying to throw their policies into reverse in an attempt to deal with the economic decline of their cities. While the urban bounty of the 1950s and 1960s provided many crumbs to distribute to the poor and disadvantaged, the stagnation of the 1970s and 1980s has left fewer resources to be divided among a much larger needy population. Desperate attempts to attract civic monuments, like a domed stadium or a convention centre, have big-city mayors falling all over themselves in a 1980s competition for prestige, believing that these grand schemes will divert attention from the fundamental ills of their cities. Good planning policies and humane social programs are being haphazardly tossed to the wind, and with them the hard-fought-for principles of citizen involvement in decision making. The 1960s and early 1970s witnessed the rise of urban reform movements, but the economic crisis of the eighties has left them bewildered, trying to sort out where to go next.

At the same time, Canadians remain largely unaware of the issues and operating principles of their municipal governments. Mythology and cynicism characterize the urban public mood. Our objective in this chapter will be to provide a brief introduction to municipal government in Canada, to discuss the range of issues and problems which will have to be faced by city councils in the coming years, and to analyze the "politics" of urban government as it is practised today.

The Mythology
The mythology of city politics revolves around two misperceptions: "Local government isn't important, being nothing more than pothole politics," and "City politics is probably the most democratic form of government which we have in Canada."

We need to clear up these misperceptions. The mythology is that City Hall merely offers mundane services like garbage collection, roads, sewers and the like, and that, accordingly, it is a level of government to be taken less than seriously. But imagine living with a million people in a city without adequate sewers, garbage collection, running water or fire protection. City governments are actually responsible for making urban areas physically habitable. Perhaps more important is the trend of the past three decades which has seen municipalities spending most of their time and money on facilities and services that everyone agrees are important: public transit, social services, policing, schools, housing and urban planning. If there was ever a time when city councils were restricted to trivial responsibilities, that day is long gone.

The second myth concerns the supposed highly democratic nature of city government. We often hear local politicians touting the unique nature of City Hall government because it is so accessible to local residents and even encourages citizen participation. This view cannot be totally discounted—there is some truth to the contention. Local politics is certainly more open to input from the average citizen than either federal or provincial governments. After all, the municipal councillors spend most of their time right in the community. City Hall is usually a short distance away from homes and workplaces. At first glance, this is the most accessible level of government.

It is also true that, in most cities (with notable exceptions such as Montreal), individuals or group delegations are given the opportunity to stand before the Council or its committees and give their views, looking their politicians right in the eye. This is not possible for most people at the federal or provincial levels. Consequently, there is a good deal of fanfare about how "government by the people" flourishes in city politics.

This view hides much of the reality of municipal politics, and there are good reasons why we should be skeptical of it. First, a pervasive combination of apathy, confusion and alienation among voters serves as a real obstacle to local democracy. Voter turnout at municipal elections is very low. On average, 30 to 40 percent of eligible voters cast ballots in local elections, in contrast to the 70 to 80 percent turnout at other levels.

Second, the electoral system in cities produces results which very poorly reflect the diverse socioeconomic makeup of urban areas. The majority of local politicians are businessmen, lawyers or other professionals. Very few are unionists, immigrants, women or people who have been unemployed. A thoroughgoing democracy would likely see a much closer reflection of the demography of a city in its elected representatives.

Worse than this, however, is the disturbing reality that many local politicians are not elected at all. Rather, they are appointed to their posts, and sometimes these posts are very powerful ones indeed. Perhaps the best example is the chairman of the regional government in Metropolitan Toronto, currently Paul Godfrey, who has held this major position for well over a decade without having to face the electorate. He is appointed every three years by the mayors and aldermen who make up the Metro Council. Other examples can be found in the many special boards and agencies which make up the local government structure: transit commissions, police commissions, hydro boards and other bodies. These important decision-making positions are almost always filled by appointment rather than election. Often the appointments are not made by local councils but by provincial governments, far removed from the local scene. The end result of an appointment process in which the electorate has virtually no say is the removal of the public accountability essential to a democratic system.

There are further problems. All politicians, including those at City Hall, are subject to pressure from special interests. Some pressure groups have considerably more resources than others, giving rise to an imbalance in the decisions made by local councils—an imbalance which favours the most powerful sectors, most notably business.

There is a final limitation on local democracy which cannot be over-emphasized: Canada's constitution gives provincial governments full control over their municipalities. The provinces can create or eliminate local governments, decide what powers municipalities exercise, prescribe procedures for local elections and decision-making processes, dictate how local taxes are to be raised, and, as if all this weren't enough, a province can ultimately veto municipal laws or policies.

All of this calls into question the traditional view that local politics is democratic, but not particularly important. Indeed, the reverse proposition seems to be more accurate. With this in mind, we will now turn to a discussion of the current state of city politics including the context within which City Hall operates, the responsibilities of city governments, the organization of local government, the various forces at work in Canadian cities and the major issues which confront city politicians. We will conclude with an analysis of political power in urban political systems.

The Context of City Politics

We do not often think of municipal government as a revolutionary phenomenon, but Canada's early city governments were born in the struggle to transform Canada from a colony to a self-governing nation. The idea that townspeople should be able to control their own affairs and not be subject to arbitrary dictates from the British Colonial Office was a central feature of reform movements in various parts of Canada throughout the nineteenth century.[1]

The "victories" of the reformers were not, however, resounding ones. While many city councils were incorporated between the 1840s and the turn of the century, they were not what one could call models of local democracy. The first restriction, which as we have seen persists even today, was the dictate that municipal governments would be "creatures of the Province." The reformers of the day were advancing the theory that "the right of the community to govern itself arose directly from the people."[2] Senior governments took a different view, arguing that local governments should only be mechanisms for administering certain delegated responsibilities and for the arbitration of selected disputes under the authority of sovereign provincial governments.

Perhaps more disturbing from today's perspective is the limitation which was imposed upon those who could vote in municipal elections. Because the role of local government was traditionally restricted to servicing property by providing and maintaining such services as roads, sewers and bridges, only male property owners were to enjoy the franchise. Women (who normally didn't own property) and tenants were not granted the right to vote, and while women were given the vote in the early twentieth century, it has only been relatively recently that tenants have been permitted to participate in local elections.

However, local governments are now involved in much more than servicing property. The advent of programs such as welfare, daycare, public housing, mass transit and public health policies, to name just a few, have expanded the work of local politicians and bureaucracies dramatically. Since the Second World War, municipalities have become increasingly preoccupied with these issues and with the constant search for funds to pay for the new services. Of course, their traditional role as suppliers of services to property (often called "hard services") has remained, but federal and provincial governments have begun to rely on the local level to deliver social services (or "soft services") because they are "closer to the people" and because it is an easy way to pass on some of the costs which provinces would have to bear themselves.

As we will subsequently explain, one of the reasons for this expansion of the municipal role was the introduction of "welfare state" policies by the senior federal and provincial governments, but another cause has simply been the burgeoning population of urban areas. The larger the population of a municipal territory, the more complex its service needs become. Services to property quickly became entangled with services to people. Roads were built near new factories to move workers to and from work and also to provide the factories with the means of bringing in raw materials and shipping out finished goods. Neighbourhoods were planned, renovated, torn down and rebuilt, in part as a social welfare measure and in part as a means of supplying services to private property. The point here is that municipalities are now involved in servicing both property interests and people generally. The extent and complexity of this mix is very directly related to the population and territorial size of the local government in question.

Responsibilities of City Governments

The responsibilities of local government can be listed in several general categories. While there is some variation from province to province, the list which follows is generally applicable to all Canada's municipalities. First are *protection services*. Police and fire services have long occupied an important position as one of the more visible and pervasive functions of local government. Local police forces enforce federal, provincial and municipal laws. Together these laws prescribe a socioeconomic order for the society, and it is the municipality's job to ensure that this order (or status quo) is maintained. Policing is a mechanism for *social control*, a central function of the state in a capitalist society. Lines of officers at worker picket lines or demonstrations as well as controversies about police treatment of minorities illustrate the phenomenon. Fire departments fulfill another important state function, the protection of private property and human life.

In any developed society the state is also called upon to provide the physical infrastructure required for the processes of production, distribution and exchange which are essential to the proper functioning of the economy. In a capitalist society, the state provides the infrastructure while the private sector by and large provides for production, distribution and exchange. In this context, *transportation services* are key elements of local responsibilities. The expressways, road networks, bus routes and subway lines which are built and maintained by city governments are nothing less than the production lines and distribution networks of the urban economy. The efficient movement of raw materials, finished products, workers and shoppers is constantly sought by the city's corporate interests. Consequently, a major proportion of the capital spending by every city hall is devoted to the discharge of this responsibility. Some of the most famous urban political battles have centred on transportation issues, for example, the construction of expressways or rapid transit lines through established neighbourhoods (the Spadina Expressway or the Vancouver LRT).

Another local responsibility designed to provide physical infrastructure is captured under the polite designation *environmental services*: sewers, garbage disposal and water supply. Initially established to respond to serious public health concerns, these services have become increasingly important as a response to urban growth. Some might consider these matters rather mundane, but the conflict between an economy which generates phenomenal quantities of waste (close to three kilograms of solid waste per person per day in Canadian cities), and the livability of the environment is becoming increasingly severe. The location of huge landfill sites, the disposal of hazardous chemicals and the need for recycling are all controversial issues on the municipal agenda of the 1980s.

Aside from physical infrastructure, cities have moved into the field of what we might call "social infrastructure." This move has been accelerated in the latter half of the twentieth century as the "welfare state" has been added to the inventory of government responsibilities. The post-Depression Canadian state found that social welfare policies were essential to maintain the capitalist social order in the face of mounting popular discontent. Municipalities have taken on the administration of a great many programs designed to keep the lid on the political fallout of urban poverty.

This category of municipal responsibility can be labelled *social and health services* and includes welfare payments, daycare and homes for the aged, as well as public health programs. In most of these categories, provincial governments maintain particularly strict control over the activities of city politicians, leaving little scope for creative or independent municipal action. Indeed, some provinces, such as British Columbia, have kept the welfare system under their own jurisdiction entirely. On the other hand, local politicians and city staff are the ones who come into direct contact with the heavy economic and personal fallout suffered by disadvantaged communities and individuals. Poverty and its associated ills are all-too-common characteristics of Canada's urban centres. Families unable to pay their rent find themselves evicted and usually contact City Hall, desperate for assistance. Inadequately fed children struggle through inner-city schools. Economic tensions breed wife-beating and child-beating crises. Most such sad situations leave city councillors at a loss; there is little beyond emergency band-aid treatment which can be provided, because provincial governments have not permitted municipalities to develop adequate policy tools to respond. Some cities have worked at the margin of existing policy to develop innovative responses to urban poverty, but because several million Canadians live below the poverty line, most of them in cities, these efforts have had limited significance. The economic crisis of the late 1970s and early 1980s has simply aggravated the situation. Social services constitute therefore a vital but frustrating area of responsibility for city governments.

An ancillary element of the "social infrastructure" is the city's responsibility for *recreation and cultural services*. Parks, community centres, municipal swimming pools, golf courses, nature trails, tennis courts and the like have become important components of urban community services. A traditional pattern of inequity has developed in most cities, however. Neighbourhoods with lower-income residents seem to receive fewer such services than the rest of the city. In part, this is due to the tendency for wealthy areas to provide private recreational facilities, but the imbalance also reflects an unequal distribution of political power between a city's neighbourhoods.

Recently, local politicians have become infatuated with "grand projects." Perhaps the first and most famous incarnation of this preoccupation is Montreal's Mayor Jean Drapeau. Projects such as Expo '67 and the Olympics required massive public investments in facilities, often at the expense of needed services such as sewage treatment or housing. The pursuit of monument building in recreational planning seems to have captured the imagination of most city governments. In part, this trend is a distorted reflection of the long-standing interurban competition for prestige and economic development. The effects of this new mania on the politics of Canada's cities will be felt during the next decade and may well precipitate a reaction by overtaxed citizens who question the benefits of these mega-projects, as was evidenced with the rise of the Montreal's Citizens' Movement.

The next responsibility in our list is perhaps the most important of all: *land use planning*. The deceptively small portion of municipal budgets allocated to planning (1 to 2 percent of the operating budget) belies the vital role played by the planning function. Indeed, decisions about the use of land in cities are by far the most politically contentious questions facing local governments.

Even with the huge geographic mass of Canada, urban land remains a scarce commodity. This is because, as we have seen, *urban* land must be extensively serviced with roads, buses, sewers, water, street lighting, parks, schools and much more. Without these services, land cannot be used for urban purposes like housing, offices, factories, universities or shopping centres. Land use planning essentially consists of determining the appropriate uses for particular parcels of land and providing required services according to the use.

Needless to say, most land in cities is already being used for one purpose or another; so planning focuses on *changes* in land uses and tries to determine which changes are appropriate and which are not. And here is the rub: there is often considerable disagreement about what should happen to a particular piece of property. The owner of the land will want to establish a use which can maximize its value. Adjacent owners will advocate a use which will enhance the value of their properties. People elsewhere in the city might have views as well. Perhaps there is a group arguing that there is a desperate shortage of affordable housing and that the land in question should be devoted to that purpose irrespective of the desires of the owner. Sometimes residents in a neighbourhood far removed from the contentious land might perceive a threat to their lifestyle. For instance, if the development of some downtown land as office towers produces a requirement for a new expressway into the heart of the city, passing through existing residential areas, opposition can be expected.

City Hall has not always been involved in land use planning. Prior to the Second World War, the urban structure of most Canadian cities was determined by the private decisions of land owners. While the city engineer might have specified a street pattern, virtually no further controls were available. However, the haphazard pattern of urban growth, combined with its post-war rapidity, highlighted the need for some sort of "rationale" for the distribution and intensity of land use. Planning acts, adopted by provincial governments, gave cities the power to regulate land use through mechanisms known as "official plans" and "zoning by-laws."

Business interests were skeptical about these measures, though the need for planned growth was generally acknowledged. Indeed, an important role of the state in a capitalist society is to manage growth in the interests of *all* capitalists, not exclusively that of a particular business. The problem for business, particularly land developers, was that planning law permitted government to interfere with what they believed to be their sacrosanct rights to do whatever they wished with their property. In this sense, the advent of urban planning constituted a dramatic intervention by the state into the affairs of private enterprise.

There was an obvious solution to this problem which was not lost on the major land developers. Clearly, they needed to ensure that the planning process produced decisions which were favourable to their objective of maximizing profit from land development. It has therefore been necessary for the property industry to attempt to "capture" control of the land use planning process. When city governments tackle land use issues in planning reports, public hearings and council debates they are subject to tremendous and usually successful pressure from developers. We will examine these pressure tactics as well as their implications later in this chapter.

A final point on planning must be made. It is important to remember that city councils cannot force a private land owner to build a certain sort of building, whether it be housing, offices or a factory. The best that politicians can do is to prohibit certain uses and permit others. Accordingly, there is no guarantee that a project desired by the politicians will ever be built. The ball always ultimately finds itself in the owner's court where the decision is made "to build or not to build." This is a serious handicap when planners and politicians are trying to accomplish their objectives.

One solution to this problem, recently adopted by some cities, is for the municipal government itself to purchase land and build projects. In the Canadian experience, this has been done primarily for the purposes of building low and moderately priced housing. The 1970s saw several major cities approach their provincial governments for permission to set up city-owned housing companies. The provinces have generally agreed, and the responsibility for housing production has now been added to the inventory of municipal responsibilities.

A similar initiative is now taking shape as cities try to reverse the flight of industry from their central cores. Toronto, for instance, is establishing a municipal corporation to purchase land and build industrial buildings in an attempt to bring industry back to the downtown. It remains to be seen if this strategy can reverse the tendency of multinational industrialists to shift production to suburban areas or, worse, to low-wage third world countries. In all likelihood a much larger "carrot" or, more likely, a "stick" will be required to reverse this trend.

This brings us to the last item on our list of municipal responsibilities: *administration*. A city government is a large bureaucracy designed to *produce decisions*. Accomplishing this requires a number of administrative components: a decision-making structure, personnel to fill the spots in the structure, funds to pay for the services provided by the city, and a management system to permit an efficient and effective operation. We will examine the structures of city government in the next section of this chapter.

The most controversial aspect of administration, as far as the public is concerned, is the financing of local government. With budgets in the billions of dollars, urban governments are faced with major problems in funding their services. Unlike federal and provincial governments, cities are not permitted to use deficit financing, virtually eliminating fiscal flexibility. Property tax, the basic source of municipal revenue, is an unfortunate instrument because of its regressive character (as incomes drop, the percentage of income paid in property tax usually increases, putting the heaviest burden on lower-income groups, including tenants).

Grants from provincial governments ease this burden to some extent but bring with them strict conditions which force city councils to spend money according to provincial priorities rather than their own. This situation has led the Federation of Canadian Municipalities to describe local governments as "puppets on a shoestring."[3] The battle between municipalities and provinces on this matter has raged for years, with little prospect of resolution. Without independent status in Canada's constitution, local governments are left without an independent financial lever to deal with urban problems. The next decade may well see a change in this situation, as it may be in the interests of both federal and municipal governments to combine forces in an effort to reduce provincial power.

Our summary of municipal responsibilities has been brief, but its purpose has been simply to whet appetites for further investigation.

There can be no question of the importance of the issues currently facing urban governments. Our next section will examine the structures and processes used in the attempt to come to terms with them.

Structures and Processes

For the purposes of our discussion, we might consider the institutions of city government as a machine for transforming raw materials (issues, problems and demands from citizens, businesses, labour or the media) into products (decisions and policies). When we examine the machinery and internal processes of a city council, wherever it may be found in Canada, a number of common characteristics can be found. While the individual structures and positions have different nomenclature, the essential elements are the same: an elected council, headed by a mayor and composed of a number of councillors or aldermen; a series of Committees of Council; and a number of bureaucratic departments. To illustrate the basic processes of decision making, an outline of the life cycle of a typical decision follows.

The machinery is fired up whenever a problem arises. The identification of this problem can come from any one of a number of sources. Perhaps a land developer wants to proceed with an office complex not permitted in the current land use legislation; or a citizen has complained about snow-clearing arrangements; or the local daily has criticized the city's policy on housing. The most frequent sources are found within City Hall itself—the bureaucracy which has uncovered some issue requiring a policy decision by Council or the politicians who have been prompted to raise some matter with their colleagues. No matter which of these sources provides the initiative, the process which follows is roughly the same, though its results can be dramatically different.

The first step is to present the issue to a Committee of Council. The committee will consist of a portion of the council members and will be responsible for a certain policy territory such as planning, hard services, social services, parks or finance. Usually, the committee will request a report on the matter from the appropriate department of the bureaucracy. This issue will come back to the committee when the report is ready. In it the staff will present an analysis of the problem and suggest an appropriate course of action in the form of a number of recommendations.

Prior to the committee meeting, the members will have received a long agenda containing the reports from staff on the assortment of issues before it. Sometimes these agendas are hundreds of pages long, and only the most diligent councillors will have studied all the material thoroughly. The most common practice is to assume that the bureaucratic recommendations are appropriate. First-time observers at these meetings are often stunned by the hundreds of recommendations which are approved without discussion. At a typical meeting, only a few items are debated. These tend to be the controversial matters, involving situations where the bureaucrats are suggesting a solution which is opposed by constituents, businesses or some councillors.

In most cities, procedures have been developed to allow people to address the committee when they disagree with proposals from the city staff. These public deputations can become lively exchanges. Whether the deputations are successful in convincing the politicians to adopt a different position from the bureaucracy will depend on the political effectiveness of the deputants. Indeed, often these deputations are mere exercises in "legitimation" through giving people the impression that their voice has been heard. Community groups are permitted to come down to City Hall and have their say, but few councillors listen to the representations of citizens. On the other hand, some deputants, developers and their lawyers for example, seem to be remarkably successful in their efforts to convince councillors.

Next, the decisions of the committee are sent along to the legal department to be cast into by-law form. A by-law is the term used to describe municipal legislation, like a "bill" in Parliament. These by-laws are constructed in the specialized language of lawyers, which means that citizens who cannot afford legal counsel are at a real disadvantage when dealing with the complexities of by-laws.

Ultimately, all committee decisions and by-laws are forwarded to the whole City Council for discussion. The members of Council have a number of options: they can approve the recommendations (which they do 95 percent of the time), they can reject the proposals (which hardly ever happens), they can amend the recommendations (a more regular occurrence), or they can delay controversial matters by referring them back to the bureaucracy for further study (a common ploy when politicians are in trouble).

With the decision of Council made, the issue may still face further hurdles. Provincial governments have the power to veto municipal decisions, and while this is rare on routine matters, some major questions may provoke provincial intervention. Most provincial governments have institutionalized a process for automatic review of municipal decisions, usually through a review board with the power to turn down or amend local by-laws. These boards are not elected but are appointed by the provincial Cabinet. Needless to say, it is most frustrating for a City Council to have its decisions rejected in this manner. A more effective reminder of the subservient status of local government would be difficult to imagine.

Councils, committees and bureaucratic departments form only part of municipal government structure. In addition there is a plethora of special agencies, boards and commissions (ABCs) designed to deal with particular policy matters. There are usually dozens of these: parking authorities, school and library boards, transit and police commissions, advisory committees on a wide range of subjects. This institutional fragmentation of decision making makes matters most confusing for the average resident. Designed initially to ensure that specialists were in charge of specific aspects of local government, these bodies have usually become repositories for political patronage appointments and have served to remove policy decisions one step further from public accountability. Despite regular recommendations from academics and formal reviews of local government structures aimed at reducing the number and variety of these special-purpose bodies, little reform has been accomplished to date.

A relatively recent development in urban government in Canada has been the introduction of "super-governments," regional governments which incorporate a number of cities, boroughs and towns under one umbrella structure. Metropolitan Toronto, established in 1954, was the first of these. The concept of regional governments has been promoted as a means of dealing with urban growth. During the post-war expansion boom, which lasted until the mid-1970s, suburban housing developments proceeded rapidly. Local councils, often little more than rural townships, found themselves faced with massive costs for the physical infrastructure to support this growth. Roads, sewers, water supply, hydro, schools—all these had to be provided to meet the needs of the new suburbanites. Developers of subdivisions were frustrated at the inability of the small municipalities to service their land quickly. Some mechanism had to be developed to utilize the strong financial base of the urban core to pay for suburban expansion, otherwise growth could well grind to a halt. Regional governments provided this mechanism, marshalling the tax base of the developed urban centre for the benefit of the surrounding suburbs, while retaining some autonomy for the various municipalities within the region.

One problem with these regional systems is that they have added yet another layer to the complex urban governments. This has created further confusion among the electorate. Indeed, the regional governments are not usually directly elected by the public. Their members are selected from among local councils. This removal of decision making from the control of the electorate has seriously undermined the democratic operation of local politics in Canada's cities.

As well, the politics of regional governments have proven problematic. The interests of the suburbs have frequently come into conflict with the urban base. Whether in Montreal, Ottawa, Toronto, Hamilton or Vancouver, downtown politicians have had great difficulty convincing their suburban counterparts to deal with many urban problems, simply because the suburbs have not yet experienced these problems directly. Neighbourhood destruction from downtown development and expressways, the need for expanded social services to deal with disadvantaged groups, and the demand for expanded public transit to reduce automobile commuter congestion have all created sharp conflicts within regional governments.

The most recent phenomenon in urban development may create a base for common interests between suburbs and central cities. Continued urban growth is gradually transforming former suburbs into more complex urban municipalities. As industry, office developments and public housing move into the suburbs, the previous power of traditional middle-class single-family suburban homeowners is being undermined. Suburban politicians find themselves confronting problems such as poverty, congestion and redevelopment schemes which were formerly exclusive to inner cities. Perhaps this trend will eventually mitigate the tensions within regional governments. There is no doubt that the politics of the "suburbs" will be quite different ten years from now.

Political Forces in Cities

In trying to understand the politics of Canada's cities, it is never enough to examine only the formal structures of local government. These are, after all, simply the components of the machine. The essential questions are: what flows into the machine, who operates it and what is done with the products?

Six major forces operate in urban politics: business, community groups, labour, the media, bureaucrats and politicians. The most influential of these, business, has, for obvious reasons, a long history of involvement in city politics. City Hall makes a great many decisions about land use, hard services and taxation which affect business interests directly. While the overt corruption of past relationships between business and city officials has largely been eliminated with conflict-of-interest legislation, there are other, more subtle and powerful techniques which have been developed to ensure that these interests are well served by civic policy makers. Indeed, the power of capitalist interests is growing in the eighties because of the depressed state of urban economies. The conventional wisdom that "what is good for our city's businessmen is good for our city" is a particularly attractive dictum in the context of recession and decline. Any policy which can encourage investment by the private sector is automatically ranked high because of its short-term benefits in increasing the tax base.

If there are negative long-term consequences of such a policy raised by critics, these are discounted. This amounts to a basic ideological congruity between the private sector and most municipal politicians and bureaucrats and constitutes the most powerful weapon in the arsenal of political power available to business. Consider the impact of a corporate executive stating to a municipal council: "If City Hall won't cooperate with me, I'll simply have to find another town that will!" Cities are highly dependent upon the investment decisions of those in control of private capital, and this dependence is accentuated by the current economic downturn being experienced by almost every Canadian city.

When it comes to specific political tactics, there are many resources available to the business sector. Most important are the funds available to hire experts, lawyers and lobbyists. These funds are also diverted into the political campaign war-chests of sympathetic politicians, enhancing the likelihood of a Council's positive response to business needs. While a small number of Canadian municipalities have implemented election expense legislation requiring the disclosure of donors, this has simply produced a more complex form of corporate donation where funds are funnelled through a number of corporate officers in small denominations less likely to be noticed.

The availability of expertise and lobbyists is actually much more significant than the relatively crass practice of campaign donations. Match a corporate lawyer against the City's own professional staff and against the wits of local politicians and the business interest is likely to come out on top. Perhaps most skilled in this area are the land developers. Practice, in this case, has made perfect. The lucrative results of a successful official plan change or rezoning has produced a small elite of lawyers, planning consultants and lobbyists in each city who have become highly skilled at extracting favourable decisions from city councils.

A final crucial political resource is "organization." No group can begin to extract what it wants from government if it is not effectively organized. Business is able to develop successful political organization because it has identified and agreed upon objectives and it can develop strategy to achieve them. The corporate sector is highly organized to deal with municipal government, through broad organizations such as Boards of Trade, Chambers of Commerce, and certain specific industrial organizations such as the Urban Development Institute or the Housing and Urban Development Association of Canada. Even the individual corporation is an organization which can be used in this way.

Thus, when the powerful political and economic resources of the private sector are combined with the predominant ideological support for business initiatives, there can be no question that capitalists receive top rank in the hierarchy of urban political power. But this is not to say that there are no instances of political loss for land developers or their colleagues elsewhere in the business world. They suffer "defeats" of two types. The first type of "defeat" occurs with sufficient frequency to be considered "normal": defeat through competition with other corporations. Occasionally the local state will be called upon to mediate these disputes within the capitalist class, with developers using their influence at City Hall to try to convince local politicians to accept their proposals over those of competitors.

A second, but rare, type of "defeat" for business comes at the hands of community or citizen groups. Attacks on urban neighbourhoods by capitalist expansion and major development projects spur residents to attempt to protect their cities. The regular success of business proposals at Canadian city halls in the 1960s and 1970s, especially those of the major developers, became so frustrating for communities who were opposing developer plans that the phenomenon of the urban reform movement emerged in response. Reformers and citizens' groups have become much more active, and in some cases successful, during the past decade. While their political resources have been much less daunting than those of their business opponents, they have had a number of important cards to play.

Not all citizen or community groups have been reformist or progressive, though. Citizens' groups come in a wide variety of shapes and sizes. Political resources and impact vary a great deal. A wealthy neighbourhood association has many of the same political advantages as a business, while a community organization in a poor neighbourhood will have few of these traditional instruments.

The involvement of citizens in municipal government is hardly a new phenomenon, but the 1970s gave a new meaning to the political clout of neighbourhoods in Canada's big cities. At the leading edge was Toronto. An informal alliance of neighbourhoods, some rich and upper class, others poor and working class, rose up to resist the unbridled armlock which the major property developers had on Toronto City Hall. Certain champions caught the imagination, including David Crombie from the middle- and upper-class areas, and John Sewell from the working-class and some middle-class neighbourhoods.

Most important was the emergence of *community* organizing as a strategy to face off against business organizations. From Halifax to Vancouver, residents were organizing to resist the destructive consequences of rapid urban growth—particularly on downtown communities. The battles were often fierce. Creative strategies were used to attract media attention and to influence politicians through the fear of the electorate's vote. While on occasion civil disobedience was added to the more traditional tactics of mass meetings, protest marches, petitions and like methods, there was a certain "properness" which pervaded these protest efforts, perhaps partly due to the fact that the movement was an alliance of middle- and working-class elements, with the middle-class providing the leadership and the major portion of the movement's membership.

As a political force, community groups have had sufficient victories to qualify as a significant factor in urban politics. However, if we were to break down these groups and victories, we would find a clear pattern. The rate of success varies directly with the class status of the group involved. A wealthy neighbourhood can often count on success at City Hall while a poor neighbourhood can almost always count on defeat. Of course even these disadvantaged corners of our cities are allowed the occasional success, thus helping to "prove" that the political process is fair to everyone, giving all an equal chance. (This is somewhat like calling an 8 to 1 hockey game score a "tie" because both sides scored.) This, again, is the "legitimation" function of the local state apparatus.

The middle-class reform movements in Canada's cities have emphasized the need for open and participatory processes in their local governments. Many of these goals have been achieved. Decisions once taken in private meetings are now discussed in public, with public deputations being heard. Of course, the improved process by no means guarantees the ultimate decision will be any different than it would have been under the previous arrangements. Indeed, many communities experience the remarkable frustration of presenting their views to a politely attentive Council Committee, views which are then summarily ignored. The citizen upheavals of the 1970s have actually done little to change the popular attitude among working-class neighbourhoods that "you can't fight City Hall."

What about labour as a political force? If workers are not successful in influencing city politics using their neighbourhood organizations, could it be that their power lies in workplace trade union organizations? Labour is not listed with the traditional list of urban political forces, but it should be. There are three ways in which unions become involved in local government. First, municipal workers in Canada's cities are unionized. They deal with city politicians as their employers, and the results of contract negotiations have a major impact on the city's budget and delivery of service. Indeed, recent cutbacks in various municipal services have met with stiff union opposition, occasionally sufficient to maintain the service. The most powerful weapon of civic employees, as with other unions, is the strike. Whenever teachers, sanitation workers or police (who cannot strike legally in most jurisdictions in Canada) walk off the job, they are able to put considerable pressure on decision makers. Most often, though, public outcry against the strike is so strong, fanned by politicians and the media, that the provincial government will step in and "legislate" the workers back to work, often with little having been gained. Nonetheless, the unionization of municipal workers, a relatively recent phenomenon, has had a decidedly positive effect on wages and working conditions.

A second way in which labour has exercised influence at City Hall is through municipal labour councils which have existed for many years in Canadian urban areas. Composed of the union locals in a particular city, labour councils are labour's watchdog on local government. Policies on a wide range of issues are developed by these councils. Economic development and jobs, housing, planning, social services, labour relations, public transit policy, property tax reform and human rights issues are among the matters most commonly raised at the meetings of labour delegates. Acting much as any other pressure group might do, though usually with considerably fewer political resources than business groups, labour spokespersons will attempt to catch the attention of the public or the ear of the politicians in an effort to produce policies which will be more favourable to working people. Nevertheless, having, as they do, few strong allies among city politicians, the success rate of the labour movement in its efforts to change the pro-business direction of urban policies has been low.

The third device which labour has used to influence city politics is the electoral process. Indeed, labour has sometimes joined forces with citizens' groups to bring forward a "united front" in contesting local elections. Most major Canadian cities have experienced this phenomenon in recent years, and despite ups and downs, these coalitions are having a major impact on the shape of urban political debate. Unions and community groups have assisted in polarizing the issues, clarifying the conflicting positions and offering voters a recognizable choice. There are many examples, some quite successful: the Montreal Citizens' Movement, the Committee of Progressive Electors in Vancouver, or the municipal wing of the NDP in Toronto, Ottawa, Hamilton and Winnipeg.

Thus, if there is a single trend for the 1980s which we can identify with some certainty, it is the gradual shift toward some form of overt party politics in Canadian cities. Labour is playing a major role in this process. If it is successful in establishing party politics in Canadian City Halls, the local arena will have received a promotion in the voters' eyes, from "pothole politics" to the serious business it really is.

Media influence on Canadian federal and provincial politics is generally acknowledged to be quite impressive. In urban politics as well, the media has helped to shape the agenda. To begin, most media outlets relegate City Hall to a low status in their coverage. Given that these are *mass* media interested in maximizing sales and profit, it is not surprising that stories with the widest geographical interest, like international or national news, will receive top or front-page billing. City issues can be found, with some searching, deep inside the newspaper or near the end of the newscast. All of this has had a serious effect on public attitudes toward local politics and politicians by reinforcing people's general apathy with respect to issues in their city.

However, certain types of local news are covered. Major private developments and public mega-projects are usually greeted with unbridled enthusiasm by the media. Whether it is a new highrise office tower, a convention centre complex or a domed stadium, the corporate and civic booster mentality dominates news stories and commentaries. A close look at the interconnections between the boards of directors of major press and electronic media outlets reveals the origin of this enthusiasm. Development companies, banks, mortgage companies and other major industries have been remarkably successful in placing their directors on these boards, effectively guaranteeing reportage consistent with their interests. The natural skepticism of reporters is often curtailed by editors not wishing to print negative stories about such pro-business ventures.

Media moguls do, however, provide one outlet for their reporters' cynicism. There is a manifest delight in presenting reports of the interpersonal attacks and sometimes silly debates between local politicians. The public quickly draws the conclusion that all municipal politicians, and city politics in general, are nothing more than trivialities, worthy of little attention and much ridicule. As a contribution to the democratic process, this tendency is extremely negative because it convinces people that there is little point in becoming concerned about the urban issues addressed at City Hall. This helps to reduce meaningful and informed citizen participation, leaving a vacuum into which other pressure groups, such as business interests, can successfully flow.

Finally, the media usually dubs critics of development "radicals" and alleges that they have adopted a "stop the world, I want to get off" approach to urban growth. This belittling of alternative viewpoints has placed a major obstacle in the path of citizens and communities in their efforts to urge different priorities on their city governments. One encouraging trend has been the emergence of alternative, community-based newspapers and cooperative radio stations. These news outlets have limited circulation because their access to corporate advertising dollars is almost nil. Nonetheless, for those willing to scout their newsstands for these fly-by-night community gems, the rewards can be substantial.

Conclusion: Uncertain Patterns of Politics

In summary, there is a marked imbalance of forces in the urban political matrix. The instruments of political influence are unequally distributed. But the picture painted here has been *static*, whereas the actual political experience of any city reveals a *shifting* picture. While there is little to indicate fundamental changes in the power structure, there is an ebb and flow. We opened our discussion with the claim that Canadian city politics was in chaos: the time is ripe for shifts. The precise direction of this movement is unclear, and will doubtless vary from city to city.

The 1970s recast the previously comfortable and effective alliance of business and the state at the local level. Growth and development had awakened a resistance among neighbourhoods of all classes. An alliance of upper-class, middle-class and working-class communities formed and placed real strains on the practice of local politics. While this tension was late in arriving in some cities, it was noticeable everywhere. New notions of the importance of community preservation and of participatory decision making spread. The alliance pushing for change was a powerful one which had considerable effect in many urban areas. "Reform movements" emerged in most Canadian cities, rallying around the concepts of open government and neighbourhood protection. A new breed of radical politicians and community organizers took leadership positions in these movements. While there was much resistance, some of the more shrewd elements of the establishment recognized that a positive response of some kind was necessary. Concessions were made, and in this way radical policies were transformed into mild-mannered reforms.

There was a sense in which reform could be afforded because of the general sense of affluence pervasive in the urban economies of the early seventies. Community organizations were even encouraged to come forward and participate. Some neighbourhoods won important victories, particularly the middle-class ones. A creative polarization between left and right, between pro- and anti-development forces, produced innovative policy structures and new "people-oriented" concepts of urban design. City governments began to tackle important problems more directly: the housing crisis through municipal non-profit housing corporations; the daycare issue through rapid expansion of facilities; urban growth through significant zoning changes; and the ubiquity of the automobile with major transit improvements.

But this state of affairs was to be short lived. Deepening recession produced a growing panic as the decade closed. Even western boomtowns watched the forest of construction cranes thin out and become idle. Reports of major development companies abandoning Canadian projects in favour of investment initiatives south of the border produced a wave of worry in every city hall. Moves to "cut red tape" (i.e., discourage citizen participation) and to attract investment through grand projects became common. City politicians returned to the boardrooms and business clubs which they had studiously avoided for ten years, looking to recultivate the smooth business–government relations of an earlier era. No longer wishing to be known as "reformers," many politicians sought to be labelled "boosters" who could lift the city's economy out of the doldrums.

Citizen movements underwent a transformation too. The alliances which made them possible in the seventies were no longer available. The middle-class had won the respect of city hall and the protection of its backyards. Working-class neighbourhoods were caught in the economic uncertainty of the recession. Unemployment and inflation replaced earlier concerns and made municipal boosters, with their promises of better times, more popular. Reform movements sputtered and foundered, their leaders seeking a new and appropriate agenda.

This is, more or less, where city politics stands in the mid-1980s. It is a somewhat depressing situation, leaving the impression that little has been learned, or that what was learned has been abandoned. This is in part because the gains of the reform movement were more symbolic than real, and could accordingly be forgotten with remarkable speed. There had been no fundamental change after all, despite the wishful claims of reform leaders to the contrary.

In the eighties, what is to be the appropriate basis upon which to construct a movement for change? The general, but highly unequal, decline in living standards in the contemporary Canadian city is the clear starting point. And no longer is this decline a matter of highrise towers casting unpleasant shadows on sedate backyards. Rising poverty, a serious housing crisis (the worst evidence being found in crowded emergency shelters and in the numbers of homeless in the streets), and record unemployment (particularly long-term joblessness among the young) are the new characteristics of the contemporary urban situation.

One problem in establishing these issues as the bases of a new urban reform movement is that they are not traditionally seen as problems for city governments to address. The policy instruments and fiscal resources necessary to tackle them lie with provincial and federal governments—at least that is what we are told. On the other hand, poverty, housing problems and unemployment are experienced by individuals, families and communities *in cities*, by the urban working class. And these problems manifest themselves in particular, distinctly urban, situations: racial tension in public housing projects, plant shutdowns, large rent increases in apartment blocks, homeless youth on downtown streets.

There is a basis for a sharply redefined progressive movement. Instead of trying to pull together the old alliances of reform, community organizing must orient itself around the pressing and painful circumstances of the 1980s. This suggests the need to sharpen the distinctions between those who benefit from the urban economy and those who do not. A more profoundly ideological approach is demanded. The new movements will have to be more self-consciously socialist and class-based. This is not to say that pragmatic policies have no place. Indeed, they must provide the concrete elements of municipal reform programs for the eighties. However, it is to say that urban conflict must be defined as having a broader social base—beyond the street and neighbourhood.

Notes

1. For a review of the history of local government in Canada see Warren Magnusson and Andrew Sancton, eds., *City Politics in Canada* (Toronto: University of Toronto Press, 1983), pp. 3–57; Donald H.J. Higgins, *Urban Canada: Its Government and Politics* (Toronto: Macmillan, 1977), pp. 15–44.
2. Magnusson and Sancton, *City Politics in Canada*, p. 7.
3. Canadian Federation of Mayors and Municipalities, *Puppets on a Shoestring: The Effects on Municipal Governments of Canada's System of Public Finance* (Ottawa, 1976).

Further Readings

Dear, Michael, and Allen J. Scott, eds. *Urbanization and Urban Planning in Capitalist Society*. London: Methuen, 1981.

Feldman, Lionel D., ed. *Politics and Government of Urban Canada: Selected Readings*. 4th ed. Toronto: Methuen, 1981.

Higgins, Donald. *Urban Canada: Its Government and Politics*. Toronto: Macmillan, 1977. This volume serves as a good introduction to institutions and processes of local government in Canada. Differences between municipal organization in various provinces are illustrated.

Magnusson, Warren, and Andrew Sancton, eds. *City Politics in Canada*. Toronto: University of Toronto Press, 1983. This book has excellent chapters on the politics of each of seven major Canadian cities as well as useful introductory and concluding chapters by the editors.

Roussopoulos, Dimitrios, ed. *The City and Radical Social Change*. Montreal: Black Rose Books, 1982.

Tindal, C.R. *You and Your Local Government*. Toronto: Ontario Municipal Management Development Board, 1983.

Chapter 19

Kaleidoscope in Grey:
The Policy Process in Ottawa
Richard J. Van Loon

At the centre of any political process is choice among policy alternatives. In Canadian parliamentary government that choice is centred squarely in the Cabinet, for it is the prime minister and the Cabinet ministers who must determine which of society's demands are to be satisfied; and it is they who are accountable to Parliament and eventually to the electorate for their decisions.

The uncertainties involved in governing a modern society make political choice a complex task. It is all the more difficult since the decisions may affect millions of people and must be made by harried men and women on the basis of information which is at best incomplete. To reduce the social and political risks involved, the prime minister—who is ultimately responsible for it all—may seek to impose order and to ensure the availability and reliability of as much information as can be brought to bear. To that end, the prime minister and the Cabinet in Ottawa and the political executive in several provincial capitals have surrounded themselves with a coterie of "central agencies" intended specifically to support the Cabinet in the process of choosing among competing priorities and ultimately imposing a semblance of order upon an often chaotic policy process.

Our title refers to a kaleidoscope. To a casual observer, the process and the constellation of organizations involved appears kaleidoscopic indeed, for the past decade has seen several major reshufflings of the roles of the central agencies which surround our Cabinet and several major changes in the process involved. However, this paper suggests that there is a direction to this change. It derives from the initial attempts by government to impose financial self-discipline on what was hitherto a rather undisciplined process—an attempt which is parallelled by many provincial governments in Canada and by the governments of other western industrial nations.

Everywhere in the West, the quarter century following the end of World War II was a time of extremely rapid growth of government. The "positive state" expanded its role in society, displacing an older economic,

412

social and cultural order and creating entirely new forms of public activity. However, early in the 1970s the feeling began to emerge that the growth of government should slow. If the growth rate of expenditures was to be slowed, then the process and planning systems which suited a period of largely unrestricted expansion would equally require change. The changes have been kaleidoscopic because the current generation of decision makers, nurtured during a period of rapid government growth, is still experimenting with various ways to operate a system which is now expanding only slowly. That the adjustments have had to be made in a time of considerable economic difficulty has certainly not made them any easier to implement.

The changes are kaleidoscopic as well because of two additional factors. First, there is not always agreement that restraint is required. As is usual in democratic politics, a rolling compromise seems to have been struck in Canada between those who believe in a restriction of government activity and those who believe that its continued growth is desirable. But such compromises are inevitably unstable. As the balance of power within a government moves back and forth, between pro-constraint and pro-growth factions, the institutions which give effect to that balance will also change.

Second, if more information is to be brought to bear on a system of rational choice, what rationality should inform the gathering of that information? Bureaucratic rationality emphasizes efficiency and systematic approaches, depends on maximum amounts of quantifiable information and demands concrete objectives and clear directions. Political rationality emphasizes the provision of maximum satisfactions for voters in the relatively short run and thereby utilizes information which makes many bureaucrats uneasy and thrives on flexible objectives. Yet the attempt to impose more order on the system of political choice is generally implemented by bureaucrats "serving" politicians. The conflict engendered by this situation is probably inevitable and perhaps even useful since it may result in the striking of a reasonable balance. But the balance is bound to be a shifting one, especially during a period of transition, and the result is, once again, bound to be kaleidoscopic changes in the structure and process of political choice.

In the pages which follow we will attempt to follow the patterns of change by first considering the Cabinet itself and then looking at the constellation of executive support agencies which surrounds it. In their current incarnation these agencies include the Prime Minister's Office (PMO), the Privy Council Office (PCO), the Department of Finance, the Treasury Board Secretariat, the Federal–Provincial Relations Office and the Ministries of State for Economic and Regional Development and Social Development. We will look at several planning systems which have emerged in Ottawa over the past decade, and we will also consider some more informal structures used to provide support for the prime minister and Cabinet and to facilitate coordination among the various policies of government. We will then consider the stages through which a policy proposal will normally pass. Finally, we will look briefly at the budgetary cycle before attempting to define in more detail the general pattern of evolution of the policy process.

Cabinet and Cabinet Committee Structures

Over the past fifteen years the Cabinet has evolved from a single decision-making body to a series of committees which possess considerable autonomy within their own spheres of activity. The full Cabinet still exists as an entity, though it almost disappeared during the brief span of the Progressive Conservative government in 1979–80. However, the bulk of its work is now delegated to a major central coordinating committee (Priorities and Planning) and to a series of sectoral or "policy"

Figure 19.1
The Committee Structure of the Cabinet
(1979 Trudeau Version)

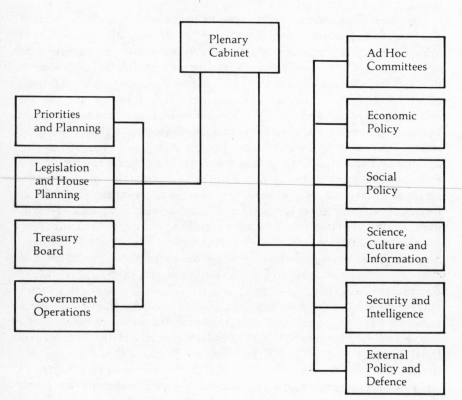

committees. In addition, the Treasury Board and the closely related Government Operations Committee act as *de facto* boards of management for government, the Legislation and House Planning Committee manages all aspects of the government's legislative program, and the Government Communications Committee attempts to coordinate dissemination of information about government programs.

Figures 19.1, 19.2 and 19.3 illustrate the committee structures of Cabinet under the Liberals prior to the 1979 election, the Progressive Conservatives in 1979–80 and the Liberals after they were returned to government in 1980. Under the first Liberal government, the Cabinet had nine standing committees, while under the Conservatives there were seven standing committees and the Inner Cabinet. The second Trudeau government maintained a reduced number of committees and replaced the Inner Cabinet with the Priorities and Planning Committee.

Each committee meets regularly, usually once a week. Ministers normally are members of two or three committees, and each committee has a small permanent secretariat which is provided by the PCO and which controls the flow of committee paper work, helps to set committee agendas, writes the committee decisions, acts as the prime minister's antenna for that sector of the government's activity and generally facilitates the flow of information from the line departments of government and the other executive support agencies to the Cabinet.

In addition to the standing committees, there are also special committees of the Cabinet established from time to time to deal with specific policy problems. For example, there is a semi-permanent Labour Relations Committee which deals with particularly serious national strikes, and from 1980 onward there was an "Ad Hoc Committee on Western Policy" which attempted to redress some of the problems attendant on the lack of Liberal support in the West.

In the Trudeau Cabinet between 1975 and 1979, the normal flow of Cabinet business was from the sponsoring minister to the PCO to be placed on the agenda of the appropriate Cabinet policy committee. Discussion there usually produced a "Committee Recommendation," which then went to the Treasury Board, in its role as the budgetary watchdog, for consideration of the financial and personnel implications. The Treasury Board recommendation together with the committee recommendation then would be presented to the full Cabinet. More often than not recommendations of the policy committees were confirmed, though major discussions might take place in full Cabinet, and policy committee recommendations could be overturned, particularly when the Treasury Board and the policy committee differed in their opinions.

The structure and operations of Cabinet were changed in May of 1979 by the Progressive Conservative government. The major structural innovations were the creation of an Inner Cabinet and of two Ministries of State, for Social and for Economic Development, while the major change in process was the creation of what came to be called the "envelope" system of financial and policy management. The Ministries of State and the envelope system will be described in more detail below. However, the normal flow of Cabinet business under this system was from the sponsoring ministry to a committee of all the deputy ministers in a particular sector. Following its discussion, the item might be aborted but more likely was forwarded to the appropriate Cabinet committee by the sponsoring minister. After Cabinet committee discussion, a decision, again called a "Committee Recommendation," was prepared and forwarded to Inner Cabinet. These were nearly always approved, for a very important feature of the system was the delegation of real decision-making authority to the committees of Cabinet. The full Cabinet seldom met and at the time of the Conservative government's defeat seemed to be well on the way to *de facto* extinction.

Figure 19.2
The Committee Structure of the Cabinet
(1979 Clark Version)

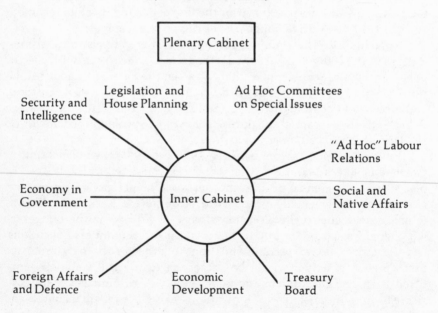

The reincarnated Liberal government of 1980 retained the basic outlines of this structure and process, though the Priorities and Planning Committee was substituted for the Inner Cabinet, and the institution of weekly meetings of full Cabinet was reinstated. Both the Conservative

Inner Cabinet and the Liberal Committee on Priorities and Planning have had memberships of about twelve ministers. The prime minister acts as chairperson. The minister of finance, the president of the Treasury Board, the chairpersons of the standing committees, and some other ministers assumed to be particularly close to the prime minister or particularly strong in other respects make up the rest of the group.

The Inner Cabinet or the Priorities and Planning Committee performs four major roles. First, it allocates budgets to the standing committees of Cabinet. These are, in effect, the cheques in the "envelopes" of the envelope system. Second, it reviews all committee decisions, though this frequently amounts simply to ratification. Third, it deals directly with particularly big or important issues or those which cut across the lines of responsibility of other committees. And finally, it has had some funds and program responsibilities of its own, such as equalization payments to the provinces.

Figure 19.3
The Committee Structure of the Cabinet
(1980 Trudeau Version)

In both the Liberal and Conservative versions of this system, the normal input to a Cabinet committee has been a "Memorandum to Cabinet" backed up by a more detailed "Discussion Paper." The memoranda are not made public, but the discussion papers (which contain the same information as that in the memoranda, often amplified with considerable technical detail but without the "political considerations")

are public documents under new Freedom of Information legislation. By far the largest number of these documents are written within the bureaucracy. They may express demands arising within the bureaucracy (for example, when officials ask for changes in departmental terms of reference or programs), they may result from demands which have been communicated from outside through bureaucratic channels, or they may represent departmental responses to ministerial requests generated by political communication channels such as caucus, the party organization or the minister's own contacts.

Items appearing before Cabinet committees may also be written by individual ministers or by the Ministries of State. Memoranda produced personally by a minister are very rare, but they may appear when ministers want to deal with politically sensitive topics. More often, however, under those circumstances a minister will simply ask that the room be cleared of officials and then will deal with the problem orally. Memoranda produced by Ministries of State may appear when the subject is a major policy change cutting across the interests of several departments, when a major statement of priorities is required, when committee procedures are at issue or when financial concerns dealing with a whole sector require Cabinet consideration.

The creation of a committee structure for Cabinet was begun under Lester Pearson in the mid-1960s. The structure was slowly elaborated and the procedures gradually formalized during the pre-1979 Trudeau government. The creation of an Inner Cabinet, of the "envelope" system, the delegation of much effective final decision-making power to committees, together with the virtual elimination of full Cabinet as a decision-making body marked another major step in the evolution of Cabinet structures. However, as we will see below, these changes, which took place on the occasion of the accession to power of the Progressive Conservative government in 1979, were evolutionary and not revolutionary. This allowed the retention of the basic outlines and all the major features of the newer system when the Liberals took office again in March 1980.

Support Agencies: The Cabinet's Advisors

Figure 19.4 presents a taxonomy of the various agencies which provide support to Cabinet in its priority determination role, classified according to their functions. The agencies are classified by their primary and formal roles, but in practice all of them are concerned to a greater or lesser degree with all of the functions. In particular, political considerations colour all of their deliberations; since their job is to provide support for political leaders, it could hardly be otherwise.

It is important, however, to differentiate between partisan considerations and political considerations. The Prime Minister's Office, ministerial staffs, the party structures and caucus provide advice and support to ministers because those ministers are of a particular partisan stripe. If the government changes, these people lose their jobs. Indeed, even if the incumbent of a position changes without a change of government, partisan advisors are likely to find themselves jobless. Their loyalty is thus to a very particular set of people. By contrast, all of the other executive support agencies provide advice for the government of the day regardless of its partisan stripe. When it is defeated, they provide similar support for the next government. They are employed on a permanent basis by the government and not by a particular party, and while, being human, they will inevitably have their private preferences as to parties and incumbents, they will generally serve as well as they are able, regardless of personal feelings, because they are career public servants.

Figure 19.4
Executive Support Agencies for Priority Determination

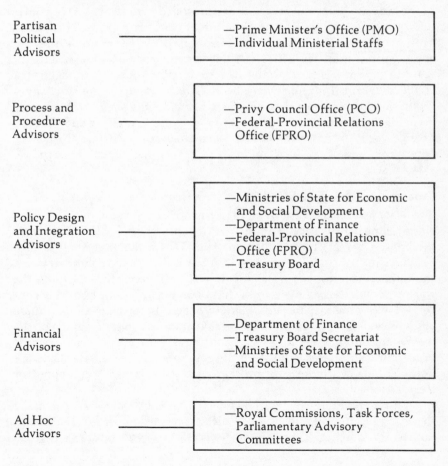

Partisan Political Advisors	—Prime Minister's Office (PMO) —Individual Ministerial Staffs
Process and Procedure Advisors	—Privy Council Office (PCO) —Federal-Provincial Relations Office (FPRO)
Policy Design and Integration Advisors	—Ministries of State for Economic and Social Development —Department of Finance —Federal-Provincial Relations Office (FPRO) —Treasury Board
Financial Advisors	—Department of Finance —Treasury Board Secretariat —Ministries of State for Economic and Social Development
Ad Hoc Advisors	—Royal Commissions, Task Forces, Parliamentary Advisory Committees

Partisan Political Advisors

The Prime Minister's Office is always staffed at the senior levels by close partisan advisors and often by personal friends of the prime minister. The staff has grown rapidly over the last twelve years and currently numbers over one hundred. By contrast R.B. Bennett had a staff of about twelve during the 1930s, while King, St Laurent and Diefenbaker had about thirty staff members and Lester Pearson about forty. However, the number of top policy advisors within the PMO has not increased nearly as quickly as these figures might imply; about half the staff of the PMO is there only to handle the vastly increased volume of prime ministerial mail.

The ways in which a prime minister will use the PMO vary from leader to leader and even from time to time. In the early Trudeau years, the PMO was avowedly the source of many major policy initiatives. Later, as an election approached followed by a minority government and another election, the PMO became much more a partisan machine devoted to the survival of the government. It has tended to remain that way since, with policy innovations being generated by other agencies. There have been important recent exceptions. In August 1978, for example, the PMO and the prime minister, acting virtually alone, produced a major series of restraint proposals and established the first national refundable tax credit program. Indeed, it may be that making major policy changes requires a sudden centralization of authority of the sort which can only occur in the federal government when the prime minister and the PMO take power into their own hands. Then they can act before the web of opposition, which can form rapidly in Ottawa, has time to materialize.

Process Advisors: The Privy Council Office

The PMO and its non-partisan first cousin, the Privy Council Office, share prime office space in a nineteenth-century office block just across Wellington Street from Parliament Hill. This symbolizes their role of serving the prime minister and, in the case of the PCO, its role of servicing the Cabinet committees which meet on the hill. Since the late 1960s the role of the PCO has evolved from that of an agency almost entirely concerned with moving paper to Cabinet, through an attempt to coordinate all aspects of government policy, to a position as arbiter of much of the machinery and process of government in Ottawa and as briefer of the prime minister on the activities of the government. These latter tasks are now combined with the function of providing major logistical support for the Cabinet.

The PCO contains secretariats for each Cabinet committee. Normally these consist of some four to eight officers headed by an assistant secretary to the Cabinet. There are also secretariats or directorates responsible for the machinery of government and for senior personnel. The whole structure is headed by Canada's highest-ranking public servant, the clerk of the Privy Council and secretary of the Cabinet.

To understand the recent evolution of the Privy Council Office and to set our later consideration of other support agencies in context, it is necessary to understand the general evolution of planning processes and the interrelationships among central agencies in Ottawa. To achieve that, we will start with the years prior to 1968, when the bureaucratic establishment dominated the formulation and implementation of policy details and when a small group of senior bureaucratic "mandarins" played a major—some would claim dominant—role in the process of policy choice.

The influence of mandarins over the determination of priorities was based on a number of factors, some related to structural features of the system and others to the personal characteristics of the individuals involved. The most important of the structural factors was simply that government was smaller and less complex. There were very few "old Ottawa hands," and it was possible for them to know each other well. When this was combined with the deputy minister's control over the flow of information within the system, and with the fact that deputies normally held office over a considerably longer time than ministers, the potential for very powerful influence existed.

It is probable that the heyday of the mandarins would have passed of its own accord. As government grew more complex, the structures of government became increasingly formal and elaborate, the number of deputies grew too large for easy direct communication, and bureaucratic power became more diffused. Moreover, informal structures of power often vanish simply because they are powerful; their power eventually makes them visible and their visibility makes them a mark for others— such as ministers and MPs—who may hold a more formal title to control over the system and who jealously guard their own authority from encroachment.

All of this coincided with, or perhaps led to, the avowed intention of the Trudeau government of 1968 to temper the influence of the senior public service by providing alternative sources of policy advice. To this end, Prime Minister Trudeau and his advisors hypothesized that the most effective counter for one institution is another with parallel responsibilities. The political advisory power of the mandarins was to be attenuated through the increase in size and influence of the PMO. Their planning functions were to be faced with competition from a revamped PCO using a more systematic approach to the divination and implementation of political priorities.

The Privy Council Office and its planning system never quite fulfilled the hopes (or fears) expressed for it in the 1970s. In part the problems derived from a tendency by the members of departments and other central agencies to view the revamped PCO as an organization of "upstarts" and "outsiders." Although in fact it was composed of regular public service personnel, this resentment was probably inevitable; any agency with a new and powerful mandate will be viewed in that light by the old hands. While that is a problem which can be overcome by time, there were larger problems internal to the PCO itself. While a considerable amount of broad system-oriented planning capacity was added to the PCO, rather little in the way of more specialized types of technical expertise was put in place. Thus its ability to conduct independent analyses and critiques of specific policy proposals emanating from departments remained limited.

The causes of most of these difficulties may well have lain simply in good intentions. The other central agencies of the early 1970s, the Treasury Board Secretariat and the Department of Finance, already conducted independent appraisals of most major policy proposals, albeit based upon different sets of premises than those used by the PCO. Thus, the pursuit of efficiency would seem to have argued against too greatly expanding another central agency even if the dictates of establishing an alternative planning system based upon political priorities might have demanded it. But whatever the reasoning, the successive heads of the PCO exhibited a definite reluctance to create another central agency "monster" in Ottawa.

Another problem also plagued the PCO planning efforts of the 1970s. They were to be based on ministerial priorities, yet the PCO found it could not effectively implement the statements of priorities that it got from the Cabinet. It was simply impossible to sort out the diverse proposals emanating from departments and to identify by reference to Cabinet priorities what should be accepted or rejected. It may be that the ephemeral nature of Cabinet's political priorities doomed such an effort to failure before it started. However, this problem was compounded by the lack of an institutional mechanism which would force ministers to trade off one proposal against another in such a way that no matter what anyone *said*, the real priorities of government would emerge and only the more politically vital of proposals would be accepted. Combined with difficulties of different sorts faced by the Department of Finance and the Treasury Board—problems to which we will turn later—the result was a predictable dispersion of government activities and a lack of coherent strategies in fields such as industrial development or social or cultural policy. We will look at more recent attempts to solve these problems in the next section.

Policy Design and Integration Advisors

Among earlier attempts to solve problems created by both a lack of information and the difficulty of defining priorities was the creation in the early 1970s of Ministries of State for Science and Technology and for Urban Affairs. These were to collect information and, if necessary, conduct research, and they were to use the power of superior knowledge to provide program integration. However, they had no direct control over departmental budgets, no large budgets of their own and no sympathetic Cabinet committee through which to report or to block unacceptable proposals. Unfortunately, contrary to the old adage, it turned out that knowledge is not power—at least not enough of it to move a large department or a determined minister set on having his or her way. At the time of this writing only one such ministry, Science and Technology, survives, and its policy role is still ambiguous.

The next stage in this evolution unfolded on the economic development front. By 1978 it appeared that if Canada was to compete successfully in the world of international trade, some coherent, national industrial strategy was required. Consequently a Board of Economic Development Ministers was created under the chairmanship of Robert Andras, one of the most powerful Cabinet ministers of the late 1970s. The Board met regularly over several months but faced persistent problems because while it discussed policy and its deliberations were supported by a strong deputy minister and secretariat, there was still no institutional mechanism to force either the integration of policies or restraint.

The solution to that problem was deceptively simple—give the Board (soon to be reconstituted as the Cabinet Committee on Economic Development) responsibility for control of the entire economic development budget. The possibility of the creation of separate budgets for various policy sectors has been considered in Ottawa on and off since at least the early 1970s. However, that implied a significant institutional alignment and, given the rigidities inherent in all large institutions, could not be implemented until the appropriate conjunction of forces appeared. This conjunction was afforded by the arrival of the new Progressive Conservative government in 1979. Newly appointed ministers, without long-established turf to defend, were much more likely to accept a new expenditure management system than was a set of ministers long in place. We have already seen that the return of a Liberal government in March 1980 did not change the trend of this evolution, except that the allocation of envelope figures was to be carried out by the reconstituted Cabinet Committee on Priorities and Planning rather than by the now defunct but functionally similar Inner Cabinet.

The new separate budgets or "envelopes" had to be administered and, more important, Cabinet committees had to be given support in the making of tradeoffs necessary to stay within the limits of the budget envelopes and in ensuring the integration of policy. This job would be most difficult on the economic development and social policy scenes. Thus two new agencies in the form of Ministries of State for Economic and Regional Development and for Social Development were created.

The ministries, created as an integral part of this new process, are relatively small, containing fewer than two hundred staff members. Each engages in long-range planning functions for its sector, administers the budgets for new programs within its area of responsibility (with the budgets for ongoing programs being managed by the Treasury Board) and attempts to ensure policy coordination throughout its sector. Each gains its primary influence by acting as a gatekeeper in the policy and financial management systems: before proposals go to the appropriate Cabinet committee they are normally widely discussed with ministry officials and considered by a committee of deputy ministers chaired by the deputy minister or "secretary" who leads the Ministry of State. The Cabinet committee is provided with written advice on the basis of these deliberations, and, in addition, the ministry briefs the chairperson of the Cabinet committee and can use that occasion to forward any reservations it may have about a proposal. Coordination and integration within the sector is to be achieved through the overview functions of these agencies and because proposals will not normally proceed to Cabinet committees before a thorough examination by the ministries. In addition the ministries themselves may initiate proposals and may retain responsibility for coordinating "events" such as national sectoral conferences or federal–provincial negotiations in their sector. A branch of the Department of External Affairs performs ministry of state functions for the Cabinet committee on External and Defense policy.

Overall policy integration with respect to federal–provincial concerns is the responsibility of the Federal–Provincial Relations Office (FPRO). In the late 1970s there was also a minister of state for federal–provincial relations, but this post has at least temporarily vanished. The place of FPRO in the policy and fiscal management system has sometimes been less clearly defined than that of the Ministries of State, for the FPRO has not performed a budgetary gatekeeper role, has no Cabinet committee of its own and has therefore relatively little direct influence over departments. It has thus at times been an agency which departments and other central agencies were prone to overlook in their day-to-day activities. However, it has had a significant role in briefing the prime minister on the federal–provincial relations aspects of issues, and it performed a major role in the constitutional discussions. Under the strong hands of its last two secretaries (deputy ministers), it has thus played an increasing role in the policy process in Ottawa.

Financial Advisors

Figure 19.4 shows the Department of Finance, the Treasury Board and the Ministries of State for Economic and Regional Development and Social Development both as policy design and integration advisors and as financial advisors. It is in the latter role that Treasury Board and Finance are pre-eminent, but the increasing integration of financial management and policy coordination means that Finance and Treasury Board have important policy integration functions while the Ministries of State have important financial management functions.

The Treasury Board is a statutory committee of the Privy Council. The Board itself is composed of the president of the Treasury Board, who is its chairperson and is also the minister in charge of the Secretariat, the minister of finance (ex officio) and five other ministers. The Financial Administration Act, which is the legislation governing the expenditure process, delegates to Treasury Board responsibility as the overseer of the budgetary process. In support of this role the Treasury Board Secretariat keeps track of current and projected expenditures within envelopes according to a common set of rules and advises the Policy and Priority Committee on envelope requirements from year to year. Moreover, the Treasury Board is coming to function more and more as the board of management for the government, having responsibility for labour relations, for many aspects of personnel policy, for "person-year" allocations to departments and for administrative and financial policy. The net result of all this is to make the Treasury Board and its large (four-hundred-person) Secretariat highly influential in both financial management and policy coordination.

The Department of Finance retains primary responsibility for advising the government on economic policy in general, for the bulk of transfer payments to the provinces and for the effect of government policies on the economy. It is the primary advisor to the Committee on Planning and Priorities when expenditure allocations are made for the various policy envelopes. Finally, it is responsible for the raising of revenues. This gives it authority over all aspects of the taxation system, including those devices intended to provide financial inducements to people and corporations to behave in certain ways—the so-called "tax expenditures." In this area it shares some responsibility for the policy aspects of tax expenditures with the Cabinet committees directly responsible for policy in these areas.

Handling Policy Proposals

Perhaps one way of understanding the processes which involve this plethora of agencies is to consider the main questions which might be asked before a major proposal could become a policy. Initially, an assessment of the quality of public demand for the proposal is required. Alternately, since many proposals are generated largely from within the bureaucracy, an assessment of the amount of public support for the policy may be what is called for at this stage. This assessment would be carried out partly by the departments and ministers most directly involved and partly by the appropriate Ministry of State.

Some of the most important questions involving a major policy decision concern the financial feasibility and the macroeconomic effects of such a step. This financial assessment constitutes the second stage in the assessment of a policy proposal. Information from economic forecasts, projections of government revenues and consequent allocations of funds to expenditure envelopes will thus become a vital part of the data required to make any major priority decision, and here the Department of Finance becomes pre-eminent. If Finance is forecasting declining government revenues, then the amount of "new" money allocated to each sector of government expenditures will be small, and barring the availability of some large expenditure reductions, a Cabinet committee will be unable to take on a big new program, however desirable it may otherwise be. Similarly, if the Department of Finance opines that a program will create critical economic problems, the Cabinet may be reluctant to assign a high priority to it. Some Cabinet ministers are not normally economists and, since they are too busy to be able to engage in extensive searches for alternative information, they are rather at the mercy of the Department of Finance when dealing with such issues. Nevertheless, countervailing opinions may be advanced by other agencies or by individual departments, and a healthy skepticism about economic projections prevails.

Closely connected to the foregoing questions are the problems of how such a program could be coordinated with current government activity in other fields and whether there are sufficient funds available in an expenditure "envelope" to finance the program. The Ministries of State for Social and for Economic and Regional Development and the Department of External Affairs, working within their respective budgetary envelopes for the next several fiscal years, must determine whether the potential increase in expenditure can be generated and whether the adoption of a new policy will necessitate the deletion of some current programs or an appeal to Priorities and Planning for additional money for the envelope. The Ministry of State must also consider the fit of the proposed program with ongoing programs in its policy area, advise ministers on the fit of the proposal with overall governmental priorities and apprise them of any administrative problems it sees in the proposal. In this latter role, it will be advised primarily by the Treasury Board Secretariat, which also retains the right to advise Cabinet independently through its minister if it feels its "management board" concerns have not been adequately addressed. The ministries may also originate program proposals themselves in order to replace older programs.

Once the financial and administrative questions have been dealt with, the issue goes to Cabinet committee and then to the full Cabinet. There, in addition to the more technical concerns, ministers will ask the political questions which return again to an assessment of the amount of demand for the policy and its political marketability. The final decisions in Cabinet committee, full Cabinet or Priorities and Planning will result from this balancing of the political and technical issues. Thus, although bureaucratic rationality informs the consideration of the "middle" questions in the policy process, political rationality has the initial and especially the final say.

The Budgetary Cycle

We have indicated that the trend of the last several years has been to create a more and more direct relationship between budgetary processes and the determination of policy priorities; hence the budgetary cycle is the final part of the policy process which requires our consideration.

Until the late 1970s, the budgetary process looked only eighteen months ahead and was used much more as an administrative tool than as an instrument to bring financial considerations into priority determination. The result was a start-stop system of policy making: if revenues were rising almost any policy proposed would be accepted by Cabinet, but when "restraint" hit, as it did periodically, no new policies would be accepted at all and adjustments could not easily be made. In an attempt to smooth out this situation more recent attempts have been made to lengthen the budgetary cycle to a multiyear process and to place priority determination within this cycle, while still leaving sufficient flexibility to deal with emergency situations as they arise.[1] The cycle begins with the preparation of four-year projections of economic conditions and hence of government revenues by the Department of Finance and the parallel preparation of expenditure forecasts by the Treasury Board Secretariat in consultation with Departments. On the basis of these projections of the overall "pie" available and of the requirements to finance ongoing commitments, the Planning and Priorities Committee of Cabinet allocates revenues to the various "envelopes" for the next four years. The making of economic projections is, of course, a risky business at best, while expenditure projections, which themselves depend on economic projections, are equally difficult to make with any accuracy. Nonetheless, if the basic objective is to determine relative priorities and to make them more explicit by assigning dollar values to them, the exercise can still be effective as long as common assumptions are adhered to throughout the system. Moreover, the revenue and expenditure forecasts are updated as time passes, and the final budgetary assessments for a fiscal year made fairly close to its start can be quite accurate.

Following the initial envelope allocations, the Ministries of State and the Treasury Board Secretariat compare the funds available to projected expenditures in order to determine how much financial elbow room the sector has for new programs over the next four years, or alternately, how much is required in the way of reductions in current programs in order to provide such room. Given the rules introduced by the envelope management systems and the usual commitment to restraint, if the government is to implement any new programs it must generally create a pool of money called a "policy reserve" to do so. It does this by reducing older programs. The bulk of expenditures—normally well over 90 percent—remains part of the "A-budget" or "A-base." Perhaps the greatest problem facing this or any other attempt to allow governments to change their priorities is the sanctity of that A-base and the consequent difficulty in creating a policy reserve of any magnitude. However, by a combination of fairly major program changes, the cutting of some small programs, the reduction of some administrative overhead and occasional transfusions from the Minister of Finance, all the envelopes have managed to create policy reserves. Then the problem becomes one of sorting out which new proposals will be accepted. At this point, the policy process described above comes into play.

The four-year expenditure cycle contains within it a more sharply focused twenty-four-month cycle. Approximately twelve months before the start of a fiscal year, the secretary of the Treasury Board and the chairpersons of the Cabinet policy committees send "call letters" to all departments and agencies asking them to prepare five-year "multi-year operating plans" accompanied by "strategic overviews." The strategic overview ideally specifies all the forces likely to impinge on departmental expenditures in the period for which the multi-year operating plan is to be valid. The forecast itself suggests what expenditures departments think will be necessary to cover their ongoing activities (their A-base) during the period. A process of bargaining and negotiation ensues among the Treasury Board (interested in keeping overall expenditures down), the Ministries of State (interested in keeping expenditures within envelope limits while providing some extra B-Budget reallocations) and operating departments (interested in keeping up expenditure levels for their activities and in maintaining maximum amounts of discretionary funds in their own budgets). The bargaining goes through numerous stages, and to it is added the selection of new policies made by the cabinet policy committees up to the limit of envelope reserves for the approaching fiscal year. The result of all of this is the completion, by the end of December preceding the April 1 start of the next fiscal year, of the Main Estimates. These, in the form of a metropolitan-telephone-book-sized "Blue Book," are tabled in the House of Commons early in the new calendar year, considered in parliamentary committees and passed, usually unchanged, in the form of expenditure "votes." These constitute authority for the receiver general of Canada to disburse the funds to departments for expenditure.

In practice this is a very complex process, and it is accompanied by procedures for supplementary estimates and for the audit and evaluation of expenditures. It is further complicated by the fact that the whole system is properly described as a "rolling cycle." As the Main Estimates are being tabled, the multi-year operating plans are being rolled forward one more year, the immediate years updated, new strategic overviews are being prepared, new policy reserves created and new policy selections made. Since most new policies are selected in the early stages of the exercise, the possibility of making adjustments becomes increasingly difficult as the time for the tabling of Main Estimates approaches. In order to deal with this rigidity, Cabinet committees also maintain a reserve fund which can be allocated in emergencies, and there is, in addition, a Treasury Board operating reserve which can be used to cover the statutory program cost increases which are encompassed in the supplementary estimates.

The image which emerges from this is one of considerable complexity and of an expenditure management system in a state of considerable flux as governments attempt to grapple with the problem of maintaining enough flexibility to permit the selection of new policies in an era when social and financial pressures appear to preclude any substantial increase in revenues and expenditures. The objectives of Canadian governments, and indeed of governments throughout the Western world, have been consistent in this regard since at least the early 1970s, and the historical threads of the attempt to achieve better integration of expenditure management and policy selection processes can be traced back to the 1920s. Whether the 1984 model will succeed where its predecessors have not remains to be seen.

Summary and Conclusions

The late 1960s saw the sunset of the mandarin system in Ottawa. The "mandarin as Prime Minister," Lester Pearson, had come and gone, and the last of C.D. Howe's boys were beginning to fade from the Ottawa scene. The growth of government was creating a system too complex to be managed over lunch at the Rideau Club or from the spacious verandahs of the Gatineau Fish and Game Club. If the mandarinate was vanishing, an alternate planning system would be required to take its place. What would fill the vacuum?

In a period characterized by a burgeoning belief in the potential of rational policy analysis and in a world characterized by the division of social science into several disparate ways of viewing the world, it was natural that the vacuum left by the departing mandarins should elicit competition among several alternate systems for the rational planning of government activities. In *How Ottawa Decides,* Richard French defined the three principal policy-planning systems which competed in Ottawa in the 1970s.

The oldest was based upon macroeconomics and was centred—one might say it dwelt almost exclusively—in the Department of Finance. Its early apostles were Keynesians, but by the mid-1970s its acolytes were coming increasingly to doubt the efficacy of Keynesian prescription and were moving, hesitantly, toward monetarism. According to French, the combination of their doubts and of a certain aloofness attributable to the fact that for many years theirs had been the pre-eminent and perhaps the only planning system in town led the Department of Finance to withdraw to a significant degree in the mid-1970s from the scrum created by the presence of other planning systems and the fact that all the line departments were rapidly developing their own planning branches.

The Finance planning system is the least changed as we move into the 1980s. In spite of continuing doubts about the efficacy for purposes of economic management of the macroeconomics on which it is based, it has managed under the leadership of Marc Lalonde to reassert at least some of its pre-eminence of the 1960s. Indeed it could be characterized as the master system, since all other policy deliberations move within the framework set by its revenue and expenditure projections.

The alternate systems were centred in the PCO and in the Planning Branch of the Treasury Board. The latter was based on microeconomics, and its watchword was "evaluation." Its precepts could be stated fairly simply: to make planning more rational it was necessary to evaluate in detail the efficiency and the effectiveness of programs and then to feed the results back to policy makers who would, when apprised of this rational input, make policy choices on the basis of this information. Reams of materials have been produced on the difficulties encountered by microeconomics-inspired and evaluation-based planning processes, much of it by former practitioners grown disenchanted with the potential for introducing rational planning into political decision making. While the Planning Branch planning system never took firm hold in Ottawa, or even managed to dominate its own agency, the Treasury Board, its precepts have not disappeared. The Planning Branch itself did disappear in an austerity move in 1978, but the evaluation function was shifted to the Office of the Comptroller General. As well, the ministries of state, as part of their role in advising Cabinet committees, routinely assess proposals with a type of evaluation which would have been quite familiar to those who worked in the Planning Branch.

We have already made the acquaintance of the third planning system of the 1970s, based primarily in the Privy Council Office. Its origins, disciplinary underpinnings and leadership were more diffuse than the other two systems, and its identity is neither as clear-cut nor as simple to trace. Its leadership is associated with Michael Pitfield more than with anyone else, but it was instigated to a considerable degree by Prime Minister Trudeau and has had several other major disciples. It relied primarily on the "softer" social sciences: sociology and political science with generous doses of law and systems analysis. Since it grew up in the PCO its source of authority was the Cabinet and prime minister, and its strength derived from its ability to claim the correct interpretation of the words of the ministers and the prime minister. That is a powerful weapon in a Cabinet-centred political system, and in spite of some significant problems it grew to be the dominant planning system of the early 1970s.

A variant of the older PCO planning system, inspired by information generated within the Finance system, is still influential in Ottawa in the early 1980s, though it is no longer correct to identify the PCO as the sole centre from which this type of planning emanates. The central body in this system is the Priorities and Planning Committee of Cabinet, which allocates amounts of money to the various expenditure envelopes and which approves decisions made by the envelope sub-committees. It is significant that "P & P" is the only standing committee of Cabinet which is regularly chaired by the prime minister, and it is there that many of the major dramas are played out.

Priorities and Planning is informed in its deliberations by a small secretariat in the Privy Council Office, by the economic projections of Finance, the expenditure projections and management precepts of Treasury Board, by the Federal–Provincial Relations Office and by the priority statements and working plans of the other envelope committees. Coordination of the bureaucracy occurs through the Coordinating Committee, the sectoral deputy ministers' committees and the Treasury Board management system.

Overall, the policy process now appears to be more decentralized *within* the Cabinet, with a major devolution of responsibility to the policy committees. However, it is also probably more centralized toward the Cabinet–central agency nexus *as a whole*, since the pooling of resources in "envelope reserves" means that individual departments now have less control over expenditure reallocations. The major procedural change from the mid-1970s has been the melding of control over expenditures within the Cabinet policy committees in the "envelope" system of management, while the major institutional change has been the creation of Ministries of State to support the Cabinet policy committees in this policy and budgetary control process. Ministers have gained in collective responsibility what they may have lost in individual authority as the titular heads of departments, so it is possible that the actual portfolio held by a minister will, in time, become a less reliable index of influence.

The 1984 model of the planning process does appear to "work" better than its predecessors, but that does not mean that it is without problems. Ministers, after all, thrive on individual recognition, and collective responsibility may sit less happily on the shoulders of the most powerful among them than the visibility and control over resources which has hitherto come from heading an important department. Too, the departments themselves are large and powerful institutions with their own clienteles and considerable ability to frustrate any planning system should they choose to do so. In the end the politics of the policy and planning process in Ottawa are really a kind of democracy among institutions, and coercion is not a particularly viable weapon within that system. The players come voluntarily or not at all.

In the end, then, we must ask what incentives there are to cooperate within any of these systems. The answer, as is true in any complex set of bureaucratic and political institutions, is power and influence. The powerful actors on the Ottawa scene will "play" within a new system if they perceive that it will enhance, or at least not diminish, their power. And since the total amount of power is basically constant, this competition means that the success or failure of a system is necessarily always a very closely balanced question.

Indeed, about all that can be predicted with certainty is that no planning system is forever: as actors come and go new positions of power and new systems evolve. Thus any description of planning processes in Ottawa has only an ephemeral value—making it incumbent on the wise reader to consult sources such as newspapers, magazines and journals for the latest grey pattern of the kaleidoscope.

Notes

1. There have been earlier attempts to introduce priority or goal setting into the budgetary cycle, most notably the somewhat abortive Planning Programming Budgeting System (PPBS) of the early 1970s.

Further Readings

Doern, G.B., and P. Aucoin. *Public Policy in Canada.* Toronto: Macmillan, 1979.
Doern, G.B., and R. Phidd. *Canadian Public Policy.* Toronto: Methuen, 1983.
French, R. *How Ottawa Decides.* Toronto: Lorimer, 1984.
Hockin, T. *Apex of Power.* Scarborough: Prentice-Hall, 1977.

Maslove, Allan M., ed. *How Ottawa Spends*. Toronto: Methuen, 1984. Published annually.

Phidd, R.W., and G.B. Doern. *The Politics and Management of Canadian Economic Policy*. Toronto: Macmillan, 1978.

Royal Commission on Financial Management and Accountability. *Reports*, DSS, 1979.

Wilson, V.S. *Canadian Public Policy and Administration*. Toronto: McGraw-Hill, 1981.

Chapter 20

Regulatory Agencies
Richard Schultz

Regulation, long a significant governmental activity, has emerged in recent years to rival taxing and spending as a primary means by which governments seek to influence, direct and control social and economic behaviour. One measure, albeit a crude one, of the growing importance of regulation is its phenomenal growth. In the past ten years, the federal government passed more pieces of regulatory legislation than it had in the previous thirty years. The total number of pages of regulations has increased from 1,849 in 1949 to 7,722 in 1978.[1] But it is not simply a matter of sheer growth. It is equally important to recognize that there has been a significant change in the functions of regulation. Previously, regulation was used to police or prohibit particular forms of behaviour or to promote or create an environment within which an activity could flourish. Today, these traditional functions are joined, and often superseded, by a planning function whereby regulation is used to direct private activities toward the attainment of publicly established social and economic objectives. In large part because of the growth and the changing role of regulation, the politics of regulation—who gains, who loses and the various processes and institutions involved—have become a subject of increasing academic and public attention.

It must be recognized, however, that the concept of "regulation" is exceedingly nebulous and can encompass virtually every form of government intervention. Given space constraints, this chapter will examine only one type of regulation, namely that which is undertaken by independent or autonomous agencies such as the Canadian Transport Commission and the National Energy Board. We find such agencies in the energy, transportation, broadcasting and telecommunications areas, where they perform a varied range of functions. They issue licences for radio and television stations, pipeline construction and nuclear reactors. They set the rates or fares for telephone calls, airline tickets and cable television outlets. They make policies and prescribe rules and regulations that govern the extent of Canadian programming on television, the quality of telephone service and the amount of gas and oil that can be exported from Canada.

Although there is a wide range of political issues associated with regulation by independent agency, we will confine ourselves to five of the more important. They are the "capture" theory, the accountability and political control of the regulators, the role of the agencies in our federal system, the general issue of public participation in the regulatory process and the limited movement to deregulation in Canada compared to that in the United States.

Regulation and the Capture Theory

If Canadians know anything at all about regulation and regulatory agencies, they know that agencies are "captured" by the very interests they are supposed to regulate. It would almost be better if Canadians knew nothing at all. The "capture theory" stipulates that regulatory agencies, which were ostensibly established to regulate economic and social behaviour in various fields, become "captured" (a later version says "bought") by the regulated and cease to regulate in the "public interest." Instead, it is claimed that they regulate to protect and enhance the private interests of the regulated. This theory is largely based on the work of an American political scientist, Marver Bernstein, particularly his influential book *Regulating Business by Independent Commission*. In this work, Bernstein advanced the theory that regulatory agencies go through a "life cycle" of "gestation, youth, maturity and old age." The end result of this cycle, "old age," finds the agency passive and apathetic and performing, not its original function of society's police, but that of "recognized protector of the industry."

Few political science conceptions have become as thoroughly entrenched as part of the conventional wisdom as the "capture theory." In part, this is because it is such a richly suggestive theory and in part because there are numerous examples of regulatory agencies which do act as protectors rather than police. Nevertheless, notwithstanding its popularity, the theory does have its critics and some significant defects. In the first place, some have maintained that far from being created to protect the public interest and, accordingly, imposed upon private economic actors, some regulatory agencies were established because of political pressures from those very actors. Thus, Gabriel Kolko, in his *Railroads and Regulation*, contends that in the United States the introduction of regulation can be traced to the demands from *within the railway industry* for the *benefit of the railway industry*. The benefits included protection from competition and for price fixing, and the costs were borne by railway users and society at large.

Other critics have argued, without adopting the negative, critical perspective of the preceding, that some agencies, like some people, were born old. Such agencies, it is argued, were not captured, but were created explicitly to regulate in such a way as to promote and protect a specific industry because this was believed to be in the best interests of society. Still others would contend that one should not be surprised by the close relationship between the regulators and regulated because it is inevitable and does not require capture. As early as 1936, during the period when many forms of regulation were introduced, Pendleton Herring maintained that in general, with greater governmental intervention in the economy, the regulated will attain leverage over their regulators. It was his argument that "the greater the degree of detailed and technical control the government seeks to exert over industrial and commercial interests, the greater must be their degree of consent and active participation in the very process of regulation, if regulation is to be effective or successful."[2] More recently, Charles Lindblom has proposed that this leverage derives from the "privileged position of business" and this, more than any "life cycle," is the dominant influence.[3] In support of this, it could be argued that the close relationships that exist between departments and their "clienteles" such as in transportation and agriculture, argue against the need for any "capture theory" and that what is involved is part of a more general phenomenon.[4]

There is no necessity here to argue the merits or demerits of the "capture theory." For our purposes, the major problem with it is that it can cloud more than it can explain if it is ritually invoked so as to end all debate about the nature of the regulatory process. If we know that agencies are "invariably" captured, what else is there to know? My answer is "plenty!" Rather than assuming away the forces behind the creation of a regulatory agency, we need detailed empirical studies of the political actors involved, the resources they possessed, the arenas in which they fought their battles, and the political circumstances which produced a regulatory agency with a specific mandate and set of powers. To date we have not had these studies in Canada. We have ignored such issues, taken for granted that they were created in the "public interest," or assumed the operation of the "capture theory."

The need for such studies is all the more pressing because in several important areas of regulation in Canada, one finds the presence of a crown corporation whose existence predates or coincides with the creation of the regulatory agency. Certainly this was the case in air transport with Air Canada (then Trans Canada Airlines), and the situation is even more complicated in broadcasting where the CBC, for a long period, was both competitor and regulator of its competition. These situations which involve regulatory instances of that staple of government intervention in Canada, namely "defensive expansion" in the face of our more powerful continental neighbour, should make one wary of simply assuming the fact of "capture."

Another important factor in shaping the regulatory process in Canada has been the nature of appointments to the agencies. In the

United States, one of the empirical supports for the capture theory is the close connection between agencies and regulated industries in terms of both appointments and post-agency employment. In Canada, the limited information available suggests that the public service is a far more important source for appointments and that regulators have longer regulatory careers.[5] Indeed, this evidence suggests the hypothesis that regulatory agencies, if they are captured, are captured by governments. Unless one equates the public interest with governmental interest, this possibility raises as many intriguing questions and issues as the assumption of industry capture.

All this is not to argue that the "capture theory" is irrelevant to the Canadian experience. It is simply to suggest that at best it offers a set of interesting hypotheses. We need to study, as I have indicated, the origins of specific agencies, the nature of the regulation that emerges, the nature of the regulatory process as a form of the larger political process that ensues. We also need to analyze the impact of different variables, such as the role of organizational forces on the interests and interactions in the regulatory process. Finally, we need to study the regulatory process over time. There are numerous examples, the obverse of Bernstein's theory, where previously quiescent regulators become social crusaders. What political forces led to such changes? How does one explain them? Are they simply aberrations from the norm or are they intrinsic to the politics of regulation in Canada? Attempting to answer such questions can fill up many political scientists' research agendas.

Regulatory Agencies and Political Control

In the preceding section we raised the possibility that regulatory agencies can be captured by governmental rather than economic forces. On the surface, this may not appear to be that significant an issue, but it becomes one when one analyses the rationale not for regulation *per se*, but for the specific variant of regulation, namely that by independent agency or commission. We are concerned in this paper with what are commonly called *independent regulatory agencies*, and in this section we want to concentrate on the nature and scope of that independence. Why are they independent? How independent are they? How can one justify giving political power to decision makers who may not be subject to meaningful political control? How can the exercise of such power be constrained and supervised? These are all important questions that are central to one of the political debates about government regulation in Canada today, namely the need to make regulators subject to effective political control and the alternative means for accomplishing such a goal.

Regulatory agencies constitute one group of non-departmental governmental bodies that Hodgetts labelled "structural heretics," though with the increasing number of such bodies the heresy involved threatens to become the orthodoxy.[6] The agencies are heretics because they involve minimally the attenuation and maximally the denial of ministerial responsibility. The objective of the system of ministerial responsibility, in theory at least, is to ensure the accountability of the government, and its members, to the House of Commons; it is premised on the convention that ministers are responsible to the House for both their actions and for those of public servants who act in their names. Ministers are not responsible for the actions of independent regulatory agencies; for their part, the agencies are independent of, or free from, ministerial control. This freedom is, of course, relative and not absolute, and below we will outline the limits.

The nature of regulatory agency independence has two basic dimensions. In the first place, the members of regulatory commissions have tenure for fixed terms, usually ranging from five to ten years. A member cannot be removed prior to the end of his or her term except "for cause," which is essentially limited to either an incapacity to perform his or her responsibilities or malfeasance in office. This contrasts with deputy ministers and other senior appointees, for example, who serve "at pleasure" and can be easily removed, as happened several years ago to the Chairman of the Canadian Dairy Commission simply because the Minister of Agriculture wanted to put his own man in the position. In this respect, although their terms are for fixed periods and not for a statutorily defined lifetime, members of regulatory agencies possess an independence of tenure similar to that which has traditionally protected the judiciary.

Of course, independent tenure would be insignificant if the agencies were not delegated important powers. It is what an agency can do, free from ministerial control, that makes independence an issue. Although we cannot survey all their powers here (the Administrative Law Series of the Law Reform Commission provides very useful studies of several individual agencies), we can outline the four major types of powers that they can exercise. The first, and the original, is an adjudicative power; that is, the power to judge specific cases involving the granting, denial or removal of licences, the approving of rates or fares and the censuring of failure to comply with terms of licences. Secondly, an agency may have legislative powers which enable it to formulate general rules or regulations applicable to classes or categories subject to the agency's regulatory authority. The CRTC, for example, has issued volumes of regulations establishing, among other things, Canadian content quotas on television and radio and the amount and types of music and talk allowed on AM and FM radio. The third power an agency usually possesses is a research or investigative power to inquire into any matter within its jurisdiction. Finally, an agency may be empowered to administer governmental programs involving subsidies or research grants.

We indicated earlier that we have not had many detailed historical analyses that seek to explain the creation of particular independent agencies. Nevertheless, several general explanations can be advanced for the resort to independent agencies. One is that the type of regulation involved required specialized regulators. The tasks were considered to be particularly complex, requiring technical training, expertise and continuous attention. Neither politicians, nor the early public service, nor the courts were deemed capable of performing such functions. The second major requirement was that regulation was to be impartial. Under the "public interest" theory, regulation, while deemed to be necessary, was, nevertheless, considered to entail interference with the freedom of private economic decision makers. Consequently, it should not be affected by partisanship or favouritism and, to meet this objective, required delegation to regulators who would be insulated from political pressures by their independence. For advocates of the various "capture theories," similar insulation is required, but for different reasons, namely not wanting any political interference with the use of public power to promote and defend private interests. Even politicians could gain from agency independence because the agencies, not the politicians, would have to take the "heat" for difficult decisions.

Regulatory agency independence is, of course, relative and not absolute and there are a number of control mechanisms, both informal and formal. Among these mechanisms are the appointment power of the government which is particularly important with respect to agency executive positions such as chairman and vice-chairman. Another is the approval of agency budgets, which can be very useful, away from the glare of publicity, to persuade agencies of the government's wisdom. This is not likely to be employed on individual cases (though its use is not entirely unheard of in such circumstances), but is more likely to be used in suggesting general directions for an individual agency.

By far the most important control mechanism is the fact that the government can normally send back and overturn agency decisions, either on appeal from an interested party or on its own initiative. In most cases the government is limited to vetoing agency decisions, while in one, the Canadian Transport Commission, the government can actually substitute its own decision for that of the Commission. Some have suggested that the "political appeal" mechanism, as it has been called, makes a mockery of agency independence. This is an exaggeration. In the first place, an appeal mechanism does not mean that the independence of the agency is undermined, but only that it does not have the ultimate decision-making authority. *Within its own powers*, the agency cannot be dictated to by political authorities. Secondly, and more importantly, the political appeal mechanism must be used sparingly if the authority of the agency is not to be undermined. Used too frequently as a means of second-guessing the regulatory agency, it would surely damage the legitimacy and rationale for having regulatory agencies. Both the government and the agencies appreciate this fact, which reinforces their general independence and freedom of decision making.

Notwithstanding the existence of the various control mechanisms described, one of the central debates surrounding independent agencies in the last decade has been their independence and the inadequacies of the control mechanisms. Although a number of explanations can be advanced for this debate, I would suggest that a central reason has been the evolution in the function of regulation and, hence, the political importance of the regulators. For most of this century, governments had no real need for continuous surveillance and supervision of independent agencies, and this was reflected in the fact that the political appeal mechanism was used extremely sparingly until the 1970s. One reason for this is that for a long time what the agencies did had no political significance, except insofar as politicians were insulated from controversial, no-win political issues.

This is no longer the case, because regulation by independent agency has increasingly entailed political decision making. This is largely because regulation is not simply negative and proscriptive, but increasingly is positive and prescriptive. Regulation entails not just policing but planning the activities and relationships of those subject to the agencies' mandates. The decisions of regulatory agencies can have an enormous impact on the allocation of resources, on the distribution of income and on the organization of production and consumption across the country. When regulation involves a planning function, it becomes inherently a political function and the regulatory process becomes deeply entwined in the political process. When one recognizes not only the changing nature of the regulatory function but also the combination of adjudicative, legislative and administrative powers delegated to regulatory agencies—a combination that leads them to be designated "governments in miniature"—one cannot avoid appreciating the political nature and role of regulatory agencies.

The political role of regulatory agencies is enhanced and reinforced by the scope for policy making that has accrued to them. This scope is primarily the result of their very vague statutory mandates. For some, their statutes contain little policy guidance other than the stipulation that "public convenience and necessity" be established or that rates be "just and reasonable." Even when statutes contain extensive policy prescriptions, these may be so ambiguous that anything is permissible. The Canadian Radio-television and Telecommunications Commission, for example, is enjoined to regulate so as to "safeguard, enrich and strengthen the cultural, political, social and economic fabric of Canada." The responsibility of the Canadian Transport Commission is to regulate so as to promote "an economic, efficient and adequate transportation system." The inevitable consequence of the "blank cheque," or lack of definitive statements of statutory policy to guide regulators, to paraphrase Lowi, is that such "broad discretion makes a politician out of a regulator."[7] Combined with the prescriptive, planning function that regulation has come to play, this broad discretion has meant that regulation and regulatory agencies have become highly politicized.

The federal government's answer to the politicization of regulation and the agencies is to propose enhanced political control. They would do this by reducing the degree of discretion delegated to regulatory agencies. The government has recognized that agencies have assumed a policy-making role, rather than being an instrument for the implementation of policy, though it has placed the blame on the nature of the policy statements found in their legislative mandates and not on the function of regulation. Rather than correcting this situation with more specific, detailed statements, the government has proposed that it be empowered to issue "policy directives" to independent regulatory agencies. This would mean that the government would be empowered to issue authoritative interpretations of the general statutory policy statements, and that the agencies would be obliged to respect these interpretations when they decide individual cases or develop sets of regulations.

There is much merit in such a proposal, though it is not without its critics, both within agencies and from outside the government. One criticism is that such a power would undermine the independence of the agency to make impartial decisions on individual cases. Some regulators maintain that one cannot separate individual applications from the statutory statements of policy, and that any attempt to do so will erode the rationale for an independent agency. Others concede that the principle of the policy directive is sound but that, as proposed by the government, there are inadequate safeguards to protect not only the rights of the agencies but those of the public and Parliament. They would argue that the government should not unilaterally be empowered to issue directives which, in effect, can amend statutes without providing for parliamentary, public and agency input.

The call for safeguards was endorsed, with specific proposals, by the 1979 Royal Commission on Financial Management and Accountability and by the Economic Council of Canada. Before the issues of how much discretion is to be delegated to independent agencies and with respect to what functions are decided, much work remains to be done. The appropriate roles and responsibilities of the central participants need to be re-examined and redefined. In addition to the "policy directive" proposal, the powers of regulation making and political appeals need to be reassessed. Finally, one may also query whether we are not asking, or allowing, regulatory agencies to do too much and whether the issue is not new political control tools, but a more circumscribed role, not just for regulators, but for regulation itself?

Regulatory Agencies and the Federal System

If the evolution of the function of regulation, combined with the inadequacy of statutory policy guidance, have underscored the political nature of regulation, much of the credit for politicizing the issue of regulatory agencies must go to provincial governments. With the growth of interdependence of the two levels of government and the economic and social interventionism of provincial governments which is so vividly captured by the concept of "province-building," regulatory agencies inevitably became embroiled in the debates that have dominated the Canadian federal system in the past decade. As provinces sought to control more of the forces affecting their environment, both by expanding their own activities and by insisting that the federal government not only consult more extensively with them but also coordinate its activities with theirs, they increasingly confronted an anomaly in an interdependent political world, federal independent regulatory agencies.

Provincial governments have contended that the nature of, and the scope for, independent action by federal regulatory agencies may conflict with the imperatives of interdependence which dominate the contemporary Canadian federal system. They maintain that regulatory independence can impede and frustrate the effective functioning of a system which demands intergovernmental policy coordination and integration.

Their concerns have focused on three main issues: regulatory appointments, procedures and policy decisions. On the question of appointments, provincial governments have argued that since regulators can play such an influential policy role, much more care must be taken to ensure that appropriate individuals are appointed, especially to the senior executive positions. More specifically, they believe that regulators must be more responsive to, and representative of, the diverse regional interests in Canada and that this has not been the case in the past. Consequently, some provincial governments have argued that they should be able to appoint members of federal regulatory agencies either directly or indirectly, perhaps through a revised Senate with provincial appointees which would confirm regulatory nominations. Other provinces have suggested that the federal government should at least consult with provincial governments on appointments, and in fact the Clark government requested provincial recommendations for the chairmanship of the CRTC.

The provinces clearly have a legitimate concern about the nature of the appointment process and the representativeness of agency memberships. It should be recognized, however, that provincial interests are not the only legitimate interests that merit representation. Moreover, the proposal for direct provincial appointments to federal agencies raises enormous potential for undermining the independence of regulators by stressing their representative obligations rather than their role as impartial decision makers.

The second point of contention for provincial governments has been the procedural practices of some of the federal agencies. There are several problems here, but the most important concerns provincial access to relevant regulatory information. In the past, and most particularly with respect to railway regulation, some provinces have felt that they have been denied relevant information with which to assess the demands of the regulated companies. This had led to accusations that the regulator has been "captured" by the railways and is insufficiently committed to protecting the public interest. Similar charges have been levelled at federal regulation of airlines and telecommunications based in part on the unwillingness of the regulator to release relevant information. In the case of railway regulation, provincial pressure was sufficient to have the federal government pass legislation requiring the CTC to provide information on a confidential basis to provincial governments. That legislation was necessary suggests the seriousness of the regulatory agency obstacle.

By far the most important provincial concern arising from regulatory independence is agency policy making. Provincial governments have argued that in many areas of vital interest to them, authority to make policy decisions rests not with the federal government but with its regulatory agencies. They cite, as examples, the CRTC's policies governing cable television hardware ownership and telecommunications interconnection and the difficulties the CTC provided for the creation of a provincially owned or subsidized airline company. The central provincial argument is that when regulatory agencies have the independent authority to make public policies, such authority inhibits provincial programs and leads to obstacles to intergovernmental collaboration and negotiation. When a regulatory agency has independent jurisdiction over a policy field, short of a legislative amendment, there may be no satisfactory system for resolving intergovernmental policy conflicts. Provincial governments have been adamant that there must be opportunity for governments to consult on the policies which regulatory agencies are to implement as well as effective binding mechanisms for transmitting such intergovernmental policy agreements. They have been strong supporters of the introduction of "policy directives." What must be recognized, however, is that, as in the case of political control within the federal government, any system devised to meet provincial concerns must also respect the equally legitimate interests of the agencies, the regulated and the general public.

Regulatory Agencies and the Public

In the first section of this chapter we focused on some of the problems with the "capture theory." Our criticisms of this theory should not be misconstrued as to suggest either that there have not been "captured" agencies or, even more generally, that there have not been instances in which the regulated interests have been the dominant participants who gain disproportionately from, and in, the regulatory process. Their influence has resulted from the disproportionate share of resources that they have possessed. Establishing a more reasonable balance so that all relevant interests are effectively represented is perhaps one of the most important issues confronting the regulatory process. This is indeed all the more imperative given the enhanced role in the policy process played by regulatory agencies and, consequently, the nature of the stakes involved.

The influence of the regulated before regulatory agencies can be traced historically to two main factors. In the first place, very simply, the regulated are always there; indeed, often they have been the only participants who appear before a regulatory agency on a matter affecting their interests. The second point, closely related to the first, is that often only the regulated interests possess the resources necessary to make the type of representation that is effective. There are several types of resources that are important. One is personnel. Attendance, let alone informed participation, is costly, especially when hearings are lengthy and complex. Often only the regulated companies can afford to be in attendance for the full hearing, and their expenses can be included as legitimate costs in any rate hearing.

Perhaps more important than simple attendance is the "informed participation" to which we referred. Information is clearly a key resource in the regulatory process, and the disproportionate influence of the regulated is normally based on unequal distribution of information. In most cases, relevant information, usually of a highly technical nature, is in the hands of the regulated. They are thus in a position whereby they can strategically employ their control over information and its flow to further their special interests. Only they may know what is or is not available and, equally critical, how to interpret it.

In the past, regulatory procedures adopted by agencies have reinforced the control of the information by the regulated. They have done this by allowing companies to file information on a confidential basis, which prevents other participants from examining and assessing it. We referred above to the difficulties the provincial governments encountered with the confidentiality of railway information, which inhibited their contribution to railway regulation. Just a few years ago, the Consumers' Association had to take the Canadian Radio and Television Commission to court in order to obtain relevant financial information on an application to raise cable television rates. Even if information is made available, if it is highly technical, participants representing general, affected interests, such as consumers or environmentalists, may not possess sufficient resources to enable them to assess it in order to participate usefully in regulatory proceedings.

Although considerable problems remain to be resolved concerning informed participation by all relevant interests, in the past few years there have been some significant improvements. In the first place, the Department of Consumer and Corporate Affairs, since the early 1970s, has funded the regulatory intervention program of the Consumers' Association of Canada. Even more importantly, the CRTC reversed the earlier position of the CTC and now awards costs to intervenors to enable them to participate effectively in regulatory proceedings. Such costs cover not only counsel but also expert witnesses who appear on behalf of intervenors. The other major change is that gradually the onus is being placed not on those who want information disclosed to justify such disclosure, but on those who seek to keep information confidential. The CRTC again stands out as the federal agency which has been the most innovative in this regard.

Although these changes do not completely establish an equitable balance between the regulated interests and affected parties before regulatory agencies, they indicate clearly a significant shift in that direction. We are nowhere near satisfying the goal of "no regulation without representation," but the recent actions increasingly recognize the validity of the principle and seek to provide means for its attainment.

The Politics of Deregulation

In the United States in the past decade, regulatory issues have been central to political debates, and the past three administrations have placed regulatory reform and deregulation high on the political agenda. The result has been far-reaching decisions to remove completely or reduce significantly regulatory activities in sectors such as telecommunications, airlines, railways, buses, trucking, natural gas and brokerage commissions. We have suggested in the preceding sections that similar regulatory issues have emerged on the Canadian political agenda, but the policy responses have been very different. Despite the faddishness of regulatory reform, Canadians have witnessed very little deregulation as a result.

It is important to determine why there have been such divergent responses to very similar, in some cases identical, policy concerns in the

446 Structures of Canadian Government

two countries. In the remainder of this chapter we can only sketch out some of the possible answers in the hope that students of Canadian public policy will be encouraged to pursue more thoroughly the questions.

In contrasting the performance of U.S. and Canadian governments in this field, we would do well to remember that the first significant act of deregulation in North America occurred in Canada in 1967 in the railway sector. However, it is important to note that recent American policies have gone much farther than Canada did in railway deregulation. Nevertheless, it is a worthwhile inquiry to determine what forces, actors and circumstances made deregulation possible in railways in the sixties but not in airlines or telecommunications in the next decade. Is the answer a simple one: that unlike the situation in the U.S., the benefits of regulation in Canada have been greater than the costs? This may well be the case, but evidence has yet to be produced to support such a conclusion.

Alternatively, the explanation may be found in our political culture. Numerous authors, commentators and regulators have noted the differences in Canadian and American attitudes toward the role of the state in the economy and toward competition in particular, and have used cultural explanations to explain why Canada has been unwilling to adopt market competition as a substitute for government regulation. John Meisel, for example, while chairman of the CRTC, took this approach when he stated in the CRTC's 1981–82 Annual Report that "deregulation a l'americaine is not an option open to us" in large part because "it is not applicable in a Canadian context. In this country, we have always tempered the desire for economic prosperity with a broad, public concern for the achievement of political and social ends."

A third explanation would examine interest group power and processes in this country. According to this approach, we have not experienced deregulation because of the lobbying power and prowess of the beneficiaries of the regulatory systems who, if the "capture theory" and its variants are to be accepted, are the regulated companies who benefit most from the current regime. An alternative approach would be to examine the power relationships not between interest groups and government but within governments and between governments. This approach would seek to identify the key intragovernmental actors who benefit from continuing regulatory regimes and policies and to explain how these actors are able to deflect calls for deregulation.

It is obvious that, given the diversity of regulatory policies and systems even within the federal government, no single-factor explanations are likely to be persuasive in accounting for the limited deregulation we have witnessed. Explanations should be developed, however, because an analysis of the policy responses to the issues could be instructive about the nature and operation of Canadian political process and institutions.

Conclusion

Regulatory agencies in the past few decades have emerged as primary instruments of governing because they perform some of the most important functions of government—functions that are critical to individual welfare and social and economic development. Their special place within our parliamentary system as exceptionally—albeit relatively—independent actors performing such significant tasks raises important issues that require scholarly attention and analysis. That these agencies, their functions and their autonomy give rise to a host of relationships between private and public power and public and private purpose should compel us to provide such attention.

Notes

1. The figures are from Margot Priest and Aron Wohl, "The Growth of Federal and Provincial Regulation of Economic Activity, 1867-1978" in W.T. Stanbury, ed. *Government Regulation in Canada: Scope, Growth, Process* (Montreal: Institute for Research on Public Policy, 1980).
2. E.P. Herring, *Public Administration and the Public Interest* (New York: McGraw-Hill, 1936), p. 192.
3. Charles E. Lindblom, *Politics and Markets* (New York: Basic Books, 1977).
4. See, for example, the evidence provided by Robert Presthus in his *Elite Accommodation in Canadian Politics* (Toronto: Macmillan, 1973).
5. Caroline Andrew and Rejean Pelletier, "The Regulators" in *The Regulatory Process in Canada*, ed. G. Bruce Doern (Toronto: Macmillan, 1978).
6. J.E. Hodgetts, *The Canadian Public Service* (Toronto: University of Toronto Press, 1973), Chapter 7. For evidence about the increase in members of such bodies, see Royal Commission on Financial Management and Accountability *Final Report* (Ottawa: Minister of Supply and Services, 1979).
7. Theodore Lowi, *The End of Liberalism*, 2nd ed. (New York: W.W. Norton, 1979), p. 304.

Further Readings

Bernstein, Marver H. *Regulating Business by Independent Commission*. Princeton, NJ: Princeton University Press, 1955.

Cairns, Robert. *Rationales for Regulation*. Technical Working Paper, Regulation Reference, Economic Council of Canada.

Doern, G.B., ed. *The Regulatory Process in Canada*. Toronto: Macmillan, 1978.

Economic Council of Canada. Regulation Reference, *Interim Report* (1979) and *Final Report* (forthcoming).

Janisch, Hudson. "Policy-Making in Regulation: Towards a New Definition of the Status of Independent Agencies in Canada." *Osgoode Hall Law Journal* 17 (1979): 46-106.

Kane, T. Gregory. *Consumers and the Regulators*. Montreal: Institute for Research on Public Policy, 1980.

Law Reform Commission of Canada. *Administrative Law Series*. Various titles which include studies of individual agencies such as the Atomic Energy Control

Board, Canadian Transport Commission and National Energy Board as well as "issue" studies on political control and public participation.

Royal Commission on Financial Management and Accountability. *Final Report.* Ottawa: Minister of Supply and Services, 1979. See especially the chapter entitled "Independent Deciding and Advisory Bodies."

Schultz, Richard J. *Federalism and the Regulatory Process.* Montreal: Institute for Research on Public Policy, 1979.

———. "Regulatory Agencies and the Dilemmas of Delegation." In *The Administrative State in Canada,* edited by O.P. Dwivedi. Toronto: University of Toronto Press, 1982.

Stanbury, W.T., and F. Thompson. *Regulatory Reform in Canada.* Montreal: Institute for Research on Public Policy, 1982.

Index